Managing Diversity

People Skills for a
Multicultural Workplace

Second Edition

Norma Carr-Ruffino

San Francisco State University

SIMON & SCHUSTER
CUSTOM PUBLISHING

Please visit our website at www.sscp.com

ISBN 0–536–00758–6

BA 98667

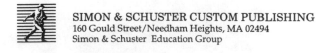 **SIMON & SCHUSTER CUSTOM PUBLISHING**
160 Gould Street/Needham Heights, MA 02494
Simon & Schuster Education Group

To Fredo, who is always there.
To Lorene, who saw good qualities in "different" people.
And to Jack, who saw through the eyes of unconditional love.

Table of Contents

HOW THIS BOOK CAN CHANGE YOUR LIFE

This book can do more for you than just provide information about changes in the multicultural workplace. It provides tools for you to change your life—if you to choose to raise your awareness, change limiting beliefs, and adopt new success strategies. Transformation, or lasting change, can only take place at the level of belief, so this book is designed to help you transform your worldview—and your relationships with people who hold quite different worldviews.

Is This Book for You?

This book is for you if you see yourself as a workplace leader—whether you're the new member of a work team, the head of the organization, or somewhere in between. This book is for you if you're ready to develop the people skills you need for managing diversity. In this book you'll get the information you need to make informed choices—as well as the processes for shifting your viewpoint and integrating new success skills into your daily interactions.

People Skills You Will Develop

Managing Diversity provides in-depth information, as well as self- awareness activities, for building the following awarenesses and skills:

- raising awareness of your own cultural viewpoints and stereotypes
- recognizing typical values, habit patterns, and concerns of each major cultural group: men and women, African Americans, Asian Americans, Euro-Americans, Latino Americans, gay persons, persons with disabilities, older persons, and obese persons
- recognizing each group's burden of myths (that reflect the stereotypes and prejudices of the dominant culture) versus reality, historical background, current demographic profile, and cultural patterns and issues
- meeting the leadership challenges and opportunities posed by the range of diverse employees in the workplace
- finding common ground upon which multicultural employees can build productive, trusting relationships
- developing strategies you can use to overcome barriers and enhance opportunities for members of each group to contribute to organizational excellence
- building productive relationships among team members, co-workers, customers, suppliers, and other business and personal contacts
- providing a work environment where all types of people can grow and thrive
- channeling diverse talents, viewpoints, and experiences toward building synergy, enhancing creativity, and developing innovative approaches and products
- functioning effectively in multicultural marketplaces—in the U. S. and globally

THE PEOPLE WHO CONTRIBUTED TO THIS BOOK

I am especially indebted to the following people who gave me feedback and moral support in the long process of developing this book:

- Ayesha Rooroh, graduate research assistant, San Francisco State University
- Chai Ha, Graduate Research Assistant, San Francisco State University
- Jane Baack, Management Professor, San Francisco State University
- Lorraine Dong, Asian Studies Professor, San Francisco State University
- John Dopp, Management Professor, San Francisco State University
- Lorene Holmes, College Administrator and Diversity Consultant
- Deborah Lowe, Marketing Professor, San Francisco State University
- Mary Pommert, Developmental Editor, Cincinnatti, OH
- Laurie Pozzi Hull, Management Consultant, National Seminars speaker, Gig Harbor, WA
- Olive James, Library Consultant, San Francisco
- Sherron Kenton, Communications Professor, Emory University, author of Crosstalk.
- Anita Silvers, Philosophy Professor, San Francisco State University
- Betty Spruill, Diversity Management Consultant, San Rafael, CA
- Barbara Smith, Diversity Management Consultant, San Francisco
- Students in Management 655, Managing Diverse Workers, San Francisco State University, who gave me feedback on the manuscript during the semesters it was used as their text
- The staff of Simon & Schuster Custom Publishing
- Many other friends and family members supported me through their willingness to listen, to comment, and to understand when for days on end I was "committed to the computer" as the project grew and developed. It is truly a privilege to do this work. Just doing it has been a powerful source of personal growth for me. May working through the resulting book be similarly powerful for you, the reader.

Norma Carr-Ruffino, Ph.D.
Department of Management, College of Business
San Francisco State University

CHAPTER 1

Changing with the Dynamic American Workplace

Whatever gets the most attention grows the strongest and lives the longest.
Jach Purcel

Are you paying attention to building a marketable package of people skills? The ability to relate well to all types of people in the workplace is an essential leadership skill these days—and becoming more important all the time. As a leader in the fast-paced, ever-changing American workplace, what do you need to know about diverse workers? What people skills must you develop? You've heard that the *way* we work is becoming more technologically based and team oriented, and that global markets affect almost all businesses. You're aware that global markets are changing almost daily, as are such American market segments as the Latino American market. These diverse markets and workplaces are increasingly made up of people from various cultures and subcultures.

What do you know about this changing workplace? Start your exploration by answering the questions posed in Self-Awareness Activity 1.1.

Self-Awareness Activity 1.1: What Do You Know About Diversity?

Purpose: To see what you know about the issues covered in this chapter.
Instructions: Determine whether you think the following statements are basically true or false—and think about why. The answers will emerge in this chapter, and the summary at the end of the chapter focuses on these issues.

1. The majority of employees entering the workplace are "white men."
2. The melting-pot theory has been a cruel myth for most minorities and women in the workplace.
3. Affirmative action programs normally include quotas for hiring minorities.
4. The goal of affirmative action programs is color blindness.
5. Affirmative action has been much more powerful than equal employment opportunity for reducing discrimination.

6. The best way to overcome problems associated with affirmative action is to revitalize the melting-pot approach.

7. A multicultural approach to managing diversity means all cultures will assimilate and integrate as one.

How is this blossoming diversity affecting workplace relationships? Think of your own relationships. You probably relate best to people you feel comfortable with. And you probably feel most comfortable with people who are most like you. Encountering new and different people can be interesting, stimulating, even exciting. But it can also be stressful, confusing, and frustrating when you don't understand where they're coming from, what they're trying to communicate, and why they do what they do. It can also be uncomfortable when they harbor stereotypes about you—and you harbor stereotypes about them, especially when those stereotypes cause you to feel and act in prejudiced ways.

Stereotypical thinking, prejudiced feelings, and discriminatory actions are what kept the doors to opportunity closed for so long. Discrimination is a typical outcome of prejudiced thinking, and we all harbor prejudices. It's just the flavor and degree that vary. For we are all products of our culture, and virtually all cultures are ethnocentric, believing "our way is the true way" of viewing reality.

Traditionally business has handled diversity by adopting the "Melting Pot Myth," but people of color and women never "melted in" because they don't look or act like the dominant majority, Euro-American men. In recent decades legal action has opened many doors of opportunity, but it has not necessarily changed the beliefs and attitudes, the thoughts and feelings that led to discrimination in the first place. Savvy leaders in forward-thinking companies value diverse employees for the unique contributions they can make to the company's success. They are crafting a multicultural approach to managing diversity, an approach that welcomes and nurtures all types of employees.

What do you need to know? As a leader in a diverse workplace, the most important knowledge you can gain is how to build multicultural skills. What skills do you need? You need those skills that will provide the basis for building productive relationships with all types of people, skills for creating a work environment that provides challenge and support for people from all cultural backgrounds.

HOW THE WORKPLACE IS CHANGING

The workplace is changing in most every way. The kinds of people we see in high powered jobs are more diverse. The way people work together and what they do are changing. And the way business is done throughout the world is changing almost month by month.

New Faces in New Jobs

People with university degrees and technical expertise come from all types of backgrounds these days. Since the 1960s more and more African Americans, Latino Americans, Asian Americans, and women have been entering college programs and technical areas that were formerly dominated by Euro-American men. And as a result, these "minorities" have been moving into managerial, executive, technical, and professional careers formerly closed to them.

The workplace is becoming more diverse in other ways, too. For example, persons with disabilities have been finding ways to use the many abilities they do have and to become productive employees. Many gay persons no longer try to hide their sexual orientation and want to be dealt with as employees who have rights equal to those of straight employees. Older employees now have the right to refuse mandatory retirement and can work as long as they are still productive. Obese persons are beginning to expect and gain some rights to be treated fairly and equally in the workplace. And people are becoming aware of the unfairness of "appearance bias" in general, especially when it is not essentially related to job productivity.

These dramatic changes in the workplace are producing some interesting challenges for everyone, from entry-level employees to top management. All must face the misunderstanding, communication breakdown, conflict, and even failure that can result when people from widely diverse backgrounds must pull together as a team or at least complete some sort of business transaction together. But these changes also offer bountiful opportunities for new levels of growth, innovation, expansion, and productivity. This book is about successfully meeting the challenges and prospering from the opportunities.

What's in a Name? The Terms We Use for "Us"

People are very sensitive about the labels others attach to them. Most prefer no labels at all. Yet how do we discuss the issues of cultures and subcultures, of diverse groups in a pluralistic society, of prejudice and discrimination based on group stereotypes? Obviously, verbal communication requires the use of descriptive terms. Such terms tend to change over time in response to social and cultural changes and interactions. African Americans were properly called "Negroes" during the 1800s, politely called "Colored" during the first half of this century, then took the term "Black" for themselves. Women were politely called "ladies" before the women's movement of the 1960s. When group labels are continually used in a limiting, demeaning, scornful, or hostile way, they eventually are resented by the people they refer to. Therefore, if we want to show respect and appreciation for others, we want to use the terms they prefer. This can be difficult since members of a particular group rarely have unanimous opinions about preferred terms.

The terms used in this book are terms adopted by a multicultural task force in a large university that met weekly for many months to work out terminology and basic policy concerning diverse groups. The terms for the largest ethnic groups are listed below and reflect the preferences of activists and leaders from those groups.

- African Americans
- Asian Americans (such as Chinese Americans, Asian Indian Americans)
- Euro-Americans
- Jewish Americans
- Latino Americans (such as Mexican Americans, Puerto Rican Americans)
- American Indians

If you got a sense of equality as you looked at these terms, you're on the right track. The major rationale for these particular terms, rather than some others that are more commonly used, is that we're all Americans, and most of us are native Americans. If we go back far enough, all of us have ancestors who came from somewhere else. And it doesn't really matter how long we or our ancestors have been here.

If your ancestors were immigrants from Europe, you're a Euro-American, often called *white*, and you're a member of the dominant majority in American culture. The terms *Asian American* and *Latino American* are used for convenience in discussing certain cultural and statistical commonalties. Most Asian Americans don't think of themselves as Asian Americans so much as *Chinese Americans* or *Filipino Americans* or one of the many Asian subcultural groups. The same is true for Latino Americans. These subcultural differences are addressed in the chapters that focus on these groups. The terms used for other diverse groups are based on discussions with various leaders of those groups and on a review of current literature. These groups include:

- Persons with Disabilities
- Gay, lesbian and bisexual persons
- Older persons
- Obese persons

When you're relating one-to-one with people from any of these groups, you rarely need to refer to the group or groups they identify with. You're dealing with the individual. However, when you deal with groups or need to discuss groups with an individual, consider beginning with questions about how the person(s) feel about the various names for the groups. Reach some agreement about appropriate labels. Become sensitive to language that some consider racist and sexist, and weed it out of your vocabulary. Every time we use such terms, we reinforce the prejudicial patterns, whether we intend to or not.

More Women and Immigrants

Since the 1960s more and more women have worked outside the home for most of their adult lives. Some are there because they want careers, even though they may be wives and mothers; some because their family needs their income; and most for both reasons.

More and more ethnic minorities are in the work force because immigration quotas were expanded in the 1960s allowing more Latinos and Asians to become citizens. In 1940 more than 85 percent of people who had come to the U.S. as immigrants were European, while in 1995, 75 percent were from non-European countries, such as Latin America (47 percent) and Asian (22 percent). These immigrants tended to be younger on average and to have more children than the Euro-American population, further expanding their numbers. Figure 1.1 shows the ethnic makeup of the population and the work force in 1990, as well as the proportions of Euro-Americans and minorities in the better-paying middle- and top-level management jobs. Although Euro-American women and minorities made up 65 percent of the work force, they held only 30 percent of middle management jobs and 5 percent of top management positions, as shown in Figure 1.1.

Income for these groups reflect the glass ceiling to higher-level jobs still in place in corporate America. In 1990, per capita (mean) income for full time workers, according to the U.S. Census Bureau was:

Per capita income, all workers		$14,421
Euro-Americans	$15,687	
African Americans	8,859	
Latino Americans	8,400	
Asian Americans	13,638	
American Indians	8,328	

Median incomes are somewhat higher overall and are shown below.

	Men	Women
Median income, all workers	$20,409	$10,371
Euro-American	22,065	10,747
African American	12,950	8,825
Latino American	13,501	8,354
Asian American	19,396	11,986
American Indian	12,180	7,310
Other Americans	12,493	7,876

The trend toward a more diverse population and work force is expected to continue. Of the 26 million new workers coming into the work force between 1990 and 2005, about 85 percent, are expected to be women and minorities, according to Labor Department estimates. A handy way to remember the proportions is to think of terms of sixths: Women will account for about four-sixths, minority men more than one-sixth, and Euro-American men one-sixth, as depicted in Figure 1.2.

Historically, men of European ancestry have run virtually all the major American organizations. They have set the rules of the game in the American culture as well as in corporate cultures. Other types of employees were traditionally kept out of mainstream leadership roles. They worked on the periphery of our organizations as the workers who were told what to do and how to do it, as temporary employees and part-timers. Some were kept out completely—the unemployed and unemployable.

Diverse Backgrounds = Diverse Issues

Whether you are an entry-level trainee, a team leader, or a top manager, your success in and enjoyment of your career increasingly depend on how well you understand and relate to a diverse range of people. If you can mentally slip inside their skin for a time and see the world through

FIGURE 1.1: Ethnic and Gender Segments of the Work Force and of Management, 1990

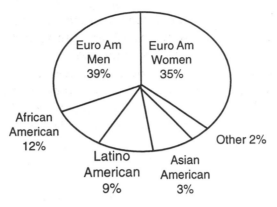

Minority Men & Women—26%
[Men 13%, Women 13%]

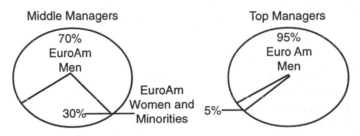

SOURCE: *U.S. Census Bureau, 1993; U.S. Dept. of Labor, 1991.*

FIGURE 1.2: New Workers Entering the Work Force, 1990–2005

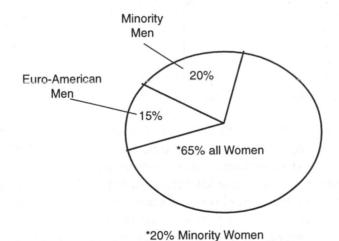

*20% Minority Women
45% Euro-American Women

SOURCE: *U.S. Bureau of Labor Statistics, 1987.*

their eyes, you'll gain great power in understanding their thinking and feeling and the issues most important to them. Here's a brief preview of some of the issues you'll learn about in this book.

Career women often find themselves in catch-22 situations. For example, people expect women to be emotional, indecisive, and vulnerable. But business leaders are expected to be in control of their emotions, decisive, and able to roll with the punches. If women project the typical image, they're not seen as potential leaders. But if they project the "business leader" image, they're often seen as too hard and masculine, even abnormal.

*Men a*re expected to be aggressive, ambitious, and proud. But many corporate cultures are changing in ways that call for leaders who are cooperative and who focus more on challenging and supporting others than on personal achievement. Many men are confused about what companies expect of them, just as they're confused about what the women in their lives expect. The dramatic changes in women's roles have had a major impact on men's lives.

African Americans who have a problem with a "brother or sister" typically take the bull by the horns and confront the issue directly. They go straight to the person, "tell it like it is," and try to work it out immediately. To them this approach is real and honest. But to most other people in a workplace, it may be threatening and may imply anger that might erupt into violence. When Euro-American, Asian American, and Latino American co-workers feel threatened by African Americans' "confrontation, rage, or violence," it's usually because they misinterpret their cultural behavior patterns.

Asian Americans are taught that one of the highest values is to control one's reactions and to become mature enough to put relationships before personal concerns. As a result they may be very indirect about expressing criticism or disagreeing. Often, they don't show or express strong emotion, especially outside the family circle. When Euro-American, Latino American, and African American co-workers conclude that Asian Americans are closed, secretive, inscrutable, and even cold, it's usually because they're unaware of Asian cultural values.

Latino Americans are often assumed to have a "mañana" (literally "tomorrow") attitude, which implies they're not ambitious, productive go-getters, as Americans tend to be. Actually, most Latino Americans are hard workers, but they tend to wait for orders from the boss. Their cultural beliefs include greater respect for authority than most Euro-Americans hold—and greater acceptance of themselves as subordinates to a powerful boss. Also, Latinos tend to be more accepting of Americans of undesirable circumstances, often seeing such situations as God's will. When Euro-Americans judge Latino Americans as lacking initiative, it's usually because they don't understand these aspects of their cultural background.

Gay persons are sometimes avoided by co-workers on the assumption that gays don't have "normal" relationships. Co-workers have made such comments as, "I just don't feel comfortable socializing with Joe (a gay man). Maybe he'll come on to me sexually," or "Maybe he'll get jealous of my friendship with a guy he's attracted to, when to me we're just hanging out." Joe would probably say, "Hey, I'm *me* first and foremost, just a person. My sexual orientation is just one slice of the whole pie that's me. What's more, I'm very sensitive to the discomforts and fears of straight guys." Studies indicate that people in the gay community have a whole range of relationships, as people in any community do, and that overall they're as likely to have "normal relationships" as people from any cultural group.

Persons with disability are thought to be a small minority by most people and are often seen as distinctly "different," even abnormal. Actually, most people have some type of disability, usually fairly minor. Persons classified as "disabled" simply have a disability that affects their ability to perform one or more major life functions, such as walking, reading, or hearing. They're not really "different" from the person who limps around occasionally with back trouble, the person who wears contacts, or the person who doesn't hear too well out of one ear. It's just a matter of degree. Even persons with a severe disability, such as paralysis from the neck down, learn to live and work independently and often to make significant contributions through their careers.

Obese persons are often as healthy as most adults, depending upon the extent of their obesity and their age. Many cruel myths and stereotypes surround obesity in our culture. The type of discrimination obese employees experience has an element of appearance bias and is related to skin-color discrimination, which is also a form of appearance bias. Obese persons also experience discrimination based on assumptions about what they cannot do, similar to that experienced by persons with disability. Recent court rulings that support the employment rights of obese persons are based on their rights to "reasonable accommodation" under laws that protect the disabled.

Older persons are often assumed to be rigid, dogmatic, and forgetful. Their younger co-workers may avoid them and may wonder why these "old folks" haven't retired or when they're going to retire. Research indicates that aging itself does not cause any significant loss of intelligence, memory, or learning capacity. However, with age one's habits tend to come home to roost. People who abuse or neglect their bodies start paying the price in their later years, while people with good eating and exercise habits tend to remain healthy and vibrant. People who habitually spend much of their time in negative thinking tend to become even more negative with age, while those who work on a positive outlook and self-growth become more delightful to be around.

Other groups that have distinct issues include American Indians, Arab Americans, Jewish Americans, and bi-ethnic persons (those whose parents are from two distinctly different cultural backgrounds). For example, the person whose mother is Euro-American and whose father is African American tends to experience a unique type of cultural conflict growing up. Because of the limitations of time and space, these and other groups are not included in this book. Resources for learning about them are provided in *Managing Diversity Skill Builder*.

Every cultural subgroup has its own unique set of values, habits, customs, life circumstances, and issues to resolve. Understanding the key cultural themes and issues of each group can give you great insight and power for building good work relationships and helping other team members do the same.

New Ways of Working Together

In the new technologically oriented companies, employees are more highly skilled and educated than ever. Old hierarchies and authoritarian bosses who dictate orders are fading into the archaic past. More common are:

- self-managing work teams
- leaders who facilitate team meetings and help teams to reach consensus
- consultants and technical experts who function more as professionals than as traditional employees.

Relationships with teammates, customers, and suppliers, and the information that flows among them, are the lifeblood of the organization. Corporations are increasingly built upon trust, collaboration, cooperation, and teamwork. In such organizations, it's more obvious than ever that people are the most valuable resource, that how we work together creates energy and innovation or decay and demoralization, that our interactions spark the knowledge and information that fuel organizational growth and success. In summary, key trends that point to the need for multicultural leadership skills are:

- A shortage of qualified, educated workers means companies must be more responsive to workers' needs and expectations.
- The U.S. work force is becoming dramatically more diverse at all levels. Workers expect more accommodation to their needs and identities than in the past. Fewer workers are willing to compromise their unique characteristics for the sake of "fitting in" with corporate cultures built on traditional values and norms.

- The global marketplace that now affects most American corporations is intensely competitive, making qualified employees more crucial than ever for providing the quality, innovation, and productivity companies need to compete.
- Growth of these subcultural groups means growth of subcultural market segments. Companies need a work force that "looks like America" to project a multicultural company image, contribute to marketing insights, and relate well to multicultural customers.

HOW APPROACHES TO MANAGING DIVERSITY ARE CHANGING

Business leaders are changing the way they manage diversity. Most realize now that the melting-pot approach was a myth so far as people of color and women are concerned. They also realize that the legal approach, which relies on meeting equal opportunity and affirmative action requirements, has been an effective tool for opening doors to all, but it does not provide an adequate basis for managing diversity. What is emerging is an approach that values diversity and develops corporate cultures that welcome and nurture all types of employees.

The Melting–Pot Approach to Managing Diversity

But America has always handled its diversity well, some say. Why, we're the Great Melting Pot. But the melting pot has been a cruel myth for aspiring career women and for non-European minorities. Who has it worked for? In society in general, for all immigrants from European countries. In the workplace, male immigrants from those countries. European immigrants were expected to learn the American ways so they could be assimilated and absorbed. The goal was to create a seamless American culture and workplace. This worked fairly well for European men because Western cultures have much in common and people from those cultures look much alike. Although the Jewish, Irish, Italian, and Eastern European immigrants experienced some distinct prejudice and discrimination, within a generation or two they blended in. As explained later, people of color actually lived in segmented and segregated subcultures and women grew up alongside men in parallel but different worlds. People of color and women simply don't look like Euro-American men, the dominant culture of the workplace, and they were never truly assimilated.

How Do I Recognize the Melting–Pot Myth in a Company?

How can you tell when a company is relying on the melting-pot myth to handle diversity? Look for the following kinds of messages:

- We (Euro-American men) are at the center of the universe here.
- Why should we bother to learn about newcomers? We're busy and we belong here.
- It's the newcomers' job to learn how to succeed here and how to fit in (become like us).
- They have to learn the ropes and speak the language correctly if they want to work here.
- If they learn to do it our way, they won't have any problems.
- Immigrants can be a nuisance to talk to because of their accent and grammar.
- Women's culture is just a subset of whatever ethnic culture they belong to; Euro-American women live in the same cultural world we do.
- The best approach is to ignore cultural differences.
- Our goal is to eliminate cultural differences.
- Managers naturally have an adversarial relationship with workers.
- Managers must do the planning, then control and check on worker performance.

This set of beliefs logically leads to a belief that the others are wrong or inferior and to relying on predominant stereotypes of people from that group, often assuming they're stupid or lazy or stubborn or sneaky. It says to the newcomer,

"Get rid of your unprofessional behavior, your odd language, your smelly food."

How Does the Melting–Pot Myth Affect People of Color and Women?

Newcomers in the past have usually bought into the melting-pot belief system, which led them to new beliefs, such as

- I must become just like the dominant group.
- My native country is inferior; America is better.
- I must fit in, no matter what I have to do.
- I won't teach the children about the old country; let them be Americans.

The immigrants' children picked up on this attitude, and many have grown up to be ashamed of their parents' "old country" ways (Simons et al. 1993).

When assimilation was either a conscious or unconscious goal in dealing with diversity, the ideal was to ignore differences and treat everyone the same. The biblical Golden Rule was the ideal:

*Do unto others as **you** would have **them** do unto **you**.*

This rule usually works in a homogeneous culture, but in a multicultural workplace life is not so simple, and a more appropriate Golden Rule would be,

*Do unto others as **they** would have **you** do unto **them**.*

People may prefer to be treated in ways you haven't even thought of—because they may have quite different values and habits than you. You must treat people differently when they are different, if you want to be fair. This is a much more complex and difficult task than treating everyone alike.

What Are the Major Problems with the Melting–Pot Myth?

You can see that the melting-pot ideal has never really been ideal. Here are some additional problems with this approach:

- Those who don't look the part can't blend in.
- Forcing everyone to assimilate leaves untapped potential.
- In a competitive environment, assimilation is stifling and deadly.
- When diverse newcomers are expected to fit in, they focus on doing the expected or accommodating the norm, or playing it safe.
- Newcomers avoid making suggestions that would make them visible.
- The more energy newcomers must expend on adapting, the less they have for developing innovative ideas and personal strengths.
- Talented newcomers tend to go and grow where they're appreciated for who they are—to companies with a more supportive multicultural approach.

Obviously, the more diverse the work force becomes, the more important it becomes for organizations to solve the problems presented by the melting-pot approach, to dismantle the traditional barriers to full productivity and contribution, and to develop an approach that's more inclusive.

The Legal Approach: Equal Opportunity and Affirmative Action

Because the melting pot approach did not provide equal opportunities for people of color and women, the legal approach was introduced by government in the late 1960s. Where people of color and women formerly faced brick walls, doors to opportunity appeared, so this legal approach has been more effective for their upward mobility than the melting-pot approach. Although most business leaders agree that the equal opportunity approach has been generally beneficial, most people don't understand it well. Euro-American men tend to resent it, and many minorities and women don't know why they need it. How did it all come about and what does it mean?

Equal Employment Opportunity

In 1964 Title VII of the Civil Rights Act established the Equal Employment Opportunity Commission (EEOC) to define and enforce acceptable employment policies and practices, especially as they affect minorities and women. EEO was an important step forward for people of color and women, because people who are discriminated against can complain to their employers, based on EEOC guidelines. If an employer doesn't satisfy such a complaint, the employee can go directly to a regional EEOC office and file a complaint there. If the employee can get other employees to join the complaint, it may become a class action. And if the EEOC cannot get the employer to resolve the discriminatory issue, the employees may be able to file a class action lawsuit. The courts then decide on the matter.

The advantage of EEO law is that it gives an employee a direct way to deal with job discrimination. The disadvantage is that it is extremely difficult for an individual to prove discrimination. Those who go outside the company to complain are usually branded as troublemakers and blackballed throughout the industry. Although such retaliation is illegal, it is almost impossible to prove when it's handled by word of mouth and never put in writing. Individuals who pursue this route usually find their career progress put on hold for years. Often they must change occupations or industries and start over.

Affirmative Action

Because EEO alone is unlikely to make a significant difference in the upward mobility of minorities and women, affirmative action (AA) was stepped up. AA law is not so obvious as EEO to individual employees. The average employee will never meet with an AA official and never file an "AA complaint." That's because AA works in the background, normally with a human resource administrator, and at times with the top management team, developing an AA program that's approved by an officer from the Office of Federal Contract Compliance Programs (OFCCP). The compliance officer periodically reviews the company's progress toward the diversity goals it has set in its AA program. Therefore, individual employees usually don't know that job opportunities were made available to them because of the company's AA plans and goals.

But what exactly is AA and how does it work? Beginning in 1967 a series of executive orders signed by then-President Johnson empowered AA by:

- requiring AA plans from firms doing business with the federal government
- randomly and periodically monitoring such firms for compliance to plans
- imposing sanctions on firms that don't comply

Specifically, all federal government contracts include provisions that prohibit employment discrimination because of race, color, religion, national origin, or sex. Any business that enters into federal contracts of more than $50,000 per year must develop an AA plan to hire and promote "under-utilized" minorities, setting goals and time targets, and periodically filing progress reports. Adequate representation of minorities and women at all job levels usually relates to their proportions in the available workforce. This focus on overall numbers, proportions, and representations takes the pressure off the individual minority person who is not given an opportunity. The individual does not have to prove discrimination. Instead, discriminatory results are implied when, for example, 40 percent of the available work force and of actual employees are women but only 5 percent are managers. The employer would then be expected to set reasonable short- and long-term goals, over a period of several years, to increase the proportion of women in the better-paying managerial, professional, and technical jobs.

The Rationale for AA

AA provoked immediate controversy and backlash, but it was fairly well established during the 1970s. However, when President Reagan took office in 1981, he signaled a desire to dismantle the system. In response, the Commission on Civil Rights issued the updated statement of principles "Affirmative Action in the 1980s." This bipartisan research body stated that the first AA principle is that a problem-remedy approach to discrimination is what is needed.

The second principle is that discrimination is a self-perpetuating process that calls for AA to break the cycle and to create new, more equitable processes when these factors are present:

- a history of widespread prejudice
- conditions of inequality with Euro-American males
- resulting barriers that have *not* been removed by measures that are color-blind and gender-neutral—that is, measures that ignore ethnicity and gender.

The main point: Under such conditions as we still have in the United States, remedies for discrimination that insist on colo*r blindness* or *gender neutrality* are not sufficient. The only effective remedy to the problem is a type of AA that responds to discrimination as a self-sustaining process and sets specific hiring and promotion goals for dismantling it. The commission went on to respond the major criticisms of AA concerning hiring quotas, lower standards, the stigma of AA hiring, and claims of reverse discrimination.

AA Is About Flexible Goals, Not Rigid Quotas. *Quotas* cannot be imposed on an employer by normal AA law. In rare cases, such as the Birmingham Fire Department, minority employees may sue. A judge *may* rule that the nature and extent of the discriminatory problem is so entrenched that the court must set quotas in order to bring about change. However, in nearly all instances normal AA law applies. This means that companies set their own numerical goals, which are then approved by a federal contract compliance officer. The goals are not quotas because they are flexible and approximate. As long as a company can show they're making a good-faith effort to create a diverse work force, they're not penalized. AA programs and goals will end when all groups are reasonably represented at all levels of the company.

AA Never Dictates Lower Standards. Nothing in the laws calls for lowering valid standards. Companies that don't use long-range planning for recruiting, hiring, and training minorities may find themselves making little progress toward a diversified work force. Sometimes, when a federal review is looming, such companies voluntarily set their own quotas and then lower their hiring or promotion standards in order to meet the quotas. But the government does not require this sort of crisis management, nor does the Civil Rights Commission condone it.

On the other hand, AA plans often require companies to examine their standards, and if standards cannot be shown to be related to successful performance, they must be discarded. The use of such invalid standards may deny opportunities to some people for reasons unrelated to merit. In situations where the use of valid standards serves to exclude women and minorities, civil rights law does *not* require the selection of unqualified minorities and women. It does, however, encourage

- the restructuring of jobs
- the development of new standards that are equally related to successful performance but do not exclude
- the development of training programs that prepare the excluded to meet valid standards.

"AA Stigma" Is Manageable. The Civil Rights Commission addressed the charge that AA further stigmatizes minorities and women when, for example, people adopt the attitude that an African American gained her position because of AA rather than because of merit. Such a woman has difficulty gaining respect and credibility. Often, the problem is actually faulty implementation of AA plans; such as, for example, when a woman is placed as a "token" in a situation where she faces open hostility and/or lack of basic support. When the resulting isolation or failure causes her to quit or be removed, the employer may cite this as the reason for not promoting other women. Company leaders set the tone by their attitudes toward diverse employees. When they signal respect, trust, and support, others are unlikely to devalue minority capabilities. Even when leadership support is grudging, many minorities and women say that an opportunity with stigma is better than no opportunity at all, which is what they had before AA. To them, throwing out AA means throwing out opportunity. They say that until some proven alternative to AA comes along, the stigmatization argument is invalid.

AA Is Not Reverse Discrimination. The remedial use of goals, timetables, quotas, and setting aside a certain percentage of government contracts to go to minorities in order to bring about workplace equity for all ethnic groups has become part of international law. In 1969 the United Nations treaty called *Declaration of All Forms of Racial Discrimination* was passed and became international law. The treaty is clear about measures designed to bring ethnic groups into the mainstream: *AA measures shall not be considered discrimination or reverse discrimination.*

The only qualification regarding such measures is that they be removed as soon as they are no longer required. By 1984, 107 nations had ratified it—more than for any other treaty that has emerged from the U.N., but the United States Senate has never seriously debated it nor ratified it (Krauthammer 1985).

A similar U.N. treaty calling for the same rights for women was passed in 1979. *The Convention on the Elimination of All Forms of Discrimination Against Women* calls for the same rights for women. It also calls for nations to "embody the principle of equality of men and women in their national constitution or other appropriate legislation." Because Congress also refuses to act on this U.N. treaty, the United States was the only industrialized democracy that had not ratified it in 1995 (Carter, 1995).

AA Made a Difference in the 1970s

The track record of AA during the 1970s, when it was enforced with fair consistency, indicates that it does open doors for minorities and women without harming business. At least four major studies concluded that the law was effective in boosting the careers and economic status of minorities and women. At the same time business suffered no loss in productivity and paid an average of $78 per employee per year for all EEO/AA related activities (Simpson 1984; U.S. Dept. of Labor 1984; Potomac Institute 1984; Leonard 1984a, b, 1985, 1986).

Bette Woody, Wellesley College Center for Research on Women, concluded that EEO/AA laws played a major role in allowing African American women who were working predominantly as cleaning women to make a dramatic shift to office positions. Clerical jobs were mostly off-limits for them before AA. In 1960 most worked as cleaning women. By 1980 only 6 percent worked as domestic maids, and 39 percent were in clerical jobs—up from 8.5 percent in 1960. The gap between African American and Euro-American women's earnings virtually closed, narrowing from 80 percent in 1967 to 90 percent in 1985 (Woody 1989).

Using figures for 1966 and 1977 regarding the change in the composition of the work force toward more women and minorities, Leonard found the following impact on the average marginal productivity of labor: Minority males in 1977 were roughly 70 percent as productive as Euro-American males at the margin and women were 1 percent more productive. The ratio of the marginal product of the average worker to the marginal product of a Euro-American male worker fell by only .007, thanks to the fact that women became slightly more productive than Euro-American males and thus offset minority males' relative performance. At the same time minority men earned about 70 percent and women about 60 percent of Euro-American male wages (Leonard 1984a). On average, then, each time a manufacturing firm promoted a Euro-American male and filled the position with a woman, it enjoyed a slight increase in productivity along with a 40 percent cut in salary expense.

A review of the relative impact that AA, the EEOC, and class action lawsuits had during the 1970s indicates that AA had the greatest impact by far—because of its power to impose sanctions that can affect the profitability of so many businesses.

AA Was Undermined During the 1980s

From 1980 to 1992 successive Republican administrations chipped away at the foundation of AA from every angle. Several studies indicate that the noticeable, but not spectacular, progress minorities and women had previously experienced became generally stalled during the 1980s (Leonard 1988). In President Bush's administration Secretary of Labor Lynn Martin commissioned a study that found the glass ceiling was much lower than predicted, existing below mid-level positions for most minorities and women and was generally lower for minorities than for Euro-American women (U.S. Dept. of Labor 1991).

Why Business Retained AA During the 1980s

While most analysts agree that the regulation and enforcement of AA and EEO laws were eroded during the 1980s, they also agree that most employers maintained a high level of interest in them, especially larger corporations that wanted to keep AA plans and reporting in place for three reasons:

- As a practical matter, in corporate political terms, AA plans provide employers with a way to integrate work forces despite internal opposition from some Euro-American males.
- AA fits with the long-term interests of some corporate human resource planners who want to streamline hiring systems, set and enforce standards, apply training requirements, and monitor progress of all workers.
- Although executives generally resist government regulation, they also understand that government regulatory positions come and go, and that eventually the pendulum would swing back in favor of AA, leaving those employers who had dropped their plans at a disadvantage.
- Many of the people who moved into positions formerly closed to them because of ethnic or gender discrimination were very productive and effective employees and were generally a bargain in salary terms.

Problems with Implementing AA

The major problem with AA is that most organizations have focused on meeting requirements, often flying by the seat of their pants, rather than focusing on valuing diversity and gradually shaping a corporate culture that reflects that value. Many companies have fallen into a frustrating AA cycle that views the workforce as a pipeline and try to fill it with minorities that "fit in," as follows:

- Recognize an AA problem, such as failure to meet targets for hiring or promoting women and minorities, or excessive turnover of these employees, their inadequate upward mobility, or their low morale.
- Respond by recruiting the kinds of minorities who will fit in with the corporate culture, rather than changing corporate systems and culture in ways that meet the needs of these minorities.

After a period of high expectations that the AA problem is being resolved, disappointment sets in when the problem remains or new related problems arise, such as:

- The new recruit doesn't progress as expected.
- Co-workers complain about reverse discrimination or preferential treatment.
- The new recruits sense that others resent them.

- Employees don't give management credit for a good faith effort.
- Discouraged, management quits trying and AA efforts are given less attention.
- After a period, a new human resource crisis appears.

We've mentioned the other major problems of AA, such as the glass ceiling, backlash, and stigma. The bottom line: AA has been the most powerful tool society has ever used to open doors of opportunity where formerly there were brick walls blocking the entry of people of color and women into upwardly mobile career paths. Because of it the United States has more women managers than any country in the world. Yet 95 percent of top managers are still Euro-American men and they're paid 30 percent more than women at every level, including vice presidents. If we as a culture want to complete our path toward equal opportunity for all, we must retain the best of AA and build on it by creating company climates that are multicultural.

From Valuing Diversity to Managing Diversity

During the 1970s, when companies were opening new doors to diverse persons in order to meet EEO/AA requirements, most of them were still using the melting pot approach in expecting everyone to adapt to the corporate culture. Since nearly all corporate cultures were Euro-American male cultures, others often had difficulty fitting in. And many who apparently fit in didn't like the price it exacted, that is, giving up important aspects of their own culture and personality. Company leaders, human resource executives, and corporate consultants looked for ways to encourage productive work relationships and to stem turnover rates of diverse employees. Meeting these needs led to the valuing diversity approach.

Valuing Diversity Approach

The valuing diversity movement is based on moving beyond tolerance of diverse others to appreciation. It involves seeing a diverse work force as an asset that offers valuable opportunities for innovation, networking, marketing savvy, and similar benefits. The approach primarily involves a shift in beliefs and attitudes away from "we're all alike (or should be)" to "we're each unique and that's the source of our greatness." The valuing diversity approach focuses primarily on educating people through experiential and informational seminars to make appropriate attitude shifts. It emerged in the 1980s and is still a part of managing diversity.

Managing Diversity: A Multicultural Approach

Beyond the melting-pot myth, the legal approach, and even the valuing diversity approach is a more action-oriented approach that's often called managing diversity. It is based on valuing diversity and goes further to find ways to shift the corporate culture itself, to make it more multicultural. The goal is to create a corporate culture that supports and nurtures all types of employees. We'll explore this multicultural approach in detail at the end of the book, in chapter 12. To grasp this evolution of management approaches to diversity, examine Figure 1.3.

FIGURE 1.3: Evolution of Approaches to Workplace Diversity

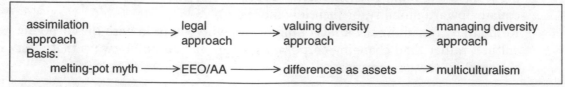

Business leaders who are using multicultural approach are discovering a surprising wealth of benefits for their organizations. Benefits accrue at all levels: personal, interpersonal, and organizational. They include:

- attracting and retaining the best available human talent
- increasing organizational flexibility
- gaining and keeping greater market share
- reducing costs
- improving the quality of management
- creating and innovating more powerfully
- solving problems more effectively
- increasing productivity
- contributing to social responsibility

We'll explore briefly why and how each of these benefits is important.

Attracting and Retaining the Best People

Attracting and retaining the best people as employees requires that organizations meet potential employees' needs, show respect for them as individuals, and use similar multicultural skills in working with them.

Attracting Qualified People. As qualified employees become more scarce, employers must become more flexible. They can no longer afford to convey the implicit message, "This is what we offer and how we do things. Fit in or leave." Now they must adapt to potential employees who say, "These are my needs and goals; they must be met if I am to stay."

Retaining High Potential Employees. To retain good employees, firms must be truly committed to treating all employees fairly and to valuing diversity. Employers who appear to favor some personal orientations and stifle others risk paying the price of low productivity due to a restricted pool of applicants, employee dissatisfaction, lack of commitment, turnover, and even sabotage. University of Alabama Professor John Sheridan's research indicates that professionals (both strong and weak performers) stay an average of 14 months longer in firms whose main focus is "interpersonal orientation" values than in firms whose focus is "work task" values. Sheridan estimates that the work task-value firms incurred opportunity losses of $6 to $9 million more over the six-year period studied than the interpersonal-value firms. Sheridan concludes that it makes more sense to foster an interpersonal orientation culture rather than to try to find individuals who will fit into a work task culture.

Meeting Employee Needs and Expectations. Nearly five-sixths of new employees will be women and minorities in the coming decade. Most are from a new generation who expect something extra from their careers, namely, meaning and a sense of making a contribution. Most, especially career women, expect to have a personal and family life and are less willing than older generations were to sacrifice all for career success. And most, especially ethnic minorities, are more resistant to fitting into a corporate culture that requires them to squelch important parts of their persona.

These better educated employees want their individual and group needs recognized and met. They want more control over their own destiny, a say in decisions that affect them, and more flexibility in the terms and rewards of employment. They want a fair, open, flexible, responsive, and responsible work environment where they can enjoy the workday as well as be productive. They want to experience the excitement and stimulation of meeting challenging opportunities and problems as well as the security and serenity that come from being appreciated and supported.

Word gets around quickly about how companies treat diverse employees and which companies are the best to work for. People are less likely to stay with employers who don't meet their needs.

Communicating Respect for Others. One of the basic principles of effective multicultural leadership is to signal respect for the unique characteristics of another's culture. Small gestures can communicate respect, such as greeting persons in their native language, taking time to chat and learn more about a person, and keeping their cultural and personal viewpoints and values in mind as you work together. Doing this effectively requires learning about diverse subgroups and building skills in relating to them.

Increasing Organizational Flexibility

Companies are teaming up, forming alliances to pool their resources and to tighten relationships with suppliers and customers. An alliance may require that two teams or units from two different companies blend together to act as a link between the firms involved. The most frequently cited source of problems with alliances is "different corporate cultures," according to a *Harvard Business Review* survey. Multicultural skills can be applied to working in various corporate cultures as well as working with individuals from various cultures (Kanter 1991).

Gaining and Keeping Greater Market Share

The spending power of African Americans, Latino Americans, and Asian Americans was about 424 billion dollars in 1990 and is expected to grow to $650 billion by the year 2000. In California these three groups make up 40 percent of the population and are expected to make up 50 percent by 2000. It is estimated that by 2000 about half of all business travelers will be women. Diverse employees can help to attract and retain minority customers.

Their experiences and perspectives can certainly be valuable in building sales. Such diversity is the best way to be sure the organization remains flexible enough to capture diverse markets and to provide adequate customer service. Having African American women on the team, for example, may motivate management to respond to growing market niches involving such customers. This happened to Avon in the cosmetics market. Also, customers tend to perceive that someone of their own ethnicity or sex is better able to serve their needs, and this can influence them in choosing one service or product over another. Using diversity to improve marketing skills within ethnically diverse domestic markets can help a company to market more effectively internationally. Learning how to be responsive to such markets and to project the right image to them will help the company sharpening skills for the international marketplace.

Diverse employees can prevent many awkward public relations problems. They can also help in those one-on-one provider-customer interactions that are becoming increasingly common as companies focus on providing services, information, and custom products to customers. It makes sense for a company to employ a work force that mirrors its customer base. Women have a special edge in tuning into women's needs and expectations and meeting them, just as African American men have an advantage in understanding and communicating with one another. Diversity can help prevent the following types of problems:

- An advertisement for a major telephone company featured a drawing of animals making telephone calls from various continents. A gorilla was making the call from Africa. Many African Americans were incensed.
- General Motors launched a major marketing campaign in Mexico to sell its Chevrolet Nova. In Spanish "no va" means "doesn't go." Almost no one bought.
- A major bank instructed its tellers, all women, to wear straw hats with a band reading "Free and Easy Banking." The word "Banking" was hidden under the turned-up brims. When women realized why customers were snickering, they were upset.

Reducing Costs

A multicultural approach saves money in the long run and often even in the short run. Diversity efforts reduce the high turnover rate of nontraditional employees and the costs that go with it. The cost of turnover per person has been estimated at $5,000 to $10,000 for an hourly worker and from $75,000 to $200,000 for an executive at the $100,000 salary level. (Auster 1988; Hinrichs

1991; Riskind 1991). When a nontraditional manager is included in a development program or gets a promotion, other nontraditional employees at lower levels tend to feel more committed to the company. Such companies are more likely to be sought out by nontraditional recruits, which reduces the costs of recruiting. They also may save money in defending grievances, complaints, and lawsuits regarding discrimination, sexual harassment, and similar problems. In addition to lost time and legal fees for dealing with such problems, other costs are job-related stress, lowered morale, lowered productivity, and resulting absenteeism and turnover.

Improving the Quality of Management

Knowing they must compete with all comers can encourage the more competent Euro-American men to perform even better, while the less competent ones are screened out. Diversity can prod managers to learn fresh approaches to business problems, to see issues from new perspectives, and to add new contacts to their business networks. Exposure to diverse colleagues can help managers develop breadth and openness. Perhaps this explains why Euro-American men who graduate from universities where African American students comprise 8 to 17 percent of the student body earn roughly 15 percent higher wages than those who graduate from "lily white" schools (Marshall 1995). Also, much of what an organization learns in trying out a special training program for diversity purposes may later be broadly applied to all employees.

Creating and Innovating More Powerfully

Traditional assembly-line industrial organizations required creative thinking from only a few, but post-industrial virtual organizations with their self-managing work teams require it of many. If people from diverse backgrounds are truly respected, supported, and appreciated, they will be willing to contribute their ideas to group sessions. This in turn gives the group a broader range of diverse ideas to choose from, increases group synergy, and prevents groupthink.

The conclusion that creativity is fostered by diversity is supported by research showing that the tolerance of diversity, defined as judging relatively few behaviors as deviant from norms, is a defining characteristic of innovative organizations (Siegel and Kaemmerer 1978).

For best results, relationships among team members must be predominantly positive. However, a certain amount of conflict is natural and inevitable, and if it is managed well, it can be constructive. Excessive group conflict interferes with productivity, closing down communication, wasting energy, and even causing people to leave. But too little conflict may signal complacency, repression, or old approaches to addressing new problems. The challenge is to stir innovation, manage conflict, and prevent breakdown (Jackson 1991).

Solving Problems and Increasing Productivity

Culturally diverse work forces have the potential to solve problems better because of several factors: a greater variety of perspectives brought to bear on the issue, a higher level of critical analysis of alternatives, and a lower probability of groupthink and therefore a higher probability of generating creative solutions.

All the benefits mentioned so far work together to generally increase organizational productivity. Specifically, an effective approach to managing diversity helps diverse teams and individuals to be more productive.

Learning about each employee's unique values, expectations, and goals is essential to effectively working with diverse team members on team projects. It's also essential for leaders in helping others with job objectives, job performance, and career plans. Job performance, dedication, and attendance are boosted when employees perceive they are valued and cared for by their organization. Employees are more productive when they enjoy coming to work, feel happy to be working where they're seen as worthy and competent, and can relax into being themselves. In addition, such employees are more innovative, even without any direct reward or personal recognition. Research indicates that groups that are diverse in terms of ethnicity, age, values, background and training are more productive and innovative than homogeneous groups (Eisenberger, Fasolo, and Davis-LaMastro 1990).

The Center for Creative Leadership identified twelve companies that showed exceptional leadership in encouraging diversity. All the companies were in the top half of Fortune magazines "most admired" corporations, and 80 percent were in the top 20 percent. Rosabeth Moss Kanter (1983) found that companies with a reputation for progressive human resource practices had more profitability and financial growth than their competitors over a twenty-year period.

Contributing to Social Responsibility

The organization can become an agent for change, to make the world a better place. If one organization can thrive by creating an environment where diverse people can work effectively together, this can serve as a model for the entire world. A Los Angeles executive said, "In this area the situation is so desperate and so in need of role models, that if we in corporations can't advance minorities so they can turn around and do what needs to be done in their communities, I don't see any of us surviving. The bigger picture we have to deal with is the minority situation in this country."

MEETING NEW CHALLENGES: GLOBAL, NATIONAL, CORPORATE, AND PERSONAL

Our diversity can be our greatest source of power, and it can also be the source of our disintegration as a culture. In biology we understand the power of a diverse gene pool, but in organizations we are just beginning to learn the power of a diverse pool of ideas, viewpoints, and talents. We see the growing crime and violence almost everywhere, and the continued divisiveness and prejudice, we begin to understand the price we must pay when we don't find ways to balance diversity with unity and harmony. Unity with diversity has always been an ideal in our nation, as has equality of opportunity. Our challenge in the workplace today is to make these ideals a reality.

The global competition of the 1990s is intensifying the need to meet this challenge. The reengineering, restructuring, and downsizing of the 1990s reflect the reality that United States business can no longer afford bureaucratic, hierarchical structures with a homogeneous group running the show. We can no longer afford the luxury of paying big salaries to layer upon layer of managers to carry information back and forth between workers, managers, and staff experts, information that all can now access through their computers. We're realizing the potential power of setting up informational networks where many workers can instantly interact. We can no longer afford to pay tiers of high-salaried managers to set goals and make plans for workers and then try to motivate them and keep them productive. We're realizing that work teams and individual workers should be setting their own goals and making their own plans and that when they do they're likely to be self-motivated and work out their own productivity issues.

The problems we're facing in our business organizations reflect problems we're facing at all levels: personal problems, family problems, national problems, and global problems. As we grow in our understanding of diversity in the workplace, of the major roles of beliefs, values, stereotypes, prejudices, relationships, and access to information, we grow in understanding ourselves, our family dynamics, and our national and global priorities. As we gain skill in establishing and nurturing relationships with the whole spectrum of diverse people in the workplace, we gain skill as a national culture in working out the problems now dividing us: violent crime, ethnic conflict, inner-city decay, failing schools. If we learn how to find greater unity and harmony as a nation, we can bring this knowledge to the arena of global culture, where as a community of nations we can apply it in meeting global challenges and creating global harmony and abundance.

No wonder workplace diversity has become a hot topic! It symbolizes the key to our power in meeting challenges and creating the world we want—at every level of existence. It symbolizes the new world beyond the year 2000 and the changes we need to make in order to meet its challenges and rise to it opportunities.

BUILDING YOUR MULTICULTURAL SKILLS

Yes, the work world is a dynamic place, and it's changing more rapidly every day. It's becoming more diverse, more technical, more global, and at the same time more dependent than ever on productive working relationships. As a business leader helping to create a multicultural work environment, your success depends more and more on building your multicultural skills. And that's the purpose of this book. In working through the book, you'll use a five-step learning process, as shown in Table 1.3.

TABLE 1.3: Process for Building Multicultural Skills

Step 1. Becoming aware of culture and its pervasive influence.
Step 2. Learning about your own culture
Step 3. Recognizing your own ethnocentricity, the ways in which you stereotype, judge, and discriminate, and your emotional reactions to conflicting cultural values.
Step 4. Learning about other cultures you encounter in the workplace, so you can recognize when cultural differences may be at the root of problems and so you can appreciate the contributions people from diverse cultures can make to the work situation.
Step 5. Building interaction skills and practicing new behaviors through exercises and cases.

You'll begin building and practicing these skills right away, and you can continue building them throughout your career. Let's review the part that each chapter plays.

Laying the Groundwork. In chapters 2 and 3 you'll work through steps 1, 2, and 3. In chapter 2 you'll start becoming aware of culture's pervasive influence, and learn some key cultural patterns that will help you compare cultures. You'll become more aware of key aspects of the American culture and of typical corporate cultures. In chapter 3 you'll begin to recognize your own biases and learn about the nature of prejudice. These chapters lay the groundwork for building your skills; they're the necessary background you'll need.

Building the Framework. In chapters 4 through 12 you'll work through steps 4 and 5. You'll build the multicultural skills framework, a structure for housing your new skills. Here you'll focus on learning about other cultures, building interaction skills, and practicing new skills. The process you'll use is based on asking the right questions, and the chapters are structured to give you some answers. The step-by-step sequence is shown in Table 1.4.

In Chapters 4 through 11 you get to learn about the cultures of others, ranging from the ways men and women live in parallel worlds within a culture to various African American, Asian American, and Latino American subcultures, to the culture-like aspects of life experienced by such groups as gay persons, persons with disabilities, and older persons. While the latter are not *ethnic* subcultures, most members rely heavily on their own networks and communities, forming a subculture in the process. You'll begin building interaction skills and practicing them.

Chapter 12 ties the leadership challenges and opportunities together from an organizational viewpoint. You'll focus on how you can influence the organization toward creating a multicultural climate in which all types of employees can be productive and comfortable.

TABLE 1.4: Process for Learning About Other Cultures and
Building Interaction Skills: Steps 4 and 5

Key Questions	Chapter Structure
• What are the key barriers to career success for this group?————————>	• Myths versus reality—that reflect stereotypes, prejudice
• How did it get that way?——————>	• Background or evolution of situation
• What's going on now?————————>	• Current profile
• What does the current profile mean?—>	• Cultural themes, patterns, issues
• What skills do I need to interact with these employees?————————————>	• Leadership Challenges and Opportunities
• How can I apply my new knowledge and practice multicultural skills?—————>	• Exercises and cases

SUMMARY

The workplace is changing dramatically, with minorities and women moving into all types of positions, including executive, managerial, technical, and professional jobs. In fact, about 85 percent of new employees are now women and minorities. Business relationships are more diverse than ever, and diverse groups have diverse issues that are important to them. Suppliers and customers are ever more international in scope, and they, along with global competition, are changing the way we do business. Self-managing work teams and more highly-educated employees call for new ways of leading.

The melting-pot myth has traditionally assumed that all employees would assimilate into a common corporate culture, but people who don't look like the dominant workplace group, Euro-American men, have never "melted in." To overcome the discrimination and workplace barriers minority employees have experienced, civil rights laws were enacted in the late 1960s.

EEO allows employees to directly complain about discrimination, but individuals find this a difficult path that usually entails severe career setbacks. AA works in the background for most employees but has proven much more powerful than EEO in opening career doors. It requires that all employers who obtain federal government contracts develop and implement AA plans for hiring and promoting minorities. Backlash and resistance to AA have been reflected in claims of reverse discrimination, lower job standards for minorities, and beliefs that minorities are hired or promoted into good jobs only to fill "quotas." The way to prevent these problems is for the leaders of organizations to make a commitment to diversity, to value diversity, and to create corporate systems and cultures that support employees from all groups.

This multicultural approach to managing diversity has many advantages for organizations, including attracting and retaining the best available human talent, increasing organizational flexibility, gaining and keeping greater market share, reducing costs, improving the quality of management, creating and innovating more powerfully, solving problems more effectively, increasing productivity, and contributing to social responsibility.

REFERENCES

Carr-Ruffino, N., et al. "Legal Aspects of Women's Advancement" in *Woman Power*. Thousand Oaks, CA: Sage, 1991.

Carr-Ruffino, N. *The Promotable Woman*. Belmont, CA: Wadsworth, 1992.

Carr-Ruffino, N. "U.S. Women: Breaking Through the Glass Ceiling." *Women in Management Review* 6, no. 5 (1991).

Carter, Jimmy. "Keeping Faith with the World's Women." *The Atlanta Constitution* (March 8, 1995) A-11.

Eisenberger, R., P. Fasolo, and V. Davis-LaMastro. "Perceived Organizational Support and Employee Diligence, Commitment, and Innovation." *Journal of Applied Psychology* 75, no. 1 (1990): 51–59.

Faludi, Susan. *Backlash*. New York: Doubleday, 1991.

Green, K.W. *Affirmative Action and Principles of Justice*. New York: Greenwood, 1989.

Jackson, S.E. "Team Composition in Organizational Settings" in *Group Process and Productivity*. Thousand Oaks, CA: Sage, 1991.

Kanter, Rosabeth Moss. *The Change Masters*. New York: Simon & Schuster, 1983.

Kanter, Rosabeth Moss. "Transcending Business Boundaries: 12,000 World Managers View Change." *Harvard Business Review* (May/June 1991): 151–164.

Krauthammer, C., "A Defense of Quotas." *The New Republic* (September 16–23, 1985): 9–11.

Leonard, J. "The Impact of Affirmative Action on Employment." Cambridge, MA: National Bureau of Economics Research, Reprint no. 535, 1984b.

Leonard, J. "Affirmative Action as Earnings Redistribution." *Journal of Labor Economics* 3, no. 3 (1985) 363–384.

Leonard, J. *Antidiscrimination or Reverse Discrimination*? Berkeley, CA: Institute of Industrial Relations, Reprint no. 457, 1984a.

Leonard, J. "What Was Affirmative Action?" *American Economic Review* (May, 1986): 359–363.

Leonard, J. *Women and Affirmative Action in the 1980s*. Paper presented at the Annual Meeting of the American Economic Association, 1988.

Marshall, Jonathan. "Minority Policy—Gainers, Losers." *San Francisco Chronicle* (July 31, 1995).

Potomac Institute. *A Decade of New Opportunity: Affirmative Action in the 1970s*. Washington, DC: Potomac Institute, 1984.

Siegal, S., and W. Kaemmerer. "Measuring the Perceived Support for Innovation in Organizations." *Journal of Applied Psychology* 63, no. 5 (1978): 553–562.

Simons, G.F., C. Vazquez, and P.R. Harris. *Transcultural Leadership*. Houston, TX: Gulf, 1993.

Simpson, Peggy. "Affirmative Action in Action," *Working Woman* (March, 1984): 104.

U.S. Commission on Civil Rights. "Affirmative Action in the 1980s: Dismantling the Process of Discrimination." Clearinghouse Publication 70, 1981.

U.S. Department of Labor. *A Report on the Glass Ceiling Initiative*, 1991.

U.S. Dept. of Labor, Employment Standards Administration. "Employment of Minorities and Women in Federal Contractor and Noncontractor Establishments, 1974–1980," unpublished final draft (The Crump Report), 1984.

Woody, Bette. "Black Women in the New Service Economy," working paper no. 196. Wellesley, MA: Wellesley College Center for Research on Women, 1989.

CHAPTER 2

Understanding Cultures: Your Own and Others

*Individuals, sharing the same belief, form a collective consciousness
that can define and shape the world.*
Harry Palmer

Culture is the collective programming of individual's minds that determines how a group of individuals perceives reality. In fact, we the people in a culture collectively agree on what reality is. We agree on the beliefs that form the foundation of the culture, on which beliefs are most important, and on what the culture values the most. We agree on the rules, the do's and don'ts, the norms by which people will live and be judged. And these basic agreements differ from culture to culture. Therefore, if you as a leader want to deal effectively with workers who come from various "realities," you must understand their cultures and your own. Cultural understanding gives you some clues about why people from various cultures and subcultures think and act as they do. It will also help you to maintain your balance and poise when culture clash occurs—and help others to maintain theirs.

What's a Value?

A *value* is an enduring belief that one way of acting or being is preferable to another. A *value system* is an organization of such beliefs along a continuum of relative importance, a prioritizing of beliefs into a set or cluster.

Culture clash occurs when an employee's sense of rightness is challenged by conflicting beliefs and values held by someone from another culture. The employee may respond with several emotions, such as confusion, frustration, disgust, and anger, which tend to block the resolution of the conflict. Typical outcomes are communication breakdown and poor working relationships. Moreover, if such emotional responses are frequent and intense and are not adequately handled, they can lead to stress and even illness. Being able to recognize cultural patterns and differences can help you handle such cultural conflict and the accompanying emotions with greater ease.

You can see that as a leader, you'll do well to move out of your cultural cave, take off your cultural blinders, and enjoy a more universal view of the workplace. In the first part of this chapter you'll learn the basics of culture: what culture is, how we learn it, and how it shapes our view of reality. You'll also learn about some basic cultural patterns that will help you understand how people from other cultures see reality.

An important part of gaining multicultural leadership skills is understanding your own cultural programming. Assuming that at least part of your cultural background is American, you need to address the question, How is being an American different from being some other nationality? The better you understand your own culture, the better you can understand people from other cultures. To function well in a diverse workplace and a global marketplace, you need to attain a worldwide perspective. It's similar to climbing the highest mountain you can find, looking around at other world cultures, and then looking at the American culture. In the second part of this chapter we'll explore some basics about American culture, as others see us, including the American business culture and some typical corporate culture patterns. So, on to the first two steps to gaining multicultural skills:

> *Step 1:* Becoming aware of culture and its pervasive influence

> *Step 2:* Understanding your own culture

Before we discuss cultures, test your current knowledge by completing Self-Awareness Activity 2.1.

Self-Awareness Activity 2.1: What Do You Know about Cultures?

Purpose: To see what you know about the issues covered in this chapter.
Instructions: Determine whether you think the following statements are basically true or false—and think about why. The answers will emerge in this chapter, and the summary at the end of the chapter focuses on these issues.

1. The most important aspects of culture are those that people don't talk about.
2. People from different cultures experience different realities.
3. Most cultures accept inequality in power and status and consider it normal.
4. Most cultures of the world value achievement over interpersonal relationships.
5. A dominant American value is putting membership in an ingroup ahead of self-interest.
6. Most Americans tend to see situations in black-or-white terms.
7. The dominant American view of humans and nature is that we must live in harmony with nature.
8. Americans in general tend to develop a few deeply committed friendships rather than many friends.
9. Corporate cultures need heroes mainly because people love a good story.
10. Strong corporate cultures are on their way out.

UNDERSTANDING THE BASICS OF CULTURE

The major goal in understanding the basics of culture is to understand that we create it and we learn it and each major cultural group creates it somewhat differently. We'll discuss the key concepts of what culture is; what we mean by the hierarchy of culture, from world culture to corporate culture; and how we learn about our own culture.

What Is Culture?

Culture is like the air we breathe: We take it for granted, rarely think about it, and assume our world viewpoint is merely the human viewpoint. We can work more powerfully with people from other cultures if we understand some key concepts of what culture is all about, how it affects our personal reality, and how we learn the beliefs, values, and rules of our culture. Culture is as pervasive and invisible as the air around us. It's our programmed beliefs, many of them hidden, our mental map, our view of reality.

Culture as Programmed Beliefs

Culture is the collective programming of the mind, the learning process that results in the members of one group of people being different from those of another. Culture is a characteristic, not of individuals, but of people who were conditioned by similar educational and life experiences. A cultural group may refer to a tribe, regional group, minority, majority, or nation. Culture becomes crystallized in the institutions that people build together: family structure, educational structure, religious organizations, associations, forms of government, work organizations, law, literature, settlement patterns, buildings, and even scientific theories. All of these structures reflect common *beliefs* that are rooted in the common culture (Hofstede 1984, 1991).

Culture is learned, but it is far more than mere custom that can be easily changed from the outside, even though it's always changing and evolving naturally from the inside. Different cultures have different ways of organizing life, of thinking, and of conceiving the underlying assumptions about the family, the state, the economic system, and of humanity itself and its role in the universe, as indicated in Table 2.1. Harvard anthropologist E.T. Hall views culture primarily as a form of communication, the link between people and the means they have of interacting with each other (Hall 1981, 1982, 1989). Many experts say that culture is very closely related to what has been defined as *mind*, and may be synonymous with it.

TABLE 2.1: Content of Culture

Consensus reality of a group
How we agree to create our reality
Ways of thinking, feeling, speaking, acting
Obvious aspects and hidden aspects
High priority beliefs = values, the roots or foundation of culture

Culture as Hidden Programming

Beneath the clearly perceived, highly explicit surface culture, there lies a whole other world, a world of hidden beliefs and motives. When we understand this world, we may radically change our view of human nature. Hall says that culture hides much more than it reveals, and what it hides, it hides most effectively from its own members.

Most people strongly believe that their cultural behavior patterns are "human nature," and resist believing that such behavior is learned and can vary from culture to culture. It is quite common to grow up and mature in a culture with little or no knowledge of the basic laws that make the culture work and that differentiate it from all other cultures. Therefore, most people are unaware of the extent to which culture is a major influence on behavior. We are socialized in our culture without much conscious awareness of the fact. We normally think about our own culture only when it comes into conflict with some aspect of another culture (Brislin and Yoshida 1994). The cultural unconscious, those "hidden" cultural systems that have as yet to be made explicit, probably outnumber the explicit, conscious systems by a factor of a thousand or more to one.

Lionel Trilling once likened culture to a prison. When we can define the prison, we can begin to plot our own jailbreak. Culture imprisons us in many unknown ways, but the bars that limit our possibilities are woven of our habits and nothing more—habitual beliefs, attitudes, and ways of thinking and feeling, along with customary actions based on long-forgotten decisions we made (Trilling 1955).

Culture as a Mental Map of Reality

As soon as we're born, our parents begin teaching us about consensus reality, helping us build the mental map we need to function in our particular culture. Anthropologists agree on three characteristics of culture:

- Culture is learned, not innate.
- The various facets of culture are interrelated. If you touch a culture in one place, everything else is affected.
- Culture is shared, and it defines the boundaries of different groups.

There is not one aspect of human life that is not touched and altered by culture. Culture is the medium or context within which humans live (Hall 1981).

Culture as Personal Reality

How we view reality and how we create our own reality is tied to how we are socialized within our culture. Putting together what many anthropologists and psychologists have discovered about reality, one way of picturing its elements is shown in Table 2.2. The psychological raw materials from which we create reality are aspects of our mind, such as our beliefs, attitudes, feelings, thoughts, choice, and action decisions. The tools for changing our reality are also aspects of our mind, namely our imagination, desires, and expectancy. Through imagination we picture, envision, and dream new, different aspects of reality. Imagination is our tool for creating new ideas and adopting innovative approaches. Our desires fire our motivation and are the basis for our purposes, intentions, and goals. Our expectancy refers to our trust or confidence that we can change aspects of our reality. We use these tools on the content or raw materials of our reality, and the most powerful parts to use them on are the belief part and the action choice part. Beliefs are at the root of every aspect of our reality, so when we change a key belief, we shift our reality. Action choices are especially powerful fulcrum points of change because actions tend to get immediate results that we can see and experience, so they may change our reality quickly.

TABLE 2.2: Elements of Reality: Mental Map

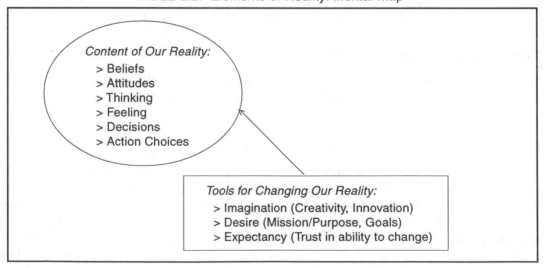

What Are Cultures Within Cultures?

In the past we thought of a culture as a relatively large group of people within a nation or geographic region who spoke the same language and embraced similar beliefs and practices. Now we recognize a diversity and hierarchy of cultures, ranging in size and scope from the whole world to a small corporation, as indicated in Table 2.3. There are about 5.5 billion people on Earth, living in about 6,000 different cultures, each with its own spoken language. Between 4,000 and 5,000 of those cultures are indigenous tribes, such as the American Indians. They number only about 200 million people, most living as small subcultures within some larger dominant society (World 1993).

TABLE 2.3: Hierarchy of Cultures

World culture	=	humanity
Major culture	=	a regional or national group with a common culture
Subculture	=	a cultural group within a major culture
Corporate culture	=	an organization within a major culture

Is there really a global culture? Humanity *does* have certain cultural commonalties, so we've always had the potential to become a global culture, but we lacked the necessary frequency and intensity of communication. We are rapidly becoming a global culture in many ways, a trend that's accelerating. Leavitt (1983, 94) states that "a powerful force drives the world toward a converging commonality, and that force is technology." Through advances in communication and transportation, most of us know what's happening in other parts of the world. For example, more than a billion people watch the television news channel, CNN. When the Chinese government clamped down on a student demonstration in Tiananmen Square in 1989, a global audience was watching. People around the world also see the commercials on such stations as MTV and CNN and are more aware than ever of new products becoming available. As a result of such global communication, governments are called upon to be more accountable for their actions. And people in formerly remote, isolated places are determined to become a part of the global marketplace.

Major regions, such as Asia, have many cultural commonalties, a Far East culture, in some ways. Yet within one small nation, Malaysia, there are many subcultures with distinct languages, religious beliefs, customs, and so forth. Likewise, in the United States, although we have a distinct American culture, there are numerous subcultures, such as Malaysian American.

To complicate matters, we have *corporate* cultures, usually established on the basis of Euro-American male values, norms, and customs, but each having its own flavor and peculiarities. These corporate cultures are changing at an increasingly rapid pace as women and people from various subcultural groups move into positions of power and influence.

All this gives us a broad-brush picture of what culture is. To fill in some of the details, we'll discuss how cultures develop in the first place.

How Do We Learn Our Culture?

Cultures have specific ways of teaching values and norms. Primary message systems communicate how the culture views the world and does things. Cultures use such techniques as symbols and *myths* within the message systems, most often communicating through networks of relationships and the grapevine. The methods used to pass on cultural values and norms are education, direction, and role modeling.

> A *myth* is a story or saying whose function is to bind together the thoughts of a group and promote coordinated social action.

The primary message systems that communicate cultural values and norms serve to tell people how to do most everything they do. According to Hall (1982) they are:

- *How we interact with our environment.*
- *How we associate with others,* the way we organize our society and its parts, the role of hierarchy, rank, and status.

- *How we meet our survival needs,* including everything from individual food habits to the economy of a country.
- *How we learn.*
- *How we differentiate male and female behavior.* (Usually when a given behavior pattern becomes associated with one gender, it will be dropped by the other.)
- *How we use space,* our sense of territoriality and personal space.
- *How we use time,* which is tied to life's cycles and rhythms. Whether we focus on a linear, circular, or present-moment approach to time involves how we emphasize the past, present, and future aspects of life.
- *How we play,* relax, enjoy ourselves, and use our leisure time, and what our sense of humor is like.
- *How we defend ourselves* against potentially hostile forces in nature and against destructive forces within ourselves. Defense includes the types of armed forces, law enforcement agencies, religions, and medical practices a culture embraces.
- *How we use things,* including money, transportation, equipment, houses, furniture, clothes, weapons, and all technology.

How we do things sends messages to everyone in the culture about our basic beliefs, values, norms, and unspoken rules. *The ways we communicate* these basics include symbols, slogans, metaphors, and myths and stories, with heroes and heroines. The *media* we most often use are networks and the grapevine, and in recent years written and electronic media, as indicated in Table 2.4. Culture has been handed down for millions of years so the traditional way is by word of mouth. According to an old Indian saying:

> *The people must tell their stories and sing their songs or the land (and culture) will die.*

Hall identifies three major teaching/learning methods that cultures use to convey primary message systems to succeeding generations. They include (1) education and training, (2) correction and direction, and (3) role modeling. We educate and train people, beginning in childhood, usually in a very conscious way. We also correct people when they do something the culture considers wrong or improper, and we direct them in the right way to think and act, also primarily in a conscious way. When we serve as role models, it's usually not in order to teach children and others how to think and act; we're just "being ourselves." But toddlers watch their parents and adults watch their heroes or heroines and learn from them and emulate them. Role modeling is probably the most powerful teaching mechanism and we're rarely aware that it's going on.

TABLE 2.4: Essentials of Communicating the Culture

How we do things communicates our:
- beliefs and values
- norms—do's and don'ts
- informal, unspoken rules

The ways we communicate include:
- symbols
- slogans
- metaphors
- myths and stories with heroes/heroines

The media we most often use to communicate are:
- networks of relationships
- the grapevine
- written and electronic means

The teaching/learning methods we use are:
- education and training
- correction and direction
- role modeling

What does this mean for you as a business leader? It means that if you want to create an environment that challenges and supports all types of employees, you must first and foremost be a role model to others. You must hold the beliefs and attitudes that value diversity. Your thinking and feeling, your decisions and day-to-day action choices must reflect your respect for people from all groups. As a leader, it's important to give effective education and training for valuing diversity. It's also important to set up organizational systems that detect and correct discrimination and other diversity problems. But most of all, you must be a role model by "walking your talk."

HOW DO CULTURES DIFFER?

When we consider all the life forms that we're aware of, it's clear that humans throughout the world are amazingly alike. Yet our differences can make it difficult or impossible to communicate and work together effectively. The purpose of this book is to help you understand where our major differences lie so that you can figure out ways to reconcile and respect differences and to find common ground for working with people from diverse backgrounds. The United States probably has the most diverse society in the world. Within our American culture we have many subcultures, each with its own unique set of values and customs. Before exploring some major ways in which cultures differ, do a brief self-analysis about your own cultural orientation by completing Self-Awareness Activity 2.2.

Self-Awareness Activity 2.2: What's Your Cultural Orientation?

Purpose: To determine your personal orientation regarding key cultural factors.
Instructions: For each of the following numbered pairs of statements, circle A or B according to which statement *best* reflects your orientation.

1. A. I create my life by what I do and by what I allow.
    B. I'm just a cog in the wheel of life. Most of what happens to me is outside my control.

2. A. My top priority is to achieve my personal goals.
    B. My top priority is to be a good son/daughter, wife/husband, boss/worker, mother/daughter, that is, to fulfill those roles expected of me.

3. A. I'm happiest when I'm ahead or winning.
    B. I'm happiest when I'm working or playing with friends, family, or co-workers.

4. A. My top priority at work is getting the job done.
    B. My top priority at work is maintaining good relationships with people.

5. A. If a top manager asked me to discuss my ideas, I'd be comfortable.
    B. If a top manager asked me to discuss my ideas, I'd be nervous and uncomfortable.

6. A. People who have talent and work hard can become very successful.
    B. People need the right family background and connections to become very successful.

7. A. My motto is "Nothing risked, nothing gained."
    B. My motto is "Stick with the tried and true."

8. A. I believe that "the exception makes the rule" and rules were made to be broken occasionally.
    B. I believe that we must stick to the rules of the game or we'll have chaos.

Follow-up: Analyze your responses by reading the answer key at the end of this chapter and the following discussion in this chapter.

Some major cultural differences include gender differences and the overriding pattern of dependence, independence and interdependence. The major factors that determine the degree of independence people in a culture tend to have are outlined in Table 2.5 and discussed next.

Gender as a Cultural Group. Do males essentially live a different culture from females? Several diversity experts say yes. Evidence indicates that the socialization of people in most societies of the world is greatly influenced by gender, and in each culture the women, as a group, hold a distinctly different worldview from the men (Cox 1993, 6; Belenky et al., 86; Tannen 1990; Fottler and Bain 1980; Rosener 1990). Here are some specific ways their socialization differs :

- Men and women have different ways of learning and creating knowledge; boys and girls play differently.
- Role modeling behaviors of fathers is different from that of mothers.
- The media portrays men/boys differently from women/girls.

Independence Level as an Overriding Pattern. Gender groups, ethnic groups, and national groups differ culturally in at least eight major areas, as shown in Table 2.5. The patterns to the left are typical of men in Western cultures, while those in the middle column are typical of most women in all cultures and of men and women in most Asian, Latino, and African cultures, in fact of most of the world's peoples. It is interesting to note that the patterns in the left-hand column all tend to correlate with a fairly high level of independence, while those in the middle and right-hand columns correlate with a dependent or interdependent worldview. An interdependent focus is typical of a post-industrial economy and contains elements of the me-first and us-first orientations. Autonomous people choose to put the work team first in order to achieve greater things together. The focus is on people-first in order to achieve together, and equality, risk taking, and direct communication are valued. See also Table 2.9 concerning the virtual corporation and Table 2.10 concerning the economic system's effect on cultural values at the end of this chapter.

I Control or I'm Controlled?

The most basic beliefs we have are probably about who or what creates our environment and causes the events within that environment. How much is caused by our own attitudes and actions? How much by a Supreme Being? How much is just chance or coincidence? Beliefs about the cause of life events tend to affect every other aspect of culture. People with an internal source of control believe that they determine their own reality, destiny, and life experiences to a great extent, either by what they do or by what they allow to happen, or both. They are therefore relatively autonomous, independent people and include most people from Western cultures, especially Euro-Americans (Rotter 1966; Spector 1982).

People with an external source of control believe that things happen to them and that they have little control over their lives. They are therefore relatively dependent on others, on fate, luck, chance and other external factors. This is sometimes called fatalism. They may often say, "It's God's will," while people in more independent or interdependent cultures may say, "God helps those who help themselves." Cultures that reflect a primarily external source of control are Latino, African, Arab, and some Asian cultures (Tse et al. 1988; Delgado 1981; Asante and Asante 1985; Redding 1982; Orpen and Nkohande 1977; Ramirez 1988; Helms and Giorgis 1980; Cote and Tansuhaj 1989).

TABLE 2.5: Overview of Major Patterns of Cultural Difference

Independent Focus	*Dependent Focus*	*Interdependent Focus*
Internal Source of Control: I control my life *Individualism:* me-first; fewer ties, loose ties with others	**External Source of Control:** life happens to me *Collectivism:* us-first; close ties with ingroup members	**Internal Source of Control:** I control my life *Combination:* independent persons choose to team up.
Achievement: competitive, masculine, focus on material things and tasks	*Personal connection:* cooperative, feminine, focus on relationships and intangibles	*Combination:* people-first in order to achieve as work teams.
Equality: democratic, give-and-take authority	*Class difference:* status, rank, defer to authority	*Equality*
Risk-taking: I can handle uncertainty; leads to openness, flexibility, focus on future change	*Security-seeking:* I must avoid uncertainty; leads to being rigid, rules-oriented, w/focus on tradition, the status quo	*Risk-taking*
Time use: linear, single-task	*Time use:* circular, multiple task	*Time use:* combination linear and circular; flexible
Space use: distant	*Space use:* close for members	*Space use:* flexible combination
Communication: direct *Economic system:* industrial	*Communication:* direct *Economic system:* agricultural	*Communication:* direct *Economic system:* post-industrial

Me–First or Us–First?

Cultures that focus on me-first are called individualist cultures because they believe that each individual must first take responsibility for her or his own life and should have the freedom to succeed or fail. Cultures that focus on us-first are called collectivist cultures because individuals are seen first as members of a family or cohesive group. It's similar to looking at a bouquet. Do you focus first on each individual flower and then notice how the group forms a bouquet? Or do you focus on the bouquet with the attitude that one flower alone would be out of context and lost?

Many analysts suggest that the me-first versus us-first aspect of culture is the single most important concept for understanding what goes on when people from different cultures get together. Whether our primary outlook is me-first or us-first greatly influences our goals and priorities. The most important difference between collectivists and individualists is the emphasis they place on the opinions and feelings of group members (what will they think?) and the psychological closeness between themselves and others (how does this affect our relationship?) (Kagitcibasi 1990; Brislin and Yoshida, 1994; Hofstede 1980; Hui 1990; Kim et al. 1994).

Individualism and collectivism refer to the degree to which people in a culture believe that a person's beliefs and actions should be independent of the group's thought and action. Us-first collectivists believe that individuals should integrate their thoughts and actions with those of a group; for example, the extended family or the work organization. Me-first individualists are more likely to pursue their own personal goals, while collectivists are more likely to integrate their own goals with those of group members. Certainly, everyone has personal desires and goals they want to pursue and everyone needs to belong to at least one group. The concept revolves around priorities and emphases. What is the relative weight we place on fulfilling the need to belong and the need to do our own thing, especially when these needs conflict?

Cut the apron strings or not? In individualist cultures, members are likely to cut the apron strings when they reach adulthood in a more complete way than do members of collectivist cultures (Hall 1979). For individualists, from birth to death, life is punctuated by separations, many of them painful. Paradoxically, each separation forms a foundation for new stages of integration, identity, and psychic growth. The newborn baby experiences himself and his small universe as one, inseparable. To be truly alive in the Euro-American culture, you must outgrow this state, and the full impact of the process comes when you leave home and establish yourself as an independent person. Conversely, in collectivist cultures, the bonds with the parents, grandparents, and even ancestors are not severed but are maintained and reinforced.

Individual Differences. It's important to remember that some people within an individualist culture may have predominantly us-first collectivist values. Women in all cultures tend to be socialized to be somewhat collectivist, for example. People in individualist cultures can also adopt collectivist values from their family, their subculture, or their religion (Brislin and Yoshida 1994).

Loose Ties = Individualist

America is one of the most loosely knit cultures of modern times. In loosely knit individualist societies, the individual is highly differentiated from others. Growing up means becoming an individual who is distinctly separate from others. Failure in life is the "sin" of the individual and may lead to guilt and separation. In such a society the collective goals of the family, ingroup, or community are often subordinated to the needs of individuals. This largely Western mind-set is held by a minority of the world's people and is most strongly held among Americans. The mind-set tends to be stronger in males than in females. Key values are autonomy, self-reliance, self-identity, emotional independence, and individual initiative. Major workplace values are job challenge, achievement, and ambition (Hofstede 1984).

In such *self-interest* cultures, people are loosely integrated (low context). Individuals look primarily after their self-interest and the interests of their immediate family. A high-quality life means individual success, achievement, self-actualization, and self-respect. In the workplace people seek the satisfaction of a job well done, especially by their own standards. When they attend a university, people are primarily motivated by a need to master their subject. Preserving self-respect and avoiding guilt are important. Job life and private life are usually sharply separated. Getting tasks done is more important than spending time on work relationships.

Many Ties That Bind = Collectivist

In more tightly-woven collectivist societies, individuals are viewed in the context of social relationships, such as the family, the organization, the community. They are less differentiated as a self in contrast with others. "We" is usually more important than "I." An individual's failure causes others to "lose face" and results in shame, so it should be covered up and not seen. This mind-set predominates in Eastern cultures, and is held by a majority of the world's people.

Key concepts are protection by the ingroup, loyalty to the ingroup, identity that stems from the group and the social system, membership in groups and organizations as the ideal mode, emotional dependence on organizations, belief in group decisions, friendships predetermined by stable social relationships, and need for prestige within these relationships. The organization or group provides expertise, order, duty, and security. Value standards differ for ingroups and outgroups. People are expected to be loyal first to their parents, relatives, and clan; and life achievement and satisfaction consists of living up to those loyalties.

Individuals perceive themselves as belonging to one or more close ingroups from which they cannot detach themselves. The ingroup may be an extended family, clan, or organization, which protects the interests of its members but in turn expects their permanent loyalty. A high quality of life is defined primarily in family and group terms. Children think of themselves as "we" rather than "I." If you gain success and wealth, you're expected to share it with your ingroup.

When they attend a university, people in a collectivist society are motivated to pass their exams in order to acquire the status of a degree. People seek the satisfaction of a job well recognized. Preserving face, or the respect from one's ingroup, and avoiding shame, are important. Job life and private life are inseparable. The company may intrude in the worker's private life and the worker expects the company to help out with family or personal problems. On the job, relationships take precedence over getting tasks done. An essential precondition for achieving a task is developing a relationship with the other person so he or she can become adopted into the ingroup (Hofstede 1984).

Some anthropologists make a further distinction among tightly woven collectivist groups: the "earthy" cultures and the "stylized" cultures. Earthy cultures include American Indian, African, Latino, Pacific Island, and most Arab cultures. Function and style are one, for they value things that are functional and at the same time express beauty or meaning and honor mythology and nature. Stylized cultures include the Chinese, Japanese, Korean, East Indian, and Thai cultures. They feature many close, irreplaceable connections and are highly structured, with strict expectations, roles, and lifestyles. They're based on the most numerous ties of all and on the closest, most binding relationships.

Achievement–First or People–First?

Some cultures value most highly a person's (or group's) achievements. Other cultures place greater value on building and maintaining strong interpersonal relationships. Some of the achievement-first values overlap with the me-first values, while people-first values often overlap with us-first patterns, for rather obvious reasons. An achievement orientation reflects traditional masculine values, while a people-first orientation reflects feminine values. However, in both types of cultures men dominate the political and work arenas.

Achievement–First = Focus on Competition and "Things" = Masculine Aspect

Achievement-oriented cultures focus on achievement for men. They define very different social roles for men and women, with a focus on clear gender roles. They tend to be patriarchal, materialistic, performance-oriented, and factual. Independence is the ideal, ambition is the motivation, live-in-order-to-work is the viewpoint, and machismo is valued. Men are expected to be assertive, ambitious, and competitive, to strive for material success, and to respect whatever is big, strong, and fast. Women are expected to serve and care for the intangible qualities of life, for the children, and for the weak. Political and corporate values stress material success and assertiveness. The most masculine culture by far is Japan's, while the United States culture is moderately masculine.

People–First = Connecting, Cooperating = Feminine Aspect

Relationship-oriented cultures focus on building and maintaining positive interpersonal relationships. They also feature gender equality and quality of life other than the material things in life. Intuition is highly valued, service is the chief motivating drive, and working in order to live is more the case than living for one's work. The most cooperative cultures are the Scandinavian ones.

In such feminine-value cultures men and women tend to focus on their interpersonal relationships with people in general (not just with ingroups, as in collectivist cultures). They allow much overlap in the social roles of men and women. Neither men nor women need be to ambitious, competitive, or focused on material success. Men and women may respect whatever is small, weak, and slow. Values within political and work organizations center around interpersonal relationships and concern for the weak.

Research indicates that while Euro-Americans, especially men, tend to be highly competitive in social interaction and in task performance, Latino Americans, African Americans and Asian

Americans favor a more cooperative approach (Cox, Lobel, and McLeod, 1991; Kagan and Madsen 1971; DeVos 1980).

Equality or Not?

Some cultures, primarily Western ones, are based on the belief that all persons have equal value and status as human beings. People are therefore entitled to equal opportunity to achieve and advance in the society. Other cultures accept the belief that some people are naturally more powerful, affluent, and privileged than others. They therefore accept the inequality of rank and status in a hierarchical or stratified society.

In the workplace, the degree of equality or rank/status is sometimes called "power distance," which is one measure of how strongly we feel the need to depend on more powerful people.

Inequality = Rank/Status Cultures

In rank/status cultures, power distance is high. Organizations tend to feature hierarchical organizational structures (picture a pyramid), power inequality, autocratic leadership, dependence on leaders, centralized decision making, and the belief that power lies with a few strong leaders. People have strong dependence needs on higher-ups. While people may aspire to democracy as an impersonal ideal, they expect superiors to behave autocratically and don't expect to be consulted. Ideal superiors are benevolent autocrats or patriarchs, good father types that subordinates can depend on. Superiors are expected to enjoy special privilege and be exempt from certain rules and laws. Status symbols are widely used and contribute to the superiors' authority in the eyes of subordinates. Organizations are identified with one or more powerful individuals. Change comes about by decree from top individuals or by revolution. Nearly all so-called Third World countries have such vertical societies. When people from these cultures move to Western countries to work, they often initially feel lost because bosses don't give them clear orders or take as much personal interest in them.

Hierarchical cultures are virtually always collectivist cultures. They value deference to authority and sensitivity to status. This is part of going along with the group. Bosses in such cultures may appear arrogant and aloof to individualists, who tend to believe that bosses and employees are basically equal human beings. Such bosses may seem to flaunt the privileges of status, such as fine cars, drivers, and elite dining rooms in contrast to workers who ride the bus and eat from a lunch box (Brislin and Yoshida 1994).

The boss-centered workplace, in which the boss calls the shots is the norm. Workers are not expected to initiate communication with the boss nor to speak up unless called upon to do so. Bosses are respected in and out of the workplace and are not to be publicly contradicted. Employees' status is higher when the status of the boss and the company is higher.

Equality = Democratic Cultures

Equality of power is referred to as small power distance. Key concepts are democratic leadership, independence or interdependence, flat organizational structures, decentralized decision making, and the belief that position power lies in the role, not in the superiority of the person. In general, women are more likely than men to manage in a democratic way (Eagly and Johnson 1990).

In moderately egalitarian cultures—such as in the United States, Japan, and most European countries—consultation is usually appreciated but not necessarily expected. Participative environments are initiated by the participative leader, not by subordinates. Ideal leaders are pragmatically democratic. Moderate status differences and privileges for leaders are acceptable. Rules and laws are expected to apply to superiors and subordinates alike. Change normally starts with the top leaders, but key people throughout the organization must buy into the change if it is to be effective and lasting.

In very egalitarian cultures—such as in the Scandinavian countries, Israel, and Austria—subjecting yourself to the power of others is seen as undesirable. Everyone should have a say in everything that concerns them. Status differences are suspect. Ideal leaders are democratic and loyally carry out the will of their groups. Change comes about through group consensus. Leaders must persuade and influence the group. Former leaders are usually comfortable with accepting new, less powerful roles, for the power differential is in the roles, not the people who fill them.

Take Risks or Play It Safe?

Cultures that value playing it safe are high in "uncertainty avoidance." This term refers to the extent to which people are comfortable with unstructured, unclear, or unpredictable situations, and the extent to which they try to avoid such situations by adopting strict codes of behavior and a belief in absolute truths.

Take risks. Cultures where people are more comfortable with uncertainty tend to be risk-taking cultures. When people don't fear "reasonable" risks, they are more open to change and more forward-looking, anticipating the payoff from their investment in future changes. New ways of doing things, new products and services, and new technology are highly valued. Mottoes may include "nothing ventured, nothing gained" and "rules are made to be broken." People in risk-taking cultures also tend to be more contemplative and tolerant, and less aggressive and emotional than those in play-it-safe cultures. The United States has a moderately risk-taking culture, and Singapore is by far the most risk-taking culture studied by Hofstede (1984).

Play it safe. In cultures where most people are intent on avoiding uncertainty, some ways they try to provide certainty include:

- focusing on rules and refusing to tolerate deviance
- providing structure through precise relationships, assignments, and schedules
- arranging life so that everyone knows what to expect

Since change creates many unknowns and uncertainties, people in these cultures resist change more than others. They focus on tradition, and therefore the past, and often become quite rigid in these matters. People in play-it-safe cultures also tend to be more active, aggressive, emotional, security-seeking, and intolerant. Greece is the most certainty-oriented culture, followed by Japan. Most European and Latino cultures fall into this pattern to some extent.

National Patterns

Hofstede (1984) found that me-first countries tended to value equality, and *us-first* countries tended to value rank/status. This was the strongest correlation for any pair of traits. Most nations are us-first, rank/status cultures. The majority of me-first, equality cultures are relatively wealthy Western countries. Some *achievement-first* countries tend to be risk-taking, while others are play-it-safe, and the same is true for people-first countries.

Values concerning independence, individualism, achievement, equality, and risk taking have proven to be powerful ways to understand cultural differences. Other important factors include how people use time and space, how directly they communicate, and the type of economy they have, which we'll discuss next.

Time: Step-by-Step or Dive-Right-In?

One framework that has proven useful in cross-cultural research for characterizing time orientations is (1) linear, single-task use of time, and (2) circular, multiple-task use of time.

Step-by-Step Time. In Western countries, especially the United States, people tend to view time as consisting of past, present, and an infinite future, with emphasis on the future. People in these cultures see time as separable into quantifiable, discrete units or steps with fixed beginnings and endings for events. They place great emphasis on scheduling appointments, specifying the starting and ending times for events, being prompt, meeting deadlines, and planning ahead. The segmenting of time leads to focusing on one task, appointment, or event at a time (Graham 1981; Cote and Tansuhaj 1989; McGrath and Rotchford 1983).

Step-by-step time is linear, like a ribbon or road of time. It's almost tangible because people talk about manipulating it, scheduling it, using it, and borrowing it. Compartmentalizing time in steps or units allows people to concentrate on one thing at a time, but it also denies them much of the context in which events occur. It permits only a limited number of events within a given period. Thus it can limit individuals' possibilities. Their business life, social life, and even sex life, are apt to be completely time dominated. Linear-time people are less likely to see things in a larger context (Hall 1982).

Dive-Right-In Time. Some people treat time more like a circle and focus on points in time within the circle. Their attitude toward time is to dive right in. Therefore, several things may be happening at once, for to these people it's more important to maintain good relationships with others and to complete transactions with others than to adhere to a preset schedule. It's as if each point is sacred but only in the sense of giving oneself fully to the relationships, events, or activities of the moment. In fact, circular-time people may view time itself as essentially irrelevant because their time-related behavior is activity driven, and an activity simply takes as much time as is needed for its completion.

You may not get the full attention of circular-time persons, and they may never get around to the most important business at hand. If you're a step-by-step person, you may think that nothing seems solid or firm with these people, particularly regarding the future. There are always changes in the most important plans, right up to the very last minute. In circular-time organizations, systems need a much greater centralization of control, characterized by a rather shallow or simple organizational structure, because the top person deals continually with many people, most of whom stay informed about what's happening.

Circular-time cultures include Latino, Middle Eastern, and some Asian and African cultures. In the United States workplace, it is likely that many African Americans, Asian Americans, and Latino Americans are circular-time people. While they may necessarily adapt to the Euro-American time orientation when they work in Euro-American-dominated organizations, they tend to return to their own time orientation for social and family events.

In some cultures, time is determined by repeated cycles of activities, such as the agricultural cycles of planting, cultivating, and harvesting. People in such cultures do not see time as stretching into the future, but focus on the past and present. This orientation is dominant in some African cultures and in the Cuban and Mexican cultures (Szapocznik, Scopetta, and King 1978; Ramirez 1988).

Space: Come Close or Back Off?

Cultures differ in how much personal space individuals expect to occupy, how close they stand or sit to one another, and how much physical contact they have. In the workplace this translates into different perceptions about comfortable office sizes and layout and requirements for privacy in work stations (Hall 1982).

Come-Close Space. In Middle Eastern cultures, business associates and friends stand close enough to be able to feel the other's breath on their face and to be able to catch each other's scent. People in Latino cultures prefer slightly more distance than those in Middle Eastern cultures, but they like to stand closer than do people in Western and Asian cultures. Latino and Middle Eastern cultures tend to be high-contact societies, with more touching permitted and expected than in other cultures. Two men will often embrace instead of shaking hands.

Back-Off Space. In most Western cultures, including the United States, we learn to stand about two or three feet, an arm's length, from people in business or social relationships. Only family members, close friends, and lovers are expected to come closer. We may stand farther away when we feel a desire to remain aloof or protect ourselves. When someone moves into our space, we normally feel uncomfortable and back away till we feel comfortable again. Western cultures are basically noncontact societies. In most Asian cultures, perhaps because of dense populations in many countries, people maintain an even greater distance for all but their ingroup members.

Communicating: Direct or Indirect?

While there are many variations in communication style, two that stem directly from the key cultural patterns we've discussed are directness and indirectness.

Going to the person; getting to the point. The direct style tends to be used in Western cultures, especially those that focus on I-control, me-first, achievement-first, equality, and risk taking. Within those cultures men are more likely than women to use a direct style of communication.

Using go-betweens and implied messages. People in most cultures use a more indirect style of communication, specifically in those cultures identified as us-first, people-first, rank/status, and play-it-safe. In all cultures, women are likely to use an indirect style. In us-first cultures with many close ties, many messages can be implied because people have been socialized alike and are on "the same wavelength." And in many cultures, go-betweens are used to broach sensitive topics.

Economy: Agricultural, Industrial, or Post–Industrial?

Hofstede's work in identifying the key factors that differ among cultures was a major break-through. Still, as John Nirenberg (1993) points out, Hofstede effectively ignores large, divergent subgroups within some countries. For example, in many countries there is a peasant-class value system that's quite different from the ruling-class value system. Nirenberg suggests that cultural beliefs, values, and norms are greatly affected by a subgroup's dominant way of making a living. He has compared the dominant values in countries that are primarily agricultural (the economically underdeveloped countries of the world), those that are primarily industrial (the developing countries), and those that are post-industrial (the developed countries).

When a country moves from a manufacturing-based economy to an information- and service-based economy, beliefs, values, and norms change, becoming reminiscent of those of the agricultural era but representing a new ethos that responds to the experiences of the new era. The overall pattern may be viewed as one that's primarily dependent on extended family and groups in the agricultural phase, independent in the industrial phase, and interdependent in the post-industrial phase. See Table 2.10 at the end of this chapter for examples of values affected by a culture's economic system.

This economic-structure approach may help explain the cultural complexity we find among people in a supposedly homogeneous nation. Within a nation, region or culture, various groups may be operating from the ethos that represents their way of making a living, undergirded to some extent by other traditional cultural values. For example, all workers in the United States share in the cultural media—television, film, radio, magazines, and books are readily available to most everyone. Farmers, factory workers, and computer technicians will therefore maintain some common values. But people immigrating from certain Latino, Asian, and African countries may have lacked access to such media and therefore were more segmented and isolated by their economic activities. For example, in China groups in fairly remote areas who may be almost entirely involved in agriculture and still adhere to many agriculture-era values. Others, in urban areas, may be focused on manufacturing and therefore on industrial-era values. A few in such areas as Hong Kong (soon to be integrated back into China) may be focused on post-industrial activities and values.

We'll return to these themes when we discuss major subcultures of the United States. For example, Latino American and Asian American subcultures retain many of the patterns of their original countries or regions. This in turn affects the motivation, work patterns, and lifestyles of employees from those groups. Leaders who have a global view of cultural patterns are better able to understand why such employees act as they do. Such leaders have an advantage in working out success strategies with diverse employees.

DISCOVERING THE AMERICAN CULTURE

You've just taken a first step toward understanding culture and its pervasive influence. You've climbed that symbolic mountain and looked down at all the cultures of the world. Now for step 2, understanding your own culture, which we'll assume is the American culture. One thing you might notice is that the American culture doesn't really look so much like a melting pot as a series of pots. Groups of people are relating mainly to those in their own subculture, all within the larger segmented society. The next thing you might notice is that people from other cultures don't always see us as we see ourselves. Many people notice that our typical beliefs, values, and worldview are quite different from theirs. As for our personal relationships, others are sometimes enchanted, sometimes puzzled, by our unique approach to making and handling friendships. First we'll focus on understanding the American culture in general. Then we'll look at the American business culture and various types of corporate culture.

What's in a Name?

America is the name given an entire hemisphere, ranging from the South Pole to the North Pole. Some people from other American nations think it odd that people from the United States apply the label *Americans* only to themselves, as if the other American nations don't exist. On the other hand, what other term would we use? *United Statesians* doesn't work, and nicknames such as *Yankees* are too informal.

A Segmented Society

A group of friends who grew up in a North Texas city during the 1940s was reminiscing about their "all-WASP" childhood. "You know, I never knew a Mexican American when I was growing up; never talked to one except for the man who sold tamales from a cart on the street. But I know there had to be a Mexican American community somewhere." Others agreed that this was a common experience. "I never had any African American friends either. Of course, that's easier to understand, with the severe segregation and all. The only African Americans I knew were the cleaning women who came to our home sometimes."

We've been called a segmented society, with groups living in separate enclaves, their lives touching those of other groups only superficially. Our diverse society has often depended on segmentation to live in peace. As the most diverse society on earth, a key American ideal has always been *unity in diversity*. We've generally managed our diversity by giving groups as much freedom and autonomy as possible. From this elementary principle emerged a pattern of beliefs and behaviors that is uniquely American.

Politically, we're a pluralistic society. Our diverse groups get to have a say through individual members' votes and whatever influence their interest groups can wield within the political system. Another of our key values is *equality and fairness for all*, and minority groups have always struggled toward that ideal value. The gap between ideal and reality has been a continuing problem for us.

What about our unity? What holds us together as a nation? Some say the major unifying forces include a common consumer market and media, a political system that lets us participate and have influence, and a political-legal system that effectively sets the rules of the game and referees it. Certainly, two primary values that have pulled immigrants to these shores and kept them here are freedom and opportunity: the freedom to pursue one's own lifestyle and religion, and the opportunity to make a decent—sometimes abundant—living.

Our common consumer desires and our legal system have forestalled most of the infighting, anarchy, and rioting that might otherwise result from significant ethnic diversity. Our political system sets the rules of the livelihood game and serves as an arena for the segments, or groups, to cooperate and compete for their share of resources and opportunities. Our legal system and its power brokers—lawyers, judges, politicians, lobbyists, and other leaders—serve as referees.

The set of values that formed the society—a commitment to a common livelihood game— was remarkably strong. But as minority groups grow larger, beliefs about equal access to the workplace and marketplace, as well as other divergent values, are tending to fragment our society. And even in the past, some of our shared values regarding individuality and privacy inherently discouraged interaction. Americans have therefore created a society with a minimum of social relationships. Public school education has tended to either bury differences in a phony American homogeneity or has pictured *"many peoples bringing many gifts to the nation like so many strangers depositing money in a collection box"* (Weibe 1975). With such poor preparation for mixing with diverse people, no wonder contact has often resulted in hardening our stereotypes.

How do we satisfy the need to overcome our segmentation and create community? Traditionally, we've only been able to do it in the face of a common enemy, such as Nazism or environmental pollution. Even then, we've usually rolled bandages or recycled our newspapers as individuals or discrete groups, relying on many independent others to do the same. We've assumed that public results don't require public processes, that the segments or groups need not interact at a local level on an everyday basis to solve the problems. We've assumed that the sum of many independent actions, a never-ending economic expansion, and our system of power brokers will do it for us. Now, events are pressuring us to change that. Increasing work-force diversity, the need for close teamwork in the workplace, and the pressures of global competition on those teams all work together in calling us to build bridges across segments, to build multicultural skills.

American Worldview, Values, and Customs

What do people from other cultures see as unique about Americans? They tend to notice that most middle-class Americans, especially the males, think of themselves as individuals first, the world as basically inanimate, nature as something to be conquered, material success as the major goal, and "doing" as the preferred state. Most value self-improvement and hard work as the way to ensure a better future for themselves and their families. Most Americans believe in scientific and technological "progress," viewing the world in rational, linear, cause-and-effect terms. People from other cultures usually see Americans as pragmatic, factual, and future oriented, with a tendency to view things in black-or-white terms rather than the many shades in between. Most Americans value work and tend to separate work activities from play activities. A summary of typical American values is given in Table 2.6.

World View: Conquering Nature for Material Progress, Using the Scientific Method

The American worldview is based on making progress by conquering nature. This is important because material progress depends on using nature's bounty for our own purposes. Because we believe in such scientific and material progress, we accept the changes that go along with progress, even welcome them. And because science is the basis of most of our progress, we value the scientific method, which has traditionally been a rational, linear, cause-and-effect approach. And of course this approach relies on gathering needed facts and putting them to work.

Conquering nature. Making progress often requires conquering nature. Most Americans tend to implicitly assume that the external, nonhuman world is physical, material, like a complex

TABLE 2.6: American Values

Individualism	Scientific method	Friendliness
Self-reliance	Rationalism	Generosity
Autonomy	Facts, practicality	Many casual friends
Achievement	Conquering nature	Few close friends
Material success	Freedom	Arms'-length closeness
Progress	Equality	Competition
Future orientation	Good versus bad	Assertiveness
Change	Work versus play	Cooperativeness
Youth	Directness	Fair play
Self-improvement	Informality	Specialized roles
Hard work		

machine with many parts, and therefore does not have a soul or a spirit. Nature, Mother Earth, is not seen as a living entity, and of course does not have a soul or spirit. The physical environment is there to be used, even exploited, for human purposes. Modern science established these beliefs, beginning in the 1600s, with the ideas and discoveries of René Descartes, Isaac Newton, and others.

We also believe in conquering human nature. While most United States religions are committed to the doctrine that humans are flawed or evil by nature, most Americans are unlikely to give the concept much thought. We are more likely to see humans as a mixture of good and bad or as creatures of their environment and experience. Most important, we stress their ability to change.

The dominant assumption in the United States is that nature and the physical world should be controlled in the service of humans, to a degree unmatched in any other major society. It is expressed by the engineer's approach to the world based on technology and applied to social spheres as "social and human engineering." This contrasts with views common in the East and among American Indians that stress the unity among all forms of life and inanimate objects. They see people as *part* of nature and the physical world instead of in opposition to them. Some cultures take a fatalistic attitude toward their environment and feel overwhelmed by it. People in cultures of poverty in many parts of the world assume that humans are subjugated by their environment (Harris and Moran 1991).

Making progress and welcoming change. Americans believe in and value progress—scientific and technological developments that improve our material world. We often use our concept of progress to evaluate ourselves and others. This concept is unknown by many in the non-Western world and may be rejected by them. We have traditionally believed that the basic problems of the world are technological and their solution will bring about economic abundance. The final criterion for what's good and desirable is how economically feasible or lucrative it is. Progress is usually tied to our struggle to increase our physical comfort, health, material possessions, and standard of living. Also tied to our concept of progress is a feeling of general optimism towards the future, that our efforts can bring about a better future in which there is enough for everyone (Althen 1988; Kohls 1988).

Progress implies change. Humans generally resist change and fear the unknown that change implies, and many Americans have their fair share of this human trait. However, Americans have institutionalized change to a greater degree than any other society. In fact, certain types of change and novelty are necessary features of things in American life; "new" and "improved" become labels for preferences. This desire for change shows up in our willingness to relocate. We are the most mobile society in the world, changing addresses more often than people in any other nation (Stewart 1992).

Using a rational, linear, cause-and-effect approach. Most Americans believe that events or actions always have a "cause" or an agent who may be held responsible; just as in the operation of a machine, everything has a cause-and-effect relationship. The notion of a natural "happening" has not been familiar or acceptable to most Americans. We see the world as rational in the sense that we believe the events of the world can be explained and the reasons for particular occurrences can be determined. Effective performance in the real world is based on experience and on training and education, which should be practical.

We tend to see the world as mechanistic and the things worthy of effort as material. The scientific method is the process we trust. We focus on facts, figures, and techniques as the means to solve problems that represent obstacles to achieving our goals. We like to develop alternative courses of action, to compare them, and to choose the one that seems best for our given purpose. We see action (and the world itself) as a chain of events, a connection of causes and effects projecting into the future.

Our action orientation leads us to look for a simple cause of events, so we can plug this cause into our problem-solving process and decide on a course of action. After we anticipate the future consequences or effects of various action plans, we then choose the plan we think will produce the best results. We like effects that are visible, measurable, and materialistic, and we like an action plan that is practical. To people from other cultures we may seem to sacrifice the end result for the means of getting there, for the scientific method is the only means we trust. Recently some quantum physicists have been collaborating with business leaders, and some are moving beyond the traditional scientific method to more holistic approaches that bring intuition and other factors into the equation (Wheatley 1992; Kohls 1988).

Getting the facts, putting them to work. Most Americans don't pay much attention to theories that don't seem to have a practical application. The role of concepts and ideas in American life is to provide direction for purposeful activity. Theories are judged and tested according to their usefulness in daily life. Traditionally, Americans haven't followed in the European tradition of evaluating ideas or systems of thought according to "intellectual consistency" or "aesthetic appeal" (Boorstin 1960).

For most Americans, the world consists of facts rather than ideas. Our thinking process generally begins with facts and proceeds to ideas, an inductive process. These ideas must then be validated by application and by becoming a part of the way business is done. We are somewhat unique in our insistence on practical applications—our continual need to organize our perceptions of the world into a form that enables us to act. We will accept a certain amount of pure science (research for the sake of curiosity), but we expect most research to result in technology or products we can use, something that represents "progress." This operational style of thinking leads to an emphasis on consequences and results, and a disregard for the purely hypothetical. Probably more than people in any other culture, we Americans tend to place our trust in the scientific method of experimental observation and measurement that has been prevalent in Western cultures since the 1600s.

We especially resist systems of thought that lose sight of the individual. For example, despite our many programs of governmental responsibility and care for the individual, we resist unifying them into a system of ideology, some sort of modified socialism. Instead, we cling to the ideal of individual enterprise, a belief that keeps the self-identity intact (Kohls 1988; Althen 1988).

Measuring things. Americans tend to stress concreteness, and the essential quality of measurability. We like to see the world in dimensions that can be quantified. Even quality and experience can be at least partially quantified, if only as first or last, least or most. Or we can assign them arbitrary values, such as "a scale of 1 to 7, 1 being the least and 7 being the most." In business, government, and academia, we tend to use statistics to measure success and failure, amount of work, ability, intelligence, and overall job performance.

Americans have managed to create unparalleled economic abundance with our combined focus on externalized achievement and on exploitation and control of the physical environment. Further, we tend to believe in unlimited physical resources, that there's enough to go around for everyone. This expansive view of achievement in a world of economic abundance contrasts sharply with the perception of limited wealth that prevails throughout most of the world. Only recently have large groups of Americans, such as environmentalist groups, begun to question the sustainability of our abundance processes. Now, with satellite television carrying pictures of our abundant lifestyle to every corner of the globe, billions of people are beginning to clamor for similar affluence. If the way of life of 250 million Americans is damaging the planet, what will happen if billions choose our way? If American belief in achievement and progress holds sway, we just may figure it out and show the way to sustainable abundance for all (Wheatley 1992; Althen 1988).

Thinking in black/white terms. When you value the scientific method, objectivity versus subjectivity, and measurable outcomes, this allows you to set a numerical cutoff point for whether something is one way or another. This may be one reason Americans tend to focus on black-or-white terms rather than shades of color. Americans draw a clear distinction between the subjective or personal and the objective or impersonal.

It is typical for Americans to ask such questions as, "Who's your best friend?" or "What's your favorite color?" People outside our culture would generally have difficulty answering such questions because the answer would depend on knowing additional factors, such as work friends or social friends, color for a room or color for a suit. Americans often make judgments or justify actions based solely on personal preference. This tendency is related to our tendency to see the world in terms of black or white, and it's related to a predisposition to action. We set up unequal dichotomies, with one element valued more than the other; for example, right/wrong, good/evil, work/play, peace/war. These polarities simplify our view of the world, prime us for action, and provide us with our typical method of evaluating by means of comparison (Kohls 1988).

Key Personal Values: Becoming an Achieving Individual

As the most individualistic culture on the planet, American culture highly values people who become responsible, autonomous individuals who make their own decisions and go out and achieve in the world. We admire people who work hard and play hard and who achieve material success.

Becoming an individual. Americans love their freedom to be autonomous individuals. American culture has emphasized the individual while accepting affiliations within groups. Some sociologists challenge the myth of the rugged individualist conquering the frontier. These myths stress a number of values that carry considerable emotional impact. One of the most important is self-reliance, which in its pure form no longer makes sense in the complex American technological culture and has given way to a search for autonomy, self-actualization, and personal growth. To the same extent that this new form of self-reliance is sought, its opposite, dependence, is avoided. We Americans like to think of ourselves as self-reliant, but we accept social security, borrow money, and in many ways show willingness to depend on government or others. However, we generally don't place as much faith in fate or luck as do people in many other cultures. The meaning of this self-reliance value is neither translatable nor self-evident in other cultures.

Closely tied to the value of individual autonomy is American belief in competition and assertiveness. We admire people who decide what they want and go for it, who are willing to compete and don't easily give up (Harris and Moran 1991; Hofstede 1984).

Making our own decisions. We encourage our children, from the earliest age, to decide for themselves, to make up their own minds. We encourage them to believe that they're the best judge of what they want and what they should do. Therefore, as adults we're likely to view bankers, teachers, counselors, and other experts as people who can give us advice, not as people who should make decisions for us. We expect to choose our own mates, careers, homes, and to some extent, lifestyles. By contrast, in many other cultures, all or part of these decisions are made by parents.

Americans are more likely than people from many other cultures to be able to express opinions and exert some influence on business and community decisions. Americans are therefore more likely than others to focus on process—on the procedures used in calling and running meetings, on agendas, and especially on voting procedures. The process should ensure fairness and equality for all and should facilitate action. Americans believe in majority rule and that people are capable of helping to make good decisions, although many men still accept the chain of command and autocratic decision making in military, government, and business organizations. In contrast, in Japan and some other Asian cultures, group decisions are reached by a system that provides for a feeling around, a groping for a voice, preferably that of the chairman, that that has proven useful in cross cultural research will express the group's consensus. They consider it offensive for individuals to urge the group to accept their opinion about what to do (Kohls 1988).

Valuing achievement. Americans tend to think they can achieve just about anything, given enough time, money, and technology. Externalized achievement has traditionally been the dominant motivation of American men, and they use competition as the primary method for driving themselves and others to achieve. Competition is seen by many as the keystone of American culture. In many nonWestern cultures, and traditionally among women in our culture, affiliation is the primary motivation and way of relating to others. A communal feeling toward each other excludes the incentive to excel over others, either as a member of a group or individually. The values in our culture seem to be changing; for example, many women are learning to accept their feelings of success and the desire to excel. At the same time, some men, and women, who formerly felt compelled to be competitive, are becoming more group-oriented and less autonomous in their behavior, as demonstrated in self-managing work teams and in many of the relationships in the virtual corporation.

In America individual identity is determined primarily by personal achievement. We believe persons should set their own goals and then make up their own minds about how to pursue them. Therefore, motivation should originate within the person. We tend to dislike it when others apply their motives to us, especially when others give us orders, injunctions, and threats. We value persuasion as the method of coordinating our organizational lives and activities. The subtle threat of failure contributes the most to persuasion and provides the basis for appeals to self-interest and reason. We want to believe that we decide what we must do.

In countries with more centralized governments, people often focus on the hierarchy, social roles, and loyalty for guidance and motivation. People in such cultures tend to accept a personal bond between subordinate and superior, which makes the authority figure an acceptable source of motivation. Direct orders, explicit instructions, and demands for personal conformity may be acceptable, and even desirable, in such cultures. In them, the American preference for persuasion may be seen as weakness on a leader's part, and self-determination may be viewed as egotism and a threat to the organization (Harris and Moran 1991; Althen 1988).

Working hard and playing hard. Americans are somewhat unique in categorizing activities as either work activities or play activities. Work is pursued for a living; it's what you must do and may not necessarily enjoy. In contrast, nonWesterners may rarely allow work to interfere with the amenities of living. For Americans, play is relief from the drudgery and monotony of work and is enjoyable in its own right. However, we often pursue play with the same seriousness of purpose as we pursue work. We tend to admire the person who "works hard and plays hard" (Stewart 1992).

Achieving material success. Most Americans consider it almost a right to be materially well-off and physically comfortable. People should have shelter, clothing, warmth, and all of the other means that make the individual materially comfortable. Each household needs its own car, house, and other physical possessions. This is an important part of the good life. Most Americans typically spend great time, effort, and money on acquiring such comforts. We expect convenient, rapid transportation, preferably under our control, a variety of clean and healthful foods, and comfortable homes equipped with many labor-saving devices, certainly including central heat and hot water. We assume that cleanliness is nearly identical with health, if not with "Godliness."

Our focus on material comforts is quite different from some traditional Asian values that stress the state of grace of the person. The American stress on material things is related to the achievement value and to the European belief in private property, one that is highly valued and upheld by an entire legal system. It's difficult for many Americans to imagine, but some cultures don't even have a concept of private property (Kohls 1988).

The American Way of Relating: Friendly, Casual, Egalitarian, Fair

Americans are seen by those in other cultures as friendly and informal, direct and casual. We have many casual friendships and few deeply committed ones. Our ideal is equality of all people, but in practice we often violate this ideal. We believe in cooperation and fair play, in specialized roles, and in positive change.

Making many casual friends. Americans are known to be friendly, informal, and generous. We tend to reject the idea of someone being special or privileged merely because of birth, and tend to defer to those with affluence and power achieved through merit. The way we dress and greet each other tends to be informal relative to many cultures. Americans are known to be generous, willing to come to the aid of people in emergencies, and to embrace a good cause.

To Americans a "friend" may be a passing acquaintance or a lifetime intimate, but we tend to have many personal relationships that are friendly and informal and to form few deep and lasting friendships. In contrast, people from many other cultures tend to be slow in forming friendships, but once committed, they tend to be friends for life and will do almost anything for a friend. To such people, Americans' immediate friendliness and tendency to form instant friendships is confusing.

Americans change friends and membership groups more easily than people in most cultures. Though we tend to spend a great deal of time in social activities, we're likely to avoid personal commitments and intense involvement except with one or two "best friends." Our exchange of invitations and gifts is within a loose, informal framework. The quality of our social interactions tends to stress equality, informality, impermanence, and personal detachment. Many Americans *need* to express friendship and to be popular in order to feel self-confident. Many tend to judge personal and social success by popularity, almost literally by the number of people who like them.

Friendships are often based on activities, on what we do together, centering around our work, hobbies, sports, children, charities, games, and political or religious interests. This specialization of friends often reflects our reluctance to become deeply involved with many people and a wish for privacy. In situations where persons from other cultures would turn to friends for help, Americans tend to search for professional help, preferring not to inconvenience friends. American adults often share friends with other friends and include their parents among their friends (Harris and Moran 1991; Stewart 1992).

Fitting into specialized roles. In our culture, traditionally, roles have been developed and filled with specialists who deal with specific functions and problems. The organizational hierarchy is like a machine with interchangeable parts; that is, people with specific skills. Until recently, we never thought of an organization as growing out of the unique qualities that people brought to it and their ability to respond to unique opportunities that unfolded in the environment. Instead, we focused on specialized roles—especially in business, the military, and government, particularly where technical skills and complicated equipment are involved. Associates from other cultures often find it difficult to understand the traditional American insistence on separating planning from implementing. That's changing with the movement toward self-directed teams, which merge these two functions.

The same tendency towards specialization of roles often occurs in interpersonal relations. We tend to think of others as co-workers, fellow tennis players, club associates, old school chums, neighborhood friends, PTA parents, etc. Our separation of social and occupational roles, of work and play, is different from the patterns found in other cultures (Stewart 1992).

Valuing equality. An important theme in our relationships is equality. Ideally, just the fact of being human gives each person a certain irreducible value, and interpersonal relations are typically horizontal, conducted between presumed equals. However, big business and big government have traditionally been hierarchical and authoritarian, run by able-bodied, straight, Euro-American males, who in practice generally considered themselves the only true equals. When one of them needed to confront another who was a subordinate, he was more likely to establish an atmosphere of equality than are the bosses in rank/status-oriented cultures. However, this value has often not extended to employees who were too *different*, particularly the African Americans, but also the Latino Americans and Asian Americans, and certainly women.

In addition to these contradictions, most Americans have further reservations about total equality: Not everyone is presumed to have equal talent and ability, even though they are entitled to equal rights and obligations. Americans tend to believe, however, that in any group there will be people of ability and leadership potential. We emphasize equality of opportunity more than equality of results or equality of individuals per se. During our history, we've blatantly violated our belief in equality and we've modified our understanding of it. But the belief remains a pervasive cultural value and the keystone for building a productive multicultural workplace (Althen 1988; Harris and Moran 1991; Takaki 1993; Wiebe 1975).

Cooperating and playing fair. Although Americans value competition, we usually compete against a backdrop of cooperation, for competition requires a considerable amount of coordination among individuals and groups. Americans can do this because we don't commit ourselves as wholeheartedly to a group or organization as those from some other cultures. We pursue our own personal goals while cooperating with others who, likewise, pursue their own. We tend to accept the goals of the group, but if our expectations are unfulfilled, we then feel free to leave and join another group. We can adjust our goals to those of other group members, if necessary, for carrying out joint action. This compromise is practical to us, allowing us to achieve a benefit we couldn't attain on our own.

We cooperate in order to get things done, but that doesn't imply that we're giving up our personal goals or principles. To ensure that we don't have to compromise more than necessary, we often focus on the process used to reach a group decision. In formal groups, for instance, we're often concerned with matters of agenda and procedure, which tend to give some formal protection to our individual rights. Most of us value processes and rules that are fair and democratic.

Most Americans believe you don't have to accept other persons in totality to be able to work well with them. Part of being practical or professional is the ability to work effectively with anyone who can do the job, even if you disapprove of a co-worker's politics, lifestyle, or religious beliefs. It is this trait that allows us to cooperate with a diversity of people in order to achieve specific goals. This is a strength we can build upon to overcome the systemic and subtle discrimination that still exists in the workplace (Harris and Moran 1991; Althen 1988).

American Time and Space

Americans typically take a linear, step-by-step view of time, keeping busy and looking toward the future. Their space orientation is more arm's-length than come-close.

Time: Looking Toward the Future

Our focus is more on the future than on the present or past. Our views of work and of doing are related to our future orientation. Americans believe that hard work pays off in creating a better future for ourselves and our families. We see any unpleasantness in our work, or any stress due to incessant activity, as necessary intermediate steps for change and as progress toward the future. In contrast, Latinos, who have a present orientation, focus on immediate events; and Chinese, who have a past orientation, focus on traditions. Americans believe we can improve on the present and that action and hard work will bring about what we want as individuals. Most Americans see time as an abstract quality, separate from self. Time moves fast. It's important to cope with time slipping away. You've got to keep up with the times. Time is something we organize, schedule, use, and save. In business time is money, so being on time and using time efficiently are critical (Althen 1988).

Time: Keeping Busy

Americans are known to be work oriented and efficient. We act upon persons, things, or situations. Others may see us as living at a fast pace, as people who are incessantly active. And most Americans fill their waking hours primarily in a *doing* mode. We seldom question the implicit assumption that getting things done is worthwhile. We like the kind of activity that results in accomplishments that are measurable by standards that our culture says are valuable. Hard work is rewarded by success, and failure usually means one or more of the following: You didn't know how to do it right, you didn't try hard enough, or you're lazy and uncaring.

Many people in nonWestern cultures fill their waking hours with a *being* or *being in becoming* mode. People who prefer the *being* mode focus on the spontaneous expression of the human personality. People who prefer the *being in becoming* mode focus on developing all aspects of the self as an integrated whole. This mode introduces the idea of development of the person, which is absent in the other two (Harris and Moran 1991).

Space: Keeping Arm's Length

Our boundaries tend to be about arm's length. When someone breaks through that boundary, we may feel invaded, and the act often carries sexual or belligerent overtones. Latin and Arab cultures value a closer proximity. The way we use space reflects our desire to have privacy and to maintain some distance in our personal lives. The large, isolated office—on the top floor, protected by a receptionist's office—signals the status and prestige of the higher level executive. Traditionally, the higher the position, the more space and privacy the employee has. This tendency is also reflected in our choice of neighborhoods and homes. More than people in most other cultures, we're willing to sacrifice to have more floor space and yard space (Stewart 1992; Harris and Moran, 1991; Kohls 1988).

American Communication: Informal and Direct

The American communication style is known for being informal and relatively direct. Most Americans stress a simple vocabulary, a relative disregard for style, and the use of slang as an expression of affiliation and social conformity. As a diverse culture, we rely more on the specifics of verbal communication, while tight-knit cultures rely more on the nonverbal. Traditionally, American immigrants have encouraged their children to become Americanized, and they eagerly accepted the language and the ways of the new country and turned their backs on the language and customs of the old. In this sense, the United States may have been the only country where speaking two languages was a mark of low status (Harris and Moran 1991; Kohls 1988; Althen 1988).

Our informal, direct approach to interacting with others can seem brusque, rude, or confusing to people of other cultures. Compared to others, we tend to make fewer discriminations among people—quickly moving to a first-name basis with all and relating with breeziness, humor, and kidding. Our friendly, personal way of treating everyone, even enemies, contributes to a depersonalization. While Americans tend to avoid confrontation, once they decide that a situation with another person must be resolved, they are likely to deal directly with the person. This contrasts with the idea of "saving face" and using a go-between or other indirect approaches that are valued by many other cultures.

Our Future: From Independence to Interdependence?

The American business culture is moving from a focus on individualistic independence to a focus on interdependence among autonomous individuals. We've mentioned that cultures tend to move from cooperative to competitive, then back to cooperative as they evolve from a primarily agricultural economic base to industrial and on to post-industrial (see Table 2.8 at the end of this chapter). In the industrial phase, people tend to take on many of the characteristics we've noted as typical in American culture, those that are independent, masculine, rational, materialistic. In America, more than in any other culture, we have focused on individual freedom and responsibility. During the industrial era this focus was used as a rationale for extreme competitiveness and ambition to acquire material things. Many leaders now believe that although this focus has brought great advantages, it imposes many personal and social limitations on us. To overcome such limitations, these leaders are shifting to a more holistic focus that balances and harnesses individual goals and group goals. As it turns out, this focus better fits our diverse post-industrial workplace.

The major difference between the group-centered cooperation of the post-industrial workplace and that of agricultural-era cultures (and of many us-first cultures today) is the degree of individual freedom and choice involved. Most traditional group-centered cultures place a heavy load of expectation on children to grow up within strict guidelines, with tightly structured responsibilities toward family and society. Parents often make many choices for their grown children. They may choose, or greatly influence the choice of mate, career, place of residence, and circle of friends. Parents normally play a large role in setting all the major life goals for their adult children.

In contrast, the typical American parent encourages children to develop a high degree of independence, free will, and individual responsibility and to make their own life choices. This means that we can now come together in work teams, alliances, networks, and other cooperative groups, each bringing greater independence and personal power to the arena. We can create greater synergistic power because we come of our own free will, as autonomous persons creating our own careers and lives, making our own choices and taking responsibility for how those choices work out. When people pursue their own goals—not their parents', teachers', or bosses'—they experience less inner conflict, clearer focus, higher motivation, and greater creativity. There is less cause for resistance, resentment, and frustration.

The American post-industrial movement toward group-centered cooperation, therefore, is not a case of the pendulum swinging back to a pattern of dependence, but of an evolutionary spiral moving up toward an interdependence that's grounded in personal autonomy and choice. The corporate culture of some of the most productive corporations feature a strong emphasis on cooperation and an equally important focus on individual performance. They harness both the competitive and cooperative drives into a very powerful combination. And they incorporate a factor that's missing in less productive organizations: trust (Peters 1992). As the most diverse culture on earth and the one with the highest level of personal independence, we have tremendous potential power to lead the world in cooperative enterprise—by effectively joining the dual drives of cooperation and competition with the key factor of trust.

AMERICAN CORPORATE CULTURES

The evolution from independence to interdependence is reflected in the American business culture generally and in the corporate cultures of leading organizations specifically. *Corporate culture* refers to the values, norms, and principles that underlie an organization's policies and practices. Every organization has its own culture, whether it's a corporation or not, so even if you work in a government agency, a school, or a nonprofit organization, you still work within a "corporate culture," more properly called an organizational culture. A corporate culture is made up of myths, symbols, heroes, legends, and rituals that are often summed up as "what we're all about" and "the way we do things around here" (Deal and Kennedy 1982). Just as the culture at large ties people together and gives meaning and purpose to their everyday lives, corporate culture is the glue that holds corporations together.

Strong and Weak Cultures

Some corporate cultures are strong, others weak. Even weak cultures influence almost everything in the organization, from who gets promoted to what decisions are made, from how people dress to what they do when they're off.

Weak cultures. In weak corporate cultures people adhere primarily to their own culture group's viewpoints, norms, and values. People have more freedom to determine how to act. However, the extreme of weak culture is organizational chaos. Some essential values must be shared by members if an organization is to be able to achieve its goals. To survive and thrive over time, organizations need strong cultures. You can identify a weak-culture firm by looking for the following signs:

- No set of beliefs about how to succeed is delineated by the leaders.
- No rank-ordered priority of values is communicated by the leaders.
- No overriding common values are held by the different subcultures in various parts of the company.
- Role models don't serve the culture well. They may be disruptive, even destructive, or don't reinforce key values and beliefs.
- Rituals of everyday work life are disorganized or contradictory. People do their own thing or work at cross-purposes, undermining each other.

Strong cultures. In strong corporate cultures leaders clearly define and enforce values and norms, giving more direction to how people should act, more reinforcement about what they should do, and perhaps higher penalties for not conforming. The result is that people are more likely to view a situation in the same way, to respond similarly, and to expect similar results. In some strong cultures, management expects people to conform to values and norms that encompass most of their activities. In other equally strong cultures management insists on conformity to only a few core values and norms but not on less important ones. This type is more suitable for diverse groups because it allows for a greater variety of behaviors. The actions of management must be consistent with corporate values, because the inconsistencies will be noticed and magnified out of proportion. Shared values act as an informal control system that tells people what's expected of them. They therefore impact greatly the organization's performance (Peters 1992).

SHOWCASE:
THE BODY SHOPS: STRONG CORPORATE CULTURE IN ACTION

During the global nineties, managers have discovered they must focus more and more on managing the corporate culture. They must build, enunciate, and promote a strong culture that bonds people together, giving diverse people a core of common beliefs and values, a sense of common purpose. An example of such a strong culture is The Body Shops, a multinational chain of retail stores selling hair and skin preparations. The founder and CEO, Anita Roddick, is the guiding heroine who enunciates the organization's key values. Her constant theme is communication. She focuses on words that are associated with feminine values and concerns: love, family, caring, nurturing, connecting, preserving.

A key value of The Body Shop is to provide quality products at reasonable prices, with honesty and integrity, using natural ingredients, without animal testing. Other key values are respecting the environment, honoring indigenous people through Trade Not Aid, and giving back to the community in creative, interactive ways. To implement its values, the company has a constantly evolving, but limited, set of humanitarian concerns addressed in a pro-active way. Some examples are (1) helping the Kayapo Indians in the Brazilian rain forest protect their way of life, (2) reducing violence against women, (3) helping the orphans of Romania, (4) supporting AIDS relief organizations, and (5) supporting education in general as well as specific educational projects.

Roddick spends much of her time traveling around the world, visiting employees of the corporate stores and owners of the franchised stores—a total of more than 900 stores in more than 40 countries. The force of her personality, her energy, and the goodwill that she projects are strong factors in bonding the far-flung shops together. She continually formulates her beliefs and values into communication themes and common causes that are adopted by people throughout the organization. Franchise owners and key employees are carefully screened, primarily to determine that their beliefs, values, and principles are compatible with those of the organization. Once on board, people are given great freedom in how they carry out the organization's plans. They also have significant input into corporate plans. Their ideas and opinions are sought out and carefully listened to.

Employee training is more aptly described as employee education in The Body Shop. Time devoted to narrow skills training is minimal. Most time is devoted to discussions of broad philosophical concepts and giving information about important developments in the world at large, as well as within the organization.

Ironically, The Body Shop is often a target of the news media precisely *because* it stands out as a model of a socially responsible, multicultural organization. A reporter might have much to gain by finding a fatal flaw in its operation. Most of the sniping is ignored, but in 1993 The Body Shop successfully sued a newspaper for false reporting. Also, some individuals respond to glowing reports about The Body Shop's unique culture by searching for negatives, criticizing and picking at its performance, apparently unwilling to believe that the founder could be sincere. As Roddick has said, it's easier to follow the herd than to break out on a new path.

Key Components of Corporate Culture

Understanding the key parts of corporate cultures can help you identify them in your company and to analyze any corporate culture. Key factors include role models and heroes, rituals and ceremonies, grapevines and networks. All of these parts of corporate culture are partly real, partly symbolic.

What's in a Name? Symbols serve an important function in all cultures. Examples of a symbol include a logo, picture, brand name, nickname, motto, song, figure of speech, treasured ritual, legendary hero, mascot, banner, or flag. Symbols may represent the essence of common values, norms, and experiences that bind people together in a common cause and may touch them deeply. A symbol can serve to trigger these communal thoughts and feelings.

The People: Role Models and Heroes

The heroes, heroines, champions, stars, and other leaders in the company are the role models who personify the core values and the strength of the corporation. They become symbolic figures whose deeds are out of the ordinary, but not too far out. People can identify with them. They become great motivators, the people everyone will count on when things get tough. They tend to be intuitive, to envision the future, to experiment, and to appreciate the value of celebrations and ceremonies.

Heroes and heroines are most often those top executives or founders who are seen as fearless leaders or courageous adventurers. They also may be top sales representatives, computer geniuses, maverick researchers, or anyone who becomes legendary in a key area. Heroes and heroines rein-

force the basic values of the culture by:
- showing that success is attainable and human
- providing inspiration
- symbolizing the company to the outside world
- preserving what makes the company special
- setting a standard of performance
- motivating employees

They are the leading actors in a strong corporate culture, but they are only part of a variety of behavioral procedures that define how work gets done. These procedures, often called rituals or ceremonies, provide the backdrop, the stage setting, in which role models can be showcased.

The Processes: Rituals and Networks

Rituals are communication forms in which there is a structured sequence of symbolic acts. The correct performance of those acts reflects respect for an important value or sacred object. *Networks* are the informal communication channels that people use to refine and modify rituals and other aspects of corporate culture.

Rituals. The customary day-to-day actions people take, their expected actions and responses, "the way we do things around here," are all rituals. Strong-culture companies communicate exactly how they want their people to act. Work rituals spell out standards of acceptable behavior and how such procedures as strategic planning and budgeting should be carried out. Recognition rituals, such as awards, are acknowledgments of valued achievement, a sign that you belong to the culture. Rituals relate to the need for belonging and for establishing common ground with others in the group. Symbolic actions such as play, rites, and ceremony incorporate ritual and are important mechanisms for establishing and maintaining common values and goals. Myths are the stories behind these ritual forms.

Play is creative, releases tension, and encourages innovation. Its form may include joking, teasing, brainstorming, strategizing. It bonds people together, reduces conflict, and helps to create new visions and corporate culture values.

Rites are rituals that are formal practices, customs, or procedures. A rite is any detailed method of procedure that is regularly followed. Most of us are familiar with religious rites and club rites but may not think in terms of corporate rites. They reflect the rules that guide behavior, little vignettes of the company's basic values.

Myths that form the basis for various rituals are those stories or legends that symbolize a central belief of the culture. Unless a ritual is connected to a myth, it's just a habit that does nothing but give people a false sense of security. Rituals provide the script by which people act out beliefs and attitudes that give meaning to corporate life, that bring order to the chaos. More about them later.

Ceremonies usually incorporate some rituals and serve as milestones or markers to focus company attention on people or groups for their heroic achievement, dedication, loyalty, and other traits or actions that reflect corporate values. Ceremonies can help companies keep values, beliefs, and role models up front in people's minds and hearts.

Core values would have no impact without ritual and ceremony. The unwritten rules of personal communication, the rituals of social interaction, govern relationships between bosses and workers, professionals and support staff, men and women, old and young, insiders and outsiders. People learn them in part through hazing rites that are often staged to dress people down before accepting them into a culture. Hazing rituals set up a conflict. Bonding and healing rituals help mediate the conflicts and misunderstandings that threaten cultural harmony.

Work rituals set up cultural boundaries that provide security during high risk activities. They also can enhance employees' sense of self-worth. It is the business of culture to provide a way for people to justify a belief in their own self-worth and that of their work. Work rituals also signal to the outside world just how effective the culture is, especially if the product is intangible. By recognizing this importance, companies can use work rituals to help build a strong culture that will produce even better results. The most important work ritual is often the staff or team meeting. All companies have them, but they vary widely as to how they're conducted and what they're designed to do.

Recognition rituals are important in strong-culture companies. There's a big commotion when someone does well and exemplifies core values. The best companies make sure everyone understands why someone gets a reward, whether the ceremony is simple or ornate. Some of the strongest corporate cultures elevate ceremonies to extravaganzas—Mary Kay and IBM are examples. Effective leaders pay great attention to rituals, not only devising them but taking an active part in them. They participate in new employee orientations, orchestrate promotion celebrations, and make sure everyone knows why the person is being promoted.

Networks. The grapevine, the informal network, is the primary means of communication within an organization. It ties together all parts of the company without respect to the organization chart. It not only transmits information, it also interprets its significance. In most organizations, only about 10 percent of business takes place in formal meetings and events. The real process of making decisions, gathering support, developing opinions, etc., happens before or after the meeting. Of course, formal networks are important too. They include the formal organization chart, task forces, work teams, professional and trade associations, and similar groupings.

Some Corporate Culture Patterns

Each corporate culture is somewhat unique, depending on the type of business, its context, and its leaders. Deal and Kennedy have identified certain patterns, however, that may help you get a handle on learning about a particular company's culture. Table 2.7 presents four typical patterns. Few companies fall completely into one type. In fact, companies organized functionally will vary in type by department.

High Risk–Fast Lane

This culture is a world where one event or decision can make or break a career, even a company, often overnight. The risk of failure is high, and you know how you did relatively quickly. Examples are shown in Table 2.7. Functional departments within companies that tend toward a high risk–fast lane subculture include marketing, especially advertising.

Timely decisions are crucial, since delaying a decision can mean losing out. The all-or-nothing nature of many decisions encourages values of risk taking and belief in oneself. The majority of these cultures, which focus on speed rather than endurance, attract young employees. High competition, both internally and externally, is the rule. In this world of individualists, the stars are the heroes. Stars are known to be temperamental, and outlaw heroes are common. They may behave outrageously as long as they keep succeeding. Procedures can become temporary havens from the fear of taking risks and making the big mistake that spells disaster. Superstitions abound. Bonding can be exclusive and exclusionary because to change the structure of a group that's been successful might break the magic spell.

The major weakness of this culture stems from the emphasis on quick feedback. The tendency is to put too many resources into short-term projects, neglecting needed long-term investments. The level of competition can also be a weakness if the need for cooperation is overlooked. If superstition gets out of hand, people may start assigning the cause of success or failure to walking under a ladder or carrying a lucky charm and may neglect to rationally analyze what went right or wrong so they can learn from their mistakes. The end result of rewarding people who focus on winning in the short run is that people whose careers might blossom over time can't last. This high turnover makes it difficult to build a strong, cohesive culture.

TABLE 2.7: Corporate Culture Patterns

Pattern	Characteristics	Examples
High Risk–Fast Lane	• tough • fast-moving • short-term • quick feedback.	Entertainment, professional sports, publishing, venture capital, advertising, construction management consulting, makers of computers, high-fashion clothing, and cosmetics; marketing departments of any firm.
Low Risk–Fast Lane	• high activity • fast-moving • short-term • quick feedback.	All retail stores. Firms that make or sell such products as food, real estate, office equipment, automobiles; sales and production departments.
High Risk–Slow Lane	• big stakes • slow-moving • long-term • slow feedback.	Firms that develop oil, minerals, etc.; insurance funds, biotech, architectural services, computer design, capital equipment; research departments.
Low Risk–Slow Lane	• bureaucratic • process culture • little or no feedback.	Government, utilities, banks, heavily regulated firms such as pharmaceuticals; support staff departments.

Low Risk–Fast Lane

These are the cultures that focus on retail markets, either making and selling or just selling. They include virtually all retail stores and sales and manufacturing departments within organizations that develop this culture. People in these companies take relatively small risks; one sale won't make or break them. They must be active—stay on the move and move fast, and they get quick feedback on whether or not they are succeeding. Sales are good or they're not. The customer bought or she didn't.

The primary values center around customers and their needs, on finding a need and filling it. Competition is fairly high, though not as tough as in a high risk–fast lane culture. The race is to the quick, and people must stay active and take initiative to even stay in the race. The super salespeople are the heroes, and people measure the worth of their activity in volume of sales, not high stakes. People tend to be friendly, fun loving, work-hard/play-hard types. The team is usually more important than the individual star because it takes a team to produce the sales volume the company needs to succeed. Rites and rituals center around contests, meetings, promotions, and conventions, all designed to bolster motivation.

A potential weakness in this culture is focusing too much on quantity volume and neglecting quality. Also, the focus on short-term results often leads to a tendency to focus on short-term goals and solutions. The quick fix is popular. Sales people are not accustomed to digging for the root of the problem when sales are off. They may become disillusioned and switch companies rather than sticking it out until they fix the problem. A strength of this culture is its ability to attract young people looking for a place to prove their stuff. They'll need their stamina in this active culture.

High Risk–Slow Lane

Big stakes, and therefore high risks, are the constant backdrop of this culture, where companies make huge investments hoping for long-term payback. Examples include companies that develop oil and minerals, provide insurance funds, biotech research and products, architectural services, computer design, and capital equipment. It includes most firms that focus on research and development, and the armed services because they spend so much time preparing for wars that may never occur.

Values focus on the future and the importance of investing in it. Because of the high stakes, deliberateness in decision making and action is a key value. The business meeting is the primary ritual. Hierarchy and rank are important.

People who thrive in this culture are as self-directed and as tough as people in the high risk–fast lane culture, but they have the stamina to endure long-term ambiguity and little feedback on how they're doing. Their moves are measured and deliberate because they need to be sure they're right. Survivors respect authority and technical competence. The heroes tend to be hunker-down heroes, and they are especially important in this culture because they provide psychological support during the rough times that people must ride out. People who will share their hard-won knowledge are valued. Younger employees depend on mentors, who are the foundation of the system. There is great respect for authority that stems from expertise and experience.

Low Risk–Slow Lane

This is a bureaucratic culture. The stakes are low—no one transaction will make or break anyone—and feedback is normally very slow if it ever comes at all. Examples include most of the government, utilities, banks, and other heavily regulated companies such as pharmaceuticals. Functional departments that often have a bureaucratic style include large support staff departments—secretarial, clerical, accounting, credit, and similar services. Typically, employees get little or no feedback on how well they're doing until someone blames them for something. This forces them to focus on *how* they do things more than on *what* they do, making it a process culture. Protecting themselves from blame often takes an inordinate amount of their time.

Values center on technical perfection, how you do things, figuring out the risks, and having solutions down pat and the details right. Survivors learn to live in this world where protectiveness and caution are the rule and where doing things (perhaps stupid or irrelevant things) neatly and completely are what's important. They are punctual, orderly, detail oriented, and have good memories. They carry out procedures according to the manual, whether the procedures make sense to them or not. Heroes tend to be hunker-down types who often win out when the political winds shift for the better. For some employees, the job position is the hero rather than the person filling it.

Rituals revolve around work patterns and procedures. Long rambling meetings may be held to talk about the way a decision should be made—the process. Reorganization is one of the most important rituals. Retirement ceremonies for those who hunkered down the longest are important. The tightly structured hierarchies are reminiscent of a class system, and title and formalities are respected. The greatest weaknesses of the bureaucratic culture can be the tangle of red tape and the difficulty employees often have of dealing with the real world of customer needs. They do provide a stability and continuity that help offset the uproar of some of the other cultures.

Virtual Corporation: A New Pattern

The virtual corporation is evolving from the demands of a diverse, post-industrial, technological, global economy. Just as virtual reality is a computerized experience that seems real but takes place in cyberspace, a virtual corporation is "like a real (traditional) corporation." However, much of the work, the meetings, and communication take place on computer screens, fax machines, car phones, voice mail, and video conferences. Work teams may include company specialists, independent contractors, suppliers, customers, and investors. They may be scattered around the globe, change from month to month, and never meet face to face. Or they may be self-managing teams that meet every day. They may work together to develop the plans, set the standards, identify and solve the problems, make the decisions, and provide the products and services. In any case, the degree of success or failure depends heavily on people's relationships with one another.

Of course, this format affects organizational structure. Old rigid bureaucratic hierarchies are melting into fluid, shifting networks of relationships among employees, customers, suppliers, and allied competitors as depicted visually in Figure 2.1. Table 2.9 at the end of this chapter shows how manufacturing corporations can fit this model; however, the virtual corporation format is also being adopted by many service organizations. Examples are custom banking, investment

FIGURE 2.1: Structure: Virtual vs. Traditional Corporations

Cust. = Customers
Dist. = Distributors

Virtual Corporation   Traditional Corporation

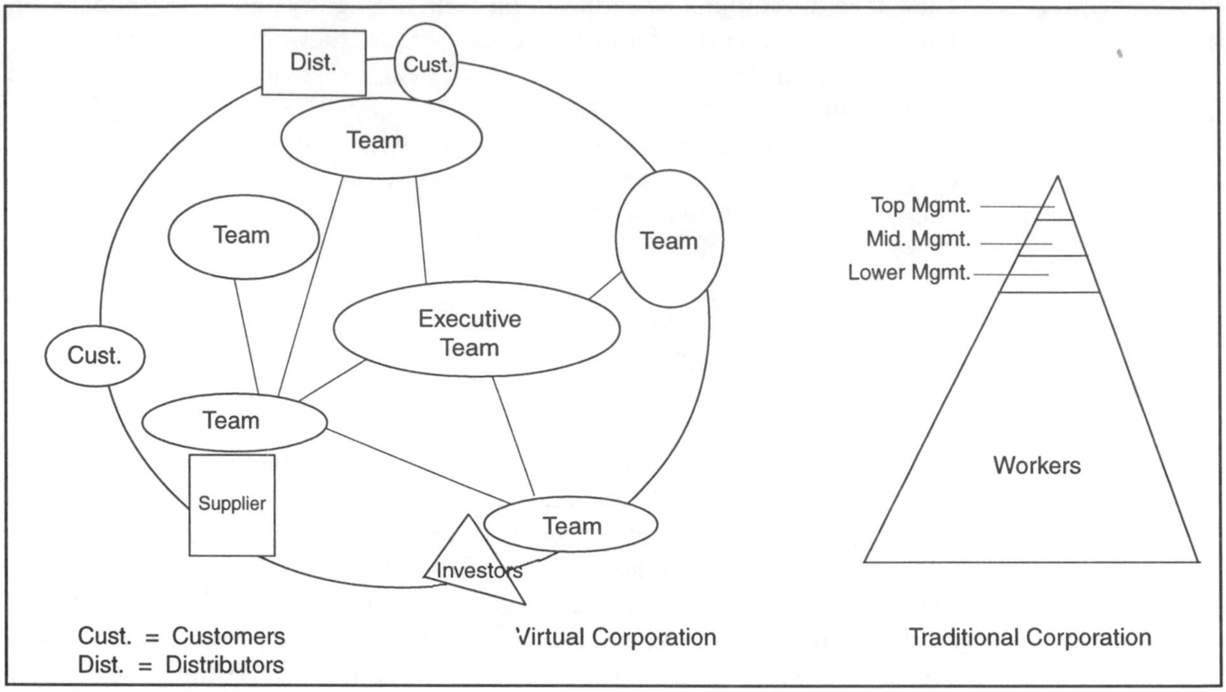

services, manufacturers' representatives, wholesale operations, and computer services (Davidow and Malone, 1992).

The virtual corporation is built upon trust, collaboration, cooperation, and teamwork, but it also relies on individual achievement and the ability to be entrepreneurial, and therefore competitive, in outlook. In such organizations, it's more obvious than ever that people are the most valuable resource, that how they work together creates energy and innovation or decay and demoralization, that their interactions spark the knowledge and information that fuel organizational growth and success. And the kinds of people moving into these new jobs are more diverse each year.

How Corporate Culture Affects Diverse Employees

The orientation process informs newcomers about the organization's goals, norms, the way we do things around here. New employees normally must develop specific work skills, learn role behaviors appropriate to their new job, and adjust to the work group's values and norms (Feldman 1981). Here's where the unspoken, unwritten, and sometimes most important information about getting along should be learned. The values and norms may be more difficult for culturally different members to learn, because minorities are usually not part of the informal social networks of the dominant group. Socialization occurs by such formal methods as training, performance appraisal, and promotion decisions, as well as by such informal methods as rituals, stories, jargon, and role modeling. The purpose of orientation, sometimes called organization socialization, is to align employees with the norms of the organization; it is closely linked to acculturation processes.

Acculturation

Acculturation is a process that occurs when new employees join an organization or when two organizations with different cultures merge. Traditionally, acculturation was accomplished through stories that express key values, and norms—stories about role models, rituals, ceremonies, myths, and symbols. Cox describes four modes of acculturation: assimilation, separation, deculturation, and pluralism (Cox and Finley-Nickelson 1991).

Assimilation. When the organization's culture is the standard of behavior for all persons, assimilation is the mode of acculturation. The goal is to eliminate cultural differences at work. New employees who are culturally different are expected to reject, or at least repress, their conflicting beliefs, values, norms, and practices. It is a one-way adaptation, similar to the melting-pot approach.

Separation. Alienation occurs when new employees are unwilling or unable to adapt to the organization culture. They maintain some separation from it. Cultural exchange is minimal. This is possible where a minority group's members are segregated by job category, and they form their own corporate subculture. To a lesser degree, minority groups from various units may cluster together, voluntarily isolating themselves from the dominant group in order to maintain some cultural autonomy.

Deculturation. A lack of enculturation that occurs when new employees are not significantly affected by either the organization culture or by their cultural group. The corporate culture is weak. New employees' own cultural identity is ill defined, perhaps because they have severed ties with their original sociocultural group but haven't formed new ties with the dominant culture. Symptoms may be: very little bonding taking place, very weak loyalty and commitment, and high turnover and absenteeism.

Multiculturalism. This is a two-way learning and adaptation process in which both the organization and new employees from various cultures change to some degree to reflect the cultural norms and values of each other. It focuses on mutual appreciation among cultures, the importance of maintaining subcultural identity, and interdependence among the corporate culture and the various subcultures. New employees assimilate a limited number of core behaviors and values, but they also maintain important differences.

Acculturation Factors

How well diverse employees are acculturated depends on many factors, especially the culture's tolerance for ambiguity, the degree to which cultural diversity is valued, the extent of conformity that's required, and how well the employees' cultural backgrounds and the corporate culture fit together.

Tolerance for ambiguity. This refers to the organization's assumptions about whether ambiguities are "legitimate and normal" (Meyerson and Lewis 1992). Organizations with high tolerance exert less pressure for conformity and tolerate more diversity. They are more likely to favor multiculturalism as an acculturation mode. Sociocultural conflict is more likely to be viewed as normal and potentially useful rather than as dysfunctional and threatening.

Degree to which cultural diversity is valued. Organizations with a strong "valuing diversity" norm tend to welcome the cultural exchange and interaction that is at the core of the multiculturalism mode of acculturation.

Demand for conformity. Cultures vary by the extent and degree of conformity they demand of members. Table 2-8 compares some tendencies of typical managers in high conformity cultures with those in low conformity cultures.

Cultural fit. This refers to the degree of alignment between two or more cultural patterns, and therefore the degree to which subcultures may comfortably exist within the organization culture. Obviously, fit is best where there is a great deal of cultural overlap between the corporate culture and an employee's root culture, where their beliefs, values, and norms are similar (De Anda 1984). Some authors have identified types of subcultures according to their degree of fit with a corporate culture (Siehl and Martin 1984). A *reinforcing subculture* is compatible with and strongly reinforces the norms and values of the organization culture. A *refining subculture* shares many of the basic assumptions and values of the organization culture but also holds some that are unique. A *counterculture* embraces basic assumptions and norms that are primarily in conflict with the organization culture and therefore challenges its validity.

TABLE 2-8: Comparison of Management Behaviors:
High Conformity and Low Conformity Corporate Cultures

Managers in High Conformity Cultures:	Managers in Low Conformity Cultures:
• Have a narrow view of behavior that's O.K.	• See many behaviors as O.K. unless they violate a few core values, such as integrity and quality
• Evaluate, judge, and criticize others	• Don't judge ideas until they clearly understand them
	• React to ideas in ways other than judging them good or bad
• Avoid taking risks	• Take calculated risks; encourage others to do so
• Are intolerant of mistakes	• View failure, within limits, as a learning opportunity
• Focus on mistakes	and part of innovation
• Ignore many positive contributions	• Pay more attention when people exceed standards than when they don't
• Prescribe the details of how to do things	• Encourage people to create new approaches
• See one right way to do most things	that work

Adapted from Cox, 1993

When cultural fit is poor, employees must pay the psychological costs of giving up some of their identity and of acting unnaturally. Their choices of how to act become more complex and ambiguous and they tend to experience stress.

Targeted acculturation. Companies can lower turnover rates of diverse employees by targeting acculturation procedures to group and individual needs. Without some special form of orientation, how can women and minorities become properly acculturated? Some companies use formal mentoring programs. Others try to manage job assignments to ensure a progression of sympathetic and supportive superiors. A third strategy is to assign them to a series of problem-solving task forces so they form a series of relationships with their peers that sustain them in their early years with the firm.

How can company leaders influence the culture to accommodate the needs of women and minorities? Some develop explicit guidelines for behavior in situations involving them, and a procedure for making everyone aware of these guidelines. Women and minorities can't become effective members of the culture if they're continually coping with embarrassing situations. Leaders must spell out standards for social behavior in relationships with these new members. They must focus on ritualistic cultural barriers to the acceptance of women and minorities and take specific action to remove these barriers. Leaders must become role models, setting an example of appropriate treatment of minorities and women.

SUMMARY

The first step in building multicultural skills is becoming aware of culture and its pervasive influence. Culture is programmed beliefs, hidden programming, our mental map, our consensus reality, and our personal reality. Cultures use ten primary message systems that communicate values, norms, rituals, and customs from one generation to the next. The message systems are embedded in the ways adults educate youngsters, direct them, and model appropriate behaviors for them.

Numerous commonalties are found across all cultures. Still, cultures can be quite diverse, and going from one to another can be like going into another world. Even within one culture, girls and boys are raised so differently it's as if they're living in parallel worlds. Some major ways that cultures differ include the degree of independence, which in turn reflects beliefs about whether I create my situation or it happens to me, and whether the focus is on me-first or us-first, achievement-first or people-first, equality or rank/status, and taking risks or playing it safe. In addition, cultures often differ in how directly they communicate and how they view time and space. Most cultures are us-first and people-first focused and most accept unequal power and status among people.

The economic base of a culture also affects what it values. In cultures with a predominantly agricultural economy people tend to be more dependent on each other and nature. Those in an industrial economy are more independent, and as the culture moves to a post-industrial economy, as it is in the United States, people become more interdependent. At this level, people are capable of being independent but choose to cooperate interdependently for greater achievement.

The United States is predominantly a me-first, achievement-first culture that values equality and risk taking. Although a key American value is equality of all persons and the melting-pot society is one of our ideals, America has been a segmented society. While various European immigrant groups have eventually integrated into the dominant society, other immigrant groups and American Indians have not. The workplace was a melting pot for men from various European countries but not for others. What has united us has been our political, legal, and economic systems. We can each have some say in government, rely on government and the courts to settle disputes, and participate in a common consumer marketplace.

Americans especially value being an individual, making individual decisions, and achieving material success and progress. We therefore believe in keeping busy and in separating work and play. Other values center on conquering nature and on getting the facts and putting them to work. The American way of thinking is predominantly a rational, linear, cause-and-effect approach that relies on measuring things. We tend to think more in black-or-white terms than in shades of gray, to welcome change more than most cultures, and to be more informal. We look toward the future and are beginning to use our individualism in an interdependent way to reach even higher levels of achievement together.

The American way of relating involves making many casual friends with less intense commitment than in many other cultures. We tend to identify people with specialized roles and to base friendships on specialized activities, such as work, sports, etc. We believe in treating others as equals, cooperating, playing fair, and being direct. We take a step-by-step, linear view of time and use it by staying busy. In physical terms, our boundary for most colleagues is about arm's length, more distant than Latino and Arab cultures and closer than Asian cultures.

Corporate cultures can be strong or weak, depending on the leaders at the top. The type of culture that works best in a multicultural workplace is a strong culture in which management insists on conformity to only a few core values and norms but not on less important ones. Heroes and heroines serve as role models that personify certain corporate values and norms. They motivate others to succeed. Corporate rituals and ceremonies indicate to everyone what the company values and the way the people in the company are expected to do things. Grapevines and networks are the informal channels for getting the word around.

Typical corporate culture patterns depend on whether the company is basically in a high risk or low risk business and whether it must produce results quickly or over time. The virtual corporation is a new pattern where people often use computers, car phones, faxes, and other electronic equipment in the field, in far-flung small offices, or in home offices, often on a subcontractor or consulting basis. Therefore the virtual corporation may not look much like a traditional corporation and the culture is accordingly much more flexible and dynamic.

Newcomers into the corporation may be acculturated or assimilated. When they're not, separation or deculturation may occur. Multiculturalism is a two-way adaptation process that values diversity. How new employees are acculturated depends largely on the flexibility and openness of the corporate culture and its leaders' commitment to a multicultural workplace.

ADDITIONAL BACKGROUND INFORMATION

TABLE 2.9: Virtual Corporation: Comparisons with Traditional Corporation—Manufacturing Example

Strategies

Virtual Corporation	*Traditional Corporation*
Post-Industrial Economic View: Manufacturing base is essential as customers of services and generator of wealth for employees to purchase services.	*Post-Industrial Economic View:* Buy products from other nations where labor is cheaper.
Result: Develop a complex, rich manufacturing and agricultural base, highly automated, few workers.	*Result:* Hollowed-out economy—manufacturing corporations as mere shells for products made in other countries.
Targeted market niches.	Economies of scale.
Engine: Information processing.	Engine: The assembly line.
Lights-out automated factories.	Large factories, many workers.
A few long-term suppliers, many customized models—targeted customers.	Many suppliers, few models of products, many customers.

Products

Virtual Corporation	*Traditional Corporation*
Virtual products are stored in minds of cooperating teams, in computers, and in flexible product lines.	Products are stored in warehouses and retail stores.
Virtual products are produced instantly and customized to customer demand.	Products supplied weeks or months after orders are placed or plans made—limited, standardized models.

Structure

Virtual Corporation	*Traditional Corporation*
Fluid, flexible, constantly changing—a web or network of informational relationships.	*Rigid, stable—hierarchical departments filled with job slots, each with a job description and lines of authority.*
Structure meets unique needs of customers.	Structure meets needs of corporation—or a broad average (mass) of customers.
Structure, planning start with customer needs and desires.	Structure, planning start with what corporation wants to do and can do.
Self-managed work teams that may include customers, suppliers, retailers, investors, distributors.	Individual workers, some internal task forces and work teams.
Corporation is a vast network of relationships to carry out ever-changing clusters of common activities.	Corporation is a discrete, separate enterprise.

Human Resources	
Virtual Corporation	*Traditional Corporation*
Most workers (85–90%) in knowledge or service jobs.	Most workers in production jobs.
Change focus to targeted production of customized products and services for "niche" customers.	Retain focus on mass production of standardized products and services for mass consumption.
Most jobs require higher education—broad, general knowledge—multicultural and technological.	Most jobs require secondary education—specialized knowledge.
Requires workers to be informed, responsible, adaptable to change, flexible. Free flow of rich information.	Requires workers to be obedient, fit a job slot, specialized. Managers have access to information they need; pass along minimal information to workers.
Managers as leaders, coaches, facilitators; power lies in people skills.	Managers as directors, motivators, evaluators; power lies in the hierarchy.
Worker freedom, power to control work.	Close supervision of workers.
Built on trust, collaboration, mutual cooperation, teamwork.	Built on protecting self-interest, confrontation between workers and management, adversarial relationships.
Rewards leaders for long-term dedication.	Rewards leaders for short-term manipulation.

TABLE 2.10: The Economic System's Effect on Cultural Values

Values Related to Achievement vs. Relationship

Agricultural-Era Values—Dependent	*Industrial-Era Values*—Independent	*Post-Industrial-Era Values*—Interdependent
Cooperative (win–win)	Competitive (win–lose)	Cooperative (win–win)
Workers as members of a family	Workers as automatons	Workers as dynamic colleagues
Static role-based relationships (place-bound)	Mechanistic organizations	Organic organizations
Community	Compartmentalization	Integration
Life is a chore—people must earn redemption	Theory X—people are lazy, must be coerced, directed	Theory Y—people can be self-motivated
Survival focus	Profit centered	Value centered
Traditions/ceremonies	Acquiring material goods for family/self	Experiencing events, life
Work relationships—focus on role	Work relationships—focus on secrecy/need to know	Work relationships—focus on openness
People necessary for family survival	People as means to organizational ends	People as ends in themselves
Feelings channeled through ceremonies	Feelings denied/relationships impersonal	Feelings expressed, relationships personal
Right brain emphasis (intuitive, feeling, holistic)	Left brain emphasis (rational, linear, factual)	Intuitive/rational balance
Role modeling (toward an ideal)	Macho modeling (winning)	Androgyny, masculine/feminine balance
Power over nature	Power over others	Empowerment of self and others
Dominance	Manipulation	Collaboration
Personal/community development	Management development	Organizational development
People as necessary components	People as expendable resources, liabilities	People as renewable resources/assets
The spiritual aspects of life most highly values	Material things most highly valued	Ideas most highly valued
Focus on traditions, values, family	Focus on bottom line	Focus on process/goal/person

Values Related to Me-First or Us-First and to I-Control or I'm-Controlled

Agricultural Economy—Dependent	*Industrial Economy*—Independent	*Post-Industrial Economy*—Interdependent
Family/community focus	Bureaucracy/hierarchy	Flexible teams/networks
Family/community hold the power	Organization centered	Organization as part of society
Family/clan centered	Class centered	Lifestyle centered
Extrinsic motivation (expectations)	Extrinsic motivation (incentive)	Intrinsic motivation
Integrated community role	Dependency at work	Autonomy at work
Social norms—universal	Social norms—universal	Social norms—pluralistic
	Shareholders/managers hold the power	Stakeholders share the power
Work as a function of life	Work as drudgery	Work as fun
Performance judged by elders, neighbors	Performance judged by boss as control factor	Performance judged by self, others for growth, learning
Submersion of self in groups	Interpersonal game playing	Authenticity
Product standard—adequacy	Product standard—planned obsolescence	Product standard—conservation
Work—rhythmic	Work—routine, often monotonous	Work—creative
Diffuse localization of power and activity	Centralization of power and activity	Decentralization of power and activity
Diverse chores	Job specialization	Job enrichment
Community oriented	Isolated, alienated	Committed
Risk averse	Risk averse	Entrepreneurial
Obedience to parent/elder	Obedience to boss	Respected associate
Workers—role/family centered	Workers—job centered	Workers—professional centered

Values Related to Time and Space Orientations

Agricultural-Era Values—Dependent	*Industrial Economy*—Independent	*Post-Industrial Economy*—Interdependent
Viewpoint tied to seasonal/life cycle	Viewpoint short-term, narrow, fragmented	Focus on the long term, the holistic
Permanence—social life static	Permanence—social life slow evolving	Transience—instant intimacy
Provincialism	Provincialism	Cosmopolitanism

Preparation for Skill Builder 2.1: What Is Your Cultural Identity?

Your cultural identity consists of the groups you identify with and the strength with which you identify with each group. When we take the time to think about it, we can easily name those aspects of our identity that are most important to us. Most people are quite aware of those aspects that make them different from the dominant majority and are considerably less aware of their other facets. For example, Euro-American women tend to focus on being a woman, expatriates focus on nationality, minority men focus on ethnicity, and nonwhite women focus somewhat equally on gender and ethnicity.

Euro-American males are more likely than any other group to focus on individual identification, according to Cox [1993], even when instructed to refer only to group identifications. As Hofstede [1980] showed, individuality is a strong cultural norm for Euro-American men. Also, because they are part of the dominant majority group, Euro-American men face the fewest workplace and socioeconomic barriers, and therefore tend to be less aware of group identities than are members of minority groups [Alderfer 1982]. The ways in which we differ from one another include gender, sexual orientation, physical ability, ethnic heritage, occupational or professional influences, educational and socioeconomic background, and religious, spiritual, or philosophical influences. You have a chance to develop your own cultural profile in Skill Builder 2.1.

The ethnic differences of immigrants tend to recede over time, and each generation born in this country is more Americanized than their parents. However, certain cultural values tend to remain strong. For example, even third-generation Japanese Americans have been found to have relatively high scores on ethnic identification with the Japanese culture, with survey scores virtually unchanged between second- and third-generation respondents [Matsumoto, Meredith, and Masuda 1970].

Skill Builder 2.1: Your Cultural Profile

Purpose: To identify key aspects of your cultural heritage and identity.

Step 1. Complete the second column of the table below by completing the statements made in the first column.

Step 2. Complete the third column of the table by determining the importance of each specific category for you. [For example, is being a college graduate a major or minor part of your identity?] Place a number, from 1 to 5, beside each category you've listed, according to its importance, using the following guidelines to assign weights:

     5 = Major, essential aspect of my identity
     4 = Very important aspect of my identity
     3 = Fairly important aspect of my identity
     2 = Somewhat influential aspect of my identity
     1 = Slightly influential aspect of my identity

Step 3. Write a brief paragraph about your cultural profile. Include any thoughts, feelings, surprises, or insights that came to you as you did this exercise.

Aspects of Your Identity

Area of Identity or Influence	Specify Categories	Weight: 1 to 5
My *gender* is: My *sexual orientation* is (hetero-sexual, homosexual, bisexual): My *ethnic group* is (ancestors' country of origin): The *nation* where I was born is: The *part of the country* I grew up in is: The *occupation* I'm in or want is: The *company* I work for is: My *religion* or philosophy is: My *socioeconomic* class is (middle, lower, upper class): My *educational* level is: My *parent's educational* level is: *Other* groups or aspects that have influenced my identity are:		

Skill Builder 2.2: Diverse Groups You Need to Learn About

Purpose: To identify those groups of people you need to learn more about, ranging from those you know almost nothing about to those you need no information about.

Step 1. In the first column below are listed types of groups discussed in this book. In the second column, you may want to set up two categories, men and women, and assign them different weights.

Step 2. The third column refers to the degree to which you lack information on each group listed in the first column. Place a number, from 1 to 5, beside each group you've listed, indicating how much you know about this group, using the following guidelines to assign weights:

    5 = I know nothing about this group
    4 = I know almost nothing about this group
    3 = I know very little about this group
    2 = I have a fair amount of information and understanding of this group
    1 = I have a great deal of information and understanding about this group
        and need little or no additional information

Groups I Need to Learn About

Type of Group	More specific identity?	Weight: 1 to 5
Arab American African American American Indian Asian American (or subgroup) Euro-American Latino American (or subgroup) Persons with Disabilities Gay/Lesbian/Bisexual Obese persons Older persons Persons from other religions Persons whose mother and father are from different ethnic groups Women's issues Men's issues Other groups		

Skill Builder 2.3: Identifying Some Perceptions

Purpose: To learn more about your way of thinking.

Step 1. Relax and focus on the following words, one at a time.

Stranger. Foreigner. Immigrant. Native. People. Family. Home. Work. Nature.

Notice what mental picture, what words, and what feelings you experience when you focus on the words. Jot down the word and note your reactions and associations with it. Do this for all the words.

Step 2. Now go back and review your list. For each word, note any judgment, attitude, or belief that came to mind when you first saw the word or that comes to mind now. Do this for all the words.

Step 3. Go back again and review your judgments, attitudes or beliefs. Where do you think each of these originally came from?

Step 4. Write down any thoughts, feelings, and insights that occur to you now that you've completed working with the list of words. What, if anything, did you learn about yourself?

Skill Builder 2.4: Your Sense of Time

Purpose: To increase your awareness about how you and others view and use time.
Instructions: Describe briefly at least one instance when you and someone from a different cultural background experienced conflict, misunderstanding, or problems about time. Use the following list to help you remember your situation:

• Being on time	• Feeling impatient over others' slowness
• Meeting deadlines	• Focusing on past events, tradition
• Feeling hurried, rushed	• Living for the moment, short-range view
• Using time efficiently	• Focusing on the present moment
• Using time effectively	• Focusing on the future, what might happen
• Being "out of sync"	• Focusing on planning, or long-range view
	• Other issues about time

Skill Builder 2.5: Your Boundaries

Purpose: To increase your awareness about how you and others view and use personal space.
Instructions: Describe briefly at least one when you (or others) experienced conflict, misunderstanding, or problems about personal space, touching, or boundaries. Use the following list to help you remember your situation.
• Invasion of privacy—yours or others
• Discomfort because of lack of privacy
• Invasion of personal body space
• Someone in your face
• Feeling crowded or claustrophobic
• Too much touching
• Invasive touching
• Too much coldness and distance
• Other issues about space, boundaries, or touching

Skill Builder 2.6: Your Values

Purpose: To learn more about yourself and what you want in life.
Instructions: Before you begin, remember that the purpose of this exercise is for you to learn more about yourself. Don't evaluate, judge, or analyze what comes up; just let what wants to come up do so.

Step 1. Brainstorm. Relax, close your eyes for a few moments and think about these questions:

• What are the aspects of my life that I treasure the most? That I wouldn't want to lose?
• That I would fight to keep?
• What are those aspects of life that I don't yet have and want most to have? That I would work hard to have?
• What are my values?

Step 2. Write. Don't try to evaluate or analyze the thoughts that occurred to you. Just write them down in whatever sequence you remember them. As more ideas come up, write them down.

Step 3. Categorize. Look over what you've written. Do the items fall into any patterns or categories, such as:

family, friends work, leisure	money, power, beauty, truth	intelligence, emotions spirituality

You'll find your own categories, not necessarily these. Work with your list till you see some logical categories; then rewrite your list of values by category.

Step 4. Personalize terms. What would you call the items on your list if you didn't call them values? (desires? goals? beliefs? issues? other?)

Skill Builder 2.7: Cultures You've Known

Purpose: To recognize the hidden aspects of your own and other cultural groups.
Instructions: For each category that is relevant to your own life, identify examples of cultural practices, as indicated in the National Symbols category.

Perhaps reviewing some obvious rites, rituals, heroes, and symbols of the cultures you've belonged to will help you recognize more subtle rites, rituals, etc., in the cultures you encounter. Remember, rites and rituals relate to the need for belonging. A *rite* is any formal practice, custom, or procedure. A *ritual* is any detailed method of procedure that is regularly followed. Be aware that in every organization, the stronger the rules, rituals, symbols, and heroes, the stronger the effect and influence the organization has on its members' lives.

National Symbols

Rites and Rituals: (What rites and rituals gave you a feeling of national unity—an overall community with common purpose? For example, the national anthem.)
Heroes: (What heroes personified key national values?)
Symbols: (What symbols served to unify, to express values? For example, the flag.)
Values: (What values are expressed by the above?)

Repeat for your school.

Repeat for your religious community.

Skill Builder 2.8: Learning More about an Organization's Culture

Purpose: To learn more about a target organization's culture, perhaps the one you work in or one you're thinking about joining, and to place it into a frame of reference for understanding what's going on. (See also Exercise 2.11 and Table 2.7 Idea Starters for Sample Interview Questions.)

Name of Target Organization: _____

Step 1. Investigate. Visit the organization and observe or ask questions as follows.
   1. *Observe the physical setting.*
      - What's your initial impression?
      - What does the physical layout seem to communicate?
      - Is the image consistent in all divisions? facilities?

2. *Collect and analyze written materials, such as annual reports, newsletters, news releases, manuals.*
   - What does the company say about itself?
   - What type of culture do written materials reflect?
   - Do you see signs of diversity at all levels in the materials?

3. *Observe reception area procedures.*
   - Formal or informal?
   - Relaxed or busy?
   - Elegant or plain?
   - What is the receptionist doing? How does she or he interact with visitors?
   - What procedures or processes are used with visitors?
   - Do visitors wait?
   - Do you see signs of diversity so far?

4. *Ask employees questions, such as these:*
   - Tell me about the history of the company. (Notice what facts seem accurate, what myths surface.)
   - What has made the company successful? (Look for company values. Do people generally agree on which company values are most important?)
   - What kind of people work here? Who gets ahead? (Look for signs of diverse role models, descriptions of role models; look for clear agreement about how to succeed. Are role models constructive, serve the company well? Do women and minorities often succeed?)
   - What's it like to work here? How do things get done? (Look for important rites, rituals, meetings, or bureaucratic procedures; do all departmental or team subcultures have some unifying values? Do rites, rules, and procedures encompass or respect the diversity found within the organization?)

5. *Observe and ask, how do people (really) spend their time?*

6. *Ask about career paths:*
   - Who gets ahead? What departments were top people once in? What positions did they hold? Do people from diverse groups get ahead?
   - What do people have to do to get promoted?
   - What does the company reward? competence in key skills? performance against objective criteria? seniority? loyalty? good team player? other?

7. *Find out how long people usually stay in jobs.*
   (Short terms usually mean people are motivated to make their mark quickly and to steer clear of longer-term, slower payback activities. They also can mean people from diverse groups became discouraged, felt they couldn't reach their career goals, and left.)

8. *Find out what people are talking about and writing about.*
   - What are memos and reports about—actual content?
   - What are meetings about? What is actually discussed, who talks to whom?

Step 2. Review and Analysis. Go over the results of your survey to determine how strong or weak, how conformist or flexible, you think the company is. Use it to help identify companies that are in danger of failing. Look for:

Patterns and themes. Think about patterns that emerged from the stories and anecdotes that people volunteered. What are the key points? Do most stories revolve around customers? political infighting? individual initiative that was rewarded or punished? This is an important indicator.

Inward focus. People don't pay much attention to what's going on outside the company with customers, competitors, new trends. They focus on placating the boss, looking good, getting one up on the people around them. They seem to over-emphasize budgets, financial analysis, or sales quotas.

Short-term focus. If people spend most of their time and energy meeting short-term goals, then sustainable business receives no support and the company is headed for problems.

Declining morale. Is turnover high or trending upward? Look at the whole company and at subcultures within the company. Look at the track records of employees from diverse groups, such as minorities. Poor morale often begins with a lackadaisical attitude, moving on to loud complaints, and finally people start leaving.

Weak culture. When a culture is weak or in trouble, people get frightened and anxious. This fright shows up in emotional outbursts in the workplace, such as condemning company policy at a meeting or getting angry with co-workers or bosses. Did you hear any stories that indicate that stress, anger, or other emotions are building up? If so, did you get any clues about the causes?

Fragmentation or inconsistency. When a division is unhappy about how headquarters is handling things or tells jokes about what goes on there, it's usually a sign that the parts of the culture are not integrated into a coherent whole. Signs that normal variations in different functions of the firm are becoming a problem:

- Subcultures (within departments, or sometimes within ethnic groups) are becoming ingrown. Regular interaction among subcultures is declining.
- Subcultures are clashing, publicly trying to undermine each other. The healthy tension among two subcultures has become destructive.
- Subcultures are becoming exclusive. One or more subculture is acting like an exclusive club. People are feeling left out and resentful, not pulling together toward company goals.
- Subcultures act as if their values are more important than company values, not giving key overriding company values top priority.

Skill Builder 2.9: Assessing Corporate Culture Fit

Purpose: To raise your awareness about how various corporate cultures fit the needs of diverse employees. (See Table 2.7 Idea Starters for Sample Interview Questions.)

Begin with how a target corporation fits your needs. Select an organization you want to study or to work in. After you have conducted a survey of the corporate culture (Exercise 2.10), complete the following exercise.

Step 1. Assessing the organization's values. In the Target Organization column, for each value, assign either an A or B, whichever best represents that organization's value, and a number from 1 to 3 that represents moderate to extreme importance placed on that value by the firm. Add any other organization values you think will affect you significantly.

Step 2. Assessing your values. In the My Root Culture column, repeat step 1 for your own values, modifying your root culture's focus, where necessary, to reflect your own values. Add any other workplace values that are important to you.

Step 3. Estimating cultural fit. Compare the target organization's profile of values with your root culture's profile, and write a brief paragraph about what this means in terms of cultural fit between someone from your culture and this organization.

Step 4. Assessing another persons's cultural fit. Think of someone from another culture that you know well. Do steps 1–3 substituting that person's profile for your own. In the paragraph write-up in step 3 include comparisons between your own fit and this person's fit and any insights that occur to you regarding cultural fit.

moderately important = 1   very important = 2   extremely important = 3

Target Org.	My Root Culture	Values: What's Most Important	
A or B? 1, 2, or 3?	A or B? 1, 2, or 3?	A Values	B Values
		Doing the work	Building relationships
		Living for the present	Working for future rewards
		Being aggressive	Being passive
		Promoting myself	Being modest
		Competing	Cooperating
		Being unemotional	Expressing emotions
		Individual goals	Team goals
		Taking risks	Avoiding risks
		Other	Other

Answer Key: Self–Awareness Activity 2.2

1. a. Internal source of control, individualism, independent
    b. External source of control, collectivism, dependent

2. a. Me-first, individualism
    b. Us-first, collectivism

3. a. Achievement first, competitive, individualism
    b. Relationships first, cooperative, collectivism

4. a. Achievements and tasks first, linear time orientation
    b. Relationships first, circular time orientation

5. a. Focus on equality, democratic orientation, direct communication
    b. Focus on class differences: status, rank, deference to authority, indirect communication

6. a. Risk-taking orientation, focus on future change, independence, individualism
    b. Security-seeking orientation, focus on tradition, hierarchy and the status quo, dependence, collectivism

7. a. Equality, risk-taking orientation
    b. Security-seeking, avoid-uncertainty orientation

8. a. Risk-taking, equality
    b. Security-seeking, deference to authority

REFERENCES

Alderfer, C.P. "Problems of Changing White Males' Behavior and Beliefs Concerning Race Relations." *Change in Organizations*. San Francisco: Jossey-Bass, 1982.

Althen, Gary. *American Ways*. Yarmouth, ME: Intercultural Press, 1988.

Asante, M.K., and K. Asante, eds. *African Culture*. Westport, CT: Greenwood Press, 1985.

Belenky, M.F., B.M. Clinchy, N.R. Golderberger, and J.M. Tarule. *Women's Ways of Knowing*. New York: Basic Books, 1986.

Boorstin, D.J. *Americans and the Image of Europe: Reflections on American Thought*. New York: Meridian Books, 1960.

Brislin, Richard and Tomoko Yoshida. *Improving Intercultural Interactions*. Thousand Oaks, CA: Sage, 1994.

Cote, J.A., and P.S. Tansuhaj. "Culture Bound Assumptions in Behavior Intention Models." *Advances in Consumer Research* 16 (1989): 105–109.

Cox, T.H., and J. Finley-Nickerson. "Models of Acculturation for Intraorganizational Cultural Diversity." *Canadian Journal of Administrative Sciences* 8, no. 2 (1991): 90–100.

Cox, T.H., S. Lobel, and P. McLeod. "Effects of Ethnic Group Cultural Difference on Cooperative Versus Competitive Behavior in a Group Task*," Academy of Management Journal* 34 (1991): 827–847.

Cox, Taylor. *Cultural Diversity in Organizations*. San Francisco: Berrett–Koehler, 1993.

Davidow, W.H. and M.S. Malone. *The Virtual Corporation*. New York: Harper Collins Publishers, 1992.

De Anda, D. "Bicultural Socialization." *Social Work* 29 (1984): 101–107.

Deal, T.E., and A.A. Kennedy. *Corporate Cultures*. Reading MA: Addison-Wesley, 1982.

Delgado, M. "Hispanic Cultural Values: Implications for Groups." *Small Group Behavior* 12, no. 1 (1981): 69–80.

DeVos, G.A. "Ethnic Adaptation and Minority Status." *Journal of Cross-Cultural Psychology* 11, no. 1 (1980): 101–124.

Eagly, A.H., and B.T. Johnson. "Gender and Leadership Style." *Psychological Bulletin* 108, no. 2 (1990): 233–256.

Feldman, D.D. "The Multiple Socialization of Organization Members." *Academy of Management Review* 67, No. 2 (1981) 309–318.

Fottler, M.D., and T. Bain. "Sex Differences in Occupational Aspirations." *Academy of Management Journal* 23 (1980): 144–149.

Graham, R.J. "The Role of Perception of Time in Consumer Behavior." *Journal of Consumer Research* 7 (1981): 335–342.

Hall, E.T. *The Hidden Dimension*. New York: Doubleday, 1982.

Hall, E.T. *The Silent Language*. New York: Doubleday, 1981.

Hall, E.T., and M.R. Hall. *Understanding Culture Differences*. Yarmouth, ME: Intercultural Press, 1989.

Hall. E.T. *Beyond Culture*. New York: Doubleday, 1981.

Hall. E.T. *The Dance of Life*. New York: Doubleday, 1983.

Harris, P.R., and R.T. Moran. *Managing Cultural Differences*. Houston: Gulf, 1991.

Helms, J.E., and T.W. Giorgis. "A Comparison of the Locus of Control and Anxiety Level of African, Black American and White American College Students." *Journal of College Student Personnel* 21, no. 6 (1980): 503–509.

Hofstede, Geert. "The Cultural Relativity of the Quality of Life Concept." *Academy of Management Review* 9, no. 3 (1984): 389–398.

Hofstede, Geert. *Cultures and Organization*. New York: McGraw, 1991.

Hofstede, Geert. *Culture's Consequences: International Differences in Work-Related Values*. Thousand Oaks, CA: Sage, 1980.

Hui, C. "Work Attitudes, Leadership Styles, and Managerial Behaviors in Different Cultures." *Applied Cross-Cultural Psychology*. Thousand Oaks, CA: Sage, 1990.

Kagan, K., and M.D. Madsen. "Cooperation and Competition of Mexican, Mexican American, and Anglo American Children of Two Ages Under Four Instructional Sets." *Developmental Psychology* 5, no. 1 (1971): 32–39.

Kagitcibasi, C. "Family and Home-Based Intervention." *Applied Cross-Cultural Psychology*. Thousand Oaks, CA: Sage, 1990.

Kim, U., H.C. Triandis, C. Kagitcibasi, S. Choi, and G. Yoon, eds. *Individualism and Collectivism*. Thousand Oaks, CA: Sage, 1994.

Kohls, Robert L. *The Values Americans Live By*. San Francisco: LinguaTec, 1988.

Leavitt, T. "The Globalization of Markets." *Harvard Business Review* 83, no. 3 (1983): 91–102.

Matsumoto, G., G. Meredith, and M. Masuda. "Ethnic Identification: Honolulu and Seattle Japanese-Americans." *Journal of Cross-Cultural Psychology* 1, no. 1 (1970): 63–76.

McGrath, J.E., and N.L. Rotchford. "Time and Behavior in Organizations." *Research in Organizational Behavior* 5 (1983): 57–101.

Meyerson, D., and D.S. Lewis. "Cultural Tolerance of Ambiguity." Working paper, University of Michigan, Ann Arbor, MI, 1992.

Nirenberg, John. "Heading Overseas? Caution, the Cross-cultural Management Literature May Be Hazardous to Your Health," *San Francisco State University School of Business Journal* (summer 1993): 47–55.

Orpen, C., and J. Nkohande. "Self-esteem: Interval Control and Expectancy Beliefs of White and Black Managers in South Africa." *Journal of Management Studies* (May 1977): 192–199.

Peters, Tom. *Liberation Management*. New York: Knopf, 1992.

Ramirez, A. "Racism Toward Hispanics." *Eliminating Racism*. New York: Plenum Press, 1988.

Redding, S.G. "Cultural Effects on the Marketing Process in Southeast Asia." *Journal of Market Research Society* 24, no. 19 (1982): 98–114.

Rosener, J.B. "Ways Women Lead." *Harvard Business Review* (November–December 1990): 119–125.

Rotter, J.B. "Generalized Expectancies for Internal Versus External Control of Reinforcement." *Psychological Monographs,* no. 80 (1966): 1–28.

Schaef, A.W., and D. Fassel. *The Addictive Organization*. San Francisco: Harper & Row, 1988.

Schein, E.H. "The Individual, the Organization, and the Career." *Journal of Applied Behavioral Science* 7 (1971): 401–426.

Schein, E.H. *Organizational Culture and Leadership*. San Francisco: Jossey-Bass, 1985.

Siehl, C., and L. Martin. "The Role of Symbolic Management." *Leaders and Managers*. New York: Pergamon Press, 1984.

Spector, P.E. "Behavior in Organizations as a Function of Employee's Locus of Control." *Psychological Bulletin* 91 (1982): 482–497.

Stewart, Edward C. *American Cultural Patterns: A Cross Cultural Perspective*. LaGrange Park, IL: Intercultural Network, Inc., 1992.

Szapocznik, J., M. Scopetta, and O.E. King. "Theory and Practice in Matching Treatment to the Special Characteristics and Problems of Cuban Immigrants." *Journal of Community Psychology* 6 (1978): 112–122.

Takaki, Ronald. *A Different Mirror: A History of Multicultural America*. Boston: Little, Brown and Company, 1993.

Tannen, Deborah. *You Just Don't Understand*. New York: Wm. Morrow, 1990.

Trilling, Lionel. *The Opposing Self*. New York: The Viking Press, 1955.

Tse, D.K., K. Lee, I. Vertinsky, and D.A. Wehrung. "Does Culture Matter?" *Journal of Marketing* 52 (1988): 81–95.

Wheatley, Margaret J. *Leadership and the New Science*. San Francisco: Berrett-Koehler Publishers, 1992.

Wiebe, Robert H. *Introduction to the Meaning of America*. New York: Oxford University Press, 1975.

World 1993, State of the. Worldwatch Institute.

CHAPTER 3

Handling Personal Prejudice

Prejudiced persons' thinking patterns tend to block their own happiness and zest for life—holding onto prejudice creates a joy drain. Researcher M.D. Kite, 1986

Prejudice is the tendency to view people who are different as being inferior. Major barriers to tapping the full potential of all persons in the workplace are prejudice and discrimination. It's been built into American institutions and systems, and it's part of our culture and subcultures. No one is completely immune to its impact, although people from historically disadvantaged groups tend to suffer the worst effects. Civil rights laws are reducing its pervasiveness and intensity, and activist groups are working against it, but groups are made up of individuals. Change begins within one person and expands person by person. Harry Palmer, author of *Living Deliberately* (1994) says:

> *Every time an individual changes his or her belief, the blueprint, by which the collective reality unfolds, changes. Even for the most isolated individual, every moment of happiness, every moment of sadness, every kindness, every critical thought adds its consequence to the blueprint for the events of the world.*

This brings us to the third step of building multicultural skills:

> *Step 3: Recognizing your own ethnocentricity*, the ways in which you stereotype, judge, and discriminate, and your emotional reactions to conflicting cultural values.

To achieve this step, we'll explore the nature of prejudice: what it is, how people become prejudiced, and how we express prejudice. You'll learn how making contact with people from other groups affects prejudice toward them and the impact of various types of contact. You'll examine the effects prejudice has on those who hold prejudices and on those who are the targets of prejudice, especially how it affects careers. Finally, you'll review suggestions for moving beyond prejudice and have a chance to work through some processes for raising your awareness of prejudice and for changing prejudiced beliefs. Before you begin Step 3, complete Self-Awareness Activities 3.1 and 3.2.

Self-Awareness Activity 3.1: What Do You Know About Prejudice?

Purpose: To see what you know about the issues covered in this chapter.

Instructions: Determine whether you think the following statements are basically true or false—and think about why. The answers will emerge in this chapter, and the summary at the end of the chapter focuses on these issues.

1. Anthropologists generally agree that there are three major races: caucasoid, negroid, and mongoloid.
2. Most aspects of our culture teach us to appreciate others and not be prejudiced.
3. People who believe in strict categories of right and wrong are unlikely to be prejudiced.
4. Prejudiced beliefs are frequently hidden, not in awareness.
5. The best way to end prejudice is simply to have contact with people from the disparaged group.
6. Being prejudiced affects the personality of the holder as well as the receiver of the prejudice.
7. Members of disparaged groups become resentful toward others.
8. Prejudiced beliefs cannot be changed, but discriminatory actions can.

Self-Awareness Activity 3.2: Examine Your Viewpoints

Purpose: To learn more about your personal viewpoint.

Instructions: Mark each item true or false.

1. I have little or no difficulty deciding what's right and what's wrong.
2. I thrive on variety and change.
3. I often enjoy being with people that some would call strange or weird.
4. I like my routines.
5. I know how I feel about most situations and don't need to keep thinking about them.
6. I need to know exactly where I'm going and when.
7. I often ask myself why I did certain things, or why I think or feel as I do.
8. I hate it when people change our plans.
9. There is only one right way to do most things.
10. Few actions are totally right or wrong; most actions stem from complex situations and have varying effects.
11. I prefer to focus on a few simple things rather than a wide variety.
12. I can feel comfortable with most situations, even if I'm not sure about what's going on.
13. I don't always agree with people from other groups, but I usually understand why they might think and feel as they do.
14. People basically create the life they have and the sooner they take responsibility for it, the better it will be.
15. I think I know my own strengths and shortcomings pretty well.
16. Most actions can be classified as either proper or improper.
17. People have different ideas about what's proper and improper; that's fine with me.

18. I don't start a job until I know exactly how to do it.

19. I'm comfortable "feeling my way" through a task, if necessary.

20. I need to know what's going on and what to expect at all times.

Follow-up: To interpret your responses, see the answer key at the end of this chapter and review the discussion in this chapter on the authoritarian personality.

WHAT IS PREJUDICE?

We've mentioned that prejudice is the tendency to view people who are different as being deficient. It's also a tendency to avoid people who belong to a different group, or to feel hostile toward them, simply because they belong to that group. It's a presumption that they'll have the "objectionable qualities" of that group. In the workplace, prejudice is the assumption, without evidence, that nontraditional managers are less competent or less suitable than traditional managers, and the refusal to accept them as equals. While prejudice refers to viewpoint, discrimination refers to actions: any behavior that systematically tends to deny access to opportunities or privilege to one social group, while perpetuating privilege to members of another group. Prejudice and discrimination can originate within an individual or be part of an institution's policies and practices. They can be obvious or hidden, intentional or unintentional (Ponteretto 1993; Allport 1954; Cox 1993).

What's in a Name?

Prejudice is the tendency to view people who are different as being deficient. It's a way of thinking.

Discrimination refers to actions or practices that result in members of a subordinate group being treated differently in ways that disadvantage them.

Workplace prejudice is alive and well. Surveys indicate that stereotypes are still prevalent and that most of the Euro-Americans who dominate the workplace tend to believe that other ethnic groups are less intelligent, less hard working, less likely to be self-supporting, more violence prone, and less patriotic than they. The Executive Leadership Council's study found prejudice to be the most serious career hurdle for African American executives. The research organization Catalyst found prejudice to be the biggest advancement barrier women face today (Morrison 1992; Smith 1990; Baskerville and Tucker 1991; Catalyst 1990).

The Major Ingredients of Prejudice

The major ingredients of prejudice are authority, stereotyping, and devaluation (Gadamer 1989; Feagin 1978).

- *Authority* includes what we've subconsciously absorbed from our culture, what we've been told by authority figures, what we've read, and similar sources.

- *Stereotyping* occurs when we're too quick to categorize, which leads to faulty, inflexible over-generalization. It's a shortcut method we take to try to make sense of the complexity of our environment.

- *Devaluation* stems from a belief that a group of people is inferior.

All are cases of failing to use our reason and to get the information we need to make open-minded, fair assessments for ourselves. For example, a Latino American woman can only be understood on her own terms, within her own context. We can understand her by learning about her cultural and personal background, and then placing ourselves into that perspective, the one in which she formed her views. When we open our minds to her perspective, we can share in the meanings she gives to events.

Some prejudice is a matter of blind conformity to prevailing cultural beliefs and customs. However, in most cases prejudice seems to fulfill a specific irrational function for people, such as making them feel superior to others or using others as scapegoats for the prejudiced persons' own resentment or guilt. Prejudice usually is tied to a person's deepest fears, although the connection is normally subconscious and therefore hidden from awareness, according to Harvard psychologist G.W. Allport in his classic work on prejudice (1954).

Discrimination usually refers to behavior that is prejudiced, the acts that have an effect on people who are targets of prejudice. Most discussions of prejudice and discrimination are based on the following assumptions (Ridley 1989):

- Prejudice is reflected in behavior.
- Prejudiced acts can be performed by nonprejudiced as well as prejudiced people.
- Prejudice is found in every ethnic group.
- The criteria for judging whether or not a behavior is prejudiced lies in the consequences, not the causes, of the behavior. (We can't prove someone is prejudiced, but we can prove that their acts have a discriminatory effect.)
- Power is a force that is absolutely essential to perpetuate discrimination.

The foregoing implies that a power imbalance is a key aspect of discrimination. As we've seen, civil rights measures are based on this premise and represent attempts to break the cycle of centuries of discrimination.

Racism or Ethnic Prejudice?

We often use the term *racism* in discussions of prejudice, which raises the question, How do I know when I'm dealing with someone of another race, and how can I be sure what race they represent? Race is usually defined as:

> *A subgroup of people possessing a definite combination of physical characteristics of genetic origin, the combination of which to varying degrees distinguishes the subgroup from other subgroups of humans.*

The major problem in dealing with race is the difficulty in finding two anthropologists who agree on racial categories. Some claim there are as few as two races, others that there are as many as 200. Anthropologists agree that there is only one human species, and there are many varieties of this one species, but they cannot agree on how to divide the species biologically into races. There is either one race—mankind—or an indefinite number of races, depending on what criteria are selected (Pettigrew 1964). Princeton professor Henry Gates speaks for most experts in the following quote.

> *"Race as a meaningful criterion within the biological sciences has long been recognized as a fiction"* *(Gates 1992).*

Those who try to distinguish between race and ethnicity say that racial traits are inborn, inherited, and given by nature, while ethnic traits are learned, cultural, and acquired through nurture. Anthropological work on race has produced two major truths:

- No one belongs to a pure stock, except a very few people found in remote isolated parts of the earth.
- Most of the variable human characteristics ascribed to race are actually due to cultural diversity and should therefore be regarded as ethnic, not racial.

Since most of the characteristics that vary from culture to culture are learned, and are not permanently fixed in our genes, they can theoretically be unlearned, modified, or otherwise changed (Allport 1954).

An ethnic subgroup is a segment of a larger society whose members have a common origin and share important segments of a common culture. They participate in shared activities in which the common origin and culture are significant ingredients (Cox 1993). An ethnic subgroup is unique because of its ancestry, language, religion, and other cultural traits. It may be a unique social group within a larger cultural and social system. Much of the "racism" discussed in the U.S. involves African Americans. Experts estimate that about 75 percent of African Americans are of mixed heritage, usually having some Euro-American ancestors.

What's in a Name?

The terms *race* and *racism* are not biologically meaningful for U.S. subcultures although they're still used by some persons as the basis for discrimination. More realistic and conciliatory terms are *ethnicity* and *ethnic prejudice*.

Targets of Prejudice

Prejudice based on gender, often called sexism, is said by some to be the root of all prejudice and discrimination, because it is a form of inequality that begins in the home. Gender inequality is normally the first form of inequality we experience. This form of inequality and prejudice does not involve a majority and minorities, since men and women are relatively equal in number, with women slightly outnumbering men in most cultures. However, women in virtually all countries are a minority in executive, professional, and political arenas.

Ethnic prejudice is also prevalent in societies such as the U.S., where there is a predominant majority and one or more minority groups. Other groups that experience discrimination in the workplace include persons with disabilities, gay persons, older employees, religious minorities, and obese persons. Certain minority groups are singled out from others in the society for differential and unequal treatment and therefore regard themselves as objects of collective discrimination. Minority status carries with it the exclusion from full participation in the society. The majority, or mainstream, group holds the balance of power, influence, and wealth in society. In the U.S. the majority group is the Euro-American population generally, and more specifically, Euro-American middle-class males (Ponterotto et al. 1993).

HOW DO WE BECOME PREJUDICED?

How we become prejudiced is closely related to why we become prejudiced. Some typical reasons are:

- the need to feel superior to someone
- fear of competition for jobs from the disparaged group's members
- general frustration because of low status and resulting hostility
- lack of education leading to a simplistic, stereotypic view of the world
- difficulty dealing with new, uncertain situations and people
- the need to be approved and included by people from the ingroup, most of whom are prejudiced themselves
- the tendency to conform to dominant beliefs and attitudes

As we explore how people become prejudiced, details of the reasons why will emerge.

Prejudice in the U.S. is probably rooted in the ethnocentric philosophy that values mainstream dominant cultural beliefs and attitudes more highly than culturally diverse belief systems. Our history is riddled with many flavors of overt and covert prejudice, ranging from slavery to segregation to ethnic and sexist jokes. Most prejudice today is of the subtle and hidden form. We might view prejudice as both a group disease and an individual disease. People become prejudiced through the following processes and sources:

- learning from the culture—family, school, church, media, workplace
- stereotyping
- developing an ethnic identity
- forming ingroups
- becoming ethnocentric
- developing certain personality traits, such as rigidity, authoritarianism
- living in a diverse, rapidly changing society

Learning from the Culture

People learn to be prejudiced first and primarily at home, but regardless of where they first adopt prejudiced beliefs, reinforcement occurs throughout the culture—within the family and in the media, the schools, the churches, the workplace, the government. Prejudice is reinforced when we see the contributions of certain groups being devalued or ignored and when we hear people use negative adjectives and stereotypes for them. It's driven home when we see people ignoring or devaluing the existence and contributions of certain groups. Prejudice is kept in place when we don't have access to a broad array of factual and suitable information about other groups—and when our contacts with people from other groups are only superficial.

Family beliefs and attitudes. Parental behaviors that facilitate the development of negative ethnic prejudice include:

- Parents avoid discussing ethnic issues because they are too touchy.
- Friends who visit regularly are all of the same ethnic group.
- When people (friends, the media) make prejudicial remarks, parents do not confront them.
- Children remain in segregated schools and play groups.
- Parents don't bother to point out the strengths and contributions of diverse cultures, including their own.

The media. Prejudice is reinforced by television and radio programs, newspaper and magazine articles, and books when the following actions occur:

- Showing minority group members in stereotypical roles.
- Failing to show minority group members in visible professional positions, such as news anchor, or in positive, leading roles in books, plays, series, situation comedies, and other programs.
- Allowing imbalanced coverage of minority communities, with more focus on criminal activities and tensions than on positive events and programs.

Schools. School systems and school cultures reinforce prejudice by:

- Allowing an administration, faculty, or student body that's not as culturally diverse as the community at large.
- Promoting a learning environment that focuses on only one value system, normally middle-class mainstream Euro-American. (For example, promoting com-

petition above cooperation, emphasizing future time emphasis over past or present, emphasizing individual achievement above group or team orientation.)

- Building the curriculum around European history and the dominant Euro-American culture, paying little attention to cultures of other Americans.
- Ignoring the need for education about ethnic and gender prejudice and discrimination.

The workplace. The workplace and its corporate cultures reinforce prejudice by:

- Allowing or imposing a glass ceiling that blocks nearly all minorities and women from top positions.
- Encouraging and rewarding only a middle-class and upper-class Euro-American-based value system.
- Tolerating subtle or overt discrimination at the workplace.

The government. Behavior by the American government that reinforces prejudice includes:

- Not passing, or watering down, equal rights legislation that is needed to promote fairness and equality for diverse groups.
- Halting or undermining affirmative action enforcement before such programs have achieved their purposes.
- Ignoring, minimizing, or downplaying harassment charges.

Religious organizations. Some people actually equate bigotry with organized religion because it's so often used as the basis for prejudice. There are differences of creed, and realistic conflicts can occur. But bigotry enters only when religion becomes the excuse for ingroup superiority and for outgroup denigration. This is done for ego-related reasons that normally extend beyond any deviation in creed between two groups.

In the 1950s and 1960s social scientists were surprised by research findings that the greater a Euro-American's commitment to religion, the more prejudiced against African Americans he or she tends to be. Some studies indicated that people with no religious affiliation show on average less prejudice than do church members. This was puzzling since virtually all denominations teach love of others. Allport, in researching this phenomena, asked, Why do people go to church in the first place? His findings revealed two basic motivations: Extrinsically motivated members use their religion, and intrinsically motivated members live their religion (Allport and Ross 1967). More specifically:

Extrinsic religious motivation refers to a self-serving, manipulative approach to religion that conforms to social conventions. The primary value is to enjoy social acceptance and belonging. Church provides members with security, comfort, status, or social support and may mean belonging to a powerful, superior ingroup. This orientation is associated with prejudice toward outgroups.

Intrinsic religious motivation refers to valuing religion as a framework that gives meaning to life, a way of understanding all of life, and guidance for day-to-day living. The primary value is to "love thy neighbor," and there's no legitimate place for rejection, contempt, or condescension. The church's basic creed of brotherhood expresses an ideal that these members sincerely believe in. This orientation lends itself to tolerance and acceptance of all groups.

Many church members incorporate elements of both orientations. Some are there primarily for social reasons, but some deeper meaning also motivates them. Others are there for life meaning and guidance but also enjoy the social and supportive aspects. In the 1990s, Herek's analyses confirmed that prejudice or tolerance toward African Americans can be predicted with some accuracy by extrinsic or intrinsic religious motivation (Herek 1994).

Herek's studies also indicate that, unlike prejudice toward African Americans, Euro-American prejudice toward gay persons can *not* be predicted on the basis of extrinsic or intrinsic orientation. The major predictor of whether a church member will harbor antigay prejudice is whether or not the church has a fundamentalist orientation. A major aspect of fundamentalism is a literal interpretation of the Bible. For example, when discussing beliefs about gay persons, church leaders and members tend to focus on Bible passages that they believe condemn homosexuality (Herek 1994).

Stereotyping

A major ingredient of prejudice, stereotyping is such an integral part of everyday thinking that it requires special attention if we're to overcome its negative effects. The process of stereotyping has several important characteristics:

- When we stereotype, we form large classes and clusters for guiding our daily adjustments. We must deal with too much complexity in our environment to be completely open-minded. We don't have time to learn all about every new person or situation we encounter. Of necessity, we associate them with old categories in our mind in order to make some sense of the world.

- We tend to place as much as we can into each class and cluster. Our minds tend to categorize events in the "grossest" manner compatible with the need for action. We like to solve problems as easily as possible, so we try to fit them rapidly into a satisfactory category and use this category as a means of prejudging the solution.

- A stereotype enables us to readily identify a related object. Stereotypes have a close and immediate tie with what we see, how we judge, and what actions we take. In fact, their whole purpose is apparently to facilitate our perception and our actions. They help us make responses and adjustments to life in a speedy, smooth, and consistent manner.

- For each of our mental categories, we have a thinking and feeling tone or flavor. Everything in that category takes on that flavor. For example, we not only know what the term "Southern belle" means, we also have a feeling tone of favor or disfavor that goes along with that concept. When we meet someone that we decide is a Southern belle, that feeling tone determines whether we like her more or less than we would if we got to know her on her own merits.

- Stereotypes may be more or less rational. A rational stereotype starts to grow from a kernel of truth and enlarges and solidifies with each new relevant experience. A rational stereotype can give us information that can help us to predict how someone will behave or what might happen in a situation. An irrational stereotype is one we've formed without adequate evidence.

- Our minds are able to form irrational stereotypes as easily as rational ones, and to link intense emotions to them. An irrational idea that is engulfed by an overpowering emotion is more likely to conform to the emotion than to objective evidence. Therefore, once we develop an irrational stereotype that we feel strongly about, it's difficult for us to change that stereotype based on facts alone. We must deal with the emotion and its ties to our deepest fear.

When people become prejudiced toward a group, they need to justify their dislike, and any justification that fits the immediate conversational situation will do. We'll use the following definition of a stereotype:

> A *stereotype* is a rigid, exaggerated, irrational belief associated with a mental category, such as a particular group of people. Although stereotypes are not identical to prejudice, they often lead to prejudice.

Stereotypes are convenient in two major ways:

* Stereotypes serve as a screening device to make perceiving and thinking simpler; they aid us in simplifying our categories

* Stereotypes are a way of justifying categorical acceptance or rejection of a group. A stereotype is a form of over-generalization and relates to over-hastiness to categorize and find meaning. Stereotypes are not identical with prejudice, since they're primarily rationalizers, so eliminating stereotypes will not eliminate the roots of prejudice. On the other hand, stereotypes may lead to prejudice, and they form barriers to building authentic relationships. Stereotypes are socially supported, continually revived, and reinforced by our mass media. Therefore, it's important that intelligent people move beyond limiting, harmful stereotypes of diverse people.

Through multicultural education, we can form some rational stereotypes, perhaps better defined as background information, as depicted in Figure 3.1. In order to avoid any limiting effects that block authentic relationship, our background information must be flexible and open to change as we get to know people on their own merits, as unique individuals. Multicultural education ideally helps us to understand individuals from other cultures, to empathize with them, and to build authentic, trusting, collaborative relationships with them (Cox, 1993).

FIGURE 3.1: Stereotypes Versus Cultural Background Information

Stereotype

Rigid, limiting

Cultural Background Information

Flexible, open

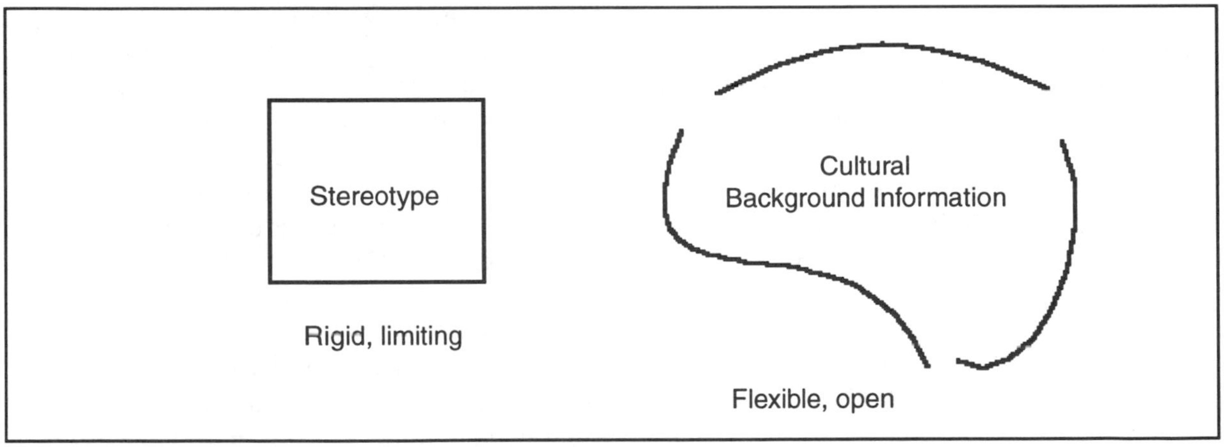

Developing an Ethnic Identity

All of us achieve our identity from a period of exploration and experimentation that usually takes place in adolescence and often continues into early adulthood. Working through this exploration, we come to solidify our decisions and commitments regarding our career and occupations, lifestyle, sexual standards, politics, and philosophy of life or religion. We'll review how most Euro-Americans develop their identity as part of the ethnic majority in American culture. We'll also see how a minority person typically develops an ethnic identity. Both are summarized in Table 3.1.

TABLE 3.1: Developing an Ethnic Identity

Euro-Americans	*Minority Persons*
Little or no ethnic awareness	Identify with Euro-Americans
Ethnic conflict about prejudice	Encounter prejudice, identity search
Reaction or retreat from conflict	Attach to own culture
Balance identity to include minorities	Integrate, internalize ethnic identity

How Euro–Americans Develop a Majority Identity

A Euro-American, or any dominant majority person, normally experiences an ethnic identity process that is different from that of the ethnic minority members. Now assume that you are a young Euro-American in the U.S. and mentally move through the stages of developing an ethnic identity.

Stage 1. Before exposure and contact with ethnic differences. In the beginning you don't even think of yourself as an ethnic person. You unconsciously identify with being "a white person" in a culture where most minorities have darker skin coloring, and you accept stereotypes about minorities without questioning them.

Stage 2. Ethnic conflict. As you mature, you become acquainted with people from other ethnic groups. You may have noticed that many or all of them don't fit the stereotypes you've held about them. Perhaps you've seen them excluded, castigated, and in many ways treated unfairly.

You may experience conflict between wanting to go along with the beliefs and actions of your biased friends and relatives and wanting to treat minorities with respect and fairness, as essentially equal human beings. So you begin to reexamine many of your assumptions and beliefs about Euro-American people, which in turn leads you to challenge your accepted set of beliefs about "being white." You come face to face with minority issues and are challenged to acknowledge the continuing reality of prejudice in American society and your role in perpetuating the status quo. Key emotions that come up during this stage are confusion, guilt, anger, and perhaps even depression, all related to your belief that you have been a part of the prejudiced establishment. Your anger may be directed inward toward yourself as well as outward toward the dominant culture in general.

If you are male, you will deal with being part of a dominant group that discriminates against women as well as ethnic minorities. You'll face contradictions about how your mother, sister, or close friends and other relatives are viewed and treated by men in the culture. If you are female, you'll get in touch with the bifurcated position of being a member of the dominant ethnic group and at the same time a member of the disadvantaged gender group. On one hand, you'll begin to deal with being part of a system where you have the power to exclude others. On the other hand, you'll probably begin to notice commonalties of women's situation with that of other disadvantaged groups.

Stage 3. Reaction or retreat. As a member of the dominant majority, you'll probably have one of two reactions to the feelings that came in stage 2.

- *Reaction.* You take a strong stand for minority issues. You begin to fight or resist the prejudice you see around you and to identify with disadvantaged groups. You feel compassion and empathy for them, which somewhat offsets the feelings of confusion and guilt you were experiencing.

- *Retreat.* You avoid situations that cause you to feel confusion and conflict. You back off from any sort of inter-ethnic contact, returning to the comfort, security, and familiarity of your own culture. You decide life is just easier and less complicated that way. You over-identify with "being white" and feel defensive about the dominant culture. You may fear minorities and feel angry about their behavior.

Stage 4. *Balancing your identity to include minorities.* At some point, you may mature into a more balanced and healthy ethnic identity, especially if you chose the reaction route in Step 3. You acknowledge that as a member of the dominant culture, you share responsibility for maintaining prejudice. At the same time you identify with the larger holistic American culture and with a nonprejudiced Euro-American viewpoint: Not all of us want to perpetuate the status quo. You can see positive and negative beliefs and actions in your own group, as well as in minority groups. You now turn your energy and attention to equality issues and become committed to fighting all forms of oppression. You feel flexible and open to learning more about all cultures, including your own.

How Minority Persons Develop an Ethnic Identity

Members of ethnic minorities are bicultural, having an American cultural identity and also an ethnic subcultural identity. Therefore, their process is different from that of Euro-American. Put yourself in the role of a young minority person and follow the typical identity development process through four stages.

Stage 1. *Identifying with the Euro-American majority.* At some point in your life, usually as a young teenager before you've had a turning-point inter-ethnic encounter, you're almost certain to identify primarily with the Euro-American majority culture. You prefer their ways of thinking and acting; that is, their standards, norms, and values. It may be that you simply view your ethnic identity as unimportant. Perhaps your unexamined preferences and commitments are based on your parents' values.

Stage 2. *Gaining minority awareness, encountering prejudice, searching for identity.* Somewhere along the line, you become painfully aware of your status as a minority in a prejudicial society. This awareness may be raised either by a single dramatic encounter with an oppressive or prejudicial experience, or it may grow out of an accumulation of more subtle experiences. This awareness triggers a period when you question your status and the values of the dominant culture. You also begin a search for your own ethnic identity.

You're likely to feel confused, embarrassed, and angry. You begin to develop positive prejudice toward your own ethnic group and negative prejudice toward the Euro-American majority. (This phase is especially difficult for children whose father is from a different ethnic group than the mother.) Your negative prejudice is just forming, so you probably don't act it out in prejudiced behavior yet. But you do become tired of the Euro-American system and you want to strengthen your bonds with your own ethnic group, to really belong and feel a part of that culture. You may feel some confusion about teaming up with members of other minority groups.

Stage 3. *Identifying with and attaching to your own culture.* If you've come into adulthood within the past thirty years, you're especially likely to have entered a phase where you committed yourself to your own ethnic group and immersed yourself in that culture. In this stage you endorse the beliefs, values, norms, and customs of your own group, while completely rejecting values and norms of the Euro-American establishment.

This stage is the most intensely emotional. You're certain to direct anger and even rage toward the majority. You feel intense loyalty and pride toward your own group, so much so that you tend to idealize and romanticize your group. Now you're more likely to act in a prejudiced way toward Euro-American than in any stage. You're likely to have a separatist attitude; you may participate in political action that calls attention to minority issues; and you may even act out your rage in a violent manner.

Stage 4. *Integrating and internalizing your ethnic identity.* At this stage you do a more realistic reassessment and reappraisal of your own minority culture, the dominant Euro-American culture, and your role in the scheme of things. Out of this reappraisal, you develop a more balanced bicultural identity that integrates the best of both cultures (your minority culture and the dominant Euro-American culture). You internalize this bicultural identity, making it a part of your belief system. If your mother and father come from different minority cultures, then you must develop a multicultural identity, integrating both minority cultures with the dominant culture.

You've run through the intense emotion of the previous phase. The major characteristic of this stage is the development of a secure ethnic identity along with an appreciation of other cultures. Now you're likely to direct your commitment toward cooperative alliances with committed people from the mainstream culture, from your own minority group, and from other minority groups in order to change discriminatory policies and practices. You're likely to work within the mainstream culture to bring about peaceful change.

Forming Ingroups

Even before we develop an ethnic identity, we identify with one or more ingroups. Part of the process of developing an ethnic identity is forming ingroups. What we're familiar with tends to become a value. The familiar provides the indispensable basis of our existence. As early as age five, children develop a fierce sense of loyalty to their ingroup. Members of an ingroup all use the term *we* with the same essential significance.

Ingroup memberships are not set in concrete. At times people have reason to claim one category of membership, and at other times a different or slightly larger category, depending on their need to look good or be accepted. No doubt, you've noticed that certain people in your ingroup squabble among themselves all the time. But if one of them is attacked by someone from outside the group, the former squabblers may join together in defending against or attacking the outgroup enemy. Likewise, two groups that formerly fought each other may join together to fight a third group, a common enemy. In this way members may modify their ingroups to fit their needs. When the needs call for hostile action, the purpose of the newly formed ingroup may be action against a hated outgroup.

The term *ingroup* indicates the sheer fact that you're a member of a group, while the term *reference group* indicates whether you cherish that membership or whether you seek to relate yourself with another group. The terms help us to identify two levels of belongingness. A reference group may be either:

- an ingroup that you're happy you belong to, or
- another group that you'd like to belong to.

Some people are always comparing themselves with groups which for them are not ingroups. Some minority persons tend to mold their attitudes around those of the dominant majority, which for them may be a reference group. The dominant majority exerts a strong pull on minorities, often forcing them to conform to majority attitudes. This conformity, however, rarely goes so far as a minority rejecting her or his own ingroup. It does explain, however, why women and minorities sometimes echo the opinions of Euro-American men even when such opinions are against the best interests of women and minorities.

Ingroup memberships are vitally important to individual survival. Through memberships we form a web of habits. When we meet outsiders who follow different customs, we tend to unconsciously say, "They break my habits." Habit-breaking is unpleasant because we tend to prefer the familiar. Most of us feel a bit on guard when other people seem to threaten or even question our habits. Attitudes partial to the ingroup, or to the reference group, do not necessarily require that attitudes toward other groups be antagonistic—even though hostility often helps to intensify the ingroup cohesion. Narrow circles can, without conflict, be supplemented by larger circles of loyalty. Allport (1954) noted that this happy condition is not often achieved, but it remains from the psychological point of view a hopeful possibility.

Becoming Ethnocentric

Ethnocentrism can lead to prejudice, but does not always do so. While prejudice assumes different groups are inferior, ethnocentrism assumes your own group is superior. It's a part of developing an ethnic identity. While ethnocentric attitudes are widespread in human society and seem to reflect a universal tendency, studies indicate that Euro-American managers are more ethnocentric than their counterparts in Britain, Australia, and mainland Europe (Ijzendoorn 1980).

> *Ethnocentrism* is the belief that your ethnic group is superior to all others.

Ethnocentrism is a form of ingroup/outgroup bias. Two related factors stand out:

* Such bias can be based on nearly any group identity, such as blue eyes or brown eyes, and does not necessarily imply a long history of prejudice.
* It's a milder form of ingroup favoritism than the more extreme forms of hostile bigotry that are usually associated with prejudice and discrimination.

In her landmark experiment with school children, Jane Elliott (1985) was able to create the main dimensions of ethnocentric behavior in a matter of hours on the basis of a group separation that was essentially arbitrary—whether a child had blue eyes or brown eyes.

Research provides evidence that dominant group members tend to believe that when outgroup people succeed, it's because they got help or got lucky, but when ingroup members succeed, it's because they deserved it, earned it, and had the right traits and skills. In other words, Euro-American males tend to think that when their own succeed in the workplace, it's because of internal traits, but when others succeed, it's because of external circumstances.

Ethnocentrism in the workplace has made it difficult for people other than Euro-American males to make it to the top. For example, several studies indicate that the major barrier is the tendency for Euro-American males at the top to be more comfortable with their own kind (Morrison, White, and Van Velsor 1987; Carr-Ruffino 1991).

Ethnocentrism is a human tendency that offers several benefits. If you decide to stick with your ingroup:

* You can better predict and understand others' behavior, because they're like you.
* It's easier to figure out why others in the group do what they do.
* It's easier to establish rapport and build a relationship.
* You're more likely to help others, because people are more likely to help others like themselves than to help "strangers."

People who are high in authoritarian and rigid personality traits and low in moral development tend to be more ethnocentric. They tend to be less tolerant toward, and hold less favorable attitudes toward, members of outgroups, especially minority group members (Ijzendoorn 1989; Brewer 1979; Clark 1975; Greenhaus and Parasuraman 1991).

People who are more open and flexible enjoy a different set of advantages. When you're comfortable and open to interacting with people from outgroups:

* You get to expand your experience and knowledge of other people and cultures.
* You make your work more interesting, exciting, and intriguing.
* You increase your ability to relate to many types of people.
* You boost your social and leadership skills.
* You become more cosmopolitan.

Developing Certain Personality Traits

The development of prejudice coincides with the development of personality. While we are all prejudiced to some extent, the degree of prejudice varies greatly. People who are rigid and authoritarian in their beliefs tend to be more prejudiced than people who are open and flexible. Business leaders who recognize key personality traits can better understand why some employees are more prejudiced than others and perhaps how to alleviate the fears that intensify prejudiced attitudes.

The Prejudice–Prone Personality

The thinking processes of highly prejudiced people are *in general* different from the thinking processes of less-prejudiced people. If you're prejudiced, your prejudice is not likely to be merely a specific attitude toward a specific group—though you may rationalize it that way. It's more likely to be a reflection of your whole way of thinking about the world you live in. You're likely to indulge in black-or-white thinking:

- Whenever you think of nature, of law, of morals, of men and women, you think in terms of good/bad, right/wrong, black/white, maleness/femaleness, etc. There is little gray in your thinking.

- You tend to be uncomfortable with categories that encompass variety, and are more comfortable if categories are limited to similar things.

- Your habits of thought are rigid, and you don't change your mental set easily, but persist in old ways of reasoning.

- You have a marked need for definiteness and don't cope well with ambiguity in your plans.

- You tend to agree with such statements as, "there are only two kinds of people" and "there is only one right way to do something."

- You divide the world into proper and improper.

- You need precise, orderly, clear-cut instructions before proceeding with a task.

In other words, you have what's known as an authoritarian personality.

The authoritarian personality involves an array of several traits, including aggressiveness, power orientation, political conservatism, cynicism, and a strong commitment to conform to the prevailing authority structure. The original work on the authoritarian personality was done in 1950, and subsequently more than 1200 studies were conducted on this topic. Dutch researcher Ijzendoorn (1989) discovered that persons with authoritarian personalities are less tolerant toward members of minority groups than are nonauthoritarian personalities. People with authoritarian personalities display the following tendencies:

- rigid in their beliefs
- intolerant of weakness in themselves and others
- highly punishing
- suspicious
- extremely respectful of authority

Research studies indicate that people who score high on an authoritarianism scale also show a consistently high degree of prejudice against all minority groups. Researchers have traced this cluster of beliefs and attitudes to early childhood experiences in families with these typical characteristics:

- Parents administered harsh and threatening discipline.

- Parents used love and its withdrawal as their major control mechanism to make the child do as told.

- The child was very insecure and highly dependent on the parents.
- The child feared the parents and felt unconscious hostility toward them.

This set of characteristics usually produces an adult with a high degree of anger and a habit of repressing the anger because of insecurity and fear of expressing it directly. Anger must go somewhere, and in this instance it takes the form of displaced aggression against powerless groups. Meanwhile the authoritarian person maintains an outward respect for law and order.

Almost invariably, when the parents of such people have been studied, they are also highly prejudiced against minority groups. This child gets a double whammy: the setup for developing an authoritarian personality and role models who specifically teach prejudice.

The rigid person is often also the one with an authoritarian personality. Rigid persons don't easily deal with situations that are unclear or difficult to interpret. They see uncertain situations as threatening, while others may see them as nonthreatening or even as interesting, intriguing or otherwise desirable. Rigidity is also referred to as intolerance of ambiguity. Cultural differences obviously create uncertainty about human behavior, and the behavior of diverse others is less understandable and predictable to us than the behavior of those we grew up with. People with rigid personalities are especially likely to view interactions with diverse others as threatening and undesirable (Cox 1993).

The less-prejudiced personality is more flexible. If you're a fairly tolerant person, on the other hand, your thinking process is likely to be more open and flexible, as follows:

- You rarely see things in black-or-white terms but see many shades of gray.
- You're usually comfortable differentiating among the variety within a category.
- You can be comfortable with people and situations you're uncertain about.
- You often empathize with those who are different; you're sensitive to their way of seeing and feeling.
- You're self-aware and assess the quality and meaning of your thoughts, feelings, and actions.
- You tend to take responsibility for what happens to you in life and for the life you create.
- You know your own strengths and shortcomings pretty well.
- You've built a great deal of inner security, have handled threats to your self-esteem with inner strength, and can be at ease with all sorts of people.
- You handle moral conflict pretty well, and so can be fairly flexible and tolerant with the ethical mistakes people make.
- You can tolerate ambiguity.
- You feel safe in saying "I don't know" and in waiting until time brings the information or evidence you need.
- You can "feel your way" through a task, if necessary.

If you're a fairly tolerant person, you're likely to fit the following profile fairly well. You were probably raised in a home with a relatively permissive atmosphere. You felt welcomed, accepted, and loved in an unconditional way. While you were reprimanded for certain behavior, you weren't rejected as a person because of that behavior. You accepted your parents on the whole but weren't afraid to criticize their behaviors or beliefs at times. You generally didn't fear or dread your parents' superior power. Of course, there are exceptions to this profile. Some persons from authoritarian homes are able to choose an open, flexible approach to life. Others, through personal growth, change their beliefs and attitudes in order to become more open, flexible, and accepting of diversity.

Investigators have failed to discover important relationships between prejudice and such variables as age, gender, or income. People with more education tend to be less prejudiced, but the connection is fairly minimal. Prejudice is clearly more than an occasional incident for many people; it's embedded in every facet of their personality. If such persons were to change their prejudiced viewpoints, it would follow that they would be changing their whole life pattern.

Being Part of a Diverse, Rapidly Changing Society

We learn prejudice from our culture, and the U.S. is a fertile ground for prejudice to grow simply because of its current situation. The following conditions provide fertile ground for prejudice to develop; they also can exacerbate or intensify existing prejudice in a culture (Ponteretto and Pedersen 1993).

- The society is heterogeneous.
- Upward mobility is allowed and valued.
- Social change is occurring rapidly.
- Communication barriers and ignorance between groups are common.
- A minority group is large or increasing.
- An increasing minority represents direct competition and a realistic threat.
- Exploitation of minorities sustains important interests.
- Customs regulating aggression are favorable to bigotry.
- Traditional justifications for ethnocentrism are available.
- Neither assimilation nor cultural pluralism is favored.

This reads like a current description of American society. We're the most heterogeneous society on earth, and a key value is the opportunity for people to move up if they learn the ropes and work hard. Social change, and every other type of change, is occurring rapidly, especially the family changes caused by women pursuing careers. We've been a segmented society and de facto segregation is still common. Barriers to communication result in ignorance about other groups, which make them easy prey to rumor, suspicion, and stereotype. This process is most likely to occur if the group is also regarded as a potential threat because it's growing and its members are competing with the dominant group in the job market. Internal colonialism has sustained privilege for Euro-American, bigotry has been a part of U.S. history, and ethnocentrism is still creating barriers in the workplace. Finally, we're in a state of flux and transition regarding assimilation versus cultural pluralism, both in our corporations and in our communities. Immigrants to the U.S. have found themselves criticized both for maintaining their cultural ways and for pressing for assimilation.

In this section, we've addressed the question, How do we become prejudiced? A review of the processes and influences may leave you wondering, How could we not be prejudiced? The legacy of the patriarchal family teaches us about the inequality and stereotyped roles of men and women just by its very existence. From the cradle, this is part of our enculturation. And the organizations we encounter when we leave our homes have virtually all been founded on the basis of inequality and stereotyped roles. Some psychologists note that prejudice and discrimination at the top level of a society, or an organization, set into motion a continuing cycle of prejudice and discrimination throughout every part (Ponteretto and Pedersen 1993). We can see, then, that prejudice is woven into the very tapestry of our culture, springing up from the grass roots of family; filtering down from the top levels of government, business, and society; and feeding back on itself at all levels in between. The people with the most influence in sustaining or breaking the cycle are parents in the home and leaders in organizations.

HOW DO PEOPLE EXPRESS PREJUDICE?

When someone is prejudiced, how do you know it? People may express prejudice by denying it or rationalizing it, by acting it out in various ways from mild to devastating, by subtly discriminating, or by using outgroup members as scapegoats.

Denying and Rationalizing

Two common ways of handling the inner conflict that arises when people discriminate against others are:

- *denial*: repressing the conflict by denying the prejudice
- *rationalization*: offering defenses for the prejudice, justifying it

People often choose denial because if they admit prejudice, they admit to being both irrational and unethical. No one wants their conscience to bother them all the time. So it's not unusual to hear the person we perceive as being quite prejudiced saying, "I'm not prejudiced, but . . . ."

The most obvious way for people to defend prejudiced beliefs is to gather evidence in their favor. People may select only that evidence that supports their stereotypes. When we rationalize, we may:

- See only those traits, actions, and events that confirm a decision we've already made, and we simply fail to notice those that don't.
- Say it must be true because other people think this way too. "Everybody thinks those people are sneaky" (. . . dirty, stupid, rude), claiming truth by consensus.
- Blame the targets or shift the blame back onto our accusers. "It's their own fault they don't get ahead" (. . . that others shun them, etc.) or "They're just as prejudiced as we are."
- Defend our thinking or action by saying it's the exception to our usual pattern. "Some of my best friends are Platians, but . . ."

Acting Out

We act out our prejudice toward people from an unfavored group with varying degrees of hostile energy. Talking against such people involves relatively little energy, while actively avoiding them takes more. Stepping up the energy level, we may discriminate against them, physically attack them, or in a rare extreme of hostile energy, participate in exterminating them. While some people would never move to a more intense degree of action, for others activity on one level makes it easier to move to a more intense level. We'll examine the talking-against and physically-attacking forms of acting out in more detail.

Talking against persons from other groups is usually done with like-minded friends, and occasionally with strangers. People sometimes disparage an outgroup in order to cement their relationship as part of their ingroup. Talking against includes joking or disparaging comments that express a mild animosity. Name-calling expresses a more intense hostility. The more spontaneous and irrelevant the talking against, the stronger the hostility that lies behind it.

Physically attacking outgroup members, and other acts of violence or semi-violence, occurs far less frequently than the milder expressions of prejudice. However, violent incidents are increasing both in the workplace and in the community, especially against women. They usually occur when people become overwrought and overemotional. However, violence may be calculated to create a reign of terror, to teach others to stay in their place, or to otherwise punish or threaten.

An FBI report cited more than 7,600 hate crimes in 1993. Director Louis Freeh said the total falls far short of the full picture because police forces representing 44 percent of the population did not report hate crimes. Crimes against people accounted for 70 percent of offenses. The most common targets:

African Americans	2,500
Euro-Americans	1,300
Jewish Americans	1,054
Gay persons	777

Offenders were unknown in 42 percent of cases. Of the known offenders, 51 percent were Euro-American and 35 percent African American (Espinosa and Pimentel 1993).

Subtly Discriminating

It's not attractive to express prejudice in many social circles, and it can be illegal in the workplace. Therefore, most prejudice today is of the covert and subtle form, sometimes classified as the avoidance prejudice of the liberals and the symbolic prejudice of the conservatives. Psychologically, if you hold your prejudiced beliefs out of conscious awareness, you can hold onto your self-concept as a nonprejudiced, egalitarian person. You can swear you're not prejudiced and define prejudice as an intentional, overt act, the old-fashioned type of prejudice (Blanchard and Crosby 1989).

Avoidance prejudice focuses on subtle prejudice among liberals, who are all for equality and consider themselves unprejudiced but who possess negative feelings and beliefs about minority groups. Because such people hold egalitarian values and see themselves as tolerant, they usually won't discriminate against other ethnic groups in situations where the policies and procedures describing appropriate behavior are clear and unambiguous. To do so would directly threaten their egalitarian self-image. When the rules of the game are weak, ambiguous, or conflicting, or if such persons can justify or rationalize a negative response on the basis of some factor other than ethnicity, many will discriminate, while holding onto their egalitarian self-image. Business leaders can reduce discrimination within the organization, therefore, by developing clear policies and procedures for the treatment of people from diverse groups. At least that portion of discriminatory behavior that is based on avoidance prejudice will be reduced.

Symbolic prejudice focuses on subtle prejudice among conservatives, who tend to believe that discrimination no longer exists and that minority groups are violating our cherished American values and are making unwarranted demands for changing the status quo. According to symbolic prejudice theory, Euro-Americans acquire negative feelings toward other ethnic groups early in life. These feelings persist into adulthood but are expressed indirectly and symbolically.

Modern conservatives tend to express their prejudice in such symbolic ways as opposition to affirmative action or sexual harassment policies, rather than directly or overtly, as in support for segregation. They reject traditional racist beliefs and they displace their prejudicial feelings onto more rationalizable abstract social and political issues, such as "family values" and "school voucher systems." People who practice symbolic prejudice, like those who practice avoidance prejudice, are therefore relatively unaware of their prejudicial feelings.

Scapegoating

Most societies seem to encourage, officially or unofficially, the open expression of hostility toward certain groups that serve as scapegoats or safety valves for anger and aggression. Scapegoating is a form of group projection that helps groups to remain ethnocentric by projecting members' shortcoming and failures upon outgroups, blaming them for the ingroup's problems. In addition, most nations have numerous chauvinistic devices that breed ethnocentrism. For example, virtually no history book ever teaches that one's country was ever in the wrong. Geography is usually taught with a nationalistic bias, and claims to achievements in science and the arts are often overblown.

HOW DOES CONTACT AFFECT PREJUDICE?

Segregation of the African American community was for hundreds of years legally enforced in the South and was a way of life in the rest of the country. Informal or de facto segregation was generally the rule for Latino American and Asian American communities until recently. We still have a great deal of de facto segregation in our cities, and even where integration has occurred, it has often been accompanied by misunderstanding, conflict, violence, and crime. Some psychologists have described the peaceful progression of contact between diverse groups as a four-step process (Ponteretto and Pedersen 1993):

1. initial contact, leading to
2. competition, which in turn gives way to
3. accommodation, and finally to
4. collaboration.

Whether or not this peaceful progression occurs depends on the nature of the contact that is established, whether it is casual contact, making acquaintances, simply living or working near each other, or working together to achieve common goals.

> *The key to moving beyond prejudice is working together toward common goals that are highly valued, in situations where people need each other to achieve their goals.*

Types of Contact

The types of contact diverse groups typically experience range from superficial contact to true acquaintance, from conflict to collaboration.

Superficial contact. Where segregation is the custom, contacts tend to be superficial, either because they're very casual or because they're firmly fixed into superior-subordinate relationships. Such contact is more likely to increase prejudice than to decrease it because we tend to selectively notice behavior that will confirm our stereotypes. Therefore, each contact may serve to "prove" that our stereotypes are true. More about superficial contact later.

True acquaintance. In contrast, most studies show that true acquaintance lessens prejudice. Specifically, contacts that bring knowledge and acquaintance are likely to engender sounder beliefs concerning minority groups, and, therefore, contribute to the reduction of prejudice.

Conflict. Clashes of interests and values do occur between groups, and these conflicts are not in themselves necessarily an expression of prejudice. Also some conflicts grow out of economic competition that is not necessarily rooted in prejudice but, again, tends to aggravate any prejudice that exists.

Collaboration. Research indicates that Euro-Americans who live side by side with African Americans of the same general economic class in public housing projects are on the whole more friendly, less fearful, and have less-stereotyped views than those who live in segregated arrangements. Merely living together is not the decisive factor. Whether people are jointly active in community enterprises is what counts. The form of the resulting communication is different and makes all the difference in the relationship that develops (Ponteretto and Pedersen 1993). For example, a public housing project in Los Angeles was converted to private condominiums, which low-income families were able to purchase. Owners established a home owners association that met regularly for the purpose of making the neighborhood as livable and vital as possible. During the Los Angeles riots of 1992 home owners took a united stand against any invasion of their neighborhood, and it was spared from vandalism. Residents who were interviewed credited the friendships built by people from various subcultures for the solidarity they displayed during the crisis (*L.A. Times* 1992).

This conclusion holds true for contact in the workplace. Only the type of contact that leads people to do things together is likely to result in changed beliefs and attitudes. Common goals are all-important. It's the cooperative striving for a goal that engenders solidarity. Participation and common interests are more effective than mere equal-status contact. Self-managing work teams hold tremendous challenge and opportunity to finally break down prejudiced belief systems and establish the unity we so need. But we must meet the challenge of overcoming the barriers to effective collaboration.

The Effects of Superficial Contact

Research indicates that superficial contact often reinforces prejudiced beliefs about the following aspects of outgroup members:

- their physical appearance
- their ability to communicate clearly
- the traits and qualities we assume they have (stereotypes and prejudice)

Physical appearance. Visibility serves as a central symbol of group differences (Allport 1954). The two most visible differences are skin color and sexual characteristics. Such differences can serve as a lightning rod for all kinds of thoughts and feelings about certain ethnic groups or about the other half of the human race. Such a lightning rod enables us to pull together and condense these thoughts and feelings and therefore to think of the outgroup as a cohesive unit. Remember, we tend to toss all we can into a category, for efficiency's sake.

For most of us, our view of others, whether favorable or unfavorable, is influenced by how we perceive their physical attractiveness. We assume that physically attractive people have more social skills, intelligence, and competence, so we're more likely to hire them. Various cultures have somewhat different views of physical attractiveness, which may change with the times, and our preferences reflect those views.

Physical distinctiveness can be a double-edged sword. If being different is viewed positively, it can be an asset that makes one stand out and be remembered. However, being too different or inappropriately different from the majority group will trigger prejudiced responses. For example, the token female sales rep in a male-dominated industry may be more successful because she's "different" and therefore remembered. But if she's "too different," she'll lose customers. Many studies illustrate the importance often placed on physical appearance in the workplace, and the dangers to career success of deviating too far from the majority norm (Cox 1993).

Communication Ability. Negative attitudes toward people who are difficult to understand has been linked with discomfort and frustration experienced by the persons who are trying to communicate with them. This applies to people who do not know the dominant language well, people who use "street language," and people with speech disabilities. As a result, others may avoid them or shorten their contact time with them (Cox 1993).

WHAT ARE THE EFFECTS OF PREJUDICE?

Prejudice dramatically affects those who hold the prejudice and those who are demeaned by it. It affects the level of trust both parties are able to build. When we stereotype, we don't give people a chance and we obviously don't trust them to behave in ways that don't conform to the stereotype. When we've been stereotyped, we find it difficult to trust those who didn't bother to get to know us as individuals or to give us a fair chance. Prejudice affects us as children, in how our personality develops, and as adults, in our career opportunities and career progression. We'll discuss career aspects in the leadership challenges section.

How Prejudice Affects Trust

Most minority group members have vivid memories of personal experiences that were triggered by their minority status. Most naturally understand the impact that their group identities have on their relationships with majority group members (Alderfer 1982). Peggy McIntosh (1988) explored the tendency of majority group members to be unaware of the effects of majority group identity on life experiences. Euro-American men are unaware of the privileges they enjoy as a member of the majority group, assuming that most share their good fortune or that they are the cause of their own good fortune. Among the 46 privileges that McIntosh lists:

- Educational materials consistently testify to the existence of my ethnic group and its contributions to the U.S.
- Anywhere I go in the U.S. I can find my own kind of foods, music, hairdressers and other services appropriate to my cultural background.
- When I take a job with an affirmative action employer, co-workers will assume I got the job because I'm qualified, not because I'm a minority.
- When I'm setting my goals and plans for social, professional, or political achievement, I don't ask whether a person from my ethnic group would be accepted in the situation.

The focus in discussions of prejudice often centers on prejudice by majority group members against minorities. However, members of minority groups may also hold prejudices against the majority. While understanding their history may give us insight into the sources of these prejudices, the fact remains that they become obstacles to effective interpersonal relations in diverse work groups. To overcome these barriers, employees from all groups must become aware of their attitudes and the sources of those attitudes. All must participate in company-wide efforts to reduce prejudice and eliminate discrimination.

How Prejudice Affects Personality

Prejudice affects the personalities of the persons who hold the prejudice and can affect the personalities of the persons they're prejudiced against. As a business leader, you can work more effectively with people who are prejudiced if you understand the ways that prejudiced thinking influences their life views and their day-to-day actions. You can more constructively deal with employees from disparaged subgroups when you understand how their life experiences may be influencing their behavior patterns.

What Happens When You Reject Others?

When you reject others as not good enough, the immediate payoff is "feeling better-than," but it's a cheap thrill. After all, the more time you spend with stereotyped, prejudiced, and discriminatory thoughts, the more time you spend in a critical, blaming, judging state of mind. It follows that you'll spend less time in an appreciative, enthusiastic, or joyous state of mind. The more prejudiced you are, the more you view life through a negative lens. The more your thoughts focus on distaste, dislike, resentment, revulsion, anger, and similar feelings, the more likely you are to experience the anxiety and fear of being despised by others, because that way of thinking is prominent in your experience. Your world becomes more hierarchical, with everyone becoming categorized as better or worse, and people always judging and comparing. You have less space in your mind and less time for the beauty, the joy, the love, the wonder of other beings. As prejudice becomes a habit, you may become more and more critical, and therefore you become more and more isolated because there are fewer and fewer people you can enjoy. You block the possibility of knowing a large part of the world's people with their fascinating variety because you choose to judge so many of them as too strange or not good enough.

What Happens When You're Rejected?

Feeling rejected and inferior is difficult to deal with, even if you're a Euro-American male. It's more difficult if you're a woman because you're told in thousands of subtle or blatant ways throughout your life that you're inferior in most life areas—just because you were born a woman. If you're a minority, you're not only told that you're inferior, you're frequently rejected—just because you were born into an "inferior" subgroup. The message that you're inferior cannot be hammered into your head day after day without doing something to your character. It may cause you to examine who you really are, to accept yourself, and to become a stronger person for it. Or it may cause you to develop defensive coping behaviors. These persecution-produced traits are not all unpleasant. Some people, even when they're in reaction to rejection, are able to overcome the human tendency to lash out against the unfairness of a dominant majority and to choose responses that are constructive and socially agreeable (Ponteretto and Pedersen 1993; Allport 1954).

Just which ego defenses people develop is largely an individual matter, often coming out of choices made at an unconscious level but sometimes decided upon consciously. At one extreme, you'll find minority group members who seem to handle their status easily, with little evidence that their outgroup affiliation is of any concern to them. At the other extreme, you'll find people so rebellious that they have developed many ugly defenses, so that they continually provoke the snubs that they resent. Most people you meet fall somewhere between these extremes, showing some mixture of acceptance and resistance to their status.

Only to a slight extent can we say that certain types of ego defense will be more common in one outgroup than in another. Every form of ego defense may be found among people of every disparaged group. Allport developed the model shown in Figure 3-2, which distinguishes between ego defenses that cause us to strike out at other persons from those that we turn inward to punish ourselves.

FIGURE 3-2: Model of Responses to Discrimination

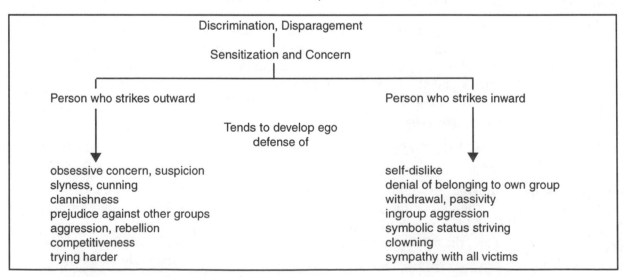

Adapted from Allport, 1954

Ego defenses that strike outward. The basic feeling of members of disparaged groups is one of insecurity, which may lead to being on guard and hypersensitive. Minorities must make many more adjustments to their status than majority members. The latter interact mainly with their own kind and only occasionally with minority group members. The reverse is true for most minorities. In addition, they are more likely to be in a less-powerful position than each of the dominant group members they meet. Preoccupation with the strain of accommodation may become excessive, so that they come to view virtually all members of the dominant group with deep suspicion.

Obsessive concern and suspicion often result in a chip-on-the-shoulder attitude based on the belief, "I've been rejected so often that I've learned to protect myself in advance by not trusting any of you."

Slyness and cunning are often responses of people who are trying to survive or get ahead in a discriminatory environment. In really hostile environments "sneaky" traits may be a passive-aggressive way of gaining petty revenge against more powerful persecutors.

Clannishness, or clustering together with other minority group members, is a natural response to being excluded by the majority group. When people are excluded in work, play, and neighborhood settings, who else can they turn to but their own kind?

Prejudice against other groups, especially less-powerful groups, is one way to gain some sense of status and power. When we start with a foundation of inequality, a pecking order naturally develops, with the strong picking on the weaker, and they in turn picking on the still weaker.

Aggression and rebellion occur when people refuse to "take it lying down," and fight back whenever they can. Their frustration breeds aggression. This can be the source of criminal activity and riots. In contrast, some members see the futility of violence and join political or activist organizations that are dedicated to improving the existing situation.

Competing and trying harder are the responses of some minorities. Examples are attending evening classes, studying harder, and working harder than others, trying to run an equal race. Dominant group members may respond with grudging admiration, but they also may accuse the minority of being *too* industrious and clever. Lower-class members of the dominant group may feel envious, resentful, or threatened.

Ego defenses that focus inward. Some minorities turn their feelings and actions inward on themselves or their group. They tend to punish themselves for being inferior or "outcasts."

Self-dislike is related to a craving to be one of the dominant group and therefore to identify more with them than with your own group. Self-dislike is not merely pretending to agree with the dominant group; it involves actually seeing the world through their eyes. A person affected by self-dislike may be ashamed of belonging to a disparaged group. For example, self-dislike can cause women to identify more strongly with male viewpoints, with the patriarchal system, and with their limited roles as being positive and in their own best interests. Normally, they are not aware of this process and would probably deny it.

In varying degrees, minorities often become *passive* and perhaps *withdraw* from life's more competitive activities. Or they may strike out at others in their own group. *Ingroup aggression* refers to attacking members of your own group because they possess the traits that you and the dominant group devalue. Aggression is sometimes related to self-dislike that extends to dislike for all disparaged persons. It sometimes occurs when two or more minority groups believe they're competing for scarce jobs and social services.

Symbolic status striving refers to attempts to gain status by pomp and circumstance, a flashy display of jewelry, cars, and clothes; pretentious use of language; obsessive interest in sexual conquests; and other ways of achieving marginal or symbolic status. It's self-punishing because it's not based on solid achievement and may include some elements of clowning.

Clowning is one way to receive good-natured, if patronizing, attention and to show that you are harmless, not threatening. Protective clowning extends into the subgroup itself. For example, some gay persons call themselves and each other *queers,* and some African Americans call themselves "niggers," saying: "If we call ourselves 'niggers,' we can harden ourselves to the sting of the insult. If we say it often enough, we'll become so hardened we won't ever feel its pain again. If we call ourselves 'nigger,' it's no longer an epithet that you can use against us."

Sympathy with all victims is considered the most positive of these inward-directed ego defenses. People who feel they've been victims of discrimination are usually either very high in prejudice or very low; they're seldom "average." Being a victim disposes you either to develop aggression toward or sympathy with other outgroups. Knowing all too well how it feels to be rejected, many minority persons reach out to other victims and offer support. Examples are Jesse Jackson's Rainbow Coalition and the number of Jewish Americans who put their lives on the line in the South during the Civil Rights era.

LEADERSHIP CHALLENGES AND OPPORTUNITIES:
MOVING BEYOND PREJUDICE

You'll encounter many leadership challenges and opportunities in the area of prejudice. First we'll discuss some leadership challenges in understanding how prejudice affects people's careers, understanding its effect on employee performance, and understanding the life experiences of minorities and women. Then we'll focus on leadership opportunities for moving beyond prejudice to collaboration and synergy.

Leadership Challenge: Understanding How Prejudice Affects Careers

Prejudice against minorities and women not only affects their career progress, it also affects employee trust, motivation, and productivity—their relationships with the rest of the workforce. Company leaders are recognizing that they can no longer afford the waste of human resources caused by prejudice and discrimination. As a leader, you need to understand exactly how prejudice affects every aspect of minority persons' careers. We'll discuss the following specific aspects:

- recruitment and hiring
- employment screening practices
- terms and conditions of employment
- tracking and job segregation
- evaluation and feedback
- training and development
- promotion practices
- layoff, discharge, seniority practices
- career alternatives

Recruitment practices. Word of mouth is still the most common way that people learn about hiring and promotion opportunities. Up to 90 percent of workers find their jobs this way. Studies have concluded that the distribution of white-collar jobs to African Americans depends heavily upon informal networks of information, radiating outward from persons currently employed in upper rank slots. Does word-of-mouth recruiting in your company happen primarily among Euro-American men? What can you do to be sure that minorities and women find out about job opportunities?

Does your company place ads for all types of jobs in minority publications—or just ads for lower-level jobs? When the company makes plans for new facilities, are they ever located at sites that are convenient for minorities and women? A Civil Rights Commission study of housing (1973) found that "despite a variety of laws against job discrimination, lack of access to housing in close proximity to available jobs is an effective barrier to equal employment."

Screening practices. Are the diplomas, degrees, and experience that your company requires of applicants really good predictors of whether those people will succeed on the job? If not, and if many minorities or women don't have them, they're discriminatory. Do the aptitude and intelligence tests that your company makes applicants pass really predict job success? The same principle applies here. Because minorities still tend to get an inferior education in the public schools, they're not as likely to do as well on screening tests as Euro-Americans. Also, most people who make the tests are Euro-American men from middle-class backgrounds. People from minority subcultures obviously are at a cultural disadvantage in relating to the terminology, examples, cases, and other aspects of such tests. However, they may be quite intelligent, capable of learning how to do the job, and likely to succeed on the job.

Does your company have a strict requirement for applicants to have clean arrest and credit records? Do such screening practices really predict job success or failure? Police department practices often discriminate against minorities, especially African American men and to some extent Latino American men. Such men are more likely to have arrest records even though their behavior may have been as lawful as many of the Euro-American fellow applicants. The same principle applies to credit records. Minorities tend to have lower incomes and to have more difficulty getting credit and maintaining good credit records.

How heavily does your company depend on cumulative employment records in making hiring decisions? Sometimes companies require women and minorities to have experience in areas where they previously had been effectively banned. How does your company conduct background investigations of job applicants? If such reports include subjective, vague, and arbitrary assessments from prejudiced persons, they may be unfair to minorities and women.

Terms and conditions of employment. Are women and minority men earning approximately the same income as Euro-American men at all levels of the company? On average, they earn about 70 percent, even at the vice-presidential level. Above the "worker" level, they also tend to receive fewer benefits and perquisites.

Tracking and job segregation. Does your company still have "women's jobs," "men's jobs," and "minority jobs," even though they're never called that? One example of tracking is the placement of women in clerical work. Do clerks and secretaries get a chance to participate in training and development for other, better-paying jobs? Do they have the chance to get to know people in management? Are they groomed and recruited for higher-level jobs?

To some extent, discrimination in every job phase from recruitment to promotion results in a dual labor market in which women and minorities work disproportionately in occupations and industries with lower prestige, status, and compensation. Within organizations, they typically work in jobs and departments that are less influential and have lower status than those held by Euro-American men. Progress is being made, but we have a long way to go (Johnson 1987; Buono and Kamm 1983).

Performance evaluation. Are performance evaluation practices in your company free of bias? Research indicates that successful performance by women on tasks traditionally done by men tends to be attributed to luck, while Euro-American men's performance is more likely to be attributed to their ability. Compared to Euro-American managers, the performance of African American managers is less likely to be attributed to ability and effort and more likely to be attributed to help from others (Deaux and Emswiller 1974; Cash, Gillen, and Burns 1977; Greenhaus and Parasuraman 1994).

Also, evaluations made by Euro-American men are often colored by their stereotyped expectations of the ways women and minorities act. As a result, Euro-American managers often hold women and minorities to a more limited range of acceptable behavior than the majority group members. Women managers often feel they must "walk a tight rope" of acceptable behavior, for example, feeling their way through the narrow range of acceptable behavior, recognizing that men can show more aggressiveness, ambition, and other traits without being criticized. African American men must show less anger and sexuality to avoid reinforcing stereotypes that cause discomfort. For diverse employees, it amounts to a double standard of acceptable behavior (Baack, Carr-Ruffino, and Pelletier 1993; Morrison, White, and Van Velsor 1987).

Training and development. Who makes the decisions about which employees will receive various types of training and development opportunities? Are these decisions open and equitable? Or are they colored by stereotypes about which types of persons have the potential and image to be groomed for certain jobs? For example, an examination of who gets picked for midcareer programs at such universities as Harvard, Yale, and Stanford indicates those selected are primarily Euro-American men. Such practices keep the glass ceiling in place for minorities and women.

Promotion practices. How open and equitable are the promotion procedures in your company? In many companies, they're secretive and very difficult for outsiders to understand. Although formal promotion policies and procedures are spelled out in writing by large companies and government agencies, unwritten, informal rules or expectations usually have a much greater impact. Many studies, past and present, indicate that Euro-American male executives and managers continue to harbor stereotyped views of women and minorities, views that shape the promotion decisions. A woman is disadvantaged if she's married ("We didn't promote her because she has children and her family responsibilities will interfere.") and disadvantaged if she's not. ("We didn't promote her because she's likely to quit and get married.") Another stereotype is that employees won't accept a woman or minority in a high position. Such subtle discrimination has kept the glass ceiling in place (Carr-Ruffino 1991; Morrison and Van Velsor 1987).

Subtle discrimination also includes passing over minority persons for "lack of initiative or aggressiveness," when the real reason is the employee's ethnic identity. Some studies have found that different standards of "getting along with others" are required for African Americans than for Euro-Americans. Tests and credentials are used to block promotions, just as they are used to block hiring. In many companies much decision making has traditionally taken place in Euro-American male-only settings, such as clubs, bars, men's rooms, and locker rooms. Newcomers of a different gender or ethnic origin are often never assimilated into these critical settings.

Indirect discrimination also occurs when Euro-American male supervisors fail to support and recommend their minority employees for promotion, even though company leaders rely on such subjective evaluations when they make promotion decisions.

Layoff, discharge, and seniority practices. What policies and practices does your company follow when they must lay off or fire people? If they use seniority to protect workers who've been there the longest, does this mean that most of those laid off are minorities and women? If not, are older workers the ones who are most likely to lose their jobs? Employees have successfully sued employers for discrimination in both types of situations.

Seniority systems often affect women and minority members more adversely because they typically have less seniority than Euro-American men. The purpose of an organization-wide seniority system is to guarantee that employees with the greatest seniority will receive the greatest protection when cutbacks or layoffs take place. Such guarantees are usually part of a union contract. Yet seniority systems operating today often result in indirect discrimination. Where women and minority persons were barred from certain occupations in the past and therefore have been hired only in recent years, they will be the first to be laid off. This situation is common in organizations with a unionized workforce, such as manufacturing firms and local fire and police departments.

In most other organizations, older workers are more likely to be laid off because they are typically the highest-paid employees. In the process of reengineering, restructuring, and downsizing, companies are often looking for ways to decrease salary expense. Also, when a company computerizes a functional area, the experience and expertise of older workers in that area may become less valuable or even obsolete.

Career alternatives. Discrimination can even make it more difficult for minorities to choose alternatives to corporate careers when they can't get hired or when they hit the glass ceiling. For example, the Small Business Administration did a study of its loans for 1990 through 1992 and declared that its loan guarantee program had been poorly serving minorities and women. The agency set a goal of at least doubling the number of loans to targeted groups during the coming year (WSJ 1994).

Leadership Challenge: Understanding the Effects of Prejudice on Performance

Prejudice and discrimination have a great impact on employee performance. At the deepest level, they undermine employee trust. They also undermine employee motivation and productivity.

Effects on employee trust. Prejudice and discrimination sabotage trust. Given the history of intergroup prejudice, trust is more difficult to build across cultural groups than it is within them. "Don't trust Whitey" has long been a motto in many African American families and communities. Minorities tend to feel less free to spontaneously express their opinions and ideas in the workplace. They tend to engage in much more internal prescreening or self-censorship in order to fit into the work group. Euro-American men tend to be unaware that this kind of self-censorship is occurring. Losses to the group generally go unnoticed.

Effects on employee motivation. Minorities generally find it more difficult than Euro-American men do to determine the cause of their events and life experiences, often asking, Was this event caused by discrimination or by other factors? This can be a major problem when they attempt to process feedback and to stay motivated: Is my boss criticizing me because my work is not up to standards or because I'm African American? Expectancy theory holds that the motivation to perform on a job is a function of three factors:

1. If I put forth enough effort, will it produce the performance level the boss wants?

2. If I achieve the performance level the boss wants, will I get what I want (praise, raise, promotion, etc.)?

3. Is it worth it to me?

Discrimination can interfere with factors 1 and 2. Even if the boss is not influenced by an employee's group identity when he evaluates performance, if the employee believes he is, then that employee's motivational level will almost certainly drop.

Effects on employee productivity. We've mentioned Jane Elliott's study of the effects of prejudice on productivity, which is described in the documentary film *A Class Divided*. Elliott separated students into blue-eyed and brown-eyed groups. On the first day, the instructor told the class that the brown-eyed "outgroup" was inferior (they wore collars for clear identification of their status). She reinforced this by various actions, such as giving certain privileges to the "ingroup." On the second day, the roles were reversed. On both days the superior ingroup discriminated against the inferiors, calling them names and otherwise ostracizing them.

The work performance of the so-called inferior group declined significantly after just a few hours of the discriminatory treatment. Test scores of the students went up on the day they were in the advantaged group and down on the day the same students were in the disadvantaged group. The change in behavior of the instructor and fellow students had an immediate impact on the performance of the students. The study highlights, among other things, the effect of leader expectations on performance.

Leader expectations are communicated to employees in several ways:

- The amount of output the leader wants signals expectations. (How challenging and desirable are the goals? To what extent does the leader believe the employee can achieve high goals? How supportive is the leader?)

- The overall climate (favorable tone, positive responses, etc.) that leaders set communicates their expectations.

- The amount of input (information relevant to getting the job done) that leaders give employees signals their expectations.
- The amount of feedback (information about how well the employee is doing) that leaders give communicates or implies their expectations.

Leaders have more influence than anyone in the work group in setting an inclusive tone. If we want top performance, there must be no outgroups. Everyone must be a member of the ingroup.

Leadership Challenge: Understanding Life Experiences of Minorities and Women

If you can meet the leadership challenge of truly understanding what makes women and minority employees tick, you'll then be able to design policies, systems, and practices that are sensitive to their life experiences. You can use approaches that help them overcome such internal barriers as lack of organizational savvy and conflict in balancing career and family demands.

Typical life experiences of many minorities and women include:

- a history of oppression
- being excluded from mainstream business (and society, for minorities)
- feelings that differ, in a negative way, from those of Euro-American men
- when moving into new roles, low self-concept, self-esteem, and self-confidence
- being positioned in a one-down status
- being prohibited from, and not encouraged to seek, a better position and status in business, and, perhaps, in society and in life
- being denied equal opportunities

The experience of being in a subordinate position typically leads to certain attitudes and behaviors that become internal barriers to workplace effectiveness. Kanter (1979) concluded from her study of corporations that many of the behaviors attributed to women were actually behaviors typical of powerless employees stuck in dead-end positions. Examples are excessive focus on detail, overconcern with rules and procedures, and excessive interest in gossip about personal lives.

Typical internal barriers include lack of organizational savvy and professional image. Most minorities don't know how to play the game of getting along, such as paying attention to office politics and the agendas of their bosses and peers. They rarely know how to be strategic about their own career development. They don't assert themselves and their views, so Euro-American men see them as subservient or passive, not willing to take a stand. Women have been reared to support men and seek their approval. Asian Americans and Latino Americans have been raised to respect authority to a greater degree and in a different way than Euro-American men. African Americans are frequently seen as too aggressive, vocal, confrontational, defensive, and pushy by Euro-Americans, though other African Americans wouldn't interpret their behavior that way. Women who are balancing responsibilities for children with a career can be misunderstood. Leaders need to understand that a slow-down or time-out phase for a woman to have a child doesn't necessarily mean that she's not a candidate for rapid career development later. Companies that are flexible enough to support women in this phase are likely to win their loyalty and commitment.

Leadership Opportunity: Strategies for Creating Synergy

Leading-edge companies are moving beyond prejudice and discrimination toward an ultimate goal of creating synergy in the workplace. Table 3.2 offers seven leadership strategies for accomplishing this type of change.

TABLE 3.2. Strategies for Moving Beyond Prejudice to Synergy

Strategy 1: Promote Tolerance

Work toward openness and acceptance of others, respect their right to have different beliefs and viewpoints, lifestyles and business images, and work styles and job behaviors.

Strategy 2: Be a Role Model of Respect and Appreciation

Be willing to listen to and learn about diverse people and groups, to examine our own ego needs, beliefs, and viewpoints that block our ability to respect and appreciate others, to work collaboratively with others to produce more creative, high-quality results. Be willing to change false beliefs.

Strategy 3: Value Empathy

Be willing to relax into your intuition and listen to its messages as you tune into others, allowing yourself to see things from their viewpoint.

Strategy 4: Promote Trust and Goodwill

Educate yourself and others about the key differences among diverse groups. Value those differences—see them as individual, colorful facets of the kaleidoscope of humanity. Expect everyone to build trust and goodwill in all their interactions—with all team members, business associates, and contacts in other countries.

Strategy 5: Encourage Collaboration

Encourage everyone to work toward common goals for the good of the whole organization, the whole industry, the whole nation, and the world. Value unity, which is not uniformity but individuated integration. See that in unity there can be great diversity. Understand that each part is vital to the integrity of an emerging whole.

Strategy 6: Work Toward Synthesis

Share a vision of people gathering together the separate elements that form the whole project, work team, organization, and industry. See them bringing the whole into active expression. Envision them acting as one to create a new reality—including new projects, processes, products, relationships, and corporate culture. Understand that synthesis is *not* assimilation.

Strategy 7: Create Synergy

Recognize that extra creative spark, that increment of information, knowledge, goodwill, or other benefit that is the by-product of collaboration and synthesis. Use it to carry the team and the organization to new heights of excellence and innovation. Celebrate that added gift, which is more than the sum of what each person brings to the group.

With input from the work of Nedra Carroll

Leadership Opportunity: Implementing the Strategies

A key multicultural skill that you as a leader can bring to the diverse workplace is to recognize your own ethnocentricity, the ways in which you stereotype, judge, and discriminate, and your emotional reactions to conflicting cultural values. Now that you've raised your awareness about the nature of prejudice and ethnocentricity, you're ready to take specific action steps that will move you beyond it. The following are action steps that serve to implement the leadership strategies presented in Table 3.2. Once you, as a leader, work through the action steps yourself, you can serve as a role model and coach for helping others work through them. These steps are listed below and then discussed in some detail.

- Uncover your personal prejudices. Become aware of the ego needs and beliefs that support them and the feelings tied to them.
- Open your mind. Be willing to listen and seriously consider other viewpoints.

- Support civil rights measures and multicultural policies and practices that bring about fairness and equity for disadvantaged groups.
- Work on your capacity to respect and appreciate diverse people and groups.
- Explore the ways that respecting diverse people and groups serves your self-interest as well as theirs.
- Be open to developing your intuition and your capacity for empathy.
- Learn ways to build trust and make it your top priority.
- Learn about diverse groups. Pursue multicultural and diversity education.
- Seek opportunities to collaborate with diverse people and groups and to work toward important common goals.

Get in Touch with Prejudiced Beliefs and Feelings

The first step toward becoming more open and accepting of diverse persons is to decide you want to. Then you can begin to notice thoughts that occur when you see certain people, judgmental thoughts that lead to feelings of aversion, dislike, suspicion, and similar feelings that prevent good interaction and block collaborative relationships. Self-awareness activities and skill builders throughout this book are designed to help you in this process. We often hide prejudiced beliefs from ourselves, so uncovering them can be challenging, but it's a challenge worth pursuing.

Open Your Mind to Other Viewpoints and Listen

Open-minded persons are relative rare. They tend to look beyond labels, categories, and sweeping statements. They usually insist on knowing the evidence for broad generalizations before accepting them as true. They are open to new evidence that might lead them to modify a category. Good listeners are just as rare. Most of us take turns talking instead of listening to get another's ideas that we might incorporate into our own. Be willing to listen with an open mind to other viewpoints and to new information that might change your prejudiced beliefs.

Support Equal Opportunity Measures

In 1954 Allport stated the belief that legal action can have only an indirect bearing upon reducing personal prejudice. It cannot coerce thoughts or instill personal tolerance. Legal restraints merely say, in effect, "You can have whatever prejudices you like, but you may not act them out to a point where they endanger the lives, livelihood, or peace of mind, of groups of American citizens." Law is intended only to control the outward expression of intolerance. Even so, outward actions have an eventual effect on inner habits of thought and feeling and can open up views of limited, stereotyped roles. For this reason, legal action has been one of the major methods of reducing private prejudice as well as public discrimination.

Have you really become informed about the major civil rights laws that affect the workplace and the equal opportunity policies of companies you've worked for? Or have you settled for basing your opinions on 30-second media sound bites or the glib opinions of co-workers? If you're serious about moving beyond prejudice, you owe it to yourself to become informed about civil rights issues, as well as diversity policies and practices.

Express Respect and Appreciation

Once you've opened your mind, the next step is to become comfortable and imaginative in expressing respect and appreciation, primarily through your actions but also through your conversations. Every time you choose to focus on goodwill and trust instead of focusing on fear and mistrust, you automatically move to respecting and appreciating instead of judging and belittling.

See Mutual Respect As Mutual Self-interest

You stand to benefit greatly from moving beyond prejudice, as does your career, your organization, and the planet for that matter. And staying stuck in prejudice, no matter how hidden or subtle, has great costs. You may have learned from bitter failure in a relationship that your stereotypes were in error or that your friends or business associates disapproved of your prejudged categories. You're fortunate if you get such a "change message," for it can help you see clearly that it's in your own interest to change your prejudiced thinking.

Even when you're not confronted by others with your prejudices, and even when you're not consciously aware of them or the effects they have, you probably believe at some level that prejudice conflicts with your deepest beliefs about human value and equality. Most of us, when we catch ourselves in prejudice, don't feel good about it, and if you stop to take a good, hard look at it, you probably don't particularly like yourself when you think and act this way. Except for making you temporarily feel "better than," it's not nearly as satisfying to dislike people and look down on them as it is to appreciate them, collaborate with them, and have fun together. Further, prejudice sets in motion a negative cycle of action and reaction that divides and separates and throws up barriers to building trust. It prevents people from having the productive and harmonious workplace and society that would benefit us all.

Open Up to Intuition and Empathy

Clearly, the ability to feel empathy for others can help us to move beyond prejudice and beyond tolerance to appreciation. When you empathize, you intuit how another person sees and feels about a situation; therefore, you're able to experience empathy when you're in touch with your intuitive side. With empathy and intuitiveness, you're better able to understand others and therefore have less need to feel apprehensive and insecure. You tend to gain confidence that you can sidestep unpleasant involvements if the need arises. Accurate perception of how others think and feel gives us the ability to avoid friction and to conduct successful relationships. In contrast, people who cannot empathize are forced to be on guard, to put strangers into categories, and to react to them as a group rather than as individuals. Lacking subtle powers of differentiation, they must resort to stereotyping.

Intuition is never wrong, else it wouldn't be intuition. To come in touch with intuition is similar to listening to your body when your body is speaking to you. We tend to tune into our intuition when we're relaxed. Give yourself permission to be intuitive, relax, ask your inner self for intuitive insight, and allow for whatever is to occur. If you're sincere, answers will come. However, the moment that you set up expectations about *how* the event may occur and *when*, you're immediately limiting your possibilities. So put forth the desire, give yourself permission to ask for it, then be watchful. Intuition is not linear and rational; answers may come in unexpected ways and times. They often come as little flashes or "glimmers" of thought or as feelings. Learn to recognize them and to use the power of insight.

Build Trust

You build trust by building authentic relationships, in which you respect and appreciate others and show it through words and actions. When you're consistent in your actions and words, keep your commitments, and show respect and appreciation, time after time, then people begin to trust you. Where there is a long legacy of mistrust, it may take years to build trust. It can be destroyed in a moment of betrayal, and the healing process may be difficult or impossible. The best preventive is to consistently choose an attitude of goodwill and trust toward other people.

Pursue Multicultural and Diversity Education

Once you begin to understand the typical stereotypes, biases, and barriers that persons from disparaged groups must cope with every day, you can begin to understand more about what their lives are like. Once you become aware of how cultural do's and don'ts affect such persons' self-image, self-esteem, and emotions, you have a better chance of anticipating how your own actions may affect them. The goal of cultural understanding is to be able to walk in another person's shoes for a while, to see the world as that person sees it, and feel what he or she feels. Or to step into a little slice of that person's life and look out at the world from that vantage point.

We've inherited the legacy of prejudice, but we've also inherited the legacy of equality, and we've recently grown to accept more and more people as qualified to be equal. We're approaching the time when Euro-Americans may become a minority in some states, and we face some confusion about our national identity and our future as one people. Euro-Americans, as the dominant majority, can insist on holding onto the past and try to further contract into a separate enclave. Alternatively, they can choose to expand into a multifaceted culture that acknowledges and values all its subcultures. As a nation that has thrived on the concept of expansion, it seems more constructive to expand our notion of cultural literacy to reflect the multicultural heritage of all our people, not just the Euro-American portion.

Work with Diverse People Toward Common Goals

We've learned that superficial contact does not help people to overcome stereotypes and prejudices toward a subgroup. What has worked to change prejudiced beliefs and attitudes is working with diverse others on projects that help all participants to achieve common goals. So continually seek opportunities to work together toward common goals.

SUMMARY

What is prejudice? Prejudice is our tendency to view people who are different as being inferior, while ethnocentricity is the tendency to think your own cultural group is superior. When we discriminate, we act out our prejudice in ways that disadvantage people from disparaged groups. The third step in gaining multicultural skills is recognizing your own ethnocentricity, prejudices, and stereotypes. Although most prejudice is called either *racism* or *sexism*, most anthropologists agree that race has little or no meaning as a practical concept. *Ethnic prejudice* is a more appropriate term. On the other hand, sexism is said by some to be the root of all prejudice because it begins in the home.

How do we become prejudiced? Virtually every aspect of our culture teaches us to be prejudiced, from the differential in mother's and father's status and other family beliefs to the media, schools, workplace, government, and religious organizations. Stereotypes are rigid beliefs about a particular group of people that often lead to prejudice. As children grow up, they develop an ethnic identity. Euro-American children usually become aware of ethnic differences after some type of ethnic conflict. They may react by defending minorities or by avoiding future contact with them. Minority children usually identify first with the Euro-American majority until they encounter prejudice and begin searching for their own identity. They may develop resentment toward Euro-Americans or become ashamed of being a minority. Most eventually identify with their own cultural subgroup and later integrate aspects of both cultures.

Prejudice and ethnocentrism are related to the human tendency to form ingroups. A reference group is either your ingroup, if you're happy you belong to it, or another group you want to belong to. People who are most ethnocentric and prejudiced tend to also be most rigid and authoritarian. The authoritarian person believes in strict categories of right and wrong, good and bad, and other black/white opposites. Such people tend to be intolerant of weakness, highly punishing, suspicious, and extremely respectful of authority. People develop either a relatively authoritarian or relatively open, flexible personality in childhood but can choose to change at any age. The U.S. provides fertile ground for prejudice to grow because it is an increasingly diverse society, still relatively segregated, and in the midst of rapid change.

How do we express prejudice? Most people are unaware of their prejudices, and denying or justifying prejudice is a typical way of handling the inner conflict that prejudice often creates. People may act out their prejudice in varying degrees of hostility, from talking against others or avoiding them to discriminating against them, physically attacking them, or even participating in programs to exterminate them. People who are unaware of their prejudices may express them quite subtly. Liberals tend to use avoidance prejudice and won't discriminate where policies and procedures are clear. Conservatives tend to resort to symbolic prejudice, opposing for example affirmative action but not advocating a return to legal segregation. Disparaged groups are often used as scapegoats so the dominant group can retain its belief in its superiority.

Superficial contact with people from disparaged groups may actually reinforce stereotypes and prejudices. The type of contact that reduces prejudice is based on getting to know people in depth and collaborating with them to achieve meaningful goals together. Work teams provide an ideal type of contact for moving beyond prejudice.

What are some effects of prejudice? It causes the prejudiced to live a more limited life than is necessary. In fact, studies indicate they have less zest for life. They block many of the possibilities for exploring diversity in the world, and the sense of curiosity and adventure that goes with it. On the other hand, prejudice causes minorities to distrust the majority because they've felt hurt, betrayed, and rejected time after time. It affects the personality of those who are targets of prejudice in many ways. Some develop ego defenses that strike out at the majority, such as suspicion, slyness, clannishness, aggression, and competitiveness. Others develop ego defenses that are self-punishing, such as self-dislike, attacking or disliking their own group, putting on a superficial show of success, and clowning. And some are motivated to succeed and to sympathize with all victims.

Leadership challenges for moving beyond prejudice include understanding how prejudice affects minorities' career paths along every step, understanding the effects of prejudice on minority employees' level of trust, motivation, and productivity. It also includes understanding life experiences typical of nearly all minorities and women and the internal barriers created by such experiences. Leadership opportunities include adopting and implementing strategies that enable employees to move beyond prejudice and to begin creating synergy.

Skill Builder 3.1: Opening Up to New Experiences

Purpose: To help you open up to all types of people. Especially helpful for people who score above average on the authoritarian personality scale.

Barriers	*Motivators*
I don't know what to expect.	It may be fun.
I don't feel comfortable.	It may be interesting.
Maybe they won't like me.	I may learn something.
Maybe I won't like them.	They may like me.
Maybe they won't treat me well.	I may like them.
I may end up looking foolish.	I may end up feeling better about myself.
I don't know what to say.	I may gain experience, perspective,
I don't know how to act.	understanding, empathy, compassion.
Others:	Others:

The barriers relate to some type of discomfort and ultimately to some type of fear. They cause us to mentally separate ourselves from others, to contract, withdraw. The motivators relate to an outgoing tendency and ultimately to some type of goodwill. They cause us to mentally reach out, to include, and to expand. They often involve curiosity, courage, and sense of adventure.

Step 1. Think of a situation where you did *not* say yes to an opportunity to experience a new situation with people you didn't know well. What were some of the barriers that held you back? Check off the barriers that apply in the list shown here. Add others that you experienced.

Step 2. Think of a situation where you *did* say yes to such an opportunity. What motivated you? Check off the motivators that apply in the list shown here. Add others that you experienced.

Step 3. What happened in the situation you said yes to? Was the experience more positive or negative in your opinion? If more negative, what lessons can you draw from this experience?

Step 4. What might have happened if you had said yes to the situation in step 1? What experiences, opportunities, advantages, lessons might you have missed? What lessons can you learn from this?

Skill Builder 3.2: Visualizing Prejudice in Your Organization

Purpose: To use the power of symbols and visuals to help you better understand your beliefs, attitudes, thinking, feelings about prejudice.

Step 1. Draw a picture of prejudice in your company (or another organization where you spend time). Draw anything you like, but do not use words in the picture. Use colors and symbols to express how people relate to one another, which groups have power, how they use power, and similar aspects.

Step 2. Put the picture away for a while. Later, when you look at your picture, pay attention to the following:

• What immediate feelings do you experience?
• What thoughts come to mind?
• What does your drawing say about prejudice in the organization?

Write a brief summary of prejudice in your organization and your thoughts and feelings about it.

Skill Builder 3.3: Process for Changing Beliefs

Purpose: For leaders who are ready for advanced personal development work.

Prejudices and stereotypes are based on beliefs. Getting accurate information leads to a thinking process that may lead you to want to change your behavior. Behavior is always based on beliefs. The beliefs that create the typical barriers to harmonious relationships are often the hidden beliefs you're not even aware you have. A powerful process for changing your behavior is to identify the beliefs that support that behavior and change those beliefs. The process of changing beliefs is primarily a process of working with your feelings, your emotions. So what begins as a thinking process must move on to a feeling process.

Be open to the idea that your hostile feelings, or feelings that separate, might be reflections of your judgments about yourself, that what you dislike in others is what you dislike in yourself. In describing this process, we'll use the term *judgment* to mean categorizing people, things, or situations, as right or wrong, good or bad, blaming or praising others, or making them wrong, bad, or evil on the one hand or right or good on the other. *Discernment* is the term we'll use for making choices.

Step 1: Find the bottom-line belief.

a. **Situation**

Think of a problem situation involving someone from a "different" group, a situation that you suspect involves prejudice on your part. Describe the situation in a few brief words. Then write in answers to the following questions.

b. **Feelings**

- How do I feel about the situation?
- How do I feel about the diverse other(s)?
- Why do I feel this way?

For each response, again ask, "Why do I feel this way?" until you sense that you are at the root feeling.

c. **Judgments**

- How am I judging the person(s)?
- How am I judging the situation?
- How am I making the person(s) wrong or bad?

d. **Beliefs**

- Why am I making this judgment(s)?
- What belief causes me to make this judgment(s)?

Keep asking, "Why? What belief?" Ask until you sense you have found the bottom-line belief underneath the judgment.

Step 2: Take responsibility for the judgmental belief and its results.

Acknowledge that you have created this reality through your beliefs. You have cocreated the situation with the other person(s) in that situation. It takes two to create a relationship problem. Allow that idea to permeate your being. Be willing to accept full responsibility for your beliefs and the actions that flowed out from those beliefs.

Step 3: Acknowledge and embrace your judgmental belief.

In your mind, you've been making the person(s) or situation(s) wrong or bad. You've been judging. That's part of being human. To create harmony, you must release your judgment, release the experience of making things good/bad, right/wrong, and move into the experience of accepting what is.

If you want to change what is, you must first acknowledge and accept what is. The only way to release judgment is to first recognize and acknowledge that you are judging. If you make yourself wrong for judging, you're still into the experience of judging, only now you're judging yourself. The change process requires you to accept the humanness of your judgment, to embrace it.

Embracing the belief. By embracing that belief you create the change. Intellectualization usually will not change a belief, but it is the first step. The change process is to say to yourself, "It's okay to believe this, but now it's time for a change." Then very gently allow the change to occur. Gather the judgmental belief from that judgmental part of yourself into your whole self, your greater self, with love and compassion. A metaphor that is powerful for some people is, "gather it into your light."

Releasing the resistance. A judgmental belief usually fits in with your bottom-line fear, and the belief is often hidden because the fear is hidden, covered over with layers of rationalizations, defenses, and other, less-painful fears. When you have great pain, you tend to handle it in an extreme way. At one extreme, you express the pain with rage, tears, or anger. At the other extreme, you suppress the pain, ignore it, pretend it's not there until you don't consciously feel it. Therefore, you'll normally have a great deal of repressed pain connected to the judgmental belief, and a great deal of resistance to feeling that pain, which for many people wants to be felt in the "pit of the stomach." The process of mentally embracing the belief with love and compassion releases the "resistance to feeling pain," so that feelings may pass through from the pit of your stomach into your heart area. Through this process, you align the judgment, bring it into balance, and neutralize it. The feeling of pain can now give way to feelings of harmony, peace, and joy.

Step 4: Feel the feelings.

Allow yourself to fully experience the joy, peace, harmony that comes when you truly acknowledge and embrace your judgment. Don't intellectualize at this point. Move your consciousness out of your head into your stomach area. Then allow the feeling to move up into your heart area. When you move beyond beliefs that hold your separateness in place, you may experience a sense of oneness, which for many leads to such feelings as peace, serenity, and joy.

With input from the work of Jani King, 1991.

Answer Key: Self–Awareness Activity 3.2.

R = Rigid, authoritarian personality
O = Open, flexible personality

Instructions:

1. To get your R score, add up all the R questions you answered true and all the O questions you answered false.

2. To get your O score, add up all the O questions you answered true and all the R questions you answered false.

3. Compare your R and O scores to assess your relative levels of openness and rigidity.

1.	R	I have little or no difficulty deciding what's right and what's wrong.
2	O	I thrive on variety and change.
3.	O	I often enjoy being with people that some would call strange or weird.
4.	R	I like my routines.
5.	R	I know how I feel about most situations and don't need to keep thinking about them.
6.	R	I need to know exactly where I'm going and when.
7.	O	I often ask myself why I did certain things, or why I think or feel as I do.
8.	R	I hate it when people change our plans.
9.	R	There is only one right way to do most things.
10.	O	Few actions are totally right or wrong; most actions stem from complex situations and have varying effects.
11.	R	I prefer to focus on a few simple things rather than a wide variety.
12.	O	I can feel comfortable with most situations, even if I'm not sure about what's going on.
13.	O	I don't always agree with people from other groups, but I usually understand why they might think and feel as they do.
14.	O	People basically create the life they have and the sooner they take responsibility for it, the better it will be.
15.	O	I think I know my own strengths and shortcomings pretty well.
16.	R	Most actions can be classified as either proper or improper.

17. O   People have different ideas about what's proper and improper; that's fine with me.
18. R   I don't start a job until I know exactly how to do it.
19. O   I'm comfortable "feeling my way" through a task, if necessary.
20. R   I need to know what's going on and what to expect at all times.

REFERENCES

Allport. G.W. *The Nature of Prejudice.* Boston: Addison-Wesley, 1954.

Allport, G.W. *The Person in Psychology.* Boston: Beacon, 1968.

Allport, G.W., and B.M. Kramer. "Some Roots of Prejudice." *Journal of Psychology* 22 (1946): 9–19, 27.

Allport, G.W., and J.M. Ross. "Personal Religious Orientation and Prejudice." *Journal of Personality and Social Psychology* 5 (1967): 432–443.

Baack, J., N. Carr-Ruffino, and M. Pelletier. "Making It to the Top: Specific Leadership Skills." *Women in Management Review* 8, no. 2, 1993.

Baskerville, D.M., and S.H. Tucker. "A Blueprint for Success." *Black Enterprise* (November 1991): 85–92.

Blanchard, F.A., and F.J. Crosby. *Affirmative Action in Perspective.* New York: Springer-Verlag, 1989.

Brewer, M.B. "Ingroup Bias in the Minimal Intergroup Situation." *Psychological Bulletin* 86 (1979): 307–324.

Buono, A.F., and J.B. Kamm. "Marginality and the Organizational Socialization of Female Managers." *Human Relations* 36, no. 12 (1983): 1125–1140.

Canby, Nicholas. "The Ideology of English Colonization: From Ireland to America." *William and Mary Quarterly*, 3rd series, 30, no. 4, October 1973.

Carr-Ruffino, Norma. "U.S. Women: Breaking Through the Glass Ceiling." *Women in Management Review* 6, no. 5, 1991.

Cash, T.F., B. Gillen and D.S. Burns. "Sexism and 'Beautyism' in Personnel Consultant Decision Making." *Journal of Applied Psychology* 62 (1977): 301–310.

Catalyst. *Women in Corporate Management.* New York: Catalyst, 1990.

Clark, C.X. "Race, Life Style, and Rule Flexibility." *Organizational Behavior and Human Performance* 13 (1975): 433–443.

Cox, Taylor. *Cultural Diversity in Organizations.* San Francisco: Berrett-Koehler, 1993.

Deaux, K., and T. Emswiller. "Explanations of Successful Performance in Sex-Linked Tasks." *Journal of Personality and Social Psychology* 29 (1974): 80–85.

Elliott, Jane. *A Class Divided* (documentary videotape). Alexandria, VA: PBS Video.

Espinosa S., and B. Pimentel. "New Fears About Racist Groups." *San Francisco Chronicle.* (August 13, 1993): A1.

Feagin, Joe R., and Clairece Booher Feagin. *Discrimination American Style: Institutional Racism and Sexism.* Englewood Cliffs, NJ: Prentice-Hall, 1978.

Gadamer, Hans-Georg. *Truth and Methods*, rev. ed., New York: Crossroad, 1989.

Gates, Henry L., Jr. *Loose Canons.* New York: Oxford University Press, 1992.

Greenhaus, J.H., and S. Parasuraman. "Job Performance Attributions and Career Advancement Prospects" in *Organizational Behavior and Human Decision Processes*, Orlando, FL: Academic Press, 1991.

Grof, Stanislav, and Christina Grof. *The Stormy Search for the Self.* Los Angeles: Jeremy P. Tarcher, 1990.

Gudykunst, W.B. *Bridging Differences: Effective Intergroup Communication.* Thousand Oaks, CA: Sage, 1994.

Herek, G.M. "Assessing Heterosexuals' Attitudes" in *Lesbian and Gay Psychology.* Thousand Oaks, CA: Sage, 1994.

Ijzendoorn, M.H. "Moral Judgement, Authoritarianism, and Ethnocentrism." *Journal of Social Psychology* 129, no. 1 (1989): 37–45.

Johnson, A. "Women Managers: Old Stereotypes Die Hard." *Management Review*, 76 (1987): 31-43.

Kanter, Rosabeth. Moss. *Men and Women of the Corporation.* New York: Basic Books, 1979.

King, Jani. *The Ptaah Tapes.* Perth, Australia: Triad Publications, 1991.

Los Angeles Times. "Neighbors Stick Together." June 2, 1992.

McIntosh, Peggy. "White Privilege and Male Privilege." Working paper no. 189., Wellesley, MA: Center for Research on Women, 1988.

Morrison, Ann, ed. *The New Leaders: Guidelines on Leadership Diversity in America.* San Francisco: Jossey-Bass, 1992.

Morrison, Ann, R.P. White, and E. Van Velsor. *Breaking the Glass Ceiling.* Reading, MA: Addison-Wesley, 1987.

Palmer, Harry. *Living Deliberately.* Palm Beach, FL: Star's Edge, 1994.

Pettigrew, Thomas. *A Profile of the Negro American.* Princeton, NJ: Van Nostrand, 1964.

Ponterotto, Joseph G. and Paul B. Pederson. *Preventing Prejudice.* Thousand Oaks, CA: Sage, 1993.

Ridley, C.R. "Racism in Counseling as an Adverse Behavioral Process." *Counseling Across Cultures*, 3rd ed. Honolulu: University of Hawaii Press, 1989.

Smith, W.T. *Ethnic Images.* National Opinion Research Center, GSS Topical Report No. 19. Chicago: University of Chicago, December 1990.

Takaki, Ronald. *A Different Mirror: A History of Multicultural America.* Boston: Little, Brown and Company, 1993.

U.S. Commission on Civil Rights. "Understanding Fair Housing." Washington DC: U.S. GPO, 1973.

Williams, Robin M., Jr. "Prejudice and Society." *The American Negro Reference Book.* Englewood Cliffs, NJ: Prentice-Hall, 1966.

WSJ. *Wall Street Journal* (June 16, 1994): B1. "SBA Sets New Goals."

CHAPTER 4

Men and Women Working Together

Men and women literally live in parallel, but different, worlds.
Deborah Tannen

Gender differences are the most basic and pervasive of all differences. Most of us are not fully aware of our beliefs, attitudes, thoughts, and feelings about being a man or woman, or about the "opposite sex." To get in touch with your opinions, beliefs, stereotypes and biases concerning gender and to play with new beliefs, complete Self-Awareness Activities 4.1 and 4.2. Then, to test your current knowledge of gender issues, complete Self-Awareness Activity 4.3. After you've finished this chapter, briefly review these activities to see if any of your responses and insights have changed.

Self-Awareness Activity 4.1: Traits of Men and Women

Purpose: To become aware of your beliefs about gender traits and roles

1. What are the traits or qualities that you like to see in men, traits and actions that you admire or feel comfortable with? List them.
2. What are the traits or qualities that you like to see in women, traits and actions that you admire or feel comfortable with? List them.

Self-Awareness Activity 4.2: What Do You Believe About Women and Men?

Purpose:
- to get in touch with your beliefs and stereotypes about this group of people
- to experience how judgmental beliefs affect your thinking and feeling processes
- to experience the ways in which your beliefs create your reality regarding other persons, even before you have any interaction with them.

Part I. What Do You Believe About Women?

Step 1. Associations

- Relax as deeply as you can: close your eyes and take a few deep breaths.
- Focus on the word "woman" and allow a mental picture to come up in your mind's eye.
- Notice the words and images that come to mind as you "see" this woman.
- Open your eyes and list 10 to 20 words in the order in which they occur to you.
- Review your list. Mark a plus beside the words that are positive, a minus beside the words that are negative, and a circle beside neutral words.

Step 2. Negative Associations

- Close your eyes and focus again on the image of the woman. Formulate a negative opinion or judgment, perhaps one you typically hold about women.
- Notice your *feelings* as you see the person in this negative way. What *thoughts* come up as you focus on the image?
- Write a few sentences about your feelings and thoughts.

Step 3. Positive Associations

- Formulate a positive opinion or judgment, perhaps one you typically hold about women.
- Notice your *feelings* as you see the person in this positive way. What *thoughts* come up as you focus on the image?
- Write a few sentences about your feelings and thoughts.

Step 4. Insights

- Focus on the differences between your experiences when you hold negative and positive judgments or opinions. What were the differences? What meaning does this have for you, for your beliefs and feelings about people from this group, and about beliefs in general?
- Write your responses in a few sentences; include anything you like about your feelings, thoughts, and insights.

Part II. What Do You Believe About Men?

Repeat the phases and steps in Part I, this time focusing on the image of a man.

Self-Awareness Activity 4.3: What Do You Know About Gender Issues?

Determine whether you think the following statements are basically true or false—and think about why.

1. The American culture is basically a patriarchal culture.
2. Men focus on reporting information, while women focus on establishing rapport.
3. About 40 percent of top managers are women.
4. Since passage of the Equal Pay Act, there is little difference in the wages of men and women.
5. The men's movement is about restoring the patriarchal system.
6. Balancing masculine and feminine strengths refers to hiring approximately equal proportions of male and female employees.
7. Sexual harassment is rare and refers to bosses giving favors in exchange for a sexual relationship.

Almost from the moment we're born, we begin learning gender stereotypes and myths. Most of us also begin learning about inequality in relationships from the patriarchal system of family, church, and culture. Although the patriarchal system is beginning to change in the U.S., boys and girls are still socialized in very different ways. Megatrends that affect all aspects of American society, such as new workplace opportunities for women, are changing our culture. For example, nearly half of all employees are women and 40 percent of all managers are women. Still, less than 5 percent of top managers are women, and women make an average of 30 percent less than men at all levels. And boys and girls still grow up in two worlds, overlapping but different. These differences cause major misunderstandings at times; for example, when men focus on reporting information while women focus on establishing rapport. Therefore, we'll discuss the way women activists view these changes, we'll compare this with men activists' views, and we'll look at how gender issues affect both women and men.

We'll discuss the impact of women's changing roles on men's lives and the emerging men's movement that welcomes most of these changes and helps men overcome the effects of the patriarchy. We'll explore the need to balance masculine and feminine strengths within ourselves as individuals and within our organizations. You'll learn what constitutes sexual harassment—that it's a complex issue that involves much more than bosses going to bed with their employees. You'll also learn how both men and women can benefit by relating to one another assertively. Finally, we'll suggest some leadership challenges in meeting the needs of women and men, and some leadership opportunities for building a more balanced work force and corporate culture.

What's in a Name?

Sex is normally defined as the property or quality by which organisms are classified according to their reproductive functions, while gender originated as a grammatical term referring to a category that includes masculine, feminine, and neuter. For our purposes here, we'll use *gender* to discuss workplace or social issues that stem from the fact that one is a man or a woman, and *sex* to discuss situations that stem more directly from one's sexuality.

GENDER MYTHS AND FACTS

As you grew up, you learned some cultural stereotypes about how men and women are supposed to be and act, their traits and roles. Self-Awareness Activities 4.1 and 4.2 were designed to give you some insight into your own gender beliefs. Compare them with the typical gender traits and roles that most people say are expected and admired, shown in Table 4.1.

Stereotyped Traits

People generally expect men and women to express different traits, and the traits they admire in men are often traits they don't admire in women and don't expect women to express. As you can surmise from examining Table 4.1, men's traits are those traditionally expected of business leaders. And these traits haven't been significantly affected by the movement of women into leadership roles since the 1970s. No wonder business women report they must walk a fine line between being considered too feminine and too masculine. The traits they need for business success are *not* the traits people expect or admire in women (Morrison, White, and Van Velsor 1987).

This "traits disadvantage" that business women have dealt with is beginning to recede as companies recognize the increasing importance of some of women's typical traits, such as a focus on personal connections, interpersonal relationships, and nurturing leadership. Men who are very aggressive and ambitious may need to develop more sensitivity and patience. All of us can benefit by becoming more well rounded and balanced, allowing the best of our personalities to emerge from both sides, the feminine and the masculine.

Developing this balance is becoming important for effective modern marriages, too. In the old survival times, men and women needed each other for a balance. Today power couples tend to develop themselves as whole persons first, then to form partnerships from preference rather than need. Later in this chapter we'll explore some traits men and women need to develop for balance.

TABLE 4.1: Opinions of Masculine and Feminine Traits: 1972, 1990

Masculine Traits

1972: Traits Most Admired	1990: Typical Traits
aggressive	aggressive
independent	strong
unemotional	proud
objective team play	confident
dominant	independent
likes math, science	courageous
not excitable in a minor crisis	disorganized
active, competitive	ambitious
logical	
worldly	
skilled in business	

Feminine Traits

1972: Traits Most Admired	1990: Typical Traits
does not use harsh language	emotional
talkative in appropriate situations	talkative
tactful	sensitive
gentle	affectionate
aware of feelings of others	moody
religious	patient
interested in her appearance	romantic
neat	cautious
quiet	thrifty
strong need for security	(Men also said *manipulative*.
appreciates art and literature	Women said *creative*.)
expresses tender feelings	

Sources: Loring and Wells, 1972, Gallup polls, 1990.

Stereotyped Roles

Myths and stereotypes about masculine and feminine roles are as rampant and misleading as the stereotyped traits.

Myth: The typical American family consists of a husband with a career and a wife who stays home and takes care of the two children.

This myth reflects traditional male/female roles. The woman belongs at home doing housework and raising children, and the man belongs in the workplace earning a living for the family. This pattern was typical from about 1900 to 1960. Now, only about 15 percent of U.S. families fit that description—and even then only temporarily while the children are very young—making the roles more myth than reality.

Myth: There are only two types of women: good and bad.

In the past "good women" were placed on a pedestal, called ladies and treated like little madonnas or dolls, while "bad women" were called sluts or whores. There was not much gray area in between. Women who had reputedly ever had sex outside of marriage were bad and the others were good. This stereotype tends to define women primarily by their sexual relationship to men.

Myth: Women's status in society is equal to men's.

The myth is that since women got voting rights, equal opportunity, and affirmative action, they've gained equal status. However, we know that less than 5 percent of the top decision makers in business and government are women. And women at all levels average 30 percent less pay than men.

If the media reflects what's going on in society, women are still seen first as sex objects—at least while they're young. Later they're seen as wives and mothers. The media frequently portrays young women as little more than dimwitted bimbos hanging onto a powerful man's arm, or sex objects that help sell cars, liquor, cosmetics, and most anything else. The idea is that buying the product will help a man to attract a young, sexy woman or help a woman to become young-looking and sexy. A 1972 study showed that the role of women in 32 percent of TV commercials is sex object/decoration and in 20 percent it's wife/mother. A 1990 survey of women's opinions of advertising indicates that things haven't changed much (Dominick and Rauch 1972; Crane and De Young 1992). Most say the few ads that feature career women tend to show them as super-women who do it all, and that advertising generally:

- shows women mainly as sex objects
- does not show women as they really are
- suggests that women don't make important decisions

Myth: Real men are in control of the situation.

In our patriarchal culture, being in control has had high value. Men have typically been told by men in authority, "You're letting things get out of control," "Control your wife," "You've got to take charge." This myth implies that men are superior. At home they should be master of the house, and in the workplace they should be the managers. More and more American women are expecting to have equal relationships at home and in the workplace. Relationship styles and management styles are changing. The trend is that people are expected to control themselves and to take control of their own lives, then come together as basic equals to collaborate on joint projects. Trying to control others is becoming frustrating and counterproductive for men.

Myth: Real men don't cry.

People in our culture typically tell little boys that "Big boys don't cry." Neither are they afraid. They are brave and confident. They may get angry and fight back, but they don't whimper or snivel. In hundreds of little ways men get the message that they should not be emotional nor show their feelings. Most boys learn to hide their feelings. By the time they grow up, many have denied their feelings for so long that they're numb to them, out of touch with them.

Once they're men, it's generally all right to show anger in certain situations, such as to get things done or to defend one's honor. And it's acceptable to show some feelings with one's mate in romantic settings. Otherwise, feelings are to be buttoned up, locked in, and kept contained. And that's the major problem with this myth. Unacknowledged and unexpressed feelings don't go away. They build and fester, contributing to stress and its related illnesses.

GENDER: PROTOTYPE OF DIFFERENCE AND INEQUALITY

Women in Western culture have traditionally been viewed as a wholly different species from men, invariably an inferior species. Those primary and secondary sex differences that exist are greatly exaggerated and are inflated into imaginary distinctions that justify discrimination. In the past most men felt an ingroup solidarity with half the humans on earth, other men, and with the other half, an irreconcilable conflict. Lord Chesterfield described the way women were traditionally viewed by men (Allport 1954):

> *(Women are) children grown large, with little reasoning ability. They are to be trifled with, played with, humored, and flattered, as with a sprightly, forward child. Few men ever consult them or trust them with serious matters, though they often make women believe that they do both, which is the source of women's greatest pride. They are mainly concerned with matters of vanity and of love.*

Let's look at how men and women activists view our traditional patriarchal social system and some of the stereotypes woven into that system.

The Patriarchal System

Patriarchy refers to the rule of a family or tribe by men, and a social system in which descent and succession are traced through the male line. It began by brute force and muscle power. Once established, men's superiority and advantage were institutionalized into every sphere of life. It's being undermined because brain power and relationship power are becoming true power. As men's superiority is undermined, some are resorting to extreme measures to hold onto it, even to physical abuse and rape.

Some men's advocates define patriarchy as the male areas of dominance, responsibility, and subservience in a culture, reinforced by both sexes for the purpose of serving both sexes' survival needs. Patriarchy has given men the authority, privileges, and responsibility that come with being in charge. Women's privileges involved being provided for and protected, if they picked the right man and all went well. Both sexes have been rewarded with "identity" when they followed the rules and punished with invisibility when they failed or sometimes even death if they rebelled. Leaders were picked from among the men who followed the rules best (Farrell 1993).

Women's groups have arisen from time to time to protest the limitations and unfairness to women and to men that patriarchy imposes. The most recent feminist movement began in the 1960s and has made significantly more progress than any previous movement. Perhaps gender equality is an ideal whose time has come. Feminists come in many political shades and stripes. For our purposes here, we'll use a simple definition:

> A *feminist* is someone who believes in equal rights for women.

Most feminists believe that the inequality inherent in patriarchy does not serve women's best interest, and that equality in the workplace will lead to equality in the family. They focus on eliminating all discriminatory barriers to women's moving up in the work world as the key to the overall liberation of women. They believe that changes in labor market conditions that women face will force changes in family dynamics. Economic power is a prerequisite to a balance of power in family relationships.

Gender Differences as Cultural Differences

All cultures differentiate between male and female behavior, and usually when a given behavior pattern becomes associated with one sex, it will be dropped by the other. One of the ten primary message systems of culture, discussed in chapter 1, is "How we differentiate male and female behavior; our beliefs about the differences in male and female roles, activities, and behavioral traits."

Recently many sociologists and anthropologists have begun to see gender differences primarily as cultural differences and have started applying cross-cultural techniques to solving gender problems. Some say that gender is not just one of many cultural differences, but *the* most important cultural difference, the root paradigm of difference, just as the inequality of patriarchy is the paradigm of all inequality among groups. Instead of seeing women's culture as a subculture within each ethnic culture, they declare that the two most basic cultural groups are women and men. Between these two groups we find the prototypical cultural distinctions, after which all other cultural distinctions are modeled. If organizations can learn to accept and deal with gender differences, all other differences can be handled in due course. On the other hand, a great deal of diversity work remains superficial when gender issues are not first recognized and managed.

Gender influences us in the most fundamental way about how to be with others and make choices in life. It influences our beliefs and attitudes, thoughts and feelings, decisions and choices at every moment. Evidence is mounting to show that misunderstanding, resentment, and violence between men and women are of the deepest, most frequent, and widespread kind.

Male Privilege in America

Patriarchy is still alive and well in American culture. While Euro-American men make up 39 percent of the workforce, they make up:

- 95 percent of top corporate positions
- 82.5 percent of the Forbes 400 persons worth at least 265 million dollars
- 77 percent of Congress
- 92 percent of state governors
- 70 percent of tenured college faculty
- 90 percent of daily newspaper editors
- 77 percent of TV news directors

They "dominate just about everything but NOW and the NAACP" (Gates 1993).

From Patriarchy to Equality

As we've moved from an agricultural economy through an industrial to a post-industrial economy, cultural values have shifted dramatically. The women's movement is a reflection of that basic shift. Marriage relationships are the most influential in a society, because children learn about life and relationships by observing their parents. Table 4.2 suggests some ways marriage relationships are changing, which in turn indicates how our culture is changing.

Traditional families are now called dysfunctional by many psychologists because they fostered codependence and abused the children by spanking them. Given the fact that survival was often at stake and that codependence was the cement in a family's foundation, much of that behavior may have been functional survival. But in industrial and post-industrial societies, most families have moved beyond survival. Leaders of both the men's and women's movements propose that we move beyond patriarchy or matriarchy—beyond hierarchy—to a system that relies on leadership that arises spontaneously from those who are willing and able to lead in particular situations.

Power Differential: From Home to Workplace

In the American culture, as in most modern cultures, we are socialized in ways that establish and reinforce a power differential between men and women. Therefore, many of the dynamics between men and women in the workplace reflect the dynamics between the more powerful and the less powerful. For example, why do some women use tears to influence men, while men tend to use logical arguments to influence both men and women? Yes, through socialization, women have been allowed to express emotions and men have not. But also, men usually have more power in male-female relationships and therefore have the upper hand. It may be that women's logic would be ignored and they feel they must resort to tears in order to have effect. One research study led to two major conclusions about gender and power tactics (Peplau, 1991):

TABLE 4.2: Traditional and New Male-Female Relationships

	Traditional Marriage Relationship	New Relationship
Major goal	Survival	Fulfillment
Relationship focus	Role mates, to create a whole	Soul mates, whole persons, to create synergy
Effect on roles	Segregated roles	Common roles
Family obligations	Must have children	Children are a choice
	Woman raises children, man makes money. Woman risks life in childbirth; man risks life in war	Both raise children and both make money Childbirth relatively risk-free; ideally no more war
Partner choice	Parental influence primary; women try to marry "up"	Parental influence secondary; both marry for love
The contract	Lifetime; no divorce	As long as both parties want to stay together
Status of parties	Neither party can end contract Woman is property of man; man expected to provide and protect	Either party can end contract; Each equally responsible for self and other
	Both are subservient to needs of family	Both balance needs of family with needs of self
Emotional expectation	Love emerges from mutual dependence I'll stay no matter what	Love is based on choice I'll stay unless you abuse me or we grow in different directions

Based on the work of Warren Farrell and Julie Matthaei, 1993.

1. *Gender affects power tactics*. Women are more likely to withdraw or express negative emotions, while men are more likely to use bargaining or reasoning. However, in a partnership between gay men, if one partner perceives himself as less powerful, he is likely to use withdrawal or expressions of negative emotions, and the more powerful partner is likely to use bargaining or reasoning. The same dynamics were found between two women in a lesbian partnership.

2. *Power, not gender, is the issue*. Regardless of gender or sexual orientation, people who see themselves as relatively more powerful in a relationship tend to use persuasion and bargaining, while those who feel they are lower in power tend to use withdrawal and emotion.

As Rosabeth Kanter (1979) found in her studies of men and women in organizations, we see once again that behaviors believed to be typical of women are actually behaviors that are typical of the powerless. Regardless of sexual orientation, a partner with relatively less power tends to use "weak" strategies, such as manipulation and pleading. Those in more powerful positions are more likely to use autocratic and bullying tactics. Signs of conversational dominance, such as interrupting, were linked also to the balance of power. Interruption is not so much a male behavior as a tactic of the powerful. Many studies provide support for the dominance interpretation of sex differences in male-female interaction (Peplau 1991; Howard, Blumstein, and Schwartz 1986; Kollock, Blumstein, and Schwartz 1985).

Now that you've completed the discussion of patriarchy, explore your own ideas about it by completing Self-Awareness Activity 4.4.

Self-Awareness Activity 4.4: Your Ideas About Patriarchy and Equality

Purpose: To explore your thinking about patriarchy and equality.

1. *Advantages of Patriarchy.* What are the advantages of the traditional nuclear family, with its segregated gender roles, and its patriarchal hierarchy
   - for men?
   - for women?
   - for children?
   - for American society?
   - for the world?

2. *Advantages of Equality.* What are the advantages of equality and role freedom within the family
   - for men?
   - for women?
   - for children?
   - for American society?
   - for the world?

CHANGING GENDER ROLES

Gender roles are changing, primarily because of changing economic realities, but also because of changing political and social values. Women have made significant progress in moving into formerly male-only jobs, the better paying, more challenging jobs, and increasing their relative pay. But they have a long way to go, and their progress was stalled by the backlash of the 1980s and 1990s. Megatrend predictions for the year 2000 and beyond are that women's leadership style is what organizations need to meet new challenges. Women still have some external and internal barriers to career success, but solutions are being found.

Megatrends that Opened Doors

Beginning in the 1960s a series of megatrends combined to accelerate the pace at which women moved into managerial, professional, technical, and leadership roles that had been almost exclusively Euro-American male territory.

Megatrends of the 1960s and 1970s

The 1960s brought major social upheavals. Those that most affected gender issues were greater acceptance of divorce, greater sexual freedom, and greater acceptance of equal opportunity for women and minorities. Such social changes allowed women more freedom of choice. The civil rights movement led by African Americans spawned the women's movement. The 1964 Civil Rights Act was mainly targeted to help African Americans. A Southern congressman who opposed the pending bill added a sexual discrimination clause to it, thinking that would surely cause its defeat. To his surprise, it passed anyway. During the 1970s women began moving into many fields of study and occupations formerly closed to them.

Economic change: more mothers must work. Prior to 1970, average family income rose an average of 10 percent per year, much of it due to men's wage increases. However, during the 1970s and 1980s, low-wage countries began selling products that competed with U.S. products in the global marketplace. This competition caused corporate profits to decrease, and many firms had to find cheaper labor sources. Many moved their manufacturing operations to low-wage countries.

Many of them began hiring women, since their pay averaged only 50 to 60 percent of men's pay. Most of this new female influx into the workplace consisted of married women. After a large number of married women entered the labor force, firms were able to limit wage increases to men. Lower wages were also a crucial aspect of meeting global competition from low-wage countries.

As a result, a growing number of husbands no longer earn an income that will support a family, and their wives must work if the family is to live above the poverty line. In addition, as divorce became more economically feasible for women, an increasing percentage of women became heads of households. For all these reasons, middle-class working mothers, once a sign of liberation, became an economic necessity during the 1980s. As the average worker's take-home pay went down, family income grew an average of less than 1 percent per year, even with many wives working, as shown in Table 4.3 (1970–1990). Buying a home became more expensive and took a larger share of family income, and renters found it more difficult to save up a down payment.

TABLE 4.3: Deterioration of Family Income

	1950	1970	1990
Purchasing power of a worker's average weekly take-home pay		(base rate)	−11%
Family income	(base rate)	+97%	113%
Home mortgage, first-time buyers		(base rate)	+50%
Mortgage as percent of income		20%	33%
Number of working mothers		10 million	33 million

Source: U.S. Dept. of Labor, 1991.

Megatrends of the 1980s, 1990s, and Beyond

The 1980s brought the further evolution and impact of social changes that erupted in the 1960s, as well as the conservative backlash we discussed in chapter 1. Trend expert John Naisbett (1982) predicted ten megatrends for the 1980s that offered exciting opportunities for career-oriented women. His prediction that large numbers of women would move into new roles turned out to be on target.

Later, in Megatrends 2000, Naisbett (1990) predicted even more dramatic changes in women's roles and careers in the 1990s and beyond, tying them in to these megatrends:

A global economy means all large businesses must compete and cooperate with businesses in other countries, and all must be multinational to some extent. Companies must be more adept than ever at identifying market niches, adopting innovative approaches, and offering top quality products and services. Leaders must think in global terms. By 1992 the European Community had become the largest consumer market in the world. The Pacific Rim is the most rapidly growing consumer market. India and China are becoming consumer societies, and the former Soviet countries are pounding at the door. Formerly communist countries are shifting to market economies and beginning to participate in global trade. These megatrends present the challenge of intensified market competition and the opportunity of huge new markets opening up.

Unity of a global culture and diversity of local cultures. A global culture is becoming more pervasive, as symbolized by such icons as MacDonald's, Levis, Bennetton clothing boutiques, the English language, and rock and roll. Naisbett predicted a simultaneous trend in reaction to this global uniformity: valuing cultural diversity, with people placing higher value on their native customs, language, music, cuisine, and other elements that make their culture unique. The result: unity of a global culture with diversity of many local cultures, a global trend that is reflected in the American workplace.

Emphasis on ethical values. The excesses of the 1980s—from the spending of a Donald Trump to the grand larceny of Wall Street dealers and savings and loan officers—brought a new respect for ethical principles. Also, biotechnology is poised to solve many of our health and poverty problems, but people are realizing a corresponding need to define ethical values to regulate the industry. Several recent surveys indicate that people believe women can bring special talents to dealing with and cleaning up ethical issues, and that people tend to trust women's ethical standards and level of honesty. This applies to both the business and political worlds. Women represent a "fresh face" without the backroom connections and long years of deal making (Naisbett 1990).

From management for control to leadership to empower individuals. The underlying theme of all the megatrends is the individual. While people are working together in more dynamic ways than ever, the trend is for power in work groups to stem from the power of individuals within the groups. Leaders who know how to empower others have an edge. This megatrend puts women at an advantage; the reasons:

- Women are usually socialized to win commitment from people rather than to give orders and apply controls.
- Women tend to adapt more naturally to the role of teacher/facilitator/coach than they do to the role of director/overseer.
- Women have historically been trained to focus on helping others achieve success, usually husbands and children.

More working mothers. Continuing the megatrend of the 1960s through the 1980s, an ever-greater proportion of women will enter the workforce and stay there, even when they have small children. This means that the largest potential source of qualified workers in the 1990s and beyond is women with children.

Women into leadership roles. The needs and opportunities posed by the new global economy and high-tech industries (further fueled by the biotech industry) mean that savvy corporations are scrambling to find highly qualified people who can produce and perform in rapidly changing, highly competitive markets.

Naisbett predicted that the U.S. would take the lead in the global economy and that women's leadership would make the critical difference. His rationale: women's numbers in business have reached a critical mass. And, as they've bumped against the glass ceiling in large corporations, women have started their own businesses— at twice the rate of men—businesses looking for new markets. Adler (1991) points to the successful track records of American women doing business in Asia. Although a culture may frown upon its own women going into business, foreign women are viewed differently. "If you have the best price, they'll buy," says an American woman based in Hong Kong.

CURRENT GENDER PROFILE

Some of the most dramatic changes in gender dynamics center around new roles for women, higher educational achievement, women as heads of households, and a continuing but slowly shrinking pay gap.

Occupations and Education

Women are 52 percent of the U.S. population and 46 percent of the workforce. While most managers, precision production workers, machine operators, and laborers are men, most clerical and service workers are women. Professionals, which include teachers and nurses as well as doctors, lawyers, and accountants are nearly half and half, as are technical and sales workers.

Nearly 60 percent of wives are in the workforce, raising family income from $30,000 to $48,000 on average. Women with dependent children are more likely to work than women with adult children. Following are the percentages of working mothers with children of various ages.

- children under age 3: 58%
- children under age 6: 55%
- children under age 18: 67%

Both men and women are more likely to delay marriage in order to finish college. And women are likely to delay having children in order to establish themselves in a career. In 1990, 63 percent of all women in their early twenties had not yet married, compared with only 36 percent in 1970.

Although there has traditionally been a male-female education gap, with more men getting degrees, the gap had closed for 1990 graduates, with women slightly outnumbering men. The fields where women graduates increased the most dramatically are shown in Table 4.4. In 1970, for example, women took only 9 percent of business degrees, 13 percent of physical science degrees, and 1 percent of engineering degrees.

TABLE 4.4: Men and Women—Occupations and Education, 1990

Relative proportions of men and women:	*Male (%)*	*Female (%)*
In total population	48	52
In the workforce:	54	46
Managers	58	42
Professionals	46	54
Technical	46	54
Sales	51	49
Clerical	23	77
Service	37	63
Production, craft (electrician, plumber, etc.)	90	10
Machine operators	60	40
Laborers	80	20
Received bachelor's degrees:	47	53
Psychology	29	71
Life sciences	49	51
Business degree	53	47
Social sciences	56	44
Physical sciences	69	31
Engineering	86	14

Source: U.S. Census Bureau; Women's Bureau, Labor Department

The Pay Gap

In 1990 women's median weekly earnings were 70 percent of men's. The pay gap was more or less 60 to 65 percent from the 1950s to 1980. The 5 percent improvement since 1980 probably reflects men's lower pay, women's higher educational achievement, their choice of formerly male-dominated fields that pay more, and the tendency to delay having children and to take fewer years off from careers once children arrive. The pay gap is especially tough for single mothers. And more families than ever were headed by single women—16.5 percent in 1990, compared to 11 percent in 1970. By ethnic group, the proportion of female-headed households in 1990 was:

Euro-Americans	12%
Asian Americans	12%
Latino Americans	22%
African Americans	44%

These women had to survive on about one-third the median income of married-couple families—about $17,000 compared to $48,000—therefore, they were nearly six times as likely to live in poverty. In fact, at all ages, more women than men live in poverty; for example, women over 65 are twice as likely as older men to live in poverty. And whether in poverty or affluence, women live about 7 years longer than men—at least those born in 1990, who can expect to live an average 79 years compared to 72 years for the average man.

CULTURAL PATTERNS AND GENDER ISSUES

Our patriarchal society still wields great influence on cultural patterns that affect gender perceptions, roles, and relationships. The movement toward more egalitarian relationships between men and women is also having great impact on our cultural patterns of behavior. This cultural upheaval and evolution has led to at least six major gender issues, which we'll explore next.

- Gender issue: Living in two different worlds
- Women's issue: Overcoming cultural barriers to workplace success
- Men's issue: Responding to new roles and expectations
- Gender issue: Balancing masculine and feminine strengths
- Gender issue: Understanding sexual harassment
- Gender issue: Relating to one another assertively

Gender Issue: Living in Two Different Worlds

Women and men are much more alike than not. Most differences are probably more cultural than physical, and individual men and women vary greatly as to their degree of typically masculine or feminine traits. Keep in mind that information about a particular group provides flexible, general guidelines only, to help us better understand people within that group. People within the group are still individuals, and we must also learn about them as individuals, keeping an open mind. The purpose here is to gain insight into general male-female differences so you can better understand why people may act as they do. Avoid a mindset that would make these differences into rigid beliefs (for example, "Hey, you're a guy, so you must be hung up on status.").

Even though women and men are more similar than not, and even though they grow up side by side, they do live in two different worlds. Because we as a culture and as individuals treat boys and girls, men and women, so differently, their experiences and worldviews are dramatically different. Social scientists tend to attribute most personality characteristics to socialization, but there could be some biological basis.

Cultural Socialization of Girls and Boys

We raise boys and girls differently in our culture. They play differently as children. They have different values and experiences as teenagers. Since we are a patriarchal culture, boys gain more respect as they grow into men. As girls grow into women, they have more difficulty being perceived as competent leaders.

Child's play. Men and women begin taking these divergent paths as toddlers. Girls are encouraged to play in small groups or pairs, often indoors. They play house, jump rope, play hopscotch or engage in other activities in which there is much sharing, and everyone gets a turn. Many activities involve no winners and losers, no rules and regulations, and are flexible, flowing from suggestions the girls make to each other: "Why don't we pretend that . . ." Boys are more likely to play outdoors and in large groups, especially when they enter school. Their team sports are more hierarchical, with group leaders dominating and giving orders. There is more focus on gaining center stage and thus gaining status, on winning and losing. The rules are more elaborate and arguments about rules abound. There is more boasting about personal skills and more focus on who's best.

Some differences in the ways boys and girls are socialized in the American culture are shown in Table 4.5. Read the table from the top down, by column, since each column represents a socialization process, by gender, not a comparison of types of experiences.

TABLE 4.5: Different Growing-Up Processes

Girls and Women	Boys and Men
Girls experience a less active childhood than boys. Girls are taught to be reactive more often than proactive. Girls learn to experience lines of power going from women to men; power is gained through men. Girls learn to think ahead about how people might respond, to "psych out" situations, to be "schemers." Girls are encouraged to believe that a man's approval is more valuable than a woman's. Teenage girls begin competing with each other for male attention. Girls and women learn they're expected to be selfless helpers, not have needs for great space, territorial or psychological. Women learn to live for and through others, to define themselves in terms of their relationships with others.	Boys lead a more active childhood, controlling their world with physical actions. Boys are taught to be self-sufficient, autonomous, a closed system. Boys learn to ignore their needs to be dependent. Eventually, males begin to deny they even have dependency needs. Males lose touch with the feelings that accompany dependency needs, than with other feelings. Boys and men become task-oriented, compartmentalized, mechanical, and highly rational. As a result men become quite dependent on women as the emotional, nurturant "translators" or bridges between men and family members, men and others.

Based on the work of Deborah Tannen, 1990

Teenage differences. Many of the old stereotypes and socialization patterns are still in place for teenagers, according to reporter and author Peggy Orenstein. In 1993–1994 she spent a year in several middle schools in the San Francisco area researching male-female differences among young teens. She found that the girls routinely reported feeling:

- resignation about the greater power that society grants boys
- resignation about society's acceptance of boys' greater assertiveness and power to disrupt
- pressure to emphasize appearance and minimize brains to win favor
- pressure to acquiesce in second-rate status
- fear of failure in science and math
- boredom with school

Orenstein was inspired to do this research after reading the 1990 report by the American Association of University Women about the discrimination girls face in school. In preteen years girls have a shining hope that all seems possible, which is dimmed with the onset of the teen years. Orenstein found that cultural expectations combine with poverty and prejudice, both gender and ethnic, to push girls into corners. Only the brave and fortunate find their way out. In spite of the fact that women outnumber men in college 53 to 47 percent, Orenstein found conditions little changed from 20 years ago (Carroll 1994).

Boys and men: more respect. As boys grow into men, their time and activities gain respect and tend to be viewed as important, while girls' time and activities are seen as less important. This tendency is tied to the fact that beginning with the Industrial Revolution, men went off to work they got paid for, while women stayed home and did not get paid. In our society income is seen as an indicator of a person's importance and value. Women are expected to be respectful of men's more important responsibilities. As little boys become adults, they take on the parent role with women, serving as their protectors. Men are thus seen as competent and tend to indulge women. On the other hand, as little girls become women, they retain much of the child role, needing to be protected and indulged, and thus they are seen as less competent than men.

Girls and women: image problems. Many studies have shown that males are considered more competent than females, at least outside the home. For example, Kohn (1988) asked people to evaluate an article, some copies with a woman's byline and identical copies with a man's byline. The article with the male byline was rated as better by 98 percent of the evaluators.

In another study of mixed-group conversations, 97 percent of interruptions were made by men. There were fewer interruptions when women were speaking with women or when men were speaking with men. In mixed-group studies of who does most of the talking, men talk from 58 percent to 92 percent of the time. Most women are unaware of this type of domination, perceiving that they did a fair share of the talking in 75 percent of the situations (Eisen 1984).

Men are allowed to take the lead and dominate in many subtle ways. For example, both men and women tend to regard topics introduced by women as tentative, whereas topics introduced by men are treated as material to be pursued. Men use humor to take the lead. They tend to remember and repeat jokes, using the opportunity to take center stage and gain control. Most women tend to forget jokes, rarely try to repeat them, and serve as supportive audience, laughing at the jokes men tell.

Different World Views

As a result of their different socialization patterns, men and women interpret and relate to their environments differently. Men tend to take more initiative, which results in their being more self-protective and assertive. They tend to be more focused, future-oriented, and objective, with a greater urge to master (Gove 1985). A summary of research studies on male and female tendencies indicates some significant differences, as shown in Table 4.6. The key word here is tendencies, as there is virtually no trait or behavior that is exclusively male or female. An awareness of these tendencies can help us to understand why men and women often see things so differently. Awareness also helps us to foresee possible misunderstandings and communication breakdowns and in turn helps us to improve male-female relationships and to communicate more effectively.

Women focus more on connection, men on status; women on establishing rapport, men on reporting information; women on cooperating, men on competing; and women on playing down their expertise, men on displaying it. We'll discuss these differences in some detail.

Connection or status? Deborah Tannen, professor of linguistics at Georgetown University, has done years of groundbreaking research on male-female ways of relating and communicating. Her best-selling books have changed Americans' thinking about this issue. Tannen's studies (1990) suggest that women live in a world of intimacy and men in a world of status concerns. Women, in their world, focus on connecting with others via networks of supportive friends. Much of their communication is aimed at minimizing differences and building on commonalties and agreements. The ultimate goal is to attain maximum consensus and to function in relationships where people are interdependent. Men certainly have their old boy networks, but their world of status places higher priority on independence, where the purpose of much communication is on giving or taking orders. The ultimate goal is to attain more personal freedom.

Rapport talk or report talk? Most communication by the typical woman could be called "rapport talk" because its major purpose is to establish or maintain rapport with others (Tannen 1990). The focus is on feelings and includes personal thoughts, reactions to the day's events, and the details of her life. Typical male talk could be called "report talk," focusing on factual information that the listener needs to know and what's going on in the world. Women tell people things mainly to increase interpersonal involvement, while men do it because others need to know. Women's major aim in listening is to communicate interest and caring; men's major interest is to get infor-

TABLE 4.6: Male and Female Tendencies

	Men's Tendencies	*Women's Tendencies*
Relationships	Self-focused	Other-focused
	Focus on individuals	Focus on group
	More impersonal	More personal
	Need more distance	Need more closeness
	Fear engulfment	Fear abandonment
	Over-identify with work	Over-identify with people
	Do what I please	Do what others approve
	More independent	Dependent/interdependent
	Like group activities more	Have more intimate friends
	More aggressive toward others	Trust each other more
	Make war	Make peace
	Define self by job	Define self by relationships
	Seek the spotlight	Prefer the sidelines
	More competitive	More cooperative
	Money a measure of masculinity	Money a tool
	Want respect for achievements	Want to be liked
	Love sports and games more	Love shopping more
Method of supporting	Challenge others	Agree with others
Method of disagreeing	Confront others	Comply with others
Thinking and Feeling	More rational	More emotional
	Express feelings less	Express feelings more
	Worry less	Worry more
	Express anger	Repress anger
	Thinking more linear, narrow	Thinking more global
		More cross-brain ability
	Focus more on facts	Focus more on intuition
	Greater visual-spatial ability	Greater verbal ability
	Less depression	Handle stress better
	Like the way they look	More concerned about looks
	Take more risks	Tend to avoid risks
Communication	*Initiate more*	*Listen more*
	Talk about things	Talk about people
	Talk more in public	Talk more in private
	Take words at face value	Search for hidden meaning
	Direct language	Circumspect language
	Interrupt women	Let men interrupt
	Decide now, on their own	Decide after group input
	Gossip about work lives	Gossip about personal lives
	Give advice for problems	Give sympathy for problems
	Make direct put-downs	Make backbiting put-downs
	Tell jokes more	Apologize more
	Figure it out themselves	Seek assistance
	Toot their own horn more	Nag more
	Intimidate more	Avoid confrontation more
	Being right is more important	Being liked is more important
	Comfortable giving orders	Uncomfortable giving orders
	Comfortable with hierarchy	Don't like hierarchy
	Don't talk about ailments	Discuss ailments more

Based on the work of Chris Evatt, Carol Tavris, Alice Eagly, Cynthia Epstein, 1992, 1987.

mation. Women will frequently reveal their weaknesses, especially when the other person is feeling discouraged. The rationale: Sharing such personal information will make the other feel equal, and thus closer. Men nearly always feel that revealing a weakness would just lower their status in the other person's eyes.

Cooperative or competitive? Women's words and actions often revolve around giving understanding, while men's are more likely to revolve around giving advice. These tendencies are probably based on the different ways men and women measure power. Women view helping, nurturing, and supporting as measures of their power. The activities they engage in include giving praise, speaking one-on-one, and private conversations. The main arenas for these activities are the telephone, social situations, and the home. Men perceive different measures of their power, such as having information, expertise, and skills. The activities they engage in include giving information, speaking more and longer, and speaking to groups. The main arenas for these activities are the workplace and public places.

In the work arena, women tend to approach decision making in a participative way: I cannot and should not act alone when it comes to important decisions. Men tend to feel they must act alone and must find their way without help. Women focus on mastering their jobs and increasing their skills, consulting and involving others in the process, and developing positive relationships with their peers. Men tend to focus on competition and power, hierarchy and status. Women may not stand up for their rights because they want to avoid conflict. Men are less likely to be afraid of conflict and more willing to confront issues in order to clear the air. Men are more likely to be intimidating to others, while women are more often perceived as approachable.

Women are more likely to be uncomfortable in taking the initiative. Because women tend to be more accommodating and self-sacrificing, they are also more likely to allow frustration to build. To overcome problems arising from these tendencies, women can develop assertiveness skills and habits. Men need clear facts in the communication process. They experience more difficulty in coping with unclear situations and expressing mixed feelings. To overcome these difficulties, they can get in touch with their emotions and intuitive side.

Expertise: play it up or down? A major source of power for managers, professionals, and other leaders is their expertise. Tannen's studies indicate that women tend to downplay their expertise, act as if they know less than they really do, and operate as one of the group or audience. Men are more apt to display their expertise and act as if they know more about their area than others in the group know. They're more likely to be comfortable taking center stage. The male expert's main goal is to persuade, and he often firmly states his opinions as facts. In contrast, when female experts speak with males, their approach tends to be assenting, supporting, agreeing, listening, and going along. They want to emphasize similarities between themselves and listeners and to avoid showing off. Their concerns: Have I been helpful? Do you like me? The male experts' approach tends to be dominating, talking more, interrupting, and controlling the topic, whether they are speaking with males or females. They want to emphasize their superiority and display their expertise. Their concerns: Have I won? Do you respect me?

The typical female response to male experts' communication is to either agree or disagree. On the other hand, male listeners usually don't understand that the female expert's main concern is to not offend, so the males often conclude that she is either indecisive, incompetent, insecure, or all of the above. They respond by offering their own opinions and information and by setting the agenda themselves; that is, they incorrectly perceive a power vacuum and try to take over.

Agreeing or disagreeing? Feedback, or listening responses, tend to be different for males and females. Women's feedback tends to be more positive and copious . They keep a running feedback loop going with such responses as "mmmm, uh huh, yes, yeah." They ask questions, take turns, and give and want full attention. They usually agree, and they laugh at humorous comments. They focus on the metamessage even more than the literal message. Men give fewer listener responses. They are more silent and listen less. They are more likely to challenge statements and to focus on the literal message.

Because women listen so attentively, they may think a man's silence implies concentration on their metamessage, when in fact he may not be listening. Later she says, "But I told you all about that yesterday!" Most men challenge any statement they disagree with, so a man tends to interpret a woman's silence as consent or agreement. Later, when her actions are incompatible with her "agreement," he concludes that she is insincere or changeable: "Women!" As we begin to understand the different worlds that men and women live in, we can begin to find ways to bridge such communication gaps.

Difference in Communication Style

With their focus on rapport, connection, intimacy, and playing down their expertise, women's communication styles tend to be more tentative than men's. Because the business world is accustomed to an assertive male approach to communication, women's credibility is undermined by a tentative, overly polite, uncertain, or indecisive approach. Several studies indicate that women perpetuate the lower-credibility stereotype with the following types of behavior (Eagly, 1987; Evatt 1992):

- *Women ask more questions*, about three times as many as men on average.
- *Women make more statements in a questioning tone*, with a rising inflection at the end of a statement.
- *Women use more tag questions*; that is, brief questions added at the end of a sentence: ". . . don't you think?" ". . . okay?" " . . . you know?"
- *Women lead off with a question more frequently*. "You know what?" "Would you believe this?" Researchers note this and other striking similarities between the conversations of men/women and the conversations of adults/children.
- *Women use more qualifiers and intensifiers*. Qualifiers or "hedges" include "kind of, sort of, a little bit, maybe, could be, if." Such qualifiers soften an assertive statement, but also undermine its assertiveness. Intensifiers include *really*, *very*, *incredible*, *fantastic*, *amazing*, especially when those words are emphasized. The metamessage tends to be: "Because what I say, by itself, is not likely to convince you, I must use double force to make sure you see what I mean."

This indicates that women tend to express their thoughts more tentatively and work harder to get someone's attention, which may in turn reflect basic power differences, or at least perceptions of power differences. On the other hand, it's not unusual for men to carry assertiveness too far and to be perceived as overbearing or authoritarian. The most effective conversational approach for leaders is usually one that conveys *both* their sensitivity as well as commitment to their beliefs and statements. We'll discuss the gender issue of assertiveness in more detail later.

Women's Issue: Overcoming Cultural Barriers to Workplace Success

Most career women must overcome both internal barriers and external barriers to workplace success that are rooted in the American culture. Internal barriers include self-limiting beliefs about women's abilities and roles. External barriers include the glass ceiling, inflexible work arrangements, and pay disparity.

Self-Limiting Beliefs

Traditions from the past affect today's career woman in two basic ways: (1) how she pictures herself and, therefore, the roles and behaviors she's comfortable with, and (2) what others expect of her—their preconceived notions of her abilities, traits, strengths, and weaknesses and their resulting beliefs about proper roles and behaviors. These traditional beliefs and expectations often lead to problems with self-limiting and conflicting beliefs. Leaders who understand how such beliefs create internal barriers are in a better position to help women overcome them.

Self-limiting beliefs many women still hold include:

- I should not be ambitious.
- I should wait to be asked.
- I should never parade my achievements and expertise, nor "toot my own horn."
- Women aren't supposed to be good in math, finance, computer, mechanical, technical, engineering, decision-making and other male fields.
- I should stay out of office politics.
- I don't need to nose around in the inner workings of the company (the hierarchy, chain of command, sources of power, career paths).
- It's best to just let others have their way rather than cause a scene.
- I need to steer clear of risky ventures.
- Criticism of my work or ideas is a criticism of me.
- All I need to get ahead is to improve myself and work hard.
- If I do good work, my boss will notice and promote me.

Some women have beliefs that cause them to personalize events, criticism, and messages of others, to react emotionally, and to act out such emotions. These are beliefs typical of the powerless, regardless of gender, and usually are picked up from the women in the family and community.

Some women have difficulty understanding how upward mobility works. If they've rarely worked on teams, they may have beliefs about self-development that prevent them from recognizing the necessity of networking and teamwork. They may neglect developing a power base, and they may not see how they can meet personal goals through helping the team achieve organizational goals.

Certain conflicting beliefs that can lead to fear of success tend to be unique to women and may include:

- I want a successful career *vs.* Men don't want relationships with strong, achieving career women.
- I want a successful career *vs.* Prince Charming may come along, sweep me off my feet, and carry me away to live happily ever after.
- I want a successful career *vs.* Good wives and mothers stay home and take care of the home and kids.

The beliefs that limit women and cause conflict all stem from cultural beliefs, values, and stereotypes about women. Therefore, even when women move beyond such beliefs, they must daily cope with people who still hold similar beliefs. Building a network of supportive friends and co-workers can help career women retain a sense of balance and self-confidence as they juggle career demands with home demands. An understanding, supportive manager can make all the difference. Sometimes the manager can take the lead in helping a woman employee recognize the beliefs that may be holding her back.

The Glass Ceiling

Fortune magazine's 1990 survey found only 19 women among 4,012 directors and highest-paid executives, 0.5 percent, not much better than in 1978 (0.16 percent). Although the U.S. leads the world in percentage of women managers, the 40 percent figure can be very deceptive for the following reasons:

- 33% of managers are women in the 38,059 companies reporting to the EEOC in 1992.

- 25% of managers were women in the 200 largest companies.

- 5% of vice presidents are women.

- 7.5% of all women employees work as managers, compared to 15% of all male employees.

- Women managers tend to be clustered in the lower paying, entry levels of management, such as working supervisor and first-line supervisor.

- Women managers' pay lags behind men's at every level, averaging about 70 percent.

- When women move into an occupation in significant numbers, the occupation goes down in status and pay and men tend to move out of it. Conversely, if an occupation loses status and pay for other reasons, women are more likely to be hired into it.

- Women are likely to hit a glass ceiling to top-level, and even middle-level, positions, according to the Labor Department studies, *The Glass Ceiling Initiative* (1991) and *Good for Business* (1995). Therefore, few women are making it beyond lower-level management, and may have little hope of doing so in the near future. The women who make up the "five percent of top managers" include women who started their own firms.

A recent survey of women managers revealed that 90 percent think the glass ceiling is the most important issue facing women managers of the 1990s (Carr-Ruffino 1991). Virtually all who did not head their companies (80 percent) said women were underrepresented at the top in their firms. The major reason given was the reluctance of the men at the top to include women. The following barriers to the top were considered the most important ones to overcome, in the order listed:

- Top management harbors stereotypes about women, especially regarding ability to gain acceptance in a top role, level of career commitment, and decision-making ability.

- Women are often excluded from key informal gatherings where information and opinions are exchanged, deals made, etc.

- Women's contributions and abilities are not taken as seriously as men's.

- Women have more difficulty finding mentors.

- Women don't get equal opportunities to serve on important committees and project teams.

Leaders who want to attract and retain the best-qualified women must eliminate the stereotypes, attitudes, and practices that create a glass ceiling. Even those women who don't aspire to the top prefer to stay in companies that have opened all the doors to qualified women and have helped them move up.

Two recent surveys of male and female managers of large American companies found that although women expressed a much higher probability of leaving their current employer than men, and had higher actual turnover rates, their major reason for leaving was lack of career growth opportunity or dissatisfaction with rates of progress (Trost 1990). Effective leaders are sensitive to career women's needs and are open to helping them meet those needs.

Inflexible Working Arrangements

Women become frustrated when the demands of work and demand for blind corporate loyalty conflict with other valuable parts of their lives and prevent their full participation in the organization. Some corporate systems and practices are designed for men whose wives handle most family responsibilities. Some are designed by men who are workaholics and expect others to be. Such expectations are unreasonable for women who can't ignore family responsibilities but are committed career professionals.

Pay Inequity

Information in the current profile section of this chapter indicates that although the U.S. leads the world in proportion of women managers, we are not as advanced in providing pay equity. Median income for full-time women workers was only 70 percent of male workers' income in 1990. Some argue that women generally have less training, experience, and job commitment than men, and that this accounts for the pay gap. However, the 70 percent figure represents every management level.

> *Women vice presidents earn*
> *only 70 percent of male vice presidents' income.*

It's highly unlikely that women who have made it to the vice-presidential level have less training, experience, and job commitment than their male peers. In fact, some studies indicate that most women who make it this far must have higher qualifications than their male peers (U.S. Census Bureau 1993; Russell 1991).

Some analysts believe that in general women are less committed to careers than men because women take primary responsibility for raising children, which requires them to interrupt their careers. A Census Bureau study (1987) indicates that the earnings were the same for women with no work interruption as those who had at least one work interruption of six months or more since age twenty-one. The author concludes that structural factors and discrimination, rather than discontinuous employment, explain the earnings gap. The study indicates that much of the female "gain" reported in some studies actually reflects declining median male wages during the 1980s.

The Equal Pay Act of 1963 has not been effective for several reasons. For example, it's easy to vary job duties so that a male and female worker are not technically engaged in "equal work." The main problem, though, is that women tend to predominate in certain occupations, all of which are low paying. We've seen that women are earning most of the college degrees these days and are as likely as men to major in business. Even though the education gap has closed, most women workers, especially those older than 40, are still clustered in "female occupations." In fact, 75 percent work in such jobs. How do certain jobs become women's jobs? In 1900 nearly all clerks were men. As new office technology, such as typewriters and adding machines emerged, employers routinized the clerical process, and women entered the new de-skilled jobs at substantially lower wages. Teachers, librarians, and bank tellers have followed similar patterns, whenever the materials, systems, equipment, or other technology made such jobs more routine and standardized. Obviously, equal pay for equal work does nothing to help women stuck in "female ghettos."

The solution most often proposed is comparable worth, also called pay equity. This approach might require, for example, that a junior secretary receive the same base pay as a journeyman electrician working in the same community. Pay scales are determined by analyzing and evaluating jobs based on such criteria as level of education and experience required, level of responsibility and difficulty, and hardships involved.

In contrast to affirmative action, which focuses on moving women and minorities into better-paying jobs, comparable worth is based on creating a labor market that values women's worth rather than moving women out of female-dominated jobs. Advocates of the concept acknowledge gender differences and accept the probability that women and men will continue to work in relatively segmented occupations for the foreseeable future. In fact, they point out that while affirmative action has had a dramatic impact on some women, opening formerly closed doors for them, most women remain in low-paid, dead-end jobs.

About half the states have implemented comparable worth for their government employees, and the others are in the process of examining the issue. The usual approach is to gradually raise wages in female-dominated occupations without lowering wages in the comparable male-dominated occupations, which does result in higher salary expense. Few corporate executives have admitted that pay equity is an issue being explored in their companies, perhaps for fear of being sued if they imply pay is not equitable now. Courts have generally been unwilling to require pay equity of employers, though it has not been tested in the Supreme Court.

Men's Issue: Responding to New Roles and Expectations

Women's and men's roles and issues evolve in tandem. Change for one gender inevitably results in changes for the other. As women and minorities have gained power, some Euro-American men fear they are losing power. Is there only a limited amount of power and resources? Is it a zero-sum game? Or, as in the case of power couples, can increased power for one actually increase the power of the other? Is it possible that women and minorities could help organizations, and nations, find creative ways to provide more abundance for all without significantly reducing it for anyone? We'll discuss men's reactions to recent demographic shifts, including perceptions of how they affect male-female power, pressure to change, career demands, and relationships with women managers. We'll also survey the recent men's movement and its questioning of traditional father-son relationships and the need for emotional support.

"The male-dominated system has failed and men haven't processed it yet," says psychologist Ronald Levant, referring to the string of scandals involving Clarence Thomas, William Kennedy Smith, Mike Tyson, Senator Bob Packwood, O.J. Simpson, and the Tailhook officers (*Time* 1993). A men's movement rose to the occasion, helping to explore what it means to be a man these days. But conservative men who want to go back to the good old pre-1960s days are joining forces, both formally with the New Right, Religious Right, and similar movements, and informally, through talk shows and "bull sessions." For example, in 1993 *Time* reported, "For the real hard core, there are 'Rush Rooms,' over 100 bars and restaurants around the country where fans gather daily to cheer on right-wing radio host Rush Limbaugh."

According to leaders of the National Association for the Advancement of Colored People, National Organization for Women, and National Federation of Business & Professional Women's Clubs, among others, Limbaugh "expresses a hateful, divisive fanaticism and disregard for minorities, calling feminists 'femi-nazis,' and bashing gays and environmentalists, as well as government leaders who support their causes." (*L.A. Times* 1994)

Promise Keepers is an all-male nondenominational religious organization that in 1994 drew nearly 300,000 men to mass meetings, as many as 50,000 men per meeting. Founded in 1991 by former college football coach Bill McCartney, its basic beliefs include:

- God says men are to take control of the family and of their house.
- Men must join to fight the moral decay that has beset the U.S. in recent years.
- Homosexuality and abortion are sins against God.
- Men should live in racial harmony.

Unlike most fundamentalist groups, Promise Keepers is racially integrated and African Americans take visible roles. In addition to the mass meetings, support groups meet on a regular basis. This "back to the basics" movement is highly controversial. At least 19 groups marched in protest outside the Oakland (California) Coliseum during a 1995 mass meeting (Chin, 1995). Louis Farrakhan, the Black Muslim leader who led the Million Man March on Washington in 1995, echoed the call for men to take charge of the family.

A *Newsweek* poll (Gates 1993) indicated that Euro-American men thought they were losing more than others thought they were losing, as shown in Table 4.7.

TABLE 4.7: Are Men Losing Power?

Question	Respondents	
	Euro-American men	All others
Are white men losing influence in American society today?	48% yes	35% yes
Are white men losing an advantage in terms of jobs and income?	56% yes	38% yes
Do white men now have less chance than others to:		
• get accepted at a university?	29% yes	16% yes
• get a union job?	24% yes	14% yes
• get a political appointment?	23% yes	13% yes
Are white men paying a fair penalty for past advantages?		
Or are they not paying a penalty?		
• Fair penalty	9%	12%
• Unfair penalty	46%	24%
• No penalty	39%	57%
Should white men fight against affirmative action programs?	48% yes	41% yes
	36% no	41% no
Are white men insensitive to the problems of others?	40% yes	54% yes
	57% no	42% no

Losing Power: Personal vs. Collective

Recent surveys indicate that the major dilemma men are wrestling with is the power problem—the profound difference between personal and collective power (Speer 1993). Most men do not feel very powerful; they report that they are:

- having a harder time making a living than their fathers did.
- dealing with a boss telling them what to do.
- trying to figure out how to be what women want: sensitive as well as strong; soft and cuddly as well as firm and "manly."

As a result, many men feel they've failed in their gender role.

Men's movement leaders say the women's movement has triggered changes for men in every life area, and most haven't adjusted to it yet. Men look around them and see that they're in danger because men are:

- 83 percent of the homeless
- 90 percent of AIDS deaths
- likely to live seven years less than women
- much more likely to die of alcoholism, heart attack, or suicide
- three times as likely to be murdered
- 94 percent of prison inmates

In fact men live in a more violent world than women. The more violent the crime, the more likely the victim is a man. Yet men aren't allowed to see themselves as victims. After all, collectively they hold the power in the U.S. And if a man is Euro-American, his complicity in maintaining the patriarchy is even greater, for the simple reason that Euro-American men continue to dominate in business, government, and the professions.

Yet, because so many men feel personally powerless, they are threatened by feminism and resist changes designed to give women more collective power. Men also live with the knowledge that women are afraid of men. Decent, protective men still know that it's men who make it dangerous for women to walk city streets alone at night, men who rape and assault and beat them so that they are forever frightened. These are some of the contradictions that men must live with; there are many others.

Feeling Pressure to Perform and Pressure to Change

When men were asked "What are the biggest pressures on men today?" answers indicated that men are feeling much pressure these days, and it's coming at them from all directions. Traditional pressures remain: to succeed in careers, to provide for families, to be strong and courageous and protective. Men also seem to feel a great deal of pressure from women to change their ways, their very natures, and they don't fully understand what's expected of them. Many don't know how to be sensitive or vulnerable and still be the strong protector, the man in control. Adding to these pressures is their sense that it's becoming harder to make a good living, the planet is being destroyed, and politics is a mess.

When males were asked "Have men been helped or hurt by feminism?" researchers got emphatic responses from both sides. The majority felt that feminism has generally helped both sexes by allowing us to see beyond traditional roles and stereotypes. About 25 percent were vehemently antifeminist, blaming the movement for promoting antimale and antifamily attitudes. Still others held that change is always a double-edged sword, and the full impact of feminism is yet to be felt.

When researchers asked men, "What are the best and worst things about women?" replies focused on empathy, support, warmth, and nice bodies. But many revealed a deep hurt and resentment for the changing roles women have assumed. And for some, women's emotionalism is a drawback.

Unemployed men commit suicide at twice the rate of employed men. Among women, suicide has no correlation to employment status. Men's self-worth is more tied to their jobs. They often feel humiliated, violated, helpless, angry, and guilty over job loss. At all ages men's higher suicide rates are likely to be tied to lack of emotional support systems. Men often bond by giving each other criticism, women by giving each other support.

Dealing with Women Managers

Working Woman magazine surveyed men in 1991, asking what they thought of women managers. Some typical comments:

- They obsess on getting one small thing right, and it's blown out of proportion.
- Some are detail-oriented, not conceptual—no sense of corporate mission, the big picture.
- They're too sensitive, take things too personally.
- Some don't get down to business fast enough. First you have to spend time with them on a personal level.
- They're harder on other women. There's more pettiness or jealousy.
- When two women are at each other's throats, it ruins the spirit of the whole team.
- When women bond together against men, it's demoralizing.
- Unmarried women bosses can make men nervous, especially if their work is their life, and they can work 14-hour days because they have no home life.
- They don't conceal anger or bitterness as well as men.
- We'd rather work for men. Getting a performance review from a woman is like being lectured by mother; it's very castrating.

Men in predominantly male workplaces are more loyal to their companies than men who work with lots of women. It's largely a matter of comfort. Men think they can be themselves around other men, so it's easier to bond. It's also a matter of status because men attach less prestige to professions that attract a large number of women. Men in traditionally male work environments, such as manufacturing plants, are more upset at the prospect of women invading their turf than are men in hospitals, where women have long been a presence (WSJ 1991).

Meeting Career Demands

A major source of male frustration, and for some resentment and envy, is that they are trapped in the provider role. A married woman with an employed husband has some choice about work—when, whether, and how much to work. If she has children, the family may need or want the money she can earn, but her decision to stay home with the children or to work part time will normally be admired by friends and neighbors. It will almost never be considered lazy, selfish, or inappropriate. Men say they don't have that luxury.

When men are asked if they would like to take six-month paternity leave to be with their newborn child, nearly 80 percent say yes, if it wouldn't hurt the family economically and if their wife approved (Farrell 1993).

Men are more likely than women workers to agree to relocate to undesirable locations and to work less desirable hours. Full-time working men work 9 hours per week more in the workplace than full-time working women, but the women work about 17 hours per week more in the home. Therefore women typically work 8 hours more per week than men.

Doing the "Worst" Jobs

Of the 25 jobs rated worst in *The Jobs Almanac*, 24 are 95 to 100 percent male-occupied. Ratings are based on a combination of salary, stress, work environment, outlook, security, and physical demands. Worst jobs include truck driver, sheet-metal worker, roofer, boilermaker, lumberjack, carpenter, construction worker, football player, welder, coal miner, and ironworker. Men are expected to brave the hazards and do the dangerous, tough jobs.

- 94 percent of workers who die on the job are men.
- We have one job safety inspector for every 6 fish and game inspectors.
- Every workday hour a construction worker in the U.S. loses his life.

The male-only draft and combat requirements are the most unconstitutional laws in the U.S. because they breach our most inalienable right, the right to life. They violate the Fourteenth Amendment's guarantee of equal protection under the law, the basis of almost all civil rights legislation. The military is the ultimate hierarchy and the individual soldier is trained in subservience to hierarchy.

Holding the "Protector" Jobs

Men protect the innocent and helpless, women and children, and the ability to protect generates respect. But men must cope with the dark side of the world in order to protect, and the price is a loss of innocence.

Men suffer the price of war more than women. The aftermath of war is devastating. After the Civil War it was called soldier's heart; after World War I, shell shock; after Vietnam, post-traumatic stress disorder. Other results are:

- More Vietnam veterans have committed suicide since the war ended than were killed in the Vietnam War itself.
- About 20 percent of all Vietnam veterans, and 60 percent of combat veterans, were psychiatric casualties.
- In 1978 more than 400,000 Vietnam veterans were either in prison, on parole, on probation, or awaiting trial.
- In 1989 more than 20,000 Vietnam veterans were homeless in Los Angeles alone.

In cultures where men must be protectors, weakness is ridiculed. Young boys search out those with weaknesses, taunting and picking on them. Valuing men as protectors gives us police brutality, the military mentality, and gangs (Farrell 1993).

Men are expected to repress their feelings. The most responsible cancer research finds that cancer is six times more likely to occur among people who repress their feelings than among cigarette smokers (Fischman 1988).

Being Groomed for Violence

Men are more likely to be subjected to violence throughout their lives. In fact, they're trained from childhood to endure and aspire to situations that include violence. Men's advocates suggest some ways in which we subject men to violence and reward them for being violent (Farrell 1993):

- unnecessary circumcision (without anesthesia) of baby boys
- violent sports (for school boys), such as football, hockey, and boxing
- approval by girls and parents when boys excel at violent sports
- government money to schools to support violent sports and military ROTC
- the draft of young men into military service
- entertainment dollars to adult males for violent activities such as rodeos, car racing, football, boxing, ice hockey, and violent movies

Ironically, we ban bull fighting because it's cruel to the bull, not because it glorifies violence for young men and the culture as a whole.

Historically, the "killer male" was essential to survival, marriage, and the family. In the future the communicative male will be essential. "For the first time in human history, what it takes to survive as a species is compatible with what it takes to love" (Farrell 1993). It's time for us to ask, How do we want our future to be and how do we adapt? All of us have the potential for killer-protector and for nurturer-connector. What will encourage males to develop the nurturer-connector within them? A good start is for each of us to notice when men and boys express nurturing-connecting attitudes, to openly appreciate men and boys who act in nurturing-connecting ways, and to reward them appropriately.

Experiencing Barren Father-Son Relationships

More and more men are becoming aware that the way they were raised affects their leadership style and therefore their careers, as well as every other aspect of their lives. For example, some men are beginning to talk about the lack of loving, touching, even liking in their experiences with their fathers. Berkeley psychologist Bernie Zilbergeld says his men's groups are less interested in discussing sex than they were in the 1970s. In his workshops business executives and professional men spontaneously start talking about their fathers.

Zilbergeld notes a very deep sadness and quite a bit of anger that their fathers had never told them that they loved them, were rarely around, and never hugged or kissed them, even when they were little kids. Along with feelings of emptiness and inadequacy because fathers didn't think their sons were "good enough" to justify their love, there was also a loss of role models: "These men just didn't know what men do. Sometimes they learned the most exaggerated male tendencies, such as adopting strict macho behavior. But they certainly didn't learn about father-child tenderness and love" (Zilbergeld 1993). The upside? These men want to avoid the same mistakes with their sons. They are trying to learn comfortable ways to express love to their own children. And they're becoming more appreciative of women's style of relating to others and its empowering aspects.

Not Asking for Emotional Support

Father-son arm's-length relationships are just one aspect of the lack of emotional support men typically give and get from one another. Most lack the powerful tool most women use to heal women friends who emotionally support one another. For men, stress often builds, sometimes leading to depression and even suicide.

From adolescence to old age, men are more likely than women to commit suicide. During adolescence, boys' suicide rates go from slightly less than girls' to four times as great. Psychologists speculate that during puberty boys begin to feel intense pressure to perform, pursue, and pay—to be daring and take risks. Boys also sense it isn't acceptable to discuss fears, anxieties, and self-doubt. In 1970 young men aged 25 to 34 committed suicide at twice the rate of young women. In 1990 it was four times the rate. Young men's suicide rate increased 26 percent, while women's decreased 33 percent.

Men older than 65 are 14.5 times more likely to commit suicide directly. They're also more likely to skip needed medication and to get inadequate nutrition and thus die through self-neglect. A husband whose wife dies is about ten times more likely to commit suicide than a wife whose husband dies. Men tend to have fewer intimate friends and family than women, so for men, the loss of love is more devastating (Farrell 1993).

An Emerging Men's Movement

Many men are confused about what's expected of them now, where the boundary lines are drawn, and how they want to be in this new era. Strong women won't put up with a dominating, dictatorial, or brutal man—but they don't want a weak man either. Men's movement leaders are filling the void with ideas about what men need and with meetings to explore the meaning of being a man today. Most participants are heterosexual, middle-class, mid-life Euro-American men (Harding 1992).

Robert Bly of Berkeley has been called the guru of the men's movement. Bly says the women's movement has been wonderful because it speaks of the pain women feel. Men feel a different kind of pain that the men's movement speaks to. Bly doesn't want to bring back the patriarchy, but prefers a new society, where male-female status resembles brother-sister more than ruling father, subservient mother (Bly 1992).

Bly says that long before the industrial revolution fathers nurtured sons and taught them intimacy and emotional resilience through a community of tribal elders. When men began leaving home every day for the workplace, their sons lost this bonding. The price men have paid for running the country is to "stop feeling, stop talking, and continue swallowing our pain and our hurt and keep dying younger than we need to" (Ferguson 1992). Bly focuses on men's need for a father figure, especially during puberty. He speaks of the importance of male initiation rites, the warrior aspect of the male personality, and the wild man inside. Men must get in touch with their emotions, with how to express caring and nurturing, and with how to ask for it. Methods of doing that include group processes, retreats, chanting, drumming, body work, and storytelling.

Sam Keen (1991) explores men's search for new personal ideals of strength, potency, and fearless hero in their lives. He confronts traditional models of manhood that "impoverish, injure, and alienate men." He describes a pilgrimage into self that moves from sunny pragmatism to the dark wisdom of dream-time, from having the answers to living the questions, from being cocksure to holding potent doubt, from numbness to manly grief, from artificial toughness to virile fear, from guilt and shame to responsible morality, from isolation to the awareness of loneliness, from false optimism to honest despair, from compulsive action to potentiality and waiting, and finally on to renewal and the rebirth of joy.

The men's movement is helping some men move into the modern relationships shown in Table 4.2 (see p. 4–8) by giving them permission to be vulnerable and intimate. Men who never learned to share their fear are allowed to do so. Talking about feelings is healing, and when the talk is heard compassionately, even more healing takes place. When men have their men's movement weekends to get in touch with the wild man and warrior parts of themselves, they acknowledge the past with its structure, discipline, and ritual that helped men overcome obstacles, protected women, and sustained human survival. The men's movement also helps men move on to the modern age. It encourages men to give themselves permission to ask, Who do I really want to become? How do I want to get there? By doing this, they can reach a deeper level of personal power.

Gender Issue: Balancing Masculine and Feminine Strengths

To reach their full potential, all humans need to develop both their masculine and feminine qualities. We all have two sides, two faces, the whole range of energies and traits that our culture labels as masculine and feminine. The balance varies for each person, depending on genes, the environment, and the decisions and choices each makes.

In a primitive survival mode, it worked well to differentiate gender traits according to gender roles. In a post-industrial society it seems to work best when we balance the masculine with the feminine—within ourselves as individuals, as well as in our homes, our organizations, and our society. Where we've done this, we've discovered that we're more well rounded, come closer to realizing our full potential, and tap more of our innate power at all levels, individual to national. To start at the individual level, do Self-Awareness Activity 4.5.

Self-Awareness Activity 4.5: (Self-Starter) Becoming More Well Rounded

Purpose: To gradually balance your masculine and feminine sides.

Step. 1 If you're a man, review the feminine strengths listed in Table 4.8. If you're a woman, review the masculine strengths. Check off the opposite-sex strengths you feel you adequately express. Are there ways you can express them more appropriately in achieving your personal and career goals?

Step 2. Select a typical opposite-sex strength that you want to develop more fully. List some ways you can become more aware of this trait, build it, and express it. Write down how it will balance some complementary same-sex trait you often express. Work on this new trait for a week or more; select a time frame that seems practical.

Step 3. During and after the time frame, jot down notes about how you expressed the trait, thoughts and feelings that came up, people's reactions, and any insights. How can developing this trait make you a stronger person or help you understand and relate better to others? How can it help you achieve career and personal goals? Get in touch with any resistance you felt about integrating this trait. Did you uncover any hidden beliefs during this process? Remember, even if you simply became more aware of the trait, you've made progress!

Step 4. Pick another strength to work on, and repeat steps 2 and 3. Keep working on strengths until you're satisfied with your own feminine-masculine balance.

The first item in each column of Table 4.8 concerns women learning to be more powerful and forthright and men learning to be more in touch with their feelings. Taking these actions helps us to move toward that personal balance that helps to heal and prevent the frustrations and resentments we often find among people in our culture.

TABLE 4.8: Balancing the Masculine-Feminine Within

Typical Masculine Strengths that Women Can Develop	*Typical Feminine Strengths that Men Can Develop*
• Learn how to be powerful and forthright. • Become entrepreneurial. • Have a direct, visible effect on others, rather than just functioning behind the scenes. • State your own needs and don't automatically back down if you meet resistance. • Make a task as important as your relationships with the people doing the task. • Build support systems with other women, share competence with them, rather than competing with them for male approval. • Build a sense of community among women instead of thinking, "I pulled myself up by my bootstraps, and you'll have to do it all by yourself, too." • Intellectualize and generalize from experiences. • Stop turning anger, blame, and pain inward—becoming angry at yourself, blaming yourself for other people's attitudes and feelings. • Stop being a victim. • Open yourself up to constructive criticism; consider the source of destructive criticism; quit taking criticism personally. • Deal directly with the source of your anger and resentments; stop allowing them to make you irritable, resistant, or a nag. • Respond directly with "I-messages" rather than blaming "you" messages. • Expand your decision-making skills by including rational fact finding, criteria development, analysis, and weighing of alternatives. • Change power-draining behaviors, such as allowing interruptions or laughing after making a serious statement. • Take calculated risks.	• Respect your feelings and others' as guides to authenticity and effectiveness. • Recognize, accept, and express your feelings. • Accept vulnerability and imperfection in yourself and in others. • Get in touch with your right to work for self-fulfillment as well as for money. • See the value of your nonwork roles, as well as your work identity. • Recognize that failing at a task does not mean failure as a person. • Accept and express the need to be nurtured. • Practice touching and feeling close to men, as well as women, without sexual connotations. • Listen actively, with empathy, without trying to solve others' problems. • Share your feelings as the most meaningful part of your contact with someone, accepting the risk and vulnerability such sharing implies. • Build or expand your support system by sharing competencies without competition and sharing feelings and needs with sincerity. • Relate to an experience or person on a personal level instead of on an abstract, rational, or objective level. • Become aware of an emotional, spontaneous, or irrational part of your self and accept it.

Working Through Gender Frustration

Men and women inevitably bring a degree of frustration to the workplace. How can a woman live all her life cast as an inferior simply because of her gender and not build up some frustration at the unfairness? The same is true for virtually all minorities, with minority women getting a double dose of denigration. Frustration has been building in many men as they see their male privilege slipping away, eroding the authority and control that society has told them "real men" must maintain. Frustration has also been building in "awakened" men who realize the price they've paid for the "real man" mystique. These men have become aware that they never felt truly loved by their fathers, they have repressed their feelings to the point of numbness, and they've been unable to develop intimate relationships with their own children, among other losses.

If we don't handle frustrations as they occur, they tend to build into anger, and even rage. Some psychologists define rage as a sense of extreme loss of power, value, self-worth, and meaning—that is often realized suddenly even though it may have been building bit by bit. When the "last straw" occurs, rage erupts, pushing you over the edge, out of control. The feelings you experience in the midst of rage can vary—anger, humiliation, shame, sorrow, meaninglessness, hopelessness, helplessness. Your actions can be quite unlike actions you would normally take, actions that lead to hurt, embarrassment, humiliation, and even disaster. Obviously, it pays to get in touch with your frustrations and work through them before they build to rage and erupt.

How do you know that rage is building inside you and needs to be addressed immediately? Here are some clues:

- You're nearly always fatigued.
- You feel cynical much of the time, assuming ulterior motives, that people just do things out of greed, ego, fear, manipulation, not out of goodwill or love.
- You often feel a sense of hopelessness—why try, nothing ever works.
- You often feel a sense of helplessness—I can't do anything about it—and retreat into a sullen silence.
- You emotionally overreact to some situations.
- You often think "Nobody *really* loves me"; denying love, intimacy, and caring.
- You rarely feel a passion for life any more.

Effective leaders—and employees—can't afford to carry around such emotional burdens. You can learn to release problem feelings and to help others do so. One way to prevent frustration buildup is to work through your feelings as they come up. Another way is to assert yourself when it's appropriate to speak up or to stand up for your rights. We'll discuss assertion in more detail later.

Creating Balanced Organizations

"Image the future in order that the future may be created."

These words were spoken more than 25 years ago by Arthur Waskow in an article "Looking Forward: 1999." He also said that one of the most powerful ways of achieving social change is to imagine in vivid detail a desirable future, and then build a part of that future in the present.

In America's traditionally segmented society, we've usually handled our differences at arm's length, through laws and agencies and courts. In corporate America we've tended to handle our differences through hierarchical power. While our governmental system is democratic, our economic system and its corporations are certainly not. All we must do to know that is to recall our various experiences as employees. In our businesses, as in the various totalitarian governments of the world, it's not at all unusual for a large majority to be ruled by a small minority. Examples are a small minority of Euro-American men controlling a textile mill or garment factory full of women employees, or a Southwestern mining operation full of Latino American men. Such companies traditionally use a hierarchical, status-oriented, masculine way of controlling. We've seen that new technology, marketplace competition, and better-educated employees with new expectations are changing all that, and a need for masculine-feminine balance in organizations is emerging.

Feminine and masculine, yin and yang—when one reaches its fullness, it subsides and the other becomes dominant. All indications are that we've reached the limits of a heavily masculine way of organizing and relating and are shifting toward a balanced masculine-feminine mode. The masculine is the active, doing, achievement aspect, while the feminine is the being, nurturing, connecting, caring aspect. Some studies indicate that a group inevitably shifts once a critical mass of distinctly different persons becomes a part of that group. How many people does it take to make a critical mass? Generally from about 20 to 35 percent. At best, women are only about 5 percent of the top leaders in big business and big government. Yet they've reached a critical mass at lower levels of management. Trend expert John Naisbett thinks that's enough to make a difference in corporate cultures.

Our strongly masculine way of relating to each other and the planet has led to deep fear of annihilation. With a highly individualistic, competitive, hierarchical, and dictatorial approach, we can destroy humanity through nuclear war, nuclear accidents, or the aggregated damage caused by overpopulation and widespread, complex, and diverse pollution of the environment. A critical mass of people recognize, at the conscious or subconscious level, that the masculine-feminine imbalance is the root problem. USSR leader Gorbechev in his own way recognized this and based his perestroika upon it in the late 1980s. From this viewpoint, it should be no surprise that the Berlin wall and the USSR broke up so quickly, nor that former political prisoner Nelson Mandela is now South Africa's president. Even in China, "where once the party and central government could dictate just about anything," the local governments are demanding a say in things (Tanner 1994).

Since the 1960s people and companies have tended to adopt one of two attitudes toward diversity. Some companies and individuals have worked toward an ever greater degree of accommodation and mutual acculturation. Others have been drawn kicking and screaming into the modern era, with a great deal of backlash and resistance, observing only the letter of the law. Yes, we've handled our differences through hierarchical power. Now it's time to draw out the potentialities of all the stakeholders in the workplace, to fully include them at every level and in every area, and to allow corporate cultures to evolve that reflect our diversity.

Not only can you balance the masculine-feminine within, as a leader or employee in an organization, you can have some influence in moving your organization toward a better balance. However, to bring about a wholeness and harmony that heals at every level, a critical mass of people and organizations in our culture must shift to values that support such change. Moving beyond patriarchy toward equality is a major part of this shift. Some examples of areas we can bring into balance include:

- a balance of male and female role models at home with preschool children; at work in preschools, kindergartens, and elementary schools; and at higher levels in all types of organizations
- male and female role models who have freely chosen a wide range of occupations and lifestyles
- an ability to move beyond wars, but in the meantime making men and women equally responsible for military defense
- men and women equally responsible for taking the initiative and paying in courtship, live-in, and marriage relationships, with each couple feeling free to work out their own balance

Society consists of individuals, and individual leaders can influence these changes by leading others to see the advantages.

Gender Issue: Understanding Sexual Harassment

Sexual harassment is a major area of concern and confusion that reflects recent changes in the workplace and in male-female relationships. Men and women need to know what sexual harassment is, how men and women view it, and what they should do to avoid it. We also need to know what to do when harassment takes place, actions the person being harassed can take, and actions the organization can take. Before we discuss these aspects of sexual harassment, test your current viewpoint by completing Self-Awareness Activity 4.6.

Self-Awareness Activity 4.6: What Do You Know About Sexual Harassment?

Purpose: To see what you know about sexual harassment.

Instructions: Determine whether you think the following statements are basically true or false—and think about why. Answers are discussed in the following paragraph.

1. Sexual harassment is always about men harassing women.
2. When a manager has an affair with one of his employees, that's sexual harassment.
3. A group of men telling each other sexual jokes is not sexual harassment.
4. If both parties agree to have a sexual relationship, it's not sexual harassment.
5. Sexual harassment is just a misunderstanding about sexual attraction and flattery.

What Is Sexual Harassment?

Wherever men and women work, there is a certain amount of sexual interaction on the job. When does it become harassment? When the behavior is unwanted, unsolicited, and nonreciprocal, when it asserts a person's sex role over her or his function as a worker, or when it creates an environment that seems hostile to the employee.

Sexual harassment can be about anyone of any gender or sexual orientation harassing an employee. When a manager has an affair with an employee, it's not sexual harassment of the employee unless it's unwelcome. However, it is sexual harassment of the employee's co-workers because it gives the lover an unfair advantage. A group of men telling each other sexual jokes is sexual harassment only if it's done within hearing range of an employee who takes offense and if it creates a "hostile environment" for that employee. When consenting adults agree to a sexual relationship and it's welcome to both, it's not sexual harassment unless one reports to the other; then it affects co-workers, as previously discussed. Sexual harassment is about misuse of power, not attraction and flattery.

Basic types of sexual interaction. Let's categorize some types of sexual interaction on the job.

- *Consensual worker-worker sex,* usually the least harmful workplace sexual relationship, but one that still gives the two workers a bond that others cannot achieve. For this reason, the fairest approach may be to reveal the relationship to co-workers, and then to keep it low-profile. This type of relationship is not viewed as sexual harassment.
- *Consensual boss-worker sex,* a form of favoritism that undermines the ability of the boss to establish boundaries because the boss often feels needy of the worker-partner.
- *Workplace flirtation,* such as suggestive dress, prolonged eye contact, or touching someone on the arm or shoulder. Whether it's friendliness or flirtation is often debatable because it depends on when and how it's done and who's making the judgment call. Generally women employees have more latitude in these areas for many traditional and cultural reasons. However if the recipient views such behavior as unwelcome advances, it may be considered harassment.
- *Workplace porn,* where employee(s) display pinups, tell lewd jokes, make sexual innuendoes in groups, and otherwise create an environment that some view as hostile.
- *Workplace prostitution,* where an employee offers to have a sexual relationship in order to gain a promotion or other favors.
- Sexual bribery, where a boss promises or implies a promotion or other favors if an employee agrees to some sort of sexual relationship.
- *Sexual extortion,* where a boss threatens to fire or demote an employee unless they have some sort of sexual relationship.

Sexual harassment defined. In 1980 the EEOC identified two types of sexual harassment: (1) the overt "put out or get out" proposition, which includes sexual extortion/bribery and

(2) behavior that creates a hostile work environment, which can include workplace porn and consensual boss-worker sex.

During the 1980s and 1990s the courts expanded the definition of a hostile environment. In the early and mid-1990s three-fourths of court cases on sexual harassment were based on the hostile environment form alone, with only about 6 percent based on the extortion/bribery form alone and 19 percent based on both forms (Hamilton and Beglahn 1992). Examples of sexual harassment from court cases include:

- physical contact such as patting, stroking, hugging, kissing
- comments on a woman's clothing, body, or appearance
- swearing, or "dirty" jokes, pinups, pictures, graffiti, and other visual depictions that are embarrassing or degrading to most women
- indirect harassment caused by being subjected to an environment where sexual harassment occurs even though you are not a target
- favoritism that constitutes a hostile environment; for example, when one employee submits to sexual favors and is rewarded while others who refuse are denied promotions or benefits.

Recent legal developments. The courts and Congress have made rulings and laws that further spell out what sexual harassment is and the legal consequences. In 1986 the Supreme Court ruled that:

- Sexual harassment can consist of nothing more than a hostile environment; no monetary loss is necessary for employees to establish a violation of Title VII of the Civil Rights Act.
- Sexual harassment can exist even if an employee voluntarily engages in sexual activity with a manager; the test is whether the manager's advances are "unwelcome."
- An employee's sexually provocative activity, dress, speech, manner, and so on can be used by an employer as evidence that sexual advances were welcomed.

A U.S. Court of Appeals ruled in 1991 that the standards of a reasonable woman (instead of the traditional "reasonable man") must be used to determine sexually offensive conduct in organizations, when the plaintiff is a woman.

The Civil Rights Act of 1991 gives employees the right to jury trials and to limited punitive damages for sexual harassment—in addition to the reinstatement and back pay formerly provided.

Sexual harassment is misuse of power. About 90 percent of sexual harassment complaints are filed by women, and in most cases the male harasser has power over the female harassee. While it's primarily a woman's issue, about 10 percent of cases are either women harassing men or gay employees harassing other gay persons.

A 1994 case filed by a legal secretary claiming that a high-powered lawyer continually harassed her typifies the power differential issue. The law partner brought in nearly a million dollars per year in revenue for the firm, and the firm was not about to call him on the carpet for bothering his secretary. "Secretaries are more expendable than partners," said the plaintiff. Her comment reveals the practical, bottom-line assumptions in many cases: A clerk is more expendable than an executive, professional, or ace salesman; a student is not as important as a professor; a nurses' aide is less important than a doctor. And the sexual harassment is ignored or swept under the rug. The power differential issue raises several questions:

- Do people who hold significant power within an organization have a responsibility to exercise it in ways that don't abuse the less powerful?
- What rights should the less powerful have to defend themselves against abuse from the powerful?
- Should restrictions against misusing power in this way become part of the law?

What Do We Need to Know About Sexual Harassment?

Sexual harassment is not just a rare or occasional problem; it's rampant in the workplace. One reason is that women and men view sexual behavior in the workplace quite differently.

Sexual harassment is pervasive in the workplace. A poll conducted by the National Association of Female Executives found that 53 percent of its 1300 members have been victims. Sexual harassment is more about power, domination, and hostility than flirting or sexual attraction. A person who is attracted to you in a positive, respectful sense does not harass you. In about 90 percent of the reported cases, women are the plaintiffs (Female Executive 1992).

Why do we need sexual harassment laws? Because men hold most of the power in the workplace, and they have never seen sexual harassment as a legitimate issue. When women have complained of harassment, just as when they've complained of rape, the men in power have tended to (1) assume the woman "asked for it," and (2) put her on trial, probing to see what problem she has that would cause her to make such an accusation.

Men and women view harassment differently. In 1991, when Anita Hill testified before a televised Senate confirmation hearing that Supreme Court nominee Clarence Thomas had sexually harassed her, the nation suddenly focused on this problem. Women became aware of the rationalizations some men use and the stereotypes they place on women who complain of sexual harassment; for example:

- **Seductress.** She asked for it. This is the oldest, most common stereotype. In the 1980s a Southern judge ruled that a five-year-old girl seduced an adult male to rape her.
- **She-Devil.** Watch that woman; she's trouble; she's trying to "demonize" him.
- **Bimbo.** She can't make it on her own merits; she has to get promotions, attention, money through a man.
- **Woman scorned.** She had a crush on him and he wasn't interested or lost interest.
- **Fantasizer.** She dreams of male attention and pretends it's there.
- **Frustrated wallflower.** She can't get male attention and desperately wants it.
- **Martyr.** She loves playing the role of victim or martyr.

Some differences in how men and women tend to view a sexual incident are shown in Table 4.9.

TABLE 4.9: Male and Female Reactions to a Boss Flirting with a Female Employee

Male Observer:	Female Observer:
It's just a sexual dalliance.	It's a power issue.
It's OK to step out of the boss role to flirt a little.	A boss can't really step out of that role with an employee.
Harassment is rare; it's just when a guy goes over the line of acceptable flirting.	Harassment is pervasive and shows a difference in how men and women see power.
(Men often exercise power without noticing it.)	Power must be earned; women often don't get power.
What's the big deal?	I feel intimidated and threatened; this touches a nerve.

Most women have some sense of the wide disparity between how men and women view sexual harassment and the stereotyped labels that may be pinned on them if they file a complaint. Understandably, most women have refused to file claims, believing that doing so would only make a bad situation worse.

Why Does Sexual Harassment Occur?

The most common causes of sexual harassment stem from people who:

- abuse power in trying to obtain sexual favors
- try to use sex to gain power
- use power to decrease the power of a victim by reference to her or his sexuality and gender identity
- are reacting to a personal crisis
- won't accept that an affair is over
- have a psychological or substance abuse disorder
- are confused about dealing with new gender roles in the workplace

The abuse of power that is part and parcel of sexual harassment probably stems from the traditional cultural view of women as inferior to men. Psychiatrists and counselors who specialize in men's abuse of women say that such abuse is woven into our culture when men are taught to believe that they are superior to women and that men should be in control. Such beliefs are carryovers from the time, not so long ago, when women were considered the property of men and when their legal rights were often in the same classification as those of children and the mentally incompetent.

With the increasing ability of women to obtain jobs, divorces, and dependable birth control, it has become less likely that the husband's paycheck can be used to enforce patriarchal authority and control. Some social scientists suggest that the declining ability of men to use their financial power to coerce women has triggered a political backlash and even an increase in violence against women. The reports of increased sexual harassment at work, physical abuse in the home, and rape outside the home indeed may be an acting-out of some men's confusion, resentment, and fear of women's increasing independence and power.

In this age of struggle for women's equality, men who believe they should be in control and authority in relationships with women can develop deep doubts about themselves as whole and complete persons when they're not controlling the relationship. In its extreme form, such frustrated expectations and deep fears are expressed as the rage that leads to harassing, raping, beating, and even murdering women. Experts estimate that each year 4 million women are beaten and 1,500 murdered by husbands or lovers (Blinder 1987). Experts in the field, such as psychiatry professor Dr. Martin Blinder and Antonio Ramirez, executive director of an agency that counsels batterers, say the key to stopping all forms of harassment and abuse is for:

- men and women to simply accept that women are equals
- women to claim their rights to dignity and safety at work, in the street, and at home
- men to support women in that struggle
- the community to say together that this is something we will no longer tolerate

How Do Men Feel About Sexual Harassment?

Most men are confused about just where the behavioral boundaries are drawn now, and at a deeper level there is an anxiety about changing norms. Men's advocate Warren Farrell believes the workplace is an easy extension of male adolescence, where boys win attention and other rewards for performing and pursuing. Many are confused by the sudden switch in rules, and some are concerned about the possibility of a woman with some ulterior motive falsely accusing them of sexual harassment.

Many men don't understand how their girlie calendars and pinups in the office constitute harassment. Some assume they merely make women feel inferior by comparison, and that's why they object to them. Women's advocates disagree, saying that pinups signal that sexiness is what counts in the workplace and everywhere else. Such symbols imply that women co-workers are viewed primarily as sex objects rather than fellow human beings and professionals.

Men's specific objections to sexual harassment laws and policies include:

- Women still play their old sexual games, without being penalized.
- Women still buy the romance formula of the man pursuing and persisting, the women attracting and resisting, until the man overcomes her resistance.
- Women still send mixed messages, saying "no, no" when they mean "yes, yes" or "maybe."
- Women still dress and behave seductively in the office. Miniskirts, slit skirts, thin blouses, plunging necklines, heavy perfume, and flirting are all provocative. These traditional indirect female initiatives are signals to most men to take direct initiative.
- Sexual harassment laws often create a hostile environment for men, where the females are like children who must be protected by law.

Some men's movement spokesmen theorize that men traditionally harass each other by hazing newcomers, picking on their area of vulnerability. The function of hazing is to train the newcomer to survive attacks to vulnerable areas and to subordinate self to the team. Men come to understand that they are replaceable if they don't fit in. Through hazing they learn to fit in or leave. The newcomer must learn to laugh and to take the criticism, even though it's personal. He learns to assess its value for self-improvement, and to not be crushed by it. Men's spokesmen say that if a woman newcomer isn't being hazed, she's not being tested. Therefore, she won't be trusted. They imply that sexual harassment is just a form of hazing (Farrell 1993).

The major concern men have is that women can now threaten men with a sexual harassment charge, and they could theoretically victimize men with false accusations of harassment. Companies can certainly set up procedures for investigating and handling sexual harassment complaints that would make it very difficult for men to be victimized and yet provide protection and fairness for women. Conservatives advocate throwing out sexual harassment laws. Liberals say that would be throwing out the baby (women's legitimate problems with men's sexual dominance) with the bath water (women's potential misuse of the laws).

Some men say that if women would communicate honestly and directly, there wouldn't be a problem. One said, "If a woman tells a man directly, with no mixed messages, that she thinks he's sexually harassing her, at least 99 percent of men will stop in that case." Actually, this is difficult for many women because they consider it direct confrontation, which they take great pains to avoid.

Men's advocates say that sexual harassment education needs to focus on the fact that for men to pursue and persist has been functional throughout history. Today, when we are struggling toward equality, it's no longer functional, at least in the workplace. Women need to understand that to attract and resist is natural because it's also been functional throughout history, but it is no longer functional in the workplace.

Men have also said they wish women would learn to become aware of the mixed signals they often give out. They could then learn how to give clear, direct, unambiguous messages. Women who give unmixed messages are more likely to be treated as equal professionals by men.

Men's advocates say that if organizations will develop clear policies regarding sexual harassment, and communicate them effectively, there will be less need for legal action. Some admit, however, that many men still resist the whole idea that sexual harassment is a problem.

Preventing and Resolving Sexual Harassment Complaints

As a leader and as a team member, you may need to know more about what individuals and organizations can do to avoid harassment problems, what you should tell a harassed employee to do, and how you should resolve complaints.

What Can Men Do to Avoid Problems?

Again, we're assuming men are the ones who worry about being the harasser, although in a small percentage of cases women are the harassers. Some suggestions to men for avoiding sexual harassment complaints include:

- *Raise your awareness.* Sexual harassment is a rather complex issue, but you can learn enough to stay out of trouble.

- *Respect the word* "No." When you're at work, it's best to forget the old idea that a woman's *no* may not really mean *no* or that it merely makes the conquest more challenging and exciting.

- *Align your attitude.* Are you still harboring the belief that women are inferior? That men should be in control? If so, work on shifting your beliefs to align with current reality.

- *Support clear policies* and training that spell out what harassment is and how the organization will handle it. If you understand sexual harassment, and your company has clear policies about its definition and consequences, you can relax and be yourself, assuming your attitude is in line.

- *Be a role model.* Now that you're savvy about sexual harassment, help other men get it by treating co-workers with respect. For example, refer to women as women, not as "girls," "chicks," "ladies," or similar names. Don't participate in story-telling and jokes that demean women as a group. Let others know you don't want to hear or see women being referred to as sex objects.

What Can Women Do to Avoid Problems?

Women can help ease the situation by becoming aware of men's confusion and complaints and, through a greater awareness, sending clear, straight messages. Some specific recommendations for women are:

- *Avoid the sexual stereotype trap.* Women don't need to automatically and unthinkingly fall into others' expectations about their role. *Sex object* is one of the age-old stereotypes that women can avoid by dressing and acting in a businesslike, professional way. Check flirtatious or femme fatale tendencies at the office door.

- *Avoid sexual liaisons at work.* The objective of the office sex game is to increase the man's status with other men. This is one of the ways a man becomes "one of the boys" who make decisions about promotions and salaries. A woman may therefore increase the status of any man she has sex with and at the same time decrease her own status.

- *Say no tactfully but clearly.* Women can let men know if they don't like being called "honey," "babe," and similar names. Women can send I-messages when they say no to requests for a drink, lunch, dinner, or date: "I like you but I don't go out socially with business friends," "I like you but I never go out with married men," "I value our relationship but my husband would be hurt if he couldn't share the occasion," "I like you but I'm not comfortable with going beyond a business relationship." The underlying message is you're not interested in sexual involvement and will always say no to such overtures.

What Can Organizations and Leaders Do?

Leaders can use their influence to make sure that the organization's policies are designed to prevent most sexual harassment and effectively handle cases that do occur. They can be sure that cases are handled professionally, so that everyone's rights are protected. Preventive actions include

- Top management establishes and publicizes a strong policy that specifically describes the kinds of actions that constitute sexual harassment and sets out the consequences for offenders.
- Top management regularly signals that it is committed to fighting harassment.
- The firm provides training seminars designed to sensitize employees to the issue.
- The firm sets up complaint procedures and mechanisms that encourage private complaints of harassment and that bypass immediate supervisors, who are often the source of the problem.

What Should Leaders Advise a Harassed Employee to Do?

Let's assume the recipient of the harassment is a woman, since that's the typical pattern. A woman in business cannot afford to allow any man to persist in actions that constitute sexual harassment. To do so would signal to other men that such behavior may be condoned and would set a poor example for the entire work team. A woman need not accept such a victim role. Here are some specific steps to take.

- *Be clear.* Say no to overtures tactfully but clearly. Mean it; give no mixed messages. Object to sexually inappropriate behavior, communication, or symbolism—again tactfully but clearly and directly.
- *Confront.* If objectionable behavior continues, tell your harasser that this behavior must stop immediately. Follow up with a memo documenting what you said and hand it to him in the presence of a witness.
- *Document.* Keep notes of what happened, when, and where. Note who, if anyone, witnessed it. Discuss the incident with any witnesses, to nail it down in their minds. Ask them to make a note about it, with a date.
- *Confide.* If you wish to keep the matter officially confidential while you try to put a stop to the behavior, tell only trusted work associates. Ask them to keep brief notes. These people can later testify on your behalf.
- *Look for a pattern.* Chances are very good that he has harassed other women. Seek out women who have worked with him. Engage in discreet, probing conversations to learn if they have been harassed. If you can establish that he has a pattern of harassment, your case is greatly strengthened.
- *Report.* If the harassment continues, find out who you should report it to, often someone in the human resources department. If you need further emotional support and advice, look for a local women's organization that provides such services.
- *Consider alternative steps.* If you don't like the way your organization handles your complaint, you can carry it further—to the EEOC or to court. Consider consulting an attorney who specializes in such cases. Local women's organizations and bar associations may recommend someone. Some courts have recently allowed class action suits where sexual harassment is common in an organization. Carefully weigh the pros and cons.

- *Be timely*. Determine the statute of limitations for reporting sexual harassment in your state. In most states you must file a claim within six months of the last occurrence.

How Should Complaints Be Resolved?

Guidelines for resolving sexual harassment complaints include:

- Take sexual harassment complaints as seriously as other grievances; investigate them as thoroughly.

- Keep such matters entirely confidential.

- Find out what the complainant wants and try to accommodate her.

- Carefully investigate. Appoint an investigative team: one man, one woman, preferably objective outsiders. Look for documentation, witnesses, confidants, observers.

- If the team cannot substantiate that sexual harassment has occurred (she says it did; he says it didn't), tell the complainant why the firm cannot take definitive action and to report any further occurrences or any instances of retaliation. Tell the accused: The organization had a duty to investigate; he is cleared; but if another complaint is filed, it will have more serious implications.

- If the team substantiates that sexual harassment has occurred, use disciplinary procedures that are similar to those used in cases of nonperformance of job duties. Normally, the first offense calls for a warning and some sensitivity training. The second offense calls for some form of punishment: no bonus, no promotion, a demotion, docked pay, temporary suspension. The third offense calls for dismissal.

- Insure that no one retaliates against the complainant, no matter what the outcome.

Now that you know the basics of sexual harassment, see how well you recognize it in action by completing Skill Builder minicases at the end of this chapter.

Gender Issue: Relating to One Another Assertively

Women often behave nonassertively and thus are viewed as weak or manipulative. Men often carry assertiveness too far and are seen as overbearing, demanding, or dominating. As a leader in a diverse workplace, you need to understand the basics of assertiveness. Relating to others assertively will improve your own people skills, and you can in turn help others to improve theirs. Women and minorities often need the encouragement to act assertively. Anyone who has been made relatively powerless in society tends to become passive. Making a habit of tactfully asserting yourself is one of the keys to preventing a buildup of frustration, resentment, and stress. It gives you more control over your life and builds self-esteem. Test your assertiveness knowledge by completing Self-Awareness Activity 4.7 now.

Self-Awareness Activity 4.7: What Do You Know About Assertiveness?

Purpose: To see what you know about assertiveness.

Instructions: Determine whether you think the following statements are basically true or false—and think about why. The answers are given in the paragraph that follows.

1. Assertion is getting your way.

2. Nonassertion is being willing to compromise.

3. Aggression is taking the initiative to get things done.

4. I-messages are self-centered messages that often violate others' rights.

5. Not asserting yourself is often desirable because it respects others' feelings.

First, we'll discuss brief definitions of assertion, nonassertion and aggression. Then we'll discuss them in more detail, with some examples.

- *Assertion* is speaking up honestly and directly about what you think, feel, or believe, in ways that respect the rights and feeling of others. It's standing up for your rights, while being considerate of others' rights.

- *Nonassertion* is not speaking up about what you think, feel, or believe, especially when your inaction bothers you when you later reflect upon it. It's allowing others to violate your rights, with no challenge from you. It's letting someone push you around, walk all over you, or not consider your feelings or rights—or to intimidate, demean, or devalue you.

- *Aggression* is carrying assertion too far. It's going after what you want in ways that violate the rights of another—or expressing yourself in ways that intimidate, demean, or degrade another person. It's pushing other people around, using them as a doormat, or not considering their rights or feelings.

As you can see, all the statements made in Self-Awareness Activity 4.7 are essentially false (I-messages are discussed later).

Respecting Your Rights and Others' Rights

The key to assertion is being clear about your rights and then standing up for them. Since people's perceptions of who has what rights in a situation can vary, what happens when rights overlap? The assertive person is willing to listen, discuss the problem, and negotiate a solution that both parties can live with.

> *Your prime assertive right might be:*
> *You have the right to judge your own behavior, thoughts, and emotions.*
> *You have the right to decide whether and how to express yourself.*
> *You have the responsibility to be totally accountable for the results of these actions.*

What are some basic rights that you believe in and that most people in our culture believe in? The Bill of Rights is probably the best expression of our common beliefs about human rights. However, it was basically intended as a list of rights of Euro-American men. Women and minorities have had to fight to be included among the people entitled to these basic rights. What rights do women have that are often violated? Within organizations, managers have certain rights and employees have rights. Think of management and employee rights that you believe in. When you have clear, firm beliefs in the rights of individuals, you have the conviction to assert yourself when your rights are violated. You also have the basis for recognizing and respecting other people's rights.

For example, what do you do when another person tries to break in line in front of you? Do you automatically give way? Do you automatically resist? Or does it depend? Maybe the person previously waited in the line, had to leave for a moment, and just returned. Maybe he or she is in the midst of a minor crisis. Sometimes it's not clear who got there first or why the person is breaking in. Therefore, the two of you have different viewpoints about who is right, and your rights may overlap or be in conflict.

People who tend to be nonassertive rarely see situations as an issue of rights, and they don't know how to stand up for their rights anyway. They may have a compulsive need to "be nice," not cause a "scene," be a martyr, and their actions imply, "my rights, thoughts, or feelings aren't as important as yours." People who tend to be aggressive just want their own way and aren't about to be pushed around. They rarely think in terms of others' rights. Their actions imply, "my thoughts, feelings, and rights are more important than yours."

People who are assertive recognize their own rights and the rights of others and are willing to negotiate, and perhaps compromise, to settle situations where rights conflict or overlap. Such compromises respect the basic integrity of both people, and both get some of their wishes satisfied. This approach helps to avoid the temptation to use assertion to manipulate others in order to get what you want. It often leads to both people getting what they want because people are most likely to become cooperative when they're approached in a respectful way.

Being Assertive

You assert yourself when you stand up for your personal rights and express your thoughts, feelings, and beliefs in direct, honest, and appropriate ways. You do this in ways that don't manipulate, dominate, humiliate, or degrade the other person. Assertion is based on respect for yourself and respect for the other person. You express your preferences and defend your rights in ways that also respect other people's needs and rights. The goal of assertion is to get and give respect, to ask for fairness, and to leave room for compromise when your needs and rights conflict with another person's.

You can assert with empathy to soften the message. "Maybe you have a good reason for wanting to break in, but I was here first." You may need to assert with increasing firmness in those relatively rare cases when people ignore your assertive message. "I mentioned that I was here first. I must insist that you wait your turn." You can use I-messages that express your inner reality without judging, blaming, or interpreting someone else's behavior. Here are some examples of I-messages, in which you take responsibility for your thoughts and feelings. Compare them to the you-messages, which tend to blame and judge the other person.

I-Messages	You-Messages
I have sensitive hearing.	You talk too loudly.
I'm not comfortable talking about sex.	You have a dirty mouth.
I'd like to meet and make plans.	You shouldn't wait till the last minute.
I'd like to go over what we want to get done this week.	You need to manage your time better.
I'd like to prepare for the meeting.	You should send out an agenda.

Your nonverbal messages nearly always convey what you really feel or think. When you're not clear and honest in what you *say*, people receive a mixed message. For example, your voice tone, facial expression, and body language might say, "I'm upset," while your words say, "Oh, it's okay; I don't mind." When you are clear about your rights and say what you really think or feel, using I-messages and other effective assertion techniques, your verbal and nonverbal expressions are in harmony. Your message comes through confidently and congruently. You can be assertive in ways that actually build stronger relationships.

Being Nonassertive

When you don't express your honest feelings, thoughts, and beliefs, or when you express them in such an apologetic, unsure, or self-effacing way that others can easily disregard them, then you're allowing your rights to be violated by your nonassertiveness. By such actions you tell others: *You can take advantage of me. My feelings aren't very important; yours are. My thoughts aren't important; yours are the only ones really worth listening to. I'm nothing; you're superior.*

Nonassertion reflects a lack of respect for your own preferences. In an indirect way it reflects a lack of respect for the other person's ability to take disappointments, to assume some responsibility, or to handle problems. For example, a typical reason people give for not asserting themselves is, "I didn't want to hurt her feelings"—or embarrass him, or upset them. The goal of nonassertion is to please others and to avoid conflict at any cost. When you're being nonassertive, you're often being a victim.

Most experts believe that nonassertion is always accompanied by some degree of resentment that is experienced at some level, whether conscious or not. You resent situations where you don't assume control for your own experience. In other words, you resent your lack of self-control. You store these resentments, small or large, inside yourself. If you don't express them in some way, they build up and you become a pressure cooker of resentful energy. Then an unfortunate person comes along who hands you the final indignity, and you blow up, out of control for all to see. Your explosive reaction is probably as much a surprise to you as it is to others. When you begin to consistently assert yourself, you gain self-control.

Passive-aggressive behavior is a variation of nonassertion. For example, in organizations there are usually some people who smile and agree with the managers, but who undermine them in subtle or sneaky ways. They find ways to quietly sabotage a manager's efforts or projects, usually by not doing their part. They always have a good reason "why not," but meanwhile nothing got done. Passive-aggressive attitudes always result in some type of hostile action.

People who are consistently nonassertive may resort to passive-aggressive behavior because they won't want to face the consequences of speaking up. It may be their way of resisting someone whom they think is trying to dominate them. They may see themselves as the victim of a persecutor. Worst of all, they may secretly stew, fret, boil, or pout—all the while being "nice" and trying to hide their real feelings.

Being Aggressive

Being aggressive is going too far. It's standing up for your personal rights and expressing your thoughts and feelings in ways that belittle the other person or violate his or her rights. Such actions and words are usually inappropriate and often dishonest. Aggressive behavior carries such messages as: *This is what I think; you're stupid for thinking differently. This is what I want; what you want isn't important. Here's what I feel; I haven't considered your feelings.* The goal is getting your way, getting things done, prevailing, winning, or dominating—regardless of the effect on the other person. It's a winner-loser approach. You win by taking needed action without consideration of others, by overpowering, intimidating, belittling, degrading, or humiliating. The result is that other people find it difficult or impossible to express their preferences and defend their rights. You don't really like yourself when you act this way, consciously or not, and others resent it.

Complete Skill Builder 4.4 to test your understanding of assertiveness, nonassertiveness, and aggressiveness.

LEADERSHIP CHALLENGES AND OPPORTUNITIES

Since gender differences are the most basic of all differences, they provide the most important challenges and opportunities to business leaders. We'll discuss leadership challenges in meeting gender needs, women's needs, and men's needs. Then we'll discuss the leadership opportunity of moving toward a gender-balanced organization.

Leadership Challenge: Meeting Gender Needs

Here are some key gender needs that we've discussed in this chapter:
- understanding one another's worlds
- understanding, avoiding, and resolving sexual harassment complaints
- relating to one another assertively

Helping Men and Women Understand One Another's Worlds

Through your own understanding and role modeling, and through formal and informal training sessions, you can help men and women in your organization to understand their differences. Since women focus on making personal connection, establishing rapport, cooperating with others, and playing down their expertise, you must help men to understand that this does not necessarily signal weakness, lack of confidence, or incompetence. It may in fact reflect personal and professional strength. Since men focus on gaining and keeping status, reporting information, competing, and displaying their expertise, you must help women to understand that this does not mean they aren't interested in cooperating and establishing rapport. Now you know that women naturally tend to communicate more tentatively and men more assertively, and that women listeners give more feedback than men listeners. You can help men and women understand the probable meanings of these style differences.

Helping Men and Women Understand and Avoid Sexual Harassment

Develop and support clear, effective company policies regarding sexual harassment. Make sure that everyone on your team understands the issues and the policies. Be a role model in the way you treat people. Help to resolve sexual harassment complaints discreetly, fairly, and firmly.

Helping Men and Women Relate to One Another Assertively

Recognize when a misunderstanding or a miscommunication is rooted in an assertiveness problem. Help employees to understand and resolve such problems. Provide assertiveness training to all employees who need it and want it. Relate to others in an assertive manner yourself.

Leadership Challenge: Meeting Womens' Needs

Here are some women's needs that we've discussed in this chapter:
- overcoming self-limiting beliefs
- breaking through the glass ceiling
- finding flexible work arrangements to balance career and family
- overcoming pay inequity

See also the chapter 5 leadership challenges section, which provides suggestions for helping African Americans move through typical issues at each career phase. Many of these issues are typical of all disadvantaged workplace groups, including women.

Women must not only deal with the stereotypes of others, but also with their own self-limiting beliefs, such as feeling powerless, taking things personally, responding emotionally, and relating in a nonassertive way. Effective leaders understand that women have valuable strengths to contribute, and these leaders support women in overcoming any barriers to using those strengths. Methods include role modeling, coaching, mentoring, and providing appropriate assignments and training classes.

Dismantling the Glass Ceiling

Dismantling the glass ceiling refers to doing your share to end or overcome all the ways, including those many small, hidden, or subtle ways, that the company discriminates against women. It includes recognizing that nearly all corporate cultures are predominantly male cultures and helping to resolve the conflicts and disadvantages this poses for women. It also includes working to bring about a balance of masculine and feminine values in the organization, which we discuss later.

Help with career planning. Support women in developing and implementing their career plans by treating women as valued individuals. Don't assume women are not as career committed as men. Ask key questions of each employee, such as:

- what do you want from your career?
- what goals do you want to set?
- what contributions do you want to make?
- what events might limit your career efforts in the foreseeable future?
- what sort of work life–personal life balance do you want?
- what can the company do to help?

Provide training. Questions about career plans can naturally lead to questions about training desires and needs. See that the training women get is geared to their particular needs, but don't assume you know what those needs are. On the other hand, be prepared to make some suggestions. You may want to encourage, challenge, and support women to gain skills in math, computer, science, and other typically male skills that are valuable in your organization. You also may want to suggest that they take these courses in all-women classes. Studies indicate that women achieve higher levels of mastery when they take such classes without men around. Also, be sure that women have equal opportunities to attend higher-level management training programs that prepare managers for promotion.

Support a variety of leadership styles. The differences in world views of men and women suggest some possible difficulties for women in male-dominated organizations. They are likely to feel pressured to change their leadership style and to experience conflict between leadership and gender roles. If they do become more directive, they are more likely than men to receive negative reactions. Discuss leadership style and communicate the belief that a variety of styles are appropriate, depending on the leader and the situation.

Providing Support to Balance Career and Family Demands

You've learned that a major barrier to women's success is inflexible working arrangements. Good employees can be retained through the child-bearing years if leaders are flexible, accepting, and supportive of family needs. Asking for flexible alternatives or family benefits should not be the kiss of death to career ambitions, but it is in many companies. For example, women who take maternity leave are 10 times more likely to lose their jobs than employees on other kinds of medical leave. In addition pregnant women are often transferred, demoted, harassed, or fired (Miller 1991). "Mommy-track" and part-time work are usually the boring, low-level grunt work that blocks chances of gaining the skills required to advance professionally. These practices and attitudes must be changed if your organization wants to attract and retain career women who also become mothers.

Women managers are in an ideal position to take leadership roles in bringing about such change. They have a special advantage in understanding the needs of working mothers and minorities: (1) They have direct experience in dealing with stereotypes and self-limiting beliefs rooted in the socialization process. (2) They have traditionally taken on most of the responsibility for children and elderly parents, as well as for the environment.

If women are to have uninterrupted careers, rather than just jobs, they need:

- adequate maternity and family medical leave

- help in obtaining affordable, quality child care and elder care

- flexible job structures and benefits, such as flextime, job sharing, part-time arrangements, contract work, and home offices.

Rather than lose competent women who go through a phase of needing more time for their small children, some companies are giving them whatever they need to do part or all of their work in a home office—fax machines, computers, car phones. Some can pack the work into three or four days instead of five. Some need to come into the office once or twice a week for meetings. Some women hire a sitter to help out while they work at home. The major advantages: They're near their children, they can handle crises and illnesses themselves, and they don't spend time and energy commuting every day.

Most companies must make significant changes to provide the type of flexibility career mothers need. For example, in 1990 only 10 percent of organizations with 10 or more employees provided such direct benefits as day care or financial assistance with child care (Rossman 1990).

Eliminating Pay Inequity

Pay inequity is endemic in our workforce, a huge problem that no leader could solve alone. However, you can become aware of the ways women have been discriminated against when it comes to pay. You can analyze the compensation packages of all the employees under your influence. And you can use your influence to eliminate inequities and to make sure that women and men receive fair compensation.

Leadership Challenge: Meeting Men's Needs

Men have their own issues that center around the profound changes occurring in the workplace and in society. As a leader, your challenge is to help meet the emerging needs of male employees. Here are some key men's needs we've discussed in this chapter:

- adapting to women's changing roles, including dealing with a sense of power loss and working for women managers
- achieving a more balanced work life–family life
- gaining more sensitivity to women's issues

Helping Men Adapt to the Changing Roles of Women

Helping men to adapt to change involves taking a leadership role regarding male-female relationships in general. It involves moving beyond gender stereotypes, and understanding women's concerns. If men are able to do this, they'll be better able to move beyond a sense of lost power and resentment over working with a woman as their manager. You as a business leader must also use your influence in managing affirmative action programs and managing diversity, so that men perceive these actions as fair and equitable to men as well as to women.

Demonstrating the advantages of equality in relationships. As a role model and coach you can help men understand the dramatic shifts in male-female relationships at work and at home. Help them to see the advantages of equality in relationships; for example:

- *Shared responsibility*, resulting in less stress for men because they now have help in making the decisions, earning the family income, and other responsibilities that can become burdensome and stressful.

- *More authentic communication* is a natural result of equality in relationships, as the research related to assertiveness training has shown.

- *Better relationships with women* can be built as aggressive tactics are replaced with assertive ones, since women are less likely to resort to passive-aggressive responses.

- *More freedom* to develop and express all facets of the self grows from going beyond the limited confines of stereotyped gender traits and roles.

Moving beyond gender stereotypes. Many men feel a loss of power, are concerned about reverse discrimination, and express difficulties in accepting a woman as their manager. Help men drop the old role stereotype about men's place and women's place. Take the lead in raising men's awareness of how such stereotypes limit men and unfairly block women. Speak up when you see men acting out the old myths and assumptions about women's traits, women's place, and women's limitations.

Gaining sensitivity to women's concerns and issues. You can help men become aware of women's concerns and issues—so men can do unto them as *they* would have men do unto them.

For example, men can learn to change sexist language, such as the use of "man" to mean all of us, "ladies" or "girls" instead of "women," too-personal terms such as "honey," "doll," or "babe." Through example and training, set a tone for treating women with the same professional respect as men.

Supporting Men in Achieving a More Balanced Work Life–Family Life

This challenge is related to helping men adapt to women's new demands. Most men feel a rising pressure to share housework and spend time with their children, since most mothers work outside the home. Men who were surveyed reported twice as many work-family conflicts in 1988 as in 1985. Conflicts include inability to find child care during overtime hours. But few men felt they could be honest with bosses about family demands and often make up excuses such as other meetings to attend. Leaders can show through their words and actions that men as well as women employees will receive understanding and support in balancing work life and family life. The most important message you can give is that they won't be taken off the fast track or considered marginal just because they express work-family concerns and accept corporate family-oriented benefits.

Be flexible about basing promotions on willingness to relocate. The days may be over when companies could insist that moving up the ladder meant moving around the country. In 1994 surveyed companies reported that 45 percent of employees turned down requests to relocate, citing family ties or spouse's employment as key reasons, up from 30 percent in 1986 (Farrell 1993). Leaders who are retaining good employees are adapting to their needs.

Leadership Opportunity: Supporting a Masculine–Feminine Balance in Corporate Culture

Changes in the American culture since the 1960s are now presenting us with great challenges and opportunities. You've been expanding your awareness of gender issues and developing skills for dealing with them. These expanded awarenesses and skills allow you and others to create more holistic, balanced organizations. Such organizations allow and encourage people to develop more of their talents and potentials and to use those talents to achieve personal and team goals.

Balancing Key Life Areas

The core gender issues, both social and professional, can only be addressed when women and men explore and create a partnership where professional and social relationships are managed out of respect for individual talents and needs and aligned with a common vision that includes more than profit making. Such a partnership balances caretaking and breadwinning and views social, emotional, and spiritual needs on a par with economic responsibility. Key areas that we can bring into balance in organizations include:

- men and women having the freedom to strike a balance between work and home

- an ability to move beyond woman as sex object and man as success object

- a balance of men and women taking paternity leaves and maternity leaves without the company stigmatizing them

- organizations that provide more flexible systems and benefits for both men and women, without stigmatizing those who take advantage of them.

Valuing Gender Differences

For many years women minimized their differences from men and stressed equality, in order to show that they could work as effectively as men and deserve equal treatment and rewards. The men who supported them tried not to notice this most noticeable of differences. Admitting one's differences in the American workplace has traditionally meant accepting inferiority.

We tend to jump to the conclusion that differences are either good or bad, rather than a source of interesting possibilities. Those who are different are commonly relegated to the edge of a work group. They may be devalued personally and their contributions ignored. Focusing on difference has been taboo because it generally led to subordination in the distribution of labor and effectively kept women from advancing in wages and promotions as most Euro-American men do. This is the tendency that a multicultural approach seeks to counteract.

Today's organizations, and those of the future, need a different mix of values, not only because women are present in larger numbers, but because of the ways work itself is changing in the age of the smart machine. Jobs require less muscle and motor skills and more information and people skills. While women continue to acquire many traditional male workplace skills, men must also now master things women have been taught to do well. What these are becomes clearer when we look at organizations run largely by women (Adler 1991). When women create their own corporate cultures by starting their own companies, the style that emerges is more democratic and less hierarchical, reflecting these values:

- the basic belief that allowing everyone to contribute and to feel powerful and important is good for employees and the organization
- the tendency to share power and information
- more emphasis on collaborative decision making
- more democratic, participative, consultative management
- more decentralization of decision making and responsibility
- greater concern with process and fairness
- more concern with quality of outcomes, while retaining a pragmatic concern for quantitative outcomes
- less autocratic, domineering, ego-involved management
- less concern with titles and formal authority, more concern with responsibility and responsiveness
- less concern for empire building, power and domination and less consciousness about one's turf

Women's leadership style also tends to shift the focus to people as the most important resource and the way to achieve higher quality and productivity, through emphasis on the following values:

- a greater responsiveness and concern for individual feelings, ideas, opinions, ambitions, and on and off the job satisfactions
- skill at enhancing other people's self-worth
- desire to get others excited about their work
- more emphasis on skills as a listener and conversationalist
- high value placed on loyalty, longevity, and interpersonal skills

This reads like a recipe for the ideal corporation of the 1990s and beyond. It represents a balance of masculine and feminine strengths, which would fit nicely in the new holistic organization.

SUMMARY

Women and men have traditionally been limited by stereotyped roles and traits that culture imposes upon them. The patriarchal system has taught babies from the cradle that people have unequal power and privilege, but marriage and family relationships are now moving toward greater equality. The cultural socialization of girls and boys has traditionally been distinctly different, so they grow into men and women who often have difficulty understanding each other's worlds and viewpoints. Research indicates that women tend to be more tentative, relationship oriented, and cooperative, while men tend to be more assertive, factual, competitive, and status oriented.

Since the 1960s a number of megatrends have resulted in major changes in women's roles. Most women now need to work, and they have greater opportunities in the workplace. Women now hold about 40 percent of management positions but less than 5 percent of top executive posts. Their pay at all levels tends to be about 30 percent less than men's pay. Women's major barriers are the external ones in the workplace, especially stereotyping and lack of support for their family demands. Some of the barriers are internal, due to socialization.

Many men are having difficulty adjusting to these major changes in virtually every area of their lives, from wives to children to work. Nearly half think they're losing power as a group. Many are no longer sure what "real men" are expected to do, nor what constitutes sexual harassment. Both men and women may experience a buildup of frustration from the pressures, demands, and uncertainties. A positive way to deal with all this is to develop both masculine and feminine strengths in order to become a more balanced person. Another strategy is to learn to interact with each other assertively, without being overly aggressive. Leaders can encourage men and women employees to achieve this balance and to move into an attitude of equality. As this occurs, a new holistic corporate culture can emerge, and in turn a better balanced society. Leaders can also focus on supporting men in adapting to gender changes in the workplace, supporting women in breaking stereotyped molds and achieving career success, and providing both with support to meet emerging family demands.

Skill Builder 4.1: The Case of New Mother Jessica

Jessica is the mother of an 18-month-old child. She is a loan officer with Trust Bank. Jessica had resigned from her previous job because the maternity leave was inadequate for her to make the adjustment to a new baby. When she went to work for Trust Bank, it was with the understanding that it would not be a high-pressure position—no expectation that she would work overtime or make business trips. However, Jessica is beginning to feel pressure to do just that.

Jessica approaches you, her manager, to tell you that she has decided she must resign in order to find a part-time job, about three days a week. She says, "My son needs more of my time and attention just now. I need to work, and I want to work, but I have decided to give his needs top priority for the next year or two."

- As Jessica's manager, what actions would you take now?

Skill Builder 4.2: Alicia Ruiz, Legal Assistant

Alicia Ruiz has been employed at Appleby Associates law firm for nearly a year. She's just been promoted from secretarial assistant to legal research assistant, and she loves her work. She gets along well with the lawyers and other assistants. The only ongoing problem she must cope with is her relationship with *Jake Barnes*, one of the law partners. Lately it's been pretty rough. Jake manages to find more and more opportunities to catch her alone and lean on her—at the water fountain, in the coffee room, and, worst of all, at the elevator in the evening. A couple of times Jake has really given Alicia a hard time, insisting that she come with him for a drink at the bar around the corner.

As a full partner, Jake is one of the most powerful men in the office, and Alicia doesn't want to turn him against her. Her way of dealing with it lately is to ask her friend *Joe* to wait for her so they can leave together, since they park in the same parking garage. She hopes that if she can avoid Jake for long enough, he'll give up.

Alicia's managing attorney, **Dale Hutchison**, is looking for a file of legal papers and remembers that he gave the file to Alicia. It's urgent that he get some information from the file at once, and Alicia's out of the office. Dale goes to her desk and finds the file on top. He can't avoid seeing a note that Alicia has written on the top sheet of her notepad:

> *"Hi, Could you wait for me again this evening? I'll leave at 5 and just take the work home with me. I don't want 'you-know-who' to catch me alone again. Yesterday when I was in the research library, he closed the door and started making disgusting remarks about "heaven between the sheets." Yuk!*

Dale is stunned. Who can Alicia be talking about? And why hasn't she told him she's having a problem with one of the guys? Back in his office, he can't get the incident off his mind. About 30 minutes later he arrives for a previously-scheduled meeting with one of the partners, *Tom Drake*. Since Dale is the first to arrive, he takes the opportunity to discuss the incident with Tom. They both agree that Alicia must file an internal complaint against her harasser.

Later that day, Dale finds time to speak privately with Alicia. "I don't mean to pry, Alicia, but when I was looking for the file on your desk, your note about being harassed was just there. The words just jumped out at me. You know, you don't have to put up with this kind of harassment—and you shouldn't. I'm just so sorry this is happening to you. Tom and I think you should file an internal complaint." Alicia is upset and angry. "Dale, you had no right to discuss this with management, especially without talking to me first. I don't want to bring a complaint. All I would do is make an enemy. It would be his word against mine, and I know who has the power around here!" She stopped, sorry that she had said as much as she had.

"Look, I'll stand behind you. You need to take action to stop this problem."

"I won't have my privacy invaded," said Alicia, "and that's that."

"But the company has to maintain an office that's free of sexual harassment, and as your manager, I'm supposed to report this. It's company policy."

"And I have too much at stake," said Alicia. "I like my job and I want to keep it. Stay out of it, Dale. Let me take care of it."

- What are the major issues here?
- What should Dale do?
- What should Alicia do?

Skill Builder 4.3: Minicases: Is This Sexual Harassment?

Purpose: To apply your knowledge of sexual harassment to specific cases.
Instructions: For each case, answer these questions:

- Do you think the actions constitute sexual harassment?
- If the person being harassed in each case brought a lawsuit, do you think he or she would win?
- If found guilty of harassment, what should happen to the harassers?
- Should the harasser be fired, suspended, reprimanded, or should nothing be done?

1. **A male supervisor** occasionally compliments his young assistant with remarks such as "You ought to wear short skirts more often" and "Sit and talk to me a little longer; I'm enjoying the view."

2. **A female doctor** is discharged from a medical residency program. She tries to understand what went wrong. She remembers that she did not react favorably to a supervising professor's invitation to go out for drinks, compliments about her hair and legs,

questions about her romantic life. He made comments that seemed to imply that he'd like to help her get through the program, but she sensed that going out with him would be part of the relationship. At first she tried to smile her way through these incidents. Later she gave disapproving looks or turned away. When he kept on, she finally told him one day that she was busy and abruptly walked away.

3. **A male journalist** willingly enters into a love affair with his female supervising editor. She has always rated his work performance as excellent. After a few months he breaks off the affair. At his next performance review, the journalist receives a less-than-satisfactory rating from her.

4. **Rosita,** an advertising copy writer, has been passed over for promotion. A colleague, Hazel, got the job. Rosita is sure Hazel is having an affair with the boss. Several times in the past year, the boss has gone on business trips which called for a copy writer to go along. Each time he took Hazel instead of Rosita, even though in at least one instance Rosita was the one who had done most of the work on the account he was calling on. Rosita has heard talk from other employees. Rumor has it this is not the first affair the boss has had, nor the first time he has promoted a girl friend.

Skill Builder 4.4: Recognizing Assertiveness

Purpose: To apply your knowledge of assertiveness training.

Instructions: Indicate whether you think each response to each of the following situations is assertive, aggressive, or nonassertive.

1. At a meeting, someone interrupts when you're speaking. You say,
    a. Excuse me. I'd like to finish my statement.
    b. Oh, excuse me.
    c. You know, it's rude to interrupt like that.

2. You enjoyed a co-worker's presentation. You say,
    a. See you back at the salt mine.
    b. Thanks for your presentation; it gave me a lot of new ideas.
    c. Well, *that's* over!

3. Your women's advocacy group has been trying to get better maternity benefits. A co-worker says, " What do you women want anyway?" You answer,
    a. To put chauvinists like you in their place.
    b. I don't get involved in these things.
    c. Fairness and equality.

4. You've been called several times by the same salesperson trying to sell you magazines. This time you say
    a. Would you please not call me again?
    b. You're a disgusting jackass. Why don't you take a flying leap.
    c. This is the third time I've been disturbed, and each time I've told you that I'm not interested. If you call again, you leave me no choice but to report this to the authorities.

5. Asking your boss for a raise, you begin,
    a. Aaah, do you think that you could see your way clear to giving me a raise?
    b. I've been overworked around here for too long, and I'm overdue for a raise.
    c. I'd like to go over this list of extra projects I've completed and work I've reorganized to produce more with less time and money. . . .

REFERENCES

AAUW. *The AAUW Report: How Schools Shortchange Girls*. Washington DC: American Association of University Women, 1992.

Adler, Nancy, and D.N. Izraeli, eds. *Women in Management Worldwide*. Armonk, NY: M.E. Sharpe, Inc., 1988.

Blinder, Martin. *Choosing Lovers*. New York: Avon, 1987.

Bly, Robert. *Iron John: A Book About Men*. New York: Random House, 1992.

Carr-Ruffino, Norma. *The Promotable Woman*. Belmont, CA: Wadsworth, 1993.

Carr-Ruffino, Norma. "U.S. Women: Breaking Through the Glass Ceiling." *Women in Management Review* 6, no. 5, 1991.

Carroll, Jerry. "The Secrets of Young Girls." *San Francisco Chronicle* (August 31, 1994): E-1.

Cherry, Robert. *Discrimination: Its Economic Impact on Blacks, Women, and Jews*. Lexington, MA: Lexington Books, 1989.

Chin, Steven. "50,000 at Oakland Rally Just for Men." *San Francisco Chronicle*, October 1, 1995.

Crane, F.G. and Susan DeYoung. "Attitudes to Portrayal of Women in Advertising." *International Journal of Advertising* (1992): 251.

Dominick, Joseph, and Gail Rauch. "The Image of Women in Network TV Commercials." *Journal of Broadcasting* (summer 1972): 259.

Eagly, Alice H. *Sex Differences in Social Behavior*. Hillsdale, NJ: Lawrence Erlbaum Associates, 1987.

Eisen, Jerry. *Powertalk!* New York: Simon & Schuster, 1984.

Evatt, Chris. *He & She*. Berkeley, CA: Conari Press, 1992.

Faludi, Susan. *Backlash: The Undeclared War Against American Women*. New York: Crown, 1991.

Farrell, Walter. *The Myth of Male Power*. New York: Simon & Schuster, 1993.

Fausto-Sterling, Anne. *Myths of Gender*. New York: Basic Books, 1985.

Female Executive. Report on sexual harassment survey, 1992.

Ferguson, Andrew. "America's New Man." *The American Spectator* (January 1992): 26–33.

Fischman, J. "The Character of Controversy." *Psychology Today* (December 1988).

Gates, David. "White Male Paranoia." *Newsweek* (March 29, 1993): 48–54.

Gove, Walter R. *A Biopsychosocial Perspective*. Vanderbilt University, 1985.

Hamilton, A. and P.A. Veglahn. "Sexual Harassment: The Hostile Work Environment." *Cornell HRA Quarterly*, 33 (1992): 88–92.

Howard, J., P. Blumstein, and Pepper Schwartz. "Sex, Power, and Influence Tactics in Intimate Relationships." *Journal of Personality and Social Psychology*, 51 (July 1986): 102–109.

Jacobs, M.A. "Men's Club." *Wall Street Journal* (June 9, 1994): A1.

Kanter, R.M. *Men and Women of the Corporation*. New York: Basic Books, 1979.

Keen, Sam. *Fire in the Belly*. New York: Bantam Books, 1991.

Kenton, S.B. and D. Valentine. *CrossTalk*. Cincinnati, OH: South-Western, 1996.

L.A. Times. "Orange Juice War Against Bad Ideas." *Los Angeles Times* (August 14, 1994): M5.

"Patriarchy: What Is It?" *Men's Council Journal*, special issue 17, May 1993.

Morrison, Ann, R.P. White, and E. Van Velsor. *Breaking the Glass Ceiling*. Reading, MA: Addison-Wesley, 1987.

Naisbett, John, and P. Aburdene. *Megatrends 2000*. New York: Wm. Morrow, 1990.

Naisbett, John. *Megatrends*. New York: Warner Books, 1982.

Peplau, L.A. "Lesbian and Gay Relationships." *Homosexuality: Research Implications for Public Policy*. Thousand Oaks, CA: Sage, 1991.

Rossman, Marlene L. *The International Businesswoman of the 1990s*. Westport, CT: Greenwood Press, 1990.

Russell, A.M. "Women Vs. Men: Where We Stand Today." *Working Woman* (January 1991): 66.

Speer, Robert. "What's New with Men?" *Chico News & Review*, April 16, 1993.

Tannen, Deborah. *You Just Don't Understand*. New York: Wm. Morrow, 1990.

Tanner, M. Scot. Expert on Chinese politics. *Business Week*, 1994.

Time. "Indecent Exposure: The Navy Takes a Heavy Rap in the Tailhook Report on Sexual Harassment." *Time*, 141 (May 3, 1993): 20–21.

Trost. "Firms Heed Women Employees' Needs. *Wall Street Journal*. (November 22, 1990): B1.

U.S. Census Bureau. "We the American Women." U.S. Department of Commerce, 1993.

U.S. Census Bureau. "Current Population Reports, Male–Female Differences." U.S. Department of Commerce, 1987.

U.S. Census Bureau. "Current Population Reports, Average Earnings of Year-Round Fulltime Workers by Sex and Educational Attainment." U.S. Department of Commerce, 1991.

U.S. Women's Bureau, Department of Labor. "Facts on Working Women." 1990, 1992, 1993.

U.S. Department of Labor. *The Glass Ceiling Initiative*. 1991.

Vanneman, Reeve, and Lynn Weber Cannon. *The American Perception of Class*. Philadelphia: Temple University Press, 1987.

Wilson, William Julius. *The Declining Significance of Race*. Chicago: University of Chicago Press, 1978.

Wilson, William Julius. *The Truly Disadvantaged*. Chicago: University of Chicago Press, 1987.

Working Woman. "How the Men in Your Office Really See You." *Working Woman* (November 1991): 101–103.

WSJ. Report on how men are dealing with women managers, *Wall Street Journal*, 1991.

Zilbergeld, Bernie. Statement by Berkeley psychologist, expert on men's groups, 1993.

CHAPTER 5

Working with African Americans

*Negroes not only raised doubts about the white man's value system
but aroused the troubling suspicion that whatever else the true American is,
he is also somehow black.* Ralph Ellison

About 12 percent of Americans are African American, or one in eight. All of us, including African Americans, can benefit from raising our awareness of this subculture that has contributed so much to the American whole. You'll learn more about the myths and realities; the background of slavery, prejudice, and civil rights struggles; and the current phenomenon of a rising middle class and a struggling underclass. You'll explore the cultural patterns of the African American community—such as typical values and customs that help explain African Americans' styles and their issues. All this will prepare you to understand and manage the leadership challenges and opportunities this group presents, from building on their strengths to supporting them at each career phase. First, check your attitudes and knowledge by completing Self-Awareness Activities 5.1 and 5.2.

Self-Awareness Activity 5.1: What Do You Believe About African Americans?

Purpose:
- to get in touch with your beliefs and stereotypes about this group of people
- to experience how judgmental beliefs affect your thinking and feeling processes
- to experience the ways in which your beliefs create your reality regarding other persons, even before you have any interaction with them.

Part I. What Do You Believe About African American women?

Step 1. Associations
- Relax as deeply as you can: close your eyes and taking a few deep breaths.
- Focus on the words "African American woman" and allow a mental picture to come up in your mind's eye.
- Notice the words and images that come to mind as you "see" this woman.
- Open your eyes and list 10 to 20 words in the order in which they occur to you.

- Review your list. Mark a plus beside the words that are positive, a minus beside the words that are negative, and a circle beside neutral words.

Step 2. Negative Associations

- Close your eyes and focus again on the image of the African American woman. Formulate a negative opinion or judgment, perhaps one you typically hold about African American women.
- Notice your *feelings* as you see the person in this negative way. What *thoughts* come up as you focus on the image?
- Write a few sentences about your feelings and thoughts.

Step 3. Positive Associations

- Formulate a positive opinion or judgment, perhaps one you typically hold about African American women.
- Notice your *feelings* as you see the person in this positive way. What *thoughts* come up as you focus on the image?
- Write a few sentences about your feelings and thoughts.

Step 4. Insights

- Focus on the differences between your experiences when you hold negative and positive judgments or opinions. What were the differences? What meaning does this have for you, for your beliefs and feelings about people from this group, and about beliefs in general?
- Write your responses in a few sentences; include anything you like about your feelings, thoughts, and insights.

Part II. Experimenting with Opinions About African American Men

Repeat the phases and steps in Part I, this time focusing on the image of an African American man.

Self-Awareness Activity 5.2: What Do You Know About African Americans?

Purpose: To see what you know about the issues covered in this chapter.

Instructions: Determine whether you think the following statements are basically true or false—and why. The answers will emerge in this chapter, and the summary at the end of the chapter focuses on these issues.

1. The Civil Rights Act of 1964 was a result of liberal Democrats' demands, led by Kennedy and Johnson.
2. Since the civil rights measures have been in force, African Americans have dramatically increased their status.
3. The best predictor of both school grades and SAT scores is ethnicity.
4. Significant numbers of African American managers and professionals are leaving corporate jobs due to the glass ceiling that prevents their advancement.
5. African Americans focus primarily on group expression rather than individual expression.
6. African American communication style tends to be more impersonal and cool than Euro-American style.
7. Most African Americans need assertiveness training to be most effective in American corporate cultures.

MYTHS AND FACTS

Most of the myths African Americans must deal with stem from the legacy of slavery and segregation that is unique to this American subculture. In order to justify slavery, a practice so incompatible with the American ideals of human freedom and equality, majority members created the most degrading stereotypes of Africans. Such beliefs are passed along from generation to generation and die hard. Although the proportion of Euro-Americans that hold the more extreme stereotypes is continually eroding, responses to a 1990 survey by the National Opinion Research Center indicate the following beliefs are still held by the majority (Thornton and Whitman 1992):

- Are they more violent than whites? Yes, 63 percent
- Are they less intelligent? Yes, 53 percent
- Are they more likely to prefer to live off welfare? Yes, 78 percent
- Do they blame everyone, but themselves for their problems? Yes, 57 percent

Myth: African Americans are more violent than others.

One basis for this myth is African Americans' preference for using direct confrontation to resolve a conflict. Most Euro-Americans, Asian Americans and Latino Americans prefer more indirect methods. African American behavior is therefore often seen as hostile and militant when it's not. This is reinforced by—and reinforces—the stereotype of African Americans as prone to violence (Foeman and Pressley 1987; Kitano 1976; Hall 1976).

Another aspect is the greater likelihood that police will arrest African American men, and that the legal system will prosecute them, as compared with Euro-American men. Numerous studies have established this type of discrimination. High-level African American business executives report that even when they're in their business suits, shop clerks tend to trail them, apparently fearing they'll shoplift. Finding a cab driver who will stop for them is almost impossible, and they're often harassed by police, who say they "fit the profile" of drug dealers and thieves (WSJ 1992).

The violent stereotype extends to the ways people communicate, often creating barriers to understanding. For example, ghetto language tends to push the emotional buttons of Euro-Americans, who associate it only with African Americans and often with implied threats of violence. There's almost a gut reaction to it, and listeners tend to discount what the speaker is saying.

African American managers and professionals cite the unfairness of this myth. One ad executive said, "I keep coming up against this stereotype of me as a guy with an undercurrent of anger that's always running just under the surface, ready to erupt." A college official said, "I've been accused of having a chip on my shoulder—many times. Maybe I do, but after all, we've been disparaged and degraded by whites every day of our lives; then we're put down for being angry about it." Another manager objected, "I'm not angry; I worked all that out years ago. I just have a different way of debating an issue, which some of these managers think is angry."

Myth: African Americans are less intelligent than others.

Recent studies indicate that school grades and grades on the SAT exam depend more on socioeconomic status than any other factor, including ethnicity. Children from low-income households, often with no father around, and whose parents have low educational achievement, tend to make lower grades. As socioeconomic status goes up, so do grades, as discussed in the Current Profile section of this chapter and presented in Table 5.6.

In the workplace and elsewhere, Euro-Americans tend to assume that even highly intelligent African Americans are less competent. An experimental study by Blanchard and Crosby (1989) indicates that when it comes to Euro-American men helping each other, the other man's ability was the determining factor, not the fact that the man was Euro-American. But when it comes to helping African American men, their ethnicity, not their ability, is the major determining factor. How can people rationalize not responding positively to competent African Americans? Follow-up evaluations indicate that Euro-Americans' behaviors may have been influenced by their perceptions of the relative intelligence or competence of others. Their ratings indicated that they accepted high-ability Euro-American teammates as being somewhat more intelligent than themselves, but they described even high-ability African American teammates as significantly less intelligent than themselves. Identical patterns of results were revealed for helping and competence ratings in a subsequent study using Euro-American women rather than African American men as the partners (Dovidio and Gaertner 1983).

Myth: African Americans are lazy and irresponsible.

As a matter of fact, about the same proportion of African Americans as Euro-Americans hold jobs, as discussed in detail in the Current Profiles section. Such stereotypes as "lazy, irresponsible, stupid" have typically created the perception among business persons that African Americans are low-productivity workers and likely to prefer welfare to working. The effect of course was to intensify the extent of job discrimination. As a result, African Americans became concentrated in jobs of low skill, low social status, low responsibility, and low pay—and in fields that require little education. Closed doors to better jobs made it appear fruitless to invest in higher education—until civil rights measures opened some doors (Young 1977).

Researchers have found that many Euro-Americans indicate they don't view people from these other groups as bad or as worse than themselves. Yet they do see themselves as better—a subtle difference. For example, in one study Euro-Americans did not rate African Americans as more lazy than Euro-Americans, but they evaluated Euro-Americans as more ambitious than African Americans. In other studies, negative characteristics were equally associated with African Americans and Euro-Americans, but positive characteristics were more associated with Euro-Americans (Gaertner and McLaughlin 1984; Sigall & Page 1971; Mayer and Schvaneveldt 1971; Rosch 1975).

The "lazy" and "incompetent" stereotypes are the two most frustrating for many aspiring managers and professionals. For one thing, many of them say they're permitted a much narrower range of behavioral styles to achieve their goals than their Euro-American peers. They also become quite frustrated when they perceive they must work twice as hard and must stay in a position longer than necessary—just to prove they're *not* lazy and incompetent and that they *can* handle the next assignment. This stereotype extends to the assumption by Euro-American colleagues that nearly all African Americans are incompetent to handle higher-level responsibilities.

The "irresponsible" stereotype often translates into limited perceptions of the jobs African Americans are fit to fill. Wherever they go, African American managers are often assumed to be sales clerks, waiters, or other entry-level or menial workers. Social interactions that they enjoy with their colleagues at work may disappear outside the office, where co-workers often literally don't recognize them on the street when they're not in corporate uniform (WSJ 1992).

Myth: They blame everyone else for their problems.

About one-third of the African American population is now considered part of the hardworking, tax-paying, responsible middle class. Obviously these African Americans are not stuck in a victim mentality. On the other hand, the cycle of entrapment, degradation, and poverty that is the legacy of slavery and segregation creates huge barriers for most who are caught in it. To demand help from one's society and government to break out seems a reasonable strategy to many African American leaders. Virtually all of them call for a combination of external assistance from society and internal bootstrap efforts on the part of underclass individuals.

Myth: Many African Americans are cocky troublemakers.

Most people in the African American community believe in speaking up assertively, especially about perceived injustices. Being genuine, expressing the feelings you are feeling, and directly confronting issues are all highly valued and typical patterns in the African American community. During the days of legal and open discrimination and oppression, African Americans did not dare to express these values outside the community, but younger generations tend to feel it's important to be genuine in all situations. The point is that expressions interpreted as cocky and troublemaking by persons outside the community may not be meant that way nor seen that way by African Americans.

A UNIQUE LEGACY OF PREJUDICE

Of all the ethnic groups in the U.S., African Americans have traditionally faced the greatest obstacles, which are built on the foundation of entrenched prejudice and discrimination. Business leaders need some background information about the specifics of this form of ethnic prejudice, how it still affects African Americans, and some typical Euro-American rationalizations around it.

What's in a Name?

Race and *racism.* In 1930 less than 25 percent of African Americans were of unmixed descent, according to a respected anthropologist (Herskovitz 1930). The Census Bureau has concurred with that estimate. Prior to the 1960s it was illegal for African Americans and Euro-Americans to marry, and yet nearly 75 percent of African Americans had Euro-American ancestors due to sexual unions outside marriage. It's likely that today the percentage of "unmixed" African Americans is much smaller. The large majority of African Americans are probably as far from the pure Negroid type as from the average Caucasoid type. Because of this fact, even though *race* is the basis for much prejudice and discrimination, we'll use the terms *ethnic group* and *ethnic prejudice* and avoid the terms *race* and *racism.*

The African American Burden

The burden of inequality placed upon African Americans in the U.S. has been the outstanding cultural contradiction in American history. African Americans grow up a part of, yet apart from, American society, in it but not of it, included at some levels and excluded at others. This duality is at the heart of the identity struggle and often generates powerful feelings of frustration, anger, and indignation. It is further complicated by their bicultural value systems, worldviews, and historical legacies. They must try to set up a workable balance between African American and Euro-American values within their lives. Completely denying either one will restrict their life choices. If they focus only on individualism, competition, emotional insulation, power, dominance, and control, they may achieve success but they'll pay a price. If they focus only on genuineness, mutual aid, the collective good, and emotional closeness, they'll enjoy inclusion in the African American community but are unlikely to achieve economic success in the workplace. (Baldwin 1992). W.E.B. Du Bois (1965, 215) described this dual cultural background as:

> . . . *this double consciousness, this sense of always looking at one's self through the eyes of others, of measuring one's soul by the tape of a world that looks on in amused contempt and pity. One ever feels his twoness—an American, a Negro; two souls, two thoughts, two unreconciled strivings; two warring ideals in one dark body, whose dogged strength alone keeps it from being torn asunder.*

Euro-Americans and African Americans operate with different definitions of ethnic prejudice. Euro-Americans tend to define ethnic prejudice narrowly as "explicit, consciously held beliefs in ethnic superiority." African Americans define it more broadly as a "set of practices and institutions that result in the oppression of a group of people" (Lichtenberg 1992). African Americans say ethnic prejudice is still their principal challenge to moving up in many firms. They say top managements look for "safe blacks" to develop and promote and are less willing to take the same risks with African Americans as they take with Euro-American males (R. Thomas 1991).

The Euro-American Rationalizations

How have we made this inequality compatible with our basic belief that all persons are created equal? The most bigoted Euro-Americans rationalized their ethnic prejudice—and a history of slavery—by denying the humanness of African Americans, viewing them as subhuman and therefore not "persons who are created equal." The less bigoted rationalized prejudice by supporting the "separate but equal" doctrine that provided the basis for segregation through the first half of the twentieth century, ignoring the fact that *separate* for African Americans was far from *equal*. At a more personal, emotional level, many Euro-Americans simply ignored the issue, as if African Americans did not exist (Stewart 1972).

Pettigrew and Martin (1987) determined that more Euro-Americans are against ethnic prejudice than are for it. The problem lies with the great majority who simply go along with the old myths and stereotypes. The specific proportions are:

- 15 percent extremely prejudiced toward African Americans
- 60 percent conforming bigots, reflecting the ethnic ideology of the larger society
- 25 percent against ethnic prejudice in ideology and behavior

Pettigrew and Martin (1987) concluded that persons in the extreme group were motivated largely by authoritarian personality needs. They found that the persons in the antiprejudice category tend to consistently support rights for African Americans. More recent studies also indicate that most Euro-American adults increasingly reject ethnic injustice in principle but remain reluctant to accept and act on measures necessary to eliminate the injustice (Ponterotto and Pedersen 1993). African American leaders often refer to this as the majority's weak will to implement real change.

Robert Terry (1990) points out two current ways that many Euro-Americans rationalize their ethnic prejudice.

- "We're all just people. I'm just a human being first and foremost." The hidden meaning is, "I don't have to take responsibility for what the dominant majority has done and is doing if I ignore my ethnicity and affirm my humanity."

- "I never even notice anyone's color or ethnicity. I believe we should be color-blind. I don't even think of you as Black," implying that if people mention someone's color, they're being racist.

The fact is that Euro-Americans have traditionally been privileged in this culture. And American culture is color conscious. Most people tend to sort others by color, to the advantage of some and detriment of others. African Americans don't have the luxury of ignoring color consciousness. Euro-Americans can choose to ignore what their ingroup has done and how they all continue to benefit from it, but that does nothing toward changing the facts.

When Euro-Americans feel the need to tell African Americans that they don't think about their color, they bring color into the picture. If color isn't important, why comment on it? Let's say Jane Doe makes such a comment to an African American co-worker. If Jane really means, "You're so white in color or in the way you act that I forget about your color," then she's not being color-blind but is absorbing blackness into whiteness. If she means, "I don't discriminate on the basis of color," then she's still not being color-blind but is trying to find a way to express her concern for racial justice.

The bottom line: Valuing diversity means acknowledging and appreciating *all* the differences, including skin color, and moving beyond using physical features as the measure of a person's worth.

SLAVERY, THE CIVIL WAR, AND THE AFTERMATH

In a 1994 television interview Marie Davis, an officer of the National Association for the Advancement of Colored People (NAACP), said:

> There's a perception among white Americans that time has erased slavery's effect. Many people think this was thousands of years ago, but it wasn't really that long ago.

Davis recalled that her grandfather was born into slavery and freed at the end of the Civil War, when he was still a toddler. She says slavery and the prejudice around it caused most Euro-Americans to accept the myth that African Americans are inferior, almost another species. The prejudice that is the legacy of slavery affects virtually all of us today. Davis gave an example:

> *Recently my granddaughter came to me, crying because she is black. I never dreamed my granddaughter would be crying like that. Then I cried, too, because I knew what she was going through. I remembered the many times I had cried as a child, cried because I was so hurt.*

Slavery: Setting the Stage for Segregation

During and just after America's colonial years, about four million Africans were brought over and made slaves. For 250 years most Africans in this country were slaves; for 150 years they have been free. Slavery had a deep and lasting effect that is clearly present today. Slavery was the culture of our African American neighbors' great grandparents, a culture that affected every aspect of their family life, beliefs about self and the world, hopes and expectations.

The culture of slavery also affected everyone else in the U.S. at the time, and most Euro-American's great-grandparents inevitably handed down the interconnecting beliefs about privilege, inequality, and prejudice—by their attitudes and actions, if not by their verbal teachings. Slavery laid the foundation for the prejudice and discrimination that African Americans must cope with today—and for the resulting social problems their leaders are working to overcome.

It began in Virginia, the first colony, which set the pattern for slavery throughout all the colonies where large cash crops were raised, primarily on the plantations of the South. By 1691 laws affecting the slaves:
- prohibited the freeing of slaves unless they were transported out of the colony
- outlawed mixed marriages
- declared that the children of mixed unions would be considered black slaves.

The few free Africans were denied the right to vote, hold office, or testify in court. The African segment of the Virginia population increased to 40 percent by 1750 (Vaughan 1989).

By the time of the Civil War, 1860, about 35 percent of all people in the South were African slaves, and only 5.5 percent were slaveholders. Most slaves provided the essential labor for raising cotton, tobacco, rice, sugar, and hemp. Kept illiterate and ignorant, they were typically told they were incapable of caring for themselves. Most slaveholders liked to picture themselves as kind masters taking care of docile, happy slaves. In reality, many owners were terrified by the threat of slave rebellion. And many slaves wore masks of docility and deference in order to hide subversive plans (Harding 1980; Takaki 1993).

For African American women, slavery held special horrors. They worked in the fields and factories just as the men did, but many masters viewed them as "breeders" and the only legal source of more slaves after importation of slaves was outlawed in 1808. Their children were not even their own, for the laws allowed masters to separate slave children from their mothers and sell them. And many slave women were used to satisfy the sexual desires of their masters. If these rapes resulted in pregnancy, the woman and her child were likely to be sold off and thus separated from friends and loved ones. Few masters would allow their offspring by a slave to stay around for them and their wives to see every day (Harding 1980; Takaki 1993).

The few slaves who managed to escape headed north toward freedom. But freedom in northern society was only a facade for the reality of caste. African Americans in the North faced segregation, prejudice, discrimination, and violence. They were excluded from the skilled and professional jobs and could find only menial labor. The North was certainly not the promised land of their dreams.

Self-Awareness Activity 5.3: How Does It Feel to Be Trapped?

Purpose: To find common ground with the people who have the experience of being trapped.

Step 1. The situation. You've read about the experience of African slaves in the U.S. They lived constantly with at least two major dilemmas: entrapment and degradation. They were trapped in situations that provided no real personal freedom and almost no alternatives. They were told in many ways that they were inferior. Can you think of a situation in which you felt similarly trapped and/or degraded—physically, emotionally, or psychologically? Write a brief paragraph describing the situation.

Step 2. Thoughts and feelings. Remember how you felt. What were some of the feelings? What were some of your thoughts? Write a brief paragraph about your feelings and thoughts at that time.

Step 3. Common ground. Can you imagine what feelings and thoughts you might have had if you were a slave living on a southern plantation around 1800? Write a brief paragraph about the feelings and thoughts that come to mind.

After Slavery: Free but Segregated

Soon after the Civil War, the African American's life in the South resembled their cousin's life in the North. The major difference was that segregation was de facto in the North and legal in the South. By the 1890s, laws provided for the "Negro's place" in neighborhoods, parks, schools, hotels, hospitals, restaurants, streetcars, theaters, and hospitals. In 1896 the Supreme Court said that such "separate but equal" segregation was constitutional. But African Americans knew that separate was never equal for them. When laws didn't keep African Americans in their "place," vigilantes did. Every year hundreds of African Americans who "stepped out of line" in some way were lynched. In 1909 the NAACP became the first African American organization with the ability to fight for justice in American courts, but its power was very limited.

During World War II there was a mass migration of African Americans from the farms and towns of the South to the cities of the North and West. Even though there was an acute worker shortage, African Americans initially were excluded from skilled jobs in the defense industry. African American labor leaders threatened to march on Washington, and President Roosevelt issued an executive order with the goal of "eliminating racial, ethnic, and religious discrimination in defense industries and in government." By 1945 more than 8 percent of all defense workers were African American. The war resulted in more industrial and occupational diversification for African Americans than had occurred in the 75 preceding years (McWilliams 1964).

Pulled by the employment opportunities in New York, Detroit, Los Angeles, San Francisco, and other urban areas, more than half a million African Americans left the South. At the outset of World War II, 75 percent of them lived in the South, and by 1970 only 50 percent were there. Over 80 percent of the ones who left went to urban areas, mainly to inner cities. This movement triggered violent backlashes, sometimes exploding into ethnic riots. When the war ended, author Maya Angelou wondered, "Can we make it through the peace?" But there would be no turning back to the old ethnic order (Takaki 1993).

The Movement Toward True Equality

Actual desegregation did not begin until the African American community began waging an open battle against oppression, now known as the Civil Rights movement. This nonviolent movement led directly to the civil rights laws of the 1960s, and the battle against oppression is still being waged today.

The simple action that ignited and united an entire community, and beyond, occurred in 1955 in Montgomery, Alabama. Rosa Parks boarded a city bus and later refused to give up her seat to a "white man," as city law required and as the bus driver demanded. Such resistance was not new, but the nation's response to it was. Her arrest led to an explosive protest and boycott of the bus system, led by Martin Luther King, Jr. One year later the court ordered the desegregation of the bus system. African Americans saw that they could transform their situation, and they felt a new sense of confidence.

In 1960 African American students declared a sit-in at a Woolworth's lunch counter, and in 1961 African American and Euro-American "freedom riders" rode together in buses throughout the South to protest segregation. Many were yanked from the buses and brutally beaten by mobs, sometimes before television cameras. In 1963 the conscience of the nation was galvanized by the famous March on Washington. Hundreds of thousands of marchers from all ethnic groups gathered in front of the Lincoln Memorial. As millions watched the event on television, Martin Luther King, Jr., gave his famous "I have a dream" speech.

CURRENT PROFILE

Business leaders need to be aware that a successful African American middle class has grown in tandem with an increasingly troubled underclass. Nearly one-third are considered in the middle class, but nearly one-third live in poverty, with the other third somewhere in between. We'll look at the interplay of this phenomenon with African American family income, career progress, entrepreneurship, and educational issues.

The Middle-Class/UnderClass Phenomenon

A central feature of African American progress since the 1960s is the simultaneous growth of the middle class and an underclass. Civil rights measures led to distinct improvement and upward mobility for many African Americans. The middle class began growing dramatically. On the other hand, the really poor tended to get poorer. The middle class began moving up and to the suburbs, earning more, sending their children to college, and living better. Meanwhile, the underclass began sinking further into intergenerational poverty, with increasing unemployment rates for young men and a dramatic rise in female-headed families. In 1990 about 27 percent of African Americans lived in the suburbs, while 57 percent lived in central cities, perhaps a fair indication of the proportionate sizes of the middle class and the less affluent.

The Growing Middle Class

Nearly one-third of African Americans are considered middle class. The emergence of a distinct African American middle class was reported in *Time* magazine in 1989. About one-third of all African American households had incomes of $35,000 or more (compared with 70 percent of all Euro-American households) in 1988. African American families living in the suburbs doubled from 13 percent in 1967 to 27 percent in 1990. Some of these people had parents and grandparents who achieved some success as entrepreneurs and professionals serving the African American community. Others somehow broke out of the poverty cycle to go through doors of opportunity opened by civil rights programs.

Closely related to socioeconomic status is home ownership. African American families who get "out of the projects" and foster "pride of ownership" in their children tend to escape the vicious cycle of drugs and crime that plague the ghetto. By 1990, 43 percent of African American families owned their homes, compared with 68 percent of Euro-Americans. The proportion has remained fairly stable for the past 20 years. The median value of the African American homes was $50,700, compared with $80,200 for Euro-American home owners.

During the 1970s and 1980s more and more industries left the cities for the suburbs, and so did more and more Euro-American families, followed by some of the new middle-class African American families. This combination of societal forces has been a major factor in the expansion of the underclass neighborhoods in the central cities. The suburban rings around cities are symbols not only of post-industrialism but also of ethnic and class exclusiveness in a traditionally segmented society. "White flight" refers to the Euro-American tendency to get away from the problems of urban living, including desegregation and other diversity issues, by moving to the exclusive "white" suburbs. Their gradual opening to African American middle-class families is a positive feature, but many of these families report feeling isolated and rejected by their Euro-American neighbors. Many say they feel estranged from the friends and families they left behind in the impoverished inner cities (Billingsley 1992).

These successful middle-class families tend to have a reverence for learning second only to their reverence for the spiritual, according to African American author Andrew Billingsley (1992). They tend to have their origins in the working class, generally in the previous generation. Most are still first-generation middle class. They tend to be more dependent than independent, more employees of others than owners and managers, and have relatively little accumulated wealth. Still, as Billingsley says, the African American middle class is "a major achievement sustained by education, two earners, extended families, religion, and service to others." Reporter Isabel Wilkerson of the *New York Times* reported in November 1990 that, "Two main things tend to distinguish black middle-class people from middle-class whites. One is the likelihood that many more of their relatives will come to them for help. The other is that they tend to lack the resources of people who started life in the middle class."

A Growing Underclass

Back in the inner city, at the other end of the scale, are increasing numbers of African Americans who are still trapped in poverty. Between 1960 and 1980 the percentage of inner-city poor families doubled, from 20 to 40 percent, compared to a small increase from 8 to 12 percent for all Euro-American families. African Americans were only 12 percent of the American population in 1980, but 43 percent of all welfare families. In fact, in 1990, 50 percent of all African American children under age 6 were living in poverty, most without fathers. Median family income ratio for African Americans as compared to Euro-Americans rose during the 1970s but has since decreased, as shown in Table 5.1.

TABLE 5.1: Median Family Income Ratios, 1960–1990

Median Family Income	1960	1970	1980	1990
Ratio: African American to Euro-American	55%	65%	58%	56%

Source: U.S. Bureau of the Census, 1993.

In 1980 the official poverty rate for all African American families was just under 26 percent, almost the same as in 1990. For Euro-Americans it was 9 percent in 1980 and 10 percent in 1990. But as Table 5.2 implies, there are differences in the patterns of African American women's lives as compared to the men.

TABLE 5.2: African American Median Income and Poverty Rate, Married and Single, 1990

	All African American families	Married couple families	Female headed families
Median income	$22,430	$33,540	$12,250
Poverty rate*	26.3%	11.0%	44.5%

Source: U.S. Bureau of the Census, 1993.
*40% of all African American children under age 16, and 32% of persons over age 65
  lived in poverty.

Why has the underclass grown despite government efforts to the contrary? Between 1960 and 1980, huge numbers of baby boomers entered the work force, and unemployment more than doubled from 2.6 million in 1968 to 7.6 million in 1980, pushing families of the unemployed onto welfare rolls, which grew from 1.4 million to 3.5 million. In 1980 about 72 percent of the African American men between ages 20 and 24 were either unemployed or earning poverty wages, compared to only 16 percent of Euro-American men this age. Those who lost their jobs were often the most recently hired in a company and frequently those with lower educational attainment.

For African American women, the problem of welfare dependency also resulted from gender inequality in the labor market. Nearly all women were crowded into female-dominated occupations, such as low-wage clerical and sales jobs, making it difficult or impossible for mothers to eke living expenses *and* child care costs out of their meager salaries.

Intensifying the middle-class/underclass disparity, the movement of plants and offices to the suburbs since the 1960s has isolated African American workers from many places of employment. African Americans have also been suffering from the effects of the "deindustrialization of America," with plants relocating to low-wage countries, such as Mexico and Korea.

The loss of blue-collar jobs hit African American men especially hard, because they were concentrated in the smokestack industries, such as automobile, rubber, and steel. Nearly 68 percent of the African American men caught in the 1980–1985 round of layoffs were unable to find comparable jobs. The plant shutdowns and economic relocations help explain why African Americans have been losing ground and why many of them have sunk into poverty. Many of the jobs available to young African Americans are in the fast-food services such as Burger King and McDonald's—dead-end minimum wage jobs.

The news media and politicians are doing an impressive job of highlighting the problems of the African American underclass, such as male drug pushers and welfare mothers. The public is quite aware of these issues. However, to focus so heavily on the problems tends to obscure the incredible successes of fully one-third of African Americans who have overcome the most onerous and entrenched barriers in American society to secure a place in the middle class. A focus on the African American strengths behind this major achievement would be productive. In the Leadership section of this chapter we'll do just that.

Career Progress

The U.S. Labor Department recently predicted that African-Americans will be about 22 percent of new workers entering the work force in the 1990s, even though the proportion of Americans who are African American is only 12 percent. From 1900 to 1970 the proportion of African Americans in the population consistently hovered around 10 to 11 percent, so such an increase would be an anomaly. One explanation may be the tendency for children of the expanded middle class to become employed. African Americans are increasingly moving into better-paying occupations, but there is still a significant pay gap, as well as glass ceiling obstacles. The changes in career opportunities and social status have been somewhat different for women than for men.

Upward Mobility

African Americans work in the same proportion as Euro-Americans but earn significantly less income. They have moved into better-paying occupations but hit a glass ceiling fairly soon, especially in private corporations. And men and women have significantly different work and life experiences.

Employment rates and pay gaps. About the same proportion of the African American and Euro-American populations hold jobs, but African Americans on average make one-third less than Euro-American men. In 1990, 63 percent of African Americans had jobs, compared to 65 percent of Euro-Americans. But this figure masks the fact that a smaller proportion of African American *men* had jobs, 66.5 percent compared to 75 percent of Euro-American men, balanced by the fact that more African American women than Euro-American women had jobs: 60 percent compared to 56 percent.

African American men's average income was only 70 percent of Euro-American men's, and the women's was 62 percent (U.S. Census Bureau 1993).

Movement into better paying occupations. From 1978 to 1990 there was a 52 percent increase in the number of African Americans who held positions as managers, professionals, and government officials. The greatest progress has been in government jobs. In 1980, two-thirds of African Americans holding jobs as managers and professionals were working for the federal government. Only 17 percent of managers and professionals as a whole work for the federal government.

The proportion of African Americans holding management and professional jobs from 1966 to 1990 is shown in Table 5.3.

TABLE 5.3: Progress in Management and Professional Jobs

African American Employees	1966	1978	1990
Percent of all managers in firms with 100+ employees	0.9%	3.7%	5.2%
Percent of all professionals	1.7%	4.0%	5.2%

Source: U.S. Census Bureau, 1993.

Since 1960 an increasing proportion of African Americans have moved into the higher-status, better-paying occupations of manager, professional, technical, sales, and administrative support. Table 5.4 shows the percentage of African Americans in each type of occupation and compares it with the Euro-American distribution. Part of this trend reflects changes in the economy as a whole, away from manufacturing and toward service and information. The decline in proportion of African Americans in service occupations generally reflects a shift out of cleaning and janitorial work into higher-status white-collar and blue-collar jobs. However, as the footnotes to Table 5.5 indicate, African Americans tend to be at the lowest-paid levels of each job category.

TABLE 5.4: Occupations: African American and Euro-American, 1960–1990

Occupation	1960 Af	1960 Euro	1970 Af	1970 Euro	1980 Af	1980 Euro	1990 Af	1990 Euro
Manager, Professional	7.4%	23.8%	14.6%	26.2%	17.9%	28.5%	16.3%	27.2%
Technical, Sales, Administrative Support	8.5	22.7	15.3	24.7	21.4	27.4	28.0	31.3
Service	31.7	9.9	26.0	10.7	23.1	12.1	21.9	12.1
Farming, Forestry	1.0	7.4	3.9	4.0	1.8	2.9	1.6	3.1
Precision Production Craft, Repairs	6.0	13.8	8.2	13.5	9.61	3.3	8.3	12.0
Operators, Fabricators Laborers	20.4	17.9	23.7	17.0	19.4	13.5	21.5	14.4

Source: U.S. Census Bureau, Statistical Abstract of the United States, 1981, 1991.

Glass Ceiling Obstacles

Progress in corporate America has not kept pace with the government picture, and the glass ceiling has resulted in virtually no African Americans in top positions of top companies. In 1979 the total *number* of African American senior managers in Fortune 1000 companies was three, by 1985 it had increased to four, and in 1990 to five. An African American reaction to the corporate glass ceiling was reported in 1988, when so many managers and professionals were leaving that it signaled a trend (WSJ, 1992). The reasons they give include:

- hitting the Glass Ceiling, lack of opportunity, and upward mobility
- feeling pressured to undermine or drop their African American identity
- having to prove themselves, over and over again, due to being African American
- dealing with the stigma of being an affirmative action hire
- coping with ethnic stereotypes

While learning the language and customs of corporate America may seem like a necessary part of playing the game for Euro-American men and women, for African Americans it can smack of selling out to get ahead. Many report feeling pressured to become "almost white" in order to be accepted, or at best to become "neutral" or to be viewed as an exception to the typical African American type. They feel the need to change their speech, their dress, their hair in order to fit into the corporate culture. If they go along, they begin to feel some degree of isolation from the African-American community. They don't really belong anywhere and feel "marginal" to all groups (WSJ 1992; Executive Female, 1992).

Men and Women: Differences in Progress and Roles

Comparisons of occupations held by African American men and women are given in Table 5.5. The largest category for women is clerical and for men, laborer. There have been significant differences in the career progress and changing status of men and that of women since the 1960s. While experts tend to agree that both men and women, on average, have improved their socioeconomic status since AA became law, and they have entered many new occupations formerly closed to them, women have made better progress than men. And both men and women have made more progress in government jobs than in corporate jobs.

TABLE 5.5: Percent of Occupations of African American Men and Women, 1990

Gender	Managerial Professional	Technical, Sales, Admin. Support	Service	Farming Forestry	Precision Production, Craft, Repairs	Operators Fabricators Laborers
Men	13.2	18.1	18.1[3]	2.8	14.2	30.5[5]
Women	19.5[1]	37.9[2]	24.9[4]	0.4	2.4	12.4

Source: U.S. Bureau of the Census, 1993.

[1] 22% of African American managers/professionals were teachers; most were elementary school teachers
[2] Nearly 30% of African American women employed in technical/sales/administrative support jobs were cashiers, secretaries, and typists.
[3] 45% of African American men in service jobs were janitors, cleaners, and cooks.
[4] Half of African American women in service occupations were nursing aides, orderlies and attendants, cooks, janitors, and cleaners.
[5] 30% of laborers were truck drivers, assemblers, stock handlers, and baggers.

Changes in Women's Status

African American women showed a dramatic increase in income, compared to that of Euro-American women, due to occupational shifts. African American women have moved from being primarily agricultural or domestic workers to being office workers. AA opened the doors of

America's offices to African American women, and huge numbers of them traded their maid's aprons for pink collars (Carr-Ruffino 1992). However, some researchers say the myth of the double-minority AA advantage is offset by the reality of double discrimination by gender and ethnicity, and sometimes by class. For example, African American women still tend to be:

- placed into training programs for traditionally female occupations
- discouraged from attempting innovative careers
- dependent upon the public sector for employment
- kept out of better private-sector jobs by rigid ethnic barriers

In 1980 more African American than Euro-American married women had outside jobs, they had more children, and they were more likely to be the sole wage earner. In 1990 these trends had not changed. Some researchers have defined a traditional nuclear family as a two-parent family where both parents have married only once and the children were all born after the marriage. In 1990 only 26 percent of African American children lived in such a family, compared to 56 percent of Euro-American children.

The trend in all subcultures is away from the traditional nuclear family: In 1970, 66 percent of all U.S. children lived in such families, compared to 51 percent in 1990. Changing the standard to "living with two parents regardless of marriage record," 37 percent of African American children did so in 1990, compared to 47 percent in 1980. Looking at Euro-American children, more than 80 percent did so in 1990, and 83 percent in 1980. The proportion of female-headed households has increased more rapidly for African Americans than for Euro-Americans. Female-headed households have lower incomes, causing the African American family income to decline independent of labor market discrimination (U.S. Census Bureau 1993).

Some economists say the rising divorce rate has been responsible for the large growth in female-headed households, and several studies indicate that rising divorce rates reflect the improved employment opportunities for women. While Euro-American marriage rates have changed very little, rates for African Americans have dramatically dropped. Historically, 90 percent of African American women were married by the age of 44. That rate dropped to 75 percent by 1975, to 67 percent by 1980, and to 55 percent by 1990. Moreover, the remarriage rate six years after a divorce was only 40 percent for African American women, compared to 60 percent for Euro-American women. African American women are increasingly delaying getting married. For example, the proportion of women in their late twenties who had never married rose from 11 percent in 1970 to 31 percent in 1990.

Changes in Men's Status

Clearly some modest employment gains were made by African American men in the late 1960s and early 1970s. African American men moved out of blue-collar and service jobs, presumably into better paying jobs, by a rate of 12 percent from 1966 to 1973, compared to a rate of 4 percent for Euro-American men (Feagin 1991). But the unemployment rate for young African American men, those from ages 20 to 24 and has remained higher than 20 percent, more than double the rates for comparably aged Euro-American men. Between 1969 and 1977, African American males' workplace participation rates fell dramatically and continued to decline thereafter. Participation rates for Euro-American men increased between 1969 and 1977 and fell only modestly thereafter.

Unemployment continues to be a major problem for African American men. Twice as many African American men are unemployed as Euro-American men; those holding college degrees are three times more likely to be unemployed than Euro-Americans. Unemployment is correlated with a host of underclass problems. For example, African American men are about eight times as likely to be homicide victims as Euro-American men, five times as likely to go to prison, four times as likely to enter a drug abuse treatment center, and nine times as likely to enter a mental institution (Mauer 1989).

Poverty and unemployment seem to be fertile ground for the birth of gangs, drug use, drug dealing, violence, and other crimes. About 25 percent of African American men ages 20 to 25 are in prison or on parole. Ethnic prejudice and discrimination play a part in all this. Studies indicate that African American and Latino American men are more likely to be arrested than Euro-American men, regardless of wrongdoing. By the early 1990s, many articles discussed the fact that young African American males were dying in disproportionate numbers because of high-risk lifestyles, and a number of African American organizations were spurred to action (Marc Mauer 1989).

Business Ownership

Within the African American community is a large and growing entrepreneurial class. While private business ownership is less well developed in the African American community than in the nation as a whole, it is substantial. And it's built on the strength of achieving, productive African American families. Its promise of future growth is reflected in the dramatic surge of interest among African Americans in attending seminars on how to start and grow a business. Beginning in the 1980s, conferences that normally had focused on upward mobility and promotions for African Americans shifted to seminars on starting a business. Some African American consultants expressed concern about this trend because, "If we are locked out of major corporations, with their enormous influence on the economy and their share of the resources, we're locked out of America" (WSJ 1992).

African American businesses currently tend to be small. The large majority of African Americans can't establish a business of any magnitude because of inadequate assets and net worth. The average net worth (assets minus liabilities) of Euro-American families was 10 times that of African Americans in 1990, and less than one-half of one percent of American assets are owned by African Americans. In spite of historical barriers, however, they now own 3 percent of America's businesses.

In 1993 total sales of all African American-owned firms was over $10 billion, although this was only a fraction of one percent of the Fortune 500 revenues of $2.4 trillion. One African American-owned firm was large enough to qualify for the Fortune 500. Beatrice Foods (4,500 workers) with a revenue of $1.7 billion equaled 238th-ranked Pet Foods. The second largest African American-owned firm was Johnson Publishing Company (2,600 workers), publisher of *Ebony* and *Jet* magazines and owner of other businesses, with sales of $294 million. Beatrice was acquired and restructured a few years ago, while Johnson was started from scratch and grew over the past 40 years (*Black Enterprise*, May 1994).

Supply-side critics point to the lack of external financing available to African American owners. In addition to having fewer assets and thus less collateral to borrow against, most are located in depressed economic areas, where banks don't want to venture. The National Black Chamber of Commerce has cited equitable access to bank loans as a major first step toward a more equitable balance. Demand-side critics say that discrimination limits the ability of African American owned firms to do business with the Euro-American majority, so they're limited to African American customers, who tend to be significantly less affluent than the majority population.

These small African American firms face huge barriers to starting out large enough and to growing large enough. However, if the new business leaders are able to establish virtual corporations in response to the fast-moving opportunities of the 1990s and beyond, smallness could become an asset (Myers 1986).

Education for Careers

Educational progress has been good and is a key to breaking out of the poverty cycle. The proportion of African Americans who have completed high school rose from 51 percent in 1980 to 63 percent in 1990. The high school dropout rate dropped from 16 percent to 14 percent, and college enrollment increased by one and one-half times. Educational attainment is about the same for males and females, but African Americans have a way to go in achieving the same level as Euro-Americans. The proportion who got a university degree in 1990 was 11 percent, compared to 21 percent of Euro-Americans.

After a significant increase in African American college enrollment in the 1980s, the total number began slowly dropping, but enrollment in African American colleges jumped. Although such schools account for only 3 percent of the nation's college enrollment, they were selected by 35 percent of African American college students in 1990. Students say the main reason is a desire for "the black experience," meaning the self-confidence boost that comes from having African American professors as role models, gaining a sense of African American history, and learning about the contributions African Americans have made to society. Most of the schools are private and expensive. Some students ask, "Why can't we get this in the typical large public university?" (NAEOHE 1990).

School achievement depends heavily on family economic status, according to a recent study. Table 5.6 shows the correlation between family income and student performance on SAT tests. The authors conclude that

- Socioeconomic status (not ethnicity or gender) is the best predictor of both grades and test scores.

- Public schools must do more to provide educational opportunity for children of low socioeconomic status, who do less well in school regardless of ethnicity or gender.

TABLE 5.6: Family Income Affects School Performance

Average Family Income	Average SAT Score
$22,000	750–800
$18,000	550–599
$14,000	350–399
$8,000	200–249

Source: American Association of University Women, 1992 Report.
Selected pairs are used, but missing pairs are consistent with these results.

It would appear that once an African American family is able to break the cycle of poverty and get good jobs, the cycle tends to stay broken for that family. The children do well in school and are therefore likely to get good jobs and earn good incomes when they grow up, which in turn increases the likelihood that their children will do well in school.

Many people have assumed that African Americans value education less than Euro-Americans, since fewer complete high school and college. However, a recent study indicates that African American high school students have significantly higher aspirations to achieve a college degree than Euro-American students whose families are at the same socioeconomic level. In both groups, the higher the socioeconomic level, the higher the educational aspirations tend to be. In addition, significantly more African American than Euro-American parents want their children to attend college, when comparing by socioeconomic class (Solorzano 1991).

Studies indicate that racially integrated classrooms tend to have positive effects for minorities. Yet in 1984 more than 64 percent of African American students were still segregated. For those who have the advantage of integrated schools, classroom studies of teacher-student relationships have indicated that minority students receive biased treatment. For example, teachers tend to give more praise and encouragement to Euro-American students and to accept and acknowledge their contributions to class discussions. Such subtle exclusion can do long term damage to children's' confidence, class performance, and educational aspirations. Although much attention has been paid to problems in the educational system that impacts African Americans, the problems have not yet been solved (Patchen et al. 1980).

A promising approach might be to study success factors. What if African American researchers were to focus on African Americans who have broken out of the poverty cycle and find patterns of factors that worked well for them? For example, are there external factors in family, school, or community that affected these members' success patterns? What kinds of internal beliefs and attitudes, thinking and feeling, decisions and choices, are common among the successful? How did successful African Americans use their imagination, desire, and expectations to avoid underclass pitfalls and move up to a better life? If some typical patterns could be found, couldn't community leaders use this information to help those who are still stuck? What if young people in the underclass could develop similar patterns in their own struggle to break out?

Political Views of African American Status

Why are so many African Americans still caught in underclass poverty? Opinions vary widely about the causes and solutions for this continuing problem.

Conservatives tend to believe that more accurate measures of jobs and income would indicate that the problem isn't very serious. To the extent that problems exist, they reflect the personal inadequacies of African American youths, compounded by the adverse effects of government antipoverty policies, including welfare and minimum wage laws. Any inequity that exists is rooted in African American laziness and disregard for law and order. The conservative prescription is for government to stay out of it because attempts to help amount to handouts, which make the poor dependent on government and are a burden on taxpayers. Poor African Americans who want to will pull themselves up by their bootstraps, and those who don't can suffer the consequences.

Liberals emphasize external causes of the problem, such as declining employment opportunities due to a weakening of economic growth and labor market imbalances. They cite the movement of jobs away from the inner cities to suburbs, Sun Belt states, and low-wage countries. The movement of middle-class African Americans to the suburbs intensifies inner city problems. It reduces the youths' access to role models and to middle-class cultural values. Liberals say that discrimination also continues to be a barrier, and as a result some African Americans naturally become discouraged and demoralized. The problems are too great for African Americans to solve on their own, and it's up to government to help bring an end to inequity.

Black nationalists tend to see the problem as pervasive prejudice. Their concern is for recognition as free human beings. They do not call for integration but rather for true equality that values diversity.

CULTURAL PATTERNS AND ISSUES

What's in a Name?

African American. The African American community is diverse, containing many complex and changing identities. Research indicates a trend among African Americans to prefer the label *African American* (34 percent and growing), while most still choose *Black* (39 percent) and a few prefer *Black American* (10 percent). Those preferring *Black* tend to be the most conservative, those preferring *African American* the most liberal, with those preferring *Black American* somewhere in between (Larkey and Hecht 1991).

Productive and dynamic business relationships are what leaders want. How can we move to the level of understanding we need, when our associate is from another culture? Learning about the culture, getting a feel for the background of the person is a key. The more skilled we become at interpreting an individual's actions against the backdrop of his or her culture, the greater success we can all achieve through working together. The African American community is diverse, and of course no one person expresses all the values and customs discussed here. You may be tempted to use this cultural information to form new rigid categories. To be fair, stay open and flexible as you interact with individual African Americans.

African Americans are always balancing at least two cultures—the American mainstream culture and their African American subculture. As a community, they've held onto key aspects of their West African heritage that are especially precious to them or that help them survive in a hostile society. Some common cultural elements are found among West Africans, Caribbeans of African descent, and African Americans. These include certain values and common ways of relating, communicating, and expressing personal style. Somewhat unique to African American culture are distrust of the establishment and strategies for coping with prejudice (Herskovitz 1958; Woodson 1968).

Many African American researchers have defined numerous African American values. We synthesize them here into seven core values that interrelate and support one another. A summary of core values is presented in Table 5.7. We'll discuss each in detail and then see how they are reflected in relationships within the community and family, in personal relationships and in coping with prejudice (Hecht, Collins, and Ribeau 1993; Rose 1982/1983; White and Parham 1990; Billingsley 1992).

TABLE 5.7: Core Values of the African American Community

> • *Sharing*, interrelatedness, interdependence, collectivism
> • *Personal style*, expressing uniqueness or individual style, who one really is
> • *Realness, genuineness*, tellin' it like it is; learning the truth from direct experience; being real; seeing the good as well as the bad
> • *Assertiveness*, speaking up, standing up; feeling and expressing emotions
> • *Vitality and resilience*, maintaining a positive attitude, bouncing back
> • *Distrust* of the mainstream establishment

Value: Sharing and Interrelatedness

Connectedness and interdependence are the unifying concepts in the African American experience base. This is a prominent theme in African American language with respect to the interactive dynamics between speaker and listener, the power of words to control, ways of thinking, timing, and communication skill (White and Parham 1990).

Sharing knowledge and endorsing the group are related to collectivism. They are expressed in the call-response pattern found in meetings of church and other groups. They're also found in the sharing of self and material possessions within the family. Interconnectedness, interrelatedness, sharing, and interdependence are seen as central and unifying values in the African American community. Sharing is expressed through touching, close physical distance, relationship intimacy, and rituals. African Americans, especially those of the lower socioeconomic class, tend to touch members of their group more than they touch Euro-Americans. African Americans tend to establish closer distances than Euro-Americans, beginning in childhood (Halberstadt 1985; Hammer and Gudykunst 1987; Hecht and Ribeau 1984).

Value: Personal Style/Uniqueness

Uniqueness in personal style and expression celebrates the individual. African Americans generally demonstrate both individuality and commonality in interactions with others (Rose 1982/

1983). For example, people may develop their own form of handslapping and dance style, using ritualized or basic forms and adding their own improvisations. Similarly, boasting serves to promote group cohesiveness but the boaster adds his or her own unique flavor to the ritual. Throughout life, African Americans are encouraged to "be real" and express their true natures through their actions and style (White and Parham 1990).

Kochman (1981) defines African American style as more self-conspicuous, expressive, expansive, colorful, intense, assertive, aggressive, and focused on the individual than the style of the majority society. He describes African Americans' expressive communications patterns as much use of direct questions, public debate and argument, more active nonverbal expression, self-presentations through bragging, boasting, and emotional intensity. Donohue (1985) observed that African Americans tend to negotiate more loudly and intensely than Euro-Americans.

A key difference between this type of individual expression and American individualism is that it's part of sharing within the group and is actually an aspect of collectivism. In contrast, American individualism refers to a more autonomous expression through personal achievement and self-reliance. It does not rely on the group in the immediate way that African American "personal style" expression does.

Value: Realness and Genuineness

You might as well tell it like it is. The natural facts, eternal truths, wisdom of the ages, and basic precepts of survival emerge from the experiences of life. You cannot lie to life. The proverbial wisdom says:

- You can't escape nothing.
- You got to pay your dues.
- If you've been through tragedy, it must be you needed it (for personal growth).

You learn the truth through direct experience. Older people, because of their accumulated experiences, are the reservoirs of wisdom, the storehouses of the oral tradition, and the keepers of the heritage. They're valued because they've been through the experiences that can only come with age. They've been "down the line," seen the comings and goings of life, and been through the cycles of oppression, struggle, survival, backlash, and renewed struggle. They've stood the test of time and adversity, paid their dues, transcended tragedy, and learned to "keep on keepin' on."

African Americans see both the good and bad in life and tend to believe that good will win out in the end. This implies they are realistic about the way things are, trust in fairness, and are positive about the future (Rose 1982/83).

Genuineness is a major issue in interethnic relationships. Kochman (1981) believes that loudness is positively valued because it communicates sincerity and conviction.

Value: Assertiveness

African Americans value standing up for personal rights and trying to achieve them without harming others. This communication style is intense, outspoken, challenging, and forward. Some label this style forceful or aggressive because they see belligerence and hostility being expressed. Assertiveness is a key symbol of standing up for yourself in the face of oppression and of taking charge of your own life. Coping with prejudice and discrimination often results in an assertive, determined, confrontational style. Assertiveness may be expressed through use of a loud strong voice, angry verbal arguments, threats, insults, way of dressing, and use of slang. It can range from calm debates to persuasion to intense expressions of anger. Euro-Americans may interpret some assertive behavior as a sign that physical violence is imminent when none is intended. Those who get to know people in the African American community learn to interpret this behavior by noting the context and observing body language.

Debating and arguing. When African Americans engage in public debate of any kind, their style is often high-key; that is, animated, interpersonal, and confrontational with the effect of expressing and generating emotion. This contrasts with middle-class and upper-class Euro-American style, which tends to be more low-key; that is, relatively dispassionate, impersonal, nonchallenging, and less likely to express or generate as much emotion. African Americans see their style as natural and sincere expressions of their thoughts and feelings. Since they're accustomed to such expression in their communities, they accept others' passionate style in the spirit in which it's intended: honest engagement, participation, and expression that helps people know each other and ultimately contributes to unity. In general, African American culture allows members much greater freedom to assert and express themselves than does the Euro-American culture, with its standards of quiet good taste and decorum as the chief restraining factors (Kochman 1981).

Expressing feelings. Euro-Americans often interpret African American expressions of anger and their verbal aggressiveness as more threatening and provocative than it's intended. The type of angry verbal disputes, even involving insults and threats, that often occur among African Americans without necessarily leading to violence, would in fact almost always be precursors to violence within the Euro-American culture.

Boasting and bragging. Most African Americans distinguish between boasting and bragging. Boasting is typically done with some sense of humor; it's usually exaggerated; and it's not intended to be taken seriously. It's done as a form of play and entertainment used to gain recognition within a group.

Bragging is a serious form of self-aggrandizement, and people are expected to back up their claims. Bragging about your ability is okay, but bragging about your possessions or social status is not.

Eye contact differences. Have you ever felt that you and an acquaintance were avoiding looking at each other in a conversation? Or staring each other down? Maybe it was unmatched eye contact. When African Americans speak, they tend to look at their partner more than they do while listening, while for Euro-Americans the pattern is reversed. Therefore, when the two get together and the Euro-American is speaking, African American listening, they may hardly be making eye contact at all. When the African American is speaking, Euro-American listening, the intense eye contact may seem like unnatural staring.

Value: Bouncing Back

Resilience and revitalization are admired and have been a key to survival. While life brings its trials and tribulations, the other side is the renewal experiences of sensuousness, joy, and laughter. Troubles will pass, the blues won't last forever, and freedom will emerge on some bright sunshiny day. In blues and gospel music, the consciousness of pain, sorrow, and hurt are not accompanied by feelings of guilt, shame, and self-rejection. The pure sadness makes it easier for African Americans to draw upon the revitalization powers of sensuousness, joy, and laughter. Oral literature also carries themes of sensuality and joy. And humor is a common weapon to confront adversity. This vitality is an essential part of African American spiritual life, and is obvious in church music, preaching, responsiveness of the congregation, and virtually all aspects of church services and events.

Value: Don't Trust the Establishment

The experiences of slavery, segregation, institutional discrimination, and ongoing economic oppression have taught African Americans to distrust the establishment. In view of this, African Americans have found it sometimes essential for survival, other times just convenient, to lie when it comes to sharing what's really on their minds with Euro-Americans. From an old slave song:

Got one mind for white folk to see, 'Nother for what I know is me; He don't know what's on my mind.

The use of a common language with culturally different meanings has enabled African Americans to make statements that have double meanings, with one level of meaning hidden from Euro-Americans but clear to other African Americans. Such deception can be used as a way of controlling undesirable psychological imagery and devaluative labels assigned by Euro-Americans. For example, "a bad nigger" to Euro-Americans means someone who is undesirable, but in African American semantics refers to a hero, someone they look up to for his courage and guts to stand up to "white folks." Double talk is sometimes called *coding* (White and Parham 1990).

Values Reflected in Community Life

Some important aspects of community life that reflect the core values are spiritual customs, the role of the church, rituals, use of a dialect often called "Black English," and certain interpretations of behavior.

Spiritual and Church Customs

Certain features of African spirituality survived and became incorporated into the religious practices of African Americans. They include the call-response patterns of interaction of the group with its spiritual leader, which is a form of participation by the entire group. We see this played out by members of congregations where the preacher "calls" and the congregation "responds" with such affirmations as "Yes," "Amen," and "Praise God." This pattern carries over into secular meetings and reflects the sharing and interrelatedness value.

The significance of music to invoke spirituality is another key custom that explains the primacy and vibrancy of the music African Americans use in their church services. The belief in the direct link between physical life and spiritual life may explain the important role that church leaders and congregations have played in every aspect of African American life.

Religious orientation is one of the greatest historic strengths of African American families. Over the centuries the church has become the strongest institution in their community. It is prevalent, independent, and has extensive outreach. In many churches a chief function of the African American preacher is to relate spirituality to current issues in the community. Most members want the strength and assurance to survive another day more than solutions to abstract theological problems. African American churches took on a major role in advocating social change in this century, with ministers becoming leaders in the Civil Rights movement.

The African American church is still at the leading edge of the African American community's push to influence the future of its families. The National Baptist Convention USA has 8.7 million members and is the largest African American organization in the nation. In 1991 they announced plans for programs to support African American businesses, provide jobs, and sell everything African American people use. "We must take care of our own."

About 75 percent of African Americans are active church members. Virtually all are Protestant, 11 million Baptists and 6 million Methodists (Blackwell 1985; White and Parham 1990).

Types of Rituals

Common rituals help make a group feel connected and comfortable. Rituals observed in African American culture, in addition to call-response patterns, include various types of jiving, playing the dozens, and toasting.

Jiving is based on improvising and on accenting behaviors that are believed to be highly acceptable. Some jivers are entertainers who sing, dance, joke, and act in ways that perpetuate the Euro-American myth that all African Americans have rhythm, can sing and dance well, and act uncouth. Some jivers use slang in a way that gets immediate favorable attention from other

African Americans. Some jivers use foolish talk and action, such as slapstick, farce, and horseplay, as a way to gain and hold a reputation for not being serious. Some rely on teasing to play tricks on other African Americans in order to get a laugh and to make a fool of the victim. Still other jivers use swing. They're often professionals or business persons who become "vigorous, vibrant, ostentatious, and often graceful in a nonserious environment" (Hecht 1993, 100). Swinging expresses the need to relax and party, partially to relieve the stresses of functioning in a Euro-American work environment.

Playing the dozens refers to a game that is an aggressive contest with the goal of ridiculing and demeaning an opponent's family members, especially the mother, often using obscene language. The dozens has been described as a strategy or method of attack that might use persuasion, legislation, justification, social pressure, play, or instruction. It's also a way that males learn to compete with one another (Garner 1983; Abrahams 1963).

Toasting in the African American style may include being sexually assertive, using four-letter words, and making fun of sentimental talk, all in ways that reinforce African American identity and connectedness.

Interpreting Behavior: If the Shoe Fits

Values and customs affect the way people in the community tend to interpret each others' behavior. For example, when African Americans express an accusation or allegation such as "the office clerks steal stamps," they typically don't intend it to include all office clerks, whereas Euro-Americans are more likely to mean everyone in that category. To African Americans, if people admit they feel accused, by that fact alone they acknowledge their guilt. An African American will make an accusation, then wait to see what happens. "If the shoe fits, wear it." If others are innocent of a general accusation, then, the natural response is to remain silent; protesting innocence is an indication of guilt. To most Euro-Americans the statement would be accusatory, and they typically protest with great anger when falsely accused. Clearly, they could misread an African American's silence in this situation. To Euro-Americans silence in response to accusatory statements implies guilt, while to African Americans it implies innocence.

Use of Black English

Social pressures, often subconscious, exist within the African American community to maintain Black English as a form of group identity and symbol of unity. African slaves developed a pidgin English that they used to communicate with their masters. They substituted English for West African words but used the basic structure and idiom of their West African language (Smitherman 1977). Over the years, the pidgin gradually became widespread among slaves and evolved into a dialect. Aspects of this dialect that survive in Black English today and that reflect West African structure include:

- My mother, she go there.
- What it come to?
- I know it good when he tell me.
- *mo* for *more* (no *r* sound)
- *souf* for *south* (no *th* sound)
- *Jus* for *just* (no consecutive consonant pairs)

Sense of Time

Africans generally have no way of expressing a distant future, which of course affects their ability to act in terms of long-range planning. Some of this time concept has survived in the African American community. Therefore, some African Americans must struggle to adapt to a corporate focus on such planning. Africans also emphasize whether something is done only at the present moment or done habitually—an either/or viewpoint. For example:

"We need to get a special shipping company for this order that's going to Alaska" versus "Orders going to Alaska typically require a special shipping company."

This either/or view contrasts with the Western view of time as linear, with an emphasis on which point on the time line an event occurs—in the past, present, or future—among infinite numbers of potential points; for example:

"During our first year of operation we relied on a special shipping company for orders to Alaska. The following year we found a shipping company that could handle all our needs, including Alaskan shipments. How are shipping needs changing and what should we plan for next year? Will projections for the next five years affect our choice of shipping companies for next year?"

Values Reflected in Family Relationships

The sharing value is probably the most prevalent you'll notice as you read about the role of extended families and child rearing practices.

Extended Families

Among African Americans, the term *parents* often refers to natural parents, grandparents, and others who assume parental roles and responsibilities from time to time. Relationships with key people who are not blood relatives are considered essential to the maintenance of the family. Studies indicate that the extended family in the African American community plays a role in modeling, validation of self, emotional support, achievement, socialization, and learning. The importance of the extended family is probably rooted both in the African American tribal heritage and in the need to withstand the stress spawned by the slavery system and its aftermath (Mann 1981).

Child-Rearing Practices

Studies indicate that African American parents tend to raise their sons to be confrontive. A typical comment from a ghetto mother: "Where we live my son has to be tough and be able to fight. I'm not going to stop that." The strict, no-nonsense discipline used by many African American parents, sometimes seen as harsh or rigid to some Euro-Americans, is actually functional and appropriate discipline by caring parents. They see it as preparation for survival in a hostile environment, one that is prejudiced and discriminatory against them (Allen 1981; Willie 1976; Young 1977).

Values Reflected in Personal Relationships

"African Americans seem to place especially high value on trust and helping one another" (Hecht 1993, 156). They also tend to develop closer, more intimate friendships than Euro-Americans. Their friendships with each other involve deeper, more intimate contact in general and in discussing the topics of school, work, religion, interests, hobbies, and physical condition. Euro-Americans tend to develop more intimacy regarding the topics of love, dating, sex, and feelings. African Americans don't necessarily develop such friendship with Euro-Americans and many may appear indifferent or uninvolved in their interactions with persons outside the community. We'll discuss first African Americans' style of relating with acquaintances and then their style with closer friends (Smith, Willis, and Gier 1980; Ickes 1984).

African American Style with Acquaintances

African Americans are guided in their communication with other African American acquaintances, such as co-workers and casual friends, by the following types of guidelines, which are somewhat similar to those used by Euro-Americans and Latino Americans (Collier 1988):

- Follow role prescriptions.
- Be polite.
- Adjust the content.
- Be expressive.

Following role prescriptions is stressed more by Latino Americans than by African Americans, and Euro-Americans stress it even less than African Americans. African Americans place more emphasis on individual roles that express each person's style than on conventional roles. This reflects their value for expressing personal uniqueness.

Being polite is seen by African Americans as being more an individual than societal trait, and they place greater emphasis on their own individual norms for politeness than do Latino Americans or Euro-Americans.

Adjusting the content refers to taking into account who you're talking with. For example, some things you would talk about with other African Americans would not be discussed with Euro-Americans.

Being expressive is more important to African Americans than to the other two groups. They especially value conversations that are supportive, relevant, and assertive, reflecting the cultural values of sharing and positivity. This holds true for relationships with African American acquaintances but not necessarily with those from other ethnic groups.

African American Style with Friends

The style used for relationships with friends stress the individual but also stress intimacy and fall into four categories (Collier 1992):

- Acknowledge or respect the individual.
- Develop intimacy.
- Appreciate the culture.
- Be supportive.

Acknowledging the individual refers to allowing others to express themselves through assertiveness and valuing individual accomplishment. It reflects the value of assertiveness and uniqueness.

Developing intimacy reflects the value of sharing and is achieved through talking about family and other personal topics. It includes the following actions:

- giving and receiving friendly advice, leading to positive feelings
- taking specific actions to establish trust as the most crucial element of relationships
- expressing sensitivity, support, affirmation, honesty, and brotherhood or sisterhood
- accepting criticisms and assertive requests without compromising the friendship

Appreciating the culture stresses similarities in beliefs, attitudes, and interests. Pride in common roots and the cultural background itself are seen as appropriate topics in conversations.

Being supportive refers to taking such actions as offering a solution for a problem, giving advice on a personal problem, seeking mutual understanding, expressing individuality, affirming the other person or the culture, and establishing trust and intimacy.

Male–Female Relationships

For African Americans, male-female relationships ideally are based on the values of interdependence, cooperation, and mutual respect. There should not be rigid sex role distinctions regarding money, household duties, and social roles. The relationships should be built on bonds of sharing, nurturance, tenderness, and appreciation. Tensions between African American males and females often prevent them from achieving the satisfaction they want in relationships. However, many have begun to talk with each other rather than about each other and are trying to understand and respect their mutual interests and individual differences. The four major issues are trust, sex and sexuality, control, and social roles.

African American culture presumes that all women have a general sexual interest in men and are sexually assertive, so they aren't considered less respectable or more available on the basis of these criteria. This contrasts with Euro-American culture that tends to divide women into the *good*, who withhold sexual interest until a certain screening process has taken place, and the *bad*, who don't. African American men are more direct in their expression of sexual interest, and the women aren't insulted by this but generally feel confident about how to reject or accept such overtures. The men are normally not offended by a rejection if it's done in good humor, only by being ignored or rejected in a degrading way.

Values Reflected in Coping with Prejudice

How do African Americans cope with the prejudice, denigration, and discrimination they face daily in the dominant society? Several researchers have contributed to the identification of specific coping strategies. Two general strategies reflect the key values of resilience and distrust of the establishment. African Americans have also devised specific strategies used from time to time in varying degrees by various groups. These include not seeking significant change, seeking a piece of the action, becoming marginal, and remaining aware but flexible (Glaser 1958; Stanbeck and Pearce 1981; Harding 1980).

Not Seeking Change

This strategy may involve accepting segregation as a preference, with African Americans valuing their own identity as an end in itself, even when this process disadvantages themselves. Or it may involve acknowledging the harmful effects of prejudice and discrimination but showing little or no strategy for coping with it. More active African Americans may call it *tomming*, or passively accepting lower status position. By not actively resisting discrimination, such African Americans may avoid such stress symptoms as ulcers and hypertension. On the other hand, if they also get in the habit of blaming the dominant society for all their troubles, they can fall into the trap of strong dependency on external solutions.

Seeking a Piece of the Action

Most middle-class African Americans have followed this strategy, gaining the skills necessary to achieve success in the mainstream. This requires assimilation, reacting only on an individual and nonethnic basis. Other African Americans may call it *passing*, or acting as a member of the mainstream group. It may be a way of desegregating through avoiding any ethnic identity. Success often comes at the price of conflicting values, especially the values of personal style and genuineness.

Becoming Marginal

This often involves shifting between self-identities and may reflect insecurity about self-identity. Examples include escaping into countercultures, adopting Black Nationalism, or identifying with an authoritarian group.

Counterculture. Some have escaped into a counterculture, trying to transcend the struggle by living outside both the mainstream culture and the African American culture. This may include heavy drug usage, involvement with religious or art forms, or the frequent use of consciousness-altering techniques. This can lead to creative and unorthodox activities, but the person may lose touch with the practical realities of prejudice and discrimination.

Black Nationalism. Some have adopted Black Nationalism, or becoming immersed in a similar movement that stresses African American identity, which can promote a positive view of African American people and culture but can be narrow and rigid in its approach to Euro-American institutions.

Authoritarian groups. Some have identified with an authoritarian group, such as Nation of Islam or Marxism, that requires allegiance to a leader or an idea. This may provide the person with direction and discipline, but the person may become overdependent on the authority and lose contact with personal viewpoints.

Remaining Aware but Flexible

This approach is the most complex but also the most promising. It focuses on being aware of the complexities of the ethnic situation while recognizing the need to struggle against prejudice and discrimination, on being conscious of alternatives but also realizing that there are no comforting or even familiar answers to the issues facing African Americans. This alternative also requires standing ready to accept new theory, practice, ideology, and therefore new hope, and recognizing the constant need to reassess and revise personal viewpoints. This approach seems to be central to the concept of the new urban village.

Integrating African Values: the New Urban Village

A growing movement is afoot in the African American community, a movement that emphasizes African heritage and values and integrates them with American values and the American dream. A comparison of the Eurocentric and Afrocentric views is shown in Table 5.8 to help explain the idea. Each of the two viewpoints builds on basic beliefs and so should be read separately, each as a belief system. Compare the systems rather than each belief.

Regarding the Eurocentric ultimate goal, Fraser (1994, 84) says that the ultimate illusion of the American Dream is that "anyone who is focused, educated, and persistent can fight his or her way to the top and enjoy the distinction of being Number One." If being number one means others are number two, and so forth, then obviously everyone cannot make it.

The urban village concept is a recent African American approach. It's grounded in the Afrocentric view and recognizes that the Eurocentric view sets the rules of the American marketplace. It incorporates the concept of Afrocentric rites of passage, especially important for inner city youth, as well as the principles of Kwanzaa, which we'll discuss. A key principle is

> *It takes a village to raise a child.*

TABLE 5.8: The American Dream: From Eurocentric and Afrocentric Viewpoints

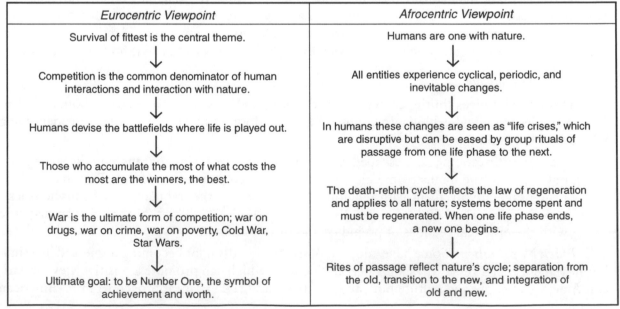

Eurocentric Viewpoint	Afrocentric Viewpoint
Survival of fittest is the central theme.	Humans are one with nature.
Competition is the common denominator of human interactions and interaction with nature.	All entities experience cyclical, periodic, and inevitable changes.
Humans devise the battlefields where life is played out.	In humans these changes are seen as "life crises," which are disruptive but can be eased by group rituals of passage from one life phase to the next.
Those who accumulate the most of what costs the most are the winners, the best.	The death-rebirth cycle reflects the law of regeneration and applies to all nature; systems become spent and must be regenerated. When one life phase ends, a new one begins.
War is the ultimate form of competition; war on drugs, war on crime, war on poverty, Cold War, Star Wars.	
Ultimate goal: to be Number One, the symbol of achievement and worth.	Rites of passage reflect nature's cycle; separation from the old, transition to the new, and integration of old and new.

Based on the work of George Fraser, 1994.

The keys to the success of the new urban village include networking, mentoring, and cooperative economics. Virtually every African American church and community organization now operates some sort of economic program, from economic literacy and job training classes to community loan funds. Weekend mentoring programs focus on bringing together urban youth and business persons and other role models. The motto of the urban village is economic empowerment.

Kwanzaa is a way of life that honors the African heritage with the purpose of encouraging a greater sense of unity, identity, and purpose among African Americans. The seven principles of Kwanzaa are rooted in Afrocentrism. Many of its symbols and terms come from African tradition, but it's the creation of African Americans. The Kwanzaa annual celebration has taken place around Christmas time holiday since its beginning in 1966. The seven principles focus on unity, self-determination, collective work and responsibility, cooperative economics, purpose, creativity, and faith.

Kwanzaa and the urban village model are approaches that recognize the realities of African American life in the American society. They are positive, empowering, practical approaches that are grounded in the interdependence and spirituality of an Afrocentric worldview.

LEADERSHIP CHALLENGES AND OPPORTUNITIES

As a leader you have many opportunities and challenges in working effectively with African Americans, in supporting their ability to contribute to work teams, and in building mutual respect and trust. You can be more sensitive and supportive if you understand the general experiences and barriers that most minorities must deal with. African American employees have some general and pervasive needs that are somewhat true of all minority or disadvantaged groups but tend to be intensified in the African American experience. One specific need is to believe in their intellectual capacity to learn and perform. As leader you can play a powerful role in meeting these needs by demonstrating a "can-do" attitude toward African American employees. You've learned about core values of African Americans, and we'll review those in terms of workplace strengths. You'll also learn about specific issues that tend to occur at each of the four career phases and how to support African Americans in each phase and help them make successful contributions.

Leadership Challenge: Meeting General and Pervasive Needs

In American society traditional prejudice and discrimination toward diverse groups results in a package of feelings and experiences that most members of these groups bring to the workplace. As a leader, you need to be aware of these factors that affect minorities in a wide range of ways. Some have managed to ignore or rise above most of them. Others may have a problem in one area and none in the others. Knowing what to look for can help you give the right kind of support. We mentioned these typical experiences in Chapter 1 and review them here because African Americans have experienced the most extreme forms of discrimination. The package may include:

- oppression
- exclusion from mainstream activities of society
- feelings of being different (in a negative way) from those in a dominant position
- low self-concept, self-esteem, and self-confidence
- being positioned in a one-down status
- being prohibited from and not encouraged to seek a better position and status in the society—or in life
- lack of equal opportunities

These factors also affect women. In fact, Kanter (1977) concluded that many of the behaviors attributed to women were actually behaviors typical of powerless employees stuck in dead-end positions.

The solutions that have been devised for the problem of discrimination and inequity have led to their own set of problems. As mentioned earlier in this chapter, the typical barriers minorities face, and therefore you as leader face in developing and retaining them, include:

- hitting the Glass Ceiling, lack of opportunity, and upward mobility
- feeling pressured to undermine or drop their African American identity
- having to prove themselves, over and over again, due to being African American
- dealing with the assumption and resulting stigma that they're Affirmative Action hire
- coping with ethnic stereotypes

You've already gained some knowledge and skills for dealing with these general minority issues from working through chapter 1. Whether your role is that of manager, team leader, or just responsible co-worker, as a leader you can identify ways to support African Americans in leaving the stereotypes behind and focusing on developing themselves for the next job promotion. The focus may be on increasing their flexibility, networking ability, bottom-line influence, computer literacy, skill in highlighting their own strengths, and other areas relevant to their career plan (Williams 1992).

African Americans must learn to pay as much attention to monitoring and developing their career strategies as they do to achieving specific job goals. They must learn to market themselves within the company and outside of it. They need to network and establish relationships with other people in other divisions. And they must learn to tap into the grapevine and keep up with what's going on. Your challenge as leader is to encourage and support them in doing all this.

Leadership Challenge: Expecting Growth and Success

Your expectations of your team members, and how you express those expectations, can push them into a failure cycle or success cycle. African American employees tend to be especially vulnerable to leader expectations. You've learned that there's a socioeconomic gap between African Americans and Euro-Americans. Howard and Hammond (1988), after studying the psychology of performance for ten years, concluded that the inferior performance of African Americans on intellectual tests was more than the result of socioeconomic disadvantage. The key factor is one that is pervasive but can be overcome: stereotyped assumptions and expectations that African Americans are intellectually inferior.

Failure Cycle

Such expectations set up a failure cycle as shown in Figure 5.1. Internalized beliefs about innate intellectual inferiority leads to low self-confidence about ability to perform intellectually-demanding tasks. Low self-confidence leads to poor performance of intellectual tasks, which causes African Americans to avoid such tasks. A major consequence of the failure cycle is that many African Americans avoid intellectual engagement and competition. We can therefore conclude that avoidance of intellectual challenge is rooted in fears and self-doubt that are rooted in a history of strong negative stereotypes that Euro-Americans hold about African American's intellectual capabilities.

FIGURE 5.1: Failure Cycle

Other's assumption that I'm intellectually inferior——⟶
My internalized belief that I'm intellectually inferior——⟶
Low self-confidence regarding intellectual tasks——⟶
Poor performance on intellectual tasks——⟶
Avoidance of such tasks

Howard (Howard and Hammond 1988) says that intellectual development is not a fixed asset that you either have or don't have. Nor is it based on magic. It's a process of expanding mental strength and reach. The developmental process is demanding. It requires time, discipline, and intense effort. In groups it often involves competition as well as cooperation and some solitary study. African Americans often place a strong negative value on intellectual competition because past performance gaps have damaged their self-esteem, and they naturally want to avoid further pain. But their retreat from competition results eventually in a widened intellectual performance gap.

Success Cycle

African Americans tend to experience greater success when they engage in sports, socializing, and entertaining others because of assumptions and stereotypes that they are "innately" gifted in these areas. This sets in motion the success cycle shown in Figure 5.2. Substitute "physical" for intellectual and you'll get the picture of African American athletic achievement. A similar cycle occurs for developing social skills or musical, comedy, and dramatic skills.

FIGURE 5.2: Success Cycle

Assumption by leader that I can master intellectual tasks——>
Internalized belief that I can master intellectual tasks——>
Self-confidence in my ability to master intellectual tasks ——>
Willingness to put forth effort on intellectual tasks——>
Development of intellectual skills

When people are able to build self-confidence, they become inspired and willing to put forth the effort necessary to achieve specific goals. Whether the goals involved physical skills, intellectual skills, social skills, or other types of skills, the effort leads to personal development; that is, learning, achievement, and growth in that particular area. That personal development becomes the foundation for increased self-confidence in the next cycle. The success cycle is a process in which success increases self-confidence and effort, leading to even more success, over and over in the upward spiral. It's circular and feeds back on itself, moving upward in a geometrically expanding spiral, as shown in Figure 5.3, Skill Development Cycle.

FIGURE 5.3: Skill Development Cycle

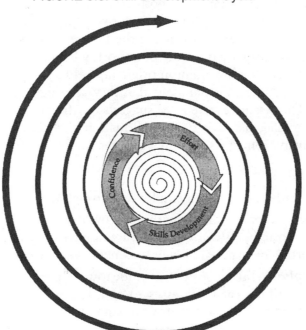

What You Expect Is What You Get

The failure cycle and the success cycle are based on expectancy theory. Expectancy communications are expressions of belief—verbal or nonverbal—from one person to another about the kind of performance they expect. They have a powerful impact on performance. The expectations of leaders for their team members have a large effect on skills development, just as expectations of teachers for students affect academic achievement. Communicated expectations cause people to believe that they will do well or poorly at a task. Such beliefs very often trigger responses that result in performance consistent with the expectation. This is just as true when expectancies are directed at an entire category of people as it is when they're directed at a particular individual.

The widespread expectation that African Americans' intellectual performance will be inferior is communicated constantly in our culture. It's projected through stereotyped images, verbal and nonverbal exchanges in daily interaction, and the incessant debate about genetics and intelligence. It's a constant background "noise" that African Americans naturally tend to internalize as reality. Expectancies apparently affect behavior in two ways:

- Expectancies affect how we perform, the sharpness and intensity required for competitive success.
- Expectancies influence how we think, the mental processes by which we make sense of everyday life.

Effect on how we perform. Credible expectancies, those from people we believe know and who make a difference, affect the following aspects of performance behavior

- the intensity of effort
- the level of concentration or distractibility
- the willingness to take reasonable risks, which is a key factor in developing self-confidence and new skills

Effect on how we think about our performance. Expectancies affect the way people think about or explain their performance outcomes, what they attribute the outcomes to. When confident people are confronted with unexpected failure, they look for what they did wrong and try to correct it. They tend to learn from the experience how to be successful next time. When people expect to fail, assume they're unable to succeed, or believe they "don't have what it takes," they're likely to take a dim view of trying again.

The combined effect of expectancy on both how we perform and how we think about our performance is what makes it so powerful. The negative expectancy tends to trigger performance failure and then influences the person to blame the failure on lack of ability (and potential or aptitude) rather than on inadequate or erroneous effort, which is correctable. By this process the person, in effect, internalizes the low opinion originally held by others.

What makes African Americans unique is that they are singled out for the stigma of genetic intellectual inferiority. This negative stereotype suggests to African Americans that they should understand any failure in intellectual activity as confirmation of genetic inferiority. No wonder many Africa Americans shy away from any situation where the rumor of inferiority might be proved true.

Action Steps for Leaders

What can you as leader do to coach employees through the success cycle?

During the confidence phase. Begin with your own stereotyped beliefs, assumptions, and expectations. Get them straight. When you're sure you have a "you can" attitude, you'll know your verbal and nonverbal messages are likely to convey positive expectations.

During the effort phase. Take a positive attitude toward performance evaluation. Encourage African Americans to attribute their successes to ability, boosting their confidence level. Help them to see their failures as either a lack of effort or some correctable error—as a learning tool for creating success the next time around. The key question is, how can I do it differently next time?

During the skill development phase. Help African American employees to assume responsibility for their own performance and development, and let them know you are there as a resource person. Pay special attention to training and development, bringing in appropriate new opportunities as skills are built. Keep the cycle going.

Leadership Opportunity: Building on African American Strengths

As a leader, you need to recognize the strengths that each of your team members brings to the organization and to build on those strengths. African Americans bring many assets to the workplace, as previous discussions imply. Let's briefly review some core cultural values and traits and how you can build on them.

- *A holistic worldview*, responding to things in terms of the whole picture instead of its parts.
- *Inferential reasoning*, concluding that something is so in light of related things being so, which is closely related to their holistic worldview. This contrasts with deductive and inductive reasoning, both of which rely on fact gathering.
- *Flexible approximations* are often used rather than insistence on exact times, numbers, and spaces. While this can be a problem in a number-specific situation, flexibility and lack of dependence on exact measurement can also be a creative asset.
- *Personal style, preference for novelty and freedom*, as shown in style of dress, communication flair, personality, and musical improvisations.
- *People focus* rather than *things* focus. People and their activities are their main interest, often shown through altruism, a concern for fellow human beings; most college students choose careers in the helping professions.
- *Nonverbal communication skills* are very strong, and they tend to rely even more on the nonverbal than do Euro-Americans.
- *Assertiveness, genuineness, directness*, preference for dealing with people, situations, and issues directly, sincerely, and promptly—fully expressing accompanying emotions.
- *Feeling mode*, in close touch with their feelings, comfortable and skilled in expressing feelings, able to manage the expression of intense feelings, facility in utilizing feelings to energize events and activities and to achieve emotional and spiritual release.
- *Keen sense of justice*, and a quickness to analyze and perceive injustice.
- *Connection with the African American marketplace*, an understanding of the African American community.

These strengths can be used in numerous ways. We'll discuss specifically how they can contribute to team processes, as well as to the development of networks and business relationships that are especially valuable for the organization, including connections with the African American marketplace.

Planning, Creating, Problem Solving

Work teams must deal with fast-paced change—by recognizing niches, developing profitable products and services, moving in on the right opportunities at the right time, solving problems, and optimizing total quality. The best work teams develop a high level of skill in generating ideas, planning, and problem solving—and they do this through synergy, creativity, and innovation as well as by discipline and application. When team leaders and members recognize the value of African American strengths—such as personal style, holistic worldview, inferential reasoning, and flexible approximation, these traits can add to the team's strengths. Some of these traits may seem foreign to those accustomed to typical business traits and approaches. But if the team realizes that a different approach can sometimes score winning points, that "differentness" can become an asset.

Building Relationships

Relationships are the name of the game in the marketplace. Business is built upon networks of relationships among team members, customers, suppliers, other departments, the community, professional organizations, regulating agencies, and others. African Americans have a special advantage when they apply their tendencies toward a people focus, sharing, nonverbal communication skills, and expression of feelings. For example, in team relationships, African American members can set a tone that could help the team avoid game playing and hidden agendas through focusing on the values of directness, emotional expressiveness, and sense of justice. To be most effective, expression of these values may need to be stepped down to an intensity that other team members can accept. Leaders can help African American members develop appropriate expressions of their strengths. Sensitive leaders can also provide guidance about expressing the justice and distrust values in ways that avoid the stereotype of the cocky African American or the troublemaker.

Connecting with the African American Marketplace

African Americans obviously have an inside edge in understanding other African Americans, the community, and the marketplace. They can contribute great strength to the organization in gaining African American market share. African Americans now represent about $300 billion a year in spending power, and the market is growing. These customers and business persons like to do business with companies that "look like America." South Africa and other African nations also represent growth market opportunities for many organizations, and African American team members provide an obvious advantage in those markets.

Leadership Opportunity: Giving Support at Each Career Phase

African Americans who enter the corporate world typically move through several phases that might be described as:

- the entry-level phase
- the adjustment and frustration phase
- the career development phase
- the mastery phase

These phases are typical for most minorities because they represent adaptations to the typical business culture. The adaptation may be most difficult for African Americans due to the results of our history of extreme interracial prejudice. African American managers Jacqueline Dickens and Floyd Dickens (1982) have described attitudes, emotions, and behaviors typical of each career phase, which will be helpful to you as a leader in helping African Americans make the best contribution from their strengths.

Many African American applicants come to the organization with a positive but naive attitude. They usually encounter personal as well as organizational prejudice and may become angry, hostile, and culturally paranoid. If they decide to stay, they then adjust and plan their growth rather than allow anger and resentment to stifle it. They find ways to recapture their earlier positive attitude, so that negative attitudes cease to be a barrier to learning. Successful African American managers somehow retain a positive attitude even in the midst of prejudiced behaviors.

In the first two phases most African Americans have great difficulty seeing themselves in a leadership position because they've been taught that Euro-American men lead, African Americans follow. They often apologize in various ways for taking leadership or initiative or for being put in even a temporary leadership position. They may have difficulty directing Euro-American males and therefore not be as directive as the norm because of discomfort with empowerment. Before they become comfortable with having and using power, their walk may be less commanding, their voice tone may lack authority, and their attitude may be more *May I?* than *This is what we can do.*

Be aware that typically minorities are required to demonstrate competence at the next level before they are promoted, whereas Euro-American males are typically promoted on the basis of their potential. Ask yourself periodically, Am I doing my share to see that people are promoted or given more responsibility on the same basis?

Even when minority persons achieve the desired results, they typically must devote extra energy to ensure that the results are properly seen by the right people. This is because the decision makers often harbor negative stereotypes that prevent them from seeing such achievements. Are you open to seeing everyone's achievements and potential?

The Entry–Level Phase: Initial Support Opportunities

During employees' entry phase, pay special attention to helping them deal with their own attitudes, emotions, behaviors, and job skills, as shown in Table 5.9.

TABLE 5.9: Phase One: Entry Level
Typical Attitudes, Emotions, Behaviors, Job Skills

Attitudes. *Typical attitudes that can cause problems for African Americans:*
- Lack of self-confidence, especially on the job with Euro-Americans.
- Attributing their job position to luck or AA instead of their own qualifications.
- Inadequate preparation for the realities of the work world, especially relationships.
- Naiveté, especially about prejudiced attitudes in the workplace.
- Belief in the Protestant work ethic, "All I have to do to succeed is work hard."
- Feelings of gratitude for job and thus being overly satisfied with their status.
- Lack of clear job goals and understanding of career objectives and advancement opportunities.
- Unawareness of civil rights issues and subtle prejudice in day-to-day interactions.

Emotions. *Typical emotions that African Americans experience and must work through in the entry phase:*
- Confusion in interactions with Euro-Americans.
- Willingness to accept responsibility for poor relations with Euro-Americans (self-blame rather than anger and hostility toward them).
- Hope that the organization will be fair and supportive.
- Internal discomfort as the only cue that something is wrong.
- High stress level from not being able to identify the source of discomfort.
- Feeling "out of sync" because of the confusion and discomfort.

Behaviors. *Some typical behaviors that African Americans display in entry phase:*
- Making great efforts to belong to the group or going to the opposite extreme and avoiding others
- Being *nice* no matter what happens—smiling, agreeing, laughing at jokes.
- Seeking support in order to feel good about themselves.
- Letting concern about others' stereotyped judgments of their personality overshadow their competence and work output.
- Focusing on job tasks with little concern for learning the organizational ropes and building support networks.

Gaps in job skills. *Typical gaps in job skills of African Americans in entry phase:*
- Managerial skills—running meetings, handling conflict, using and managing resources, expressing emotions appropriately, managing others' prejudice.
- Organizational savvy—understanding how organizations function.
- Opportunities to obtain training and development in job.
- Ability to translate Euro-American training material into effective use.
- Realistic expectations of job and people; sometimes there's just wishful thinking, other times no real expectations.
- Future orientation for career; for example, finding African American or substitute role models, to get a picture of how to move up in the organization.
- Communication savvy—understanding the grapevine, the networks, and how to use them.
- Knowledge of how to get the resources, information, and skills they need for survival.
- An understanding of the styles of the managers who will evaluate them.

The Adjustment and Frustration Phases: Crucial Support Opportunities

After an entry or orientation time, employees begin to make the necessary adjustments to the corporate culture. The attitudes, emotions, behaviors, and skills gaps are shown in Table 5.10.

TABLE 5.10: Phase Two: Adjustment and Frustration
Typical Attitudes, Emotions, Behaviors, Job Skills

Attitudes that are typical during the adjustment phase:
- Low self-confidence, often as a result of running into much criticism.
- Readjustment of expectations about the organization to fit new perceptions.
- Better picture of how prejudice affects progress; identification of barriers.
- Reality testing.

Emotions that are typical during the adjustment phase:
- Disappointment in the results of the work ethic.
- Disillusionment about company fairness and support.
- Frustration—uncertainty about who is responsible for barriers; trial-and-error reality testing.
- Stress at a deeper level.
- Anger or rage.

Behaviors that are typical during the adjustment phase:
- Struggling to identify and learn appropriate behavior.
- Establishing an informal communications network, often with other African Americans.
- Learning to identify own skills.
- Reacting negatively to Euro-American males, perhaps having many arguments with them, perhaps taking business events and criticism "personally."
- Speaking out more, often inappropriately by Euro-American norms.

Job skills will progress during the adjustment phase, to include:
- Developing a positive perception of own competence.
- Struggling to acquire needed skills.
- Continuing to notice that Euro-American male peers get better jobs and more responsibility. Dealing with the issue of potential versus proven competence. Asking, "How do they know what I can do if they won't give me a chance?"
- Perceiving little job movement and few results, picking up the message, "You've got to prove yourself again and again."
- Beginning to see that how well they manage or collaborate with others determines how their job competence will be evaluated.

For African Americans, the adjustment phase normally includes a frustration period because of cultural conflict. African Americans often become very sensitive to people and resistant to certain uses of organizational power. Historically, beginning with slavery, they have needed to be sensitive to other's needs and wishes in order to survive. This sensitivity became a cultural trait handed down from generation to generation. Also, African Americans often resist Euro-Americans' organizational power to position them in roles that fulfill Euro-Americans' negative and prejudicial stereotypes. They enter the organization armed with their own cultural behavioral patterns, which they may soon find they cannot fully use in the organization to achieve results. In fact, they usually find it necessary to repress normal responses that are considered inappropriate, too emotional, too flashy, too ethnic, or in poor taste. They see that they must develop additional behavioral styles and skills.

At this stage African Americans need to learn the more subtle aspects of getting their jobs done.

Often African Americans don't understand the corporate culture or its norms because they're just starting to learn how to tap into and use organizational resources. They often test and probe their organizational environment, using trial and error, to determine specific behaviors that trigger approval or disapproval.

They must learn acceptable ways, by Euro-American norms, to master frustration, anger, rage and other emotions, manage interactions with other people, manage conflict, and read organizational cues. A common complaint by Euro-American managers is that African Americans are too emotional, and they do tend to display and use emotions very openly. They normally restrain their emotions during the entry-level phase, which results in a buildup of frustration that's ready to blow during the adjustment and frustration phase. They may become frustrated because they have high job interest and energy but can't seem to achieve job goals.

This is the most turbulent and active phase because African American employees are becoming aware of the realities and the barriers they face. If their experience is that they're treated differently from the way Euro-American males are treated, they begin to push back on the organization and to test it. This testing helps them build a more realistic picture of the situation and to gain confidence—if they don't push too hard. The key to helping them move on to the career development phase is to suggest how they might organize their experiences, learn quickly from them, and grow as a result. The danger is allowing them to thrash around in frustration till they burn out.

Leadership opportunities are abundant during the adjustment and frustration phase. Actions you can take as a leader to help African American employees include:

- Be aware that their adjustment phase differs from that of their Euro-American male peers.
- Take extra time to discuss their needs for information gathering and to help with difficulties.
- Open doors for them by introducing them into the informal communications network.
- See that they are included in work activities where corporate information is discussed.
- Don't take their behavior personally and overreact to it.
- Coach them in avoiding the powerless response of personalizing business adversity, criticism of performance, and similar business events.
- Understand why they behave the way they do.
- Provide an additional perspective by sharing your interpretations of behavior.
- Be creative in helping them through this phase.
- Help them learn to convert the energy generated by anger or rage to productive activity.

The Career Development Phase: Building Trust

In the third phase, career development, the most important issue is overcoming mistrust of the Euro-American establishment. Typical attitudes, emotions, behaviors, and job skills issues are shown in Table 5.11.

Overcoming African American mistrust of the input from Euro-Americans is still an issue for most African American employees, even at the career development stage. They may establish one-to-one relationship with their manager, but they rarely expand this to a generalized attitude toward all Euro-Americans. During this phase African American employees usually keep their misgivings to themselves, choosing instead to behave in a manner of trust. They need to identify and access one or more mentors. They must develop and use a network of supporters, whether the members are prejudiced or not. A commitment to succeed becomes the prime goal of successful employees. By now they should understand that waiting to be adopted by a Euro-American mentor is risky, so they may need to take the initiative to locate potential people in the organization and find a mentor.

TABLE 5.11: Phase Three: Career Development
Typical Attitudes, Emotions, Behaviors, Job Skills

Attitudes that are typical during the career development phase:
- Clarifying ambitions; realizing they need to shine, to move up the ladder.
- Being willing to expend more energy than Euro-American peers to succeed.
- Evaluating personal style and removing style barriers; perhaps shifting from low-key to quietly assertive; projecting a competent image through style of dress and walk; channeling emotions into intellectual aggressiveness rather than explosive anger.
- Relying more on African American support to balance lack of support from other sources

Emotions that are typical during the career development phase:
- Acquiring a sense of determination.
- Building a feeling of pride.
- Using anger as a selective strategy to achieve certain goals.

Behaviors that may develop:
- Avoiding knee-jerk reactions; using *protective hesitation*.
- Learning to make proper demands on the organization as part of career planning.
- Using strategy to position people and the company in a way that also meets personal needs.
- Setting and meeting goals.
- Consciously acting to remove barriers under own control.
- Seeking mentors.
- Learning to effectively network with Euro-Americans.

Job skills that are typically added during this phase:
- Learning and using multicultural management skills to neutralize others' prejudice.
- Making continued use of communication networks.

In this phase, two of the most important job skills to be acquired are conflict management and the management of prejudice. If African Americans can't deal with conflict constructively, they're likely to be blamed as a *cause* of any conflict they become embroiled in. African Americans tend as a group to be more open and straightforward in their interactions than do Euro-Americans. They typically want to confront conflict directly and solve the problem quickly. In many organizations however, the norm is conflict avoidance. If so, the African American's style will be seen as inappropriate. African Americans are more likely to confront the other person as soon as they're aware of a conflict situation. If that's inappropriate, they'll do it later in private. Euro-Americans in many corporate cultures will tend to discuss the situation with the other person's boss, and may talk about it with others before they'll openly confront the person involved in the conflict.

Management of prejudice involves a range of skills most African Americans must develop in order to counteract and neutralize Euro-Americans' demeaning, prejudicial actions. For example, *protective hesitation* is a common African American strategy for dealing with prejudice and the hostile situations it engenders. It's based on the value of distrust of the establishment. The strategy consists of deliberately hesitating before interacting or preparing to interact with Euro-Americans, in order to think about how to protect oneself from possible psychological assault or to avoid reinforcing negative stereotypes about African Americans. Such preventive hesitation involves using caution and preplanning. This behavior has been handed down from parents to children through generations and so comes naturally to many African Americans by the time they're adults. It can be especially helpful at the career development phase when the employee is being assessed for promotion potential.

The Mastery Phase: Mutual Support

One of the key insights needed in the mastery phase is that making mistakes or failing is not an option for African American managers. When they fail, they fail for the entire group of African American employees. Those who've succeeded report that they use protective hesitation as a way of life in the corporation. Preplanning, careful thought, and caution in relying on Euro-Americans as resources is part of their style. Through trial and error, they take their rage and use its energy to help them achieve productive results. Typical attitudes, emotions, behaviors, and job skills issues are shown in Table 5.12.

TABLE 5.12: Phase Four: Mastery
Typical Attitudes, Emotions, Behaviors, Job Skills

Attitudes *typical during the mastery phase*:
- Accepting the additional burdens of minority status that go with first promotion.
- Realizing that failure is not an option; they must not reinforce stereotypes or let down other African Americans.
- Using protective hesitation as a strategy.
- Being aware that success probably depends on remembering they're African Americans and that's how they're seen by the organization.
- Continuing awareness of how subtle prejudice works.
- Being sensitive to prejudicial cues, but responding only to those that threaten or offer opportunities.
- Seeking less praise; being results-oriented and getting satisfaction from within.

Emotional *aspects of this phase*:
- Channeling emotions constructively.
- Feeling high confidence.

Behaviors *that are typical*:
- Using formal and informal communication networks effectively.
- Continuing to refine and smooth personal style.
- Confronting Euro-American males in a way that leaves them their dignity.
- Continuing to set and meet goals.
- Producing high quality results.
- Displaying a success image: confident, knowledgeable, in charge.

Job skills *that are typically added for this phase include*:
- Using a higher level of interpersonal and behavioral skills than required of Euro-Americans.
- Using skills to resist power from above that puts them in a subservient position.
- Continuing to develop multicultural management skills.

SUMMARY

The 12 percent of Americans who are African American must deal with myths and stereotypes about violence, anger, intelligence, initiative, and style, all part of a heritage of slavery, segregation, and discrimination. African Americans led the Civil Rights movement that opened doors for all disadvantaged groups in the U.S. workplace. As a result, there is a growing affluent African American middle class, about one-third of African Americans, but also a growing underclass of about one-third, which has an especially devastating effect on the young men. Leaders are establishing cooperative economic programs in the new urban villages to cope with this problem. African American educational achievement tends to be lower than that of Euro-Americans. Studies indicate that higher socioeconomic status is the best predictor of school grades and SAT scores, so the solution to this problem may lie in finding ways to help more African Americans reach middle-class status. Meanwhile, for those who have achieved such status, there's still a glass ceiling to advancement for African Americans in corporate America, and many who hit it are leaving to form their own businesses.

The core values of the African American community are sharing, personal style, genuineness, assertiveness, vitality, and resilience. Relating in a way that's personal and emotional is typical. The community is close-knit, and their ways of confronting one another assertively are part of being genuine. This trait is often misunderstood by Euro-Americans as being combative and even a prelude to violence. But it can be a strength, just as vitality and resilience are strengths, that African American employees bring to the workplace and marketplace. These strengths can be especially helpful in team projects and in building networks of relationships. Leaders can help

African American employees build on these strengths as they develop other skills and strengths they need to achieve job and career goals. Leaders must be especially sensitive to the value of distrust of the establishment, and special care must be taken to build trust.

Skill Builder 5.1: The Case of Jason, African American Manager

Jason has applied for an assistant manager's position at Drysdale Corporation. He's looking for opportunities to learn and grow in his career and wants to leave his current job because such opportunities are lacking. His ultimate career goal is to become CEO of a large corporation. With his degree in business administration and plans to complete an MBA, he thinks he has a chance—if he can find the right firm—even though he's an African American. When Jason is escorted around the Drysdale offices, he sees no African Americans, a few Asian Americans, and one Latino American. Nearly everyone is Euro-American, and they mostly seem too busy to pay much attention to Jason or spend time with him. But Jason really believes in the Drysdale Corporation and decides to accept their job offer.

Soon after he begins work, he notices that ethnic jokes and comments are common at Drysdale. Jason doesn't look like a typical African American because his mother is Euro-American. He speaks up several times, saying he doesn't appreciate jokes and comments that belittle people from any ethnic group. Most of the comments stop, but so does the already-sparse friendliness of Jason's co-workers. While the environment is not particularly warm at Drysdale, Jason still believes he can achieve career success here because he loves the work itself.

Jason knows he's a rapid learner and a responsible person, one who works effectively and efficiently. His performance evaluations during the next year and a half are all excellent and his manager *Ken* seems to be encouraging.

In fact, Jason believes he is one of the most productive workers in the company. He meets his time targets and maintains high work quality. But Jason is getting restless. His work is becoming routine to him and therefore boring. He has asked Ken several times about a promotion and expanded job responsibilities. Ken has been vague, telling Jason to "hang in there and I'll keep an eye out for job opportunities for you." In the meantime, several management positions have opened up at Drysdale and been filled by others.

- What do you think is going on here?
- If you were Jason, what would you do?

Skill Builder 5.2: The Case of Karla, African American Salesperson

Karla is a salesperson at Ellison's Furniture, the only African American on the small sales force of 20 persons. She has been very successful in selling furniture, makes a good salary plus commission, and during the year she has been at Ellison's has made top salesperson of the month three times. Karla enjoys her work but feels isolated from most of her co-workers. Most of them are Euro-American men, and five are Euro-American women. The manager *Daniel* is Euro-American and has been very supportive of Karla's training, development, and sales work. He often praises her work and encourages her to "keep it up."

Rachel is the only salesperson who has seemed willing to spend much time with Karla during coffee breaks or at lunch. While Karla doesn't think of Rachel as a close personal friend, she does view her as more than just a business colleague. She's also a friend.

From time to time Karla has overheard comments of her co-workers about the good times they've had together at various parties and outings that they plan. She can't help thinking about the fact that she is never included. Last week as Karla approached the employees' lounge, she heard someone saying, ". . . at Rachel's party last Saturday. . . ." Karla stopped dead in her tracks. She felt as if someone had punched her in the stomach. What a blow to discover that even her friend, her only "real work friend," had thrown a party and had excluded her.

Daniel has noticed that during the past week Karla has seemed quieter and more withdrawn than usual. He is concerned because he believes that Karla's success as a salesperson is largely due to her outgoing, cheerful personality. When he gets a chance to talk privately with Karla, he says, "Is everything okay, Karla? You've been awfully quiet the past few days."

- If you were Karla, what would you do?
- If you were Daniel, what would you do?

Skill Builder 5.3: The Case of Assistant Manager Doug

Doug is assistant manager of the Nashville branch of Angelo Shipping Company. He's been an employee there for 12 years, since he was 23, and he was promoted to assistant manager a year ago. Last month Doug learned of an upcoming opening in the Atlanta headquarters and applied for it. He believes he has all the necessary qualifications for the position as well as an exemplary performance record. Although there are many African American men working as manual laborers for the company, none are full managers or executives.

John, an executive in the headquarters office, is interviewing applicants for the management position and will make a recommendation to the executive team. Of the four qualified applicants, all but Doug are Euro-American men. John, also a Euro-American, has never worked with an African American manager.

When Doug arrives for his interview with John, he's left waiting in the lobby for an hour. Then a secretary comes in and tells him that John is still interviewing another candidate and will be with him in a while. About 45 minutes later, John appears in the lobby with *Mike* of the Memphis branch. John is talking warmly with Mike, then thanks him and shakes his hand before turning to welcome Doug. They walk to John's office, where John waves toward a chair across from his desk, and Doug seats himself. John and Doug talk for about 10 to 15 minutes, mainly about how Doug feels about his current job and the company. The phone rings. John takes the call, puts his hand over the receiver, and says to Doug, "Thank you for coming in. Could you show yourself out? I must take this call." Doug was shocked, but he found his way out.

A few days later, Doug receives a telephone call from John, who tells him the executive team has selected Mike for the job. He says the executive team felt the position called for someone with Mike's experience. Later, Doug says to his friend Jan, "I know I've been with the company at least as long as Mike, and I've been employee-of-the-month here eight different times. I heard Mike has only won it twice. I don't understand how his experience could be any better than mine. What would make it better?"

- What is your opinion of John's actions and the executive team's decision?
- What do you think Doug should do?

Skill Builder 5.4: The Case of Sales Rep Evelyn

Evelyn has been one of the outstanding sales representatives for McCord Foods' West Coast region for the past three years. Her immediate supervisor *Rosalie* is in a quandary about what to do. The Houston office needs a sales supervisor with just the kind of experience and qualities that Evelyn has. However, the last time an African American was transferred into a management position at the Houston office, he faced many problems. The major issue was that key customers didn't accept him and he lost a number of accounts. These accounts were with large, traditional food processing and manufacturing firms.

McCord sells spices, flavorings, and other additives to the food industry. The field is very competitive, and accounts are often won and lost on the basis of the personal relationships between sales manager, sales rep, and purchasing agent. The sales manager periodically travels with sales reps to call on major accounts and potential accounts. The sales manager also enters the picture when thorny customer problems arise.

Louis, who is head of the Houston office, was enthusiastic about Evelyn's resume until he heard that she was African American. He called Rosalie and talked over the touchy situation with her. "Maybe it wouldn't be fair to Evelyn to ask her to move all the way down here and then be faced with a no-win situation," he said.

Now Rosalie must make a decision. She knows that two other well-qualified candidates are being recommended for the position, but actually Evelyn is better suited to the job than the others. Shall she recommend Evelyn for the position? Evelyn has a child in the fourth grade, who would have to adapt to a new school and the Houston environment. If it didn't work out, Rosalie would feel responsible.

• What do you think Rosalie should do?

REFERENCES

AAUW. *The AAUW Report: How Schools Shortchange Girls*. Washington DC: American Assn. University Women, 1992.

Abrahams, R.D. *Deep Down in the Jungle*. Chicago: Aldine Press, 1963.

Allen, W.R. "Moms, Dads, and Boys." *Black Men*. Beverly Hills, CA: Sage, 1981.

Baldwin, J.A. "The Role of Black Psychologists in Black Liberation." *African American Psychology*. Thousand Oaks, CA: Sage, 1992.

Billingsley, Andrew. *Climbing Jacob's Ladder: The Enduring Legacy of African American Families*. New York: Simon & Schuster, 1992.

Black Enterprise (May 1994).

Blackwell, J.E. *The Black Community: Diversity and Unity*. New York: Harper & Row, 1985.

Blanchard, F.A., and F.J. Crosby. *Affirmative Action in Perspective*. New York: Springer-Verlag, 1989.

Carr-Ruffino, "Legislative Measures for Women's Advancement." *Womanpower*. Thousand Oaks, CA: Sage, 1992.

Carr-Ruffino, Norma. "U.S. Women: Breaking Through the Glass Ceiling." *Women in Management Review*, 6, no. 5, 1991.

Collier, M.J. "A Comparison of Intracultural and Intercultural Communication Among Acquaintances." *Communication Quarterly*, 36 (1988): 122–144.

Collier, M.J. "Ethnic Friendships." Manuscript submitted for publication, 1992.

Dickens, Floyd, Jr., and Jacqueline B. Dickens. *The Black Manager: Making It in the Corporate World*. New York: Amacom, 1982.

Donohue, W.A. *The Politics of the American Civil Liberties Union*. New Brunswick: Transaction Books, 1985.

Dovidio, J.F. and S.L. Gaertner, eds. *Prejudice, Discrimination, and Racism*. Orlando, Fl: Academic Press, 1986.

Du Bois, W.E.B. *The Souls of Black Folk*, reprinted in *Three Negro Classics*. New York: Avon Books, 1965.

Executive Female. A survey on the glass ceiling, women and African Americans, 1991.

Feagin Joe, "The Continuing Significance of Race: Antiblack Discrimination in Public Places." *American Sociological Review*, 56 (February 1991): 101–116.

Foeman, A.K. and G. Pressley, "Ethnic Culture and Corporate Culture: Using Black Styles in Organizations." *Communications Quarterly*, 35 (1987): 293–307.

Fraser, George. *Success Runs in Our Race*. New York: Wm. Morrow, 1994.

Garner, T.E. "Playing the Dozens." *Quarterly Journal of Speech*, 69 (1983): 47–57.

Glaser, D. "Dynamics of Ethnic Identification." *American Sociological Review*, 23 (1958): 31–40.

Halberstad, A.G. "Race, Socioeconomic Status, and Nonverbal Behavior." *Multichannel Integrations of Nonverbal Behavior*. Hillsdale, NJ: Lawrence Erlbaum, 1985.

Hall. E.T. *Beyond Culture*. New York: Doubleday, 1976.

Hammer, M.R. and W.B. Gundykunst. "The Influence of Ethnicity and Sex on Social Penetration in Close Friendships." *Journal of Black Studies* 17 (1987): 418–437.

Harding, Vincent. *The Other American Revolution*. Atlanta, GA: Institute of the Black World, 1980.

Hecht, M.L., and S. Ribeau. "Ethnic Communication: A Comparative Analysis of Satisfying Communication." *International Journal of Intercultural Relations* 8 (1984): 135–151.

Hecht, M.L., M.J. Collier, S.A. Ribeau. *African American Communication*. Thousand Oaks, CA: Sage, 1993.

Herskovitz, M.J. *The Myth of the Negro Past*. Boston: Beacon, 1958.

Herskovitz, M.J. *Anthropometry of the American Negro*. NY: Columbia Univ. Press, 1930.

Howard, Jeff, and Ray Hammond. "Rumors of Inferiority: The Hidden Obstacles to Black Success." *The New Republic*, September 9, 1988.

Ickes, W. "Composition in Black and White." *Journal of Personality and Social Psychology* 47 (1984): 1206–1217.

Kanter, R.M. *Men and Women of the Corporation*. New York: Basic Books, 1979.

Kenton, S.B. and D. Valentine. *CrossTalk*. Cincinnati, OH: South-Western, 1996.

Kitano, H. *Japanese-Americans*. Englewood Cliffs, NJ: Prentice-Hall, 1976.

Kochman, Thomas. *Black & White Styles in Conflict*. Chicago: The University of Chicago Press, 1981.

Larkey, L.K., and M.L. Hecht. "A Comparative Study of African American and Euro-American Ethnic Identity." Paper presented at the International Conference for Language and Social Psychology, Santa Barbara, CA, August 1991.

Lichtenberg, J. "Racism in the Head, Racism in the World." *Report from the Institute for Philosophy and Public Policy* 12, no. 1 (1992): 3–5.

Lynch, F.R. *Invisible Victims: White Males and the Crisis of Affirmative Action*. New York: Praeger, 1989.

Mann, W. "Support Systems of Significant Others in Black Families." *Black Families*. Thousand Oaks, CA: Sage, 1981.

Mauer, Marc. Research report on African American problems, 1989.

McWilliams, Carey. *Brothers Under the Skin*. Boston: Little, Brown and Company, 1964.

Myers, Samuel L., ed. *Economic Issues and Black Colleges*. Chicago: Follett Press, 1986.

NAEOHE, National Association for Equal Opportunity in Higher Education, 1990.

Patchen, Martin, et al. "Academic Performance of Black High School Students Under Different Conditions of Contact with White Peers." *Sociology of Education* 53 (January 1980): 33–51.

Pettigrew, Thomas F., and Joanne Martin. "Shaping the Organizational Context for Black American Inclusion." *Journal of Social Issues* 43, no. 1 (1987): 41–78.

Pinkney, Alphonso. *The Myth of Black Progress*. Cambridge: Cambridge University Press, 1984.

Ponterotto, Joseph G., and Paul B. Pedersen. *Preventing Prejudice*. Thousand Oaks, CA: Sage, 1993.

Rose, L.F. "Theoretical & Methodological Issues in the Study of Black Culture and Personality." *Humboldt Journal of Social Relations* 10 (1982/1983): 320–338.

Smith, D.E., F.N. Willis, and J.A. Gier. "Success and Interpersonal Touch in a Competitive Setting." *Journal of Nonverbal Behavior 5* (1980): 26–34.

Smitherman, G. *Talkin' and Testifyin': The Language of Black America*. Boston: Houghton Mifflin, 1977.

Solorzano, Daniel G. "Mobility Aspirations Among Racial Minorities, Controlling for SES." *Social Science Review 75* (July 1991): 182–188.

Stanbeck, M., and W.B. Pearce. "Talking to 'the man.'" *Quarterly Journal of Speech 67* (1981): 21–30.

Stewart, Edward C. *American Cultural Patterns: A Cross Cultural Perspective*. LaGrange Park, IL: Intercultural Network, Inc., 1972.

Stienstra, Tom. "A Dramatic Turnaround for State Parks." *San Francisco Examiner* (January 22, 1995): D-12.

Takaki, Ronald. *A Different Mirror: A History of Multicultural America*. Boston: Little, Brown & Company, 1993.

Terry, Robert W. (Detroit Industrial Mission). *For Whites Only*. Grand Rapids, MI: William B. Eerdmans Publishing Company, 1970, 1990.

Thomas, Roosevelt. *Beyond Race & Gender*. New York: AMACOM, 1991.

Thornton, Jeanne, and Davis Whitman. "Whites' Myths about Blacks." *U.S. News & World Report* (November 9, 1992): 41–44.

U.S. Census Bureau, *Current Population Reports. 1991*. "Average Earnings of Year-Round Fulltime Workers by Sex and Educational Attainment." February 1991.

U.S. Census Bureau, Department of Commerce. *We the American Children,* 1993.

U.S. Department of Labor. *A Report on the Glass Ceiling Initiative*, 1991.

Vaughan, A.T. "The Origins Debate." *Virginia Magazine of History and Biography*, 97 (July 1989): 354.

West, Cornell. *Keeping Faith*. New York: Routledge, 1993.

West, Cornell. *Race Matters*. Boston: Beacon Press, 1993.

Whitaker, Mark. "White & Black Lies." *Newsweek* (November 15, 1993): 53–63.

White, J L., and T.A. Parham. *The Psychology of Blacks: An African American Perspective*, 2d ed. Englewood Cliffs, NJ: Prentice-Hall, 1990.

Wilkerson, Isabel of the *New York Times* reported in November 1990.

Williams, Walter. "Career and Opportunities." *Black Enterprise*, February 1992.

Willie, C.V. *A New Look at Black Families*. New Bayside, NY: General Hall, 1976.

Woodson, C.G. *The African Background Outlined*. New York: Negro Universities Press, 1968.

Woody, Bette. "Black Women in the New Service Economy." Working paper no. 196. Wellesley College Center for Research on Women, 1989.

WSJ. "Black Managers Leaving the Fold." *Wall Street Journal* (May 6, 1992): 1A.

Young, V. "Family and Childhood in a Southern Negro Community." American Anthropologist 72 (1977): 269–299.

Resources

Major organizations set up to fight the Ku Klux Klan, neo-nazis, and other groups that foster hate crimes:

Southern Poverty Law Center, 400 Washington Ave., Montgomery, AL 36104.

Anti-Defamation League, 823 United Nations Plaza, New York, NY 10017-3560.

CHAPTER 6

Working with Asian Americans

I keep the harmony and pay honor and respect to the manager.
Why didn't he talk to me about the new supervisor job?
Asian American worker

About seven million Americans are Asian Americans, or around three percent. In this chapter we'll examine some common threads running through the major Asian American subcultures, from myths and stereotypes, to background and current profile, to cultural patterns and issues. Then we'll review unique aspects of various Asian American groups based on their country of origin—China, Japan, the Philippines, Korea, Vietnam, India, and the Pacific Islands. Each of these groups has their own immigration patterns, current profile, and cultural issues. Most important, you'll examine how the wide-ranging talents and values of Asian American employees can contribute to the organization. First, explore your opinions and knowledge of Asian Americans by completing Self-Awareness Activities 6.1 and 6.2.

Self-Awareness Activity 6.1: What Do You Believe About Asian Americans?

Purpose:
- to get in touch with your beliefs and stereotypes about this group of people
- to experience how judgmental beliefs affect your thinking and feeling processes
- to experience the ways in which your beliefs create your reality regarding other persons, even before you have any interaction with them.

Part I. What Do You Believe About Asian American Women?

Step 1. Associations
- Relax as deeply as you can: close your eyes and taking a few deep breaths.
- Focus on the words "Asian American woman" and allow a mental picture to come up in your mind's eye.
- Notice the words and images that come to mind as you "see" this woman.
- Open your eyes and list 10 to 20 words in the order in which they occur to you.

- Review your list. Mark a plus beside the words that are positive, a minus beside the words that are negative, and a circle beside neutral words.

Step 2. Negative Associations

- Close your eyes and focus again on the image of the Asian American woman. Formulate a negative opinion or judgment, perhaps one you typically hold about Asian American women.
- Notice your *feelings* as you see the person in this negative way. What *thoughts* come up as you focus on the image?
- Write a few sentences about your feelings and thoughts.

Step 3. Positive Associations

- Formulate a positive opinion or judgment, perhaps one you typically hold about Asian American women.
- Notice your *feelings* as you see the person in this positive way. What *thoughts* come up as you focus on the image?
- Write a few sentences about your feelings and thoughts.

Step 4. Insights

- Focus on the differences between your experiences when you hold negative and positive judgments or opinions. What were the differences? What meaning does this have for you, for your beliefs and feelings about people from this group, and about beliefs in general?
- Write your responses in a few sentences; include anything you like about your feelings, thoughts, and insights.

Part II. Experimenting with Opinions About Asian American Men

Repeat the phases and steps in Part I, this time focusing on the image of an Asian American man.

Self-Awareness Activity 6.2: What Do You Know About Asian Americans?

Purpose: To see what you know about the issues covered in this chapter.

Instructions: Determine whether you think the following statements are basically true or false—and think about why. The answers will emerge in this chapter, and the summary at the end of the chapter focuses on these issues.

1. Asian Americans are too passive in temperament to be effective business leaders in American corporate cultures.
2. Most Asian Americans in the workplace are more Asian than American.
3. Asian Americans tend to be more unemotional than people from other groups.
4. Early Asian immigrants were considered nonwhite and had to cope with segregation and other forms of discrimination.
5. Most Asian Americans are from China.
6. Asian Americans expect the manager to be "one of the guys."
7. The "model minority" label reflects the idea that Asian Americans adapt to the American workplace better than African Americans or Latino Americans.

Let's examine some common threads among all Asian American groups. Asian Americans have been in America for over 150 years, before many European immigrant groups. But because they were "different," they were often stereotyped as heathen, exotic, and unassimilable. The

Chinese were the first group to arrive in significant numbers, seeking gold, and what happened to them influenced the treatment of the Japanese, Koreans, Filipinos, and Asian Indians, as well as the Southeast Asian refugees who have come since the end of the Vietnam War. Most must cope with similar myths and stereotypes, experience generational differences as new generations become Americanized, hold some common cultural values and behavior patterns, and are affected by some common political issues, including the model minority stereotype.

MYTHS AND FACTS

We'll focus on a few of the most common myths that Asian Americans must deal with. These myths reflect some typical Asian stereotypes, and they contribute to the flavor of prejudice and discrimination that Asian Americans face.

Myth: Asian Americans are too passive and polite to be good managers.

Here's another career-bashing myth with not even a kernel of truth. One implication is that they're polite and therefore lack the conviction and backbone to stand up to the heat a supervisor must take. Another implication is that they're compliant, therefore passive, which means they don't have the ambition it takes to move up the competitive corporate ladder. This contradicts the Asian American small-business success record, which we'll discuss. It also contradicts studies of assembly line workers, which reveal that even at this level the women are surprisingly assertive and persistent beneath their "face" of compliance and cooperativeness. The behavior of Asian Americans is often misread by people who don't understand their cultural values and training.

Myth: Asian Americans are unemotional and inscrutable.

Euro-Americans often complain that they can't tell what Asian Americans are thinking or feeling, so they're seen as unemotional and inscrutable. In fact, Asian Americans experience the same emotions as other people. As we'll discuss later, their cultural values call for self-discipline in expressing emotions and for indirectness in communicating. When they disagree with you, say no, or convey unwelcome information, they often do it so indirectly and subtly that a Euro-American doesn't know they've done it. Later, if the Asian Americans' actions reflect a lack of agreement, Euro-Americans may conclude that the Asian Americans were evasive, sneaky, dishonest, or even corrupt, when perhaps they were merely being polite. You'll learn more in our values discussion.

Myth: Asian Americans tend to retain their foreign ways so it's difficult for them to fit in.

This myth creates what Asian Americans call "the perpetual foreigner barrier." To fully understand the experience of Asian groups in America, we must view them as immigrants, as minority groups, and as people of color. As immigrants, many of their struggles have been similar to those of European immigrants. But as minorities and as people of color bearing distinct physical differences, and coming from a culture and lifestyle that is just "too different," they've been viewed as "perpetual foreigners" who can never be completely absorbed into American society and politics. Discriminatory laws and practices have reinforced this separateness.

Myth: Asian Americans have learned how to make it in American society by working hard and being thrifty.

The model minority myth is pervasive in American society and is a double-edged sword for Asian Americans. On the one hand, it gives them a productive-worker image that makes them more acceptable in business and in society in general. On the other, it ignores the complexities and difficulties of their situation. It sets up unrealistic expectations that they'll gladly make major sacrifices for their work. It assumes that there are no pressing Asian American issues that need addressing. And it causes undue resentment from other minorities. Later we'll discuss the complexities of this myth as a cultural issue.

Myth: Asian Americans can't seem to master English grammar and pronunciation; they have communication problems.

Asian languages are about as different from English as a language can be. Therefore, becoming fluent and proficient is a long, arduous process for Asian Americans. Most work diligently and continually to improve their communication skills. Nearly all Asian Americans believe that English should be the only official language in the United States. Third- and fourth-generation Asian Americans tend to be fluent in English and may not be fluent in an Asian language. We'll briefly discuss these and other communication issues later in this section.

Myth: Asian Americans are good in technical occupations, but they don't have leadership potential.

This myth can create a huge barrier to career mobility. It's related to the idea that Asian Americans are technical coolies, computer nerds, or memorization whizzes, great at crunching numbers but short on people skills and creativity. As a group, Asian Americans do score better than any other group on math tests. But as a matter of fact, Asian American students demonstrate a broad range of aptitudes and talents. Many second-generation members have overcome the communication barriers entirely, and certainly most all third- and fourth-generation members have done so. Most immigrants, of course, must get through the English-as-a-second-language process. At times some Asian American students have found themselves somewhat isolated by language barriers and discrimination barriers. They resorted to what they *could* do well, which was study diligently, practice, and memorize. They naturally preferred courses of study in which this learning style could succeed, such as quantitative and computer courses.

Myth: Asian Americans just want to own their own businesses and acquire real estate; they don't care about social problems or politics.

Results of a recent survey seem to contradict this myth. For example, Asian American responses indicate they attach far more importance to political freedom than to buying a home. They're as happy to work for a U.S. corporation as to be self-employed. And, as we'll see, Asian Americans have viewed the establishment of small family businesses as the only way to survive and get ahead, not necessarily as a choice that's preferable to working for a large corporation. The survey also indicated that Asian Americans *are* concerned about social problems, especially the plight of the homeless (Viviano 1990).

Myth: Asian Americans know about all things Asian.

Some Euro-American business persons tend to look upon the company's "token" Asian Americans as the resident experts on all things Asian American—and Asian, for that matter. This assumes they know everything about the country their parents or grandparents immigrated from, its culture, adaptation of its people to the American culture, and which local restaurants are the best source of its cuisine. For some Asian Americans, this stereotype has become a pet peeve.

BACKGROUND:
FROM IMMIGRATION TO AMERICANIZATION

Understanding the Asian American experience requires understanding the processes of their acculturation, how overt and subtle prejudices have constrained their choices, and how each generation has changed the community. Although they become increasingly Americanized and acculturated, Asian Americans have also retained much of their Asian cultural heritage.

Acculturation Processes

Asian immigrants to America have experienced two major processes of acculturation:

- They've had to acquire the values and behavior of Euro-Americans.
- They've had to learn to accept their standing as ethnic minorities.

Many report that they've been seen as people who, because of the skin color and physical appearance, were not allowed to enjoy the rights and privileges given acculturated European immigrants and Euro-American native-born citizens. If they wanted to stay and survive in the U.S., they had to learn to "stay in their place" and to act with deference toward those of higher ethnic status; that is, Euro-Americans. Therefore, many of the choices they have made, such as becoming small-business owners or majoring in accounting, have been made within those limits. To fully understand Asian Americans' background as a group, we must be aware of these constraints.

Overt Prejudice from the Beginning

The 1882 Chinese Exclusion Act was the first law that prohibited the entry of immigrants on the basis of nationality. The Chinese condemned this restriction as racist and tyrannical. The precedent later provided a basis for the restriction of European immigrant groups such as Italians, Russians, Poles, and Greeks. The western states, where most Asian Americans lived, passed Alien Land Acts in the early part of this century that barred them from owning land because they were "aliens ineligible to citizenship." Asians were legally classified as "nonwhite" for many purposes, catching them in the segregation net cast around African Americans. Restrictive covenants were written into many deeds making it illegal to sell the property to a "nonwhite." State laws prohibited intermarriage. Asians were usually required to sit in the balcony or on one side of theaters, and some public pools and beaches were off limits to them. And school segregation was practiced in districts that had significant numbers of Asians, such as in San Francisco (Kitano and Daniels 1988).

The Japanese painfully discovered that their achievements in America did not lead to acceptance, when during World War II they were placed in internment camps.

Early Immigrants and Second and Third Generations

First-generation Asian Americans often refers to those who immigrated from China or Japan in the early years of this century. By the end of World War II second-generation Chinese Americans and Japanese Americans finally outnumbered their immigrant parents. Two immigrant groups that were much smaller, Asian Indian Americans and Filipino Americans, often intermarried with other ethnic groups. Their second-generation children, many of bi-ethnic parentage, tried their best to fit into the mainstream. For all Asian American groups, the second generation was mostly born in the 1940s to 1960s. Now mature and aging adults, they're primarily a low-profile group.

Young and inexperienced though they were, members of the second generation began to find a voice of their own and to become distinct from their parents' generation. First-generation Asian Americans tended to be relatively isolated in their ethnic communities and to retain their old cultural ways. Second-generation members are of course more Americanized but still strongly affected by their Asian cultural heritage. Studies indicate that even third-generation Asian Americans, while increasingly molded by the American culture, still retain certain aspects of their Asian community's worldview and values. A recent survey indicates that 47 percent think it's more important to move their family into mainstream American life, while 42 percent think it's more important to maintain traditional Asian ways (Baldassare 1990).

The great changes initiated in the 1960s affected Asian Americans, as they did everyone else. Laws forbidding intermarriage were overturned by the Supreme Court in 1967, and "mixed marriages" have become more common. Occupations previously closed to Asian Americans, such as public school teaching, began to open up, so the phenomenon of second-generation college graduates working at fruit stands began to disappear. College degrees began to mean something and career choices could be planned with some reasonable hope of fulfillment. Most private social clubs were closed to the second-generation, and housing segregation was still a reality. But higher education opened up, and streams of second-generation students poured in, most choosing safe majors in the professions, such as accounting, education, dentistry, or pharmacy. Employment patterns tend to be less discriminatory in professions, where credentials open doors and private practice can be lucrative, especially within one's minority community.

Third and Fourth Generations

Those Americans born in the 1970s and thereafter are of course the most Americanized of any generation. Many of them have never faced overt discrimination, and some have never had close ethnic ties or friendships with other Asian American families. Most go to the university and are eager for good jobs, especially in the professions, such as medicine, engineering, and law. They're entering occupations and fields once considered closed to them, such as advertising, the performing arts, journalism, and broadcasting.

They're more likely to reflect the influence of their surrounding communities than a strictly ethnic one. Those raised in California are likely to be more Californian than Asian. Nearly all live in urban areas in the West, especially in California and Hawaii. Although third- and fourth-generation young people question the lifestyle and values of their parents, they're the beneficiaries of the material success of the second generation.

Recent Immigrants

The contemporary Asian immigration and the refugee influx have been shaped by changes in U.S. immigration legislation and by the political, economic, and social agreements made between the countries of origin and the U.S. since the end of World War II. The U.S. has favored escapees from communism above all others.

Regardless of their reasons for coming, as soon as they arrive, most Asians have quickly made themselves productive. This ability to find niches for themselves is a double-edged sword. Their very success has resurrected some deeply ingrained prejudices and hostility. These contradictions that have characterized Asian American history continue to limit the lives of many Asian Americans today (Takaki 1992).

CURRENT PROFILE:
WHO ARE THE ASIAN AMERICANS?

In 1990 about seven million Asian Americans comprised nearly three percent of the U.S. population. Their country or region of origin varies widely, as follows:

Chinese	24%
Filipino	20%
Southeast Asia	16%
Japanese	12%
Asian Indian	12%
Korean	12%
Other	4%

Pacific Islanders living in the mainland U.S. are a relatively small group that were reported separately for the first time in 1990. We'll discuss each of these groups, beginning with the largest. But first let's review some information that applies to all Asian Americans.

The 1990 census gives some interesting information about the current status of Asian Americans—who they are, where they live, and how they're doing. The following are some key facts (U.S. Census Bureau 1993).

- *They doubled in number* between 1980 and 1990, due primarily to immigration.
- *Most live in the West*, 54 percent, compared to 21 percent of the total population.
- *Many are foreign born*, 66 percent, with Southeast Asian Americans having the highest percentage and Japanese Americans the lowest.
- *Some are recent immigrants*. Thirty-eight percent entered the U.S. during the 1980s, mostly refugees. Most live in the West, especially in California.
- *They're relatively young*. Thirty is the median age, compared with the national median of 33.
- *They have larger families*, an average 3.8 persons compared to 3.2 for all U.S. families. Hmong families (refugees from the Laotian hill country) average 6.6 persons, while Filipino, Vietnamese, Cambodian, and Laotian average over 4 persons per family. Japanese had 3.1.
- *They have more high school graduates*: 78 percent, compared to 75 percent nationally. Averages range from 88 percent for Japanese Americans to 31 percent for Hmong.
- *They have more college degrees*: 38 percent, compared with 20 percent for all Americans. Asian Indian Americans have the highest rate and Hmong the lowest. Asian Americans do better on quantitative exams than any other group.
- *Most speak another language*. Sixty-five percent speak another language at home, 56 percent don't speak English well, and 35 percent are linguistically isolated. Asian Indian Americans have the lowest proportion speaking another language at home, Hmong the highest.
- *More have jobs than any group*: 67 percent, compared with 65 percent nationally. Groups with an employment rate higher than 70 percent are the Filipino Americans, Asian Indian Americans, and Thai Americans. Asian American women's employment rate is 60 percent, compared to 57 percent nationally. Twenty percent of Asian American families contain three or more workers, compared with 13 percent nationally.
- *More hold high-status jobs than average*. Thirty-one percent are managers and professionals, compared to 26 percent nationally, due primarily to higher education levels and the tendency to start their own business or practice.
- *They make slightly less money than average:* $13,806 per capita (mean income person) compared to $14,143 for all Americans. Earning above the national average are Japanese Americans and Asian Indian Americans. Chinese Americans and Filipino Americans earn close to the national average, and Thai Americans and Korean Americans earn somewhat less. Groups from the Indochinese peninsula include large proportions of recent immigrants and thus earn dramatically less, as shown in Table 6.1. Because more of their family members work, the median income of Asian American families is $41,583, compared to $35,225 nationally.
- *Slightly more live in poverty:* 14 percent, compared to 13 percent nationally. Southeast Asian poverty rates ranged from 35 to 64 percent, with Chinese American and Korean American rates at 14 percent, and rates for Filipino Americans, Japanese Americans, and Asian Indian Americans under 10 percent.

- *They live longer* than Euro-Americans, whose mean life expectancy is 76, compared to 80 for Japanese Americans and Chinese Americans.
- *They have less crime.* FBI reports indicate that arrest rates of Asian Americans for serious crimes between 1980 and 1985 were well below their proportion in the population. Since the 1930s Asian Americans in California have had lower rates of crime and delinquency than the general population.

These statistics can help us sort through the controversy surrounding the model minority stereotype of Asian Americans, which we'll discuss later.

TABLE 6.1: Per Capita Income of Asian American Groups, 1990

Total Asian American	**$13,806**
Japanese American	19,373
Asian Indian American	17,777
Chinese American	14,876
Filipino American	13,616
Thai American	11,970
Korean American	11,177
Vietnamese American	9,032
Laotian American	5,597
Cambodian American	5,120
Hmong American	2,692
Other Asian American	11,000

Source: Census Bureau, 1990

COMMON THREADS: CULTURAL PATTERNS AND ISSUES

There is not one Asian culture; there are at least six or seven major cultures and hundreds of subcultures. The extreme variations in Asian Americans' ways of life make it impossible to identify precise patterns for all. Still, many Asian cultures, and therefore Asian Americans, share a number of characteristics that help describe, but not define, them.

Asian Americans have no common language or religion. Each major Asian ethnic group has its own language and dominant religion, and some groups have several languages and religions. Chinese, Japanese, and Koreans are physically and culturally very similar, with many of their cultural similarities stemming from Confucianism. The Vietnamese culture has been strongly influenced by the Chinese culture. India has its own culture, with major influences from the Hindu religion and the British culture, while the Philippine culture has been greatly influenced by the Spanish culture and Catholicism. Even so, both India and the Philippines reflect many common Asian values and cultural patterns.

Individuals are also affected by socioeconomic class and education, by region, by generation, by individual life experiences, and by individual choice. The following information about Asian American cultural patterns is meant as background information. Resist any temptation to use the information to form rigid categories, and remember to be open and flexible as you interact with individual Asian Americans.

Common Cultural Themes

With that reminder, let's examine some common threads in Asian cultures, a number based on the Confucian ethic. We'll discuss some typical values and behaviors that flow from these threads, including emotional expression, communication patterns, and view of the managers' status (Brislin and Yoshida, 1994). Key values include:

- *Collectivism,* which is interdependence of beliefs and actions with one or more closely knit ingroups.
- *Give and take* or reciprocity, which is a natural result of interdependence
- *Other-directedness,* which is expressed through extreme sensitivity to others' feelings and wishes, giving second place to one's own feelings and wishes.
- *Maintenance of harmony and avoidance of open conflicts,* which includes the avoidance of conveying unpleasant messages, or doing so very indirectly. Directness in the Asian sense would still be considered indirect from an American perspective. An indirect message from an Asian is so subtle that it usually goes unnoticed by an American.
- *Conformity,* which is valued because it maintains harmony, not because there is never internal conflict between what persons want and what they think they should do. It's part of becoming self-disciplined, which is a personal asset in itself.

Many of these traits are true for some Latin American, African, and South European cultures and women in all cultures. Even in the U.S., many people in small towns and rural communities, and many women everywhere, hold similar values (Tannen 1990).

The Confucian Influence on Relationships and Education

Most Asian cultures, especially the Chinese, Japanese, Korean, and Vietnamese, are strongly influenced by Confucian ethics. The major life areas that are affected are obligation to family and state, hierarchical status in relationships, great respect for elders, and sanctity of education. Everyone is expected to honor certain binding obligations to immediate family, relatives, clan, province, and state. Society has been structured to minimize deviations from these obligations. Customs relating to status, harmony and family/community obligations flow from the belief that interpersonal bonding and devotion are the basis of all conduct. Sons are subordinate to fathers, younger brothers to older brothers, wives to husbands, and everyone to the state. Elders are especially respected, even revered.

Education is also revered. In Asian countries, scholars are given the greatest respect and have the highest rank, and they are often among the most powerful and wealthy in society. Being educated is a high moral virtue and is a rigid prerequisite for moving up from lower to higher political and social standing.

When the Chinese and Japanese came to the U.S. during the last century and early in this century, their exclusion and resulting isolation reinforced these traditional values. It led to group solidarity and reliance on mutual aid and mutual dependence.

Typical Values

Some typical values that further define the common themes and stem from them are reviewed next (Harris and Moran 1991).

The Group. Members are expected to honor the group by:
- Seeing the group as the most important part of society.
- Focusing on a group of people who are working toward a goal as more important than focusing on each one as individual.
- Valuing group recognition and group reward above individual reward.
- Emphasizing a sense of belonging to the group, and security.
- Extending tight, strong family ties to other relatives and close friends.
- Placing central emphasis on a strong network of social relationships.
- Making public service a moral responsibility.

- Viewing personal saving and resource conservation as more important than consumption.
- Placing fairness above gaining wealth.

Harmony. People are expected to put group harmony first by:

- Placing higher value on saving face and achieving harmony than on achieving higher sales and profits.
- Believing that harsh words, scolding, temper flares, and similar affronts cause a loss of face to the listener and a loss of listener's respect for the speaker.
- Avoiding personal conflicts.
- Being flexible, deferring, and complying with the wishes of others in order to maintain harmony, which reflects maturity and self-discipline.

Modesty. Everyone, especially females, is expected to show modesty by:

- Avoiding statements that can be perceived as boasting or self-congratulatory, as in overuse of the words "I," "me," and "mine."
- Being reticent to talk about themselves or their own accomplishments.
- Avoiding drawing attention to themselves.
- Responding to compliments by belittling their abilities.

Education. Unique emphasis is place upon education by:

- Valuing education and position.
- Through education, striving for some financial security and a decent standard of living, though not focusing especially on the materialistic.
- Seeing education as an moral virtue.
- Considering education as an investment in family status.

Status. Indicators of the importance of protocol, rank, and status are:

- Valuing a sense of order, propriety, and appropriate behavior between persons of varying status.
- Basing status on occupational position, education, wealth, and family background.
- Upon meeting, establishing quickly which person is older and has the higher status and is thus shown more deference.
- Addressing people by their title and first name in all but informal or family situations.
- Respecting seniority and the elderly.
- Preferring sons to daughters. Sons are much freer socially; daughters are protected. Among recent immigrants, parents often expect to arrange matches for children.

Customs. Some typical customs are:

- Beckoning for someone to come to them by holding out the arm with the palm down, using a scratching movement. Beckoning with the fingers up is rude.
- Meals are often more ritualistic, communal, and time consuming. The talk is considered more important than the food.
- Colors and numbers often have different meanings than they have in Western cultures.

Typical Behaviors

Some typical behaviors flow from these common cultural themes (Brislin and Yoshida 1994, Harris and Moran 1991)

Self-effacement. It's often appropriate for persons to act as if they are of lower status in order to show selfless humility and give honor to others. Highly respected people often assume an attitude of self-effacement in social and business contacts. Putting yourself forward is usually viewed as proud arrogance and invites scorn. To make a joke at someone else's expense and to cause embarrassment is highly resented.

Respect for elders. Older people are always honored, respected, pampered, and appeased. Their every wish and desire is catered to whenever possible. Every home, no matter how poor, provides the best room for the honored grandparent.

Disciplined emotional expression. Asian Americans experience the same range and intensity of emotions as other cultural groups, but often mask expression of feeling due to social control and self-control. Therefore, Euro-Americans often view them as expressionless and inscrutable.

In face-to-face relations, Asian Americans tend to maintain the amenities and cordialities, no matter how they are feeling. To show your anger is the same as admitting loss of control and therefore a lapse in training and self-discipline and loss of face—that is, unless things have gone too far. It's almost impossible for people outside the culture to estimate when things are about to go too far. The key message for managers to remember: When an Asian American gives in to another person, it's not necessarily a passive or weak gesture, but is often a sign of tolerance, self-control, flexibility, and maturity (Kumagai 1981, Markus and Kitayama 1991).

Respect for the manager's status. In the U.S., it's appropriate at certain times for a supervisors or managers to roll up their sleeves and work alongside the people to get things done. Pitching in when there's an emergency is the sign of a good sport, one of the guys. Many Asian Americans, especially the immigrants, would interpret this as an insult to the workers, a signal that they can't get the work done the way they should. If it recurs or is handled badly, the loss of face could result in an Asian American's resignation. In addition, the worker might lose respect for the manager because managers are supposed to be above doing manual labor or other work below their station.

Communication Patterns

Because of the extreme difference in Eastern and Western language patterns, first-generation Asian Americans usually experience serious communication barriers. Cultural patterns of vagueness and indirectness, listening and silence, can be confusing to Westerners, as we'll see.

Language barriers. Misinterpretation and misunderstanding are possible between two people speaking within a culture. They are more likely when one of the persons was raised speaking another language, and they are even more intense problems when the first language is one of the Asian tongues. This is because Asian languages are so different from English or other Latin-related languages, not only in structure and pronunciation, but also in the nonverbal gestures that typically accompany certain verbal messages. For example, a competent Japanese American product development researcher persists in pointing to the flip chart with his middle finger instead of his index finger. This distraction could prevent his idea from being transformed into a multimillion dollar product. To further complicate matters, since the "l" sound is not used in many Asian languages, he may seem to say, "This is a wrong project," when he's actually saying, "This is a long project."

First-generation Asian Americans tend to have heavy accents because of profound differences in the sounds of Eastern and Western languages. Studies indicate that an Asian accent tends to be a barrier, but a British or French accent is a plus in the U.S. (Morrison 1992). However, Asian Americans expect to learn English. Nearly all who responded to a recent survey indicated that English should be the only official language of the U.S. (Viviano 1990).

Vague indirectness. Being indirect and vague are more acceptable than being direct and making specific references. Ambiguous terminology is preferred. In homogeneous cultures, such as the Japanese, the significance or meaning of the conversational details may be left to the listener to interpret. Sentences are frequently left unfinished so the listener may mentally conclude them. In many instances, it would be presumptuous and even impolite for the speaker to be specific and complete because it might insult the listeners' intelligence or sensitivity. When these tendencies carry over into the U.S. workplace, co-workers can become quite confused and communication can be blocked.

Saying no. To say no is an insult, could damage feelings and disrupt harmony, and is therefore bad manners. Asian Americans may say *yes*, meaning "I heard you," and then go about doing the opposite with little sense of breaking an agreement.

Listening and silence. If you were listening to someone and didn't understand something they said, would you wait, expressionless, until they had finished a long explanation, expecting the speaker to take responsibility for your understanding? Hardly. But if all the people you know believe that's the way to listen, then your behavior would be normal. For many Asian Americans not interrupting is basic courtesy that is essential for conversations to proceed.

When you finish speaking, how do you react when your listener is silent for a minute or more? Most Americans view such long silences as extremely uncomfortable and feel compelled to fill them in with comments or questions. For many Asian Americans, Japanese Americans for example, a few moments of quiet contemplation after listening may be essential, and comments are distracting.

Issue: The Model Minority—Good or Bad?

In the 1960s, reporters began writing about the high education attainment, high median family income, low crime rates, and absence of juvenile delinquency and mental health problems among Asian Americans. The publicity served an important political purpose at the height of the civil rights turmoil. Proponents of this model minority stereotype were in effect asking Latino Americans and African Americans, Why can't you folks succeed like this? They were telling minority activists that their groups should follow the Asian Americans' example. They should work hard to pull themselves up by their own bootstraps instead of using militant protests to demand their rights.

By gaining an understanding of the model minority issue, you as a business leader will understand a great deal about the background of your Asian American employees.

Some Euro-Americans tend to lump together all Asian Americans and criticize them for being "too successful." Virtually all the Silicon Valley managers interviewed in a recent survey said that Asian Americans make the best production workers (Hossfeld 1994). They gave the following reasons:

- investment in and commitment to higher education, even at the cost of financial hardship
- dedication to hard work
- willingness to work unusually long hours
- a frugal lifestyle
- saving small amounts of money until they can invest in a small business
- employing family members in their businesses, to keep labor costs down
- a cultivated tradition of perseverance
- cultural identification with the American Dream

Like most stereotypes, the model minority image has some basis in reality, but it's controversial because numerous studies have resulted in two viewpoints. One viewpoint sees a rosy picture of Asian Americans, while a second perceives that the statistics can be misleading and that many Asian Americans still suffer from considerable discrimination in the labor market and in other areas of public life. We'll review some extenuating circumstances that help explain Asian Americans' apparent success and affluence despite continuing barriers. We'll also examine some advantages experienced by Asian Americans that African Americans, and in some instances Latino Americans, haven't experienced. Finally we'll explore why some outsiders see a model minority, while others see a mixed picture.

Extenuating Circumstances

Several variables that add to the complexity of the model minority stereotype are receiving lower return on education, living in higher-cost-of-living geographic areas, holding lower-paying occupations, having more workers per family, experiencing more underemployment, and being a recent immigrant.

Lower return on education. The socioeconomic status of Asian Americans has undeniably improved since the early 1940s. About twice as many Asian Americans as Euro-Americans hold degrees. Relatively more Asian Americans than Euro-Americans have white-collar jobs, but Asian Americans' per capita income is lower: $13,806 compared to the national average of $14,143. Three times as many Asian Indian Americans as Euro-Americans hold degrees, but their median income of $18,000 does not adequately reflect this huge education gap.

Return on education more clearly reveals the existence of discrimination than does educational level alone. Several 1970 studies showed that U.S.-born Chinese American and Japanese American men had higher median incomes than Euro-American men. However, this was not the case in California, where 58 percent of Chinese Americans and 45 percent of Japanese Americans live. In California, these groups had significantly more years of schooling than Euro-Americans, but their median incomes were no higher because their return on education (the additional income derived from increased years of schooling) was lower. So the Asian American-to-Euro-American parity in income was made possible mainly by the Asian Americans' higher levels of education. Even in 1990, these returns were still not on a par with those received by Euro-American men.

Higher cost of living. More than half of all Asian Americans live in only five areas: Honolulu, San Francisco, Los Angeles, Chicago, and New York. Of these, more than 90 percent are found in areas that feature high incomes and high costs of living. Even though Asian Americans and others living there may earn more, they also have to spend more.

Lower-paying occupations. In geographical areas with the highest density of Asian Americans, the percentage of Asian Americans in low-status, low-income occupations (service workers, laborers, farm laborers, and private household workers) is considerably higher than among Euro-Americans.

Throughout the economy, professionals cluster in accounting, dentistry, nursing, health technology, and engineering. They are underrepresented in law, teaching, administration, social services, and the higher level of the medical professions. Managers are more likely to be self-employed than employees of large, powerful firms. Salespersons tend to be retail clerks but seldom brokers or insurance agents. Clerical workers are mostly file clerks, typists, or office machine operators, not secretaries or receptionists. Few Asian Americans hold jobs in heavy-machine, electrical, paper, chemical, or construction industries. Most female operatives are garment workers. In summary, Asian Americans are concentrated in occupations that do not pay as well as other jobs in the same industries.

A major complaint has been the lack of upward mobility into positions of power in corporate America. In 1985 Asian Americans held only one-half of one percent of the officer and director positions in the largest 1,000 corporations, even though they hold about three percent of all jobs (Corporate 1000 1985).

More workers per family. The high labor force participation rate of Asian American women is a reflection of the fact that more of them are compelled to work because their mates earn low wages. Working Asian American women earn a higher median income than do Euro-American working women, but they also have better educational qualifications and live in localities with higher wages. Compared to Euro-American women, a larger percentage of them work full time. They also receive lower return on education than do Euro-American women, and the disparity between their return and that of Euro-American men is, of course, even greater.

Underemployment. The lower unemployment rate of Asian Americans tends to camouflage high underemployment. Apparently, Asian American workers are more averse to "going on welfare" than other workers. They are therefore more willing to accept low-paying, part-time, or seasonal jobs, to avoid the "humiliation" of receiving public assistance. This is less so for recent immigrants from communist countries, who have been influenced by the communist belief that the government should provide for all.

Some professionals have not been able to find professional jobs, so they have bought small businesses, thereby increasing the number of Asian American "managers," particularly Korean American. However, many of them operate only small mom-and-pop stores with no paid employees, very low gross earnings, long work hours, and few benefits. Such businesses are a disguised form of cheap labor. The owners run a high risk of failure, and many couldn't stay afloat without the unpaid labor of family members. Still, small business is an important channel of upward mobility open to immigrants who face obstacles in getting well-paying, secure jobs.

Problems of recent immigrants. Recent immigrants, especially those from Southeast Asia, do not share the improved economic standing of Japanese Americans and Chinese Americans. Korean Americans' per capita income averaged $11,000 in 1990, compared to the national average of $14,000. Vietnamese Americans averaged $9,000, Laotian Americans and Cambodian Americans $5,000, and Hmong Americans $2,700. In California, where about 40 percent of Southeast Asian Americans live, about half were on public assistance (U.S. Census Bureau 1993; Chan 1991).

Cultural Strengths

Asian Americans as a group have several advantages that African Americans, and in some instances Latino Americans, have not had in our society. They include a high-productivity image in the mainstream culture, an unusually strong preference for education as a virtue in itself, and success in sustaining small family businesses over time.

High-productivity image. Attempts to exclude Asian Americans from jobs has generally been based on the fear that they're too competitive in the labor market and too willing to work for far less than Euro-Americans. If anything, they were seen as too productive. As mentioned elsewhere, their tendency to work hard and be productive even when forced to work for less, their success in small businesses, and their higher educational attainment have all enhanced the perception by mainstream business persons that Asian Americans are highly productive.

Preference for education. Asian Americans have tended to overinvest in education, given their lower return on education than Euro-Americans. Asian Americans probably place a higher value on education than any other cultural group, as a result of the Confucian belief that education is a worthwhile pursuit in itself, not just as a means to an economic end. They are therefore willing to make great sacrifices in order to provide a good education for their children. Return on education is not as important as in other cultures because education in itself is considered a high moral virtue. In addition education has been seen as one of the few tools for upward mobility in a hostile environment. Compared to most Asian countries, education in the U.S. is an incredible bargain, with tuition-free community colleges and low-tuition state colleges often available to them.

Small business ownership. Small family enterprises have traditionally been common in Asian countries; therefore many immigrants arrived with some skill, know-how, or at least comfort with the idea of starting a small business. Because they experienced significant discrimination in the regular job market, many Asian American families resorted to small business as an alternate way to survive. Asian communities established their own forms of credit unions, which financed many of these businesses.

Most Asian American small family businesses succeeded over time in the American business culture because they employed the following success strategies:

- *Specialization and small scale.* They tended to specialize in limited areas and were small in scale and therefore not threatening to the majority.

- *Preferential hiring.* Jobs went first to members of the immediate family, then to members of the extended family, clan or neighborhood, and ethnic group, in that order.

- *Job security.* Employers looked after workers and rarely laid them off. Often, most of them were members of the family or extended family and others tended to become part of the extended family.

- *Long-range goals.* The primary goal was to sustain the business over the long term. Working long hours to attain a certain minimum income was common.

- *Mutual aid and cooperation.* Nearly all businesses belonged to at least one mutual aid association and didn't compete with one another. Association functions typically included serving as employment agencies, fixing locations and prices for each business, loaning capital, and helping members in distress.

- *Efficient labor use.* They typically scheduled employees to work during peak periods of the day or year and freed them to go to school or to work at jobs in the open labor market during off times.

On the downside, owners' language problems and dependence on ethnic customers have limited the growth and expansion of many Asian American small businesses. Concentration in traditional minority areas where per capita wealth is lower is another limiting factor, as is reluctance to go outside the Asian American community to get money that would be needed for business expansion.

Benefits from small business ownership. Asian American families who have managed to build and hold onto at least a minimal level of business success have achieved the following advantages:

- *Protection from discrimination.* For most of this century approximately half the Asian American male population worked for such small businesses, effectively shielding themselves from the open labor market with its discriminatory practices.

- *Higher educational attainment.* Owners were able to accumulate money to send their children to college. Between 1940 and 1960 there was a dramatic increase in the percentage of Asian Americans who completed high school and went to college.

- *More opportunities.* Small business success and higher educational attainment enhanced Euro-Americans' perception of Asian Americans as productive workers. Some Euro-American business persons are therefore somewhat more open to hiring Asian Americans than they are to hiring African Americans or Latino Americans (Young 1977).

Differing Viewpoints

Why do some scholars and reporters so eagerly focus on Asian American success, while others keep stressing discrimination? The debate is not just over economics but also over political viewpoint. Those who depict Asian Americans as the model minority tend to be conservatives who believe that American society is indeed an egalitarian one, with opportunities for all people who make the necessary effort to achieve a measure of material well being. If an individual or group does not make it, it's their own fault. Liberals who focus on continued inequality believe the problem lies primarily within the social, economic, and political system. Before the minority groups can improve their status, some aspect of the system must change. But systemic change can occur only with a shift in the present balance of power between different groups. Therefore, those who perceive reality in this manner advocate greater political activism.

The answer obviously lies somewhere between those extremes. We each create our reality in a very important sense. The Asian American woman who has certain attributes and who does the right things, makes the right moves, can indeed overcome all barriers and achieve the success she wants. Connie Chung is one of the few Asian American women who has achieved national prominence. But should it be so much more difficult for her than it might have been for a Dan Rather? Put another way, why must a Connie Chung be such a "rare bird" in appearance and talent in order to make it, when a Dan Rather can be more "ordinary" and still make it? To what extent can and should we try to level the playing field?

Issues of Male–Female Dynamics and Differences

Most Asian cultures are extremely patriarchal and women are significantly more subjugated in these cultures than in the American culture. Confucian principles place women in subordination to men in virtually all aspects of life. A key aspect is the patrilineal extended household, where women marry young and enter the husband's parents' household, and are isolated from their birth families.

Family Culture Clash

Culture clash affects husband-wife dynamics in ways that are typical among immigrant families, especially those who came after the 1960s. That's when women's pay and work status began improving and traditional male jobs in manufacturing plants began deteriorating. Problems often arise when wives find better-paying jobs than husbands, upsetting the male status in a hierarchical family structure. Further problems arise when the wife must learn to be assertive, decisive, and efficient on the job, which conflicts with her role as a shy, patient, and resilient wife and mother. Children are also caught in bicultural conflict, being expected to keep quiet and do as they're told at home, while they must speak up, express opinions, and ask why in order to succeed at school. This conflict is most intense for girls who are supposed to be more reserved and compliant than boys.

Workplace Stereotypes

Women who don't have the educational credentials to land better paying jobs often take manufacturing assembly line jobs. They typically encounter myths, stereotypes, and other barriers to upward mobility and job satisfaction. For example, research indicates that the formula used by many hiring managers in California's Silicon Valley for entry level manufacturing assembly line operatives can be summarized as "small, foreign, and female" (Zinn and Dill 1994). This means they recruit and hire primarily Asian and Latina immigrant women. Reasons employers give for the hiring policy are based on stereotyped and prejudiced beliefs:

- Immigrant women are more likely to be content with such jobs.
- They're unqualified for better-paying jobs.

- They have a man who earns more than they do (in fact, about 80 percent are the main income earners in their families).

- Their patience and superior coordination better suits them to assembly line repetition of a small set of tasks requiring constant concentration and intensive eye-hand coordination in manipulating tiny, intricate circuitry.

- Their small size makes it easier for them to sit quietly for long periods, doing small detail work.

- Most U.S. citizens would not be content for long with such boring, low-paying jobs.

- The seemingly obedient and submissive character of Asian American women makes them good candidates for the type of control imposed in assembly line settings. Their strong task orientation, high achievement motivation, and hard work qualify them as reliable production workers (Zenn and Dill 1994; Chow 1994).

These assembly line workers have little chance at upward mobility. Most upwardly mobile jobs, especially those in the higher ranks, are middle class in nature and require middle-class educational credentials and such cultural resources as the values, mannerisms, lifestyle, language, and symbols of the dominant middle class. Many Asian American women, especially immigrants, have not acquired these resources and cannot quickly attain them through acculturation. Even third and fourth-generation Asian American women may find the inner circle is so tight that it's almost impossible to break through. Moreover, Euro-Americans tend to hold gender and ethnic stereotypes about them that block their ability to present an appropriate image. Many see them as childlike, possessing little managerial potential, feminine, possessing weak qualities of women.

Beneath the Passive Surface: Active Achievement

The stereotype of Asian American women as passive and submissive has been challenged by studies of resistance that indicate they are often active, goal-oriented doers. Chow's study links women's resistance to the conditions women find in the workplace and to their types of work adaptation. She specifically identified ways that Asian American women struggle at work to ensure family survival and to cope with ethnic oppression, patriarchal domination, and economic exploitation within the work bureaucracy. Asian American women are disadvantaged in these three aspects of the social structure, that is, being an ethnic minority, a woman, and within a lower socioeconomic class.

Their coping responses seem to be a combination of their Asian cultural learning and their American acculturation. Many challenge supervisors and co-workers who threaten their survival, with about half using an assertive style. They fight back to protect their work rights and set boundaries to maintain their individual integrity and personal lives. Sometimes even their silence signals not submissiveness but inner strength, resourcefulness, and perseverance. They often form alliances with Euro-American women based on gender (Chow 1994).

Asian American Women's Style

Since Asian women are brought up in a tradition of deferring to authority, their supervisors represent figures with such omnipotent authority that they have difficulty challenging them. The relatively powerless women depend on the goodwill of their supervisors and they act mainly with compliance and conformity. Nearly all the supervisors are Euro-Americans, part of the ethnic and class hierarchy. The problems these women workers experience stem primarily from the following:

- supervisors' perception of their inabilities
- disrespect for Asian women
- unreasonable work assignments
- unfair performance evaluation

• accusation of job errors
• inappropriate decisions regarding promotion
• intolerance of language accents
• apparent discrimination

Asian American women often seem dependent, passive, and submissive, and to some extent this appearance reflects their powerless position in society. However, co-workers and leaders should not equate their gentleness for passivity, their docility with timidity, nor their kindness with weakness. Doing so blinds leaders to reality. Behind their apparently docile and demure manner, many Asian American women clearly possess inner strength, firmness, resourcefulness, tenacity, and courage, which they summon in order to resist unfairness and discrimination.

In Chow's study about half the women said they have no difficulty challenging their supervisor regarding these problems. However, well over half have difficulty in expressing anger and in demanding their fair share from supervisors. This was especially true of Asian American women of higher occupational status, as they had more to lose. Only 6 percent said they choose to say nothing to offensive co-workers or to ignore incidents they think are unfair.

Almost all the women attempted to establish congenial working relationships with people at all levels of the organization. Two-thirds of the women said they had little difficulty in protesting unfair treatment by their Euro-American *co-workers* (as distinguished from their supervisors). They had more difficulty protesting to Euro-American women than to the men, since they tend to consider the women as natural allies and hesitate to break that feeling of camaraderie. Typical styles for dealing with workplace situations are confrontational, assertive, affiliation, and indirect or situational adjustment.

Confrontational style is a somewhat aggressive method of fighting prejudice and discrimination at work. The women directly protest against those co-workers they view as insensitive and threatening to their survival. They fight back in the face of apparently overwhelming odds in order to protect their work rights and to show they won't compromise themselves to what they see as others' unreasonable demands. Some even go as far as quitting their job rather than be pushed around, the ultimate form of resistance. They see it as affirming self-respect and human dignity over job security.

Assertive style is a direct approach to claim certain work rights and independence. It includes negotiating their time, effort, intellect, commitment, and personal involvement with other workers. About half the women use this style, and they're more likely to do so when they deal with Euro-American male workers than with females. It includes expressing their viewpoints and judgment of a situation, demanding explanations from offensive workers, and focusing their efforts on problem solving. This approach is active, goal-oriented, and a way of taking charge of their own lives. Women using this approach expect mutual agreement and reinforcement in the process of negotiation. For example, they want agreement about clear boundaries between work and personal life.

Affiliation style is used sometimes to show the importance of willingness to be congenial in solving workplace problems. The approach involves personal consideration, friendliness, and candidness to achieve some kind of equity with co-workers. Women using this style may emphasize commonalties, such as being women or being Asian Americans, in order to establish rapport, to dispel issues of inequity, and to neutralize feelings of injustice. They are more apt to use this style with Euro-American women than with men.

Indirect or situational adjustment is essentially an indecisive and passive way of dealing with co-worker problems. Instead of facing the problem directly, some women sometimes take a defensive stand, protecting themselves from the hurt by pushing their tolerance to the limit. Variations of the approach include avoiding problem situations as much as possible, doing little about them, or hoping the problem will go away. It might include writing to the supervisor, telling a supervisor about the offensive co-worker, or making an impersonal telephone call to the co-worker, all in hopes of finding a solution to the problem. The ultimate solution here is to quit, but in this case it's a defeatist choice, implying that they blame themselves rather than affirming their self-respect.

Silence is sometimes a temporary reaction in the process of coping. Although women often choose the indirect or situational adjustment reaction in the beginning, they frequently shift to other strategies later.

Political Issues

Some issues that unite Asian Americans across political and ethnic lines include discrimination, the increase in hate crimes, university quotas against Asian Americans, and the maintenance of Asian American studies programs on campuses.

Discrimination

Most Asian Americans say that prejudice and discrimination is not a problem in their local area, with 64 percent of Filipino Americans and 51 percent of Chinese Americans saying it's not a problem. However, when asked if qualified members of their ethnic group can rise to the top in local companies, 56 percent of Filipino Americans and 37 percent of Chinese Americans said it was a problem. Less than 31 percent of Filipino Americans said the glass ceiling was not a problem, and 44 percent of Chinese Americans agreed.

Hate Crimes

Since 1980, increased instances of physical assault, harassment, vandalism, and anti-Asian racial slurs are being reported. In 1986 the U.S. Civil Rights Commission issued a report saying that "the issue of violence against Asian Americans is national in scope." They identified victims in three categories: Southeast Asian Americans, immigrant entrepreneurs (especially Koreans), and various individuals. Many instances of hate crimes against Vietnamese are reported in Texas, California, and Massachusetts. Tensions have built between Korean merchants and residents of mostly African American or Spanish-speaking neighborhoods where many Koreans own stores. They have accused the Koreans of treating them rudely, even roughly. Some have responded with firebombings and vandalism.

University Quotas Against Asian Americans

The ability of Asian American young adults to get a first-rate college education has become an issue. In the mid-1980s community leaders, parents of college-bound students, and many straight-A students who had nevertheless been refused admission by some of the nation's most prestigious public and private universities, alleged that informal quotas were being imposed on Asian American university admission. At the same time major news and business magazines were running stories about the outstanding academic achievements of Asian American students. Administrators at some of the Ivy League schools and at the University of California at Berkeley have, under intense public pressure, released figures that indicate that the admission *rate* of Asian American applicants has been lower than that for any other ethnic group. This revelation seemed to substantiate charges that informal quotas must have been imposed on Asian American university admissions for a number of years. No university has admitted any discriminatory intent, but officials at several have acknowledged that existing policies and practices may have had an unintentional adverse impact on Asian Americans.

Asian Americans have united to ensure that their educational rights will not be abridged, because access to quality higher education, perhaps more than any other issue, is something they feel very strongly about. Many Asians immigrate to the U.S. precisely to allow their children to receive such education. Most Filipino Americans, 56 percent, favor affirmative action programs that set quotas for minority admissions to college. Chinese Americans are almost evenly divided on the issue, with 41 percent favoring affirmative action and 43 percent opposing it. Interviews indicated that nearly all Chinese Americans are concerned about discrimination, but many are uncomfortable with using government regulation to alleviate the problem (Baldassare 1990).

Asian American Studies Programs

The appearance of an increasing number of Asian American college students has influenced another education issue: the growth of Asian American studies courses and programs, established at many West Coast universities in the late 1960s and early 1970s. Those at San Francisco State University and at the University of California at Berkeley began as part of the settlement of two long and militant student strikes. What that generation of students, as well as succeeding generations who filled the classes, wanted was a more "relevant" education. By that they meant a curriculum that included the history of prejudice and discrimination in the U.S., an accurate portrayal of the contributions and struggles of people of color, and practical training to enable graduates to bring about fundamental social change in their ethnic communities as well as in the society at large. Because of their radical agenda, the programs encountered stiff resistance from curriculum and personnel review committees. A number failed, while others managed to survive but did not grow.

In the late 1980s these programs took a new lease on life when students began demanding a more multiethnic curriculum. Dozens of campuses, including five of the eight University of California campuses, now have some version of an ethnic studies requirement. Students at East Coast and Midwestern universities are also insisting that Asian American studies programs be set up. One reason for this is a new cultural awakening among Asian American students, along with a rising political consciousness. Instead of choosing between an Asian heritage and American culture, some young Asian Americans are forging a new culture of their own, one that goes beyond a simple blending of East and West. This culture directly reflects the historical experience and current life circumstances of Asians in America. In university courses about Asian Americans, they may get a glimpse of this emerging culture and even be encouraged to help create it.

We've seen some common threads running through all Asian cultures and the Asian American experience. Next we'll look at some unique patterns of major Asian American cultures, including Chinese, Filipino, Southeast Asian, Japanese, Korean, Asian Indian, and Pacific Islander.

CHINESE AMERICAN WORKERS

About one-fourth of all Asian Americans are Chinese Americans, the largest of the Asian groups. Because of their greater numbers and more extensive history in the U.S. than other Asian American groups, we'll spend a little more time on this group than the others. We'll review some background information about their immigration experiences, differences among generations, and facts from their current profile.

Background: From Gold Mines to Laundries

The Chinese were the first sizable group of Asians to immigrate to America and most settled in the West. Most had been farm peasants in China. However, most who came after the 1940s were more affluent business and professional persons escaping from communism. The earliest immigrants came to California soon after the 1849 Gold Rush to work in the gold mines. Later they were the primary workers who built the railroads and the irrigation canals and levees of the river deltas, laying the groundwork for the agricultural industry.

For many years nearly all the Chinese immigrants were men, who came to earn a nest egg and return to China. But most stayed and since there were so few Chinese women, they formed a bachelor society. The workers were nearly always targets of Euro-American labor resentment, especially during hard times. Ethnic antagonism in the mines, factories, and fields forced thousands of Chinese to set up small stores, restaurants, and service shops, especially laundries, which took little start-up cash. By 1890 the Chinese represented nearly 70 percent of all laundry workers. The "Chinese laundryman" was an American phenomenon. There were no laundries in China. The women there did the laundry, and men in China would have lost social status if they had done it (Ong 1983).

Euro-American workers often referred to the Chinese as "nagurs," and they were often stereotyped as oriental vampires with slanted eyes, a pigtail, dark skin, and thick lips. Like African Americans, they were perceived as heathen, morally inferior, savage, childlike, and lustful. The Chinese were seen as inferior colored people, along with African Americans and American Indians.

In 1880 Congress passed a Chinese Exclusion Act that prohibited further Chinese immigration, even though they represented only 0.002 percent of the total U.S. population. The exclusion act, which was extended indefinitely in 1904, also denied naturalized citizenship to the Chinese already here. Euro-American workers complained about competition from Chinese who would work for less. Many Chinese complained that the "cheap labor" cry was always a falsehood. They said that employers preferred Chinese workers because they were so much more honest, industrious, steady, sober, and painstaking. They said they were persecuted, not for their vices, but for their virtues (Chew 1906).

Second-Generation Chinese Americans

By the 1920s and 1930s Chinese Americans had become more concerned than ever about their status because they were bringing up an increasing number of American-born children. As in other immigrant families, a generational conflict existed in many Chinese American families over parental authority and the freedom of the children coming of age. Many American-born teenagers and young adults, especially females, resented the restrictions on their social lives most of all (Chan 1991).

Identity Crisis

Chinese American children reared in America experienced an identity crisis that was intensified by the prejudice that permeated many areas of public life. They were barred from public recreational facilities, such as swimming pools, and forced to sit at the back of movie theaters. Those who participated in athletics usually had to join Chinese teams. One Chinese American gave a typical interview response, "At times I have been called a 'Chink' and I have resented it bitterly and would at times answer back, but recently I have not replied" (Chan 1991, 113). Most troubling, very few second-generation college graduates could find jobs appropriate to their education and training.

Distinct Socioeconomic Classes

By the 1960s Chinese Americans were drifting into two categories. One was educated, relatively affluent, and becoming acculturated to American society. The other was largely uneducated, not affluent, and still retained much of traditional Chinese culture. Many Chinese had either much education or none. Given the number of well-educated adults, however, the income figures for Chinese Americans was quite low. Although well trained Chinese Americans could find suitable employment with relative ease, it was still very difficult for them to gain promotion to supervisory and higher administrative positions. Many were clearly overqualified for the jobs they held, and the only conclusion was that employers were reluctant to place Chinese Americans in positions that gave them power over Euro-Americans (Kitano and Daniels 1988).

Since 1960 the most notable developments have been the rapid growth of the Chinese American population, the degree to which it came to be seen as a model minority, and movement to the suburbs. The population increased four fold between 1960 and 1985, due primarily to expanded immigration quotas. The model minority phenomenon was discussed earlier.

Movement to the Suburbs

A major development during the 1980s was the movement of Chinese Americans out of Chinatowns into the suburbs. This move reflects their ongoing acculturation and Americanization. The so-called "miniature Chinatowns" sprouting up in suburban cities are actually small shopping malls, each usually anchored by a large American supermarket. These malls are often financed by Chinese Americans, who may also be some of the shop owners. The homes bought by Chinese Americans who frequent one of these malls tend to be scattered throughout the neighborhood, a different pattern than the dense homogeneous Chinatown pattern.

Current Profile

Chinese Americans are the largest group of Asian Americans; in fact, until recent decades they were the only large group of Asian Americans. Now they make up 24 percent of Asian Americans, with Filipino Americans running close behind at 22 percent. In 1990 nearly 70 percent of Chinese Americans were foreign born, so most are strongly influenced by Chinese cultural values and practices. Statistical averages of factors that purport to indicate Chinese socioeconomic status can be misleading due to the existence of the two distinct classes discussed earlier. When these two are averaged together, their profile is very similar to that of the average American.

One distinct difference however lies in educational attainment; nearly twice as many Chinese Americans hold bachelor's degrees as the national average, 47 percent of men and 35 percent of women. Such educational attainment is remarkable given the language problems. About 83 percent speak Chinese at home, 60 percent speak English "not very well," and 40 percent are linguistically isolated. Their per capita income does not reflect their higher educational attainment. At $14,900 it's only slightly higher than the $14,100 national median. Their family income is near the national average because more family members work. Nearly 20 percent of families have three or more members in the workforce compared to the national rate of 13 percent.

FILIPINO AMERICAN WORKERS

Filipino culture encompasses a diverse, multilayered mix of subcultures. Its complex indigenous culture has strong Malay and other Asian influences, and this is combined with Spanish and American colonial cultural influences. The Spanish ruled the Philippines for 300 years, and the Americans for 50 years, but since 1950 a clear Filipino cultural identity has been developing.

Current Profile

Most Filipino Americans are hardworking, well educated, and foreign born.

Hardworking. Filipino Americans tend to be very industrious, having the highest percentage of employment (75 percent) of any ethnic group. They also have the highest percentage of families with three or more members working (30 percent), and the lowest rate of poverty (6 percent). Their families average 4 persons, more than the national average of 3.2 (U.S. Census Bureau 1993).

Educated. Filipino Americans are the only Asian American group with more women holding degrees (42 percent) than men (36 percent). This is nearly double the rate of Euro-American men and more than two and one-half times the rate of Euro-American women. In spite of higher education levels, Filipino American per capita income of $13,600 is below the national median of $14,100.

Foreign born. Nearly 65 percent are foreign born, so Filipino values and practices are a strong part of their heritage. Language is not a problem for most. Only 13 percent are linguistically isolated, although 66 percent speak other than English at home. Most Filipino immigrants come from a rural, agricultural environment to urban areas of the U.S. and must adjust to the differences.

Cultural Values and Practices

Because of the historical Spanish influence, about 85 percent of Filipinos are Roman Catholic, and more than 90 percent have a Christian Malay heritage. The most dominant cultural values are:

- maintaining face or self-esteem
- saving face and avoiding shame
- meeting obligations and reciprocating others' generosity
- cooperating
- respecting authority and elders
- placing the extended family first

Other important cultural values include:

- Personalistic view of the universe and fatalistic view of the future.
- "God will help," a fatalistic reliance on powers beyond self.
- Good luck determines success.
- Sex and marriage are religious concerns; marriages are expected to last.

Let's discuss further the most dominant values.

Maintaining face and avoiding shame. From the Spanish comes a special sense of self-esteem called *amor proprio*, meaning self-love. To maintain self-esteem, some Filipino Americans put great energy into displaying appropriate dress, modesty, and good manners. Shame, called *hiya*, is felt when self-esteem is damaged, and nothing is worse than being shamed. An adult worker may withdraw, becoming less cooperative. If questioned, he or she may feel frustrated and too embarrassed to respond. As a result, Euro-Americans may conclude that they're oversensitive and can't take criticism.

Meeting obligations and reciprocating others' generosity. When a person does something for someone, reciprocal action is usually implicitly expected. When Filipinos don't reciprocate and meet their obligations, they may be shamed. To be called shameless is a serious insult.

Cooperating. Filipinos value cooperation, the ability to get along with people, and are usually very receptive and willing to accept tasks on the job. They may cooperate with the work group at their own expense, and yet be too shy to make friends within the group. They tend to agree with those around them rather than express disagreement, to avoid confrontation, and to be cooperative and compliant. As a result their true feelings may remain hidden from outsiders.

Respecting authority and elders. Respect for authority and elders and obedience to authority are strong cultural values. They believe older people should be shown respect and allowed to take the lead. They generally seek out elders or other authority figures for approval and protection and for support or advice in making decisions. Filipino American employees, in return for the respect, obedience, and politeness they give the boss, may expect protection and favors, due to the value of reciprocity. Also, they may expect the boss to have an authoritarian management style and may therefore interpret a participative style as evidence of weakness or indecision.

Placing extended family first. Large extended families are common in the Philippines, which has one of the highest birth rates in the world. Family needs and status are placed above individual needs, reflecting the interdependence among family members. Filipinos don't think in terms of accumulating wealth and prestige for themselves, but for their families. Education, which is highly valued, is seen as an investment, primarily to benefit the family.

Communication patterns. Although Tagalog is the major language, most speak English, reflecting the U.S. influence, Filipino Americans follow the pattern found in many Asian cultures of indirectness and the use of a mediator or go-between as a tool of indirectness. To get directly to the point with a supervisor might be seen as disrespectful. They also tend to use flowery language, based on the belief that an impressive command of language is the sign of a cultivated person and enhances one's image, which is similar to the Latino viewpoint.

Use of time. Immigrants from the Phillipines often must adjust to punctuality and use of time in the American workplace. In the Phillipines, social events begin an hour or two after the appointed hour. According to Euro-Americans, Filipinos rarely complete things on time despite deadlines. They do get things done in their own time; many Euro-Americans say they do things "almost, but not quite."

On the other hand, most Filipino Americans readily adjust to the punctuality required in the U.S. workplace, as long as expectations are made clear. Their desire to cooperate, respect for authority, and fear of shame impel them to meet the supervisor's expectations regarding punctuality and meeting deadlines.

Expression of feelings. Filipino Americans place great emphasis on feelings or emotions, and generate warmth and friendliness. In this they're more like Latinos than other Asians. Supervisors must be especially careful in giving performance evaluations, critiques, and feedback. It's very difficult for most Filipinos to objectively separate the task at hand, the product, or their performance from themselves as subjective persons. They're likely to interpret a supervisor's objective analysis as a personal attack.

View of nature. Traditional Filipino culture sees humans as part of nature, not dominating it as much as conforming to it and interpreting their experience of nature through religion, family, and other means.

SOUTHEAST ASIAN AMERICAN WORKERS

About one-sixth of the Asian American group emigrated from Southeast Asian countries since the 1960s, most of them escaping the Vietnam War and communism. We'll discuss the unusual conditions of their emigration, their current profile, and the key issue, acculturation.

Background: Refugee Flight

About a million refugees have recently entered the U.S. from Southeast Asia as a result of the Vietnam War. The war created many political refugees from Vietnam, Cambodia, and Laos. The conditions of emigration may include:

- a recent past marred by years of war, chaos, and political persecution
- panic, fear, crisis, distress
- evacuating under a state of emergency with inadequate time for planning
- problems in transit, perhaps even becoming a "boat person," attacked by pirates and turned away by various governments
- life in temporary centers
- for many, transition from a rural, agricultural society to a modern, industrial or post-industrial society

Because of U.S. involvement in the Vietnam War in the late 1960s and early 1970s, the U.S. withdrawal in 1975, and the subsequent communist takeover of those countries, the U.S. has taken some responsibility for these political refugees. Immigration legislation in 1975 and 1976 expanded Asian immigrant quotas, and the 1980 Refugee Assistance Act further expanded quotas and provides for federal aid to states during refugees' first few years of residence.

Differences and Similarities Among Groups

The first wave of refugees consisted primarily of middle and upper-class South Vietnamese who got out in the 1970s before the U.S. withdrew, while the second wave contained many more Hmong, Cambodians, and Laotians. People of the first wave are generally more accustomed to Western ways, better educated, more affluent, and better equipped to enter the U.S. workforce than those of the second wave. Many among the second wave are having a difficult time.

Vietnamese

Vietnam is largely an agricultural country, but it has more large urban centers than Laos and Cambodia and more people, with a population of 55 million. Many Vietnamese refugees were middle- and upper-class citizens, wealthy or well-connected, and were able to leave South Vietnam before the communist takeover. Most came as family groups, some with large bankrolls and others with only the clothes on their backs.

Laotians and Hmong

Laos is small, mountainous, rural, undeveloped and sparsely populated with only 3 million residents. Most of the refugees are the Hmong, one of the largest hill tribes of northern Laos. They lived apart from mainstream Laotian society, subsisting as seminomadic slash-and-burn farmers. They're generally described as industrious, independent, and peace-loving people who were swept up in the Vietnamese War because of their strategic location. By 1970 two-thirds of Laos had been bombed, creating more than 600,000 refugees. The fall of Vietnam and the withdrawal of American forces forced many Hmong to flee Laos to different parts of the world, including the U.S. Although most Laotian immigrants are Hmong, others include urban government workers and ex-soldiers and their families, and single young men.

Perhaps the most unique feature of the Hmong, and the most important for their transition to a U.S. workplace is their traditionally oral form of communication. They had no experience with written language until 1960 when missionaries came to the Laotian highlands. Adapting to a high-tech workplace that's based upon quite sophisticated uses of written information presents a formidable challenge.

At first the resettlement programs attempted to scatter them throughout the U.S., but most voluntarily moved to warm-weather states. A group of perhaps 10,000 did settle around Minneapolis. In 1985 about 20,000 of the 60,000 Hmong were reported living in the San Joaquin Valley of California, 15,000 of them in the town of Fresno.

The Hmong came as an immigrant group with very few tools for adapting to American society. Most strongly believe in evil spirits, trust their shamans, and distrust modern medicine. Nearly 90 percent were on welfare in the 1980s. Their clustering in certain areas strained social services in those locales and created ethnic ghettos. Fresno is the home of agribusiness and not the site of the kinds of small family plots found in the Laotian highlands. In those highlands there were no taxes and few bills. In Fresno everything comes due the first of the month. Hmong are now forbidden to directly resettle in the Fresno area, but about half will probably end up there. Prejudice against them runs high among the dominant majority as well as among minority groups, triggered by the large number of Hmong, their extremely different ways, and their dependence on expensive social services.

They have a strong family and clan system, and families are traditionally large. They follow a pattern of male dominance, where the role of the wife is to be devoted to her husband and where clan and kinship ties are strong. The household, rather than the individual, is the primary unit, and clans serve as mutual aid associations. The major problem facing most Hmong immigrants is gaining facility with the English language.

Cambodians

Cambodia is a small, primarily agricultural country, with a population of about 7 million. In 1979 Vietnamese Communists invaded Cambodia, creating more than 3 million refugees. Cambodians who fled to the U.S. are mainly farmers, although some are skilled tradespersons and a few are educated young people.

Current Profile of Southeast Asian Americans

Before 1970 there were about 20,000 Vietnamese in the U.S. and the number of other Southeast Asians was too small to count. In 1990 more than one million Southeast Asian Americans made up about 16 percent of the Asian American population. Although the U.S. government attempted to scatter them throughout the country, many migrated to the West, especially California.

Large families. They have the highest birth rates of any U.S. group; Hmong American families average 6.6 persons, while Filipino Americans, Vietnamese Americans, Cambodian Americans, and Laotian Americans average more than 4 persons per family, compared to the U.S. average of 3.2.

Less education. The Southeast Asian Americans have the lowest educational level of any U.S. cultural group. Causes probably include the chaos and disruption of years of war in the area they emigrated from, the rural agricultural background of many, language barriers, and their relatively destitute status as political refugees. The differences between educational level of men and women is significant, as indicated in Table 6.2.

TABLE 6.2: Educational Achievement of Southeast Asian Americans by Gender, 1990

Group	Percent holding a high school diploma or higher		Percent holding a bachelor's degree or higher	
	Male	Female	Male	Female
Hmong	44	19	7	3
Cambodian	46	25	9	3
Laotian	49	30	7	3
Vietnamese	69	53	22	12
U.S. Total	76	75	23	18

Language barriers. More than 90 percent speak their native language at home. More than 70 percent of Hmong, Cambodians, and Laotians don't speak English very well, and more than half of them are linguistically isolated. About 65 percent of Vietnamese don't speak English very well and 44 percent are linguistically isolated.

Less income. Fewer refugees have jobs than the national average of 65 percent. Only 29 percent of Hmong have jobs, 58 percent of Laotians, 46 percent of Laotians, and 65 percent of Vietnamese. They have dramatically lower per capita incomes than the national average of $14,000. The Hmong average only $2,700; Cambodians, $5,000; Laotians $5,600; and Vietnamese $9,000. It follows that a greater percentage live in poverty: 64 percent of the Hmong, 43 percent of Cambodians, 35 percent of Laotians, and 26 percent of Vietnamese. Surveys of Vietnamese indicate that 92 percent of families with two or more workers are above the poverty line. As recently arrived groups acquire job skills, become employed, and have two or more workers in a family, they too should move out of the poverty category.

Cultural Patterns and Issues

Many Southeast Asian American values and practices are found in other Asian cultures. The primary religion is Buddhism, which is expressed more as a traditional philosophy of values and social relations than attendance at services or professions of belief. The following are general beliefs and behaviors that are especially emphasized by some Southeast Asian Americans, representing tendencies rather than rules:

- Having large, close-knit families, sometimes three generations in one house; it's very common for an extended refugee family to work together and pool resources to attain goals.

- Avoiding public displays of affection between men and women, especially between unmarried couples. Holding hands or touching among women and among men is a sign of close friendship. Greeting by hugging and kissing is not done. Sexual topics are not openly discussed, especially in mixed company.

- In Vietnam, people are introduced by their last name followed by their first name. A married woman retains her own last name, but is often called by her title and husband's last name.

- Being quiet around outsiders. Most Southeast Asian Americans are quite talkative, especially among themselves. The fact that they usually are perceived by Euro-Americans as unusually reserved probably reflects their unfamiliarity with the American culture and their natural reticence as "newcomers."

- Shaking hands upon meeting—for men, not women.

- Viewing a perceived unfairness or betrayal of trust as difficult to forgive or forget.

- Respecting teachers highly, even above parents. They are always referred to and addressed as teacher, never as he, she, or you.

Key Issue: Acculturation

Surveys taken a year after the first wave of refugees entered the U.S. indicate that major problems in adapting to the American culture were:

- breakup of the family and extended family units
- limits placed on the number of people who can live in one home
- lack of respect by Americans toward the elderly
- absence of friendly American people
- hectic pace in the American workplace
- dependence in America on the automobile and public transportation (difficult to walk or ride bikes from place to place)
- high value Americans place on work and achievement over interpersonal relationships

Factors that affect the acculturation of Southeast Asian refugees include the coercive aspects of their emigration, their need for a cohesive community, culture clashes that affect family cohesion, compatibility with American culture, reactions of other Americans, and occupational and educational fit.

Plans to return or stay. Because they are pushed out of their homes, many refugees hope to go back when conditions change. Those who plan to return have a strong incentive to retain their old cultural ways and less incentive to adapt to American ways. Younger refugees are acculturating more rapidly than the older ones. Many want to become American citizens and are more hopeful about their future in the U.S.

Need for a cohesive ethnic community. U.S. policy was to scatter refugees to avoid backlash from American workers who compete for jobs. Another goal was to settle the refugees as quickly as possible so they could adapt and become self-sufficient. The scattering policy generally didn't work, and most moved to the warm climates they're accustomed to and to urban areas where they could network with other Asian groups. Since 1975 more than 500 mutual assistance associations have been created within refugee communities. They provide support, education, language development, job training, and cultural orientation. Some want to eventually provide economic assistance in the form of business opportunities and jobs (Baldwin 1984).

Refugees who arrived in family units had the advantages of emotional support and multiple incomes. However, Vietnamese couples have experienced culture clashes that typically occur in families that recently immigrated from Asian cultures. Working wives' new status and children's Americanization can cause problems, reflected in the rapid rise in the divorce rate among Vietnamese couples in America.

Compatibility with the American culture. The Vietnamese culture encourages responsibility, discipline, and hard work. Vietnamese value facing adversity with courage and stoicism, and they place a high value on education. Like other Asian cultures, they fit into a dominant society through conformity and avoiding confrontation and conflict. Most want a better life for their children and have a high degree of achievement motivation. The Hmong are most unlike Westerners and adaptation for them has been more difficult.

Reception by other Americans. Some researchers have identified groups who tend to feel threatened by new immigrants: (1) downwardly mobile workers, those who once had more than they now have; and (2) disadvantaged people, the unemployed or underemployed who have always lived on the fringes of society. In this era of civil rights and valuing diversity, overt prejudice against Asians is relatively rare. However, in an era of deindustrialization and restructuring, job competition can be fierce. American fishermen have clashed with incoming Vietnamese fishermen, some minority farm workers and assembly line workers resent the competition for jobs, and some underclass minorities have complained about the special aid given to refugees. Some middle-class workers seem worried about further erosion of their take-home pay, saying refugees "must be getting a government handout," and therefore they, the taxpayers, must be supporting them.

Asian immigrants cannot merge into the dominant culture as easily as European immigrants. Because they're easily identifiable by their looks as Asians, they don't have the luxury of choosing whether or not to partake of the advantages and disadvantages of being of a distinct ethnic minority.

Refugees have many specific needs that are different from the typical immigrant's needs. However, the things they generally need from the dominant culture are similar to the needs of all minorities:

- sensitivity to their culture and life experiences
- recognition of both the similarities and differences among groups
- understanding that their communication patterns and feelings may not be expressed in the American way, so assumptions may be misleading
- the use of culturally relevant frames of reference for understanding each other
- competent people to process their papers and help them meet governmental requirements

Occupations and education. The language barrier is the most immediate problem for the refugees, who need to gain the education and skills necessary for job success. Lack of child care has also been cited as a major problem. Because these cultures value hard work and education, most authorities think they will eventually overcome the barriers and become self-supporting citizens.

The most obvious goals for any migrating group are to find good jobs and get a good education for their children. Vietnamese have had the most success in finding jobs because of their urban background. Many are working as assembly line workers, technicians, machine operators, and office workers. Underemployment has been a real problem, as has a lack of Vietnamese in supervisory positions. When previously low-status employees in the home country are given higher job positions than former high-ranking army officers, or when women are in higher positions than men, conflicts occur, especially when directions and orders are given directly.

JAPANESE AMERICAN WORKERS

The Japanese were the second group of Asians to arrive in the U.S. in significant numbers. Their experiences have both similarities and differences to the Chinese experience.

Myths and Facts

Japanese Americans must cope with the myths and stereotypes that all Asian Americans face, which were discussed earlier, but they face at least two other myths that are specifically held about Japanese Americans.

Myth: Japanese Americans are greedy and acquisitive.

This is a variation on the myth that Asian Americans only care about starting their own businesses and buying real estate. The Japanese twist for this myth may reflect the fact that Japanese Americans are the most financially successful of Asian American groups. As mentioned earlier, results of a recent survey refutes this myth. Japan today is extremely competitive with the U.S. in several key industries, and the greedy, acquisitive stereotype is often applied to Japanese business persons. It may be projected onto Japanese Americans, most of whom have virtually no ties with Japanese business.

Myth: Japanese Americans are prejudiced toward African Americans.

This myth apparently is based on reports that African Americans who go to Japan to do business report difficulties in dealing with Japanese discrimination. Japan is a very homogeneous society, and few persons of African heritage live there or do business there. Unfamiliarity seems to be part of the problem. More important, most Japanese Americans were born in the U.S. and do not necessarily have the same viewpoint toward African Americans that Japanese in Japan have.

Background: The Japanese American Experience

The first large group of Japanese that arrived in the U.S. first migrated to Hawaii as laborers in the late 1800s, later moving on to the U.S. West Coast. In 1900 about 25,000 Japanese lived on the West Coast, mostly men who came to get ahead and planned to return to Japan. By 1920 there more than 100,000, about two-thirds of them in California. Like the Chinese immigrants, most were men working at physically strenuous, low-status, low-paying jobs, mainly in farming and building railroads.

Unlike the Chinese, the Japanese came from scattered rural areas all over Japan and Okinawa. As a group they were somewhat better educated and skilled than the Chinese immigrants. Some were quite skilled in intensive farming, such as truck gardening. Unlike China, Japan had begun the transition toward a modern industrial era. Although the Chinese presence in agriculture diminished after the 1880s, the Japanese became more heavily entrenched as farm owners and tenant farmers.

Community Growth

Due to pressure and negotiations of the Japanese government, immigrants' families were allowed to join them during the period from 1900 to 1924. This balanced the gender ratio and led to the establishment of families. By 1940 the nearly 80,000 second-generation Japanese Americans outnumbered the 47,000 immigrant parents. By 1940 Los Angeles had the largest Japanese

American settlement, numbering 37,000, but San Francisco with only 5,000 was the headquarters for the major organizations of each generation.

War and Concentration Camps

The major issue for pre-1940 Japanese Americans was prejudice. Euro-Americans simply did not accept Asian Americans as equals. When war came between the U.S. and Japan, all persons of Japanese ethnicity on the West Coast, regardless of citizenship, age, or sex, were herded into concentration camps, called relocation centers. The rationale was, apparently, to protect the U.S. from Japanese spy and saboteur activity, linked to a possible attack on the West Coast by Japanese submarines. The camps were surrounded by barbed wire and were patrolled by armed soldiers, who shot and killed several of the Japanese they were guarding. While they were not death camps, they were concentration camps by most commonly accepted definitions.

Japanese Americans are the only group of U.S. citizens ever to be deprived of their constitutional rights without a trial. Yet no individual Japanese American was ever found guilty of espionage nor were any so charged. Italian Americans and German Americans were not confined, even though their homelands were also our war enemies. More than 150,000 Japanese Americans living in Hawaii were left alone, as were the 10,000 who lived east of the Mississippi. Those who were sent to the camps lost virtually all their assets except those they could take with them. Their greatest economic loss was the income they weren't allowed to earn during their internment.

This wartime exile and incarceration was and still is the central event of Japanese American history, making their history unique among Asian Americans. The violation of Japanese American trust, and the extreme level of distrust expressed by the government of their homeland, the U.S., was traumatic for those who lived through it. The U.S. government has recently formally apologized to these families and set up a process for reparations.

Current Profile

By most measures of success, Japanese Americans are the most successful of any Asian American group. They have the fewest foreign born (32 percent) of any Asian American group, and the oldest average age, 36 compared to 30 for Asian Americans in general, and 33 for the total U.S. population. Most speak English at home (57 percent) with only Asian Indian Americans at 85 percent having a greater percentage speaking English at home. However, 33 percent are still considered linguistically isolated.

Japanese American educational attainment is high. Nearly twice the percentage of men hold degrees as the total men, 43 percent compared to 23 percent. Only Asian Indian American men have a significantly higher educational level. A significantly greater proportion of Japanese women hold degrees than total women, 28 percent compared to 18 percent. Still, among Asian American women only the Korean Americans and Southeast Asian Americans have a lower percentage with degrees.

They have the highest per capita income of any Asian American group, at $19,400, well above the national median of $14,100. The poverty rate of 7 percent is just a step above the lowest for all Asian American groups, with the Filipino Americans at 6.4 percent. They have the smallest families, 3.1 compared to the Asian American average of 3.8 and the U.S. average of 3.2. And a relatively small percentage (15 percent) have three or more family members working, compared to the Asian American average of 20 percent and the U.S. average of 13 percent.

Cultural Values

Surveys indicate most Japanese American young people still believe in traditional Japanese cultural values, most of which are typical Asian cultural values. The following values seem to be especially meaningful in the Japanese American culture:

- self-confidence
- sympathy and compassion for others
- fun-loving approach
- craftsmanship, pride in work

KOREAN AMERICAN WORKERS

The Korean American population has increased significantly since 1965. During the Korean War in the early 1950s, millions of peasant refugees fled from their farms to South Korean cities. Many of their children who got professional degrees found inadequate opportunities in their developing economy. When U.S. immigration law was liberalized for professionals in 1965, they flocked to the U.S. to escape political instability and high unemployment in Korea. They were one of the few immigrant groups in American history that was predominantly urban, educated, and from one generation. Most were Christian, a result of missionary efforts. Most also had some personal savings, military training, and a willingness to work hard.

Current Profile

Nearly 800,000 Korean Americans comprised about 12 percent of the Asian American population in 1990. About 73 percent were foreign born and the average age is 29. More than twice as many Korean American men have degrees as the total population, 47 percent compared to 23 percent. Among women, 26 percent have degrees compared to 18 percent of the total population. About 63 percent hold jobs, compared to 65 percent of all Americans. They have the highest percentage of all Asian Americans in technical, sales, and administrative support jobs. Per capita income is $11,000, somewhat under the $14,000 national median. Poverty rates and families with more than three workers are about the same as the national average.

Cultural Values and Practices

The major religion is Buddhism and there is a strong underlying ethic of Confucianism and Shamanism. Confucianism has especially affected cultural values and practices, and most of these are discussed under Asian American cultural patterns (Harris and Moran 1991).

Inner feelings, mood. A concept that is important to understanding Korean Americans is that of *kibun,* literally "inner feelings," with the closest English translation probably being "mood." When the kibun is good, the person functions smoothly and easily and feels great. If the kibun is upset or bad, transactions may come to an abrupt stop, and the person feels depressed, awful. Part of the intention of business people is to enhance the kibun of all parties. To damage the kibun could end the relationship and even create enemies. Class or status is intimately involved in the nurturing of kibun.

Nonpersons. Koreans who fail to follow the basic rules of social interaction are considered by other Koreans to not even be a person—to be a nonperson. Foreigners in a certain sense and to a certain extent are considered by Koreans as nonpersons. Koreans show very little concern for nonpersons' feelings, their comfort, or whether they live or die. Nonpersons are simply not worthy of much consideration. Korean Americans obviously must modify this attitude in order to function effectively in a diverse society; however, some variation of it probably survives and affects relationships.

Use of names. Newly arrived Korean Americans must adapt to the American use of first names in business situations. To the Confucian, a name is something to be honored and respected, not to be used casually. Therefore, to call someone directly by her or his name is an insult in most social circumstances. A Korean is addressed by her or his title, position, trade, profession, or some other honorary title.

Flattery and patience. Flattery is an intimate part of doing business among Korean Americans. An important or delicate business matter is always approached gradually. To begin discussing it directly and immediately is considered mere stupidity and will almost always result in failure. A highly skilled business person moves with "deliberation, dignity, and studies motions, and senses the impressions and nuances" that others are signaling.

ASIAN INDIAN AMERICANS

About one-eighth of Asian Americans are of Asian Indian heritage. They are the most highly educated group in the U.S. and nearly all speak English. We'll discuss the two waves of immigrants that came from India, their current profile, and some cultural values and practices.

Background: Sikhs and Professionals

Asian Indians came to the U.S. in two waves, the first around the turn of the twentieth century and the second after 1965. The first wave were Sikhs from rural areas, and the second wave were educated professionals from urban areas.

The First Wave

About 10,000 Asian Indians emigrated to the U.S. around 1900. Most were from one region of Punjab, a fertile, prosperous region in North India. Nearly all were Sikhs, a religion that combines aspects of the Hindu and Muslim religions. Highly visible religious customs for males include wearing a long turban, a dagger, and an iron bracelet, and never cutting their hair. About half the immigrants settled in eastern and midwestern cities, especially New York, and worked as merchants and middle-class professionals.

The other half settled in the fertile valleys of California. Following a typically Asian pattern, most were married men who left their wives in India, planning to make money to send back home to buy land. A few of the men took wives after arriving, mostly women from Mexican American farm worker families. Because of cultural differences, these marriages tended to be conflict ridden, and at least 20 percent ended in divorce. They generally experienced the same kind of discrimination as other Asians. For example, the alien land laws made it impossible to own farmland.

From 1914 o 1946 few Asian Indians entered the U.S., due to tight immigration laws, and the Asian Indian population in California declined from a high of more than 5,000 to about 1500. About 7,000 immigrants arrived between 1948 and 1965, mostly close relatives of American citizens. They did not establish new ethnic communities but rejuvenated those in existence.

The Second Wave

Since 1965 a much larger wave has established new communities with few connections with the old ones. Most are not Sikhs, are not farmers, and do not live in the Far West. The 1980 population of nearly 400,000 doubled by 1990 to more than 800,000. Asian American Indians are not dispersed around the country. About a third live in the Northeast, a fourth in the South, a fourth in the Midwest, and a fifth in the West.

Current Profile

In 1990 about 840,000 Asian Indians comprised about 12 percent of all Asian Americans. About 75 percent were foreign born, and the average age was 30. They are the most highly educated ethnic group in the U.S. with over 65 percent of the men and 49 percent of the women holding bachelor's degrees or higher, compared to the total population figures of 23 and 18 percent respectively.

Because of India's history as a British colony prior to 1950, most immigrants from India speak English. It's the major linking language in a nation of many languages and dialects. They have the least language difficulties of any Asian American group.

Asian Indian Americans are industrious and are heavily represented in high-status occupations. More than 72 percent of them have jobs, compared with 65 percent of all Americans, and 18 percent have three or more family members working, compared with 13 percent nationally. Nearly half of all foreign-born Asian Indian workers are managers and professionals. This is twice the proportion for all Americans, which is 24 percent, and significantly higher than any other Asian American group.

It follows that Asian Indian Americans have relatively high incomes and few live in poverty. Per capita income was nearly $18,000, compared to about $14,000 for all Americans. Among Asian American groups, only Japanese Americans earned more. Asian Indian Americans had one of the lowest poverty rates, 10 percent compared with 14 percent nationally.

To summarize Asian Indian Americans tend to be:

- strongly committed to maintaining family connections
- highly educated
- concentrated in the professions
- well paid
- trained in India, many part of a "brain drain" during the 1980s, caused by India's training more professionals than its businesses could profitably employ.

Cultural Values and Practices

The predominant religion in India is Hinduism, which of course strongly influences the values and practices of the people. In Hindu marriages, the woman is expected to show absolute dedication, submission, and obedience to her husband. Her traditional status in the household is low until she produces a male child. Other traits include:

- Family and friends are much more important than in the West.
- Extended family living is highly valued.
- Friends sense each other's needs and do something about them.
- Speaking your mind to a friend is a sign of friendship.
- Most believe that there are no accidents, that all things are interrelated in a cosmic order.
- Indian women do not expect to be spoken to by men who are strangers; nor is it appropriate for such men to help women out of a car, up steps, etc.
- Women who dare to dance do so only with their husbands.
- People don't address others outside the extended family by first name. The equivalent of *Mr. Bill* or *Miss Linda* is appropriate, as are such titles as *Teacher* and *Doctor*.
- People are expected to be on time.
- Public displays of affection are considered inappropriate.

While Asian Indian Americans have much in common with other Asian Americans, their culture is probably the most distinct because of the influence of Hinduism. There is also a strong Muslim influence, especially in Pakistan and Bangladesh, and this affects the values of practices of immigrants from those countries.

PACIFIC ISLANDERS

Pacific Islanders who live in the mainland U.S. are a relatively small ethnic group, but still more than 1 percent of the U.S. population. Business people in the West are most likely to encounter Pacific Islanders, since most of them live there, especially in California. We'll review their current profile and some common issues. Then we'll explore the background of the largest population within this group, the Hawaiians.

Current Profile

In the 1990 census, for the first time Pacific Islanders were identified as a distinct group of about 365,000 people living in the mainland U.S. Their islands of origin are as follows

Hawaii	58 percent
Samoa	17 percent
Guam	14 percent
Other	11 percent

Most live in the West and a few (13 percent) are foreign born. The median age is 25. Many came to the U.S. to pursue an education, and 76 percent are high school graduates, while only 11 percent are college graduates.

Most speak English, but 33 percent don't speak it very well, and 11 percent are linguistically isolated. The average family size is four. Most have jobs, but their income is significantly less than the national average and their poverty rate is significantly higher. More than 70 percent have jobs, with 18 percent holding managerial or professional jobs. Their per capita income averages $10,342 and their poverty rate is 17 percent.

Issues Common to Pacific Islanders

Some issues shared by many Pacific Islanders include:

- Education and skills gaps representing the major differences in surviving in their island culture and the high-tech U.S. culture
- Loss of status, rank, and prestige of people who were leaders in the islands
- Low wages and high expenses
- Role and identity problems—hierarchical roles of males are threatened, and identity closely tied to the family is weakened
- Stereotyped as islanders, who are exotic, romantic, heavy-drinking revelers
- Stereotyped as Asians, whose patterns are decidedly different in many ways

What is functional in a small island economy may not be helpful in an urban, technological society. Pacific Islanders' numbers are too small and their resources too slim to develop a separate community and that could develop opportunities for its members. Strong family ties and the belief in helping one another have been an asset for the immigrants.

The Hawaiians: A Multicultural Group

Two hundred years ago Hawaii was the home of a rich, distinct culture, but today it is more multicultural than Hawaiian.

From Distinct Culture to Multiculture

When Captain James Cook, the English explorer, came upon the Hawaiian islands in 1778, he found a thriving, highly stratified culture of more than 300,000 Hawaiians ruled by a class of chieftains. Other Europeans soon followed, including Christian missionaries from New England. By 1890 the great "white man's diseases" had decimated the population, leaving only about 35,000 Hawaiians.

The event that most dramatically changed the Hawaiian social system was the 1848 pact that permitted private persons to buy the land. Much of the land, formerly under the king and chiefs, ended up in the hands of a few Euro-American plantation owners who wanted to grow sugar, pineapple, and similar crops. The sugar and pineapple industries grew rapidly, and the demand for cheap labor changed forever the cultural mix of people on the islands. Most of the Hawaiians were dead, and those who were left generally did not make good laborers. The plantation owners brought in Chinese, Japanese, Korean, and Filipino laborers, many of whom stayed, creating a multicultural population. Today there are almost no "pure" Hawaiians left.

In 1898 the U.S. annexed Hawaii as a territorial possession. By that time Euro-Americans owned most of the land, were in control of the economy, and ran the political system. The cultural aspects of plantation life were primarily Asian: The languages, games, worship, and attitudes toward family, property, and authority reflected Asian cultural themes. Although Asians were the majority of the population, they were divided by ethnicity and were economically dependent on the plantation owners. What little remained of the native Hawaiian culture was found in the more remote villages.

Twentieth-Century Hawaii

Of all the groups found in twentieth-century Hawaii, the native Hawaiians had the most difficulty in adjusting to the competitive Euro-American culture, and a retreat to the past left them further behind. They began blaming the Asians for their plight and helped the Euro-Americans write land laws discriminating against the Chinese and Japanese, which of course further entrenched Euro-American dominance.

In 1959 Hawaii became a state. The actual numbers of immigrants since then has been difficult to assess. Most who come to the mainland are of mixed ancestry, and their experiences are as diverse as the diversity that they represent. Because of this background, Hawaii is the most multicultural of all the states in the U.S., and the culture has both Euro-American and Asian American themes.

LEADERSHIP CHALLENGES AND OPPORTUNITIES

Asian Americans are faced with some typical barriers to success in the American business culture, and they also possess some distinct strengths. Effective leaders devise ways to help Asian American workers to overcome the barriers and to build on their strengths. We'll also review some suggestions for working most effectively with Asian Americans.

Leadership Challenge: Meeting Asian American Workers' Needs

Leadership challenges include helping Asian Americans to overcome workplace barriers, avoiding typical assumptions and stereotypes, and helping employees get to know their Asian American co-workers (Dong 1992; Baldwin 1984).

Provide Support in Overcoming Barriers

Some typical barriers to job success faced by Asian Americans include:

- Being typecast as technologists (technical coolies) and therefore not being considered for higher level positions
- Being discriminated against because Euro-Americans are uncomfortable with their cultural style, which is considered too "foreign and strange."

- Communicating and verbalizing, problems especially crucial with first-generation immigrants
- Being misunderstood because of their values and behaviors, such as humbleness and passiveness. Such behavior is not necessarily an indicator that they are not qualified for leadership roles.

Avoid Typical Assumptions and Stereotypes

You've learned about the most typical myths, stereotypes, and assumptions that can hamper good working relationships. Here are a few reminders.

Remember, they're Americans, not foreigners. Non-Asian Americans have a tendency to look upon Asian Americans as foreigners because of their Asian appearance. Most of Asian-appearing workers you'll encounter will be Asian Americans. They're Americanized in varying degrees and possess varying language skill levels. Keep in mind that they aren't foreigners.

Determine generational status. There tend to be significant differences between first-generation immigrants and second-, third-, and fourth-generation Americans. By open, direct, but tactful conversations, you can share information about your background and learn about each worker's background. Be sure that your tone or manner is not in any way condescending or patronizing. Such information can help you to understand the worker's values, viewpoints, and actions. Keep in mind that information you've absorbed about such groups as third-generation Japanese Americans or recently arrived Hmong Americans can only provide general guidelines. Keep an open mind, get to know each individual, and avoid the tendency to use such information to form rigid stereotypes about these people.

Ascertain citizenship status. For workers who are not American citizens or permanent residents, find out about their status, which can help you better understand their background. For example, some initially come as foreign students, then get work visas. Their values and actions therefore tend to stem from Asian values and practices, and they are less Americanized. Companies must sign papers for Asians to keep their work visas, which frequently makes such workers feel dependent on the company. Such workers may be more submissive, obedient, and compliant, a situation some companies prefer and capitalize upon. Take the lead in respecting such workers.

Don't make assumptions about language ability. Some leaders assume Asian Americans are fluent in an Asian language and have problems with English. When Euro-Americans make such comments as "You speak very good English" or "Where did you learn to speak English so well?" Asian Americans who were born and raised in the U.S. may be understandably taken aback. It's one more reminder that even though they consider themselves as American as anyone, others tend to see them as foreigners.

Asian Americans are often embarrassed or frustrated when others expect them to be bilingual. For example, a worker who is third-generation Chinese may speak little or no Chinese. Let multiple language skills emerge and be used as an asset after you establish the facts.

Most important, when discussing an Asian American employees' skills, qualifications, and career goals, you as a leader can identify any communication skills or problems that he or she has and provide remedial training, if possible.

Don't assume they're cultural ambassadors. Don't try to make an Asian Ameircan worker your token Asian expert. Asian Americans appreciate people who don't assume they're experts in their ancestors' culture, just as they appreciate those who don't assume they're bilingual. For example, Japanese Americans who were born and raised in the U.S. are not necessarily experts in Japanese cuisine, culture, or politics. They do not necessarily agree with economic or political developments in Japan. Chinese Americans do not necessarily know about all the Chinese restaurants in the area. Again, it's better to ask about special bicultural expertise than to make assumptions.

Avoid such labels as "Oriental." For many Asian Americans the term Oriental, meaning Easterner, conjures up old Hollywood stereotypes (such as Charlie Chan and Tokyo Rose) depicting mysterious, unknowable, exotic Asians. It brings up unpleasant memories for many. Also, some consider it Eurocentric, since it describes Asia as east of Europe. A case can be made that it's west of the Americas, and that the Americas are the East to Asians. See exercise 6.2 for further ideas.

Remember, people with Spanish surnames may be Filipinos. Many types of people may have Spanish-sounding names. For example, many Filipinos took Spanish surnames during the era of Spanish colonialism. They are not Latinos, although their values and practices probably reflect a Spanish influence.

Help People Get to Know Asian American Co-workers

Leaders can influence others in the workplace by providing information and training about Asian American myths and realities, their cultural patterns and strengths, and guidelines for building productive relationships with them.

Leaders can include Asian American employees on team projects, thereby providing for in-depth contact with other employees and increased comfort levels. Perhaps most important, leaders can look beyond surface behaviors and get to know each Asian American team member personally in order to help them develop their talents and make appropriate career plans.

Constantly Question Your Assumptions About Behaviors

Keep in touch with the diversity of values and practices we've been discussing. Do further research on your own. Always question your assumptions about why an Asian American acts a certain way. For example, in the American business culture "silence is consent," and if someone doesn't speak up about a decision being made during a meeting, we assume he or she has no objections. But in Asian cultures "silence is golden," and "maintaining harmony is virtuous." Check your assumptions, and then ask.

Leadership Opportunities

To work most effectively with Asian Americans and to help them contribute their talents to the organization, build upon their strengths, apply some leadership strategies that relate to their cultural values, and help them make their own unique contributions (Chow 1994; Harris and Moran1991).

Build on Typical Asian American Strengths

Some Asian American characteristics that are especially important in business include:

- They emphasize trust and mutual connections.
- They stick to their word.
- They're interested in long-range benefits.
- They're punctual.
- They generally don't like being touched; a slight bow or brief handshake is appropriate.
- Once they decide upon who and what is the best choice, they are steadfast.
- Most are a little more reserved than Euro-Americans, often showing less emotion and greater physical distance when conversing.

Recognize Asian American Values as Strengths

Nearly all values and behavior patterns represent a two-sided coin in the workplace. One side is the advantages these can bring to the career achievement and organizational contribution of the employee. The other side is the barriers they could erect. Effective leaders recognize the cultural and individual values and behaviors of team members and figure out ways to enhance them and bring them into the work situation in constructive ways. Here are some ideas.

Respect their values regarding hard work and cooperation. Some managers take advantage of the Asian American tendency to value hard work and cooperation by piling on the work. Asian Americans are patient, but not stupid. Eventually such exploitation will backfire.

Understand their values of modesty and humility. By American corporate culture standards, many Asian Americans may appear to be too passive and too lacking in self-confidence and ambition to be given tough assignments that call for traditional leadership skills. In Asia such qualities are seen as positive, and the American standards are likely to be seen as egocentric and arrogant, as pushing or imposing oneself on others. First- and second-generation Asian Americans often reflect the traditional Asian traits of modesty and humility, while later generations are more likely to have adapted such values to American views.

Properly used, such values can be quite appropriate for facilitative team leaders. Further, such values do not mean that the worker lacks self-confidence, ambition, or assertiveness, qualities that vary among Asian Americans, just as they do among Euro-Americans. Asian Americans merely tend to express them in a more low-key, indirect manner. Similarly, we usually reward employees who tactfully question the status quo, speak up, take initiative, or find a better way of doing things. Asian Americans do not necessarily behave in this manner. The leadership challenge is to find ways to reward and motivate Asian American employees who are not as verbal or assertive as Euro-Americans.

Understand the values of indirectness and respect. Instead of assuming that that they are devious, uncommunicative, or dishonest, get to know them as individuals so you can reach a deeper understanding of the values of indirectness and respect in their communication patterns.

Understand their expression of emotion. Asian Americans feel the entire range of emotions, just as other human beings do. Certain values lead to less public expression of certain emotions; for example, maintenance of harmony and avoidance of open conflicts repress tendencies to openly express anger, resentment, jealousy, and similar emotions. Also, when any person feels vulnerable, intimidated, or threatened because they're perceived as a minority or foreigner, they're likely to hide their emotions as a protective device.

Work with the value of strong obligation to family. In most American corporate cultures, workaholics are rewarded and people who do not consistently put the company first are viewed as lacking commitment. While most Asian Americans place high value on hard work and perseverance, when family members need them, family obligations must come first. Managers who understand Asian American priorities regarding family and work are likely to win the respect and loyalty of these employees.

Apply Leadership Strategies

Here are some strategies that may be especially appropriate for Asian American workers. See also leaderships strategies discussed in Chapters 5 and 12.

Explain deviations from traditional boss-worker practices. Asian cultures tend to be more hierarchical and status-oriented than the current American culture. If you familiarize yourself with the expectations and traits of the traditional U.S. manager of the era prior to the 1960s, and still detectable in some corporate cultures today, you'll come close to the Asian expectation.

Have a conversation with the Asian American workers in which you share your ideas of the leader-worker relationship. Once you understand the workers' expectations, you can help the worker to understand your own deviations from that a expectation. For example, if the worker expects the boss to make all decisions, you can explain why workers in this company participate in decision making. And if the worker would be personally humiliated if you pitched in to help her or him complete a task, you can explain how this is viewed in the corporate culture and what it means.

Provide assertiveness training. We've seen that Asian American women are assertive on the job when they believe it's necessary or desirable to be assertive. Because Asian cultures focus on humbleness and subordinating personal desires for group interests, Asian American employees often need some training about the role of assertiveness in the American workplace. For more than 20 years, Euro-American women have benefited from such training. Asian American employees also respond well to assertiveness training and can reap similar benefits.

Build trust. Trust is a factor with Asian Americans, just as it is with African Americans. Be aware that centuries of prejudice and discrimination may have created some trust barriers in interethnic leader-worker relationships. When Asian Americans perceive that a Euro-American boss is trying to "buddy up" to them, they may respond internally with some distrust and suspicion. If you're a Euro-American leader, you must find ways to overcome this barrier. Begin by raising your awareness of the ways in which messages can be misunderstood or misinterpreted, and give special attention to clear communication. Then be very consistent in your messages and positions, and always follow through on agreements. Trust is built through the experience of another person as honest, fair, consistent, and reliable.

Help bring issues to the surface. One Asian American tendency that could be a double-edged sword is the focus on harmony and compliance. The other side of this behavior pattern may be an unwillingness to confront relationship problems. Most Asian Americans are taught that in troublesome situations, they should act as though nothing has happened. If they acknowledge a relationship problem, then they must take action, and action may be extremely serious. As a result, they tend to be long-suffering and patient, but resentment may build.

In team situations it's usually important to bring problems and troublesome feelings to the surface and to deal with them—if they're important enough to an individual to eventually create communication and relationship barriers. Leaders can work with all members in developing such team-related skills.

Express sincere personal concern. Get to know Asian American workers as people and to understand their goals and needs, which are usually tied to family status and needs. In this way you show that you understand the value of cooperation and want to establish a cooperative relationship. Cooperative relationships are normally personal ones.

Communicate clearly and check for understanding. Requests, assignments, expectations, and explanations must be clear and unambiguous. Instead of saying, "You might want to think about doing xyz," say "Please do xyz before you leave today. Can you do that?"

Use the team approach. One way to bridge the gap between Euro-American emphasis on individual initiative and Asian American emphasis on obedience to authority is to structure tasks to be performed by teams. Gradually introduce independent decision making by doing it as a group.

Choose motivators and rewards according to employees' values. Such motivators as individual recognition may not be as effective with Asian American employees as with Euro-Americans. The same is true for perks and benefits. Talk to them about their values, goals, and expectations. Together you can develop effective systems of motivation and reward.

Help Asian Americans Make a Contribution

Many companies are realizing the potential of the growing Asian American market, and nearly all U.S. companies are doing more and more business with Asian countries. Asian American employees tend to have a special touch with such clients and also are an invaluable resource in developing strategies and action plans for doing business in such markets.

Connections with the Asian American marketplace. Asian Americans have greater consuming power than their share of the total population. Companies such as Coca-Cola and AT&T have established Asian American marketing departments and have tried to reach Asian American communities with donations and advertisements. Companies are targeting the rapidly increasing Asian

American clientele. They are putting more Asian American models in their television commercials and advertisements. Some are looking to Asian American culture—art, music, dance, clothing designs, movies, and food—for inspiration and to make connections with the Asian American markets. Asian American employees can provide a valuable resource and connection in such efforts (Min 1995).

Connections with Asian countries. Virtually all economists expect Asian countries to play a more important role as American economic partners in the twenty-first century. Some locations that are emerging as economic tigers are Singapore, Taiwan, Hong Kong, and South Korea. New trade relations with China are opening up a market of over a billion people. Asian Americans employees obviously provide insights into and links with these global markets (Min 1995).

SUMMARY

Asian Americans must deal with many stereotypes and myths, such as they're too passive to be good American leaders, they're unemotional and inscrutable, they're "foreign," good at math, and "technical coolies." Actually Asian Americans are assertive when it's important and acceptable to be assertive, and they respond well to assertiveness training. Asian Americans have the same emotions as other people, but their values and training determine how they express themselves. Consideration for others' feelings and concern for harmony cause them to limit their emotional expression. Many have focused on technical skills until they could overcome language difficulties, but third- and fourth-generation Asian Americans tend to have good language skills.

Asian Americans have dealt with overt prejudice since Chinese immigrants first came to the U.S. about 150 years ago. The segregation and discrimination imposed probably reinforced their tendency to retain tight-knit families and communities. They've therefore retained many of their cultural values and patterns. Still, third- and fourth-generation Asian Americans tend to be quite Americanized. As a group, they have higher educational achievement than average. Although they holder higher-status jobs than average, they make less income. This apparently reflects some workplace barriers that still remain.

Common cultural themes of all Asian cultures are us-first, give and take, other-directedness, emphasis on harmony, and conformity to group norms. Education is highly valued, and rank and status are important. Communication patterns tend to be indirect and subtle.

The model minority stereotype has been a double-edged sword for Asian Americans, creating a belief that they are productive workers but leading to unfair expectations that they'll work harder for less than other employees. The myth has been used to blame African Americans and Latino Americans for their lower socioeconomic achievement. The model minority image is misleading and complex. On average Asian Americans do have higher educational and income levels than other groups. However, more of their family members must work to achieve these levels, and their education does not given them payback in income at the same rate as Euro-Americans. Asian Americans' success in small business has helped them to achieve higher education and some financial security in spite of discrimination. Women are expected to be especially modest and compliant, but most are strong and will be assertive and even confrontational when necessary.

Chinese Americans are the largest of the Asian American groups and have been here the longest. In fact they were the only Asian American group of any size for 100 years. They established Chinatowns in several cities, with their own small businesses and mutual aid associations. Filipino Americans are the next largest group. They retain many Asian cultural patterns, as well as patterns similar to Latino Americans because of several hundred years of Spanish rule. Most Southeast Asian Americans arrived since the 1960s as refugees of the Vietnam War. Their backgrounds range from urban professionals to Hmong hill people. Japanese Americans began arriving just after the Chinese and are considered the most successful of the Asian American groups by most measures. Korean Americans are from a predominantly Confucian culture but most are

Christians. Most have come since 1965. Asian Indian Americans are mainly urban professionals. They have the highest educational achievements of any group in the U.S. and most hold degrees. Pacific Islanders are a relatively small group that live primarily on the West Coast.

Leadership challenges include helping Asian American employees overcome the traditional workplace barriers, especially the myths and stereotypes. Opportunities include recognizing their values as strengths, explaining corporate cultures that may be confusing to them, and helping them to bring their issues out in the open to discuss. Their understanding of Asian cultures can be invaluable in doing business in Asian marketplaces.

Skill Builder 6.1: The Case of Doug Fong, Asian American Manager

Doug Fong is a restaurant manager for Jollytime Corporation. Jollytime consists of a chain of over 250 fast food restaurants throughout the U.S. Its corporate mission is to provide quality fast food at competitive prices and quality service. One of its strategies for quality control is to send "mystery shoppers" to every restaurant at least twice a month. These employees check on quality of food, cleanliness of restaurant, and quickness of service. Two managers operate each restaurant, a day manager and a night manager. Restaurants are categorized as low-level, medium-level, or high-level based on the following criteria: gross sales, annual profit, percentage of increase in sales and in annual profit, and scores assigned by mystery shoppers.

Doug Fong is a first-generation Asian American who lives in the San Francisco area. He's been with Jollytime for ten years and is respected by the other managers. Seven years ago he was promoted to manager of a low-level restaurant in the East Bay suburb of Concord, whose residents are primarily Euro-American but are also somewhat multicultural.

After two years he was transferred to a medium-level restaurant in the Hunter's Point area of San Francisco, an area dominated by African Americans. Restaurant profits increased 13 percent the first year and 15 percent the second year. The top executive team was impressed with Doug's ability to handle the challenging Hunter's Point location, and at the end of two years transferred him to a "less hectic" restaurant in the Sunset district, where he has been working for three years. Doug told a colleague, "I was sad to leave the Hunter's Point location because I had built a trusting relationship with my employees and my customers. There were a few trouble makers around, but I really didn't have any problems."

Residents in the Sunset are primarily Euro-American but also multicultural with a significant Asian American population. During the following three years under Doug's leadership, the Sunset district restaurant is ranked third, then sixth, and then second on the top 50 list of all Jollytime restaurants. Profits increased in each of these three years, and mystery shopper ratings have been outstanding. Doug has done well in managing a diverse group of employees. They speak well of him. For example, Kevin, a Euro-American food server, says, "Doug is a great manager; he treats everyone fairly." And Ruben, a Latino American cook says, "I've worked with Doug for nearly three years and he knows how to motivate people."

Doug's career goals include moving up to district manager and then to division manager. He's become more and more devoted to his job, often working 12-hour days. This is rather ambitious given the fact that Doug's educational background includes only a high school diploma. However, he's a rapid and avid learner. For example, he does all the accounting for his restaurant, and the auditors have always approved his work and even praised it.

A district manager oversees 10 to 12 restaurants. In an average day, the district manager may go over current operations and improvement plans with several restaurant mangers. The job requires good interpersonal communication skills and knowledge of accounting principles, including budgeting.

Doug has never asked for a promotion. He has operated on the belief that his hard work and excellence speak for themselves and that he'll be offered a promotion when the time is right. In the past two years, two district manager positions opened up, and the outgoing managers picked their successors. All the district managers that Doug has met are Euro-American men with college degrees.

Jim Davis was one of the outgoing district managers. His job had been to oversee restaurants in Oakland, which is predominantly African American. Doug decided to overcome his reticence and speak to Jim about the possibility of taking his place. Jim told Doug, "You're an extremely well-qualified manager—no doubt about that. But maybe the Oakland area is not the best place for you." Jim obviously doubted that Doug was assertive enough to handle the employees there. He said, "Let's wait for an opening in an area that's predominantly Asian American or Euro-American. That would be a better fit." A few weeks later *Jordan Jones*, a Euro-American, was named new district manager for the Oakland area.

Now, a year later, the buzz is that Jones has failed miserably in overseeing the Oakland restaurant managers and he'll be replaced soon. *Jack Barnes*, the division manager will name the replacement.

- What are the key issues in this case?

- If you were Doug Fong, what would you do?

- If you were Jack Barnes, what would you do?

Skill Builder 6.2: The Case of Linda Vuong, Asian American Cashier

Linda Vuong has been working for two years as cashier for Computer City, one of a chain of retail electronics stores. It is located in a neighborhood populated primarily by Chinese Americans. In fact, all of the 20 employees, including its managers, are Chinese American, except Linda, who is Vietnamese American. Most of the employees are in their early twenties, attend college, and help support their families. Linda is majoring in business administration and hopes the company will soon promote her to assistant manager. She takes her job seriously, is very customer oriented, and cooperates well with co-workers.

Wallace is one of the store's three assistant managers and is Linda's immediate supervisor. One of the assistant managers is leaving next month, and Wallace is recommending Linda for the job. In his written evaluation that he submits to *Guy*, the manager and co-owner of the franchised store, Wallace includes the following:

- Linda has continuously demonstrated quickness and efficiency in performing job tasks, which include taking customer orders promptly, packaging smaller items properly, and maintaining a clean work environment

- Linda has good customer skills

- Customers praise her performance

- Linda is a team player, helping her co-workers and offering advice on how to improve communications with difficult customers

Guy seldom interacts with Linda and in fact spends minimal time communicating with employees except to exchange greetings. The exception is that he loves to gossip about the local Chinese American community with a few "insider" employees who speak Cantonese. He rarely speaks English to people in the company except to those at an equal or higher level than he. Guy is a concerned employer, paying attention to salaries, work loads, work schedules, and career opportunities within the company, especially for those employees he feels closest to. However, Linda has never had a chance to discuss her career ambitions with Guy.

Linda has not received a pay increase in 16 months. Guy recently instructed Wallace to delegate more work duties to Linda in order to relieve some of the other employees from job tasks. Not only is Linda expected to do more work without an increase in hours worked, her schedule is often changed to accommodate the requests of other employees who want to attend to personal matters. Linda is hoping all these problems will be solved if she can just get an assistant manager position. This promotion would also allow her to expand her skills and abilities.

Max, one of Linda's co-workers, also wants the assistant manager job. He's definitely in the running even though Wallace has rarely given him high performance ratings. Wallace has had to talk with Max several times about excessive tardiness. However, Max gets along well with Guy, often chatting and gossiping with him in Cantonese about mutual friends and acquaintances.

Today, Guy calls Wallace to his office and says, "I know you've recommended Linda for the assistant manager position, but I don't think she's quite ready for it. You know, Max has great communication skills, and I think he's better equipped to supervise our employees. Max reads people well, he knows how to get close to people, and that's what we need."

- What are the key issues in this case?
- If you were Guy, what would you do?
- If you were Linda, what would you do?

Skill Builder 6.3: The Case of Office Whiz Connie

Connie has been working for six years for Crystal Fizz, a manufacturer of drink mixes. She is one of six employees in the plant office, the youngest at age 27 and the only Asian American. Connie has learned how to do most all the major functions in the office and likes her job. However, she's become disillusioned with the work environment. If it weren't for the good pay and benefits, she'd be gone. In fact, she's thinking about looking for a job elsewhere.

Bob, the owner and manager, a year ago hired *Jim*, who performs duties similar to the ones Connie does. Soon Jim was making comments that disturbed Connie, such as "I can't understand what you're saying half the time," and "Why don't you do things the American way—whatever the American way is?" Connie's response has been to ignore and avoid Jim as much as possible. However, Jim was soon being consulted by Bob about various company decisions. Bob sometimes takes Jim with him to important business meetings. Connie is never included in this way, and she recently discovered that Jim makes about 10 percent more than she.

Company employees get four weeks of vacation. Before Jim came, Connie never took all four weeks at one time because of office demands. It was typical for her to come into the office even when she could have taken some time off, simply because there was much important work to be done. Now she finds she doesn't care about that any more. She came back from a four-week vacation last month, and she plans to take all the time off she has coming to her. She feels that she is being treated unfairly and has no real chance of advancement.

- What do you think are the major problems here?
- What should Connie do?
- What should Bob do?

REFERENCES

Baldassare, Mark. "Ethnic Groups Slow to Assimilate." *San Francisco Chronicle* (March 27, 1990): A1.

Baldwin, Beth C. *Patterns of Adjustment*. Orange, CA: Immigrant and Refugee Planning Center, 1984.

Blinder, David, and Catherine Lew. "Asian Americans: Exit Poll." *San Francisco Chronicle* (November 6, 1992): A1.

Brislin, Richard W., and Tomoko Yoshida, eds. *Improving Intercultural Interactions*. Thousand Oaks, CA: Sage, 1994.

Chan, Sucheng. *Asian Americans: An Interpretive History*. Boston: Twayne Publishers, 1991.

Chew, Lee (interview). "Life Story of a Chinaman." *The Life Stories of Undistinguished Americans as Told by Themselves*. New York, 1906.

Chow, Esther Ngan-Ling. "Asian American Women at Work." *Women of Color in U.S. Society*. Philadelphia: Temple University Press, 1994.

Corporate 1000: A Directory of Who Runs the Top 1,000 U.S. Corporations. Washington, D.C.: The Washington D.C. Monitor, Inc., 1985.

Dong, Lorraine. Professor of Asian American Studies, San Francisco State University, interview, 1992.

Harris, Philip R., and Robert T. Moran. *Managing Cultural Differences*, 3d ed. Houston: Gulf Publishing Co., 1991.

Hossfeld, Karen, "Hiring Immigrant Women: Silicon Valley's 'Simple Formula.'" *Women of Color in U.S. Society*. Philadelphia: Temple University Press, 1994.

Hurh, Won Moo, and Kwang Chung Kim. *Korean Immigrants in America*. Cranbury, NJ: Fairleigh Dickinson University Press, 1984.

Kenton, S.B. and D. Valentine. *CrossTalk*. Cincinnati, OH: South-Western, 1996.

Kitano, Harry H.L. and Roger Daniels. *Asian Americans: Emerging Minorities*. Englewood Cliffs, NJ: Prentice Hall, 1988.

Kumagai, regarding emotional expression, 1981.

Markus & Kitayama. Comments on emotional expression and values, 1991.

Min, Pyong Gap, ed. *Asian Americans: Contemporary Trends and Issues*. Thousand Oaks, CA: Sage, 1995.

Morrison, Ann. *The New Leaders*. San Francisco: Jossey-Bass, 1992.

Nguyen, Liem T., and Alan B. Henkin. "Refugees from Vietnam." *Journal of Ethnic Studies,* 9, no. 4 (1982): 101–116.

Ong, Paul. "Chinese Laundries as an Urban Occupation in Nineteenth Century California." *The Annals of the Chinese Historical Society of the Pacific Northwest*. Seattle, 1983.

Russell, John. "Narratives of Denial: Racial Chauvinism and the Black Other in Japan." *Japan Quarterly* (Oct.–Dec. 1991): 416–428.

Stuart C. Miller. *The Unwelcome Immigrant: The American Image of the Chinese, 1752–1882*. Berkeley, CA: 1969.

Takaki, Ronald. *A Different Mirror: A History of Multicultural America*. Boston: Little, Brown and Company, 1993.

Tannen, Deborah. *You Just Don't Understand*. New York: Wm. Morrow, 1990.

U.S. Census Bureau, Department of Commerce. *We the American . . . Asians*, and *We the American . . . Pacific Islanders*, 1993.

Viviano, Frank. "Poll Contradicts Stereotypes." *San Francisco Chronicle* (March 27, 1990): A1.

Wang, Gungwu. *The Chineseness of China*. Oxford, New York: Oxford University Press, 1991.

Wei, William. *The Asian American Movement*. Philadelphia: Temple University Press, 1993.

Young, Jared. *Discrimination, Income, Human Capital Investment, and Asian-Americans*. San Francisco, CA: R & E Research Associates, Inc., 1977.

Zinn, M.B., and B.T. Dill. *Women of Color in U.S. Society*. Philadelphia: Temple University Press, 1994.

CHAPTER 7
Working with Latino Americans

Latino Americans love their Spanish language and value the warmth and romance of their culture, even as they aspire to the American Dream.
Jack Forbes

About nine percent of Americans are Latino Americans. Numbering 22 million, Latino Americans are the second-largest and fastest-growing minority group in the U.S. While virtually all Latino Americans have in common the Spanish language and certain Latino cultural themes, each subgroup has its own profile and issues. First, we'll review the typical myths and the current profile of the Latino American group in general, along with common cultural themes and patterns that reflect their rich cultural heritage. Then we'll explore the specific profiles and issues of the largest subgroups—Mexican Americans, Puerto Rican Americans, and Cuban Americans—and take a brief look at workers whose roots are in Central America, South America, and the Dominican Republic. Finally, you'll learn about leadership challenges and opportunities in working with Latino Americans.

But first, remember the warning about keeping cultural influences in perspective. There are dozens of major Latino cultures throughout the world, and individuals are also influenced by socioeconomic class, region, generation, individual experiences, and individual choices. Although extreme variations in Latino Americans' ways of life make it impossible to define a precise pattern for all, many do share a number of values and customs that may help you understand why they think, feel, and act as they do. We must always keep in mind that group patterns are not necessarily an individual's pattern. Use the following as background information, and resist any temptation to form rigid categories. It's important to be open and flexible as you interact with individual Latino Americans. First, get in touch with your beliefs and knowledge about Latino Americans by completing Self-Awareness Activities 7.1 and 7.2.

Self-Awareness Activity 7.1: What Do You Believe About Latino Americans?

Purpose:

- to get in touch with your beliefs and stereotypes about this group of people
- to experience how judgmental beliefs affect your thinking and feeling processes
- to experience the ways in which your beliefs create your reality regarding other persons, even before you have any interaction with them.

Part I. What Do You Believe About Latino American Women?

Step 1. Associations

- Relax as deeply as you can: close your eyes and taking a few deep breaths.
- Focus on the words "Latino American woman" and allow a mental picture to come up in your mind's eye.
- Notice the words and images that come to mind as you "see" this woman.
- Open your eyes and list 10 to 20 words in the order in which they occur to you.
- Review your list. Mark a plus beside the words that are positive, a minus beside the words that are negative, and a circle beside neutral words.

Step 2. Negative Associations

- Close your eyes and focus again on the image of the Latino American woman. Formulate a negative opinion or judgment, perhaps one you typically hold about Latino American women.
- Notice your *feelings* as you see the person in this negative way. What *thoughts* come up as you focus on the image?
- Write a few sentences about your feelings and thoughts.

Step 3. Positive Associations

- Formulate a positive opinion or judgment, perhaps one you typically hold about Latino American women.
- Notice your *feelings* as you see the person in this positive way. What *thoughts* come up as you focus on the image?
- Write a few sentences about your feelings and thoughts.

Step 4. Insights

- Focus on the differences between your experiences when you hold negative and positive judgments or opinions. What were the differences? What meaning does this have for you, for your beliefs and feelings about people from this group, and about beliefs in general?
- Write your responses in a few sentences; include anything you like about your feelings, thoughts, and insights.

Part II. Experimenting with Opinions About Latino American Men

Repeat the phases and steps in Part I, this time focusing on the image of a Latino American man.

Self-Awareness Activity 7.2: What Do You Know About Latino Americans?

Purpose: To see what you know about the issues covered in this chapter.

Instructions: Determine whether you think the following statements are basically true or false—and think about why. The answers will emerge in this chapter, and the summary at the end of the chapter focuses on these issues.

1. Most Latino Americans are too emotional and excitable to be leaders in American corporations.
2. Most Latino Americans are originally from Mexico.
3. The largest Latino American population is found in New Mexico.
4. The value that's most important to Mexican Americans is achievement.
5. *Machismo* refers to being the boss.
6. *Simpatico* refers to giving sympathy to poor persons.
7. When communicating, Latino Americans tend to speak indirectly.
8. Latino American workers tend to buddy up to the boss.

MYTHS AND FACTS

Latino Americans can bring a special worldview and way of relating to the workplace, a warmth and camaraderie that are especially valuable in team situations. However, myths and stereotypes often support the barriers of prejudice and discrimination. Leaders need to understand what they are and how to counteract them.

Myth: Latino American workers are only qualified for menial jobs.

Related myths are: *They can't speak English well; They have only the most menial-level skills; They're not productive; They have a mañana attitude.*

Latino Americans are a diverse group. Many of them have been in the U.S. for generations and may be highly educated. Some groups, such as Cuban Americans, have business qualifications comparable to Euro-Americans. Recent immigrants frequently have language, education, and skill barriers to qualifying for better jobs. Some companies operating in urban areas with large Latino immigrant populations have found that providing remedial education and job training results in a pool of skilled, loyal workers. When Latino Americans feel they are part of an ingroup, they tend to be extremely loyal. Studies indicate that most identify with the American Dream of getting ahead, which means that most are willing to learn the skills and approaches it takes—including how to be productive and meet time requirements.

Myth: Latino Americans are too emotional and excitable to hold leadership roles.

Latino Americans generally hold views about expressing emotions that are different from Euro-Americans' views. More on this later. The point is, the resulting behavior is a difference in style, not substance. It need not affect Latino Americans' ability to lead, as long as Euro-Americans learn to understand various leadership styles. Also, after Latino Americans have been in an American corporate culture for a while, they naturally tend to modify their style a little.

Myth: Latino Americans are too passive, polite, and lacking in conviction to be good leaders in the workplace.

This myth looks only at surface behavior that reflects key cultural values and fails to take into consideration the values themselves and the contribution they can make to an effective leadership approach. Again, the myth focuses on style, not substance. The values of harmony and positive interpersonal relationships have always been important in the workplace and are increasingly crucial to business success. Euro-American leaders can learn what Latino Americans' behavior really means and can open up ways for them to assert their ideas and opinions. Latino Americans can learn to adapt to American corporate cultures and how to be appropriately assertive in that arena.

Myth: Latino American men are macho men.

Although Latinos generally are viewed as passive and polite, the men are often stereotyped as being macho with their women and with each other in bars and similar settings. have a machismo viewpoint. They're said to have a quick smile and quick knife and love to fight.

Most modern cultures are based on some form of patriarchy. Latino cultures have their own brand. The "quick knife" stereotype is mainly a phenomenon of youth gangs, and most every U.S. cultural group has some youth gangs. In all cases they're a small minority of the total population and have little to do with employee relationships. As a matter of fact, Latino Americans, especially the largest group, Mexican Americans, tend to be one of the most cooperative, accepting groups in the U.S., and getting along is one of their highest values. In addition, the machismo style is changing along with changing economic realities and new job opportunities for Latino American women.

CURRENT PROFILE: WHO ARE THE LATINO AMERICANS?

Around the turn of the century there were fewer than 250,000 Latino Americans in the U.S., fewer than the number of Swiss immigrants. By 1990, there were more than 22 million or 9 percent of the U.S. population, equivalent to the entire U.S. population of 1850. In America's 10 largest cities, an average of one in very four people is of Latino origin: more than 55 percent in Miami and San Antonio, 40 percent in Los Angeles, and 24 percent in New York (U.S. Census Bureau 1993]. The major Latino American subgroups are shown in Figure 7.1. The largest subgroup by far is the Mexican American, followed by the Puerto Rican American, and Cuban American.

FIGURE 7.1: Major Latino American Subgroups: By Country of Origin

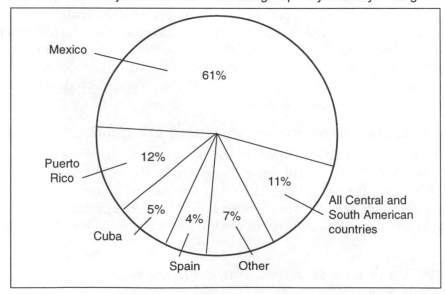

Source: U.S. Census Bureau, 1993.

Latino Americans include about a million descendants of Spanish and Spanish American settlers. Many of them have ancestors who lived in the West before it became part of the U.S. As a group, they don't have the same profile or issues as the other subgroups because they were never immigrants to the U.S.

The following are characteristics of the Latino American population as a whole.

Fast-growing. The Latino American population grew by 53 percent between 1980 and 1990, over seven times as fast as the rest of the nation. This followed on a growth of 61 percent between 1970 and 1980. A higher than average birth rate and substantial immigration are the major reasons. The Census Bureau's 1992 middle series projections suggest that the Latino American population could rise to nearly 50 million by 2020.

Concentrated in a few states. Most Mexican Americans live in California or Texas, most Puerto Ricans in New York, and most Cuban Americans in Florida. The way the Latino American population is distributed among the states is shown in Table 7.1.

TABLE 7.1: Latino American Population by State, 1990

State	How Latino Americans are Distributed (%)	Proportion of State Population That's Latino (%)
California	35	26
Texas	20	26
New York	10	10
Florida	7	10
Illinois	4	—
New Jersey	3	—
Arizona	3	20
New Mexico	3	10
Colorado	2	10
Other states	13	—

Source: U.S. Census Bureau, 1993

Predominantly in cities. The tradition of the Latino American has been that of a rural peasant. But by 1980, most were urban dwellers, including 95 percent of all Puerto Ricans and Cubans and 80 percent of all Mexican Americans. About 66 percent of the general U.S. population lived in urban areas.

Young. Their average age is younger, 23 compared to 30, than for the U.S. population at large. Youthful population groups are more likely to bear children than aging groups, so even if no future immigrants came, Latino Americans would probably increase at a faster rate than average for the next few years.

Educational levels that vary by subgroup. While educational levels have improved significantly since 1970, they are still well below the national average of 77 percent with high school diplomas and 21 percent with bachelor's degrees or higher. In the Latino American population as a whole, 50 percent hold high school diplomas and 9 percent hold degrees.

Least educated are those from Mexico, Central America, Dominica, and Puerto Rico, with 45 to 55 percent holding diplomas and 6 to 10 percent holding degrees. Best educated are Spaniards and South Americans, with more than 70 percent holding diplomas and about 20 percent holding degrees. Cubans fall into two classes: While only 57 percent had diplomas, 17 percent had degrees.

Fewer in well-paying occupations. The most typical occupations for men are laborer/operator/fabricator (28 percent) and craft/repair/production (20 percent). Only 12 percent of the men hold managerial or professional positions, compared with 27 percent of total males.

Latino American women are making slightly more progress; 17 percent hold managerial or professional jobs, compared to 28 percent of non-Latino women. In U.S. companies of 100 or more employees, Latino American women held less than one percent of all management jobs in 1988, according to EEOC records. The most typical jobs for the women are administrative support, sales, and technical (39 percent) and service jobs (24 percent) (U.S. Census 1993; Mackowski 1991).

Lower median family income. Median family income is $25,000, lower than the national median of $35,200. Puerto Rican female householders with no husband present had the lowest income, $9,000. Family incomes by subgroup, from lowest to highest are:

Puerto Rican	$22,000
Mexican	$24,100
Cuban	$32,400
Spaniard	$36,700

Median family income of subgroups tend to reflect educational attainment.

Many Mexican Americans and Puerto Rican Americans, the largest subgroups, remain at a persistent, substantial disadvantage, which is reflected in the overall Latino American earnings patterns. After some modest gains during the economic boom of the 1960s, most Latino Americans became stuck at their relative earnings levels. In fact, the earnings ratio of Latino Americans to Euro-Americans is in a decline, with the pay gap widening at a rate of one-half percent per year.

Higher-than-average poverty rates. The average poverty rate for all Latino American families is 22 percent, compared to 13 percent for all Americans and 5 percent for Euro-Americans. Poverty rates for subgroups generally reflect education levels, ranging from 30 percent for Puerto Ricans to 10 or 11 percent for Cubans and Spaniards. Some sociologists think that the major causes of urban Latino American poverty are:

• decreased employment opportunities for the less skilled and educated

• severely depressed wages among the employed

• restricted or non existent welfare benefits, except for Puerto Ricans

Declining proportion of married couple households. About 70 percent of Latino American families consist of married couples, compared to nearly 80 percent of Euro-American families, 82 percent of Asian American families, and 50 percent of African American families. About 9 percent consisted of a male with no wife present, and 22 percent of a female with no husband present. More than 36 percent of Puerto Rican families are headed by a female. In 1990, 64 percent of Latino American children lived with two parents, compared to 71 percent in 1980. For Euro-American children the proportions were 80 percent in 1990 and 83 percent in 1980. Only 38 percent of Latino American children lived in traditional nuclear families in 1990, compared to 56 percent of Euro-American children (U.S. Census Bureau 1993).

Language barrier. Latino Americans are evenly divided between those who speak English very well and those who don't. All speak Spanish. Since the arrival of recent immigrants, Puerto Ricans have the largest proportion (nearly 60 percent) who don't speak English very well. Educational level is directly related to English language skills.

By 1980 more than 11 million Latino Americans spoke Spanish at home, although 75 percent of them also used English. In San Antonio 40 percent of the people spoke Spanish, in Miami 36 percent. Spanish-language television and radio stations now serve large audiences in New York, San Francisco, Los Angeles, San Antonio, Miami, and Chicago. Spanish-language television and radio, films, and music have been instrumental in transcending national barriers of Latino American audiences.

Most U.S.-born but increasing immigration. About 65 percent of Latino Americans were born in the U.S. Of the 35 percent who are foreign born, about half came to the U.S. during the 1980s. Prior to 1970 Latino Americans comprised from 20 to 30 percent of legal immigrants entering the U.S. During the 1970s this proportion leaped to 40 percent and during the 1980s to 47 percent. In addition, many illegal immigrants cross the U.S.-Mexican border every year. Many work for a while and return, but many stay.

COMMON THREADS: CULTURAL VALUES AND PATTERNS

The most important values to most Latino Americans are the focus on family, ingroup loyalty, and getting along with family and ingroup persons. They love their culture, their language, and their tradition, so most have strong feelings about holding onto their ethnic heritage. In a 1980s survey, most Latino Americans expressed a deep desire to pass on to their children their cultural and religious traditions, especially the Spanish language and respect for elders. Passing on the tradition of commitment to the family ranked high, but not as high as passing on the language.

You'll better understand Latino personal values if you first understand their basic worldview—how they see reality. Basic to what Latino countries have in common is the influence of Spanish culture, which includes an aristocratic hierarchy based on a powerful patron who protects his subjects. They in turn serve him and owe him their loyalty. Therefore, the societies that developed in the Latino countries normally consisted of a small, privileged group of the served and a mass of underprivileged servers (Gann and Duignan 1986). Some common themes we'll explore are:

- *Worldview*: maintaining the status quo of the powerful and powerless and patriarchy, with a focus on the present moment, the future's up to God's will.
- *Relationships*: the highest values are family, ingroup loyalty, and getting along.
- *Spiritual life*: fatalism, destiny; a thin veil between physical world and spirit world.

Values: Worldview

Latino Americans have their own view of hierarchy and status. This view in turn leads to beliefs about getting by in the world, expressing emotions, being physically close, and seeing the present moment as more important than an uncertain future (Harris and Moran 1991; Hofstede 1980).

Hierarchy and Status

A sense of hierarchy and status is a strong element in virtually all Latino countries. People are born into an upper or lower class, and the middle class in most countries is small but growing. Traditionally the masses live in destitute poverty and the elite live with great wealth. The upper classes are more formal and elaborate than in the U.S. The work you do is directly related to your social class; therefore, to do manual labor, such as helping out as a house guest or pitching in to help an office worker would be undignified and inappropriate.

In recent years nearly all of the political unrest, upheaval and terrorism in Latino countries has centered around attempts to break down the hierarchy. Opposing groups try to break the hold of the rich aristocracy and multinational corporations on the wealth of the land.

Showing respect or respeto. People show respect for someone of superior status by their voice tone and manner. The traditional belief is that the reason people are poor or rich, have power or don't, is because of God's will. A patron is a man of power or wealth who receives loyalty from people of lesser status. He may be the boss, a politician, a landowner, or a businessman. The patron makes the decisions, and others don't question him. Where Americans attempt to minimize differences between persons due to status, age, sex, etc., Latino Americans tend to stress them.

Accepting the powerful superior. Those in positions of authority maintain their leadership by their ability to dole out resources to their followers and to help and protect them when they need it. The relationship is reminiscent of a parent-child relationship. The authority figures tend to set clear standards and boundaries for compliance with their policies and rules.

Patriarchal values may explain why Latino Americans tend to express less tolerance for gays and lesbians than do Euro-Americans in recent surveys. On the other hand, Latino Americans tend to be more tolerant regarding skin color. Social class is not tied to skin color in Latin American countries as it has been historically in the U.S.

Accepting one's social place. Latino Americans tend to accept their social status, even when it's extremely inferior to that of the ruling class. They tend to value the stability that comes with everyone knowing their place and staying in it, living up to societal expectations. Social climbing is frowned upon, and people who are seen as "trying to get ahead" are not admired. Such attempts, if successful, are seen as disturbing and disruptive, threatening the relative social position of many people. Climbing also appears as crass materialism and greed to many, and it shows disdain for sensitive human relationships.

Trusting the government. The acceptance of social status, so traditional in Mexico and most other Latino cultures, is reflected in most Latino Americans' view of government's role. In a recent survey most Latino Americans agreed with most Euro-Americans that individuals are responsible for providing for their own needs. However, nearly twice as many Latino Americans as Euro-Americans felt the government should provide jobs, and significantly fewer Latino Americans expressed distrust of government.

Power Distance

Related to the values around status and hierarchy is the tendency to perceive greater distance between authority figures and their subordinates. Latino Americans tend to show greater deference and respect than Americans toward certain respected or powerful groups of people, such as the rich, the educated, the older, and toward certain professions, such as doctors, priests, teachers. They place a higher value on conformity and obedience, and they support autocratic and authoritarian attitudes from those in charge of organizations or institutions. People generally fear disagreeing with those in power. The less powerful try to meet all the expectations of the powerful.

Getting By in the World

Latin American cultures hold a special space for certain Spanish archetypes or heroes. These heroes include the idealist, the defender of honor, and the opportunist. In Spain the military landed class could theoretically be joined by any man who could prove that his ancestors were "old Christians," and who had a sword, a shield, a horse, and the ability to gain the favor of the king by brave exploits. Virtually every man who could do so aspired to this status and behaved as though he was entitled to it.

The idealist. This aspiration for noble status led to an attraction to the idealist, the Don Quixote who tilts at windmills, dreams the impossible dream, and is willing to do battle and even die for a noble cause.

The defender of honor. The aspiration for noble status also led to an extreme sensitivity to personal and family honor. Many Latin Americans still experience this "touchiness" about their personal honor, especially the honor of their good name and their family. Remember, family ancestry was a prerequisite to gaining status.

The opportunist. The Spanish culture also values the colorful character whose circumstances force him to live by his wits, and sometimes, as part of the process, by other people's suffering. When Latino Americans attempt to model some behavior after the idealist and other behavior after the opportunist, they often experience inner conflict, for obvious reasons.

Emotion or Passion Factor

The fiery, romantic Latino who passionately expresses his or her feelings is one facet of the Latino American image. This tendency is reflected in many Latino plays, films, soap operas, and other theatrical productions. To Euro-Americans the acting may be seen as overacting and the emotional content of the production may seem too melodramatic and overwrought to be sincere.

Several studies seem to confirm that this passionate, fiery tendency still exists in Latino Americans. For example, studies indicate that Latino Americans who respond to surveys are more likely to choose the extreme response categories (strongly agree, strongly disagree) than the middle categories, to a greater extent than Euro-Americans. Overall, the less time Latino Americans have spent in the U.S., the more they prefer to make extreme choices. They see the use of the middle categories (somewhat agree) as a way of hiding a person's real feelings by presenting them in moderated terms. This indicates that Latino persons value their feelings, are encouraged to fully experience them, and have fewer restrictions about expressing them—especially the ones that reflect caring and passion for life—than Euro-Americans. The research results also imply that that the longer Latino Americans live in the U.S., the more they tend to modify the way they express emotion.

Personal Space

In general Latino Americans like to be physically closer to others than do Euro-Americans, and so they stand closer together when they converse. This preference is related to their close, mutually dependent relationships, and their frequent expression of warm feelings. They are a contact culture that feels comfortable when physically close to others. Therefore, when they brush close to another, moving into what Americans would consider personal body space, there would be no reason to say, "excuse me," as most Americans would. Latino Americans are also more likely to touch each other during a conversation.

Differences in personal space affect the emotional reactions of people in interactions. Latino Americans may seem too pushy as they close in on Euro-Americans, who in turn may seem cold and distant as they back away.

"Mañana" and Other Time Attitudes

Mañana (literally, "tomorrow") doesn't refer to procrastination or laziness, but to the concept that the future is indefinite. In Latin countries it's not unusual for a business person to promise to give you a product or service by the deadline date you want even though they're unlikely to be able to meet the deadline. The main reason for agreeing is to make you happy in the moment. The backup reasoning is that the future is very uncertain, and some miracle may occur that will enable them to meet the deadline. Therefore, they know they can make you happy now, and they might be able to make you happy then. Latino Americans typically focus more on the present moment than do Euro-Americans. Latino Americans spend less time thinking about the future and planning for it, partly because they see the future as too uncertain to do much planning. This view is related to their sense of fate.

Latino Americans tend to be more conditioned by the past than are Euro-Americans. The typical Euro-Americans approach is to start with *now* and project your thoughts into the future; the past is past; it doesn't need to get in the way. Latino Americans are more concerned with tradition and more willing to continue with things as they have traditionally been. An example is the willingness of the poor masses in Latin American countries to accept their lot in life, although this view has been changing somewhat in recent years.

Meeting time deadlines and being on time for work and business appointments is generally the same for Latino Americans as for Euro-Americans. The main difference in attitudes toward promptness is in social situations, where it is typically less important for Latino Americans. The focus there is on relating to people in the moment, so the passage of time is not in immediate awareness.

In summary, Euro-Americans are considered to be generally future oriented because they stress planning for the future, being able to delay gratification, being on time, and making efficient use of time. Present-oriented Latino Americans put less emphasis on these traits and tend to have a more flexible attitude toward time. They feel they are on time even if they arrive 15 or 20 minutes after the appointed time. They place greater value on the quality of interpersonal relationships than on the length of time in which they take place. Highly efficient or time conscious people may be perceived as impolite or insulting (Marin et al 1991).

Education

Latino Americans place a high value on education, even though they have the lowest educational level of any U.S. group. Studies indicate that Latino American high school students report significantly higher aspirations to get a college degree than Euro-American students whose families are at the same socioeconomic level. In both groups, the higher the socioeconomic level, the higher the educational aspirations tend to be. About the same percentage of Latino American and Euro-American parents want their children to attend college, again controlling for socioeconomic status (Solorzano 1991).

Values: Personal Relationships

Latino Americans tend to place the highest priority on relationships. Family comes first, extended family next. There's a much stronger sense of mutual dependence and loyalty than among most Euro-Americans. Gender relationships tend to be less equitable and gender roles more segregated (Triandis 1984a; Triandis et al 1982; Cohen 1979; Grebler et al 1970; Mannino and Shore, 1976; Valle and Martinez 1980).

Familismo

The Latino culture is collective, and family and group closeness is their most important priority. *Familismo* includes three types of value orientations: (1) feeling obligated to provide material and emotional support to extended family members, (2) relying on relatives for help and support, and (3) constantly checking with relatives about the way they see various behaviors and attitudes and being influenced by their perceptions and feelings.

Mutual dependence. Latino Americans typically have high levels of mutual personal dependence, sensitivity to relationships, conformity, readiness to be influenced by others, mutual empathy, willingness to sacrifice for the welfare of the family or ingroup members, and trust of the members of the ingroup. It's expected that members will ask others for any assistance they need and that they'll give it when asked. While Euro-Americans expect to repay favors quickly, Latino Americans are comfortable with being indebted to those in their ingroup. For them, if you were to repay a friend's favor too quickly, they might see it as almost an insult, as though you think your friend's help was grudging or done out of expectation for gain.

This value helps to protect each person against physical and emotional stress by providing natural support systems. As a result, Latino Americans place highest value on building interpersonal relationships in ingroups that are nurturing, loving, intimate, and respectful. In contrast, Euro-Americans see value in more confrontational and segmented relationships (Hofstede 1980; Marin and Marin 1991).

Extended family first. The family is the center of personal existence, more so than for most U.S. families. Latino Americans' identities are closely tied to that of their family and its members. The tight bonds of love and loyalty may exclude outsiders to a greater degree. The family may include many more members than most Euro-American families: Grandparents and great-grandparents stay close and aunts, uncles, and cousins may be almost as close; even some close friends may be included. Family business is considered private, and to discuss it with outsiders would be a betrayal. Families are inward-focused and members rely on these relationships for their emotional security. Within the family, members tend to be quite open, honest, and communicative. Parents exercise strong authority.

Undying loyalty. Latino Americans have incredibly strong ties and loyalties to family and friends. If one person loses his job, the whole family may quit. As a result, disputes can have a more complex quality than Euro-Americans are accustomed to. The net effect is for the Latino American to hold back until he can stand it no longer and then strike out. Therefore, he may go to great lengths to avoid disputes, and using a third party to intercede or to mediate a dispute is one method.

Getting Along

Getting along with others is extremely important to Latino Americans. They tend to acquiesce to the wishes of others and to agree with them in order to maintain *simpatico*, a Latin form of harmonious relationship. Most try to do what's expected by the culture and to be courteous.

Acquiescence and agreement. The acquiescence response set, or agreeing regardless of personal opinions and feelings, is a type of extreme response set in which respondents agree with statements presented to them or answer yes to questions regardless of their content. Acquiescence is frequent among Latino Americans and is closely related to educational and acculturation level, with the less educated and less acculturated respondents being more likely to acquiesce than the better educated, more acculturated. There seem to be no significant differences in acquiescence overall between men and women (Landsberger and Saavedra 1967).

Simpatico. Closely related to acquiescence is the tendency to respond in socially desirable ways in order to be *simpatico*. The Latino cultural value of *simpatico* encourages these responses in order to promote smooth, pleasant social relations. *Simpatico* persons are polite and respectful and don't express criticism, confrontation, or assertiveness. They show a certain level of conformity and empathy for the feelings of other people, try to behave with dignity and respect toward others, and value working toward harmony in interpersonal relations. Latino Americans therefore are more likely to give socially desirable responses and to perceive aggressive and assertive behaviors differently than Euro-Americans do. Small talk before and after discussing business is extremely important for building empathetic relationships.

Latino Americans tend to report that they carry out socially desirable actions and avoid reporting less desirable attitudes and behaviors. They tend to provide the "correct" answer as they perceive it, independent of their actual experiences. Mexicans residing in Mexico are more likely to express socially desirable responses than are Mexican Americans. Also more likely to acquiesce are those in lower socioeconomic levels, indicating that acculturation may modify this tendency (Ross and Mirowsky 1984; Triandis et al 1984b).

Doing what's expected. The willingness to conform to others' expectations is highly valued in Latino cultures, but so is the willingness to rebel at those rare times when too much has been too much for too long. Latino Americans conform because they want to please and support important others and because they want others to think well of them and accept them. In a high context culture a frequent concern is, "What will they say?"

Courtesy. Latino Americans place greater importance upon courtesy than do Americans and tend to offer profuse thanks, praise, and apologies. Elaborate courtesies are common and constant among the upper and middle classes. Lower class people may reserve such treatment for special occasions and for "superiors" and strangers.

Personalismo: Relating in a Personal Way

To relate well to people from a Latino culture usually means relating everything to them on a personal level. Instead of talking in generalities, you would talk in terms of them as persons, their families, their town, and most of all their personal pride. Especially for the male, the more the communication is personalized, the more successful it tends to be. In fact, Latino Americans tend to trust only those with whom they have a personal relationship, for only those persons can appreciate their soul, or inner self, and therefore only those persons can be trusted. For these reasons, it's difficult or impossible to do business with a Latino without establishing a personal relationship.

Reluctance to Self–Disclose

The need for *personalismo* means that Latino Americans are less likely than Euro-Americans to self-disclose. They're reluctant to reveal their thoughts and feelings to mere acquaintances. When people reveal personal information, they become vulnerable to how the listener will use that information, and their *amor proprio*, or personal honor, could be damaged.   Males are even less likely to self-disclose than females, especially with someone they are likely to interact with in the future and in culturally alien situations. When Latino American males do self-disclose, it's usually with Latino American females, who pose the least threat of responding with scorn, rejection, or other blows to self-respect (LeVine and Franco 1981; Franco et al 1984; Constantino et al 1988).

Business Relationships

When doing business in Latino countries, Euro-Americans find they must spend more time building rapport than usual before they can move to discussing the business at hand. This tendency has some carryover, of course, to Latino Americans who immigrated to the U.S. Latino Americans tend to avoid at all costs having face-to-face confrontations or unpleasantness with business associates, co-workers or friends. We'll discuss this trait more fully later (Cox 1993; Zurcher et al 1965).

Gender Relationships and Roles

Most agree that sex roles are more strictly defined in Latin cultures than in the U.S. Men's higher status is more noticeable, their sexual behavior is more broadly defined, and the division of labor is more pronounced.

Machismo. The macho pattern of behavior represents male power and an attitude toward the world, especially toward women. While Latino men have a poetic, romantic side, the macho aspect is aggressive and sometimes insensitive. The *machismo* image consists of virility, courage, competitiveness, a readiness to fight, and a determination to conquer. In business it means that a man should be forceful, confident, unafraid, and take the lead. Both boys and girls are socialized to admire this image, and Latino husbands virtually always "wear the pants" in interactions with the outside world. However, if the wife is a strong Latino woman, she may actually control the home, children, and husband.

The dark, extreme side of machismo involves wife-beating, excessive gambling, fighting, heavy drinking, and a tendency to have children with other women. Some sociologists think the underlying roots of machismo lie in male-male relationships: how men "traffic in honor and how men negotiate status with one another, how men hammer out the measurements of their standing as a man" (Lancaster 1993). Tannen's work regarding the male focus on status seems to support this idea.

The *machismo* stereotype is that the male is strong, in control, and provides for his family, while the woman is submissive and lacking in power and influence. However, this stereotype has not been fully researched, and some studies indicate that male dominance in marital decision making is not the rule among Latino American couples (Condon 1985).

Women at home. More Latino Americans than Euro-Americans believe that mothers should not have outside jobs. In an extensive survey of Latino Americans, a little more than half said they didn't think married women with children should have the opportunity to pursue their own careers, even if they were able to look after their home and family while doing so.

Men are less likely to participate in household and child care responsibilities. Insofar as their social standing will allow, they avoid any manual or menial work, which is considered degrading for men of the middle or upper classes. A man is supposed to protect and defend the honor of the women in his family, but women in other families are fair game for sexual advances. This obviously leads to a conflict of values and some tense situations. Men are expected to be assertive, to be leaders, to be in control, and to earn the respect of other men by their masculinity. The degree and importance of these values varies from one Latin culture to another.

Women as good or bad. Women are significantly limited by what some call the "Madonna or whore system," in which every woman is classified as either a good woman or a bad woman. The good woman marries as a virgin and martyrs herself to her family. She accepts men as the dominant ones and experiences her lot as saintly suffering. The bad woman is an essential figure if men are to make their sexual conquests outside marriage, but afterward she may be seen as little more than an unpaid prostitute. This viewpoint is held to some extent in most cultures, and tends to be especially strong and have a special religious flavor in the Latin cultures.

Women's boundaries. Assertive women within the culture are generally disliked, often more by other traditional women than by men. Women are expected to be reserved and modest with men outside the family. Women who work usually have a greater say in family decisions than those who don't.

Values: Spiritual Beliefs and Practices

Latino spiritual beliefs are closely tied to the Catholic church, a belief in fate, and a unique attitude toward the relationship between life and death (Harris and Moran 1991; Gann and Duignan 1986).

The Roman Catholic Church

The Roman Catholic Church remains one of Latin America's major cultural institutions and has played a large role in shaping the various cultures of all Latin nations. Priests tend to be more involved in the family lives of Catholic churchgoers than in other denominations. Most professing Christians in Latin America are Catholics, as are about 80 percent of Latino Americans. Their religious commitment varies widely, from indifferent to highly committed. Most are nonpracticing. About 30 percent of those who live in New York go to church. The poor tend not to stress duty to the church and parish as much as Irish Catholics do. About 60 percent could not name a single one of the seven sacraments in a recent survey.

Erosion of beliefs and practices increases with the second-generation Latino Americans. In recent years an increasing number are joining Protestant churches, primarily those of an evangelical, fundamentalist nature (Gann and Duignan 1986).

Fatalism

Latino Americans tend to let chance guide their destiny. This stems from an ancient mysticism combined with a Latino interpretation of church teachings. Many believe that outside forces govern their lives, for life follows a preordained course and human action is determined by the will of God. Those who hold this belief are therefore willing to resign themselves to the "inevitable," bow to fate, and take what comes. This is in direct contrast to the typically Euro-American belief that "God helps those who help themselves," or that people cocreate their own reality. Fatalism can result in an attitude that Americans often perceive as passivity, procrastination, or laziness and that they attribute to a *manana* tendency (tomorrow's good enough for me). After all, if it's God's will, if it's written in the stars, why fight it?

Closeness to the Spirit World

The spirit world lives alongside Latino Americans, particularly Mexican Americans, in their everyday lives. They perceive less distinction between the living and the dead than do most Euro-Americans. They believe the dead are just beyond the veil of physical reality and there's nothing to fear from these spirits of relatives and friends.

They celebrate afterlife and death symbols—such as ghosts, skeletons, and skulls—in their holidays. They wear the symbols as costumes, similar to some of our Halloween costumes, and use them as themes in toys, confections, songs, and dances. Latino Americans tend to think of death as "passing on" and treat it as an old friend or special person. They frequently joke about death and include the theme in their play. This theme is related to their fatalistic sense of life and death, and draws on some aspects of a worldview that originated in their ancient Indian past.

The Mexican American relationship with death and the dead may be better understood by studying how they observe the Day of the Dead in early November as part of a three-day celebration. First, they observe Halloween, along with other Americans. The next day is known as All Saints Day, and they observe religious rites. The following day is the Day of the Dead, the most important of the three days. Rituals may include altars set up in churches, homes, and shop windows, an all-day picnic in the cemetery, a candlelit procession in costume, and an all-night vigil in the cemetery. Many Latino Americans believe that the spirits of family and friends who have passed on are present at these events and that their spirits in fact move in and out of the physical world all the time.

Behavior Patterns

We've explored some of the typical values and beliefs of Latino American cultures. Next we'll look at some behavior patterns that emerge from these values, including acculturation and communication patterns.

Acculturation Patterns

First-generation Latino Americans tend to be less Americanized or acculturated than those in the second generation, for obvious reasons, but certain aspects of the Latino culture tend to be important over generations. As people live in a new culture, a process of culture learning and behavioral adaptation takes place in six areas: language use, cognitive style, personality, identity, attitudes, and stress (Barry 1980; Padilla 1980).

The process includes a stage of crisis or conflict, followed by the acceptance of an adaptation strategy, such as assimilation, integration, or rejection of the host culture's pattern. In terms of language use, for example, Latino Americans may assimilate by:

- speaking English almost exclusively
- integrating the old and the new by becoming bilingual
- rejecting the new by continuing to speak Spanish almost exclusively

In fact, use of language has become a reliable shorthand measure for evaluating level of acculturation, which in turn affects Latino Americans' mental health status, levels of social support, level of social deviance, alcoholism and drug use, political and social attitudes, and health behaviors such as consumption of cigarettes and the use of preventive medical practices. Higher acculturation level also seems to correlate with higher education level (Szapocznik and Kurtines 1980; Griffith and Villavicencio 1985; Graves 1967; Padilla et al. 1979; Alva 1985; Marin et al. 1989; Marks et al. 1987).

Communication Patterns

The Latino American style of communication includes speaking indirectly and using speech to impress, while exhibiting less clarification, high concern for feelings, high sensitivity to criticism, and some unique patterns of communicating nonverbally and of saying hello and good-bye.

Speaking indirectly. Latino Americans are frequently indirect in their communication with strangers and outsiders. It may appear evasive, but it's intended to be courteous.

High concern for feelings. Latino Americans may tell you what you want to hear, regardless of the "truth" out of great concern for your feelings. This reflects their belief that their own opinion doesn't matter as much as respecting your feelings and giving you the response you'd like to have. This conflicts with the American value of "telling it like it is."

High sensitivity to criticism. How Latino Americans take criticism is closely tied to the relative status of the people involved. Usually if criticism comes from a higher-status person, it's accepted sheepishly; if it comes from an equal it may be treated with humor; and if it comes from a lower-status person, it may not be tolerated since this would signal weakness and invite more criticism and even derision.

Using speech to impress. The better educated tend to display their vocabulary and style in order to impress, and any Latino American may use it to tease equals and intimates. Men may use this type of speech to size up each other and to establish dominance or leadership in relationships.

Nonverbal signals. As in all cultures, most nonverbal language is not sent consciously. When Latino Americans are in the presence of higher-status persons, their posture usually shows deference: head and shoulders slightly lowered, and hands behind the back or out of sight. To call someone with your forefinger is generally seen as very rude, and in some places this is an obscene gesture. Most any type of pointing at people should generally be avoided; in some places it's associated with the evil eye. However, you may gesture with your hand, palm upturned, toward a person you're talking to or about. In some places, when people want to accuse another of being stingy, such as when bargaining over price. they touch the palm of their hand to their elbow. Therefore, you'll probably want to remind yourself of this gesture and avoid it.

Saying hello and good-bye. If several people are in a group when you arrive, you're expected to go around and greet everyone, shaking hands, or if you know them well enough, embracing them. The "Hi, everyone" greeting would be considered rude. Likewise, upon leaving, you're expected to say good-bye to each person individually. A general "See you later" or equivalent is also considered too breezy or abrupt.

MEXICAN AMERICAN WORKERS

Mexican Americans are the largest of the Latino American groups, 61 percent, or more than 13 million people. They are the largest minority group in the Southwest, where their influence on culture and society is quite visible. Today most Mexican Americans have immigrant roots; they or their parents or grandparents came from Mexico to *El Norte* in search of a better life. Los Angeles has more people of Mexican origin than any city in the world except Mexico City (Camarillo 1979).

Background

After the Mexican-American War in the 1840s, the border between the two countries was moved, and many residents of northern Mexico were suddenly told they were living in the Southwest U.S., foreigners in their own land. They were caught in the path of the "manifest destiny" to expand U.S. territory to the Pacific Ocean. During the first decade of this century, many Mexican farmers lost their land, leading to a civil war in Mexico that devastated the economy and triggered a migration of peasants to the U.S. The Mexican population grew from about 175,000 to more than a million between 1900 and 1930. These immigrants were generally segregated and exploited as cheap labor by the Euro-Americans. During the Great Depression, Mexicans became the target of deportation programs designed to rid the country of illegal aliens. The purpose was to reduce the labor pool and preserve the few remaining jobs for legal citizens.

Current Profile

Mexican Americans are the fastest growing segment of the population, increasing by 147 percent between 1970 and 1990, compared with a 114 percent growth for all Latino Americans and 16 percent for non-Latinos. They have the lowest educational level: Only 44 percent hold high school diplomas and 6 percent hold degrees. Compared to other Latino American groups, they have the largest proportion of native-born citizens (67 percent) except for the Spaniards (83 percent). About 7 percent are foreign born who became citizens, and 26 percent are foreign-born residents who are not citizens. In most other regards, their profile is the typical Latino American profile. About half speak English very well and half don't. Three-fourths live in family households, and median family income in 1990 was $24,100, compared to $25,000 for all Latino Americans and $35,200 for all Americans. More than 23 percent of families live in poverty, compared with 22 percent of all Latino Americans and 10 percent of all Americans (U.S. Census Bureau 1993).

Cultural Themes and Issues

Mexican Americans have a strong cultural heritage. It's extremely important to them. They love their Spanish language and value the warmth and romance typical of their culture. But is it predominantly Spanish, Indian, or a unique blend? Anthropologists who have studied Mexican Americans seem to agree that approximately 95 percent are at least part Indian, and that the Spanish cultural influence is strong (Forbes 1977). Mexican Americans have nourished and sustained Mexican cultural characteristics to a greater extent than other ethnic groups, keeping alive their language, identity, and values. This stems partially from the fact that the Southwest was the home of some before it was part of the U.S. Another factor is the common border, over a thousand miles long, with continual flows of people back and forth. The most noticeable ethnic feature of Mexican Americans is the pervasive retention of the Spanish language.

Key Value Themes

One study found that the cultural values of Mexican Americans have been strongly influenced by a folk or rural culture in which organized and continuous striving for future monetary gains plays little part (Bullock 1971). This folk pattern of living, especially among the poor, promotes a mixture of individualism and family unity that leaves little room for an interest in the broader community. The welfare of the family is a key focus, along with the duty of older children to help support the family, even if it means dropping out of school. Mexican Americans generally focus less on involvement in the schools and other societal institutions than do Euro-Americans. Class has been a binding influence for the masses: "We're all the same—poor."

Mexican Americans' cultural values and patterns are virtually the same as the Latino American values discussed earlier. Special importance may be given the following values (Ramirez 1972).

- *Relationships* between individuals are more important than competitive, materialistic, or achievement goals. Latino Americans in the Southwest have a high context, highly involved culture, where people constantly monitor members' emotional states.

- *Family* ties are especially strong.

- *Machismo* and a patriarchal family and social structure are strong but they're changing along with changing economic demands and women's new job roles.

- *Ethnic loyalty*, a sense of solidarity and pride in their unique heritage, is strong.

Changing male-female dynamics. Male dominance of the family traditionally emphasized physical occupations as opposed to intellectual endeavors. Women were discouraged from competing in male-dominated occupations. However, beginning in the 1970s some women began organizing and supporting one another in breaking out of some of these traditional limitations (Bullock 1971). And wives are often able to find jobs more readily than the men, sometimes at higher pay.

Religion. Religion in Mexico is a unique blend of Catholicism and ancient beliefs handed down by the Mayans and Aztecs. God is deeply personal, caring for each person through specific saints. Home altars are decorated with *santitos*, images of saints dear to the family. Mexicans believe that the Virgin Mary, Virgen de Guadalupe, has a particular concern for Mexicans and protects them.

Valuing the American Dream. Mexican Americans as a group tend to be law-abiding citizens who love their Latino heritage but identify primarily with Euro-Americans and value the American Dream. Despite the prejudice and discrimination that have resulted in segregation and lower socioeconomic status than the mainstream, most believe they're better off in the U.S. than they would be in Mexico.

The Chicano movement of the 1960s and 1970s confronted discrimination and its effects. The movement sparked a new interest in the Latino American culture, but it did not succeed in its original objective of converting the Mexican American masses. The early Chicano intellectuals had underestimated their own people's belief in the American system, identification with Euro-American values, and their conservatism. The average Latino American voter simply did not view U.S. society as one of the most repressive, intolerant, and prejudiced in the world.

Nor did most Mexican Americans identify themselves with the American Indian, and they had never done so in the past. The cultural mixture of Indian and European elements that occurred in Mexico also blended with the Euro-American in the U.S. to produce a value system within the Mexican American community that is itself a blend. The rejection of Euro-American values by the Chicanos, therefore, is seen by some Mexican Americans as a rejection of one element of their own culture (Gann and Duignan 1986).

Above all, Chicano activists didn't seem to understand the strength of the social conservatism that inspires the mass of ordinary people in the barrios. Most parents who work hard to send their children to college have no desire to see them become rebels. They want them to learn a profession and become solid citizens. In fact, a 1983 poll showed that only a small percentage of Mexican Americans choose to identify themselves as Chicanos. While Latino alienation, anger, and rage exist, overall the Mexican Americans identify themselves with the U.S. Only about a third of them identify themselves as Mexicans or Latinos first and Americans second. In 1983 a *Los Angeles Times* poll showed that only about half of California Latino Americans were even aware of the Chicano movement, about the same rate of awareness as other citizens.

Overview of Current Issues

Major issues for Mexican Americans, especially for recent immigrants, are overcoming job discrimination, improving workplace status, improving knowledge and skills, and dealing with immigration backlash. What do Latino Americans need in order to overcome workplace barriers? De Freitas (1991) suggests adopting active public and corporate policies that aim to:

- increase access to affordable schooling, language instruction, and job training
- relocate and retrain mature workers
- stimulate job creation
- eliminate ethnic discrimination

As the Latino American share of the American labor force grows, the payoffs for helping these members develop their talents and make contributions become greater.

Issue: Overcoming Segregation and Discrimination

The long history of discrimination against Mexican Americans, together with the antagonism toward Mexican culture expressed by many Euro-Americans, has served to heighten the alienation from the dominant culture felt by many Mexican Americans (Bullock 1971).

Occupational segregation. Discrimination against Mexican Americans has never been as formally overt as that against African Americans and American Indians. Informal discrimination, however, has often yielded very similar results. The historical tendency in the Southwest has been for Mexican Americans and Mexicans to be employed in work gangs, crews, or families by large growers, ranchers, mine companies, and railroads. Few business owners and managers were concerned with these workers as individuals, only as groups. Within these industries, Mexican Americans have been relegated to the worst jobs, ones that are heavily manual, dirty, seasonal, and dead-end (McWilliams 1975). Where unions existed, they tended to exclude them, and to establish work rules that effectively barred them from opportunities to compete with Euro-Americans for better jobs. The better paying craft unions, in particular, were closed to Mexican American workers. These patterns became self-reinforcing over time. Because Mexican Americans were hired in large numbers for the worst jobs, they became stereotyped as being only good for those types of jobs.

During World War II, President Roosevelt's executive order regarding fair employment practices was mainly in response to African American demands. However, some Latino American writers say that had the government been pressed to recognize "a single minority group as facing the greatest potential for mistreatment on each of the four bases proscribed by the order, that group would have been workers of Mexican ancestry" (Daniel 1991). The bases were religion, color, national origin, and race. The three million Mexican Americans living in the U.S. during the 1940s were virtually all of Catholic religious affiliation, with skin colorings reflecting their Indian/Spanish ancestry and a national identity that generations of denigration had made burdensome. To confuse the issue, the government couldn't decide whether Latino Americans were fellow "whites" or a race apart. Three separate government studies conducted in 1942 found that Mexican Americans were probably the "most submerged and destitute group in the U.S.—economically, intellectually and socially" (U.S. Government 1942).

Residential segregation. Occupational patterns determine residential patterns. Prior to 1950 most of these jobs were in isolated rural areas. Mexican Americans in urban areas could only afford to live in camps or the worst parts of town. Occupational barriers meant they could hardly hope to ever afford much better. As a practical reality, therefore, most were segregated in Mexican American barrios and schools, just as African Americans were segregated in African American ghettos and schools. The path by which they arrived and became trapped in a barrio situation was different from that of African Americans, but the results were strikingly similar.

Immigration patterns. Since 1950 the Mexican American population has rapidly urbanized. The industrial base of the Southwest has greatly diversified, but the legacy of employment discrimination remains. Between 1940 and 1975 Mexican American workers made some progress in shifting away from the lowest paid laborer and farm worker jobs into more white-collar jobs. However, in recent years, the large influx of unskilled immigrants who must settle for such jobs has affected the overall picture.

Clearly, were it not for federally sponsored manpower training programs, Mexican American unemployment rates would stand in an even more unfavorable ratio to the Euro-American rates than they do. The stereotyped work attributes, along with the prejudice that is built into the institutions of society, have tended to block complete equality and fairness for Mexican Americans. They remain disproportionately concentrated in blue-collar occupations, especially in the laborer and operative classifications, and in such industries as manufacturing, mining, and agriculture, where employment opportunities are declining. Overt discrimination has declined, but covert, or hidden, business practices often result in discrimination that blocks upward mobility.

The unnoticed minority. Latino Americans' concentration in the Southwest, one of the most intense concentrations of national minorities in the U.S., reduced their visibility in the population at large. In 1940 about 90 percent of Mexican Americans lived in five states: Texas, California, Arizona, New Mexico, and Colorado. People in the other forty-something states rarely encountered Mexican Americans and were hardly aware of their existence. Even in the Southwest, they were isolated from the mainstream of American life. In the 1940s Mexican Americans for the most part held the status of "servants to a Euro-American-American community that could not do without them but refused to assimilate them" (Daniel 1991).

It was not until the twentieth century that vast numbers of Mexican immigrants came to the U.S. Sheer numbers are important to the ability of any group to make its presence felt. By the 1970s the Mexican American population was large enough to have some impact, and the Chicano movement was instrumental in voicing the concerns that were finally heard by U.S. policy makers. To attract the national attention that is crucial in overcoming the problems of group discrimination, Mexican Americans pressured the federal government for recognition as a separate and distinct racial group. As mentioned earlier, the Mexican American community has at times been divided over this issue, with many clinging to the designation of "white." Chicanos won the separate designation battle in 1970, but lost the terminology battle. Court rulings and federal government compliance directives now recognize *Hispanics* as a distinct racial group for civil rights purposes.

Difficulty in gaining access to adequate labor market statistics has been another barrier for Chicano advocates trying to get national attention and political action. To document the degree and nature of discrimination, they must be able to adequately assess both the present patterns and the trends over time. To make such assessments, they must have reliable statistics. Only since 1950 have relatively reliable census statistics been available for Latino Americans. Not until 1970 did the U.S. Department of Labor begin publishing statistics on its manpower programs with a Hispanic category.

Significance of the Mexican American labor supply. Today a sizable portion of the labor supply in the Southwest is Mexican American. In some areas, such as south Texas and southern California, Mexican Americans are a rapidly growing proportion of the labor force, and in some areas they are the largest segment. The huge disparities in wage levels and worker expectations between the U.S. and Mexico motivate Mexican workers to migrate to the U.S. Such disparities also motivate U.S. manufacturers to build plants in Mexico in special industrial zones called *maquiladores.* In return, U.S. firms agree to not compete with Mexican manufacturers by not selling these products in Mexico. The U.S. government has cooperated by treating the products as only partially manufactured goods for purposes of levying import duties when they're brought into the U.S.

Issue: Improving Workplace Status

Mexican Americans have the largest number of recent immigrants, which intensifies workplace problems for this group. Although many Mexican Americans have achieved middle-class status, many are caught in the poverty cycle, especially recent immigrants. Most workplace problems, such as unemployment and underemployment are tied directly to their lower socioeconomic status, which in turn is tied to other factors, such as discrimination and educational disparities, which feed back into lower status and unemployment. It's a vicious cycle of poverty similar to that experienced by underclass African Americans. When we compare the workplace issues of Latino Americans to those of Euro-Americans, several major factors stand out: higher unemployment, lower economic status, problems of new immigrants, educational discrimination, the need for job skills, and employment discrimination.

Unemployment. Studies have tried to account for unemployment differentials among Latino American groups. For Mexican Americans, their low educational attainment dominates all other factors. Also playing a substantial role is the employers' differential treatment of Latino American work traits, which reflects the persistence of ethnic stereotypes and discrimination (DeFreitas 1991).

Lower socioeconomic status. The causes of socioeconomic disparities are related to average age, schooling, family composition, migration, and language ability. Latino Americans have made impressive progress since the 1950s in educational attainment and occupational mobility. However, many Mexican Americans remain at a persistent, substantial disadvantage.

Welfare benefits are rarely available to needy Mexican Americans because most of those who need it are either illegal immigrants or noncitizens (Aponte 1991). Recent immigrants tend to earn the lowest incomes and have the most barriers to upward mobility. Most are either linguistically isolated or don't speak English well. They tend to be from rural areas and have difficulty adapting to urban life. They rarely have the job skills needed to gain stable employment and make adequate wages. And many lack a high school diploma. Because of male underemployment and unemployment, an increasing percentage of mothers now work (Santiago and Wilder 1991).

Employment discrimination. Workplace discrimination persists because, even if employers do not themselves hold discriminatory attitudes, the practice of using stereotyped beliefs that minorities have lower-than-average productivity will result in employers ranking individual minority group members lower than other job applicants. Inside the company, employer discrimination usually involves the confinement of minorities to less skilled, more unstable job titles and slower promotional tracks, rather than differential treatment of minorities and Euro-Americans in the same jobs.

Most Mexican Americans rarely complain about discrimination. Most in the San Francisco area, 60 percent, say that prejudice and discrimination are not a problem, and 35 percent say they are. Nearly half believe that qualified Latino Americans can rise to the top in local companies, but 35 percent say there are discriminatory barriers. Surveys taken in other states might produce different results, since San Francisco firms have a reputation for being less discriminatory than the national average (Viviano 1990).

Issue: Improving Knowledge and Skills

The lower educational achievement of Mexican American workers accounts for a far larger share of their earnings differential than is true for other groups. Continuing high dropout rates and low college enrollment indicates that Latino Americans will be the group most damaged by the shift to a better educated, highly skilled workforce. A 1989 study found that the Latino American high school dropout rate had risen to 36 percent, almost triple the Euro-American rate and more than double the African American rate. As the economy continues to shift from manufacturing to services, education becomes increasingly crucial (U.S. Department of Education 1989; De Freitas 1991).

But why are Mexican Americans experiencing an education gap? For one thing, Mexican immigrants who arrived in the first half of the 1990s were much less likely to enroll in high school than immigrants from previous years. Key factors that undermine Latino Americans' high school enrollment and graduation are:

- recent immigration
- poverty-level family incomes
- early marriage
- early pregnancy
- higher unemployment in the family
- English not spoken in the home

Similar factors determine whether they will attend college and earn a degree. Reasons given for not attending college are:

- inability to afford a college education
- immigrants' deficient education in home country
- language barriers and difficulties
- segregated schools
- biased treatment in integrated schools

Education and its associated credentials are a primary hurdle to better jobs and upward mobility. With the possible exception of American Indians, no ethnic group has fewer high school and college graduates than do Mexican Americans. For Mexican Americans, education may also be a hurdle to exercising power in the political system. Mexican Americans, despite their solidarity and pride of heritage, have been less forceful and articulate than African Americans in seeking redress of their grievances against the larger society. We bring about change through the American political process. And for those Mexican Americans with inadequate education, English literacy deficiencies, no citizenship papers, and uncertain legal status, full participation is impossible.

De facto segregation. Although overt segregation against Mexican Americans was not part of the laws of any of the southwestern states, it occurred as a matter of standard practice in California and Texas. The separation of Euro-American and Mexican American students in Texas was reinforced by the widespread practice of local school boards not enforcing compulsory school attendance for Mexican Americans. In California the segregation policies were not so overt. School districts were gerrymandered, transfer policies allowed students to be shifted from one school district to another, and in some cases, students from designated ethnic groups were required to attend specified schools within the school district. By these means, school segregation was the unwritten policy of numerous local school districts throughout the Southwest before 1950.

In 1970 the U.S. district court held that Mexican Americans were a separate class covered by the Brown vs. Board of Education decision (1954) that forbade segregation of any group of children in public school because of race, color, origin, or ethnic characteristics. The decision made it clear that the relevant issue was discriminatory treatment, not whether Mexican Americans were a majority or a minority of the school district's population. The judge stated that "when a group, as a whole, is politically impotent and economically disadvantaged, it invariably will find itself subordinated, in one respect or another, to those who are politically and economically stronger" (Cisneros 1970).

Court rulings and federal government compliance directives since 1970 have recognized Latino Americans as a distinct racial grouping for purposes of achieving integration. The more conservative Mexican American organizations have grudgingly joined with the more militant Chicano organizations in accepting the need for a separate racial classification.

In many parts of the Southwest in the 1970s the problem of de facto segregation, as well as unequal quality of educational opportunity for Mexican American students, was still a real issue. They were significantly isolated in de facto segregated schools throughout the region and experienced severe "cultural exclusion" with respect to curriculum, textbooks, and instructional methods.

Separate and not equal. The U.S. Commission on Civil Rights wrote three volumes in the 1970s on the plight of Mexican Americans. They found that in 1970 there was a difference of five years in the median years of school completed by Spanish-surname and Euro-American persons age 25 and over. Differences among the states in this education gap were considerable. In California the gap was 2.1 years, but in Texas it was 5.6 years.

The commission concluded that schools throughout the Southwest had reflected and reinforced a caste system prevailing in the larger community. The dominant Euro-American majority harbored a caste consciousness that assigned inferior status to Mexican Americans. This relegation to inferior status was impressed on students by the school, intentionally or otherwise, in ways that are now carefully documented, but which for generations went unchallenged.

Ethnic isolation, both by district and by school, was the rule, not the exception. Part of the perceived mission of the public schools in the Southwest was to "Americanize" the Mexican Americans. The strategies were, at worst, a demeaning and uprooting of the language and culture of Mexican Americans and, at best, an ignoring of their cultural differences as though they were of no consequence.

The commission recommended extensive reliance on bilingual education in the early years, using Spanish with Spanish-speaking children for teaching the basics. The focus on gaining English language skills should be postponed until the children reached the upper elementary grades. The commission also recommended the addition of course materials that discuss the Mexican American heritage and its contribution to the cultural development of the region.

Issue: Overcoming Immigration Backlash

Nearly a third of Latino Americans are first-generation immigrants with limited English proficiency that significantly hinders their socioeconomic progress. Controversy rages over the cost to taxpayers of providing social services to these immigrants, but studies indicate that the long-run economic benefits they generate for the average U.S. worker outweigh any short-run costs.

During the 1980s more than 8.6 million immigrants entered the U.S. from Mexico, more than in any decade since 1900–1910. This figure does not include the regular flow of illegal immigrants across the U.S.-Mexican border, nor those given temporary work permits. About 11 percent of these immigrants settled in Los Angeles, intensifying the job competition that flared up during the recession of the early 1990s. Immigration became a hot political issue as the U.S. declined into this deep recession.

Opinions began changing in the 1990s, when unemployment increased and tax dollars for social services drastically decreased. Many U.S. citizens became concerned. By 1993, 70 percent of the general public and 80 percent of Mexican-born U.S. residents, said there were too many immigrants crossing the borders. Generally people were worried about overpopulation straining the country's resources and illegal immigrants not paying income taxes or property taxes even though they use the services those taxes provide (Polls 1993).

PUERTO RICAN AMERICAN WORKERS

Puerto Ricans are now the second largest Spanish-speaking community in the U.S. They number nearly 2 million and constitute 12 percent of the Latino Americans on the U.S. mainland. The population of their homeland, the Caribbean island of Puerto Rico, was only 3.5 million in 1980.

Background

Puerto Rico was a Spanish colony for 400 years, and shortly after 1900 became an American affiliate, its citizens American citizens. The island is shifting from an agricultural to an industrial economy. Spanish is still by far the strongest cultural influence, which has only slightly waned during this century. The island culture is a microcosm of Latin America, a culture in transition. Therefore, many Puerto Ricans "swing between extremes of apathy and frantic activity, hide hostility and frustration, and lean on fantasy" (Harris and Moran 1991, 86).

The migrations to the mainland began in the 1930s, most immigrants coming from the poverty level. They're primarily Catholic, from low-skill rural backgrounds, and many are dark skinned. On the island, about 20 percent of Puerto Ricans are considered African American and 16 percent "mixed blood." Those who emigrate to the U.S. tend to have better educational and employment credentials than the average African American on the island, but most experience downward mobility after they arrive in the U.S.

In earlier decades nearly all Puerto Ricans landed in New York and stayed there. In 1950 about 80 percent lived in New York, but they've become more dispersed in the past two or three decades. In 1970 about 65 percent lived in New York and in 1980 only 50 percent. The other half live primarily in New Jersey, California, Florida, and Illinois. When they moved out of New York, most moved up, both socially and economically. Still, the majority of Puerto Rican adults in the U.S. are first-generation immigrants, and they remain the most ill-favored of all Latino American groups (Gann and Diugnan 1986).

National Profile

The Puerto Rican American population grew 76 percent between 1970 and 1990, greater than the non-Latino population growth of 16 percent, but less than the Mexican American growth of 147 percent and the total Latino American growth of 114 percent. Educational attainment was close to the Latino American average, with 53 percent holding diplomas and 9.5 percent holding degrees. After the Spaniard group, they have the largest proportion of members who speak English well (59 percent).

Puerto Rican Americans have the smallest number of members living in family households (56 percent) with 37 percent living in female-headed households. Only 7 percent are headed by men without wives at home. Puerto Rican women have the lowest median income ($8,900) of any Latino American group, and median family income is also the lowest ($22,000). While only slightly lower than the Mexican American median of $24,100, it's significantly lower than the Cuban American median of $32,400. It's not surprising the Puerto Ricans have the highest poverty rate, 30 percent for families and 35 percent for females.

Relatively high unemployment among Puerto Rican men is also a factor in the poverty picture. Puerto Ricans workers' concentration in declining manufacturing industries in the Northeast seems to be the major factor. Their below average schooling and English fluency, and their limited ability to afford job retraining and job searches have hampered their ability to compete for new jobs in more stable, expanding industries (De Frietas 1991).

New York Profile

New York Puerto Rican Americans are mainly a youthful community. In 1980 their median age was 20, compared to 30 for the general population. The Puerto Rican birthrate was high, with women having children at a younger age than any other ethnic group. The number of children under five among Puerto Rican Americans in 1970 was double that for the general population. In 1980 only 42 percent of Puerto Rican American children in New York were living in families where husband and wife lived together, and 47 percent lived with a single mother. In contrast, 58 percent of all New York children lived with husband/wife families and 31 percent with a single mother. Seventy percent of all New York families were married couples, compared to only 50 percent of Puerto Rican American families.

Puerto Rican American households are large. In 1980 the average New York Puerto Rican household contained more persons than any other group, 3.08 persons as compared to 2.5 for the general population. Their families are more overcrowded. According to the standard of one person per room, 16 percent of all Puerto Rican households are overcrowded, compared with 8 percent for New York City as a whole (Gann and Duignan 1986).

Issue: Prejudice and Discrimination

On the surface, it appears that Puerto Rican immigrants would have an easier adjustment than the Europeans who immigrated to New York earlier. Puerto Ricans are U.S. citizens. They don't experience the traumatic shock of being illegals, like many Mexicans, or being "screened" at

Ellis Island, as were Europeans in the past. (After screening, families were sometimes split up and the sick or "unsuitable" sent back home.)

Puerto Ricans seemed well adapted to fit into America's multicultural society because the Puerto Rican community contains persons of every possible color and complexion: people of European appearance, people with light-brown skin, and people with dark or black skin. The Puerto Rican upper and middle classes are generally more light skinned than the rest but by no means universally so. Most of the poverty-stricken people in the mountain towns are of European descent. There are no iron-bound distinctions, as is typically true in the U.S. Intermarriage is common, class counts for more than color, and there is less concern over skin color than in the English-speaking world.

Once Puerto Rican immigrants arrive in the U.S., all that changes. Discrimination based on skin color has encouraged dark-skinned Puerto Ricans to place special emphasis on their Spanish linguistic legacy in order to differentiate themselves from African Americans. There has often been rivalry between the two groups for jobs, between opposing neighborhood gangs, and between welfare recipients. They've had to cope with a cold climate dramatically different from their island warmth, and with a cold people, in contrast to the interpersonal warmth so common in their Latin culture. A common complaint is, "The weather is very cold here, just like the people."

Many Puerto Ricans, therefore, have great difficulty adjusting to New York, even when they're healthy and able to work. They often feel unwelcome and more discriminated against than Cubans and Mexicans. In New York City more than a million Puerto Ricans live in some of the city's most undesirable conditions. They are widely stereotyped as muggers and troublemakers and suffer from ethnic discrimination, especially those with darker skin tones (Gann and Duignan 1986).

Issue: Breaking Out of Poverty and Gaining Skills

Puerto Ricans often lack fluency in English, transferable skills, and formal education. Unskilled Puerto Ricans tend to benefit economically by leaving the island and settling in New York. But upwardly mobile Puerto Ricans often do better by returning home and many do after a while.

By 1960 half the Puerto Ricans families in New York were receiving welfare, and one-fourth of their children received some form of welfare assistance. Most didn't want to go on welfare when they arrived on the mainland. They have always preferred to work, and they place high value on dignity, independence, and self-respect.

By 1970, whatever the stereotype, the bulk of Puerto Ricans in America did not belong to the underclass, and they neither shunned work nor broke the law. High fertility rates were concentrated among those who didn't finish high school. While the Puerto Rican Americans were one of the youngest and more poorly educated groups, they earned comparable incomes when compared with people of the same age and education. Those who did move up did it through education. Many second-generation Puerto Ricans went to college, then into various professions or public service. Many attained distinction in sports, entertainment, business, and academia. The proportion of semiskilled and unskilled workers declined significantly between 1950 and 1970, and the percentage in skilled and white collar occupations went up.

During the early 1980s more and more professional people began to settle on the mainland. For example, more than half the engineering graduates on the island took jobs in the U.S. in 1983. The popular stereotype of the unskilled or semiskilled Puerto Rican immigrant has less and less relevance to the facts. Still, many Puerto Ricans are heavily dependent on New York City's welfare economy.

CUBAN AMERICAN WORKERS

Cuban Americans are the smallest, 5 percent, of the three major Latino American groups. They are also the best educated and most affluent. Most Cubans in the U.S. arrived since 1960, when there were only about 30,000 here. Now there are over a million.

Current Profile

Cuban Americans tend to be either high school dropouts or professionals with degrees. While some 43 percent do not have a high school diploma, 17 percent hold degrees. Compared to other Latino American groups, they have the largest proportion of members living in family households (78 percent) and the highest family income ($32,400) almost equal to the national median of $35,200. It follows that their poverty rates are the lowest (11 percent). More than 55 percent speak English very well and the others do not, but virtually none are linguistically isolated.

Most were born in Cuba (72 percent) and about half of those have become citizens. Nearly half the Cuban-born entered during the 1960s to escape Communism, and nearly all the others have entered since 1970. Most settled in the Miami area. Many also moved to the eastern U.S., especially to western New York state, Jersey City, Newark, and Bridgeport, and to a lesser extent to Los Angeles and Chicago.

Soon after Fidel Castro came to power in Cuba in 1959, people of the middle and upper classes began leaving, more than a million or about 10 percent of Cuba's population. The overwhelming majority came to the U.S.

The early emigrants in the 1960s were from varied backgrounds but many were business or professional persons, and entrepreneurs. Those who left were far more likely to be relatively well-educated urban professionals than was the average island resident. They averaged three more years of schooling than Mexicans immigrating at the same time. About 11 percent were professionals or business owners, compared to 1 percent of Mexicans. Meanwhile 12 percent of Mexicans were farm workers compared to 2 percent of Cubans. There were many skilled blue-collar workers from both countries.

The first wave was soon joined by disillusioned members of the revolutionary regime as Castro became more aligned with the USSR. By the end of the 1970s there was a substantial Cuban American community in the U.S., with Cuban Americans numbering more than legal immigrants from the whole of Latin America. Immigrants during the 1970s were primarily from the working class, including many skilled workers. Most had to settle for lesser jobs during their first two years in the U.S. The Cuban American population swelled from about 30,000 in 1959 to about 600,000 by 1980 to 1,070,400 by 1990 (U.S. Census Bureau 1993).

Where Cuban Americans have created their own communities and established a middle-class or upper-class lifestyle, they've experienced little discrimination. However, Black Cuban Americans apparently believe that racial oppression in the U.S. is more severe than in Communist Cuba. In the 1950s about 72 percent of Cuba's population consisted of people of European heritage. In the U.S. Census of 1970, almost 95 percent of Cuban Americans in the U.S. were of European heritage.

Revitalizing Miami: Little Havana

Most Cuban Americans live in urban areas, and their capital is Miami, often called "Little Havana." By 1980 almost 60 percent of Miami's population was of Latin American origin. On average, Cuban Americans living outside Miami have a better formal education and higher income than those in Miami. But far from placing a burden on the city, the immigrants transformed its economy.

Before 1959 Miami depended mainly on tourism and money spent by retired persons who moved to Florida from the Northeast. The Cuban Americans used their enterprise and skills to turn Miami into the "new capital city of Latin America." Increasing numbers of Latin American tourists fill the city's hotels. Latin American businessmen are investing huge sums in real estate, about $1 billion a year by 1980. Miami became "the banking center" for investors from Central and South America. More than 100 multinationals doing business with Latin America have established headquarters in Miami. By 1982 international commerce was generating more than $4 billion a year in state incomes and had created 170,000 jobs.

By 1980 nearly half the Cubans in Miami worked for Cuban-owned firms and 21 percent were self-employed. Their wages were somewhat higher than those who worked in non-Cuban firms.

Cuban Professionals

In Miami and elsewhere educated Cuban Americans lost no time in moving up to the status they had enjoyed in their native land. By 1978, about 30 percent of Cubans worked in middle-class occupations as professionals, administrators, managers, and proprietors, as compared to 20 percent in 1970.

Cuban Americans are making an important contribution to American cultural life as artists, university professors, journalists, and other professionals. But they haven't tried to build a new Cuban American culture, comparable to Mexican American culture. Most consider themselves exiles who will return to their homeland after its liberation but are grateful for their freedom and prosperity in the U.S. The mass emigration of these intellectuals became a cultural disaster for Cuba. Most of them are not right-wing conservatives but people of every shade of opinion, including many who had originally supported Castro. Most regard socialism as morally superior to capitalism, at least in the abstract, and continue to regard the U.S. as a bastion of reaction.

OTHER LATINO AMERICAN WORKERS

During the 1970s and 1980s, more than 1.2 million people emigrated from Central and South America and the Spanish-speaking Caribbean Islands, swelling their numbers in the U.S. to 2.2 million, or one in nine Latino Americans (U.S. Census Bureau 1993).

Central Americans

About 6 percent of all Latino Americans, 1,380,000 people, are originally from Central America. Nearly half are from El Salvador, 20 percent from Guatemala, and 15 percent from Nicaragua. These are among the smallest and poorest countries in Latin America. Most Central American immigrants are young men, married but traveling without their families, planning to work and save for a couple of years before returning. Most take minimum-wage blue-collar jobs, but these earnings are four times what they could earn at home. Nearly 90 percent work in crews composed of legal and illegal Latino aliens. Most intend to return again to work in an American city (Gann and Duignan 1986).

South Americans

More than one million immigrants from South America live in the U.S., comprising 5 percent of all Latino Americans here. Colombians are by far the largest group of South Americans in the U.S., comprising over a third, or nearly 400,000 people. Those arriving in the U.S. appear to be heavily urban, with educational and occupational levels well above the Colombian average. Significant numbers of people have also emigrated from Ecuador, Peru, Argentina, and Chile.

Dominican Americans

More than half a million people in the U.S. are from the Dominican Republic, and more than half arrived here during the 1980s. Only 15 minutes by air from Puerto Rico, Dominicans have a close relationship with their Puerto Rican neighbors. Over half the current population of Dominican Americans entered during the 1980s due to political unrest on the island. Many are unskilled workers from rural areas, and they have replaced the Puerto Ricans as the most disadvantaged group of Latino Americans. They are among the least educated: only 43 percent have high school diplomas, and 8 percent have degrees. The elimination of many low-wage manual manufacturing jobs in the U.S. has created severe employment problems for these immigrants. They have the largest percentage of female-headed households (41 percent), the lowest family income ($19,700), and the highest poverty rate (33 percent).

LEADERSHIP CHALLENGES AND OPPORTUNITIES

Latino American culture offers a wealth of values and insights to enrich the workplace. And Latino American workers sometimes have needs that present challenges to leaders. We'll explore some of these challenges and opportunities.

Leadership Challenges

Leadership challenges that may be presented by Latino American workers include:

- providing the flexibility they need to meet family obligations
- helping them understand the necessities of accurate information and goal achievement
- turning conflict avoidance into greater sensitivity in conflict resolution
- helping them overcome promotion anxiety

We'll briefly discuss each of these challenges.

Family Obligations

Work is important to most Latino Americans. They want the American Dream. But family comes first. Therefore, when it comes to the following kinds of issues, the Latino American is more likely than the American worker to put family concerns before work concerns.

- job relocation that requires the family to move
- overtime work that conflicts with family obligations
- the need to be absent in order to deal with family problems, illnesses, or emergencies

American managers must put this in perspective in order to understand the true dynamics of the situation.

Latino American workers will generally consult with the family when deciding to take a job, to seek or accept advancement, and whether to leave a job. For managers to understand and work with Latino American employees, they must know and understand about their family concerns that impact work decisions and performance.

In Latino cultures people are hired and promoted based primarily on family and personal ties. Latino American employees may expect the company to give their relatives and close friends preferential treatment. Managers may need to explain differences in company policy and in U.S. corporate cultures.

Attitudes Toward Information and Goals

Latino cultures tend to value accurate data less highly than the American business culture. Most Latino business persons see nothing unusual or harmful in withholding information in order to gain or maintain power. While goals are important, the process of achieving the goals and the symbolic messages implied by various aspects of the process may be more important.

The success of U.S. corporations often hinges on effective and efficient goal achievement, doing what works, getting accurate data and passing it on to those who need it to do the best job. These values are so pivotal that Latino American employees may benefit from special training sessions on these topics.

Conflict Avoidance

The Latino value of simpatico compels most Latino Americans to avoid interpersonal conflict on the job. They try to emphasize positive behaviors in agreeable situations and de-emphasize negative behaviors in conflictive circumstances. This affects methods of conflict resolution and needs to be addressed in work team situations. Latino American employees need to understand why conflict is being addressed openly instead of ignored. They need to be reassured about the expectation and value of their openness. Also, the team needs to respect Latino American members' sensitivities and find ways of resolving conflict that all can accept comfortably. Latino American workers may lead others in finding ways to combine openness with sensitivity and compassion.

Promotion Anxiety

Career development has some unique aspects for Latino American employees. For one thing, the employees, especially the men, may see more risk than Americans in applying for a promotion. If they don't get it, they not only experience a loss but their self-respect will suffer. Also, they may believe they'll be seen as competitive and too ambitious by their peers. Latino Americans tend to view competition as disruptive, leading to imbalance and disharmony. To overcome such barriers, leaders can begin working on career development with employees from the beginning. At periodic one-on-one meetings, career goals and ways of meeting them can be discussed. In this way, each step of development and advancement comes about naturally and the threats are diluted.

Leadership Opportunities

Leaders have valuable opportunities to help Latino American workers contribute to organizational excellence and productivity and to enrich the workplace through such approaches as:

- using their love of group affiliation to enhance work teams
- being sensitive to their sense of honor and good name
- appealing to their idealist side in creating a vision, goals, and standards
- adopting a leadership style that respects Latino American values and traits
- valuing their understanding and connections with Latino communities

Team Activities

The tradition of small group loyalty among Latino Americans offers a valuable opportunity for leaders to organize employees into work teams. Latino Americans place a very high value on belonging to a group and on cooperation and harmony within the group. Once they feel they are an accepted part of a work team, they are very comfortable functioning in this structure. For best results, Latino Americans need to feel personally close to the people in the group; otherwise, their first loyalty will lie elsewhere. Once they're committed to the team, motivational appeals and rewards geared to the team and the employee's contributions to the team can be the most powerful motivators. Latino Americans tend to feel extreme loyalty to their ingroups. On the other hand, they may have more difficulty adapting to an impersonal culture and to large groups in which individual recognition rarely occurs.

Latino Americans' reluctance to self-disclose can pose a problem for optimal team functioning. Members often must know what's going on inside each others' heads in order to solve problems and keep operations flowing smoothly. When the corporate culture respects and values Latino Americans, their culture, history, and beliefs, then they are more likely to reveal their thinking and feeling to other team members.

In Latino cultures those in authority make the decisions, and subordinates don't pass judgment on leaders' ideas or question their decisions, as this would imply a lack of confidence in their judgment. Sometimes U.S. managers think they've communicated to Latino American workers that they can make certain decisions, only to find that the decisions are simply not made. U.S. managers may need to explain in detail the decision-making process. They may need to reassure employees about when they can make certain decisions, when the team expects them to participate in making decision, and when managers expect their input, feedback, or questioning of ideas and decisions.

Remember, that Latino Americans tend to give higher importance to relationships than to tasks. Ask yourself, on a regular basis, how you can make this tendency an asset. Look for opportunities for these employees to work on tasks together, to share projects. When delegating, coaching, and giving feedback, speak to them in terms of relationships where possible.

Honor and Good Name

Managers and team members who offer feedback, evaluation, comments, or criticisms of Latino Americans' work would do well to understand and remember the importance of personal dignity, honor, and good name. If this is violated, the employee may feel compelled to leave. If in doubt, see that feedback is given in private. It should always be offered in a supportive, warm, concerned way. Separating the work or the end result from the person is often futile with Latino Americans. Since they're likely to take criticism personally no matter how objective you try to be, make it personal but supportive and offered with great understanding and empathy.

Visions, Goals, and Standards

The idealist aspect of Latino culture can be an advantage when it motivates Latino American employees to support the organizational vision and mission, and to achieve the goals and standards set by the group or the company. Their idealism can inspire and energize other employees. On the other hand, the trickster aspect may impel them to test the boundaries to see how strict the work team or the managers will be about holding them to performance standards.

Leadership Style

Values around hierarchy and status, personalismo and simpatico, are important in leader-employee relationships. Also, women managers need to understand effective ways of interacting with Latino Americans, especially the men.

Respeto and status. Respect for status and authority runs deep in Latin cultures, but respect for the person, regardless of position, runs even deeper. Latino American employees generally expect that the boss will be demanding. They often expect the boss to tell them what to do and to exercise fairly close direction until it's done. On the other hand, they can be led to use their own initiative if the leader makes it clear what types of initiative are expected and that this does not conflict with the leader's authority. The combination of challenge and support can help them to be productive and feel comfortable on the job. Such an approach is likely to establish an effective working relationship and engage the Latino American's sense of strong loyalty.

Personalismo. When the leader is generally warm, friendly, and encouraging, that deeper personal respect tends to develop. When the leader is not warm, employees may conclude that he or she is displeased with them. Rudeness or insensitivity in a leader tends to be shocking to people from a Latino culture. To them courtesy is synonymous with education, and they would wonder how such a rude person could ever be given a responsible position. On the other hand, they greatly admire leaders who can get the job done while exercising smooth social skills that boost the employees' self-esteem and honor.

Simpatico. A certain charm is seen as crucial for dealing effectively with others and that simpatico is a quality that increases one's status. Latino Americans tend to feel a greater need than Euro-Americans to express their personality in order to do business. Being seen as simpatico is the surest form of acceptance in Latino culture. Since almost all relationships are more personalized in Latin American than in the U.S., Euro-American leaders may have difficulty understanding the implications of simpatico. In American business cultures, people tend to value the separation of business matters from personal relationships and concerns. However, it's quite possible to balance the Latino Americans' need for their leaders to show personal understanding and warmth and the Euro-Americans leaders' need for some professional distance. The reverse is also true. Euro-American employees can understand that the Latino American manager's concern for their personal and family matters is not intended as a prying or controlling ploy. It's the leader's way of showing proper concern for each person.

When you're in the leadership role, and when you must give instructions or feedback, be especially aware of honoring and respecting the employee as an adult. Supervisors with warm, personable personalities who are good conversationalists tend to be especially appreciated by Latino Americans.

Women managers. Latino American men may have more difficulty than Euro-American men in dealing with a female manager. They are likely to react negatively to being corrected or criticized where other men can hear, since this would be seen as a major attack on their honor. The more assertively the woman comes on, the more difficult it is for the employee. Therefore, women managers need to be especially sensitive to these feelings of Latino American men and to search for gentle ways to achieve their purposes.

Some men may seek out Latino American women managers as allies or patrons because they think it's safer to approach a woman than a man, that they're more likely to be received favorably or at least to be rebuffed gently. Whether or not you can help them beyond the relationship, you can certainly help by nonjudgmental listening, just letting them pour out their concerns.

Occasionally a Latino American employee will make sexual overtures. It's important for the manager to keep in mind the implications of the Latino good woman-bad woman concept. She can nip such advances in the bud with clear I-messages, such as "I never get romantic with another employee; it wouldn't be fair to the others." She can then continue to be warm and friendly, making sure she is also businesslike and professional, sending the clear nonverbal message, "I like you and respect you and I will not have a romantic or sexual relationship with you."

Latino Connections and Understanding

Latino Americans obviously understand Latino cultures better than anyone. They can be of invaluable help in dealing with those markets, customers, suppliers, and other associates. Latino American market's spending power is at $XX billion and growing. Latino Americans are apt to have key connections in the community. NAFTA and other trade agreements are opening up greater-than-ever trade opportunities in Mexico and other Latin American countries. Corporate representatives who can speak the language and know the customs can provide the company with a valuable edge.

SUMMARY

Nearly one of every ten of us is a Latino American. This is the fastest growing minority group because of immigration and fertility rates. Myths and stereotypes center around traditional roles as menial workers, emotional temperaments, and tendency to be perceived as passive or docile. The large majority are Mexican Americans who live primarily in the Southwest, followed by Puerto Rican Americans in the New York area, and Cuban Americans in Florida. New immigrants usually have a language barrier, are young, and often have low educational achievement.

Latino American values center around the family, including extended family, and mutual dependence is expected. Relationships are of the utmost importance. The Latino American worldview is built upon acceptance of a social hierarchy consisting of a few privileged elite and a mass of relatively powerless workers.

Simpatico refers to getting along and is extremely important. People are expected to acquiesce, agree, and do what's expected in order to promote smooth social relations. Everything is translated into personal terms and personal relationships. Emotions are honored and expressed, and close, warm relationships are expected. Outside such personal relationships, Latino Americans tend to be reserved. Therefore, the idea that they're too emotional to hold leadership roles is mistaken. Machismo refers to male domination in male-female relationships. This is changing along with changing work roles for men and women.

The present moment is to be appreciated because the future is indefinite and unknown. Only God knows, and death hovers around the other side of a thin veil, as do the spirits of those who have passed on.

Latino Americans love the Spanish language but encourage their children to learn English also. They tend to speak indirectly, sometimes use flowery language to impress, and are highly sensitive to direct criticism since they're accustomed to indirectness.

Mexican Americans, the largest Latino American group, tend to identify with Euro-Americans and to value the American dream. Their current issues center around overcoming a tradition of segregation and discrimination—in workplaces, schools, and housing. Improving their educational opportunities and upgrading their knowledge and skill levels are crucial to achieving other goals. A recent issue is overcoming immigration backlash.

Puerto Rican Americans are following two divergent paths. Some are becoming highly educated and moving into well-paying, responsible business and professional positions. Others seem trapped in a poverty cycle, with many single mothers, and a high crime rate among young men. Their main issues involve overcoming discrimination, breaking out of poverty, and gaining skills.

Skill Builder 7.1: The Case of New Manager Luis

Luis has been manager of the claims department for three months. He's on his way to the office of his immediate supervisor, *Gale,* for their monthly planning and evaluation session. Walking down the hall, his mind is filled with events of the past few months and what he wants to discuss with Gale.

When Luis applied for the management job, he had five years' experience with National Life Insurance. He had taken the screening exam for the new position and did well on both the written and oral portions. One of Luis' co-workers, Richard, also took the test and told Luis that he had done great on it.

Richard had come to National about a year before Luis and had trained Luis in some claims department procedures. Luis learned quickly and they soon had a friendly rivalry going. When their boss Gale was recruited from outside the company, Richard told Luis he heard it was because of pressure to place more women in higher positions. He said the company had recently gone through a government review of its affirmative action program and was found lacking. Richard said, "They brought Gale in mainly because she's a woman." Luis agreed with Richard at the time because he didn't really know the story and he didn't want to argue about it.

Four months ago, Richard told Luis that he really expected to get the claims department manager's job because he had such a good track record with the company and he also had more seniority than the other seven candidates. When Luis got the job, he became Richard's immediate supervisor. Luis felt uncomfortable giving Richard direction. He knew Richard was probably at least as well qualified as he to be boss. He worried about it quite a bit the first month. But he told himself that he must be the most qualified for the job; otherwise, he wouldn't have been selected.

During the second month, Luis noticed that Richard and several other employees seemed reluctant to follow his instructions. Luis attempted to meet them halfway by asking why they weren't doing certain things as he had directed, what they felt should be done, etc. Sometimes it seemed as if these few employees didn't take him seriously. He could see that efficiency and productivity were beginning to be affected by their resistance and balkiness. Time and time again Luis told himself that it would take time for his former co-workers to get used to him as their manager and for him to become adjusted to his new role and responsibilities.

Then just last week, Luis overheard a conversation in the lounge. Richard was talking with a co-worker and didn't realize Luis was in the next room:

> *I don't know about this affirmative action. Why would anyone want to use the past as a reason why they haven't gotten ahead educationally or economically? I think it's time we all stood up for ourselves and accomplish or fail on our own merit, instead of some people falling back on excuses. Why should we American males be discriminated against just because of past history? If people want everyone to be treated equally, then they can't be given an extra advantage at the same time. I know my test scores were higher than some of these people who are being promoted, but they get promoted anyway—just so some job-climbing administrator can brag about his political correctness and make his track record look good. Worst of all, it just amazes me that Luis actually thinks he deserved that promotion.*

Luis was stunned at the time. He started thinking about the number of Latino Americans in company management. He could think of only one. Maybe Richard was right. Maybe he really wasn't qualified enough to handle the new job.

- What do you think are the major problems in this situation?
- If you were Luis, what would you do?
- If you were Gale, what would you do?

Skill Builder 7.2: The Case of Evelyn Sanchez, Supervisor

Evelyn Sanchez is a Customer Services Supervisor for Buckman's, a large mail order house. Her duties include making sure that work is distributed and completed under strict deadlines, approving certain transactions, and reviewing employee's work. She is required to set quarterly goals for herself and to train employees to cross-sell to customers in ways that meet their needs.

Evelyn's team includes ten employees of diverse backgrounds, including African American, Euro-American, Latino American, and Asian American. Most of the employees are bilingual. *Rosita,* a Latina American, is hired as a new member of Evelyn's team. One day when Evelyn stops by to check on how Rosita is doing, they lapse into speaking their native Spanish. *Ophelia,* an African American team member, is working nearby. She feels uncomfortable because she doesn't know what the two were saying. It's no big thing, and she tries to forget her discomfort. However, Evelyn comes by almost every day and has a brief conversation in Spanish with Rosita. Finally, Ophelia mentions her discomfort to Evelyn. She says, "I feel really left out when you two speak on and on in Spanish—and it keeps happening. I wish we could all speak the same language around here."

Evelyn replies, "Lighten up, Ophelia, we're not talking about you nor are we sharing secrets. We're just chatting, and it's good for our heart and soul to be able to converse in our beautiful *Castellano* now and then."

Ophelia becomes more disturbed each day as Evelyn and Rosita have their little Spanish conversations. She decides to complain to Gene, the general manager.

- What are the key issues here?
- If you were Gene, what would you do?

Skill Builder 7.3: The Case of Gino George, Sales Rep

Gino George, is a sales rep for Delcor, a telecommunications company. Five years ago he completed a degree in business administration and went to work in the finance department of Delcor as a junior accountant. He was the only Latino American in his department, and he got along well with his co-workers. He earned good performance reviews and merit increases and two years ago applied for and got the sales rep job.

Gino likes being a sales rep. He especially likes getting a commission on every sale he makes. Because he's a good salesperson, his salary is significantly higher than it was as an accountant. Gino is proud of the fact that he can help his Euro-American co-workers when they must deal with Spanish-speaking clients. In fact, Spanish-speaking clients have learned to ask for Gino, making him a valuable asset to Delcor.

On the other hand, being the only Latino American makes Gino feel somewhat isolated. For example, co-workers frequently "forget" to inform him of meetings or to invite him to group events. Few of them talk with him about anything outside of business matters.

Recently Gino was going over some files in the office. A couple of sales reps entered the adjacent cubicle and Gino overheard their conversation. Jeff said, "I heard that Dave's raising our sales quotas for the spring quarter. Business is always slow in the spring. How are we going to sell more than last year? If we don't meet that quota, we won't get our bonus." Ralph replied, "I think it's Gino's fault. He just gives Dave ideas. If he weren't such an eager beaver, Dave wouldn't start thinking that the rest of us should do better." "Yeah," said Jeff, "Any ideas on how we can send Gino back to the accounting department? Let him count beans!"

Gino is very upset by the news that his co-workers view his achievements so negatively. He hates being viewed as a trouble maker and difficult person. He decides to pull back on his sales efforts and to be satisfied with barely meeting his quotas.

Today Dave receives the news that he's being promoted and that he should recommend a replacement to take over his job. As Dave goes through the performance evaluations of all his team members, he narrows the choice down to Gino or Jeff.

Jeff has a high school diploma, experience as a salesperson with one other company, and has been with Delcor for three years as a sales rep. He gets along well with co-workers and is well accepted as "one of the gang."

Gino is better qualified, with his bachelors degree that includes technical expertise in the telecommunications field. He has been building a better track record as a sales rep than Jeff has, but the co-workers don't seem to be as receptive to him as they are to Jeff.

Dave calls Gino and Jeff into his office. He tells them that they're both in the running for the job and sets up times to interview each of them separately. Gino is concerned. He really wants the promotion, but he's worried about being accepted in the managerial role. On the other hand, if Jeff gets the job, he'll probably offer Gino little or no support and encouragement. He'll probably make it tough for Gino.

- What are the key issues in this situation?
- If you were Gino, what would you do?
- If you were Dave, what would you do?

REFERENCES

Alva, S.A. "Political Acculturation of Mexican American Adolescents." *Hispanic Journal of Behavioral Sciences* 7 (1985): 345–364.

Aponte, Robert. "Urban Hispanic Poverty: Disaggregations and Explanations." *Social Problems* 38 (November 1991): 516–528.

Barry, H. "Description and Uses of Human Relations Area Files." *Handbook of Cross Cultural Psychology*. Boston: Allyn & Bacon, 1980.

Briggs, Vernon M., Jr., Walter Fogel, and Fred H. Schmidt. *The Chicano Worker*. Austin: University of Texas Press, 1977.

Bullock, Paul. "Employment Problems of the Mexican-American." *Mexican Americans in the United States*. 1971.

Burdman, Pamela. "Divided We Stand." *San Francisco Chronicle* (March 29–31, 1994): A-1.

Camarillo, Albert. *Chicanos in a Changing Society: From Mexican Pueblos to American Barrios in Santa Barbara and Southern California, 1848–1930*. Cambridge, MA: 1979.

Cisneros et al. *vs.* Corpus Christi Independent School District, Southern District, Texas, Civil Action Number 68-C-95, June 4, 1970.

Cohen, R. *Culture, Disease and Stress Among Latino Immigrants*. Washington, DC: Smithsonian Institution, 1979.

Condon, J. *Good Neighbors: Communicating with the Mexicans*. Yarmouth, ME: Intercultural Press, 1985.

Constantino, G., et al. "Folk Hero Modeling Therapy for Puerto Rican Adolescents." *Journal of Adolescence* 11 (1988): 155–165.

Cox, Taylor. *Cultural Diversity in Organizations*. San Francisco: Berrett-Koehler, 1993.

Daniel, Clete. *Chicano Workers and the Politics of Fairness: The FEPC in the Southwest, 1941–1945*. Austin, TX: University of Texas Press, 1991.

De Freitas, Gregory. *Inequality at Work: Hispanics in the U.S. Labor Force*. NY: Oxford University Press, 1991.

Duran, R.P. *Hispanics' Education and Background*. New York: College Entrance Examination Board, 1983.

Forbes, Jack D. *The Chicano Worker*. Austin: University of Texas Press, 1977.

Franco, J.N., et al. "Ethnic and Acculturation Differences in Self-Disclosure." *Journal of Social Psychology* 122 (1984): 21–32.

Gann, L.J., and Peter J. Duignan. *The Hispanics in the United States: A History*. Boulder, CO: Westview Press, 1986.

Graves, D.T. "Acculturation, Access, and Alcohol in a Tri-Ethnic Community." *American Anthropologist* 69 (1967): 306–321.

Grebler, L., et al. *The Mexican American People*. New York: Free Press, 1970.

Griffith, J., and S. Villavicencio. "Relationships Among Acculturation, Sociodemographic Characteristics and Social Support in Mexican American Adults." *Hispanic Journal of Behavioral Sciences* 7 (1985): 75–92.

Harris, Philip R., and Robert T. Moran. *Managing Cultural Differences*, 3d ed., and *Instructor's Guide*. Houston: Gulf, 1991.

Hofstede, Geert. *Culture's Consequences: International Differences in Work-Related Values*. Thousand Oaks, CA: Sage, 1980.

Kenton, S.B. and D. Valentine. *CrossTalk*. Cincinnati, OH: South-Western, 1996.

Lancaster, Roger N. *Life Is Hard*. Berkeley, CA: University of California Press, 1993.

Landsberger, H.A., and A. Saavedra, "Response Set in Developing Countries." *Public Opinion Quarterly* 31 (1967): 214–229.

LeVine, E., and J.N. Franco. "A Reassessment of Self-Disclosure Patterns Among Anglo Americans and Hispanics." *Journal of Counseling Psychology* 28 (1981): 522–524.

Mackowski, Maura J. "Where's the Fast Track?" *Hispanic Business* (February 1991): 26.

Mannino, F.V., and M.F. Shore, "Perceptions of Social Support by Spanish-Speaking Youth with Implications for Program Development." *Journal of School Health* 46 (1976): 471–474.

Marin, G., et al. "The Role of Acculturation on the Attitudes, Norms, and Expectancies of Hispanic Smokers." *Journal of Cross-Cultural Psychology* 20 (1989): 399–415.

Marin, Gerardo, and Barbara VanOss Marin. *Research with Hispanic Populations*. Newbury Park, CA: Sage, 1991.

Marks, G., et al. "Health Behavior of Elderly Hispanic Women." *American Journal of Public Health* 77 (1987): 1315–1319.

McWilliams, Carey. *North from Mexico*. 1975.

Morales, Rebecca, and Frank Bonilla. *Latinos in a Changing U.S. Economy*. Thousand Oaks, CA: Sage, 1993.

Morrison, Ann. *The New Leaders*. San Francisco: Jossey-Bass, 1992.

Padilla, A.M. "The Role of Cultural Awareness and Ethnic Loyalty in Acculturation." *Acculturation*. Boulder, CO: Westview, 1980.

Padilla, A.M., ed. *Hispanic Psychology*. Thousand Oaks, CA: Sage, 1995.

Padilla, E.R., et al. "Inhalent, Marihuana, and Alcohol Abuse Among Barrio Children and Adolescents." *International Journal of the Addictions* 14 (1979): 943–964.

Polls: Latino National Political Survey, 1993; *Wall Street Journal–NBC*, 1993.

Ramirez, Henry M. "America's Spanish Speaking: A Profile." *Manpower* (September 1972): 33.

Ross, C.E., and J. Mirowsky. "Socially-Desirable Response and Acquiescence in a Cross-Cultural Survey of Mental Health." *Journal of Health and Social Behavior* 25 (1984): 189–197.

Santiago, Anne M., and Margaret G. Wilder. "Residential Segregation and Links to Minority Poverty: The Case of Latinos in the U.S." *Social Problems* 38 (November 1991): 492–515.

Shorris, Earl. *Latinos*. New York: W.W. Norton Co., 1992.

Solorzano, Daniel G. "Mobility Aspirations Among Racial Minorities, Controlling for SES." *Social Science Review* 75 (July 1991): 182–188.

Szapocznik, J., and W. Kurtines. "Acculturation, Biculturalism, and Adjustment Among Cuban Americans." *Acculturation*. Boulder, CO: Westview, 1980.

Triandis, H.C. "Role Perceptions of Hispanic Young Adults." *Journal of Cross-Cultural Psychology* 15 (1984a): 297–320.

Triandis, H.C., et al. "Simpatia as a Cultural Script of Hispanics." *Journal of Personality and Social Psychology* 47 (1984b): 1363–1375.

Triandis, H.C., et al. *Dimensions of Familism Among Hispanic and Mainstream Navy Recruits*. Chicago: University of Illinois, 1982.

U.S. Census, Department of Commerce. *We the Hispanics* and *We the American Children*, 1993.

U.S. Department of Education. *The Condition of Education*. Washington, DC: GPO, 1989.

U.S. Government reports: (1) David J. Saposs. "Report on Rapid Survey of Resident Latin American Problems and Recommended Program." Office of the Coordinator of Inter-American Affairs (April 3, 1942), p. 1, in Reel 28, HQ Files, FEPC Records. (2) "Spanish-Americans in the Southwest and the War Effort," p. 1, June 1, 1941, Reel 48, HQ Files, FEPC Records. (3) "Report on the Spanish-Speaking Peoples in the Southwest, Field Survey March 14 to April 7, 1942," p. 13, in Reel 70, HQ Files, FEPC Records.

Valle, R., and C. Martinez. "Natural Networks Among Mexicano Elderly in the U.S." *Chicano Aging and Mental Health*. Washington, DC: GPO, 1980.

Viviano, Frank. "Poll Contradicts Stereotypes." *San Francisco Chronicle* (March 27, 1990): A1.

Weber, David, ed. *Foreigners in Their Native Land: Historical Roots of the Mexican Americans*. Albuquerque, NM, 1973.

Zurcher, A.L., et al. "Value Orientation, Role Conflict, and Alienation from Work." *American Sociological Review* 30 (1965): 539–548.

CHAPTER 8

Working with Gay Persons

Gayness is not the illness; judgment is the illness.
Scott Stewart

Gay men, lesbians, and bisexuals, referred to collectively as gay persons, are often called the invisible minority because they don't *look* different from others in their ethnic group. About two percent of Americans, five million, are gay persons. Gay men and lesbians are invisible in many occupations simply because they don't identify themselves as gays, since gays are not easily tolerated in those occupations. They speak of the "gay stigma," which comes out only when *they* come out. But not coming out creates its own anxieties and terrors. Therefore, the main concern of these invisible minority is whether to become visible, and how to manage the gay stigma if they do. We'll explore the specifics of gay stigma, the changing perceptions of gay persons, and their current profile. You'll also learn what it's like to be part of the gay community, theories about whether people are born gay or choose that orientation, what their major concerns and issues are, and some leadership challenges and opportunities with gay employees. First, test your opinions and knowledge by completing Self-Awareness Activities 8.1 and 8.2.

What's in a Name?

The American Psychological Association's (APA) Committee on Lesbian and Gay Concerns in 1991 adopted the following guidelines for terminology recommended to psychologists:

- *gay male* and *lesbian* rather than *homosexual*
- *gay persons* when referring to lesbians and gay men as a group
- *antigay prejudice* instead of *homophobia*
- *bisexual* when referring to persons attracted to both same-sex and opposite-sex partners

The term *homophobia* is still used by many persons when referring to prejudice and discrimination against gay persons. Homophobia originally meant an irrational fear of same-sex eroticism, an appropriate use of the term. But in the 1970s it came to mean a fear or dread of gay persons, a prejudice against gay persons, or a general intolerance and disapproval of gay persons. The term *phobia* is not descriptive of such emotions.

Self-Awareness Activity 8.1: What Do You Believe about Gay Persons?

Purpose:
- to get in touch with your beliefs and stereotypes about this group of people
- to experience how judgmental beliefs affect your thinking and feeling processes
- to experience the ways in which your beliefs create your reality regarding other persons, even before you have any interaction with them.

Part I. What Do You Believe About Lesbian Women?

Step 1. Associations
- Relax as deeply as you can: close your eyes and taking a few deep breaths.
- Focus on the word "lesbian" and allow a mental picture to come up in your mind's eye.
- Notice the words and images that come to mind as you "see" this woman.
- Open your eyes and list 10 to 20 words in the order in which they occur to you.
- Review your list. Mark a plus beside the words that are positive, a minus beside the words that are negative, and a circle beside neutral words.

Step 2. Negative Associations
- Close your eyes and focus again on the image of the lesbian woman. Formulate a negative opinion or judgment, perhaps one you typically hold about lesbians.
- Notice your *feelings* as you see the person in this negative way. What *thoughts* come up as you focus on the image?
- Write a few sentences about your feelings and thoughts.

Step 3. Positive Associations
- Formulate a positive opinion or judgment, perhaps one you typically hold about lesbians.
- Notice your *feelings* as you see the person in this positive way. What *thoughts* come up as you focus on the image?
- Write a few sentences about your feelings and thoughts.

Step 4. Insights
- Focus on the differences between your experiences when you hold negative and positive judgments or opinions. What were the differences? What meaning does this have for you, for your beliefs and feelings about people from this group, and about beliefs in general?
- Write your responses in a few sentences; include anything you like about your feelings, thoughts, and insights.

Part II. Experimenting with Opinions About Gay Men

Repeat the phases and steps in Part I, this time focusing on the image of a gay man.

Self-Awareness Activity 8.2: What Do You Know About Gay Persons?

Purpose: To see what you know about the issues covered in this chapter.

Instructions: Determine whether you think the following statements are basically true or false—and think about why. The answers will emerge in this chapter, and the summary at the end of the chapter focuses on these issues.

1. You can always tell gays by the way they act, dress, and talk.

2. Gay persons tend to influence young people to becoming gay.

3. The American Psychological Association takes the position that gays are mentally disturbed and need therapy.

4. With the proper therapy and motivation, gays can become heterosexual.

5. Boys raised by domineering mothers and weak or absent fathers usually become gay.

6. If a person has one or two sexual experiences with someone of the same sex, he or she is gay.

7. Most researchers conclude that gay persons are born with a gay orientation.

8. Gay persons are protected from workplace discrimination throughout the U.S.

MYTHS AND FACTS

Gays must deal with some of the most vicious and degrading myths and stereotypes, and they probably suffer from more distorted or invalid myths than any group. The effects are devastating, and antigay prejudice ranges from trivial snubs to violence. While most Americans still do not approve of a gay sexual orientation, they are against discrimination and for equal treatment in the workplace.

Many of the stereotypes reflect beliefs about outgroups in general, usually portraying outgroup members as both threatening and inferior to members of the dominant ingroup. Adam (1978) and others found that gays, African Americans, and Jews all are perceived as animalistic, hypersexual, overvisible, heretical, conspiratorial, and inclined to physical and mental disease.

Myth: Gays cluster in certain occupations.

Many people believe that gay men flock to the occupations of hair stylist, designer, dancer, and similar creative, "feminine" jobs. In fact, the gay men who happen to choose such occupations are more likely to come out for the simple reason that gays are more accepted in those jobs. Meanwhile, people are unaware of the gay men in the more masculine occupations because most stay in the closet in order to survive. Evidence suggests that gays and lesbians do not cluster in a few occupations but are found in a wide range of different occupations as diverse as the general population. A survey of 4000 gay persons found more gay men and women in science and engineering than in social services; 40 percent more in finance and insurance than in entertainment and arts, 10 times (1000%) more in computers than in fashion [*Fortune* 1992]. The true part of this myth is that some gay employees feel forced to cluster in certain jobs or departments because they feel safe there and unsafe in other, perhaps more appropriate, areas (McNaught 1993).

Myth: People who associate with gays are probably gay themselves.

This belief is sometimes called "courtesy stigma" or stigma by association. When heterosexuals associate with gays, only to be suspected of being gay themselves, they may respond with anger or they may back off. Courtesy stigma, therefore, can create barriers to gays' establishing the support networks and mentor relationships they need for career success. It can block competent researchers from addressing gay issues because of the tendency of the general public to assume that heterosexuals would not be interested in these topics. Closet gays' reaction to courtesy stigma is frequently fear of disclosure and thus avoidance of association with other gays.

Myth: Gays in sensitive or high-level jobs are a security risk.

This stereotype is downright vicious in its impact. No evidence has appeared to support the belief that gay persons represent an increased security risk. But the myth persists in this form: Gay employees try to keep their homosexuality a secret; therefore, they are easy blackmail targets for con artists and spies, which in turn makes them a security risk, so they shouldn't be hired or promoted into sensitive or high-level jobs. Author G. Herek reasons that if this were true, the fair solution would be to remove the stigma from homosexuality and protect them from discrimination, not to use the "potential blackmail target" rationale for inflicting further discrimination (Herek 1993). In 1995 President Clinton signed an executive order barring the use of this criterion for personnel decisions involving placement of federal employees.

Myth: Gay Persons don't have normal, lasting relationships.

This myth depicts gay persons as people drift from one sexual liaison to another, ending up alone when they're old. Studies indicate that most gay persons very much want to have enduring, close relationships and many do. Between 40 and 60 percent of gay men are currently involved in a steady relationship, and between 45 and 80 percent of gay women are so involved. In fact 75 percent of gay women are so involved according to most studies. The few studies that have included older gay persons have found that relationships lasting 20 years or more are not uncommon.

Research also indicates there are no significant differences between heterosexual and gay persons on any of the measures of relationship satisfaction. Further, when couples were asked the best things and worst things about their relationships, researchers found no significant differences in the responses of gay and heterosexual couples, all of whom reported a similar range of joys and problems. The point is not that all gay couples are happy and problem-free but that they are not any more prone to relationship dissatisfactions and difficulties than are heterosexual couples.

Another aspect of this myth is that gay persons don't have normal relationships with friends and therefore don't have strong support networks. While they do experience psychological stress from social rejection and stigma, most have made significant progress in overcoming these obstacles and creating rich, satisfying social networks. Overall levels of support received by gay men and women were similar to and slightly higher than those reported for heterosexual men and women. (Peplau 1991).

Myth: Gay men act feminine and lesbians act masculine.

Most heterosexuals believe that gay persons possess the characteristics of their opposite sex. They also believe the reverse side of the coin, that men who act feminine are likely to be gay and women who act masculine are likely to be lesbian. In fact, gayness itself does not establish the types of sexual roles and behavior people will adopt. The expression of sexuality is diverse and functions along a continuum, rather than in an either/or manner. To refute the myth we can recall how the late film star Rock Hudson shocked the world when he came out, especially the women fans who idolized him as the essence of masculine attractiveness.

A conflicting myth is that gay partners take on clear husband and wife roles, which seems unlikely if both gay male partners act feminine, and likewise if both lesbian partners act masculine. In fact, masculine-feminine roles have sometimes been important in the past, but in recent years gender-linked roles have sharply declined. In fact, most gay couples today actively reject traditional husband-wife or masculine-feminine roles as a model for enduring relationships. Most are in dual-earner relationships, with neither member the exclusive breadwinner and each having some economic independence. Any specialization of activities is based on individual skills or interests rather than sex-role stereotyping. While many partners report that there is some sense of a masculine-feminine or husband-wife fit, it's subtle. The most common relationship pattern is the friendship model that emphasizes companionship, sharing, and equality.

Myth: Gay sex is immoral and gay persons are promiscuous.

This is a religious or philosophical belief and therefore cannot be rationally proved or disproved. Constitutional rights concerning the separation of church and state provide some protection in the legal system and in the workplace against discrimination based on such personal beliefs.

A percentage of the population engages in promiscuous sex, at least during a certain phase of their life, regardless of sexual orientation. The sexual behavior of gay persons who are in the closet, especially married persons, usually stems from their fear of discovery and the resulting need for secrecy and anonymity.

Related to the belief that gay sex is immoral is the belief that AIDS is God's punishment for gay persons. In fact, anyone can contract AIDS; it just happened to gain a foothold in the gay community first. Ignorance about the disease has led to the myth that people who come into contact with gay persons are exposing themselves to AIDS. However, AIDS can only be contracted through sexual intercourse or through the bloodstream. Therefore, casual contact in the workplace is not a threat.

Myth: Gay persons are a bad influence on children.

The extreme form of this myth is that gay persons tend to be child molesters, which may be based on the idea of sexual perversion. The flawed thinking process is: Child molesters are sexually perverted and so are gay persons; therefore as sexual perverts, gay persons are prone to be child molesters. Scientific studies have repeatedly disproven this myth. A small percentage of the population are accused of child molestation, and sexual orientation is not a factor in the tendency toward this type of behavior.

One aspect of this myth is the idea that gay men are looking for very young men and boys as partners. Research indicates that a majority of gay men aged 18 to 24 prefer a male partner who is older, a majority of those aged 25 to 34 prefer a same-age person, and of those older than 35 about half prefer a younger partner. It was found that the degree of emphasis on youthful partners varied with the social setting and reflected the diversity of the gay community. It also probably reflects the tendency of older men in the larger American culture to prefer younger partners (Harry and DeVall 1992).

Another twist is that gay persons will influence children and youth to become gay. This false fear is the basis for trying to bar gay persons from becoming teachers, counselors, and youth group leaders—and to deny gay parents their child custody rights. Since the preponderance of evidence suggests that sexual orientation is fixed by biology early in life, this myth has no basis in fact nor experience. No evidence exists that a gay teacher or parent could convert a child, even if he or she tried.

Myth: Gay persons can't or shouldn't be parents.

Until recently most people assumed that gay persons could not be parents. This is based on some of the myths just discussed. In addition, some courts have denied parental rights to gay persons on grounds that children of gay parents will be teased and stigmatized by other children and adults. Chief Justice Burger once said that the Constitution "cannot control such prejudices but neither can it tolerate them. Private biases may be outside the reach of the law, but the law cannot, directly or indirectly, give them effect" (Palmore 1985 p. 62).

New ideas about family life have opened up the idea of gay persons having an active family life that includes children. Research on gay parents clearly indicates that their lives are remarkably like those of heterosexual parents. Far more similarities than differences are found.

Specific myths about lesbians as parents include:

- They don't care for children in maternal ways.

- They hate men and deny their children access to positive male roles models.

- Their lesbianism is a sort of illness that makes them unfit to be parents.

Studies indicate that lesbian mothers do not differ significantly from heterosexual mothers in maternal attitude, self-concept as parents, attitude toward marital and maternal interests, current lifestyles, and child rearing practices. Lesbian mothers are more likely than heterosexual mothers to be child-centered (as compared to adult centered or task centered). There is no evidence that a lesbian mother is more likely to negatively influence her child's development, nor that the child is more likely to become gay.

ANTIGAY PREJUDICE

Gay persons experience a unique brand of prejudice, based on the myths and stereotypes we've just discussed. To better understand their experience, we'll discuss why people feel antigay prejudice, which people tend to be the most prejudiced, some of the effects of prejudice, and whether prejudice is increasing decreasing.

Why Do People Feel Antigay Prejudice?

People express antigay prejudice in many ways, from "I never met a gay I liked" to "I don't know any" to fear of not being masculine or feminine enough myself. Antigay prejudice is more dominant in certain regions and among certain socioeconomic groups. It ranges from mild disapproval to violent hate crimes. The National Gay and Lesbian Task Force noted a 42 percent increase in reported hate crimes against gay persons in 1990 compared to 1989. More than 7,000 incidents ranged from verbal abuse to murder. Many were attributed to increased teenage gang violence, usually in large cities and associated with drug traffic.

Varying Reasons

People can hold similar attitudes for very different reasons. Attitudes toward gayness can be influenced by:

- adherence to traditional sex roles
- fear of contact with gay persons
- past interactions with gay persons, whether they were rewarding or punishing
- personal benefits from expressing the attitude, such as affirming self-identity, increasing self-esteem and maintaining a sense of belonging to a group with antigay beliefs.

An example of personal benefits is the feeling, "I felt like a real man when I compared myself to that gay man. I felt strong and normal." Prejudice against gay persons is widespread, so people who want to boost their own egos by putting down gay persons are likely to get social approval. Gay persons are an easy target in most communities.

The Arm's–Length Syndrome

Some people have no gay persons in their family and no friends who are openly gay. In keeping with the discussion of prejudice in chapter 3, heterosexuals who report that they don't know a gay person are more likely than others to have negative attitudes toward gayness. Gay persons are less likely to reveal their gayness to such prejudiced persons, perpetuating their isolation from gay persons and creating a sort of arm's-length syndrome. Their only sources of information about gay persons will therefore be hearsay and the media. Gay persons are rarely seen in films or TV programs; when they are, they are usually playing a stereotyped role, having problems, or dying. Such limited information about gay persons may perpetuate negative attitudes. On the other hand, heterosexuals who are not prejudiced toward gay persons are more open to interacting with them and therefore gain more experiential knowledge of them. This serves to counterbalance negative stereotypes presented by the media or by acquaintances.

The more eagerly a person endorses traditional sex roles, the more negative he or she tends to be toward gay persons. Gay persons are disliked by such heterosexuals at least in part because of their perceived sex-role deviance. When getting acquainted, intolerant men tend to describe themselves as higher in assertiveness and independence and lower in feminine attributes than do tolerant men. This suggests that intolerant men want to make certain that others know they're not sex-role deviant. It also helps explain their intense resistance to women's new career roles that in turn produce a need for husbands to help with household and child-care responsibilities (Rothblum 1988; Storms et al 1981; Deaux and Lewis 1984; McDonald et al 1973; Newman 1989; Whitley 1987).

Who Are the Prejudiced?

People with antigay attitudes are more likely than others to have the following characteristics:
- male
- older
- less well educated
- reside in rural areas, the Midwest, or the South
- members of a conservative religious denomination
- strongly religious

Men tend to be more prejudiced than women, and the gender gap may result from the strong cultural belief that masculine men are heterosexual and heterosexual men are masculine. Men feel considerable pressure to affirm their masculinity by rejecting that which is not culturally defined as masculine, such as gayness, and that which is perceived as negating the importance of men, such as lesbianism. In contrast, women rarely perceive that rejecting homosexuals has anything to do with their own gender identity and therefore feel less pressure to do so.

What Does Antigay Prejudice Do to People?

The picture of prejudice is not pretty. When gay persons are excluded, ridiculed, or assaulted due to antigay prejudice, the impact on their lives can range from the mild to the devastating, from difficulty adapting to the workplace culture to deep psychological damage. The people who hold onto antigay prejudice are affected too. They typically experience more guilt, discomfort, and a draining away of joy than do less prejudiced people.

How Gay Persons Are Affected by Others' Antigay Prejudice

Because of antigay stereotypes, beliefs, and attitudes in the culture, virtually all children learn to disapprove of gayness. More than 2 percent of those children are gay, but until a certain age they're not aware that they're gay. Once they become aware, these internalized beliefs about gayness complicate the process of self-acceptance and often have devastating effects on self-esteem, at least until some coping strategies are mastered.

Many institutional policies stigmatize and discriminate against gay persons, and gays experience considerable violence. In 1992, 17 percent of gay persons reported being physically assaulted because of their lifestyle, 44 percent said they had been threatened with violence, and 80 percent said they've been verbally harassed. Gay activists claim that gay persons experience more open hostility than any other stereotyped group. Research also reveals a general pattern of treating gay persons differently, and usually more harshly, than nongays. People tend to speak more rapidly to gay persons, and are less likely to help them. Gay persons infected with HIV are evaluated more harshly than heterosexuals infected with HIV, and people tend to be less willing to interact with gay persons who have AIDS than with heterosexuals who have AIDS (Berrill 1990).

How People Who Hold onto Prejudice Are Affected

When intolerant people interact with gay persons, they tend to experience increased discomfort, anger, disgust, and tension, along with decreased happiness and excitement. In contrast, tolerant people tend to have no emotional response to the mere fact of gayness, unless they treat gay persons in a discriminatory manner, in which case they feel uncomfortable and guilty. Let's review some research on this (Kite and Deaux 1986; Kite 1990).

When asked about interactions with gay persons, all heterosexuals in a major study reported a difference between how they thought they *should* act and how they actually would act; that is, they said they probably *would* act in a more discriminatory manner than they thought they should. These heterosexuals had been classified as either tolerant or intolerant persons. The tolerant persons reported that the realization that they would not live up to their ideals of tolerance made them feel generally uncomfortable, guilty, and self-critical. Intolerant persons reported feeling discomfort only.

Thought and behavior scenarios were added to the situation, such as: If you think a masculine woman must be a lesbian, would you move to another seat to distance from her? Again, many respondents realized that they probably *would* move, even though some thought they should not move, and this realization produced antigay feelings of anger and disgust. Tolerant persons used their own principles to decide how to respond to the scenarios, while intolerant persons responded in the way that they believed important others would expect them to respond. This finding suggests that one way to move beyond prejudice is to educate people, beginning in early childhood, to develop their own standards and to think for themselves. Such education would include consistent rewards to those who follow their own ethical principles in dealing with others.

In several experimental studies, persons who were rated as intolerant on a Homosexuality Attitude Scale registered greater dislike than did tolerant persons toward all the teammates they interacted with, including teammates with unknown sexual orientation. This pattern is consistent with findings that intolerant people are generally prejudiced against others. Also, intolerant persons especially disliked known gay teammates. Tolerant persons liked their teammate regardless of sexual orientation. Neither the men's nor the women's liking was affected by their teammates' gender, but heterosexual men tended to hold more negative attitudes toward homosexuality than did women. Intolerant persons were less happy and excited and more disgusted and tense when they believed a teammate was gay than when sexual orientation was unknown, but tolerant persons' happiness and excitement was not affected by the sexual orientation of their partners. This research finding suggests the following:

> *Prejudiced persons' thinking patterns tend to block their own happiness and zest for life—holding onto prejudice creates a joy drain.*

Is Antigay Prejudice Decreasing?

National opinion surveys suggest that people's attitudes toward civil rights for gay persons are often independent of moral judgments about homosexuality. Even though the gay lifestyle is unacceptable to 53 percent of Americans, according to a 1992 Gallup poll, Herek (1991) reported that most agree that gay persons should have equal employment opportunities and free speech rights. Other research indicates that about half the people would be uncomfortable working with gay persons and from 35 to 45 percent would be comfortable (Roper 1987; *Los Angeles Times* 1985).

One research study that tested people for level of prejudice and tolerance indicated that both tolerant and intolerant persons are usually willing to *meet* a gay person, though the intolerant ones were uncomfortable working with gay persons. About half the gay persons in a 1989 poll said they have experienced some form of discrimination because they're gay. Table 8.1 indicates how people's attitudes toward certain gay rights, including employment rights, are becoming more accepting.

TABLE 8.1: How People Feel About Gay Rights

	1977	*1985*	*1989*
For equal rights for gay persons	56%	59%	71%
Against equal rights for gays	33%	28%	18%
For guaranteed equal treatment under the law in jobs and housing	60%	66%	
Against guaranteed equal treatment under the law in jobs and housing	28%	22%	
For hiring gays as elementary teachers	27%		42%
For allowing gays in the clergy	36%		44%
For allowing gays in the military	51%		60%
For allowing gays as doctors	44%		56%

Source: Herek, 1991.

EVOLUTION OF BELIEFS ABOUT GAY PERSONS: FROM MENTALLY ILL CRIMINAL TO SOLID CITIZEN

During the past 20 years beliefs about gay persons have rapidly evolved from ,"They're mentally ill sexual deviants whose lifestyle is depraved and illegal," to "They have a right to express their sexual orientation and many are solid citizens." How did such a dramatic reversal come about? The following dates are milestones in recent gay history (Rutledge 1994).

- 1952 American Psychological Association classifies gayness as a mental illness rather than a choice to be sexually perverted and depraved.
- 1969 Stonewall riots and first Gay Power meeting, New York.
- 1970 Gay pride parade in New York attracts 10,000 gay persons.
- 1973 American Psychological Association announces that homosexuality is no longer considered a mental illness.
- 1974 First openly lesbian state representative elected: Elaine Noble, Massachusetts.
- 1977 Anita Bryant, former Miss America, begins national campaign against gay rights on behalf of religious conservatives.
- 1977 First openly gay person elected to city government: Harvey Milk, San Francisco supervisor.
- 1978 California voters defeat a statewide proposal to remove gay teachers from schools.
- 1981 Kaposi's sarcoma, a rare cancer, is diagnosed in 41 gay men; tennis star Martina Navratilova comes out.
- 1982 Gay Olympics, later called Gay Games, begin (and by 1994 was one of the largest sporting and cultural events in the world).
- 1986 The U.S. Supreme Court upholds Georgia's anti-gay-sex law.
- 1992 President Clinton proposes removing military's ban on gay persons.
- 1993 Gay persons hold third and largest civil rights march in Washington, DC.

Before 1952 the general public viewed gay persons as sexual perverts, morally depraved persons who engaged in immoral, criminal sexual activities. Most professionals also viewed gayness as immoral and criminal behavior until the American Psychological Association (APA) classified it as a mental illness. This was a giant step toward greater acceptance of gayness by the general public. The next giant step came in 1972 when the APA declared that psychologists no longer viewed gayness as mental illness.

Understandably, prior to the 1970s almost no one admitted to being gay, especially if they lived in a typical small to midsized town. Many people today, most of them conservative or fundamentalist Christians, still hold to pre-1950s beliefs about gayness. The majority of Americans, however, believe gay persons have a right to privacy regarding their sexual orientation and should have the same rights as other citizens.

Prior to the 1950s virtually all gays kept their sexual orientation "hidden in the closet." The few exceptions were those who gravitated to the largest metropolitan areas. In the 1920s being gay came to be considered chic for a few bohemian types in New York City. Gay subcultures emerged in Harlem and Greenwich Village among African American and Euro-American gays.

In 1950 the Mattachine Society became the first national gay group in the country. In a world that viewed gay persons as criminals and perverts, the society provided a safe space to meet. It stressed the importance of discretion, and its goal was the ultimate assimilation of gay persons into society at large.

In 1969 the incident known as Stonewall changed the emerging gay community forever. Stonewall refers to four days of gay riots that occurred in New York in response to a routine police raid on a Greenwich Village gay bar called Stonewall Inn. Since then, Stonewall has become the symbol of gay resistance to oppression and gay empowerment around the world. To gay persons, it marks the birth of the modern gay political movement, "that moment in time when gays and lesbians recognized all at once their mistreatment and their solidarity" according to gay author Martin Duberman (1993).

By the early 1970s San Francisco had become the heart of the newly formed gay nation, and Castro Street was the gay Main Street.

From Extremism to Reformism

Within months after Stonewall, a liberation movement emerged. Gay persons formed the Gay Activists Alliance, the Gay Liberation Front, and the Gay Academic Union—and other organizations sprang up later. Liberationists were political extremists who wanted to radically change American culture by changing or eliminating common concepts of gender and sexual orientation. They viewed "coming out of the closet," in which their sexual orientation had been hidden from public view, as an intermediate step in a process of releasing the ambisexual potential in everyone. They said that antigay prejudice is just heterosexuals' rejection of their own latent homosexuality or homosexual desires. Liberationists declared that for heterosexuals to move beyond such prejudice, they needed to confront their own sexuality. In summary, liberationists said to heterosexuals, All persons can go either way, gay or straight, and your rejection and fear of gayness are rooted in your denial that this is true for you. As a matter of fact, scientific research results since the 1970s have not supported the viewpoint that everyone is potentially bisexual.

Most gay persons came to see the liberationists as enraged persons lashing out at all straights, overreacting to the pain and rejection they had experienced as gay persons. Most gay persons were more attuned to the reformist movement. Reformists adopted a strategy of minority group politics that envisions gay persons as members of a subculture with its own needs, goals, and interests that deserve to be recognized and met within the larger culture. A major goal is protection from employment discrimination. Reformists view heterosexuals' antigay prejudice as a rejection of members of an outgroup, similar to ethnic prejudice. Change involves challenging heterosexuals' misconceptions about gay persons and prejudice toward them.

Evolvement of a Lesbian Subculture

The national lesbian subculture was born during World War II. Many lesbians joined the military and were stationed at the large ports in such metropolitan areas as New York, Boston, and San Francisco. Military lesbians established the beginnings of the lesbian communities that flourish in those cities today. In the 1950s butch and femme roles for lesbians became common, and the patterns for lesbians in those roles were very specific. Middle-class and wealthy lesbians tended to avoid these roles, so it was the poor and working class lesbians that the dominant culture came to recognize on the street and in the media. In the 1970s most lesbians gave up the butch and femme dress, and both members dressed in a similar manner, usually masculine-looking slacks, shirts, and haircuts. Even though studies indicate that 95 percent of lesbians have rated themselves or been rated by others as either butch or femme, most dismiss these archetypes. By the 1990s it was more common for all gay persons to dress according to individual taste and business concerns rather than gay culture expectations (Loulan 1990).

CURRENT PROFILE

As a group, gay persons tend to be highly educated, and in spite of workplace discrimination many are in responsible, well-paid occupations.

About two percent of the population. What proportion of the population is gay? This has been debated for decades, and was frequently said to be 10 percent. It's still debated but recent research indicates about 2 percent. An extensive, well-respected survey of Americans aged 17 to 60 indicates that 2.8 percent of men and 1.5 percent of women identify themselves as gay, lesbian, or bisexual, for a combined rate of 2.15 percent. Gay persons are found in virtually every demographic group. The gay community encompasses a wide range of diversity that cuts across all cultural ethnic, economic, social, age, and other lines (Michael et al, 1995).

Higher educational levels. Studies show that gay men achieve significantly higher educational levels than the population at large, that significantly more of them hold jobs requiring creativity and innovation, and that they are the highest paid group in the U.S. because of their professional achievements. About 62 percent of gay men are college graduates, compared to 24 percent of all U.S. men; for lesbians it's 59 percent, compared with 17 percent for all U.S. women.

Better-paying occupations. Higher educational levels normally mean better-paying jobs and higher income. Gay persons therefore do tend toward the high end of average income, compared to most groups.

During the 1980s, according to one survey, average income for gay men was $42,000 and for lesbians $39,000, nearly twice the U.S. average at the time. About 15 percent of gay households, and 4 percent of all households, earned more than $100,000 (Green and Herek 1994).

A 1994 survey concluded that mean household income of gay men was $37,400, or only $2,000 more than the mean income for heterosexual households; for lesbians, it was $34,800, or only $400 more than for heterosexual households. Part of the difference in the 1980s and 1990s comparisons could lie in the dramatic increase in working wives and mothers, which increases heterosexual household income. The drop in gay persons' income could reflect a wider range of persons who admit to being gay, including many from the lower-paid occupations. (Yankelovich Partners 1994).

CULTURAL PATTERNS AND ISSUES: WHAT'S IT LIKE TO BE GAY?

Most people who identify themselves as gay or lesbian say they first became aware of same-gender attraction before adolescence, and the attraction became established before sexual activity actually began. For some gay persons, sexual orientation remains the same throughout life. For others, a gay orientation may be adopted after many years as a heterosexual, which is called sequential bisexuality, and which may simply reflect a valiant effort to fit into a heterosexual world. Obviously, parents and society don't socialize children to be gay, and gay youngsters are not prepared to deal with antigay prejudice and the wounding of self-esteem. Once they are able to accept their sexual orientation and "come out," they can join gay support networks and have access to healing acceptance within the gay community.

Growing Up Gay

For most gay persons, growing up gay involves a process of becoming aware of gayness. This process has several stages, including denial of their gayness, recognition of it, sexual experimentation, and coming out of the closet. The process is somewhat different for gay men than for lesbians (Gonsiorek and Rudolph 1991).

Denial. In the initial stage, gay persons tend to block recognition of same-sex feelings in a variety of ways. Some maintain these defensive strategies indefinitely and hold back their same-sex feelings, consuming huge amounts of psychological energy in the process. Constricting such a major area of strong feelings tends to result in some restriction of all feelings and to damage self-esteem.

Studies indicate that gay persons who are more open about their sexual orientation have higher levels of psychological well-being.

Recognition. For many gay persons, a gradual recognition of same-sex interests emerges. They begin, by stages, to gradually tolerate the fact that they're having significant same-sex feelings.

Experimentation. Next comes a phase of experimentation, emotionally and behaviorally, with homosexuality. Some gay persons increasingly feel that same-sex feelings are normal for them.

Gay identity, coming out. As gay persons begin to accept their same-sex feelings, they develop a sense of identity as gay persons. Ideally, this gay identity is successfully integrated and accepted as a positive aspect of who they are. The unfolding of this developmental process is generally unpredictable, with stops, starts, and backtracking being quite common. For example, denial of same-sex feelings may weave in and out, sometimes halting development. The coming out process represents a shift in the person's core sexual identity and may trigger intense emotional distress.

Male-female differences in the process. The process for gay men tends to be more abrupt and more likely to be associated with emotional symptoms, while the process for gay women tends to be more ambiguous and yet more fluid. Women, in their relationships with other women, are allowed a wider range of behaviors and emotions, such as hugging, crying, and kissing, without homosexuality being implied. They may therefore view emerging sexual and emotional intimacy with other women as "mere friendship." Men who long for emotional and physical contact with other males are likely to be clearly perceived as gay, and therefore to recognize their same-sex feelings as gay. During the coming-out process, women are more likely to handle distress through reflection and self-absorption, while men are more likely to handle it through sexual activity.

Gay women are more likely than gay men to attach emotional, romantic meaning to same-sex relationships before actually having sex. Some researchers have concluded that lesbians have more in common with heterosexual women than they do with gay men.

Self-Esteem Issues

Gay persons, like heterosexuals, are raised to have antigay prejudice. Such prejudices bring into play other psychological processes.

Self-Esteem in the Denial and Recognition Phases

Children who eventually learn that they are gay or bisexual often develop an awareness of being different at an early age. They often don't understand the precise meaning or the sexual nature of their differentness, but they soon learn that it is considered "bad." These negative feelings are often incorporated into their self-image, resulting in varying degrees of internalized antigayness. Negative feelings about their sexual orientation may be generalized to negative feelings about the entire self, ranging from mild self-doubt to overt self-rejection and even self-destructive behavior. The ironic result is that they are taught as children to shun and despise the type of person that they are destined to become. Most gay persons are naturally socialized in a middle-class environment, yet the adoption of generally accepted middle-class values tends to trap them.

Becoming aware of gayness is therefore a wounding of the self-esteem that usually begins in mid- to late childhood and is often a progressive wounding through adolescence. Gay persons' sexuality is devalued and rejected by society generally, and more personally by parents, friends, and teachers. For all of us, sexuality is a fundamental aspect of the self, of the core of the personality. Gay persons see that their parents and others do not admire or respond favorably to their sexuality. All around them, gay persons see their friends' heterosexuality being anticipated, embraced, and cultivated, while their homosexuality is not. Dating, becoming engaged, marrying, and having children hold joyous implications for others, but not for them. The result of this devaluation and neglect is often a sense of loss: loss of self-esteem, loss of initiative, and loss of the belief that they're entitled to a full life.

Dealing with self-rejection. Internalized antigay attitudes, or self-rejection, refers to attitudes in the culture at large that are learned and accepted by gay persons from infancy and are later turned inward when they discover they are gay. Almost all gay persons adopt negative attitudes toward homosexuality early in life, and this set of negative attitudes is incorporated into their self-image, causing a fragmentation of sexual and emotional facets of themselves that interferes with the development of a healthy self-image. Studies suggest that between 33 percent and 25 percent of gay persons, and probably a larger proportion of African American gay men, report conscious, negative attitudes or feelings about their gayness at some point in their lives (Bell and Weinberg 1978)

High levels of self-rejection are associated with overall psychological distress and specifically with lower self-esteem, as well as isolation and loneliness. Self-rejection also creates barriers to developing effective coping strategies and interpersonal relationships, and generally impedes personal growth. It encourages distrust and self-sabotage.

Dealing with closet stress. Concealing a gay sexual orientation is referred to as being in the closet, closeted, or "passing" as a heterosexual. Passing can be an adaptive coping strategy when used strategically to survive. When gay persons use the closet as a long-term survival tool, they lose the spontaneity we all need for authenticity in relationships. The constant pressure to conceal parts of the self and the constant dread of being found out creates stress. When gay persons believe that gayness is an illness and sign of inferiority, self-hatred is an inevitable result, creating further stress. Such stressors increase their vulnerability to psychological distress and physical illness.

Self–Esteem in the Coming–Out Phase

Coming out is a great relief for gay persons, but the downside is facing direct antigay prejudice. This can lead to lower their self-esteem, self-rejection, and new types of stressors. At least four cultural influences affect the self-esteem of gay persons:

- *Personal shame and denial.* Gay persons experience shame for their sexuality. This is dramatically different from the experience of most heterosexuals, where choice of partner and sexual behaviors are celebrated, as long as they stay within socially-approved boundaries.

- *Partner shame and denial.* Gay persons have partners who have also experienced shame and denial, while heterosexuals are likely to have partners who take pride in their sexuality.

- *Equality and self-esteem.* Gay persons do not have a power difference based on gender built into their relationships, which for lesbians might increase self-esteem.
- *Liberation and self-esteem.* Lesbians are likely to be feminists, and the liberation from traditional views that subordinate women tends to lead to increased self-esteem.

These viewpoints suggest that while lesbians are at a distinct disadvantage in having been born female in a male-dominant culture, they may access more tools for building self-esteem than gay men. In comparisons of levels of self-esteem for gay men to heterosexual men, and of lesbians to heterosexual women, lesbians have some relative advantage.

One of the most stressful aspects of coming out for most gay persons is telling the family. When families in the 1950s were told that a son or daughter was gay, they immediately went into fear that the gay member would be arrested, lose his or her job, become a social outcast, and be isolated. By legal definition gay persons were mentally ill criminals. Disclosure to family is still difficult, but family fears are easing now that there's increased cultural acceptance, more positive imagery in the media, and support within the gay community. On the other hand, there are still many problems. Gay persons are not protected from discrimination in employment, housing, parental matters, military service, and other areas. In nearly half of the states consensual sexual activity between gay persons is still illegal. Withdrawal and passive aggressiveness can easily develop in response to such social stigma.

When they come out, the major way most gay persons handle self-esteem issues and the stress of antigay prejudice is by building support networks and joining the gay community. In addition, they may turn to a gay counseling center. These organizations are usually staffed by counselors and psychologists who affirm gay persons' homosexuality and then proceed to treat them as individuals. Psychological researchers have found no significant difference in the incidence of mental health problems of homosexual and heterosexual men; in other words, gay men are generally as mentally healthy as heterosexual men (Silverstein 1991).

Healing Self–Esteem and Empowering Self: Support Networks

Many gay persons end up "banging on the door of American society in the hope of fading into the mainstream of social life" (Silverstein 1991, 113). Some even have children, buy houses, strive for success, and in general maintain households that seem identical to those of married friends and family. Yet in most American neighborhoods, they are not accepted. On the other the hand, the APA decision to treat the societally induced ills of gay people and to assist in their integration has had reasonably successful results. Gay people now participate in all levels of society, and in those arenas where acceptance permits, they do so openly as gay persons.

The coming-out process can help to heal the wounded self-esteem and to restore integrity and functioning to the damaged self. Coming out means a person can join or develop a support network of other gay persons, receiving guidance and comfort. Newly-out gay persons tend to view the established, already-out support network as wiser and more powerful, though later a generation gap may develop. In identifying with the network, and through it with the larger gay community, gay persons begin to feel empowered and more certain, instead of feeling confused, afraid, and powerless. Within a gay support network, young gay persons can for the first time be with others like themselves. Through this affiliation, they can observe and then use their various skills and talents to succeed socially, sexually, politically, and otherwise in the larger gay community. New members tend to view friends in the network as benevolent and as willing and able to meet their needs.

The support network mirrors and admires the gay behaviors of gay persons who are coming out. In time, gays internalize the approval of their support network, representing the larger gay community, as pride in their sexual orientation, as self-esteem, assertiveness, and self-acceptance. Also in time, gay identity is internalized as feelings of vitality and motivation for gay activities and concerns, and beyond. As they develop greater inner strength, young gays tend to view the support network as less necessary and to rely less heavily upon its strength and stabilizing influence. As they heal and mature, young gay persons gradually incorporate into their personalities the values and ideals of the larger gay community, especially the value of self-determination.

Gay Culture and Lifestyles

Gay persons have as wide a variety of lifestyles as the rest of the population. They have close friends in support networks that loosely form a gay community, as well as heterosexual friends and associates outside the community. Singles may frequent a gay bar scene, while couples tend to focus on their relationships and sometimes on parenting roles. Some have had heterosexual marriages and must deal with the complications of that. And all must eventually deal with the process of aging. In order to understand what it's like to be a gay person, we must know something about these various aspects of the gay community.

Wide Variations in Gay Lifestyles

Sexual expression is multifaceted, with wide-ranging behaviors, emotions, and preferences and therefore a variety of lifestyles. Writers on this topic provide us with at least five categories in which gay persons, like heterosexuals, vary greatly in their preferences, choices, and experiences:

- sexual attraction
- social preference
- emotional and affectional preferences
- self-identification
- lifestyle choice

In the area of sexual attraction, for example, members of both groups sometimes have sexual relations because they've "fallen in love" and other times because they've "fallen in lust," often not being sure which is the case when they're first attracted. Lifestyle choices are the most all-encompassing, reflecting preferences and tendencies from the first four categories. Lifestyles range from the gay singles bar scene to the lifetime-committed, pillar-of-the-community gay couple.

Gay Communities

Forming community with other gay persons is an important part of self-acceptance. For gay persons, it relieves their sense of being uniquely different and allows them to jointly form a set of beliefs about sexuality that counter the negative beliefs of the dominant culture. The main function of a gay community or group is psychological, to provide a social environment of acceptance and support. Because this is usually the only environment in which openly gay persons can find acceptance and support, they tend to develop a deep emotional involvement with their group, to readily accept its norms and dictates, and to subject themselves to its behavior patterns. Gossiping about the sexual experiences of others is a major form of recreation, which can create sexual rivalry and hostility (Loznoff and Westley 1992). The meeting places for the gay community in most urban areas fall into two categories:

- *sexually oriented*, the locales for making sexual contacts, such as bars, bathhouses, and certain areas of parks or beaches. These are frequented primarily by young men, although there are some lesbian bars.
- *socially oriented*, locales where gay persons join together to achieve certain social, political, civic, or spiritual goals, such as gay rights organizations, social clubs, and gay churches and spiritual groups. Both women and men congregate here, and a large majority of lesbians prefer this arena.

One of the major differences between gay men and lesbians is that lesbians are somewhat more likely to establish a steady relationship, to parent their own or adopted children, and to make a commitment to socially oriented organizations. As gay men get older, they're also likely to adopt a more settled lifestyle.

When women who are gay are compared with those who are not, both groups hold very similar values about the importance of social support, receiving similar amounts of support from both their social networks and their personal relationships. They may receive support from different sources. Lesbians depend more on their partner and friends and less on relatives. Comparing gay men and women, no differences are found in their sources of support or in their level of satisfaction with the support.

The gay community consists of many distinctive groups. Friendship binds the members of each group together in strong, relatively long-lasting relationships. Between the groups, members are often linked by tenuous but repeated sexual contacts. As a result of these bonds and their relatively small numbers, gay persons within a city tend to know of each other. They have a number of common interests and moral norms. Such communities are linked throughout the U.S. and Canada because of the mobility of members.

Gay persons tend to spend at least half their social life with other gay persons, according to one survey. A common pattern is to have two sets of friends, one heterosexual and the other gay (Ashworth and Walker 1992).

Gay Couples

A steady relationship is claimed by between 40 and 60 percent of gay men and between 45 and 80 percent of lesbians, and many establish lifelong partnerships. Within the gay subculture couple relationships are given a status similar to that of marriage. The two partners are sexually available to each other on a continuing basis, expect that the relationship will be relatively long-lasting, and present themselves as a social couple. Studies by Harry and Lovely (1992) indicate that those gay men who are committed to the gay community are more likely to:

- be interested in emotionally intimate relationships
- be more sexually exclusive during the term of a relationship
- share a common home with their partner
- like socializing with other gay couples
- be affiliated with community organizations
- place a greater emphasis on sexual exclusiveness

The level and type of relationship satisfaction is very similar for gay and heterosexual couples. For both types, couples who are satisfied say the relationship has high rewards and few costs. They also tend to rate high in interpersonal competence, such as low neuroticism and high expressiveness.

Gay and heterosexual couple relationships show similar changes over time, each phase having a different focus (Peplau and Cochran 1990; McWhirter and Mattison 1984):

- Phase 1: absorption in each other and near exclusiveness
- Phase 2: power struggles and strategies for dealing with conflict
- Phase 3: increasing independence, trust, and security in the relationship

Gay Bars

Gay persons have had to develop their own social institutions that serve as their cultural gathering places. Urban gay men usually choose gay bars, and lesbians choose small, nonpublic informal groups or women's communities. Couples are less likely than singles to frequent gay bars.

Gay males congregate in gay bars as the primary center of their community. People who live in the gay subculture need an opportunity to get together. Bars reflect the diversity of the gay world. Gay persons who frequent "leather bars" tend to be the exaggeratedly masculine type who wear motorcycle jackets and boots. Effeminate "queens" congregate in queen bars. More discreet, luxurious bars cater to affluent gay male professionals. Some lesbian bars are known as *butch bars*. The types of bars reflect the varied lifestyles of the gay singles community, and they change as the community changes (Achilles 1992).

Gay Husbands

Gay persons sometimes marry in hopes of denying or curing their gayness, as discussed earlier. What causes gay husbands to come out of the closet? The most common impetus is falling in love with another man. Once this happens, the husbands tend to move from covert, highly compartmentalized lifestyles with all the surface appearances of suburban married life, toward openly gay lives. Divorce is a part of this movement, but most men retain a commitment to their children and responsibility for them to the extent that the courts will allow (Miller 1992).

When gay husbands leave their wives and become openly gay, they may initially become deeply involved in the gay singles community and not be so closely bonded with their children. Another pattern, or later development, involves recognizing that their marriages were deeply unhappy, struggling to achieve a gay identity, and finally reaching some level of contentment. At this stage they're likely to have custody of their children and be living with a lover. This group tends to be fairly sedentary and to have a close circle of gay friends.

Older Gay Persons

Most older gay persons (ages 40 to 72) that Berger studied prefer to associate with peers of a similar age and have active sex lives with age-appropriate partners. Discrimination in both housing and employment is a major problem (Berger 1992).

A study of older lesbians found that serial monogamy was the dominant life pattern (Raphael 1992). Each of the women in the sample had had at least one major relationship during her life, and most preferred couple relationships to the "swinging single" lifestyle. Some expressed interest in nonmonogamous, supportive, and collective-type friendship networks. Sexuality continues to play an important part in the lives of older lesbians. Most prefer older lesbians as partners, and their level of sexual activity depends upon the availability of such partners. Most who were not in couple relationships had realistic expectations of finding new partners and expressed little difficulty in finding sexual partners in their own age group. Those with high self-esteem tend to have weak ties with their sisters and brothers and strong ties with friends. There are three major differences between those who claim to be feminists and those who don't:

- Feminists tend to be active in organizations, while nonfeminists are not.
- Feminists tend to be single, and nonfeminists tend to be in long-term monogamous relationships.
- Feminists are interested in the idea of collective living, while nonfeminists are not.

Most gay persons function in two cultures—the larger heterosexual culture and the gay or lesbian community—and may be considered bicultural. Ethnic minorities who are gay have an even more complex socialization process and more cultures to integrate.

Gay Parents

Most gay parents acquired their children through a previous heterosexual marriage. Why would a gay person marry? Several reasons are offered:

- They are in the denial phase of the coming-out process.
- They hope the marriage will "cure" their homosexuality.
- They think of themselves as bisexual and want a marriage and children.
- They want a child or children.

Almost all parents reported that their children seemed to be developing normal gender-role identification and were not noticeably different from other children of their age and gender. Most have positive relationships with their children. Gay parents try harder to create stable home lives and positive relationships with their children, probably due to their fear of loss of custody or visitation rights. They tend to be less conventional and more androgynous or egalitarian in their roles than heterosexual parents. One study found that the only major difference was the gay parents' greater effort to provide an opposite-sex role model for their children (Green and Bozett 1991).

Male and female gay parents were compared in another study. Gay fathers are more likely than lesbian mothers to live with lovers, felt more satisfaction with their first child, had fewer disagreements with their partner over discipline, and were more likely to encourage play with gender-typed toys. Lesbian mothers were more likely to realize the benefits of their gayness, such as increased empathy and acceptance and appreciation for others (Green and Bozett 1991).

Gay fathers. Comparing gay and nongay fathers, a study found gay fathers were:

- more convinced of the importance of setting and enforcing limits
- more likely to consistently emphasize those limits
- go to greater lengths to promote their children's cognitive skills by explaining rules and regulations
- more apt to act as a resource for activities with children

On the other hand, nongay fathers were more willing to be demonstrative with their female partners in the children's presence—for rather obvious reasons.

Fathers who are more public in their gay identities tend to be less authoritative than closeted fathers and to use less corporal punishment. They express stronger desires to raise their children with nonsexist, egalitarian standards. Closeted fathers who remain in their marriages tend to spend less time with their children, to have father-child relationships that are more tense and rushed, and to shower their children with expensive gifts. It's not uncommon for such fathers to become workaholics.

Lesbian mothers. Social and personal development among children raised by lesbian mothers proceeds in a way that's very similar to that expected among children of heterosexual mothers, according to psychologist Charlotte Patterson's research (1994). The children showed normal social competence, behavior, and sexual identity. Their self-concepts did not differ from those of children with heterosexual parents except in one area. Children of lesbians reported that they experienced more reactions to stress—such as feeling angry, scared, or upset—and also a greater sense of well-being, feeling joyful, contented, and comfortable with themselves. We could conclude that these children actually encounter more stressful events and conditions than do children with heterosexual parents, but how then could we explain their greater sense of joy and satisfaction? A more plausible explanation is that they are more able and willing to identify and report their whole range of emotional experiences, from fearful and contracting to love-based and expanding.

The idea that lesbians' children have more experience with the discussion of feelings in general—and therefore more openness to expressing negative as well as positive feelings—is supported by at least two other studies. Rather than experiencing more stress, they may simply be more open to emotional experience of all kinds, positive and negative, and more skilled at verbalizing their feelings (Pollack and Vaughn 1987; Rafkin 1990).

The lesbian mothers in Patterson's study were primarily Euro-American, well educated, and relatively affluent. For all practical purposes, the children, ages 4 to 9, were growing up in homes with either one or two female parents. Patterson concluded that the presence of a father figure is not crucial for young children's successful development, which is consistent with research findings on other nontraditional families. These studies indicate that certain family processes are more important than the family structure, such as traditional nuclear family, in predicting child outcomes. Many of these family processes have not been studied yet (Eiduson and Weisner 1978; Emery 1982; O'Leary and Emery 1984; Weisner and Wilson-Mitchell 1990).

The Plight of Bisexual Persons

A small percentage of gay persons identify themselves as bisexual, being neither exclusively heterosexual nor gay. Bisexual persons may well be born without strong tendencies toward heterosexuality or homosexuality. Some bisexual persons have both types of relationships during a given time of life. Others have only one sexual relationship at a time, and the sex of the potential partner could as easily be male as female. Bisexual persons not only experience all the stresses and problems of gays, they may find themselves the objects of hostility from gays themselves. Gays may view them as people who are denying their true gayness. Heterosexuals may have the same negative stereotypes and judgments about bisexuals as they do about gays. In fact, bisexuals *seem* to choose their orientation, rather than be naturally pulled or driven by it and may therefore be denounced more harshly than gays. This may leave a bisexual person with no built-in supportive community except for other bisexuals, who may be scarce and difficult to identify.

Core Issue: Why Are Some People Gay?

Do gay persons choose to be gay or are they born that way? Or does the answer lie somewhere in between? This question has become a raging controversy in some quarters. If researchers could prove that gay persons are born gay, they would undermine the belief of many church members that people choose to be gay and that doing so is a sin against God. Such proof would also validate the APA's view that gayness is not a form of mental illness. It would vindicate gay persons who say that in the long run they never really had a choice. And it would bolster the argument of gay rights activists who ask, Why would so many law-abiding, productive citizens *choose* a sexual orientation that's so repugnant to society?

Although the origins of *any* sexual orientation are not certain, most researchers now think that genetics, hormones, and environment each plays a role. They say the nature theory, which proposes that gays are born that way, is most likely the predominant explanation for most gayness. Even so, the nurture theory, which proposes that it's some combination of environmental influences and personal choice, is probably a small part of the explanation for some gays and bisexuals.

The Layers of Sexuality

Sexuality could be viewed as having layers of depth, the deeper layers being more innate, an unchanging part of us, and the superficial layers being potentially changeable. In this viewpoint, as shown in Figure 8.1:

- *Sexual identity* is the deepest, core layer, and refers to whether we identify ourselves as male, female, or transsexual.
- *Sexual orientation*, which is wrapped around the core sexual identity layer, refers to *who* turns us on, men, women, or both.
- *Sexual preferences*, the next layer, refer to *what* turns us on, the particular types of scenes, fantasies, or body parts.
- *Sexual roles*, the third layer out from the core, refers to those ways of being and doing that are adopted primarily by males and those adopted by females.
- *Sexual performance*, the most superficial layer, is how we behave when the time seems right for making love.

At the sexual identity level, Seligman (1994) describes transsexuals as persons who are physically indistinguishable from average men or women but who believe they're trapped in the body of the wrong sex. He views transsexuality as a problem at the identity level, one that's based on a core belief that simply won't go away. Second only to this core aspect of whether we're male or female is sexual orientation, which includes gayness, a very deep aspect of sexuality (Gonsiorek and Weinrich 1991).

FIGURE 8.1: Layers of Depth in Sexuality

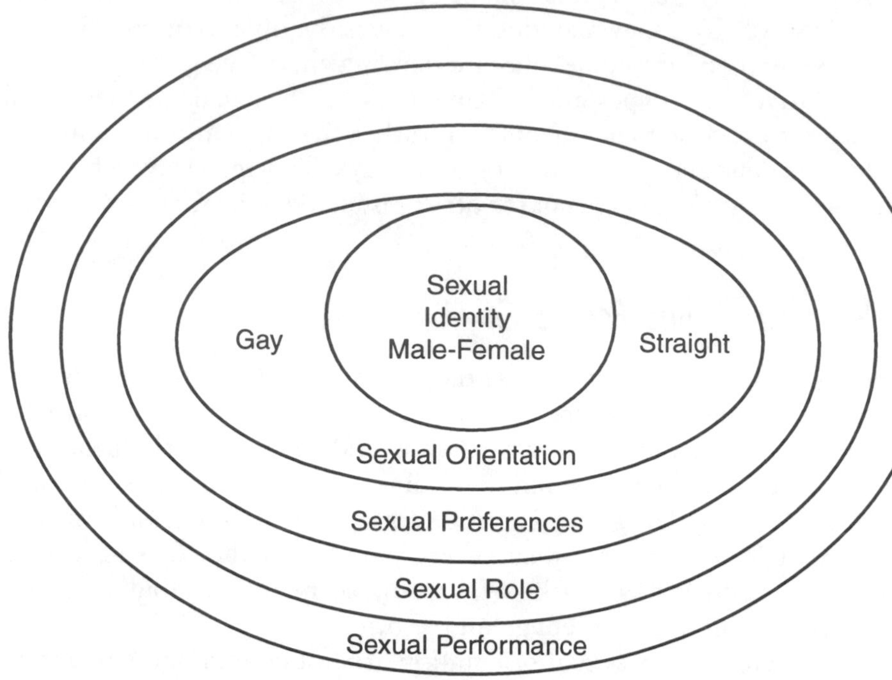

```
                    Sexual
                    Identity
        Gay       Male-Female      Straight

               Sexual Orientation

               Sexual Preferences

                  Sexual Role

               Sexual Performance
```

Based on the work of J.C. Gonsiorek and J.R. Rudolph, 1991.

Degrees of Sexuality: The Continuum Concept

For each aspect of sexuality, people fall somewhere on a continuum, according to some researchers. This is opposed to the more common idea that there are only two choices for some aspects. For example most people tend to assume that everyone is either male or female, gay or straight. At the next-deepest level, one's sexual orientation is either gay or heterosexual. But we all know people who seem extremely masculine or feminine and those who seem almost androgynous.

Similarly, some people are more confirmed in their gayness than others. Researchers have defined a gay sexual orientation as the desire for physical, sexual contact with a person of the same gender and/or conscious sexual arousal from thinking of or seeing such persons. The Institute for Sex Research devised a seven-point scale to represent the continuum of homosexuality, with 0 indicating exclusive heterosexuality, 4 or 5 predominant homosexuality, and 6 or 7 exclusive homosexuality. We could reverse the definition and the scale for determining degree of heterosexuality.

One way of visualizing the continuum of sexual identity and sexual orientation, is shown in Figure 8.2. In the case of the deepest core, sexual identity, people who are extremely masculine or feminine would fall at either end, with many people in between and transsexuals at the center, indicative of their core belief that they're trapped in the body of the wrong sex. At the next level out from the core, sexual orientation is shown as a continuum, with the large majority of the population at the straight end, about two percent who are exclusively gay at the other end, and in between bisexuals and people who've had some homosexual experiences.

Many straights have homosexual experiences. Surveys lend support to the continuum theory although little experimental research has been done on the concept. Many people who don't identify themselves as gay nevertheless report they've had a number of homosexual interactions. Although less than three percent of adult men consider themselves gay, nearly one-third have had overt homosexual experiences, primarily during their adolescent years, and one or two percent of married men are predominantly gay. Although only 1.3 percent of adult

FIGURE 8.2: The Continuum Concept at Two Levels of Sexuality

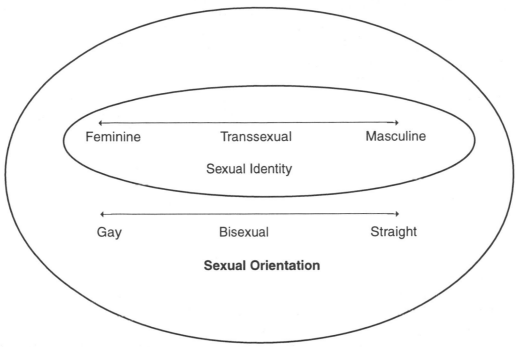

Based on research reviews by Seligman (1994) and Haldeman (1991).

women consider themselves to be lesbians, about 10 percent report they've had homosexual experiences (Gebhard 1992).

Lesbians' degree of gayness varies. Lending further support to the continuum concept are two studies of lesbians (Ponse 1978; Golden 1987). The results indicate there are three distinct types of experience regarding how fixed or fluid lesbians' sexual orientation is.

- *Most always knew.* Group one members, the most numerous, expressed the belief that they had always been lesbian, that their sexual identity was lesbian, and they had difficulty imagining being heterosexual.

- *Many denied for a while.* Group two members had discovered their lesbian tendencies only after attempting to fit in as heterosexuals. Looking back, their heterosexual phase seemed "a poor fit, unreal, or uncomfortable." These women believe they were born lesbians and had made a more valiant effort than some to deny that fact. It's understandable that many gay men and lesbians would take this route, given the censures and punishments society inflicts on them.

- *A few just prefer lesbianism.* Group three members did not view sexual attraction to women as an essential and unchangeable aspect of who they are. However, most expected to continue having their primary or total sexual relationships with women. Some in this group said their sexual feelings were bisexual, fluid, and potentially changeable over the course of their lives. Some said that even though their sexuality was fluid, they choose to act as if it is fixed. Living so many years as part of a lesbian culture and community, they couldn't imagine starting a different life outside of it.

The human development view supports a continuum. Some researchers point out that people develop and change over the entire course of their life span. At all ages we are influenced by social expectations and rewards combined with physical factors and other factors. That sexual and affectional feelings can change in varying degrees over the course of life must be assumed. According to this view sexual orientation is not necessarily fixed for life.

Some gay persons identify themselves as gay in early adolescence, despite social barriers to expressing this identity. For far more, a sense of consolidated gay identity occurs in late adolescence or early adulthood. Some gay persons don't fully appreciate their feelings, some consciously choose to deny them, and others learn to focus on other aspects of their lives. Individuals are unique in their development over the life span. Nature theory advocates point out that even though sexual interest may blossom early or late, most people are destined to be gay or straight by the time they're born. And though they may deny and resist it, that destiny will express itself sooner or later. Nurture theory advocates say the continuum theory supports their belief that people are influenced by their environment and use their free will to choose their sexual orientation.

Nurture Theory

Nurture theorists fall into two camps. The traditional ones think gayness is caused strictly by environmental influences and personal choice. Modern ones tend to think it's some combination of nurture and nature.

Strictly nurture. In the 1950s most people agreed that passive fathers and emotionally domineering mothers were the universal cause of gayness, usually referring to gay men. Strict nurture theory is based on the belief that homosexuality occurs because of environmental factors that influence a person's perceptions and preferences. Many believe that being exposed to gay persons, a gay lifestyle, and gay roles, such as butch, femme, drag queen, and leather stud, creates an attraction for some young persons that causes them to become gay. Others believe that gay persons, especially men, are attracted to young persons, even very young boys, and seduce them into having sex, which may lead to their becoming gay. In addition, nurture theorists point to bisexuals as clear proof that anyone can choose to engage in sexual acts with either sex.

Although environmental influences are strong, they can be overcome. In the final analysis, people choose to adopt a gay sexual orientation and lifestyle. Therefore, they could choose not to adopt it. Many nurture theorists therefore advocate psychological or spiritual counseling and treatment in order to change gay persons' experiences and help them shift to a "normal" sexual orientation.

Nature—critical period—nurture. Some modern nurture theorists are not strict "environmentalists" but believe that all behavioral expressions are both biological and social, a process of nature—critical period—nurture. These researchers point out that research using identical twins indicates that while genetic structure may account for half of the homosexual tendency, it doesn't account for all of it. Therefore, experiences after birth must account for the rest. In this view, people are born with relatively high, moderate, or low degrees of masculinity or femininity, with some falling toward the middle of the continuum, as shown in Figure 8.2. These nurture theorists think that most critical programming and sensory stimulation that affects sexuality probably takes place during infancy and early childhood, rather than at puberty. Sexual rehearsal play occurs in childhood, and by adulthood sexual preference has become fixed for most.

We know that some left-handed children can be coerced into using the right hand for such basic activities as eating and writing, while others can't, and all who are coerced tend to pay a price. According to this modified nurture view, the same is probably true for sexual orientation.

Do gay persons choose a gay role? Some professionals have explored the nurture theory claim that gay persons choose a gay lifestyle or role. Some of these researchers point out that despite the absence of a homosexual *role* in society, by age 17 nearly all men who later identify themselves as gay are aware of attraction to other males. The roles that emerge in the gay community—such as husband, drag queen, or *auntie*—do not *cause* homosexuality. By the time gay persons have contact with the gay subculture, they know they're gay. A minority of gay persons live out their lives without active involvement in the gay subculture, although they may be vaguely aware of its existence.

No known society socializes children into a homosexual role. American parents, after years of teaching their little boys about male sex-ways and their little girls about female sex-ways, are usually shocked and disappointed when they discover their child is gay. How can we explain the universal emergence of homosexuality when there is a universal absence of a homosexual role? Many professionals now believe that children are neither socialized (nurtured) into a "homosexual role" nor do they rationally choose it. Most researchers have concluded that homosexuality is not a role but rather a sexual orientation.

If persons are not socialized into the role of homosexual, then it stands to reason that gay persons choose it because they become aware of their gay sexual orientation. It does not seem likely that we choose our sexual orientation. If this is true, then persons who are predominantly homosexual can no more will themselves to become heterosexual than heterosexual persons can will themselves to become homosexual.

Nature Theory

The idea that homosexuality is fixed before birth and is probably biologically based seems most prominent today, and is sometimes called the nature theory. Some research indicates a genetic basis for homosexuality, other research points toward hormonal influences before birth. Most researchers, medical doctors, psychiatrists, and psychologists lean toward a nature theory of some type. Some researchers focus on biological processes, some compare the incidence of gayness in twins, siblings, and other relatives. Still others look to the actual experiences of gay persons for clues (Green 1988; Seligman 1993).

Development in the womb: the hormone bath. Martin Seligman (1994) suggests how sexual identity and orientation may occur before birth. A human embryo has the potential to be either male or female. The sperm that fertilizes the egg determine whether the egg becomes a male or female fetus, but sexual identity requires another crucial process. When the male fetus is about three months old, he normally secretes two masculinizing hormones from his testes. This causes the internal female organs to wither, the internal male organs to grow, and the external male organs to develop. If for some reason the male hormones are not secreted, the fetus will become a female. The internal male organs will wither, and female internal and external organs develop.

Seligman speculates that the masculinizing hormones also produce a "hormone bath" that washes over the fetus, having the psychological effect of producing male sexual identity. In the case of transsexuals some disruption of this sexual-identity process occurs even though the organ-development phase is normal. That's why transsexuals with the normal organ development of a man feel as if they are really a woman. They did not complete the male-identity process in the womb.

For males this "hormone bath" includes the masculine hormone androgen. The condition called androgen-insensitivity syndrome refers to cases in which a normal male fetus with male internal organs is not affected in the usual way by the androgen in the "bath," and is feminized psychologically. Therefore he is born psychologically female but with a working penis and so is declared a boy. He will be attracted to men and will therefore become a gay man. The extent to which he is drawn to feminine roles may depend on *how* insensitive he was to the androgen in the hormone bath. As for bisexuals, it may be that the hormone sensitivity of fetuses who eventually become bisexual persons falls somewhere in between normal sensitivity and the insensitivity of fetuses who become gay men. Some variation in these processes might cause a fetus to eventually become a lesbian.

Destiny at conception: the gay gene. Recent research indicates that there are probably genetic aspects of sexual orientation. Dean Hamer, molecular biologist with the National Cancer Institute, found for gay men the gene lies hidden in the X chromosome, which they inherit from their mothers. Hamer doesn't claim that a "gay gene" is solely responsible for homosexuality, nor that any gene can dominate any behavior trait. He says that genes influence behavior through indirect and complex paths that require inputs from the physical body, the environment, and the culture. Nor does Hamer claim to have isolated a "gay gene," only to have detected its presence (Hamer and Copeland 1994).

Gayness in twins and siblings. Research using identical twins seems to support the belief that genes have much to do with sexual orientation. In a study of lesbian women, of those who were identical twins, about half had twin sisters who were also lesbians. For fraternal twins, the incidence fell to 16 percent, and for adoptive sisters it dropped further to 6 percent. Each pair was raised in the same home and so had similar environmental influences. The similarities among twins indicates a genetic basis for homosexuality. It also indicates that the cause is not entirely genetic; otherwise, the incidence in identical twins would be 100 percent (Bailey 1993). The results are similar to studies of gay male twins.

Gay awareness patterns. The large majority of gay persons say they've always known they were "different," which supports the Nature Theory. Gay persons' emerging sexual attraction to people of the same sex parallels heterosexuals' patterns of initial sexual attraction to the opposite sex, according to some studies. Nearly half of gay men say they were sexually attracted to males before they learned there were such sexual relations in the adult world. About 91 percent of gay men experience attraction to other males before age 17 (Whitam 1992).

Can gay persons change their orientation? Before the 1970s, nearly all psychiatrists and psychologists who treated gay clients apparently accepted the nurture theory, for they focused on helping gay clients convert to a heterosexual lifestyle. The diagnosis of gayness as illness has changed since those days, but "conversion therapies" are still used by some, most notably certain church-connected groups who believe homosexuality is a sin against God. The American Psychological Association, referring to a review of research, recently released this statement (Welch, in Haldeman 1991):

> *These findings suggest that efforts to repair homosexuals are nothing more than social prejudice garbed in psychological accouterments.*

If the nature theory is correct, then virtually all "change" of homosexuality is a change in conduct or behavior, not in basic sexual orientation, which must then be suppressed at a high price emotionally and psychologically. Psychiatrist D. Haldeman has noted that "gays have a right to choose conversion therapy but should do so with the awareness that such choice is virtually always based on the self-hate that results from their family's hostility toward homosexuality and an intolerant society" (Haldeman 1991, 143).

What's the Answer?

What can we conclude from all this? Probably that being male or female, straight or gay, is not always a fixed, either-or, black-or-white condition. For people at one end or the other of a continuum it may seem that way, but for those near the middle it's not that way. It seems clear that a strongly masculine person with a strongly heterosexual orientation cannot change. It may well be that the androgynous bisexual person cannot really change either. And even if such persons do change as their lives progress, it may be essential for their psychological and physical well-being that they be allowed to develop naturally, going through all the phases that want to unfold at the time they arise and demand expression.

Issue: Acceptance in the Workplace

Discrimination toward gay persons is alive and well in the workplace. Yet few companies have any formal policy for protecting the rights of gay persons. Ask a corporate executive about the company policy on sexual orientation and most will respond, "Sexual orientation? Oh, you mean our policy on sexual harassment?" or, "Well, all our policies are in line with EEOC requirements." The myth is that the workplace is essentially asexual. The reality is that heterosexuality is seen and discussed everywhere in the workplace. Gay activists point out that there is actually a double standard for expressing sexuality, one for heterosexuals and another for gay persons.

The Realities of Discrimination

The most problematic form of prejudice for most gay persons is job discrimination. About one in three gay persons who have come out say they have experienced some form of job discrimination, according to some two dozen studies conducted since 1980 (Woods and Lucas 1993). Most who have identified themselves as gay persons in their private lives remain in the closet at work. In fact 81 percent of lesbians and 76 percent of gay men fear they *would* be the victims of job discrimination if they came out at work (Gross and Aurand 1992). About 18 percent of employers in Anchorage, Alaska, said they would fire someone they thought was gay, 27 percent wouldn't hire gay persons, and 26 percent would not promote them (Brause 1989).

Some gay persons refer to the "lavender ceiling," the gay version of the glass ceiling, where they reach a certain level of responsibility and never go higher. Many say that the executives above them feel uncomfortable with bringing gay persons into the inner fold. Some executives rationalize that clients or employees won't accept a gay person at a high level, that relationships are more sensitive at that level, and that the company image might suffer. This barrier is real but invisible. About 86 percent of management jobs are filled by word of mouth and are not advertised in public media. Managers tend to pass the word to and about others like themselves, and as a result top managers tend to clone themselves (Woods and Lucas 1993).

The Sexual Double Standard

Outside of fairly recent sexual harassment policies, most companies do not have formal policies about workers engaging in sexual affairs or marrying. The myth is that people will be judged on the quality of their work alone and that sexuality does not enter into it, meaning the workplace is essentially asexual. Gay persons would love for the myth to become reality.

The sexual double standard is that it's acceptable for heterosexuals to discuss their sexual partners, such as husbands, wives, and lovers, and the children produced from such unions, but it is not acceptable for gay persons to do so. This is based on the belief that being heterosexual is normal and desirable, but being gay is not. Questions about marital status are a matter of course in professional circles, part of getting acquainted. When a woman speaks of her husband at work, others interpret this as a statement about her social role as wife, not about her sexual performance as a heterosexual woman. People typically inquire about how she met her husband, how long they've been married, and similar facts. Her sexual relationship is so socially acceptable, it is treated as asexual. When a lesbian speaks of her woman partner at work, the focus tends to be on "unnatural sex."

The double standard compels gay persons to remain silent while others talk about family life. Gay persons must mask and repress their sexuality while heterosexuals do not. For example, many gay persons won't entertain co-workers at home because it's too risky, especially if they haven't come out. Some say, "I'd love to invite people from work, but I can't because I don't know that their reaction would be."

One reason gay persons like working in San Francisco or New York is the tendency for people who live there to mind their own business. They simply view what others do outside of work as those persons' private business, which they may choose to discuss or not. Many gay persons say they love the indifference; it's so much better than judgment or pity. Because of their early experiences with censure and worse, their sexuality is always an issue with them, a perpetual threat in the heterosexual world, something to be constantly monitored there. A central career focus for gay persons is managing their sexual identity (Woods 1993).

Issue: Managing a Gay Identity in the Workplace

Because of workplace discrimination, managing their sexual identity is an issue for all gay persons. Strategies vary. For those who haven't come out, vigilance is constant. They must devote great energy to pretending they have a lifestyle they don't or avoiding the lifestyle issue altogether. The fear of disclosure is ever present, resulting in anxiety and stress. Those who do come out experience great relief, but they must still deal with the gay myths and stigma, the prejudice and discrimination, as well as tokenism. Many cope by overachieving and building support networks. Virtually all say that coming out is worth it.

Counterfeiting a Heterosexual Identity

How do gay persons manage to stay in the closet without raising suspicion? Many create fictitious spouses or opposite-sex lovers. They note that many corporate cultures and local cultures make heterosexuality a prerequisite for acceptance and involvement (Rich 1990). They may complain about their status as a confirmed single, as someone unlucky in love, as a man with an old war wound, or as a woman with an inconsolable broken heart from an early tragic love affair. Many invitations to business-related events include mates. If gays accept these invitations, they must make up an excuse for not having a mate or bring an opposite-sex mate to keep up the pretense. If they shun such events to avoid the discomfort, important career opportunities can be lost. The "couple expectation" is culturally driven and people inherit and adopt the cultural bias.

The goal is to escape the usual penalties against gay persons in a heterosexual workplace. But the pretenders pay the penalty of enormous wasted energy from the effort needed to keep up the pose and the anxiety over possible discovery. They also must cope with the ethical problems implicit in living a lie. Perhaps most crucial, they must deal with the feelings of isolation and detachment that result from not being "who you really are."

Dodging the Issue

Gay persons who evade the issue of gayness tend to avoid all discussions of sexuality and to insist that others respect their privacy. They withhold the sexual information that people usually exchange in conversations, information about wives and husbands, girlfriends and boyfriends. They try not to answer such personal questions without people *realizing* they're not answering. Strategies include changing the subject and asking the questioner a question, perhaps softening their evasions with humor.

The dodges can be stressful. About half the gay persons in a recent study said that co-workers frequently talk about sex, 30 percent said social obligations were common at work, and 34 percent said that socializing with co-workers was necessary at least some of the time (Woods, 1993). Gay persons who avoid the subject of their sexuality have no way of knowing what conclusions others have made about it. They wonder, but never know, if others think they are gay.

Gay persons who counterfeit a heterosexual identity, leading others to think they're probably heterosexual, often complain that their social lives don't reflect their inner reality. Not surprisingly, they feel they're treated as if they are "someone else." On the other hand, those who dodge the issue may have no social contact at all, leaving them feeling alone and separate. Most eventually bump into a glass ceiling imposed by their social isolation. They just don't quite fit in with upper management; the comfort level is not high enough.

Coming Out: A Process

Coming out is anxiety filled and liberating at the same time. Gay persons say that when their sexual orientation is disclosed, whether by choice or not, their first response is apprehension and anxiety about their job and the workplace. They don't believe their homosexuality affects their work performance but that prejudice against them does. Most believe their career progression will be slowed or blocked. In fact, about one in three gay persons who have come out say they have experienced some form of job discrimination, according to some two dozen studies conducted since 1980 (Hall 1989; Woods and Lucas 1993).

Calculating the risk. As the awareness and coming-out process unfolds, gay persons' natural tendency is to want to end the deception. They calculate the probable effects of coming out on their job security. Those who are most likely to come out are those who work directly with customers, so their dependence is dispersed across many persons outside the company. No single boss or team is responsible for their job security or mobility. Self-employed gay persons are more likely to come out, for the same reason. Job security is also protected by formal credentialing processes, such as the degrees and exams required for most professions. Similarly, jobs that have concrete measures of success mean that performance evaluations are less vulnerable to the bias of an antigay boss. Unique, irreplaceable skills can also bolster job security, as can mobility within an industry. The belief that "They can't do without me now" or "I can always find another good job" helps to provide the security some gay persons need to come out.

Facing the reactions. What kinds of reactions do gay persons actually face when they come out? The most immediate reactions can include being fired or demoted, becoming the target of verbal abuse and nonverbal hostility or being heaped with effusive sympathy and support. They're likely to experience a backlash of negative attitudes, and they report increased stress levels stemming from harassment by co-workers. The harassment that gay and lesbian employees experience is well documented in the media, and the U.S. Hate Crimes Act of 1990 mentions gay men and lesbians as frequent targets of unprovoked attack. Professionals may find their effectiveness compromised and their authority undercut. Teachers often feel that they must always be on guard. For example, they may think twice before giving a student a hug and saying "Great job," because it could be misinterpreted (Woods and Lucas 1993).

Once out, gay persons must wage the battle for acceptance that other groups of stigmatized employees must fight. Coming out is a change in direction, the first step down a different but difficult road, a process more than a single event. The concern for secrecy becomes a concern for how their sexuality should be communicated in the workplace. In the long run, they must still spend much energy managing their gay identity, and most of them must also deal with being a token gay in a heterosexual work group. The most important strategy gays adopt is to build a support network, although being gay makes this more of a challenge. Strategies for managing the fact that they're admittedly gay include minimizing their gayness, making it seem normal, and offering it as an asset to the firm.

Minimizing gayness. Some minimize the visibility of their sexuality with the goal of lessening their vulnerability. They fear that if they become too visible, or if gay persons in the organization appear too numerous, they will trigger hostility. They say there's a big difference for most heterosexuals in knowing about a gay's sexuality and actually engaging in conversations on the subject, seeing them with a gay partner, and especially seeing them touching, dancing, or embracing. Most gay persons feel safer behind veiled comments and insinuations.

Normalizing gayness. Gayness *is* normal for more than two percent of the population, but most Americans don't think of it as normal. Therefore, many gay persons use a strategy of making the "abnormal" seem normal. They talk about their relationships and lifestyle in terms that highlight similarities to heterosexual life, speaking of family, romance, civil rights. They speak of many of the same concerns as co-workers, such as making house payments, dealing with "in-laws," and finding a date. Their purpose is to transform the unusual into the commonplace and acceptable and to give co-workers a framework for thinking about gay lifestyles. In doing this, they get away from the focus on their "different" sexual orientation so they can relate as a normal person. Gay persons know that beneath their sexual self is a core self that is more essential and encompassing, a more complete and complex self. "Whether I'm gay or not, I'm still *me*," said one.

Making gayness an asset. A few gay persons are able to use diversity-valuing strategies to assert control over the terms by which co-workers come to understand their homosexuality.

Instead of ignoring the differences, their goal is to transform them into assets, such as their rich connections with the gay community and marketplace. This is also one of your opportunities as a leader.

Heaving a sigh of relief. Despite the hassles of discrimination, stigmatization, tokenism, and pressure to compensate for being "less than," virtually all gay males who have come out say they don't regret the decision. The most important result is an overwhelming sense of relief at being finally open, followed by reduced stress, enhanced self-image, and feelings of freedom. Research evidence indicates that gay persons who come out experience less anxiety and depression, have more positive self-concepts, and feel better able to fully experience their emotions and interests (Schmitt and Kurdek 1987; McDonald 1982).

Issue: The Struggle for Legal Rights

Gay persons probably make up the largest minority group facing workplace discrimination that is not protected under federal civil rights statutes. Their legal rights to equal opportunity and fair treatment in the workplace are in a developmental process. Gay activists have made some progress in getting political representation and in getting some laws passed, but they're also coping with backlash, primarily from the religious right. Gay activists are not only struggling for workplace protection, but for equal rights in the legal system itself. For example, no state law provides for gay employees' partners to have access to the same benefits married partners enjoy. In their personal lives, gay persons in many states must still cope with their sexual orientation as a crime and most face formidable barriers to parental rights. These personal rights issues deeply affect many gay employees; therefore, leaders need to understand these issues (McNaught 1993; Woods 1993).

Struggling for Equal Employment Rights

The most crucial issue, in the effect on gay persons' daily lives, is employment discrimination. Gay persons must either stay in the closet and live in constant fear of being found out or come out and suffer the prejudice and discrimination that may ensue.

The employment-at-will doctrine holds that employer and employee enter an agreement as legal equals because the employee can quit "at will" and the employer can fire "at will." There are three limitations on the employer's ability to fire "at will."

- Federal law, which supersedes state law, prohibits employment discrimination on the basis of gender, race, nationality, age, and handicap.
- Union workers are protected by a "just cause" requirement in the union contract.
- Employers may enter into an express or implied contract with the employee regarding the terms of discharge; such contracts are rare and usually occur at top organizational levels.

In most states the employment-at-will doctrine remains a serious obstacle to worker protection from arbitrary and "at whim" personnel decisions. For gay persons who work for private employers, protections are virtually nonexistent. Federal law provides no protection. Gay union workers are protected in theory, but unions have traditionally been lethargic about actual protection for gays.

Some laws actually require discrimination against gay persons; for example, military regulations. Congress has repeatedly refused to include sexual orientation in the antidiscrimination legislation of the Civil Rights Act. In several states, laws have been proposed that would bar local governments from protecting gay persons from discrimination on the basis of sexual orientations.

Making legal progress. Gay activists are slowly making progress and often suffering setbacks. In recent years a few openly gay persons have been elected and appointed to public office, ranging from local representatives to heads of federal government agencies. Their work increases the probability that laws protecting gay persons' rights will be passed.

Although gay persons are largely unprotected from job discrimination, some states and cities have passed protective laws, as indicated in Table 8.2

TABLE 8.2: Employment Discrimination Rights for Gay Persons, 1995

Type of Protection	Protection
Federal protection in all organizations	none
Federal protection for federal government workers	none
State Protection in all organizations	4 states
State protection for state government workers	9 states
City or county protection in all organizations	a few
City or county protection for local government workers	130

The federal government offers no protection to gay employees working in private business nor those working as federal government employees. States that have passed gay rights laws specifically forbidding job discrimination in all organizations that operate within the state, both private business and government, include: Wisconsin (1982), Massachusetts (1989), Connecticut (1992), and Hawaii (1992). In at least nine states, by 1995, governors had issued executive orders prohibiting discrimination against gay persons employed by the state government. By 1992, more than 130 cities and counties had added sexual orientation to the protected categories of city and county employees. A few cities, including Washington, D.C., and San Francisco, had local laws that made it illegal to discriminate on the basis of sexual orientation in all organizations that operate within the city.

Fighting backlash: new antigay measures. Gay persons say they are often persecuted on the basis of the dominant majority's religious beliefs. Members of certain denominations say that laws prohibiting discrimination against gay persons would require them to violate their personal moral standards. In their capacity as owners or managers of businesses, they would not hire or promote gay persons on moral grounds, but nondiscrimination laws would require them to do so on legal grounds. On this basis, antigay political groups have sprung up in many states with the purpose of blocking laws that establish civil rights for gay persons (Herek 1991; Paul 1982).

Antigay groups persuaded Colorado voters to pass a controversial antigay measure in 1992. It called for banning protectionist laws for gay persons. However, gay rights activists got a court injunction against the antigay measure, and in 1994 the Colorado Supreme Court invalidated it. The Court said the measure singled out a class of people for denial of basic rights and thereby violated the equal protection clause of the Constitution. This marked the first time a state supreme court had validated gay rights. Meanwhile, antigay groups in at least eight states prepared similar initiatives. The issue is expected to go before the U.S. Supreme Court.

Resisting Private Sex as a Crime

In 1991, same-gender sexual conduct—private, adult, and consensual—was still a crime in 24 states, in many instances, a felony punishable by up to 20 years in prison. The right of states to enforce such laws was upheld by the U.S. Supreme Court in 1986. The gay community was stunned when the Court upheld Georgia's right to criminalize private gay sex by consenting adults. The Court relied on Judeo-Christian history and literature and characterized gay persons as a threat to the American family and not a legitimate alternative to traditional patriarchal family life. This in spite of the fact that opinion polls in the 1980s showed that most Americans believed that both gay and nongay persons have a fundamental right of privacy for adult, consensual sex.

Pursuing Family Rights

Gay partners cannot file joint income tax returns. Gay employees usually cannot include their partners in their health plans as can heterosexual employees. When gay persons become seriously ill or die, their partners can't legitimately take time off to attend to the illness or funeral.

Their partners may be barred from their bedside by hospital staff because a gay partner is not a legal member of the patient's family.

Common law marriages are a way of recognizing unmarried heterosexual couples as a family unit; gay activists are fighting for a similar status. They point to rights being granted in other countries and in certain cities and corporations. Some of these laws establish a basis for gay persons to ask employers to include their partners in health insurance and other benefits, just as married employees do. Some also provide a basis for claiming certain legal rights if their partner becomes seriously ill or dies.

When gay persons seek custody of children from previous heterosexual marriages, they're likely to come up against myths that we discussed earlier. Courts are changing their views in some regions. In recent years, some gay couples, predominantly women, have been able to adopt children.

Speaking Out in the University

A tradition of academic freedom in public universities has provided gay students with more protection when they're on campus than most any other place. Gay persons on university campuses have a right to meet, create formal student groups, advocate gay rights, and socialize together. Federal and state courts have ruled that these are constitutionally protected free speech and free association rights. Courts have also required state universities and colleges to provide equal space and equal funding to gay student groups, as they do to other types of legitimate student groups. About 100 universities have policies forbidding discrimination based on sexual orientation, and 46 schools have programs in gay and lesbian studies, according to the National Gay and Lesbian Task Force.

LEADERSHIP CHALLENGES AND OPPORTUNITIES

As an invisible minority, gay persons present some of the most formidable challenges to identifying and providing for the needs of a major workplace group. On the other hand, they offer a treasure trove of very marketable skills and talents that is overlooked in many industries.

Leadership Challenges: Meeting the Needs of Gay Workers

When gay persons perceive the corporate culture to be hostile, they may seek refuge in a safe job or position. They may find a protected niche in a large organization, stay out of the spotlight that goes along with high-visibility assignments, broad decision-making responsibilities, and major promotions. They may gravitate to departments that have a reputation for tolerance or in which other gay persons are clustered.

Gay activists have identified some specific needs of gay employees, which must be met if they are to be most productive and motivated to stay with the company.

- Gay persons need to be seen as normal persons. Sexuality is only one dimension of our being. Although it is certainly a major dimension, time spent in actual sexual activity is very small in the whole scheme of things. Gay persons are as highly individualistic as the population at large, with the same variety of interests, abilities, and traits.

- Gay persons most need to work in a corporate culture that accepts them as valuable persons, one that values nonjudgmental caring of one human being for another.

- Gay persons need to "come out" at the time of hiring in order to be most productive within an organization. If they feel they must come in as closet gay persons, they may gain respect and credibility as straights in the organization, based on their skills, creativity, and competence. This credibility may be decimated if they later come out because co-workers may think they've been deceived all along and trust is shattered.

- Co-workers need to understand that HIV and AIDS are immune disorders that affect all persons, not just gay persons. Everyone needs valid information about the safety of working with people who have contracted the virus.

We'll discuss the leadership challenge of meeting these needs, as well as the leadership opportunity of providing a corporate environment that helps gay employees, and all employees, make an optimal contribution. This effort revolves around curing antigay prejudice and moving on to building synergetic work relationships. The bottom-line result of workplace prejudice is to create walls of silence and mistrust, which in turn lowers productivity.

Prejudice poisons work relationships and fosters misunderstanding. In its presence many gay employees feel forced to either deceive, disengage, or resign, taking with them whatever investment the company has made in their development. For heterosexuals, prejudice sets up limited behavioral boxes that may seem comfortable and safe but that stifle ways of thinking and behaving that might fall outside the boundaries. What a waste!

Stemming the Productivity Drain of Antigay Prejudice

Antigay prejudice creates an expensive diversion of human resources. Gay persons must learn to suppress ideas and actions that might invite suspicion, to monitor the way they dress and every word they say. Managing their identity at work consumes enormous amounts of energy, time, and personal resources. Gay persons who must disguise their lifestyles, who avoid the issue of sexuality altogether, or who go public with their sexual orientation all must deal with various types of prejudice and discrimination. They must cope with high levels of stress that could be eliminated in a supportive work environment. For gay professionals, the drain on productivity is clear. For leaders, the first challenge to be tackled is to influence the corporate culture in ways that begin to eliminate antigay prejudice, or at least the acting out of prejudice in the form of antigay discrimination. Most of the other challenges will be solved when prejudice and discrimination are eliminated.

Tearing Down the Walls of Silence that Deaden Synergy

Like all forms of prejudice, antigay prejudice creates barriers between different groups of people, ensuring that they'll have a distorted, insufficient understanding of one another's needs and talents. The bottom line is an atmosphere of mistrust. Prejudice denies gay persons and co-workers the kind of trust and rapport that would enable them to discuss problems frankly. The result is a "spillover of silence," with the communication habits that people adopt for avoiding sensitive, sexual topics spilling over to business topics. Such walls of silence tend to deaden relationships, and they deaden the synergy and creativity that can spring forth from lively interactions (Woods and Lucas 1993). They expand the productivity drain from gay employees to their co-workers. Leaders must cure the prejudice and discrimination that builds these walls in order to bring them down.

Creating Antidotes to the Stigma that Poisons

Gay persons' sexual orientation, by itself, is disruptive only when others despise them for it. When homosexuality is feared and despised, people become fearful that their actions might be viewed as symptoms of gayness. When any type of same-sex affection and closeness may be viewed with suspicion, spontaneous collaboration among employees is inhibited. This is especially true for men, where standards of "manliness" compel them to remain relatively distant, competitive, and independent. Where men's tendencies to express their feelings or to nurture others might be devalued, men tend to be suppress them. Masculinity can become a burden when men perceive they must constantly take charge of situations, speak their minds, and view compromise and accommodation as signs of weakness. The solution is simple but not always easy to implement: Accept gayness as normal for about two percent of the population. When gay persons are as valued as anyone else, people don't need to worry about appearing gay.

Reducing Workplace Tokenism

Savvy leaders understand the problems inherent in being a "token" employee. Tokens carry the burden of the few interacting with the many. Their actions are often interpreted symbolically. Token gays typically represent all gay persons to co-workers, and their failures prove that "gays don't fit in here," while their successes show that "gay persons can contribute after all." Token gays are likely to become lightning rods, targets for co-workers' attitudes toward the entire category of gay persons. Their mere presence may raise related issues beyond their immediate work performance. Gay professionals are thus often treated as community spokespersons. Some view this as an opportunity.

Over half the gay persons in a recent survey said that their desire to educate others about gay lifestyles was a major reason they came out. Others refuse to come out precisely because they don't want to do "all that explaining." Some find that being a symbol or token means they can't quite be themselves after all, even though they're "out." They sense that co-workers are probing, testing their attitudes about gayness in general. Some token gays feel they're being dissected and examined, and that they're "on," performing, instead of just being themselves.

Whether gay persons are in the closet or out, fear of discrimination, together with impaired self-esteem, can motivate them to work harder and be better. Some become overachievers, star performers, top salespersons, or award-winning professionals. In their insecurity they try to be the model professional or the consummate team player. They compensate by working longer and harder than their co-workers. Some suffer from double or triple stigma, such as also being a woman and an African American, and work even harder to compensate. Tokens' visibility is higher than average. The downside is that people are more aware when tokens know less or do less, and people remember. But they're also more aware when tokens know more and do more, so overachieving pays off (Woods 1993).

What can you as a leader to? Set an example, be a role model, by treating gay employees as individuals whose achievements and failures reflect the person, not the gay community. Help educate others about the unfairness of viewing people as tokens.

Eliminating the Need for Gay Ghettos

Minority ghettos refers to places where gay and other minority employees tend to cluster for relative safety from discrimination; for example, in such staff areas as public relations, human resources, or maintenance. Ghettos are more likely to include support staff and sales clerks than line managers or technical experts, more likely to be skilled workers than broad-based decision makers. In ghetto-type jobs, the required skills are tangible, and performance can be measured more objectively in terms of sales figures or concrete tasks completed. Therefore, these jobs are safer, more secure and can provide a haven of tolerance in a larger, more biased organization. But comfortable niches nearly always have glass ceilings and walls all around them, in this case lavender glass (Woods and Lucas 1993). Leaders can eliminate gay ghettos by creating a corporate culture that values and welcomes gay persons along with people from all types of groups.

Stemming the Major Talent Drain

Gay persons look for workplaces where it's safe to be themselves. When they don't find it in one company, they tend to leave for a better environment in another. Leaders can stem this major talent drain by examining the corporate culture and modifying it where needed and by breaking open the lavender glass ceiling.

Examining the corporate culture. Gay persons tend to move away from large companies with unwelcoming cultures, from companies with traditional, family-oriented cultures, especially when they require extensive socializing; from vaguely defined managerial roles that stress hetero-sexual social skills; and from cultures that they consider antigay. They naturally move toward gay ghettos in such companies where they can socialize with others who are on the edges rather than in the mainstream. Many leave large organizations in order to work for smaller companies, gay-run businesses, or to form their own business. This means quite a large talent pool is leaving corporate America. Leaders who want to retain this talent are analyzing the corporate culture to determine how it disadvantages or welcomes gay employees. You have an opportunity to influence your company to modify the culture in ways that accept and welcome gay persons, which we'll discuss in more detail later.

Breaking open the lavender glass ceiling. As managers and professionals move toward the top, reputation is everything. Careers are ruined by the perception that people are not "playing on the team." Leading-edge companies don't fire people for being gay, but most gay persons are sure that gayness creates a lavender ceiling at some point. And, knowing your job is safe is not the same as having a "warm, fuzzy environment" where people accept you as you are and therefore give you an equal chance. Blocked gay employees usually leave if they can find a more open organization. Some leave to find work in nonprofessional fields or to start their own professional firms (Woods and Lucas 1993).

Leadership Opportunity: Finding and Keeping Gay Workers

Gay persons consistently say that homosexuality itself is not self-limiting, but negativity toward homosexuals is and creates most of the problems they report. The corporate culture or local culture makes all the difference. Research indicates that a tolerant and accepting atmosphere at work is conducive to coming out, but coming out is less likely in high-paying jobs. It follows that highly productive and high-potential gay and lesbian employees will tend to leave prejudiced corporate cultures to accept employment within more tolerant or supportive corporate environments (Schneider 1987).

You and your organization can look at what leading-edge companies are doing to encourage qualified gay persons to join their firms, to stay there, and to thrive. In dozens of major companies across the nation, management is taking the following types of actions:

- building an inclusive corporate culture
- valuing the talents and contributions gay persons make
- formally banning discrimination on the basis of sexual orientation
- raising awareness of the sexual double standard
- providing the same types of benefits, attention, and support for gay persons that they provide for other minority groups
- helping gay employees build support networks, including supporting gay employee associations
- adding sexuality issues to diversity training programs, including AIDS awareness programs

Providing an Inclusive Corporate Culture

Gay advocates say the workplace issue should not be one of denying sexual orientation but rather respecting all persons' rights to privacy and to a harassment-free environment. Those organizations that have faced the gay workplace rights issue have been forced to look squarely at themselves and to rethink the basic assumptions that underlie their objectives, values, and boundaries. The transition to a more inclusive organizational environment is most difficult for traditional, hierarchical corporate cultures (Woods and Lucas 1993). You as a business leader can use your influence to bring about these changes in the corporate culture.

Recognizing that Gay Persons Have High–Value Skills

As a practical matter, nearly all companies must have business reasons for focusing attention on a problem and for spending time or money on solving it. Companies are most likely to combat prejudice when they have economic incentives for doing so.

The reverse side of the myth that gay persons cluster in a few "feminine" occupations is the myth that few gay persons work in basic industries, government service, or such classic professions as medicine and law. A recent survey of more than 6,000 gay persons indicates that more gay men and lesbians are found in science than in food service and more work in finance than in the arts. The three most common job categories for gay men are management, health care, and education. In fact, no field is devoid of gay workers. Gay men are disproportionately drawn to white-collar, professional jobs, so many of them are found in corporate America. Relatively few work in blue-collar or manual jobs. (Overlooked 1991).

More than two percent of the population is gay and gay persons are overrepresented in the pool of highly educated, well-qualified employees, possibly representing 5 to 10 percent of such workers. This is precisely the type of worker that's getting harder and harder to find and keep. Companies need a reputation for diversity in order to be able to hire and keep high-potential gay employees. So long as prejudice, and double standards block their career paths, the collective creativity, knowledge, and energy of millions will be lost to companies (Woods and Lucas 1993).

Gay employees have much to offer in business situations where a knowledge of the gay community is needed. They are likely to have an inside track on how to market products to gay customers, how to provide services to them, the implications of AIDS, and other business issues that involve gay persons. In addition, they can energize work teams. Most have experiences and insights that don't come with conventional lives—a cutting-edge sensibility, freedom from marital responsibilities, and a sensitivity and compassion for members of outgroups.

Formally Banning Discrimination

We've discussed the devastating impact of antigay prejudice—and of all kinds of prejudice based on group stereotypes. The first step is for the company to establish clear policies that ban antigay discrimination and specific procedures for implementing such policies. Leaders, of course, must serve as role models, setting the example of being as fair as possible in all interactions and making personnel decisions based on individuals' work performance and potential.

Raising Awareness of the Sexual Double Standard

The sexual double standard was discussed earlier. Any kind of double standard is perceived as unfair by those it discriminates against. Gay employees, to feel as valued and accepted as others, must feel free to discuss their personal lives in the ways that other employees do. The sexual double standard is based on the myth that the workplace is asexual. When managers are asked about sexual orientation and protection for gay employees, many will say that sex has no place at work, that the workplace is the arena of professional, not private, life and is therefore basically asexual. This mythical workplace would be ideal for gay persons, for it would be much easier for them to fit in.

The fact is that personal and professional roles are not at all separate in most corporate cultures. The interactions there are colored by sexual possibilities, expectations, and constraints. Sexuality is always on display, explicitly or implicitly, in dress and image, jokes and gossip, looks and winks, fantasies and affairs. Sexuality is there in the range of persuasive behaviors we call flirtation or seduction and those coercive behaviors we call sexual harassment. Actual sexual contact at work is rare. Yet we humans *are* sexual creatures, even though we're much more than that, and our interactions are always colored by sexual possibilities. We can't help but bring our sexuality to work. It underlies such intangible assets as rapport, familiarity, charisma, and "chemistry." It can be the source of intense feelings of personal commitment and loyalty to the work team.

Then there are the peripherals and accouterments of our sexuality, such as husbands, wives, girlfriends, boyfriends, children, and grandchildren. They show up in pictures on desks and in conversations anywhere and any time. They show up in person at company parties, client dinners, and supplier events. Even traditional male activities, such as golf, fishing, hunting, and spectator sports, are accompanied by male camaraderie and sexual banter in which gay men simply don't fit in, at least in most corporate cultures. On the other hand, lesbians tend to fit in pretty well in with heterosexual women at work, unless the talk turns to "my man."

Does your company have a "couple expectation," meaning people should be in heterosexual relationships, bring their partners to social events, and discuss important family events at work? We know this is culturally driven and to change it, we must start with the corporate culture. Leaders can help others in the organization to become aware of the asexual workplace myth and the sexual double standard. The next step is to bring about change in the attitude that being gay is abnormal and undesirable. When gay relationships are seen as normal for that percentage of the population that is gay, people tend to be comfortable discussing such relationships.

Extending Benefits to Partners

To the gay or lesbian who is in a loving, long-term relationship, working for a company that provides benefits to state-recognized spouses but not to same-sex partners creates an atmosphere that devalues their couple relationship. Also, corporate antidiscrimination policies regarding gay and lesbian employees would almost certainly have a positive psychological impact on them. The change would probably trigger some negative backlash among certain heterosexual employees in the short term. Top management support for an accepting, nonprejudiced environment, however, can produce positive results for all employees in the long run. Clearly, an accepting environment is likely to result in higher productivity for gay workers.

Providing Education About Gayness, AIDS, and Other Issues

Most employees base their opinion of gay persons on common stereotypes and myths. Leaders can provide educational seminars for all employees to inform them of the facts and to initiate discussions of concerns and of new attitudes. A frequent concern is AIDS anxiety, a key fear many people have regarding gay persons. The antidote is facts and figures. For example, AIDS is no longer a predominantly gay disease; it infects all segments of the population. It's not normally contagious and is spread only through very specific types of activities, almost none of which normally occur in the workplace. Savvy companies are building AIDS awareness into company policy, providing informative training sessions for all employees, and giving them written materials that explain the issue.

Helping Gay Employees Build a Corporate Support Network

Gay persons can have the same problems in building support networks as other minorities. People are most comfortable with others like themselves. Therefore, it may be difficult for gay persons to make key connections and to find mentors. This may be especially true in nonaccepting corporate cultures because other gay employees tend to hide out in order to avoid backlash, and other employees tend to avoid guilt by association. However, in flexible corporate cultures that encourage minority employee groups, gay employee associations tend to spring up. Such groups are providing many of the same benefits provided by support networks within the gay community at large, as well as specific workplace benefits (Scandura 1992; Hetherington, Hillerbrand, and Etringer 1989).

Following the Lead of Savvy Companies

Business leaders are recognizing that antigay prejudice creates a talent and productivity drain. Many companies are now enticing potential gay employees with promises of a diverse work environment, among other company attributes. Gay professionals are finding more incentives than ever for favoring those employers who treat them well. Such leading-edge companies as Apple Computer, AT&T, Digital, DuPont, Hewlett Packard, Oracle, and Xerox, as well as smaller software firms, now have gay employee organizations and nondiscrimination policies. These high-tech companies are painfully aware that their most talented employees can easily switch jobs and go to competitors that provide a more tolerant social atmosphere and better benefits. Competition is the newest reason for companies to offer domestic partners benefits. Top managers also know the high cost of replacing highly trained engineers and other technical workers. Companies that fall behind can expect a talent drain.

Fortune magazine became the first mass-circulation business magazine to run a major feature story on gay issues, "Gay in Corporate America," on December 16, 1991. The author called for granting gay persons minority status and placing them in the same category with women, African Americans, and other groups who are now protected by nondiscrimination laws and policies. Gay activists say that gay persons in fact constitute a cultural minority, suffering many of the same predicaments as other oppressed groups. Also in 1991, several hundred consultants, trainers, and managers met for the first national conference on gay and lesbian issues in corporate America.

Specific philosophies, strategies, and programs devised by some of the most successful companies offer ideas for making the most of gay employees' talents.

Microsoft. "When we lose a viable employee, we've probably lost . . . upward of two million dollars," said Microsoft's diversity director. Microsoft, the world's largest computer software company, set a goal in 1990 of making sure that gay professionals have everything they need to stay productive, and their diversity program is an integral part of that strategy.

Lotus. Another software company, Lotus, was one of the first to recognize that gay persons don't have the choice to legalize permanent and exclusive relationships through marriage and so cannot legally share financial, health, and other benefits with their significant partners, as married couples can. Lotus began in 1991 to recognize such relationships by including them in company policies and benefits. It was the first major publicly-held U.S. company to do so. Since then a number of large companies have made similar changes in their policies.

Levi Strauss. In 1992 Levi Strauss became the largest employer to recognize gay partners for purposes of employee benefits, such as health care and life insurance. In 1990 gay employees at Levi Strauss formed a gay employees' association. Of the 2,000 employees of the San Francisco Levi Strauss facility, about 170 were known gay persons at the time. Gay employees' association members estimate that about 400 are actually gay. Each year gay persons in the company hold a Gay Pride Celebration in the headquarters atrium, which top management attends. The gay community is an important market segment for Levi Strauss. Levi's 501 jeans are known in the gay community as queen jeans. Many gay men wear them, but not everyone who wears them is gay, of course.

Bank of America. In 1991 the Bank of America and several other San Francisco area corporations canceled their annual donations to the Boy Scouts of America in response to Scout policy statements that barred gay persons from participation in Scout activities. Corporate policy of these companies bans donations to organizations that discriminate against any minority group. In August 1992 the Republican Party platform criticized Bank of America and others for their withholding of donations. After the criticism, Bank of America backed down, saying the Boy Scouts "have clarified that now they are open to all boys." But the Scouts' national spokesman said the official interpretation of the Scout oath phrase "morally straight" means "not homosexual" and that gay youths are "not eligible" for the Scouts (*Chronicle* 1992).

Regional consortiums. Gay rights advocates in at least one area have formed a consortium of representatives from companies who are changing their policies toward gay persons. Gay Rights in the Workplace is a San Francisco-based organization that has gained acceptance in most of the large corporations in the metropolitan area, including Levi Strauss, Pacific Bell, AT&T, Hewlett

Packard, Apple Computer, and Wells Fargo. The major corporate viewpoint toward gay persons expressed by these companies: Management must respect diverse backgrounds; there will be no discrimination based on sexual orientation; we value the creativity of all people.

SUMMARY

Gay persons must cope with many stereotypes and myths, such as gay men act feminine and lesbian women act masculine, which is untrue. Gays don't cluster only in certain occupations, though they naturally gravitate to companies, businesses, and jobs where they feel most accepted. Gay persons tend to be better educated and to earn better incomes than average. People who associate with them are no more likely to be gay themselves than those who don't associate with gays.

Gay persons have a wide range of relationships, including long-term, committed ones, and ones in which gay couples raise children. Research indicates that children raised by gay parents have no major problems and are not more likely than other children to become gay adults. Gays are not more likely than heterosexuals to molest children.

The people most likely to harbor antigay prejudice are older, less well-educated men who are strongly involved with fundamentalist religious groups. Antigay prejudice has many negative effects on gay persons and on the persons who hold the prejudice, but there is increasing acceptance of gay persons in the workplace. In the 1950s gayness was considered a mental illness often caused by domineering mothers and weak, or absent fathers. But in 1972 the American Psychological Association took the position that gays are not mentally disturbed nor in need of therapy to change their sexual orientation.

Growing up gay is a confusing, painful process for most gay persons, and cultural prejudice creates self-esteem problems for them. Most initially deny the fact that they're sexually attracted to same-sex persons. However, those who come out are able to identify with the gay community, which is a healing and empowering process. The gay community is as diverse as the heterosexual community.

The core gay issue in American culture is, Why are some people gay? This brings into play the continuum theory, the nurture theory, and the nature theory. According to the continuum theory, there are degrees of maleness or femaleness, degrees of heterosexuality or homosexuality, and degrees of every other layer of sexuality. People in the Nurture Theory camp think that people become gay primarily because of their environment, experiences, and role choices. Most conservative religious leaders adhere to the nurture theory, which, if correct, upholds their belief that the Bible condemns homosexuality. This means that it's a condition that can and should be prevented or cured. Nature theory advocates think gay persons are probably born gay, even though they may not realize this until adolescence. Their gayness may be due to hormone conditions in the womb, being endowed with a "gay gene" at conception, or some combination. Most researchers tend toward the nature theory, which, if correct, means that it's perfectly normal and natural for about two percent of the population to be gay.

The struggle for acceptance in the workplace is a major issue. Gay workers must deal with prejudice and discrimination in every career aspect. They must cope with the sexual double standard that allows straight workers to discuss wives, children, and family events, while gay workers' personal lives are "off limits." This, combined with the "couples expectation," is especially difficult when advancement depends partly on social skills. Managing their gay identity is an ongoing issue for gay workers, whether they're in the closet or out. Pretending they're heterosexual or dodging the issue brings on the problems of "living a lie." Those who've come out often use such coping strategies as building a support network, minimizing their gayness, making it seem as normal as possible, and making their gay connections and insights a marketing asset to the company.

Struggling to gain equal rights is also an important issue. In 1995 there was no federal protection from discrimination for gay employees, whether they worked for private business or the federal government. Four states prohibited discrimination in both private and government jobs, and nine states prohibited it for their government workers. In addition, a few cities provided protection in both private and government jobs, while 130 cities and counties provided it for their government employees. Sexual conduct between same-sex persons was a crime in 24 states, gay partners could not legally marry, and in most areas they had few or no family or parental rights.

Skill Builder 8.1 The Case of Gay Rumors

You are a supervisor in the computer section of a large bank. One of your best computer technicians, *Diane*, has worked there for three years. She has been an excellent worker up to now. Lately, however, her productivity has fallen off and she has called in sick several times. The other day you noticed a cartoon about lesbians stuck on the wall near Diane's desk. You've also overheard some gossip in the restroom implying that Diane might be a lesbian.

- What actions, if any, should you take?
- Outline at least two scenarios and the follow-up actions you would take in each instance.

Skill Builder 8.2 The Case of Clients' Comfort Zone

Carmen studies the file folder on her desk. As head of the Western Regional office of the Hartford Company, a lending and investment firm, she must decide how to handle a touchy situation. She's thinking about *Jayson*, one of her most productive employees. Jayson has been in the special customer department for two years, dealing with customers who have a net worth of $200,000 to $1 million. He has done an excellent job of handling these customers' needs to invest their available cash and to get loans for business or home-buying purposes.

Don, in the custom portfolio department, is being promoted and transferred, and Carmen has been considering who should take his position. Don deals only with customers who have a net worth of over $1 million. This is a different group, mostly older and more conservative than the customers Jayson has been working with. The only problem Carmen worries about is the fact that Jayson is a gay man. Carmen knows that at least one or two of Don's customers have made antigay comments. She's concerned not only with the possibility of losing some customers, she wonders if it's fair to Jayson to throw him into such a sensitive situation.

- If you were Carmen, what would you do?
- If you were Jayson, how would you view this situation?

Skill Builder 8.3 The Case of Frank, a Gay Assistant

Frank is hired in February as an administrative assistant at Graphics Express, a Palo Alto, California, software firm. He considers it an excellent opportunity because the company has made a commitment to provide him with career development opportunities and to give him the backup resources he needs to carry out his projects. The resources include clerical help. Frank and his supervisor *Bradley* hit it off well, and Frank looks forward to a successful, rewarding career at Graphics Express.

Frank makes no secret of the fact that he's a gay man—because he prefers to start off on an honest basis with his co-workers. Soon after he comes to work, however, one of his co-workers, *Jennifer*, begins making derogatory comments about gays to him.

Frank tries to ignore these put-downs, but Jennifer escalates them to direct insults about Frank's sexual orientation. The comments upset Frank. He discusses them with his partner, saying "It hurts to be treated this way in this day and age. I thought that in this city and this company I would be left alone." Frank and his partner agree that the best response is to continue ignoring Jennifer's negative comments and to focus on doing a good job.

The situation takes a turn for the worse, however, when *Katie*, who works closely with Jennifer, brings some disturbing news to Frank. Katie says that Jennifer frequently complains about Frank to others when she's in the employee dining room-lounge. Katie says, "Frank, I hate to be the one to tell you, but I think you should know. Jennifer's saying you're unfit to represent the company to customers because you're gay. She says you tarnish the company and all of us with your perverse lifestyle."

This time Frank decides he must take action. It's one thing to put up with remarks directed solely at himself, but mudslinging in the presence of all his co-workers is more than he can take. He schedules a meeting with *Jeff*, the human resources director, and informs him of the situation. Jeff promises to look into it. This meeting takes place in early May.

In late May, Frank's supervisor Bradley is promoted. Frank shares Bradley's elation over the promotion, but when he hears who will take Bradley's place, his heart sinks. His nemesis Jennifer will be his new supervisor. Frank decides to try to make the best of it, to ignore Jennifer's hostility, and to do the best job possible.

By the end of June, Frank can see that his goals are becoming more and more difficult to achieve. Jennifer is giving Frank more and more assignments, often menial and tedious ones, and makes it clear that Frank is expected to complete them by deadline without receiving additional clerical help or overtime. The final straw comes when Jennifer tells Frank he can no longer depend on the help of Deborah, the clerk who has worked most closely with him in the past.

This occurs in late July, and Frank immediately goes to Jeff, the human resources director. Frank brings Jeff up to date on the situation, saying: "Jeff, you said you'd look into this problem of Jennifer's hostility toward me. It was difficult enough when she was merely slandering me. Now she's in a position of direct power over me, and she's setting up impossible performance standards for me. The situation has become so stressful that I have great difficulty sleeping, and I've been putting in such long, hard, tension-filled days that I'm beginning to feel drained all the time. What can you do to relieve this situation?" Jeff promises to investigate the situation but makes no further commitment.

Now, in August, Frank is trying to decide his next move. He feels exhausted, he's had a respiratory infection for six weeks, and his doctor tells him he must get more rest.

- What are the key issues in this situation?
- If you were Frank, what would you do?
- If you were Jeff, what would you do?

Skill Builder 8.4 The Case of Edna, Lesbian Employee

Edna has been working for Whizware, a Silicon Valley software company, for two years. She is 26 years old and for a long time refused to believe that she was a gay person. She married her high school sweetheart but the marriage ended in divorce after a year or so. Now Edna is living with her lesbian partner *Janice*. The relationship is good, and Edna finally feels comfortable about her sexuality. However, she has not told anyone about her sexual orientation except a few close lesbian friends.

Whizware has many liberal policies, including flextime, three-week vacations, and a relaxed dress code. Most of the employees are under age 40. Recently the company encouraged a gay support group to form. Edna was astonished that out of about 350 employees, 52 attended the first meeting. While this turn of events is heartening to Edna, the response of many co-workers is not. Most of what she hears is pretty nasty and hateful, with few accepting or supportive comments.

Having a divorced status has helped Edna to pass for a heterosexual. She says, "I don't deliberately lie, but when my colleagues talk about child care and how hard it is to find reliable help, I can safely murmur something about being glad I didn't have children when I was married. But at the same time I can be sympathetic to their problems, which of course I am."

The longer Edna is employed by Whizware, the more difficult it is for her to maintain her counterfeit identity. The workers tend to know a great deal about each other's lives outside the office. Edna knows, however, that most people are more interested in talking about themselves than hearing about other's lives, so she staves off friendly curiosity by showing more interest of the details of their lives than she actually feels. She says, "Most of my co-workers respect my privacy and assume I'm mourning my failed marriage."

Edna periodically travels to Vancouver and Dallas as part of her job of training clients in the use of Whizware products. Occasionally a colleague or executive will travel with her. Recently *David Southam*, Vice President, accompanied her to Vancouver. As Edna says, "He had a little too much to drink and definitely became too friendly. I had a tough time convincing him that 'no' means 'no.'"

Edna has never heard any office gossip about Southam being a womanizer, but she's concerned that he may seek revenge for her rejection of his overtures. If he does, and if her lesbian relationship with Janice becomes known to him, she would be especially vulnerable. Southam made several antigay remarks while under the influence and clearly was against the gay support program recently instituted at Whizware. After thoroughly bashing the program, he said, "*#* faggots, who needs 'em?" He also made several nasty cracks about *Jane Goodman*, one of the founders of the gay support program. Edna is terrified of the prospect of being regarded in the same devastating way by Southam. On the other hand, when Southam is sober and on the job in Silicon Valley, he's well respected. However, Edna wants to avoid traveling with him in the future.

Edna's partner Janice suggests that Edna could file a sexual harassment complaint against Southam, which could solve any future travel problems. This prospect horrifies Edna, who says, "I'm just gonna try to get out of traveling with him." She knows this might not be possible because one of Whizware's best clients is located in Dallas. The strategy for keeping this client satisfied depends on Edna's technical knowledge combined with Southam's customer relations skills.

- What are the key issues in this situation?

- If you were Edna, what would you do?

REFERENCES

Achilles, Nancy. "The Development of the Homosexual Bar as an Institution." *Sociology of Homosexuality*. New York: Garland, 1992.

Adam, B.D. *The Survival of Domination: Inferiorization and Everyday Life.* New York: Elsevier, 1978.

American Psychological Association. Minutes of the Council of Representatives. *American Psychologist* 30 (1975): 633.

Ashworth, A.E., and W.M. Walker. "Social Structure and Homosexuality: A Theoretical Appraisal." *Sociology of Homosexuality*. New York: Garland, 1992.

Bailey, J. Michael. Northwestern University, *see* Archives of General Psychiatry, March, 1993.

Bell, A.P., and M.S. Weinberg. *Homosexualities: A Study of Diversity Among Men and Women*. New York: Simon & Schuster, 1978.

Berrill, K.T. "Anti-Gay Violence and Victimization in the United States." *Journal of Interpersonal Violence* 5, no. 3 (1990): 274–294.

Brause, Jay K. "Closed Doors." *Identity Reports*. Anchorage: Identity Inc., 1989.

Chronicle, The San Francisco (August 19, 1992): A1

Deaux, K., and L.L. Lewis. "Structure of Gender Stereotypes: Interrelationships Among Components and Gender Label." *Journal of Personality and Social Psychology* 46 (1984): 991–1004.

Duberman, Martin. *Stonewall*. New York: Dutton, 1993.

Eiduson, B.T., and T.S. Weisner. "Alternative Family Styles." *Mother/Child Father/Child Relationships*. Washington, DC: National Association for the Education of Young Children, 1978.

Emery, R.E. "Interparental Conflict and the Children of Discord and Divorce." *Psychological Bulletin* 92 (1982): 310–330.

Fortune. "Chicago Research Firm Surveys Gays." December 16, 1992, p. 45.

Gebhard, Paul H. "Incidence of Overt Homosexuality in the United States and Western Europe." *Sociology of Homosexuality*. New York: Garland, 1992.

Golden, C. "Diversity and Variability in Women's Sexual Identities." *Lesbian Psychologies*. Urbana, IL: University of Illinois Press, 1987.

Gonsiorek, J.C. and J.D. Weinrich, eds. *Homosexuality: Research Implications for Public Policy*. Thousand Oaks, CA: Sage, 1991.

Gonsiorek, J.C., and J.R. Rudolph. "Homosexual Identity: Coming Out and Other Developmental Events." *Homosexuality: Research Implications for Public Policy*, Thousand Oaks, CA: Sage, 1991.

Green, Beverly, and G. M. Herek, eds. *Lesbian and Gay Psychology*. Thousand Oaks, CA: Sage, 1994.

Green, R. "The Immutability of (homo)Sexual Orientation: Behavioral Science Implications for a Constitutional (legal) Analysis." *Journal of Psychiatry & Law* 16 (1988): 537–568.

Gross, Larry, and S.K. Aurand. *Discrimination and Violence Against Lesbian Women and Gay Men in Philadelphia and The Commonwealth of Pennsylvania*. Philadelphia: Philadelphia Lesbian and Gay Task Force, 1992.

Haldeman, D. "Sexual Orientation Conversion Therapy for Gay Men and Lesbians: A Scientific Examination." J. Gonsiorek and J. Weinrich, eds. *Homosexuality: Research Implications for Public Policy*, Thousand Oaks, CA: Sage, 1991.

Hall, M. "The Lesbian Corporate Experience." *Journal of Homosexuality* 12 (1989): 59–75.

Hamer, Dean, and P. Copeland. *The Science of Desire: The Search for the Gay Gene and the Biology of Behavior*. New York: Simon & Schuster, 1994.

Harry, Joseph, and Robert Lovely. "Gay Marriages and Communities of Sexual Orientation." *Sociology of Homosexuality*. New York: Garland, 1992.

Harry, Joseph, and William DeVall. "Age and Sexual Culture Among Homosexually Oriented Males." *Sociology of Homosexuality*. New York: Garland, 1992.

Herek, G. "Sexual Orientation and Military Service." *American Psychologist* 48 (1993): 538–549.

Herek, G. "Stigma, Prejudice, and Violence Against Lesbians and Gay Men." *Homosexuality Research Implications for Public Policy*. Thousand Oaks, CA: Sage, 1991.

Hetherington, C.E., Hillerbrand and B.D. Etringer. "Career Counseling with Gay Men." *Journal of Counseling and Development* 67 (1989): 452–454.

Kennedy, E.L., and M.D. Davis. *Boots of Leather, Slippers of Gold: The History of a Lesbian Community*. New York: Routledge, 1993.

Kite, M.D. "Age, Gender, and Employment." Paper presented at the meeting of the American Psychological Association, Boston, 1990.

Kite, M.D., and K. Deaux. "Attitudes Toward Homosexuality." *Basic and Applied Social Psychology* 7 (1986): 137–162.

Loulan, J.A. *The Lesbian Erotic Dance*. San Francisco: Spinster, 1990.

Loznoff, Maurice, and W.A. Westley. "The Homosexual Community." *Sociology of Homosexuality*. New York: Garland, 1992

McDonald A.P., Jr., J. Huggins, S. Young, and R.A. Swanson. "Attitudes Toward Homosexuality." *Journal of Consulting and Clinical Psychology* 40 (1973): 161.

McDonald, G.J. "Individual Differences in the Coming Out Process for Gay Men." *Journal of Homosexuality* 3 (2982): 47–60.

McNaught, B. *Gay Issues in the Workplace*. New York: St. Martin's Press, 1993.

McWhirter, D.P., and A.M. Mattison. *The Male Couple: How Relationships Develop*. Englewood Cliffs, NJ: Prentice-Hall, 1984.

Michael, Robert T., J.H. Gagnon, E.O. Laumann, and G. Kolata. *Sex in America: A Definitive Survey*. New York: Little, Brown and Company, 1995.

Newman, B.S. "The Relative Importance of Gender Role Attitudes to Male and Female Attitues toward Lesbians." *Sex Roles* 21 (1989): 451-465.

O'Leary, K.D., and R.E. Emery. "Marital Discord and Child Behavior Problems." *Middle Childhood: Development and Dysfunction*. Baltimore, MD: University Park Press, 1984.

Overlooked Opinions, a Chicago market research firm, in a 1991 study.

Palmore, 466 U.S. at 433. For an application of Palmore in a lesbian mother case, *see* S.N.E. v. R.L.B. 699 P.2d 875 (Alaska, 1985).

Patterson, C.J. "Children of the Lesbian Baby Boom." *Lesbian and Gay Psychology*. Thousand Oaks, CA: Sage, 1994.

Paul, W. "Minority Status for Gay People: Majority Reactions and Social Context." *Homosexuality: Social, Psychological, and Biological Issues*. Thousand Oaks, CA: Sage, 1982.

Peplau, L.A., and S.D. Cochran. "A Relational Perspective on Homosexuality." *Homosexuality/Heterosexuality: Concepts of Sexual Orientation*. New York: Oxford University Press, 1990.

Peplau, Letitia Anne. "Lesbian and Gay Relationships." *Homosexuality: Research Implications for Public Policy*, Thousand Oaks, CA: Sage, 1991.

Pollack, S., and J. Vaughn. *Politics of the Heart: A Lesbian Parenting Anthology*. Ithaca. New York: Firebrand, 1987.

Ponse, B. *Identities in the Lesbian World*. Westport, CT: Greenwood,1978.

Rafkin, L. *Different Mothers: Sons and Daughters of Lesbians Talk About Their Lives*. Pittsburgh: Cleis, 1990.

Rich, R. "Compulsory Heterosexuality and Lesbian Existence." *Signs* 5 (1990): 631–660.

Rothblum, E.D. "Introduction: Lesbianism as a Model of a Positive Lifestyle for Women." *Women and Therapy* 8 (1988): 1–12.

Rutledge, Leigh W. *The Gay Decades*. New York: Penguins Books, 1994.

Scandura, T.A. "Mentorship and Career Mobility." *Journal of Organizational Behavior* 13 (1992): 169–174.

Schmitt, Patrick J., and L.A. Kurdek. "Personality Correlates of Positive Identity and Relationship Involvement in Gay Men." *Journal of Homosexuality* 13, no. 4 (1987).

Schneider, B.E. "Coming Out at Work." *Work and Occupations* 13 (1987): 463–487.

Seligman, Martin. *What You Can Change and What You Can't*. New York: Knopf, 1994.

Silverstein, C. "Psychological and Medical Treatments of Homosexuality." *Homosexuality: Research Implications for Public Policy*, Thousand Oaks, CA: Sage, 1991.

Storms, M.D., M.L. Stiver, S.M. Lambers, and C.A. Hill. "Sexual Scripts for Women." *Sex Roles* 7 (1981): 699–707.

Weisner, T.S., and J.E. Wilson-Mitchell. "Nonconventional Family Lifestyles and Sextyping in Six Year Olds." *Child Development* 61 (1990): 1915–1933.

Whitam, Frederick L. "The Homosexual Role: A Reconsideration." *Sociology of Homosexuality*. New York: Garland, 1992.

Whitley, B.E., Jr. "The Relationships of Heterosexuals' Attributions for the Causes of Homosexuality to Attitudes Toward Lesbians and Gay Men." *Personality and Social Psychology Bulletin* 16 (1987): 369–377.

Woods, J.D., and J.H. Lucas. *The Corporate Closet*. New York: The Free Press, 1993.

Yankelovich Partners. Income survey, 1994.

CHAPTER 9

Working with Persons with Disabilities

*Persons with disabilities are in a **different** situation,*
not necessarily a less fortunate one—in the deeper, eternal sense.
Carolyn Vash

About 49 million Americans are persons with disabilities. One-third are employed, meaning 16 million persons now have some protection from workplace discrimination under the Americans with Disabilities Act (ADA). To raise your awareness of your perceptions of persons with disability, and to determine what you already know about them, complete Self-Awareness Activities 9.1 and 9.2.

Self-Awareness Activity 9.1: What Do You Believe About Persons with Disabilities?

Purpose:
- to get in touch with your beliefs and stereotypes about this group of people
- to experience how judgmental beliefs affect your thinking and feeling processes
- to experience the ways in which your beliefs create your reality regarding other persons, even before you have any interaction with them.

Part I. What Do You Believe About Women with Disabilities?

Step 1. Associations
- Relax as deeply as you can: close your eyes and taking a few deep breaths.
- Focus on the words "disabled woman" and allow a mental picture to come up in your mind's eye.
- Notice the words and images that come to mind as you "see" this woman.
- Open your eyes and list 10 to 20 words in the order in which they occur to you.
- Review your list. Mark a plus beside the words that are positive, a minus beside the words that are negative, and a circle beside neutral words.

Step 2. Negative Associations

- Close your eyes and focus again on the image of the woman with a disability. Formulate a negative opinion or judgment, perhaps one you typically hold about such women.
- Notice your *feelings* as you see the person in this negative way. What *thoughts* come up as you focus on the image?
- Write a few sentences about your feelings and thoughts.

Step 3. Positive Associations

- Formulate a positive opinion or judgment, perhaps one you typically hold about women with disabilities.
- Notice your *feelings* as you see the person in this positive way. What *thoughts* come up as you focus on the image?
- Write a few sentences about your feelings and thoughts.

Step 4. Insights

- Focus on the differences between your experiences when you hold negative and positive judgments or opinions. What were the differences? What meaning does this have for you, for your beliefs and feelings about people from this group, and about beliefs in general?
- Write your responses in a few sentences; include anything you like about your feelings, thoughts, and insights.

Part II. Experimenting with Opinions Men with Disabilities

Repeat the phases and steps in Part I, this time focusing on the image of a man with a disability.

Self-Awareness Activity 9.2: What Do You Know About Persons with Disabilities?

Purpose: To see what you know about the issues covered in this chapter.

Instructions: Determine whether you think the following statements are basically true or false—and think about why. The answers will emerge in this chapter, and the summary at the end of the chapter focuses on these issues.

1. The definition of a person with a disability is "anyone with a physical impairment that limits the range of tasks he or she can accomplish."
2. Employees with disabilities tend to have better records of punctuality, attendance, and turnover, but they're somewhat less productive than other employees.
3. Society has always attempted to rehabilitate and integrate persons with disabilities.
4. The large majority of persons with disabilities, even those with severe disabilities, can become independent and productive.
5. Only about 30 percent of persons with disabilities are currently employed.
6. The federal Americans with Disabilities Act requires employers to make special accommodation for the disabled, which is proving very costly for employers.
7. Job applicants with disabilities must provide a medical history to potential employers.
8. If you see that a person with a disability needs help, give it at once.

Strictly speaking, everyone has some type of impairment, perhaps a missing toe or finger, mild nearsightedness, or difficulty learning advanced mathematics. The people classified as disabled have a greater degree of impairment. For some, the difference this makes in their lives is relatively minor; for others, such as quadraplegics, it's enormous. Virtually all persons with disability want to live as normal a life as possible. Most want to work, regardless of the extent of their impairment. When they do hold jobs, they tend to be productive and to have better-than-average attendance and turnover records (Myths & Facts 1992).

Persons with disabilities must cope with a wide range of myths and stereotypes, prejudice and discrimination, from mild to devastating in impact. Like the other groups we've discussed, some of them have become activists and are bringing about changes. Doors that were formerly closed are opening, and chances for a normal or near-normal life are improving. Like other groups, persons with disabilities have their support groups and networks that are connecting to form a subculture. We'll explore all this, along with their current profile, the issues most important to them, and some guidelines for you as a leader who wants to empower this committed group of employees and utilize their rich and varied skills.

> *What's in a Name?* Labels can hurt, especially when their effect is to isolate people from the rest of society. The terms we use to refer to persons with disabilities can be loaded with unintended meanings. Most activists prefer terms that are descriptive rather than euphemistic, emotionally neutral rather than charged, and words that don't elicit negative stereotypes (Longmore 1985a).

Preferred Terms	*Terms to Avoid*
• Persons with Disabilities	• Differently Abled
• The disabled (as a protected class)	• Physically Challenged
• Sight Impaired, Blind	• Handicapped
• Mobility Impaired	• Crippled, Lame, Gimpy
• Hearing Impaired, Deaf	• Deaf and Dumb
• Emotionally Impaired	• Insane, Crazy
• Neurologically Impaired	• Moron
• Mentally Impaired	• Retard

The term *persons with disabilities* is preferred when referring to the group as a whole because it focuses on them as persons first, rather than on their disability. The use of the term *the disabled* is acceptable when referring to them as a protected class. Such terms as *differently abled* and *physically challenged* are not descriptive and attempt to avoid the issue. They're politically correct in the worst sense. *Handicapped* was considered acceptable for a time, but the word stems from the phrase *cap in hand* and carries a connotation of begging. Now most persons with disabilities avoid it. Such terms as *hearing impaired* or *sight impaired* are specific and descriptive. They're often more accurate than deaf or blind because they refer to those with varying degrees of impairment, as well as those with total loss of an ability. The worst terms carry emotionally devastating stereotypes and tend to focus on the negative: deaf and dumb, crippled, limp, lame, gimpy.

Who are the persons with disabilities? If they're protected under the Americans with Disabilities Act, they are persons who fit one or more of these descriptions:

• They have a physical or mental impairment that substantially limits one or more of the major life activities.

• They have a record of such an impairment

• They are regarded as having such an impairment.

To help you imagine what it's like to have a disability, complete Self-Awareness Activity 9.3.

Self-Awareness Activity 9.3: What If You Became Impaired?

Purpose: To increase your awareness of the experiences of persons with disabilities.

Step 1. Various Activities. List some barriers you would face in a typical day if you lost your ability to walk, your vision or your hearing. Consider how you would manage the activities shown in the column to the left if you had each of the impairments shown on the right. What barriers would you have to overcome in each case?

	Mobility Impaired	*Visually Impaired*	*Hearing Impaired*
• getting up in the morning, getting ready			
• getting to work or school			
• doing your work, communicating, etc.			
• having lunch			
• using the restroom			
• other activities? (list)			

Step 2. Getting Dressed. Put on a tight blindfold, or close your eyes and don't peek. Go through the motions of getting dressed. What problems do you experience? Which are the most difficult?

Step 3. Sight and Sound. While watching a television drama, try the following experiments.

• Wear a blindfold for 5 or 10 minutes.

• Mute the sound for 5 or 10 minutes.

What are the key differences between no-sight and no-sound? What insights does this experience suggest to you about visual and hearing impairments?

MYTHS AND FACTS

Myths about persons with disabilities reflect cultural stereotypes, beliefs, and attitudes. They form invisible barriers between people, more powerful even than the steep steps and narrow doorways that block persons in wheelchairs. People usually don't openly express their attitudes of avoidance or discomfort toward persons with disabilities. For example, most people don't voice their pity or distaste, nor avoid *all* eye contact, conversation, touching, or proximity. Avoidance attitudes are more likely to be expressed indirectly in the form of exclusionary practices, sometimes said to be necessary for the safety or convenience of persons with disabilities, or of people in general. The result is that people don't have persons with disabilities around, which relieves them from feeling uncomfortable or distressed (Myths & Facts 1992; Longmore 1985b).

> *Myth: Employees with disabilities create safety risks, increase costs, and are less flexible and productive than other workers.*

In fact, a review of 90 hands-on studies reveals that compared to other employees, persons with disabilities (Cox,1993; Green and Johnson 1987):

• have better safety records

• do not normally cause increased health care costs

• have equal or better turnover and absentee rates

• have equal or better job assignment flexibility

- are productive; more than 90 percent of 1,451 workers at DuPont rated as average or above average on overall job performance
- have better average attendance records than those of nondisabled employees.

Myth: Employees with disabilities are more difficult to work with than others.

Two large surveys of managers and co-workers of persons with disabilities indicate the following (Harris 1986, 1987):

- Eighty percent of managers say they are no more difficult to supervise than others.
- Fifty percent of managers rate the following quantities as *better than* those of other workers: willingness to work hard, reliability, punctuality, and attendance.
- Eighty percent of co-workers say they are just as productive as others.

Myth: Persons with disabilities are unable to lead normal lives.

Most persons with disabilities can live relatively normal lives and want to do so. Most are impaired in only one functional area. They tend to compensate for their impairment in numerous ways. They're able to do most things as well as anyone and usually can do some things better. Many people with disabilities view their limitations as a fact of life but go to work and participate as actively in society as they can. Persons with disabilities are increasingly better educated, with 75 percent completing high school in 1994, compared with 60 percent in 1986 (*Business Week* 1994).

Myth: Persons with disabilities can only do menial or entry–level jobs, and most don't want to work.

In fact, persons with disabilities are successfully employed at almost all levels in nearly every field. More than 90 percent of net new job openings in the 1990s are in information-intensive and service occupations, and at least 90 percent of persons with disabilities are capable of filling such jobs.

In fact, most see work as a major route to self-fulfillment. They want to find work that draws on their skills and talents and helps them live a more abundant life.

Myth: Persons with severe disabilities are childlike, dependent, and in need of charity or pity.

In fact, many persons with severe disabilities have a great deal to contribute and are able to work and to manage their own lives through the Independent Living Movement.

A related myth is that a disability is a constantly frustrating tragedy. In fact, many persons with disabilities say that a disability need only be an inconvenience *if* it is dealt with as an inconvenience. Developing intelligent accommodations is one way to accomplish this. Although severe disabilities pose huge challenges, even they can be viewed primarily as a challenge to be overcome rather than a hopeless tragedy.

STEREOTYPING AND DEVALUATION

People tend to shun, be prejudiced against, or devalue people who are different. This is especially true when the persons are different because they have less of something than most people have. But people who have more than most others may also be devalued. People who are exceptionally rich, brilliant, beautiful, or even kind are suspected and punished by some people. Most every culture seems to display this tendency.

Most devaluation refers to regarding someone as inferior, a lesser being, not very capable, not very useful, possibly burdensome, not beautiful, and generally one down. Devaluation follows close behind outright oppression when it comes to psychologically damaging consequences. It is the most common and devastating attitude facing persons with disabilities. They consistently experience devaluation in the eyes of others, and therefore their own, whether their disability is physical, sensory, or mental in nature.

The form and degree of devaluation is heavily influenced by the surrounding culture. Devaluation can be blatant or subtle. The Nazis blatantly killed disabled people. Most societies are so subtle that their devaluative practices have gone unrecognized as such for many years until the new breed of activists began to call attention to them. In both the East and the West, for example, it has been common to segregate the disabled into their own schools and workplaces.

Personal Beliefs that Affect Devaluation

The prevailing philosophical or religious beliefs of the culture have a distinct effect on how people view persons with disabilities (Vash 1981).

Western. Most Western religions and philosophies hold that we each have only one life to live. Therefore, being disabled has other implications, from "It's just God's will and we can't know why" to "It's God's punishment for something the victim did or something the victim's parents did" to "It's a tragedy because we're here to enjoy life."

Western cultures, such as the dominant culture of the U.S., place a high value on standard modes of reasoning, a cultural model of physical beauty, and the physical, material world. Such values tend to create barriers to good relationships and to communicating with persons with certain impairments (Vash 1981; Althen 1988).

Many people in our culture view people as a personality inside a body. When one or both of those has been damaged "permanently," not much is left. Societies and individuals who are more spiritually oriented understand that the spirit is not damaged just because the body or personality is damaged.

Materialistic people are especially likely to believe that persons with disabilities continually mourn their misfortune, perhaps as long as they live. This is simply not the case for most persons with disabilities. Therefore, the implied belief that persons with disabilities are sad victims of terrible life circumstances erects a communication barrier between the believer and those persons.

Eastern. Some Eastern philosophies and religions include the idea of reincarnation into multiple lives. Many believe that before coming into a new lifetime, at a spiritual level we choose our parents, our body, and our total life situation. We do this in order to learn certain lessons and have certain experiences that deepen our awareness and understanding and promote our spiritual growth. Disability thus becomes a growth experience. This is not to say that all Asians view disability in this manner. It is to say that some persons with disabilities have found this viewpoint to be more constructive and empowering than the Western view.

When persons without disabilities believe they're more fortunate than persons with disabilities, they tend to feel pity, which implies superiority. People with this viewpoint may feel threatened when a co-worker with disabilities excels, or they may assume that the co-worker was excused from meeting the usual standards. On the other hand, some people view persons with disabilities as merely being in a *different* physical situation, not necessarily a less fortunate one—in the deeper, eternal sense. Such viewpoints allow us to relate to persons with disabilities as peers, colleagues, and equals.

Media Influences

In the past, films and television programs often presented persons with disabilities as villains, criminals, monsters, and tragic figures. All these stereotypes express the idea that disability involves the loss of an essential part of the person's humanity. The figures were often portrayed as almost subhuman. Think of Captain Hook, the hunchback of Notre Dame, mentally impaired Lennie in *Of Mice and Men.* Here disability implied the loss of moral self-control, often through bitterness and isolation that results from the fear and bigotry of others. During the 1970s and 1980s we saw persons with disabilities in the media who chose suicide as an escape from their "living death," or "vegetable existence," even though they retained many functions. In these films disability implied total physical dependency and separation from the community. In nearly all these dramas the victims were unable to adjust to their disability, and death was presented as the only logical and humane solution to a horrible situation. The role of social stigma and discrimination in these tragedies was not the issue, and society was generally let off the hook.

Other dramas have focused on bitter, self-pitying victims whose families eventually got tough in order to help the person with disability adjust and cope. In a similar vein, the focus is often on victims who have worked courageously and have achieved remarkable feats. Both types of stories featured overcoming adversity, based on the concept of disability as primarily a problem that requires the person with the disability to accept the situation and find the emotional resources to cope and overcome. Social stigma and devaluation were still not the issue.

A few recent productions have directly dealt with the issue of prejudice. Others have presented persons with disabilities as normal persons who happen to have some functional impairment. Deaf and paraplegic persons have been portrayed as attractive and sexual, entering relationships out of the strength of their own identities. Certain activist groups are trying to influence media decision makers to focus on these more realistic aspects of disability.

Fear of Becoming Disabled

People don't like to think about losing control of their destiny or that the hand of fate could strike them as well as the person with a disability who they see before them. This fear can lead to extreme discomfort and distress upon even seeing persons with disabilities, much less spending time with them. What people fear, they tend to shun and stigmatize. Fear can also lead to blaming the disabled for their predicament. Some people find comfort in believing that persons with disabilities must have brought it on themselves through sin, carelessness, or self-sabotage. In turn, they can tell themselves that they would never bring such a disaster upon themselves, and this makes them feel more in control and safer.

Unfamiliarity and Discomfort with Persons with Disabilities

When people have had little or no experience with persons with a certain type of disability, the unfamiliarity can be disconcerting. People are frequently confused and uncertain about how to act and what to do. Some avoid making eye contact with such persons because they got punished for "staring" when they were children. How many mothers have grabbed their child's arm and snapped, "Don't stare! It's rude." How many have said, "Shhh! Don't ask!" when their naturally curious child blurted out questions and concerns upon seeing a person with a disability? Parents' comments are well meaning, but they teach their children to ignore anyone with a disability.

Unfamiliarity can cause people to focus on the equipment surrounding some people—braces, crutches, wheelchair—and keep them from really seeing and tuning into the person. It can cause people to look at an interpreter, leaving out the hearing-impaired person, instead of viewing the translator as a mechanism for communication and focusing on the person they're communicating with. In all these cases, the person with the disability gets little or no eye contact and becomes something of a nonperson.

EVOLUTION: FROM VICTIM TO ACTIVIST

Persons with disabilities say that the most serious barriers to living reasonable lives and doing their work are not necessarily their own physical or psychological disabilities. The worst barriers are external: other people's stereotypes and attitudes and the buildings, vehicles, walks, steps, and restrooms they must negotiate. Cultural attitudes and policies toward persons with disabilities have changed dramatically in this century (Longmore 1987). Some highlights of historical change include:

Before 1850   Traditional moral attitude: take care of the disabled.
1850s   Provide special schools for the trainable.
1880s   Institutionalize the disabled in large centers.
1880s–1920s   Involuntary confinement and sterilization.
1930s   Rehabilitation for some. Sight-impaired advocates fight for
                   participation in society.
                   F.D. Roosevelt, who uses a wheelchair, is elected U.S. president.
1940s   World War II opens doors to disabled workers because of manpower
                   shortages; March of Dimes, Cerebral Palsy associations are
                   formed.
1950s   Focus on rehabilitating and adapting to the environment.
1960s   Disabled-rights advocates organize to change their environment;
                   Urban Mass Transportation Act, Architectural Barriers
                   Act encourage access.
1970s   Federal law requires access and accommodation from some
                   employers and organizations; some states pass similar laws;
                   Independent Living approved by Congress and some states.
1980s   Independent Living Movement; Air Carriers Access Act.
1990s   Federal ADA requires access and accommodation from most
                   employers and in nearly all public buildings.

From Institutionalizing to Rehabilitating

The traditional moral attitude toward adults with disabilities was to take responsibility for their care. Social reform efforts of the 1850s sought to establish special schools for those children with disabilities who were considered trainable. In the 1880s there was a move to switch from small centers to large, more economical institutions that could accommodate more people, with the attitude that defective persons should be removed from the mainstream of society. Subsequent legislative drives from 1880 to 1925 focused on enforcing involuntary confinement and sterilization to prevent "defective" persons from having children.

Rehabilitating

The Rehabilitation Act of 1918 focused on World Ward I veterans with disabilities. Proponents of vocational rehabilitation assumed that people with disabilities could overcome them and become wage earners if given training. The major goal was to prepare people to work so they could pay back the government's investment; it did not seek to offer generalized assistance.

Rehabilitation became a part of the solution for persons with some types of disabilities, but after rehabilitation, they were given only the most menial jobs. During World War II, because of the extreme manpower shortage, workers with disabilities filled a variety of jobs. Studies indicated they incurred less absenteeism and tardiness than other workers and that their productivity was good. After the war, these work reports "got lost" and it was back to the old "moral" attitudes.

From Accepting Disability to Adapting

By the late 1950s it became unfashionable to talk about *accepting* disability. *Adapting* to or *coping with* became the preferred terminology. This thinking led in part to the disabled-advocates revolution. Some saw that counseling would not solve the problem if, in the end, people with disabilities still could not get from one point to another because there wasn't an accessible bus service or they couldn't get up the stairs. The world was not a very reasonable place to live for the disabled, so advocates began to shift the emphasis from modifying the disabled to modifying the world around them.

Adapting While Changing the Environment

"Persons with disabilities" became a movement in the 1960s. They also became a minority group with culture-like features, such as dominant values, cultural themes, and key issues. Emerging from their former victim roles, disability activists brought about important legislative changes. Looking to the future, their goal is to remove as many of the barriers to a normal life as they can.

Transformation: From Victims to an Activist Minority

A new day dawned for persons with disabilities in the late 1960s, as it did for many groups. Many of them began viewing themselves as part of a minority group that must manage its own brand of stereotypes and discrimination from others, develop and affirm its own values and issues, and take charge of its own destiny (Longmore 1985a, 1985b, 1987). Once the disabled started talking to each other, most of them concluded that:

- Other people with disabilities are valuable and worthwhile.
- They themselves weren't the only exceptions to those negative stereotypes that they had previously accepted.
- All persons with disabilities have valuable experience and information to share.
- In unity there is strength.

They began to fight in the civil rights mode of other minorities, to formulate their rights, and to demand protection for those rights. They campaigned for and won new laws during the 1970s. A 1973 federal law addressed the issue of making some public places accessible to persons with disabilities and eliminating discrimination, but it applied only to organizations receiving federal funds. It did not include most stores, restaurants, and theaters, nor did it include private corporations, except those involved in federal contracts. Soon after the 1973 law was passed, several states passed similar laws. California's law, considered an outstanding model, deals mainly with providing physical and program access to the disabled. School administrators began installing ramps and elevators instead of counseling people with disabilities to stop wanting to attend classes held upstairs. Managers began to remove discriminatory hiring practices instead of advising applicants with disabilities to start liking the few jobs they would be allowed to do.

Breakthrough: The Americans with Disabilities Act

The Americans with Disabilities Act (ADA), which was passed in 1990 and became fully effective in 1994, expanded accessibility to jobs and activities in virtually every major arena. It's an amendment to the Civil Rights Act, not a part of affirmative action law that stems from executive orders. It's therefore enforced by the EEOC. Complaints not resolved through the EEOC may be resolved in the courts through EEOC lawsuits.

Future Aspirations: To Bring Down Barriers

Now activists are clear that if the disability cannot be changed, then it must be accepted, as must any other reality, pleasant or unpleasant, if the person is to survive and grow. What they don't accept is the unnecessary handicapping imposed upon people with disabilities by a poorly designed or unaccommodating world or by their own failures to accept what is and go on from there. Nor do they want to be dependent from cradle to grave because this can severely limit their growth and contributions. Activists have made significant progress toward reducing all types of barriers to a quality existence: barriers that existed in the legal, welfare, and educational systems, barriers created by modes of architecture, transportation, employment, housing, shopping, and recreation. Most important, activists initiated the Independent Living Movement (ILM), which we'll discuss later. The U.S. is the most highly individualistic of nations, so independence has the highest value here, and the ADA and the ILM reflect that.

CURRENT PROFILE

In 1992 the U.S. Census Bureau estimated that there were 49 million Americans with disabilities that fell under the ADA definition, about 24 million of whom are severely disabled. About 16 million persons with disabilities were employed. The ADA definition is broad and includes such chronic conditions as diabetes, heart disease, HIV, AIDS, past (but not present) drug addiction and alcoholism, and mental and emotional illnesses. It could potentially cover 25 percent of all workers. However, it's directed mainly to those who are hearing-impaired, sight impaired and mobility impaired, which is about one percent of working-age adults (Minton 1994).

The U.S. Census Bureau does not recognize persons with disabilities as a separate category yet. We may get some sense of the types of disabilities people experience at various ages by examining information regarding people who receive disability payments. Business leaders need to be aware that persons with disabilities who have been working all or much of their adult lives are not eligible for disability payments unless their disability becomes significantly worse. Managers should not assume that if they lay off persons with disabilities, they'll be able to collect disability payments.

The great majority of persons receiving disability payments suffer from four broad health conditions—mental disorders, heart disease, musculoskeletal disease (primarily arthritis), and cancer—as shown in Table 9.1. The ADA is expected to benefit older workers the most, since that group has the highest percentage of persons with disabilities. About 22 percent of people 55 to 64 years old receive disability payments, compared to 6 percent of people 25 to 34 years old.

TABLE 9.1: Breakdown of Reasons People Receive Disability Payments

	All (%)	Younger <50 (%)	Older 50–64 (%)
Mental disorders	28	40	17
Heart disease	18	7	25
Arthritic disease	19	12	23
Cancer	3	3	4
All other	32	38	31

Source: Mitchell, 1993.

The two-thirds of adults with disabilities who are not working represent the highest unemployment rate of any minority. About 80 percent of those who aren't working say they would rather have a job. Dissatisfaction with life is reported by four times as many adults classified as having disabilities as other adults (WSJ 1994).

CULTURAL PATTERNS AND ISSUES

The community of the disabled is emerging as a subcultural group. It began with the Independent Living Movement and the activism of the 1960s. As a leader, you need to have some insight into what it's like to be a person with a disability, what inner resources are most crucial to them, how women's experience differs from men's, and which aspects of the environment impact them the most. You need to understand their major issues, such as the struggle to become more independent.

What's It Like to Be a Person with a Disability?

Being a person with a disability is like being any other person, only with an impairment that prevents you from performing one or more major functions. It's having normal reactions to abnormal situations. Human beings are more alike than different, regardless of variations in their physical bodies, sensory capacities, or intellectual abilities. Some abnormal situations are biological, such as having multiple sclerosis, which involves progressive nerve deterioration. Some are environmental, such as inaccessible entrances. Other abnormal situations are social, such as having a salesperson ask your companion, not you, what size you wear. Not being able to get a job is an economic example. Some abnormal situations are obvious, such as a restroom door you can't get through. Others are subtle, such as people using or not using the word cripple when you're around. Some may be pleasant, such as being allowed to board the airplane first. Others are unpleasant, such as not being allowed to board at all. Persons with disabilities are continually perceiving and experiencing things that the majority of people around them cannot validate. Unless they are in regular contact with people who are similarly disabled, their sense of isolation and the lack of consensus for their ideas and feelings are added to the list of abnormal situations.

What's it like to be disabled? That depends on the following types of factors:

- *Type of disability*: severity, stability
- *Inner resources*: temperament, self-image, self-esteem, gender, education, skills, creativity
- *Environment*: family support, cultural attitudes, available technology, government funding

Type of Disability

The type of disability refers to the time and type of the onset of the illness or accident, which abilities are impaired and which are not, the severity and duration of the affliction, and the way society views it (Vash 1980).

Time and type of onset. Some persons are born with disabilities. They grow gradually to recognize that they are different from most other people in negatively evaluated ways. Others become disabled after a short or long lifetime of being "normal." The disability may occur in a catastrophic moment or over a period of illness.

To some, having been born disabled seems somehow less respectable than acquiring a disability later on. Such persons are more likely to be subjected to isolation, unusual child-rearing practices (such as overprotection or rejection), and separation from the mainstream in family life, play, and education.

Many become disabled after a close brush with death, which often has a powerful influence on their life. Some feel guilty for having survived to be a burden. Others feel an intensified faith and sense of purpose.

Functions impaired. The extent to which the disability interferes with physical attractiveness is a key determiner of the disability experience. Sensitivity to its lack or loss can exceed the pain felt about the functional disability.

The functions impaired directly affect other experiences the person has. For example, deaf people describe the loneliness of being "left out" even when physically present in a group. Blind persons may speak of their terror of pitfalls they can't see, and wheelchair users of curbs they can't get up or down.

Severity, duration, and status. There is not a direct, consistent relationship between severity of disability and the intensity of reaction to it or quality of adjustment to it. One person can assimilate total paralysis with fair equanimity, while another is devastated by the loss of a finger. Varying degrees of severity do create different kinds of situations for people to respond to, somewhat independently of personal dynamics.

Some people are temporarily disabled, others are permanently disabled, and some fall into a gray area where some day their impairment may be reparable. For those people, the most depressing influence is often the not knowing. One spoke of living a "provisional existence of unknown limit," saying, "I was convinced that I would eventually walk, but the uncertainty of how long it would take was a most depressing factor."

Persons who are disabled perceive a status hierarchy of disabilities, with polio and spinal-cord injury at the top and mental retardation and cerebral palsy at the bottom. When a disability causes you to walk and talk like a drunk, you get a lot of rejection.

Inner Resources

To learn how inner resources affect the disability experience, we might ask such questions as:

- What kinds of temperaments do persons with disabilities have?
- What is the spiritual or philosophical base in their lives?
- What personality traits do they have that will influence the type and intensity of their reactions to being disabled?

The inner resources of persons with disabilities dramatically affect how they experience their disability. They include ability to adapt to the disability, self-confidence built in early childhood, personal interests and values, ability to express emotions, gender, and other personal variables.

Ability to adapt. How well a person is able to adapt to the loss of abilities and to enjoy the abilities that remain is an important inner resource. Whether key activities can be continued obviously plays a big role in what inner resources can be tapped. What alternate activities are available is also an important factor. Inner strengths that help people to adapt may include high energy level, strong career motivations, life history of emotional stability, many artistic talents, social poise, and leadership ability or potential.

Psychological support. Inner resources and emotional stability are established early in life. Those who are disabled as children need more psychological support than most children. When they are taught to believe that they're "as good as anyone else and can do anything they want to do," they gain self-confidence to disregard the taunting of other children. The early years of confidence help them combat the doubts and rejections they experience later on.

The hit movie *Forrest Gump* was an exposition of this idea. Forrest was mentally impaired, but his mother made sure that he joined mainstream society. She repeatedly told him that he was not inferior. One of the many mottoes she taught him was, "Stupid is as stupid does." She taught Forrest to do good deed because actions speak louder than words and to value the goodness of his inner self.

Interests, values, and goals. People tend to adjust more easily if they have a wide range of interests, such as physical interests, intellectual pursuits, vigorous activity, rigorous creativity, passive pastimes, and active involvements. For one thing, they're more likely to find some things they can still do that interest them. People who sustain spinal-cord injuries through adventurous, potentially dangerous activities are apt to be most intolerant of a physically inactive life. People from cultures that highly value physical or sexual prowess are more devastated by this disability than those whose traditions stress scholarly or other sedentary pursuits.

Ability to express emotions. What emotions do persons with disabilities tend to feel? Disability has the power to elicit the full range of human emotions, from fear, anger, and sorrow to relief and even joy. Chronic depression is the worst. Periodic fear, embarrassment, or righteous indignation are improvements over that.

Almost all persons with disabilities experience anxiety about survival as well as episodes of rage. Some rage against themselves, their own incompetence to do what others take for granted. They may rage against the universe for being unjust. Some turn their rage against other people for not helping or for helping inappropriately. Some of today's disabled peopled have been called an "angry generation," expecting change to come faster than it ever does and seething inside when it doesn't. Some say that even justified anger isn't good for them over the long term, but they feel they need its impetus to sustain their demands for change.

The ways of expressing and acting out emotions are unlimited. The specific trigger to feelings varies from one person to another. Because disability normally brings strong emotions, being able to express them is important for mental and physical health.

Gender considerations. Being male or female does not imply better or worse reactions, only different ones. It's more acceptable for women to be helpless in our culture because of the greater social acceptance of a passive, dependent lifestyle for women than for men. Women also tend to have the advantage of being more in touch with their feelings and expressing them more freely. However, women's advantage is virtually destroyed by the far greater demand placed on women to be physically perfect specimens, beautiful in face and figure. By definition, women with physically disabilities cannot hope to meet this social ideal.

Other personality variables. Such variables as flexibility, adaptability, maturity, and their opposites influence reaction to change generally, and this includes the changes imposed by disability. Personality variables will affect what meaning persons with disabilities give to the fact that they're disabled. The person who views disability as a punishment from God for past sins will feel differently about it than the person who views it as a test or an opportunity for spiritual development.

Reactions that people with disabilities have to their disability continue as long as the persons and the disability do. There is not some point in time when the person has "adjusted." Reactions simply change with each step in the learning process.

The Environment

At the most primitive level of existence, the ability to get around to find food and shelter is the basic requirement for independent survival. In civilization we must also be able to communicate with other people who are essential for our survival. We're dependent on our immediate environment as well as the greater cultural environment. Persons with disabilities are especially dependent on adequate funds, programs, laws, and technological developments to provide what their impairments prevent them from providing for themselves.

The immediate environment. The financial assets of persons with disabilities make a crucial difference in the type of experience they have. Money can solve many disability problems. With enough money, persons with disabilities can buy all the equipment and gadgets available to help them do what they need to do. And they can pay other persons to do what's left. A major problem with disability is that it's often difficult to make money. A person's welfare and experiences are therefore greatly influenced by the family's social standing and power base in the community, parental acceptance of the person's disability, and their willingness and ability to offer practical and moral support.

Cultural context. We've discussed the importance of cultural beliefs and attitudes toward the disabled. Predominant beliefs and attitudes are the direct cause of psychological and physical barriers on the one hand and their removal on the other.

Mastering the physical environment. The main issue for mobility-impaired people is accessibility, and safety is the main issue for the visually impaired. Inaccessibility has implications for survival. For example, if wheelchair users cannot get into a building, they can't get a job there. If they can't get over the curbs, up the stairs, or into the restrooms, they literally cannot function even though they have many other abilities. The most typical ways people with disabilities cope with problems of inaccessible or unsafe facilities are by:

- minimizing their own disabilities by developing every possible adaptive skill
- keeping up the good fight to get remaining environmental barriers removed

Some wheelchair users are interested in the development of wheelchairs that climb steps. Most prefer to see ramps and elevators wherever steps are used. What do wheelchair users do if they're working in an upper floor of a skyscraper and fire breaks out, rendering all the elevators unusable? Some feasible plans do exist, but they're rare. When deaf passengers take an unknown bus route, how can they know when they're reached their street destination? These are the crucial emergencies and everyday problems that disabled-rights advocates are trying to resolve.

Community and regional influences. The size and location of the community where the person lives are important. A small town may offer a quality of human support that is lost in the big city, but it may also lack the equipment and services that persons with disabilities need. Also important are the extent to which the community has been willing and able to eliminate mobility barriers, to mainstream children with disabilities into the public schools, and similar actions.

Other factors that affect the quality of life include the services that local voluntary organizations make available, television and telephone services available for the hearing impaired, the type of transportation that's available, and whether activist organizations are around. The climate and typical building styles also can have a significant impact on how persons with disabilities fare.

The bureaucracies. The various bureaucracies that persons with disabilities must deal with may include live-in institutions and social service agencies.

- *Institutions.* Living in an institution has a profound impact on the disabled person's experience. Few, if any institutions, are ideal. By their very nature they tend to restrict residents' freedom and violate their privacy. Few people go there by choice. Giving up one's autonomy, even for a time, can have long-lasting, negative effects. In an institution, the staff tends to make most of the crucial decisions about the patients' lives. Those patients who are most willing to cooperate with the staff, therefore, may eventually be the least prepared to resume effective, assertive autonomy when they return to the outside world. Those who have been in institutions say it's the attendants who make the most difference in their quality of life while there (Vash 1980).

- *Socials Service agencies.* The disabled must often interact with agencies that provide vitally important services. These interactions can be supportive, but they can also be stressful. According to disabled advocate Carolyn Vash, when dealing with agencies "in order to receive the benefits they need, disabled people must tell all, hand over the reins, and oftentimes swallow much, possibly for a very long time" (Vash 1980, 36).

Technological support. How well the culture is able to provide the latest in technological tools, aids, therapies, cures, and other responses to the cause and aftermath of the disability makes a great difference in resolving functional problems. The U.S. culture provides a great deal of independence and convenience through motorized wheelchairs, powered lifts, electronic magnifiers, talking calculators, portable teletypewriters, computers, and similar aids.

Recent technological breakthroughs. Motorized wheelchairs have opened up dramatic new opportunities for the mobility impaired. For the sight impaired, Braille, audiotape, specialized computers, and other electronic or optical devices have greatly reduced the need for personal services, such as readers. Hearing-impaired persons' communication problems are yielding more slowly to technological intervention than those of the blind. They continue to need interpreters to convey information that's presented orally. Signing is a tiring activity and is ideally done by one person for not more than an hour at a time. What's needed is a portable device that will decode speech and turn it into a visual readout. There is still much televised information with no closed captioning for the hearing impaired.

Public transportation is making strides in assisting users with both short-distance and long-distance travel. The kneeling bus, which lowers a wheelchair-sized platform to curb level, has opened up many opportunities. Many housing functions are becoming computerized. In education, computers provide self-paced learning and easy access to libraries of information. Computers have also made employment more feasible, including home-based employment. Flexible work schedules, job sharing, and other programs to accommodate parents and older workers can also accommodate persons with disabilities.

Future technological probabilities. Technology holds enormous potential for easing and enriching the lives of persons with disabilities. For devices and equipment to be affordable under current business methods, they must be standardized, mass produced, and mass marketed. Individual needs often require unique technological solutions, and devices developed on a problem/solution basis cannot be standardized. Therefore, it's nearly impossible to mass produce and mass market such devices. However, under new business methods using computer-assisted design and manufacturing, customizing, or creating variations on a theme, is becoming economically feasible. New strategies to meet global competition by customizing can also be applied to the equipment or medical-device needs of persons with disabilities.

Technology will affect all aspects of a disabled person's life, such as education, health care, transportation, housing, occupations, and recreation. Some specific trends include:

- increased diversity among people, resulting from more individualized education and media
- easier access to all kinds of information
- decreased routine labor and physical labor
- less reliance on mass production of products and more access to custom-made products
- better communication devices, including computers with multimedia (screen, keyboard, and voice) input and output, resulting in a reduced need for physical transportation
- fewer large organizations and buildings and more use of the home as a place to learn and to work

Each of these trends will influence the future of persons with disabilities and their ability to live productive, independent lives.

Issue: Becoming More Independent

Throughout most of our history, people who were so severely disabled as to need an attendant had only two options:

- to be cared for by family or friends
- to live in a maintenance-care institution

The alternative of being provided with funds to live as an independent adult did not yet exist. By 1980 independent living was becoming the standard as a result of laws that recognized the human and monetary needs of the disabled.

Disability activists are owning their problem, saying they would rather take care of it themselves, and are demanding their rights. They have made their needs known to government entities at all levels. Their thesis is that people with disabilities, as the ones who share the needs, are uniquely qualified to plan ways of meeting those needs. They want to predominate in the advisory boards of professionally run agencies. They want to take over the key jobs of providing services to the disabled. The new type of service organization consists of independent living programs operated by and for the disabled (Crew and Zola 1983).

Self-Determination as Keystone

The independent living program is a community-based program with significant consumer involvement that provides services that persons with severe disabilities need in order to increase their self-determination and to minimize their dependence on others.

Persons with disabilities are now running many of the programs that offer a wide range of services never before offered to persons with all types of impairments. Some disability advocates, for example, help others find their way through bureaucratic red tape and regulatory obstacles. Others help severely disabled clients locate, select, and supervise personal attendants. Housing counselors help the disabled locate appropriate, accessible places to live. Transportation counselors, interpreter services, support groups, and peer counseling services are other types of programs that are found in some cities.

Other services include readers, advocacy or political action, financial counseling, training in independent living skills, equipment maintenance and repair, social or recreational opportunities, and information about other necessary services and products. The services are designed to serve the needs of persons in a particular community so that they need not move to a regional, state, or national facility. There are residential programs and transitional programs, as well as independent living centers. Persons with disabilities do most of the directing and managing and much of the staffing.

Independent Living Arrangements

The independent living setup can be as large and formal as an apartment complex of several hundred accessible, fully equipped units that offer extensive personal services and are planned along with adjacent accessible shopping and employment facilities. It can be as modest and informal as one person with a disability living in an ordinary apartment and having an agreement with a neighbor to provide needed morning and evening attendant care. Many in the disabled community believe that the full range of possibilities should be made available to allow for individual choice.

Individual choice is the keystone of independence. The independent living concept specifically includes the provision of needed assistance from other people that, when given, allows even very severely disabled people to live free from the control or determination of others. The goal is for persons with disabilities to take charge of their own lives and to allow them to contribute to an improved destiny for all people with disabilities.

Training for Assertive Communication

Assertiveness training offered by community organizations is becoming common for persons with disabilities. They are learning to speak up for their rights rather than leave the job to professional rehabilitators and other concerned advocates who are not themselves disabled. For example, they learn as patients how to interview physicians who say little or say it in technical jargon. They learn to get necessary information upon which to base their own decisions. They learn as students how to get helpful cooperation from teachers when they are physically unable to fulfill course requirements in the usual ways. As citizens, they learn to get the help that they're entitled to from agencies, without triggering resistance from agency workers. Persons with disabilities often rely on funds and services from public agencies, and failure to get what they need can mean poverty or institutionalization.

Training to Supervise Personal Service Employees

Supervisory training is essential for tactfully and assertively dealing with personal service employees, and community service organizations often provide this training. Many persons with disabilities must hire and supervise attendants, readers, drivers, or interpreters. Abuses are reported regularly, such as mistreatment, unreliability, exploitation, quitting without notice, and subtle cruelties of withholding help. This occurs when disabled employers don't know how to screen out poor risks during the hiring process or how to create a rewarding job for those they do hire. They must make the job intrinsically rewarding because the public funds provided often don't constitute a living wage. To survive, psychologically as well as physically, people using personal service providers must develop skill in their selection and supervision.

Education for Career Success

During the past few decades, public education for young people with disabilities has progressed from no education at all, to special education in segregated classrooms, to a concerted effort to integrate students with disabilities into mainstream schools. Major problems resulting from segregating disabled students from the mainstream include:

- Employers cannot imagine that job applicants with disabilities could function in their work settings because they never saw them functioning in school.
- Employees have trouble relating to co-workers with disabilities because they had no opportunities for contact from their earliest years.
- Students with disabilities do not get an equal education.
- Orientation toward college preparation is usually virtually absent.

The ILM recognizes that persons with disabilities must have access to optimal educational experiences in order to become self-sufficient.

Integration into Work and Community Life

The goal of the inner and outer struggles of the disabled is to break out of poverty and restrictive environments that offer nothing to do and no one to do it with. The goal is to stay out of institutions and back bedrooms and break into the mainstream of everything—school, work, politics, and love affairs. The ultimate goal is to live a more or less normal life in a fairly normal community. Integration into the workforce can be managed in a variety of ways, often in a gradual, step-by-step manner. An emerging trend is for employers to participate in this process by giving on-the-job training to the disabled. These trends are discussed in the last part of this chapter. A related goal is to change society's image of persons with disabilities—from that of pathetic victims to a more positive image of "people like you and me, who happen to have a disability." As such, they're entitled to basic human rights. The disabled have the right to participate, to give and receive, and to take risks like anyone else. The ADA, which we'll discuss next, is based on this belief.

SHOWCASE
Ed Roberts: Success Story of a Person with Severe Disability

In 1962, when Ed Roberts, paralyzed from the neck down, applied for help from the California Department of Rehabilitation, they said no. The counselors argued that it was "infeasible" to think that Ed would ever be able to work. But Ed was persistent; he was accustomed to fighting such battles. At age 14 he had polio and heard the doctor tell his mother, "It would be better if Ed died because he's going to be a vegetable." Right then Ed decided that if he was going to be a vegetable, he'd be an artichoke: prickly on the outside, with a tender heart. His motto was "I'm paralyzed from the neck down, not from the neck up." He used his tough mind and soft heart to fight for disabled persons' rights and to change forever their place in society.

Ed had to persuade his high school principal at Burlingame High to give him his diploma even though he had not completed required classes in physical education and driver's education. He won that battle, and in 1962 he won the battle to get into the University of California at Berkeley, one of the top-ranking U.S. universities. On Ed's first day he was lifted out of his wheelchair and carried up the steps to Room 201 of Cal Hall. A local newspaper headline read, "Helpless Cripple Attends UC Classes."

Later, he organized a group of mobility-impaired students who called themselves the Rolling Quads. They in turn started the Physically Disabled Students' program at UC Berkeley, with the main goal of solving all problems that created barriers to academic achievement. They provided such services as finding attendants, accessible apartments, and 24-hour emergency wheelchair repair service. A broken wheelchair could mean weeks of missed class sessions.

When Ed graduated from UC Berkeley in 1972 he and fellow students founded the Center for Independent Living. It became the model for similar centers across the nation. Ed also founded the Independent Living Movement. In 1975, he became the head of the California Department of Rehabilitation, the very same state agency that had at first opposed helping him go to school. He held that position for seven years, until 1982.

In 1984 Ed Roberts was awarded a MacArthur Foundation "genius" award of $225,000, which he used to establish the World Institute on Disability, an influential policy and research center based in Oakland, California. When he died at age 56 in 1995, colleagues called him "the Gandhi of the disability rights movement."

LEADERSHIP CHALLENGES AND OPPORTUNITIES

Workers and applicants with disabilities offer some of the greatest opportunities and challenges to business leaders. Leaders can help to integrate them into the workforce, gaining an important asset and performing a service to the community. Leaders can participate in various job training programs and design on-the-job training that helps persons with disabilities use their abilities. Leaders can adopt positive attitudes toward workers with disabilities and encourage others to do the same. They can make sure the Americans with Disabilities Act is followed both in letter and spirit. They can go beyond ADA requirements in helping to change the corporate culture to one that is friendly and accommodating to employees with disabilities.

Leadership Challenge: Making Reasonable Accommodation

Leaders are beginning to realize that it makes good business sense to accommodate persons with disabilities, for they usually make excellent employees. In addition to complying with the law, companies enrich their talent pool. The 1990 federal ADA is aimed at virtually all government and private business operations. Its main provisions are set out in five sections or titles, as shown in Table 9.2 (Bureau of National Affairs 1990; McGovern 1991; Potter 1991).

TABLE 9.2: Major Sections of the 1990 Americans with Disabilities Act

Section	Purpose
Title I Employment	Prohibits employment discrimination
Title II. State and Local Governments	Requires accessibility and prohibits employment discrimination, similar to the 1973 law.
Title III. Public Accommodations	Requires accessibility to restaurants, theaters, stores, etc.
Title IV. Telecommunications	Requires accommodations, such as telephone relays for the deaf.
Title V. Miscellaneous	Catchall section with a variety of technical provisions.

Most large corporations have set up ADA task forces to ensure that all the provisions are met. Some smaller business owners have formed regional groups by type of business, such as restaurant, clothing store, or grocery store owner associations. Such associations plan their response to the ADA with the help of professionals, such as consultants and attorneys, and take the large-corporation viewpoint in handling the changes. For example, some send newsletters to employees to inform them of the provisions of the act, proper etiquette in dealing with persons with disabilities, hiring techniques, what the business is doing to adhere to the act, and other helpful information.

Keystone: Equal Opportunity and Reasonable Accommodation

The major stated goal of the ADA is for organizations to manage their affairs in a manner that includes all groups of applicants and workers with disabilities, where reasonable accommodation can make inclusion possible. The major factor that determines if an accommodation is reasonable is whether it imposes an undue hardship on the employer. Another ADA goal is to increase the employment rate of persons with disabilities in order to reduce the cost of government subsidies to them and to enable them to enjoy a more productive, satisfying lifestyle.

The major provisions of the ADA are (1) to require employers to clearly state bona fide job requirements, (2) to provide equal opportunities for qualified persons with disabilities who can meet the job requirements, and (3) to provide reasonable accommodations that will allow otherwise qualified persons with disabilities to do the job, as long as such accommodations don't cause undue hardship for the employer.

Clearly Stating Job Requirements

Job descriptions are a key factor in preventing unnecessary discrimination against the disabled. Essential job functions must be clearly spelled out. If physical ability is essential, the exact activities must be specified; for example, "lift a 5-pound packet 5 to 10 times a day." Requirements that are not truly necessary to do the job must be eliminated.

Providing Equal Opportunity

The ADA states that a job candidate may not be discriminated against on the basis of disability, history of disability, or perception of disability. In the past, most employers would not consider hiring candidates who have been in mental institutions, who have a history of epileptic seizures, who have attended classes or schools for the mentally retarded, or have similar indications of disability. The tendency was to see only the potential problems and ignore the positive contributions such persons can make.

The ADA bars discrimination in all aspects of employment, including hiring, compensation, training, and promotion. Employers also must give disabled employees equal access to employee benefits, including medical insurance.

Providing Reasonable Accommodation

Title I of the ADA focuses on "reasonable accommodation" by employers for disabled workers, where such reasonable accommodation will allow them to do the work. All employees must be given reasonable accommodation, whether they're new employees, have been with the company for some time, or become impaired after being hired.

Reasonable accommodation can occur during the recruiting and hiring phase and includes accommodation in job descriptions, medical tests, employment tests, job interviews, and all other pre-employment activities.

Human resource professionals must determine ways to make testing and interviewing procedures realistic and fair for all persons. Persons with disabilities who are fully competent to meet the demands of a job may have difficulties in completing the normal job-screening process successfully. Be sure that testing procedures actually measure those performance capabilities that are required by the target job and that tests are required for bona fide job requirements only.

Medical screening. Companies cannot perform medical screening prior to hiring a person. That means they cannot require applicants to provide a medical history, nor can they require them to pass any short of medical test. After hiring, medical screening and other types of screening are permitted only if all workers are included. Those who are thought to be disabled cannot be singled out.

Employment tests. Reasonable accommodation must be provided for persons with disabilities. For example, reasonable accommodation for visually impaired persons might include reading the test to them or providing the test in large print or Braille. Tests must truly measure whether or not candidates have the ability or potential to be successful on the job.

Job interviews. Interviewing procedures must protect persons with disabilities from discrimination. For example, interviewers cannot legally ask job applicants about such matters as physical or mental impairments, medical history, drinking habits, or phobias. What if an applicant voluntarily discloses a disability? The interviewer is not legally allowed to follow up with questions about the disability. It is *not* all right to ask directly about a disability, but it *is* all right to ask persons with disabilities whether they can and would do a particular type of work or job and how they would manage the job. There is a fine line between legal and illegal questions here, for *the interviewer cannot ask what kind of accommodation the applicant might need to perform the job until a conditional job offer is made.* After this point, applicants can be asked to demonstrate or describe how they would do the job. If applicants indicate the need for an accommodation, the employer must either provide reasonable accommodation for the demonstration or allow the applicants to merely describe how they would perform this function.

On-the-job accommodations. The key questions for employers are:

- What are the one or two things I must do as an employer in order to give this person an opportunity to succeed?
- How can I level the playing field for this person?

Reasonable accommodation for some jobs, especially professional or technical positions, might be as easy as providing an amplified telephone receiver or larger computer screen. It is frequently an action as simple as providing flexible scheduling for work arrival and departure. It might include providing an interpreter for a hearing-impaired worker to attend a training session on reassigning job functions so that a wheelchair user handles telephone calls while another employee stores and retrieves folders in file cabinets.

Protection from Undue Hardship

The ADA states that employers are not required to make accommodations that would cause them undue hardship. This exemption applies when the measures necessary to allow a disabled person to do a job are unduly expensive or interfere with a business necessity. The major test is how the accommodation would affect the entire budget of the organization. Most cases of undue hardship occur in small businesses. Some don't have the profit margin, cash flow, or capital cushion to take such measures as remodeling a building or providing readers or interpreters. What constitutes undue hardship is decided on a case-by-case basis, since the range of disabilities and types of jobs are so vast that no set of legal formulas could begin to cover them. Some guidelines may eventually be worked out through precedents set in court cases.

No-Cost and Small-Cost Accommodations

Most accommodations cost nothing at all (Berkeley 1992; Shapiro 1994). The great majority of accommodations are easily made by even the smallest businesses. Often it's as simple as allowing more flexible times to arrive and depart from work or rearranging a work area. Studies of costs in 1992 indicate the following:

- Fifty-one percent of all accommodations cost nothing
- For the other 49 percent, the average cost of an accommodation is $300.
- Less than 1 percent of accommodations cost $5,000 or more.

Many companies are discovering that just by being flexible and opening up their attitudes toward persons with disabilities, they gain workers who are highly committed, productive, and loyal.

Leadership Challenge: Clearing the Barriers

Persons with disabilities report that major problems they face as employees are (WSJ 1994):

- Transportation to work is inadequate or difficult.
- Employers are insensitive to their disabilities.
- Co-workers tend not to socialize with them.

Transportation barriers are probably the simplest to overcome. Major cities now must modify their public transportation systems to provide lifts and ramps for persons with mobility impairments. Also, managers can work with these employees to solve transportation problems. The sensitivity and socializing issues are related to corporate culture and to level of employee awareness. Companies that have taken a leadership role in disability issues are providing training sessions for all employees in order to raise their awareness and provide skills for working effectively with this group. Influencing corporate culture change can open up many opportunities to utilize the talents of persons with disabilities—as well as other groups that are disadvantaged in the workplace. We'll discuss this later.

Taking a broad view of how to integrate persons with disabilities in the mainstream workplace, disability advocate Carolyn Vash (1980) has identified five levels on an ascending scale of increasing integration:

- home-based or homebound employment, which is being upgraded with the advent of computer and telecommunications technology
- sheltered workshops that hire predominantly workers with disabilities
- semi-integrated units in mainstream industry that offer some disability-related accommodations and some shelter
- fully integrated employment in mainstream industry with some disability-related accommodation
- competitive employment with no disability-related accommodation

We've discussed some of the ways in which technology can substitute for sensory and motor capacities. This opens up occupational options previously considered unavailable to those with given disabilities. They are therefore able to engage in higher-level and more demanding kinds of work. With computer modems, fax machines, and similar technology, many computer-based types of work can be done at home, which eliminates the transportation barrier.

Sheltered workshops and semi-integrated units of workers with disabilities are approaches used by the *crews* programs (Community Rehabilitative Employment Work Sites). This type of training program provides a gradual shift from rehabilitation training to on-the-job training to regular employment. About 70 percent of trainees in *crews* programs have mental disabilities, such as learning problems or retardation. They work in groups at workshops located in centers for persons with mental impairments. They are trained and supervised by trainers familiar with the skills needed by particular industries, such as assembling and packaging skills. Once trainees become productive, they are paid by the center to perform work for affiliated private businesses, who in turn pay the center.

Cooperating with On-the-Job Training

Sheltered workshops and semi-integrated work units can be provided by companies that need committed workers. The growing trend in such work preparation programs is to use mainstream industry as the setting for work training, evaluation, and adjustment, instead of using rehabilitation facilities. The trainees get acclimated to actual business situations, and employers and employees get to know the trainees through the relatively nonthreatening training process. Actual job performance sampling is also the best predictor of job success and the best way to identify problem areas and needs for further training.

Providing for Ongoing Training and Development

Some studies indicate that most organizations are less likely to provide training and development opportunities to employees with disabilities than to other employees. This reinforces a tendency for persons with disabilities to define their viable career options rather narrowly. Leaders can encourage broader definitions of career goals, help persons with disabilities to develop career plans, and provide the appropriate training and development opportunities. Reasonable accommodation in the training function can pay off handsomely (Stace 1987; Curnow 1989).

Leadership Opportunity: Opening Up the Corporate Culture

Highly qualified persons with disabilities are most likely to apply to companies that have corporate environments that are friendly to them. They're most likely to be productive in such companies and to stay with them. Environments are likely to change when leaders recognize the many benefits that employees with disabilities bring to the organization, from skills and commitment, to connection with a multibillion-dollar marketplace.

The most important step in changing the culture is for top management to attend training sessions that provide information and encourage opening up attitudes about persons with disabilities. When top management makes a commitment to providing an environment that welcomes persons with disabilities, the next step is to provide similar training for every employee. Other steps include actively recruiting persons with disabilities as job candidates, providing those who are hired with mentorship programs, and encouraging them to form their own employees' organizations and networks.

Providing Diversity Training for All Employees

Employee training should include exploring the beliefs, myths, and stereotypes that lead to devaluation of the disabled; giving accurate information about current facts, trends, issues, and profiles; and developing approaches that help co-workers appreciate all persons with disabilities and work effectively with them. Training should include positive attitudes and language as well as specific information on how to relate to and assist people with various specific disabilities. As co-workers become better able to see beyond a person's abilities or disabilities and to form relationships with the "normal" core person within, the quality of work life is further enhanced. Training should include some guidelines for personal interactions with the disabled. For example, helpers should not rush in and take over when they think a person with disability needs help, such as finding the way or getting through a door. They should ask whether and what type of help is needed. The Additional Background Information section at the end of this chapter gives extensive guidelines and suggestions for assisting persons with various types of impairment.

Adopting Positive Attitudes Toward Employees with Disabilities

The following are some constructive attitudes that business leaders can adopt for working with the disabled, attitudes that leaders can encourage among all employees.

Realize that people with disabilities are not all alike. They have some common experiences and they are also highly diverse. On the one hand, many ask to be considered in the same vein as an ethnic minority. Most belong, in varying degrees, to a disabled community, with distinct cultural values, vocabulary, in-jokes, mutual support, and common issues. On the other hand, they ask that we also think in terms of diversity, for their disabilities and abilities range widely. Each person has his or her individual strengths, weaknesses, and peculiarities.

Focus on what people can do. The traditional tendency is to focus on the impairment. Cooperate with these employees in taking a can-do attitude. Focus also on what people, disabled and nondisabled, can do together. See persons with disabilities as basically normal people who happen to have lost some function. Recognize that this does not define their character. They are people first, and their disability is only something they must cope with; it's not who they are.

Move through fear of disablement. Be aware of the fear of many people, perhaps your own unconscious fear, of being around persons with disabilities. Others typically do not want to be reminded, "There but for the grace of God go I. This could happen to me." Almost everyone has fear around the issues of body image and brain power.

Accept persons with disabilities as normal persons. Don't think of them as sick, as patients, as victims, or as abnormal. Remember that we all have some disability; it's just a matter of degree. Most persons with disabilities can marry, have sex, have children, and live many aspects of a "normal" life. The key is that they must work in order to have a full life. Their resources must be used in order for them to gain the sense of purpose, meaning, and achievement that all people want in life.

Explore possibilities for persons with mental retardation. Even the mentally retarded can usually do some sort of meaningful work. Some are classified as "high functioning mentally retarded" or "high functioning Down's syndrome."

Never treat persons with disabilities as if they're childlike or childish. Some persons with disabilities, especially the mentally impaired, may appear childlike to some people because of certain mannerisms that go along with their impairment. Respect for them as adults is essential. So are realistic assessments of their capabilities and the tailoring of assignments, expectations, and guidance to fit their level of ability.

Focus on the benefits. Research indicates that employees with disabilities tend to be:

* very enthusiastic—because they're happy to have real employment
* eager to succeed—they're adaptable and cooperative
* absent and tardy less
* a terrific resource—one that has been wasted in the past

This adds up to highly committed, loyal employees.

Using Positive Language

Certain language habits tend to focus on a person's disabilities rather than to focus on the person and to support stereotypes.

Avoid shorthand terms, such as *the disabled* except when referring to them as a protected class. In most contexts *the disabled* doesn't acknowledge the persons at all and focuses only on the disabilities. The term *disabled persons* at least acknowledges that persons are being discussed, but *persons with disabilities* is even better because it puts persons first. Where appropriate, more specific terms are better yet; for example, *persons with visual impairments*.

Avoid such phrases as "John is a diabetic," and use instead "John has diabetes." When you say that someone *is* an alcoholic, arthritic, drug addict, or mental retardate, the implication is that he or she is nothing more than that. More realistic language is "Sue has a drinking problem" or "Jan has a learning impairment."

Prefer the active to the passive, such as "person who uses a wheelchair" instead of "person confined to a wheelchair," or "He is a wheelchair user" instead of "He is wheelchair bound."

Use tact in dealing with disabilities. In some cases, persons with disabilities do not want to deal with their disability. They don't want to talk abut it or be reminded of it. This presents the greatest challenge for the manager.

Making Marketplace Connections

Employees with disabilities are a valuable resource for understanding this market of nearly 50 million consumers. They can help the company create communication bridges for marketing to persons with disabilities. In 1994, disabled persons' incomes came to over $700 billion. Yet many companies have made no efforts to target this huge market. Those who do are likely to find some profitable niches.

Companies that design products and services for disability markets often find an even larger general market for the same or similar products and services. This principle is sometimes called *universal design*. Designs that work for persons with disabilities are also frequently more workable for the rest of the population. Examples include big-buttons telephones, voice-recognition and voice-output computers, safer bathtubs, easier-to-open boxes, and easy-to-grip tools. Special service designs can also apply to larger markets. For example, personal services targeted at disability markets, such as grocery shopping and home meal delivery, can also fill a need for working mothers and others.

Following the Lead of Successful Companies

Hewlett Packard is on the top ten list of corporations that actively recruit from a pool of disabled workers. Executives say that the "HP Way" is to treat persons with disabilities with dignity and respect. Hewlett Packard was among the first large corporations to set policies for a disability-sensitive workplace. The company holds seminars to inform all employees about various types of disabilities. It also has a mentorship program and employee network for employees with disabilities.

SUMMARY

Persons with disabilities are those who have a physical or mental impairment that substantially limits one or more of the major life activities, or a record of such impairment, or are regarded as having such an impairment. They're generally stereotyped as posing difficulties as workers, but managers and co-workers report that they are just as productive and cooperative as other workers and that they tend to have better records of punctuality, attendance, and turnover. Most want to work and to lead lives that are as normal as possible. Their abilities and motivations to work are as wide-ranging as that of the general public with the exception of their having an impairment in one or more activities. Before the 1930s most persons with disabilities were confined to institutions. Disability activists have brought about a realization that when certain accommodations are made, most persons with disabilities can become relatively independent and productive.

About 49 million Americans fall under the ADA definition, and about 16 million of these are employed. Leaders and co-workers need to understand what it's like to be a person with disabilities, to become aware that they are normal persons except for a specific impairment, and they want more than anything to lead a normal life. They want to be viewed as a person, not as "a disabled." The ILM was founded to help persons with disabilities take charge of their own lives, to form their own subculture, and to remove barriers to living and working on their own. New technology, especially computer-based technology, is helping more and more persons with even severe disabilities to achieve these goals.

Leaders need to understand the basic requirements of the ADA and to make sure that company policies and procedures are in line. During the job recruitment phase, companies can no longer do medical screening or require medical histories. After hiring, workers with disabilities cannot be singled out for medical tests and screening. Reasonable accommodation must be made for applicants taking employment tests, and such screening tests must truly predict the likelihood of job success. The heart of the ADA is the requirement that employers make "reasonable accommodation" that will allow persons with disabilities to do a job.

The major challenge for leaders is finding ways to help employees with disabilities to eliminate and overcome barriers to their productivity and effectiveness. The experience of other companies in making reasonable accommodation indicates that this usually costs nothing. It only requires an open, inquiring attitude and a willingness to cooperate with these employees. Accommodations that would work a hardship on a business are not considered "reasonable accommodation" and are therefore not required. The main thing to remember when you want to personally assist a person with disability is to first ask what kind of help they would like, as the guidelines in the next section indicate.

BONUS:
ANSWERS TO FREQUENTLY ASKED QUESTIONS

Leaders and employees usually have limited experience in working with persons with disabilities, and therefore questions arise as day-to-day interactions occur. Questions range from, "When should I help an employee using a wheelchair?" to " How do I plan staff meetings that include a deaf employee?"

The "help issue" affects persons with many types of disabilities. The key concept is *respect*. Always remember that the person with the disability is the one who makes the decisions about whether help is needed, what kind, how, when, where, etc. Respect her or his autonomy; don't take over or join with others to run the show. Other general principles that can provide guidance in giving help include (Maloff and Macduff 1988):

- Offer help; it's never the wrong thing to do. It can always be declined if not wanted.

- Always ask first if the person wants you to help.

- Be prepared to take no for an answer, and take no offense.

- If your offer to help is accepted, then ask specifically what needs to be done and how to do it, or suggest something and get agreement.

- If someone is already helping and it appears that additional assistance may be needed, get instructions from the person with disability, not from the helper.

- Handle the helping situation as unobtrusively as possible. Keep any surrounding commotion to a minimum.

Use this section as a reference manual for those relatively rare occasions when you will be working with the following types of employees:

- mobility impaired co-workers

- visually impaired co-workers

- hearing- and/or speaking-impaired co-workers

- hearing-impaired co-workers

- speaking-impaired co-workers

Mobility–Impaired Co-workers: Guidelines

Q: How do I show consideration for people who use crutches, braces, canes, or wheelchairs to get around?

- Never grab disabled persons or their appliances except in cases of obvious immediate physical danger.

- After helping, stay a moment and make sure matters are in hand before leaving. Be sure the person knows you are leaving, so you don't leave them stranded.

- Respect the personal space. Wheelchairs, crutches, or other appliances should not be touched without permission.

Doors may be a difficult barrier. Everyone can use help with doors, including elevator doors, at times, and persons with mobility impairments are no exception.

- Hold the door itself rather than trying to grab an arm or push a wheelchair.

- Hold the door open until all parts of the person and all related appliances are totally inside.

Wheelchair users have a specific set of needs and considerations.

- Avoid blocking aisles, passageways, and other spaces that a wheelchair user needs to access; use tables or desks for depositing briefcases, etc.; push chairs under tables or desks; be aware.

- When having a conversation with a wheelchair user, position yourself so that it will be comfortable for the person to look at you. Try to seat yourself in front of the person, so you can talk eye to eye. If you must stand, step back so the person is not required to look up to you.

- Reaching elevator buttons may be impossible for a wheelchair user; offer to help.

- Users of non-motorized wheelchairs sometimes need help getting up hills and inclines or around barriers; offer to help.

- Never begin pushing a wheelchair without first asking the occupant's permission.

- Never release the chair without first making this intention known so the wheelchair user is always in control.

- Be sure you know exactly where the person wants to go.

- Begin pushing a wheelchair cautiously if you are not familiar with it. Go slowly at first; wheelchairs can gain surprising momentum.

- Note the size and protrusions of the chair, such as protruding foot plates. Pay attention to the terrain, such as soft spots, potholes, and stepdowns, and watch where you're going.

- When entering a crosswalk in a street, remember the wheelchair user's feet may be further out than you think and may be dangerously close to passing traffic.

- Going up steps, lean the chair back to raise the front wheels and push the chair up frontwards.

- Going down steps, ask if the person prefers going down frontwards or backwards. Either way, raise the front wheels and keep them up until the entire chair is down the step. The occupant should always be tilted toward the back against the backrest instead of toward the front where there is no support.

Q: How do I show consideration for persons who walk with difficulty?

- When approaching steps with a person who walks with difficulty, walk at his or her side and extend an arm to be used for support and balance. If more help is needed, put your arm around his or her waist as you go up or down.

- Do not grab a mobility-impaired person by the arm; this offers little support and may throw the person off balance.

- If the person wants to negotiate the stairs unassisted, get out of the way.

- Any time a person falls, ask if assistance is wanted, or offer your arm for the fallen person to take if he or she needs it. Don't grab the person.

Q: What should I consider when I'm planning activities that require mobility-impaired persons to go to unfamiliar places?

- Mobility-impaired persons need to know in advance whether they will encounter a difficult barrier. The most common areas of difficulty are parking places, steps, and restrooms. Learn to observe these three important architectural features.

- Find out if the person needs extra space for their vehicle and for maneuvering a wheelchair in and out of a vehicle. Must they park near the building?

- Wheelchair users must have access to restrooms with hallways and doors wide enough for the chair. They must have sufficient space inside the stall to accommodate the chair. They may need a hand bar by the commode.

- Never insist on simply carrying a disabled person over, around, and through obstacles. They may find it demeaning, unpleasant, or even scary—and it could be dangerous for both of you. All of us prefer to be independent and self-possessed.

- When in doubt, ask the disabled person for some tips on restaurants and other public places that are accessible and comfortable.

VISUALLY IMPAIRED CO-WORKERS: GUIDELINES

The single most useful thing you may be able to do for visually impaired persons is to furnish relevant information about the immediate surroundings. Often just a few words will do.

Q: What should I consider when giving directions to visually impaired co-workers?

A: Here are some general principles:

- Furnish simple information without hesitation, anytime it seems appropriate.
- For a more active form of assistance, always ask first whether help is wanted.
- If your offer is accepted, be sure you understand what needs to be done before taking action.
- Follow through to the natural conclusion; don't leave the person hanging and perhaps worse off than when you began.

B: Here are some specific principles for giving directions:

- Be sure you really know where the target location is. If you don't know, you may try to get assistance from someone who does know. If that's impractical, admit you don't know rather than send the person on a possible wild-goose chase.
- Find out what types of directions are most helpful; this will depend on what the person can see or not see. Use numbers, where possible. Ask yourself, How many blocks down the street? How many doors down the hall?
- Give directions that are as specific as possible. Describe turns or curves as *left, right, clockwise,* etc. Terms such as north or south will probably be irrelevant.
- Describe anything out of the ordinary along the way, such as possible safety hazards, one-way traffic, sidewalk construction.
- Tell persons with some vision about noticeable landmarks, such as large trees or buildings.
- Be as complete as necessary without overloading the person with information.
- If you think the place is simply too hard to find, offer to act as escort, if possible.

Q: What should I do when I'm walking with a visually impaired person?

- City streets pose one of the biggest hazards for visually impaired persons. Offer your arm, but do not clutch the person's arm. Before giving any assistance at an intersection, be sure you understand which street the person wants to cross.

- Don't leave the person until she or he is safely up the opposite curb.
- If the person does not take your arm, walk closely enough for her or him to reach over and touch you. Avoid getting separated in crowds.
- If the person takes your arm, walk slightly ahead to guide the way and proceed normally. Never push the person ahead of you.
- When walking with a visually impaired person, avoid sudden turns or jerky movements.
- Tell the person when it's time to step up, step down, or step around some obstacle.
- Remember to watch for overhead obstacles, especially with a taller companion.
- When approaching steps, elevators, or other possible barriers, pause and briefly describe what's ahead.

Canes are sometimes used by visually impaired persons to help them avoid obstacles.

- If a person touches your foot with a cane, step aside and let her or him pass.
- Don't touch a cane without permission, and never grab a cane while the person is using it.
- When walking with a person who uses a cane, offer your arm.

Guide dogs are used by a minority of visually impaired persons to help them get around. Dogs that are used by mobility impaired persons to perform certain tasks are called service dogs. In both instances they're likely to be either Labrador retrievers or German shepherds. The same behavioral principles apply to interacting with both types of dogs and their masters.

- A guide dog is on duty any time it is wearing a harness.
- Take care to do nothing that will interfere with the dog's performance. Have faith in the dog and do not interfere unless there is a genuine emergency.
- Don't disrupt the routine and training by touching, feeding, petting, playing with, or otherwise distracting such a dog, unless you're encouraged to do so.
- Don't speak to the dog or attempt to give it commands. If you have pets in the area, keep them away from the dog.
- When walking with someone who is using a dog, offer your arm.

Q: What should I consider when I'm communicating with visually impaired persons?

A: Be aware that they rely on sound and touch to know what's going on; here are some suggestions:

- When you first meet a visually impaired person, feel free to shake hands. You might say, "May I shake your hand?" to cue them that you're extending your hand. When you meet the person thereafter, identify yourself; if you're with other people, identify them as well.
- When you would normally hand a business associate a business card, brochure, or other written material, give the visually impaired person the option to accept or to refuse. If the person accepts the material, you might offer to stay a moment and help deal with it.
- When you need to communicate with persons who are so visually impaired that they cannot see to read written material, keep in mind that someone will have to read any written message you send and format it accordingly. For most messages, use the telephone. Consider dictating an audiotape.

- When you enter the presence of visually impaired persons, speak to them and let them know you're there. Otherwise they may be unduly jolted when they hear you make some noise. Also, let them know when you're leaving.

- When leaving in a public place, say how long you'll be gone. Consider whether you need to offer to guide the person to a chair, wall, or post where he or she can wait comfortably.

- When visually impaired persons hear your voice, they may be unsure whether you are talking to them or to someone else. They may remain silent rather than respond to comments they think might be meant for someone else. Address them by name when you're in a group or in public. If you don't know their name, stand directly in front of them and begin speaking. You may also gently touch their arm or repeat yourself to be sure they understand.

- Offer to describe visual sights. Although people with visual impairments learn to use their other senses to get in touch with their surroundings, most enjoy descriptions from their sighted friends when there are interesting things to see.

- Don't yell. It's not necessary or desirable to speak loudly to visually impaired persons, unless they also have a hearing impairment.

- One of the most helpful things a friend can do for visually impaired persons is to speak up when some aspect of their grooming seems unpremeditated. The sooner they're informed of the matter, the sooner they will be able to correct it.

- While sudden or pervasive loud noises are a problem for visually-impaired people, the normal sounds of living give them valuable information. It's not necessary or desirable for bystanders to quit talking when a visually impaired person comes near.

When making plans that include visually-impaired persons, consider the following:

- If you're planning to meet outside the office, the key issue is likely to be transportation. If an invitation does not include provision for transportation, visually impaired persons are likely to appreciate some advance notice so they can arrange for a ride.

- If you're planning an activity and are not sure whether a visually impaired person would be able to participate or would want to be included, ask. Invite them and allow them to make the decision; then respect their wishes.

- If you go to a restaurant with visually impaired persons, remember to offer help in reading the menu. During the meal, help flag down the server if they need something. When the server arrives, let it be known, and, of course, allow them to make their own requests.

Hearing- and/or Speaking-Impaired Co-workers: Guidelines

Hearing and speaking impairments are not apparent to the casual observer, making this group one of the most invisible subgroups of disabled persons. A common misconception about communication impairments is that hearing and speaking impairments always go hand in hand. In fact most people with speaking impairments have normal hearing. Many hearing-impaired persons have excellent speech skills, particularly those whose hearing impairment is not of long standing or is not severe. Here are some guidelines:

- When you initiate a direct conversation with communication-impaired persons, begin by asking, orally or in writing, how best to communicate.

- Communication may be difficult at first but usually improves with a little patience and experimentation.

• When introducing communication-impaired persons to others, make every effort to introduce only one or two persons at a time. If possible, steer the persons to a quiet spot. Pronounce names slowly and distinctly, or use whatever type of communication is appropriate. Tell the people involved a little about each other and stay a few moments to help get the conversation started.

If you are asked to make a telephone call for a communication-impaired person, be sure you understand ahead of time what needs to be accomplished by the call. If necessary, have the person write key pieces of information. Before you hang up, check with the sender to be sure the message is complete. After you hang up, give the person a complete report on the transaction.

Hearing-impaired and speaking-impaired persons have some common problems and ways of solving them. For example, the methods or devices used by both may include the following.

Lipreading, or speechreading, is a skill developed by many hearing-impaired persons to augment their ability to understand speech by watching mouth movements. It involves observing the visible sounds and using skillful guesswork and reading nonverbal signals to fill in the blanks. Lipreading is most effective when combined with partial hearing.

When talking to persons who use lipreading and have partial hearing, position yourself about three or four feet directly in front of them. Try to have the light falling on your face. Be sure that your mouth is clearly visible and that your voice carries well. Face them squarely without looking down or turning your head. Keep your hands away from your mouth and avoid eating, smoking, chewing gum, and other activities that inhibit lipreading.

Be aware that lipreading and listening are tiring for many persons. Don't run them ragged with long monologues. Use a give-and-take format. For long conversations, ask them if they would like a rest period now and then.

Reading nonverbal messages, such as gestures, body language, and facial expressions, is crucial for the hearing impaired. Be aware of the increased importance of using these nonverbal forms of communication. Your eyes are especially expressive, so remove dark glasses, hats, or any other impediments. Maintain a natural and relaxed manner without straining to exaggerate. Anytime nonverbal communication does not seem to be getting the idea across, use other methods. When both speaking and using gestures, be sure the gestures correlate with the speech. Random motions throw the listener off balance trying to sift them from the real clues.

Sign language and finger spelling are related methods of communication that use the hands. In sign language, entire words and phrases are expressed with a single hand symbol. In finger spelling, each letter of the alphabet is represented by a certain hand symbol, and words are spelled out. The two methods are usually used together. Names and unusual words are spelled out, while others are signed. Many hearing-impaired people are skilled at this type of communication. Learning sign language is difficult and time-consuming. Finger spelling involves learning only 26 symbols and can be mastered in a few hours. It is a useful skill for people who occasionally deal with the deaf.

Writing out messages is slow but is sometimes used. Be creative when you communicate in writing. Often a simple diagram, picture, or map is most effective. Watch the person's face as he or she reads your message, just as you would do if you were speaking, so you can gauge his or her understanding and reaction. When persons begin writing to you, don't talk or otherwise distract them until they finish. Allow them to finish writing before you try to read the message, and read the entire message before you begin to answer. In a group, you can help by offering to read the person's written message aloud to others.

• Avoid engaging the interpreter in side conversations that exclude the person with the impairment.

• Remember that with any translation process certain subtleties may not quite survive intact. Choose simple, specific words to be as clear and direct as possible, avoiding slang.

Professional interpreters may be used by people with severe impairments. Interpreters have normal hearing and speaking abilities plus a special communication skill, usually sign language. When you speak through an interpreter, your key goal should be to respect the dignity and autonomy of the impaired person who is the "listener." The interpreter is merely a device in this situation, a tool. Face the hearing-impaired person and speak as though no interpreter were present—as if the interpreter were a computerized voice synthesizer, for example. Direct all your comments to the listener, the person with whom you have business, saying, for example, "Your project is being reviewed." The interpreter will relay these exact words to the person. Never direct comments intended for the listener to the interpreter, saying "His project is being reviewed." This has the effect of excluding the listener, implying that he is a helpless bystander. Remember to look at the listener, not the translator, and to speak to her or him in direct address, using *you*, not *he* or *she*.

A telecommunication device for the deaf (*TDD*) is used by many people with speaking or hearing impairments for communicating by telephone. The device has a keyboard for typing messages and a screen for viewing them. Both parties of the conversation must be using a TDD device for the system to work.

If you don't have a TDD, you can still communicate through the device by going through a voice exchange system, available in most cities. The voice exchange operator will speak and listen to you over one telephone line and communicate with the other person via TDD on another line. You should speak slowly so the operator has time to type your message to the other party, then wait while the other person types a response and the operator reads it to you

With telephone relay systems, two deaf persons can communicate with each other via telephone, and of course a nondeaf person could also communicate with a deaf person. Here's how the system works: A deaf (or nondeaf) person (person A) wants to place a call to a deaf (or nondeaf) person. He or she calls the operator and requests translator equipment. The operator routes the call through the equipment and then connects the caller with person B. The translator equipment allows the two persons to communicate as follows:

Person A—>Telephone Operator—>Translator equipment—>
—>Person B—>Translator equipment—>Person A

Telephone communication with a hearing-impaired is often possible without translator equipment, if the person has enough hearing ability, but even then it poses some special challenges. Avoid calling just to chat, unless you have been encouraged to do so. When you do call, try to quiet the noise at your end. Organize your message ahead of time so you can convey it in a concise, direct manner. Talk directly into the receiver clearly and firmly. Speak moderately slowly and pause at the end of a sentence. Be prepared to spell, rephrase, or use more creative ways to get your message across. If you have trouble hearing or understanding, ask for clarification as soon as you start getting lost. Keep the conversation short unless you are encouraged to extend it.

Staff meetings and similar meetings pose special problems for the communication-impaired persons. If you are in charge, use the following guidelines:

- Select a room with good acoustics and a minimum of extraneous noise.
- Check ahead of time to determine what devices, such as interpreters, are needed. Offer the people with impairments preferential seating, where they will have a good view of speakers. Ask what they prefer. The best spot may be in the front row or at the head of a rectangular table; on a panel, it may be near the center.
- Ask speakers to stay in one spot rather than pacing the floor, for lip-readers.
- Pay special attention to the use of visual aids, handouts, charts, illustrations, and other communication aids. Write down new words or terms as you introduce them; it is almost impossible to lipread an unknown word. Write down

important facts. Repeat all comments or questions from other people in the room before you respond to them.

- If you sit next to a hearing-impaired person in a meeting, be as quiet as possible. If you must communicate with the person during the meeting, write a brief note. Allow the hearing person to observe any notes you're taking, and offer to fill him or her in afterwards on any points that were missed.

- Make occasional eye contact with speaking-impaired persons, to see if they have anything to contribute to the discussion. If they can't speak up quickly, creating a break in the conversation for them may give the encouragement they need.

- If you set next to a speaking impaired person, offer to ask questions for her or him during the meeting.

Hearing-Impaired Co-workers: Guidelines

Hearing-impaired persons may have any degree of hearing loss, from mild to complete. Once you become aware of the disability, tactfully inquire about the best way to communicate in order to establish the extent of the disability.

When communicating with hearing-impaired persons, the first step is getting their attention. Stand in front of them and say their name loudly, but don't shout. If they don't respond, tap them lightly on the arm or shoulder. If you're not in touching range, wave your hand and try to make visual contact. You may also get attention by knocking on the desk or rapping on a nearby wall. Many hearing impaired people are sensitive to vibrations generated by rapping. Flipping the light switch will get the attention of everyone in the room, so use this method with greater selectivity.

Effort and concentration are needed by hearing impaired persons in order to understand the speech of others. Conversing at length while walking down a hall or street may be impossible. At best, trying to have a discussion when conditions are poor may exhaust them.

Giving needed information that the hearing-impaired person may not have been able to hear is one of the most helpful things you can do. This includes information that comes over public address systems, radio, and other sources where lipreading is impossible. You may be able to help as an interpreter when a hearing-impaired person is trying to understand someone with a foreign accent or a child with a high-pitched voice. Remember to tell a hearing-impaired person about any sound that may spell danger, such as honking horns, sirens, and alarms.

If you don't know their name, stand directly in front of them and begin speaking. You may also gently touch their arm or repeat yourself to be sure they understand.

Background noise is the bane of the person who relies to some degree on hearing but is hearing impaired. When you need to communicate and the area is noisy, consider moving to a quiet, well-lit room with good acoustics. Find a place where there are no nearby distractions demanding attention. The ideal conversation is held sitting down. Other considerations that can guide you include:

- Speak up, but do not shout. Shouting makes words sound less distinct and distorts lip movements.

- Avoid dropping your voice at the end of a sentence. The last two or three words can be the most important.

- Talk a little more slowly than usual. Pause slightly at the end of a sentence to allow time for its meaning to sink in. Pause an extra moment when you change the subject.

- Make an effort to speak clearly and pronounce every syllable, but don't exaggerate your mouth movements because this interferes with lipreading.

- Fuller explanations with a certain amount of redundancy are easier to understand than short, terse sentences. Using examples can sometimes aid understanding.
- If the message is long, get some occasional feedback to be sure the listener is understanding.
- If you are asked to repeat something, repeat it verbatim, Then, if necessary, rephrase the message. Sometimes breaking a complex sentence into a couple of short simple ones helps.

Speaking–Impaired Co-workers: Guidelines

Speaking-impaired persons often have had severe hearing impairment since an early age. Because children learn to speak by listening, those who can't hear have difficult forming the sounds that others easily understand. Most learn to speak but are somewhat difficult to understand. Others don't speak at all, relying on other means of communication. Here are some points to keep in mind:

- Be aware that the conversation will not move along as rapidly as usual, and don't try to rush it. Speaking-impaired persons may speak slowly, and if they are also hearing impaired, they have the additional task of trying to understand you.
- Find a quiet place to talk, if possible. Noise forces speaking-impaired persons to raise their voice, often a difficult or impossible requirement. It also increases the likelihood that they will miss what you say.
- Face the person, maintain easy eye contact, and give the conversation your full attention. If the person speaks for some time, nod now and then, or interject a few words, to let the person know you are still listening and understanding.
- When you think the person has finished, pause a moment to be sure. Then speak moderately slowly.
- If you do not understand, never remain silent, hoping to make sense of the conversation as you go along. This strategy virtually never works. You simply become more mired down as the speaker progresses. Instead, ask for clarification.
- If you are aware of a barrier to understanding that can be eliminated, let the person know.
- Repeat key pieces of information, such as names or phone numbers, to be sure you understand correctly.
- Alternate speaking and listening. Do not barrage the person with one question after another. Communicating may be stressful and tiring for the person.
- Keep the conversation of moderate length unless encouraged to continue. Understand that, as a practical matter, the speaker may want to stick to the business at hand and dispense with small talk.
- Until you get to know the person, listen to the words and not the way they are said. Try not to draw conclusions based on tone of voice or manner of speaking because these may be misleading with a speaking-impaired person.

At times speaking-impaired persons will pause, seemingly struggling to finish expressing a thought. Your normal reaction may be to speak up and help them complete the sentence. A suggestion: Until you are familiar speaking-impaired Alfredo's feelings on the matter, always allow him to finish his own sentences. Even if you know he won't take offense at such help, be sure you know what he's trying to say before you say it for him. Never make random guesses about what the end of his sentence might be.

Group conversations are difficult for most speaking-impaired persons, and the tend to prefer one-to-one conversations. Groups are noisy, and members often must raise their voices to be heard. It may be difficult or impossible for the speaking impaired person to speak loudly enough to be heard. The conversation moves quickly, making it difficult for the speaking impaired to gear up in time to get a word in edgewise.

Devices that a few speaking-impaired persons carry include small typewriters, computers, or similar devices in lieu of writing. The message may be printed on paper, displayed on a screen, or broadcast by synthesized voice. High-tech devices often intrigue others who ask for explanations, demonstrations, and even permission to play with them. This gets tiresome. The best policy: Don't ask and don't touch.

Skill Builder 9.1: Relating to Wheelchair Users

Purpose: To raise your awareness of your reactions and attitudes toward persons who use wheelchairs.

Instructions: Have paper and pen handy. Follow the directions for each step and jot down brief answers to the questions.

Step 1. Person in a Wheelchair

a. Relax by closing your eyes and breathing deeply. Think of a person in a wheelchair and focus on this mental image. Notice the thoughts and feelings that come up.

b. Open your eyes and write a few brief sentences about the thoughts and feelings that came up, as well as your answer to this question:

   • What did you see first when you pictured a wheelchair user: A wheelchair? A person within a wheelchair? Or a person?

Step 2. Person in an Easy Chair

Repeat Step 1, but this time think of a person sitting in an easy chair. When you write about your thoughts and feelings, answer this question:

   • What did you see first when you pictured an easy chair user: An easy chair? A persons within an easy chair? Or a person?

Step 3. Person in a Wheelchair and Person in an Easy Chair

Repeat Step 1, but this time think first of a person in a wheelchair and then think of the same person in an easy chair. Shift the mental image back and forth several times. When you write about your thoughts and feelings, answer this question:

   • How did shifting the mental image affect your thoughts and feelings about the person? How did it affect the way you position the person within your own mind and therefore how you're likely to relate to such a person?

Skill Builder 9.2: The Case of Severely Disabled Judy

Judy was paralyzed from the neck down. She must have help getting out of bed, getting dressed, and getting into a motorized wheelchair. Judy says that she still has the greatest ability of all: her mind, which is as sound as ever. She says if she can find a way to attend the university, she will get a degree in public administration and she wants to have a career in that field. She has come to you, a vocational counselor at the state Department of Rehabilitation as the first step in getting the funding she needs from the state in order to pursue this educational and career goal. Your responsibilities are:

- *Regarding education*: to predict the possibility and probability that an applicant will actually complete the educational program he or she enters.
- *Regarding occupation*: to predict the possibility and probability that an applicant will actually get and retain a job in the proposed field.
- *Regarding funds*: to allocate scarce state funds for rehabilitation in a manner that produces the best results for persons with disabilities and for society.

Considering Judy's situation and your responsibilities:

- What will your decision be?
- *What will you say to Judy?*

Skill Builder 9.3 The Case of Paul, Who Becomes Disabled

Paul works for the San Francisco AIDS Foundation as a developmental system associate. He's been there for nearly three years and his work has become an asset to the foundation. He is solely responsible for overseeing the data base system, which he helped create. His responsibilities include tracking donations and generating the foundation's budget reports and income statements. Paul's performance evaluations have always been excellent.

A little over a year ago Paul was diagnosed with Aggressive Liver Disease. This disease eventually results in liver failure. Paul is waiting for a liver transplant and hopes a donor will make one available within the next three to five years. Last year Paul took a four-month medical leave of absence to get his disease under control. Since his return, he has managed to keep his performance up to par, even though he must miss work for his doctor's appointment each week. The main physical problems that Paul is currently experiencing are fatigue and the nausea caused by the drugs he must take.

Paul knows he cannot continue working forty-hour weeks, and the commute to and from work is an energy drain he'd like to avoid. Paul starts thinking that he could do most of his work at home. He would need a computer, modem, and dedicated telephone line. He researches this idea and determines that this would require an initial investment of $2,500 plus about $20 per month in telephone charges. Paul is thinking about asking for a meeting with his manager *Claudia* and requesting that the foundation provide him with the equipment for a home office. As far as he knows, no other employee has ever asked to do most of their work from a home office. However, Paul is concerned that if he doesn't make better use of his failing energy, he'll be required to go on disability leave until his liver transplant comes through.

- What are the key issues here?
- If you were Paul, what would you do?
- If you were Claudia, what would you do?

Skill Builder 9.4 The Case of Visually Impaired Manager Jill

Jill Dovetsky is the Human Resource Manager of Spirit Clothing Co. She has been visually impaired since a very young age and in fact is almost totally blind. In spite of this, Jill earned a degree in business administration and worked her way up to Human Resource Manager within five years of joining Spirit.

Jill has had a positive influence on the company's policies toward persons with disabilities, and Spirit's workforce includes one of highest proportions of employees with disabilities in the industry. Last month, on November 15, the Accounting Department Manager announced his retirement plans. Jill has met with the Spirit executive team and determined that they want a manager who will bring in "new blood," someone fairly young with recent university training but also a good track record in the field. They want someone with new ideas, new energy, and hopefully someone who will stay with the company for many years.

Jill has interviewed many applicants for this job and is leaning toward **Amy** as the probable best fit. She's now in the process of interviewing three finalists for the position and would like to make the selection before the Christmas holidays. She schedules a 5:30 p.m. meeting with Amy. The interview goes well. Amy seems to have most of the right answers to Jill's questions and responds satisfactorily to the few concerns that Jill has about Amy's qualifications.

They've been chatting for well over an hour when **Rick**, Jill's assistant knocks on the door and enters the room. Rick says, "Hey, why are you two sitting here in the dark?" As Rick turns on the lights, Amy lets out a sigh of relief, and it seems to Jill that a heavy weight is lifted from Amy's shoulders. Jill responds, "Well, you know me, Rick, lights or not, it's all the same to me. Amy, I must apologize for forgetting the time of day. But surely you know it's okay to remind me?" Amy seems quite flustered and stammers, "Oh, that's okay, it's . . . it doesn't matter."

Later, when Jill discusses the incident with Rick, he said, "Amy seemed very nervous and uncomfortable when I came in. I saw a definite sense of relief when I turned on the lights." Jill said, "Mmmm, too bad. We have several persons with disabilities in the Accounting Department—and in fact many throughout the company. The person we hire for this management job must know how to deal with disability situations and issues."

- What are the key issues in this case?
- If your were Amy, what would you have done?
- If you were Jill, what would you do now?

REFERENCES

Althen, Gary. *American Ways*. Yarmouth, ME: Intercultural Press, 1988.

Berkeley, CA, City of. Survey of ADA Costs, 1992.

Brown, S.E. "Creating a Disability Mythology." *International Journal of Rehabilitation Research*, 15 (1992): 227–233.

Bureau of National Affairs, Inc. "The Americans with Disabilities Act: A Practical and Legal Guide to Impact, Enforcement, and Compliance." Washington, DC, 1990.

Business Week (May 30, 1994): 63–93. "The New Competitive Advantage."

Business Week (April 12, 1993). "Business Has to Find a New Meaning for 'Fairness.'"

Cox, Taylor, Jr. *Cultural Diversity in Organizations*. San Francisco: Berrett-Koehler Publishers, 1993.

Crew, Nancy M., and Irving Kenneth Zola. *Independent Living for Physically Disabled People*. San Francisco: Jossey-Bass, Inc., 1983.

Green and Johnson, 1987.

Hahn, Harlan. "The Politics of Physical Differences." *Journal of Social Issues* 44, no. 1 (1988): 39–47.

Hahn, Harlan. "Toward a Politics of Disability." *Social Science Journal* 22 (1985): 87–105.

Harris, 1986, 1987.

Hopkins, Kevin, and Susan Nestleroth, supplement in *Business Week* (October 28, 1991): 24.

Longmore, P.K. "A Note on Language and the Social Identity of Disabled People." *American Behavioral Scientist* 28, no. 3 (January/February 1985a): 419–423.

Longmore, P.K. "Screening Stereotypes: Images of Disabled People." *Social Policy* (Summer 1985b): 32–37.

Longmore, P.K. "Uncovering the Hidden History of People with Disabilities." *Reviews in American History* (September 1987): 355–364.

Maloff, Chalda, and Susan Macduff. *Business and Social Etiquette with Disabled People.* Springfield, IL: Charles C. Thomas Publisher, 1988.

McDonough, Hugh H. "Hiring People with Disabilities." *Supervisory Management* (February 1992): 11–12.

McGovern, John. "Justice Department Publishes Final Rules on the ADA." *P&R* (November 1991): 12–73.

McKee, Bradford. "Achieving Access for the Disabled." *Nation's Business* (June 1991): 31–34.

Minton, Eric. "Implementing a Can-Do Attitude." *Hemisphere* (July 1994): 31.

"Myths & Facts: About People Who Have Disabilities." Chicago: National Easter Seal Society, 1992.

Mitchell, Olivia S., ed. *As the Workforce Ages.* Ithaca, New York: ILR Press, 1993.

Potter, Edward E. *A Compliance Guide to the Americans with Disabilities Act.* Washington, DC: Employment Policy Foundation, 1991.

Shapiro, Joseph. "The New Civil Rights." *Modern Maturity* (November–December 1994): 28–35.

Shapiro, Joseph. *No Pity: People with Disabilities Forging a New Civil Rights Movement.* New York: Times Books, 1993.

Stace, S. "Vocational Rehabilitation for Women with Disabilities." *International Labour Review* 126, no. 3 (1987): 301–316.

Vash, Carolyn. "Sheltered Industrial Employment." *Annual Review of Rehabilitation.* New York: Springer, 1980.

Vash, Carolyn. *The Psychology of Disability.* NY: Springer Publishing Co., 1981.

WSJ. "Labor Letter" in *Wall Street Journal* (June 7, 1994): A-1.

Resources:

The Disability Rag & ReSource, ed. Joseph Shapiro.

The World Institute on Disability, 510 16th Street, Suite 100, Oakland, CA 94612, phone (510) 763-4100.

Stepping Stones, Growth Center, 1720 Adeline St., Oakland, CA 94607. (Mission: bringing persons with developmental disability into the mainstream of society.)

We magazine, 372 Central Park West, Suite 6B, New York, NY 10025. Phone: (800) we mag 26, e-mail: editors@wemagazine.com, website: www.wemagazine.com. A monthly magazine that focuses on issues of persons with disabilities.

CHAPTER 10

Working with Older Persons

*What if we began to value older persons as fountains of wisdom, support,
and vitality . . . and to expect that they would continue to
grow, develop, and unfold as they did earlier in life?*
—Betty Friedan

Nearly half of all Americans are older than 40 and so are included in federal and state laws designed to protect workers from age discrimination. Nearly one-third are older than 50, and the older we get, the more devaluation and discrimination we face. Discrimination based on age is called *ageism*.

Older workers who lose their jobs face more intense problems than their younger counterparts with unemployment, underemployment, and lowered wages—primarily because of false myths about age. Those who keep their jobs must deal with ageism, the barriers some managers have to investing in training for older workers, and the resulting lack of new job skills. They must cope with the generation gap that can occur as new generations of younger workers enter the workforce. Older workers must also deal with retirement expectations—their own, their organization's, and the culture's expectations. They also face many issues and decisions around retiring, not retiring, or partially retiring.

Perceptive business leaders are learning the facts about older workers and how to help them stay motivated, growing, and contributing to the organization. As a leader, you can learn how to utilize their wealth of experience, knowledge, and talent. Before we explore these fascinating aspects of working with older persons, complete Self-Awareness Activities 10.1 and 10.2.

Self-Awareness Activity 10.1: What Do You Believe About Older Persons?

Purpose:

- to get in touch with your beliefs and stereotypes about this group of people
- to experience how judgmental beliefs affect your thinking and feeling processes
- to experience the ways in which your beliefs create your reality regarding other persons, even before you have any interaction with them.

Part I. What Do You Believe About Older Women?

Step 1. Associations

- Relax as deeply as you can: close your eyes and take a few deep breaths.
- Focus on the words "older woman" and allow a mental picture to come up in your mind's eye.
- Notice the words and images that come to mind as you "see" this woman.
- Open your eyes and list 10 to 20 words in the order in which they occur to you.
- Review your list. Mark a plus beside the words that are positive, a minus beside the words that are negative, and a circle beside neutral words.

Step 2. Negative Associations

- Close your eyes and focus again on the image of the older woman. Formulate a negative opinion or judgment, perhaps one you typically hold about such women.
- Notice your *feelings* as you see the person in this negative way. What *thoughts* come up as you focus on the image?
- Write a few sentences about your feelings and thoughts.

Step 3. Positive Associations

- Formulate a positive opinion or judgment, perhaps one you typically hold about older women.
- Notice your *feelings* as you see the person in this positive way. What *thoughts* come up as you focus on the image?
- Write a few sentences about your feelings and thoughts.

Step 4. Insights

- Focus on the differences between your experiences when you hold negative and positive judgments or opinions. What were the differences? What meaning does this have for you, for your beliefs and feelings about people from this group, and about beliefs in general?
- Write your responses in a few sentences; include anything you like about your feelings, thoughts, and insights.

Part II. What Do You Believe About Older Men?

Repeat the steps in Part I, this time focusing on the image of an older man.

Self-Awareness Activity 10.2: What Do You Know About Older Persons?

Purpose: To see what you know about the issues covered in this chapter.

Instructions: Determine whether you think the following statements are basically true or false—and think about why. The answers will emerge in this chapter, and the summary at the end of the chapter focuses on these issues.

1. Older workers are no more forgetful than younger ones.
2. Older workers have more difficulty adapting to change.
3. Older workers are prone to frequent absences because of age-related conditions and illnesses.
4. Older workers have fewer work accidents than younger workers.
5. Extensive training for older workers doesn't pay off because they don't learn as well and they'll retire soon anyway.

6. Older workers have more job security and higher pay than younger ones.

7. Workers who retire before age 65 tend to live longer than those who don't.

MYTHS AND FACTS

We tend to view old age quite negatively in this culture, often equating it with loss of abilities, vitality, and attractiveness and with illness, nursing homes, and death. It's not surprising that many younger people prefer to avoid older people and the depressing thoughts their presence may trigger. Older persons must cope with a huge number of myths and stereotypes, most of which tend to devalue and exclude them. Some contain a kernel of truth, a few are basically valid, and most are distorted or outdated.

Myth: Older people have higher absenteeism and accident rates.

The accidents myth is totally false. Bureau of Labor Statistics data shows that occupational injuries occur at a lower rate for older workers. In many instances older workers are better risks than younger workers across a variety of jobs even when risk exposure is controlled. Some studies indicate that their accident rate is less than half that of younger workers. All managers agree that older workers tend to be more careful.

The absentee myth is essentially untrue. The kernel of truth is that older workers are more likely to be absent for unavoidable absences such as illness. What offsets this is that their overall attendance record is much better than that of younger workers. This is because younger workers tend to take days off for "mental health" reasons, for going to the beach, for dealing with love affairs, or for caring for family members. Most older workers have outlived their responsibilities for dependent children and elderly parents and are free to concentrate on their careers. In fact, people older than 65 are less likely than those who are younger to suffer from the acute illnesses that require hospitalization. The older we get, the more likely we are to develop chronic diseases and to become disabled, primarily because of heart disease, arthritis, or cancer, but most older persons remain healthy until the last few months of their lives. In a massive Swedish longitudinal study, 95 percent of seventy-year-olds were without serious disabilities, as were 80 percent of eighty-year-olds. In the U.S. 95 percent of persons older than 65 live independent lives (Salzberg 1983).

The absentee myth is based on an image of age as inevitable decline and deterioration, which in turn is tied to a dread of aging and of dying. It causes people to deny that old age even exists for them. And the more age is denied, the more terrifying it becomes. Prejudice and discrimination toward the elderly are actually created by the American culture's obsession with and idealization of youth and by our refusal even to look at the reality of age on its own terms. Subconsciously, we think that if we can keep old people out of sight, we can keep the illusion of eternal youth and rarely have to face the fact that we all age and die.

Myth: Older workers are more rigid and dogmatic.

Evidence indicates that dogmatic behavior is unrelated to age. What is related to age is a tendency to become more caring, accepting, and mellow. This means that older persons tend to handle crises better than younger workers and to see the humor in life's slings and arrows.

Nurturing, accepting. People are more likely to mentor others and become more accepting of life as they age. Studies indicate that men and women tend to change their behavior during middle age to focus more on mentoring younger persons, showing more concern for guiding the next generation and feeling more of a sense of responsibility to younger persons. Beyond middle age, people tend to become more accepting of life, to adapt to the triumphs and disappointments of being human, and to view past events as inevitable, appropriate, and meaningful (Ryff 1985).

While basic character traits tend to be stable, people's experiences and personal development become more varied with age.

Respect. An implication of the rigid myth is that older workers resent being told what to do by younger managers. In fact, no one really likes being told what to do, and younger workers are more apt to respond negatively. Older workers do appreciate receiving some respect for their years of experience. When managers get them on their side, they're less likely than younger workers to be vying for the manager's position, to quit, or to be disloyal. Their accumulated wisdom can be very helpful to managers.

Creativity. Also implied in the rigid myth is that older workers are not very creative. In fact, creativity and intellectual activity is still vital in persons older than 100, according to a Social Security Administration survey of such people. When creativity is encouraged and rewarded, and when the environment is structured to enhance it, older workers bring a greater richness of ideas, stemming from their abundance of life experience (Friedan 1993).

Myth: People quit learning when they get old

One of the most untrue and degrading myths is "You can't teach an old dog new tricks." It's common and career-devastating for management to ignore training for older workers—and for older workers to believe training won't pay off for them. In fact, while the most rapid rate of learning occurs at very young ages, the capacity to learn remains high throughout life. Older workers bring a lifetime of experience to the learning situation. That's why they tend to be better at problem solving, to draw on more information for decision making, and to be good mediators. They're trainable and retrainable.

Intellectual performance remains robust throughout life for healthy people. From age 30 onward there is a slight mental slowdown, such as in reaction time, but older workers compensate by increasing their speed on certain complex repetitive tasks. Other functions, such as vocabulary choice, get better with age, and the brain continues to develop throughout adult life. Some brain cells die each year, but connecting branches between them—pathways for the nerve impulses that create thought, feeling, and memory—keep sprouting and spreading, more than compensating for the loss of cells. Studies show that intellectual challenge normally enhances brain growth. Physical exercise helps brain function too.

Forgetting names and poor concentration are not connected with normal aging. They're often connected with new priorities, more years of information, more names to sort through, and heavy work loads. Actually, 92 percent of persons older than 65 show no significant mental deterioration. Only about 8 percent have such symptoms as partial memory loss and slowing reaction time.

Research indicates that we will not deteriorate in either basic mental competence or intelligence, even in our eighties, if we continue to be physically and mentally active and stimulated and remain healthy. In fact, current research indicates age brings some positive changes in certain mental abilities. In addition, we can compensate for age-related declines through practices that enhance certain muscular, sexual, and immune processes. For example, through mental activity, we can continue to develop vital new brain connections until the end of life and even reverse deterioration. The type of intelligence that involves experience, meaning, knowledge, professional expertise, and wisdom continues to increase even though speed in completing IQ tests may decline. Yet the false stereotypes of the elderly may keep older people from seeking or getting continuing education and the right kind of health care.

Myth: Older workers are not as attractive to clients.

This myth contains the kernel of truth implied by our discussion of the American tendency to be obsessed with youth and fearful of old age. However, it overlooks the truth that beauty is in the eye of the beholder. Since women's value is more firmly tied to looks than men's, women stand to lose the most as they age. If a man is old, ugly, and wise, he's a sage. If a woman is old, ugly, and wise, she's a hag, a witch, a crone. But in prepatriarchal societies the elder women were generally considered founts of wisdom, law, healing skills, and moral leadership. Their wrinkles would have been badges of honor, not of shame. By contrast, our society regards elder women as relatively unattractive and useless.

When men are considered in their prime, in their fifties and sixties, women are considered to be over the hill. The aging woman is often surprised and hurt by the unexpected hostility she encounters as she slips into old age. The combination of sexism and ageism turns older women into invisible citizens of the modern world. We make them invisible by rarely featuring them in films or television programs, and generally passing them by as social and professional leaders.

The Gray Panthers' nationwide volunteer force called Media Watch concluded in the late 1970s that older people are generally pictured as "ugly, toothless, sexless, incontinent, senile, confused, and helpless," and that old age was so negatively stereotyped that "it has become something to dread and feel threatened by." The sales pitches for products that promise to stop or cover up aging send the message that age is acceptable only if it passes for or acts like youth. A multibillion-dollar beauty industry exploits women's well-founded fear of looking old. Many proclaimed a real breakthrough in the 1980s when the female stars of the TV series *Dynasty* were considered still attractive and employable at age 50. A 1993 consumer survey found that most consumers older than 35 now believe that a woman can be beautiful at 40, or 50, and *even* past 60. This was hailed as great progress, even though it implies that women past sixty-something have no chance (*Advertising Age* 1993).

Yet the U.S. population is about one-third older persons, one-third youngsters under age 20, and one-third adults in between. Assuming youngsters are not potential customers for most products, people 50 and older represent half the potential customers that most companies should target. Companies who project an image of older persons in a positive way, with attractive, natural older role models may hit pay dirt.

Myth: Most older workers are less productive, just coasting to retirement.

Research refutes the myth that older workers slow down and have lower performance and productivity. Indications are that there is no significant performance decline that's caused by aging in the case of engineers, scientists, blue-collar workers, clerical workers, and production workers. Several studies suggest that older paraprofessionals and clerical workers outperform younger workers. U.S. Department of Labor studies reveal that age has little effect on manual-labor workers through age 50, and declines in productivity after age 50 never exceed 10 percent, on average. A study of 1,700 managers working in diverse organizations showed that when managerial performance is measured in terms of such bottom-line indicators as return on total capital, growth of stockholders' equity, earnings per share, and sales growth, no significant differences in performance could be related to the age of managers.

There is some age-related decline in speed and accuracy of movement, perception, hearing, vision, and certain types of problem-solving skills—for some older persons, but not all. Researchers have concluded that these declines would affect performance in only a few jobs requiring extremely high levels of sensory or cognitive skills. Drawing on years of experience and good judgment, workers older than 60 are functionally able to excel in most occupations.

Overwhelming scientific evidence indicates that older workers (*Retirement Living* April 1976):

- enjoy higher morale
- have a greater sense of organization commitment
- are more involved in their jobs
- rate work as more important to their lives
- have the highest job satisfaction of any age group
- rate needs for job security as more important
- are less likely to report an intention to leave the organization
- are much less likely to leave the organization

Age stereotypes depict older people as frail and fragile, as having lost the vitality and energy necessary to make a full commitment to a career. Actually, large differences exist with respect to the health and well-being of persons in every age category. While some people remain very healthy in their eighties, and even in their nineties, others become mentally and physically old at 40. Recently, changes in lifestyles, dietary habits, and exercise patterns, along with the better medical interventions, have dramatically changed the health picture for older persons.

In summary, evidence on the performance of older workers and managers generally indicates that they perform as well as their younger counterparts on almost all criteria. Chronological age is a poor indicator of a person's mental and physical well-being and an inadequate basis for predicting vocational performance. Individual differences within age groups accounts for much more variation in performance than does age. Managers should carefully assess each employee's capabilities with an eye toward matching them to job requirements.

Myth That's true: you're only as old as you feel.

Remember, a myth is a symbolic saying or story whose function is to bind together the thoughts of a group and promote coordinated social action. Some myths are essentially true, and this is one of them. Scientists are discovering that aging is mainly in the mind. The best ways to slow the mental aging process are:

- maintaining a positive attitude
- remaining mentally and physically active

Myth That's very true: use it or lose it.

This myth is not only true, it's a key to staying healthy and alert as we grow older. We can retain our vitality and health best by using our minds and bodies. Physical and mental exercise, along with a healthy diet, are the specific keys. Energy levels peak in the early thirties and normally drops about 7 percent per decade, primarily because people tend to become more sedentary. But physical exercise can dramatically slow the energy drop.

Aging decline has in fact been reversed with changes in diet, exercise, lifestyle, and environment. People who reach age 65 in the 1990s are more likely to be healthy, active, and financially self-sufficient than any previous generation (Campbell, Abolafia, and Maddox 1985). We must learn to view age as continued human development, a continuation of personal growth, not of decline and decay. Staying independent and connected to people in the workplace, community, and family are crucial to vital aging and longevity. The key is to move on to new growth in the last third of life.

Moving Beyond Stereotypes

We're entering an era when old age will be a full one-third of life for most people. Youth is the first 30 years of life, middle age the second 30 years, and old age the third 30 years, from 60 to 90. Many people today are retaining great vitality throughout the third age. Our society needs to use their "wisdom and large visions and truthtelling to confront its own problems of polarization and decline" (Friedan 1993, 611). Older persons in turn can embark on a new adventure during old age and find new wholeness. A burning need of those who are vital during these years is to be part of the community, part of an enterprise larger than self, to contribute to humanity, to pass on something to the next generation.

It's especially ironic that a culture should devalue so cruelly its members who survive to a ripe old age. In one survey, 70 percent of younger people said the stereotyped image of older people is unfair, but only about half the people older than 65 said it was unfair. How can we explain that one (Retirement Living 1976)?

What if we reexamined our devastating stereotypes of age as do-nothing retirement, deterioration and decline, and changed our beliefs? What if we began to value older persons as a fountain of wisdom, support, and vitality—a slow-burning, steady energy rather than a flash fire? What if we began to allow and expect that they would continue to grow, develop, and unfold in the last third of life as they had during the first two-thirds? Might we have much to gain and little to lose (Friedan 1993)?

HOW AGEISM EVOLVED

Before the Civil War older people were admired and respected, and young people were put in their place and kept there. New generations adopted the occupations and lifestyles of parents and grandparents, so older people's knowledge and experience were indispensable. They were at the center of economic and social life, from trade and commerce to finance, political organization, and religious training. By the 1930s most who lived to old age faced poverty, loneliness, and ageism. What happened in between?

Some sociologists say we've become more ageist in this century because of the way industrial capitalism unfolded in the U.S. (Hushbeck 1989). Between 1860 and 1920 our occupational structure changed in ways that were devastating to older workers. During those years we moved from an agricultural to an industrial economy. In 1860 the old were less than 3 percent of the population but they had great economic and political influence relative to their proportion. They dictated the behavior of younger family members because they owned the farm or family business and they knew more than anyone about making money from it.

Although negative conceptions about old age didn't suddenly appear after 1860, such conceptions had little power over older people's economic security. Younger people may have resented the older for the privileges they monopolized, but discrimination against them was not an issue before the Civil War. Economic discrimination against older persons couldn't exist until their hold on valued resources had been loosened. Their lost edge meant that age became an impediment, even a barrier, to employment.

The institutional changes in the American economy between 1860 and 1920 that had the greatest impact on older workers were:

- Agriculture and small family businesses, which were ideal for people who wanted to work as long as they were healthy, were substantially replaced by manufacturing and finance.
- A system of regional economies was essentially replaced by a national economy, made possible by westward expansion and such advances as the railroad and telephone.
- People lived and worked in cities rather than in rural areas and small towns.
- Wage work for corporations became the norm, and self-employment declined.
- Rapid technological advances made many skills obsolete, encouraging specialization and assembly line work.
- The business cycle came to predominate, making workers vulnerable to its ups and downs.

Mass Production and the Older Worker

Mass production, the assembly line, job specialization, and scientific management techniques led to de-skilling and to workers' loss of autonomy and individuality in the workplace. Economies of scale meant that most manufacturing firms had to be large in order to be profitable. Businesses could best make use of large numbers of culturally diverse workers by minimizing skill requirements and developing uniform production processes. What an individual worker had to offer became irrelevant; the worker's ability to adapt to prescribed work processes was what mattered most. Even highly skilled work became ever more finely divided until workers knew very little about the overall work processes, only their small part. In effect workers traded off their autonomy and security for a rising standard of living—at least as long as they were in the workforce.

The rapid pace of work in mechanized industry, often combined with the need for great stamina and a rapid wearing-out of laborers, led firms to prefer hiring younger, healthier applicants. Labor de-skilling was the strategy used to drive down the cost of labor in production and to further encourage the substitution of unskilled and semi-skilled work for labor power that required years of skill development. This put older workers at a physical and technological disadvantage.

Survival in the City

As people moved to cities to get jobs, the nuclear family became the norm, housed in small quarters. The older generation was separated from the younger. Floods of immigrant workers pushed many older workers out of jobs. Immigrants wanted more for their children, and many parents sacrificed for future generations at the expense of saving for their own long-run needs. So older immigrant parents often became poor immigrant parents. The decisive factor was not whether or not the elderly lived in an urban or rural environment, but whether they were able to be self-supporting or economically productive. This was increasingly not the case. Many were faced with no property, no job, and uncertain family support. Industrial pension plans tended to be unilateral, voluntary, underfunded, poorly administered, and generally nonexistent or inadequate when it was time for a worker to retire.

Some sociologists say that our ageism is basically economic because our culture values "doing" in a world of paid employment. Those who "do" little or nothing are implicitly devalued and often suffer feelings of inadequacy. Before industrialism, older people served as role models and leaders, which gave meaning and value to their lives. Older people are now often excluded from a system that equates success with employment. "They've been moved out of established, recognized, productive positions into roles that are generally poorly defined, marginal, and without prestige" (Hushbeck 1989, 8). Although the current generation of retired persons may have the money to live better than their grandparents did, most will be socially isolated, ghettoized, and ignored.

Economic discrimination has fed our cultural stereotyping of older people, our dread of aging, and our aversion to the old that this dread generates. Today, older workers who have the skill and knowledge their company needs tend to be better paid and more secure than younger workers. However, those older workers who lose their jobs acquire many of the characteristics of a minority group. Older Euro-American male job applicants often find themselves in the same marginal position as African Americans have traditionally been: a secondary labor force, the last hired and the first fired. Whether and when they work depends on the overall scarcity of labor.

CURRENT PROFILE: WHO'S OLD?

How old is old? For business purposes, we might say it's older than 40 because that's when protection from discrimination kicks in.

> *The Age Discrimination Employment Act (ADEA) protects employees between the ages of 40 and 70 from workplace discrimination, and even those older than 70 cannot be forced to retire from most occupations.*

Other government sources seem to disagree about how old is old. For example, the Bureau of Labor Statistics says it's 55, but the Census Bureau says it's 65. Gerontologists say that because people live longer and remain healthier than in the past, it's now more realistic to use two age categories:

- *young-old*, currently 65 to 75, soon to be 75 to 85
- *old-old*, now older than 75, soon to be older than 85.

How many are there? About 13 percent of Americans are currently older than 65, a huge increase during this century, and the trend is expected to accelerate in the coming 25 years, as shown in Table 10.1.

TABLE 10.1 Proportion of Americans Over Age 65

	1900	*1990*	*2015, Projected*
Americans older than 65 than 65	4%, 1 in 25 3 million	13%, 1 in 8 31 million	17%, 1 in 6 54 million

Source: U.S. Census Bureau, 1993.

Which subgroups had the largest population older than 65 in 1990?

- Euro-Americans   13 percent
- Asian Americans   8 percent
- Latino Americans   8 percent
- African Americans   6 percent
- American Indians   6 percent

The Euro-American population had the highest proportion of elderly because they have higher survival rates to 65 years old and lower recent fertility rates.

- Who lives the longest? Euro-American women, who average age 80 at death.
- Who die the youngest? African American men, average age 45 at death.

Currently, persons who make it to age 55 without chronic illness will normally remain healthy to age 85.

About two-thirds of people older than 65 are women. The older they become, the less likely the women are to be married because their husbands die before they do. Therefore, older women are more likely to live alone, in contrast to older men, most of whom are married and living with their wives. And the women are twice as likely to live in poverty, with 16 percent classified as poor. Nationally, about 10 percent of older persons live in poverty, but in nine southern states, the rate is 20 percent or more (U.S. Census Bureau 1993).

Increased life expectancy has led to a larger population of older Americans. In addition, the Baby Boom population will soon move into the older category. Demographers call the Boomer phenomenon the "pig in a python," as depicted in Figure 10.1. The back part of the python symbolizes the relatively small generation of babies born during the depression and World War II. The pig in the middle of the python represents the baby boom after the War and during the 1950s. The front part of the python represents the relatively small Baby Bust Generation of the late 1960s and early 1970s.

FIGURE 10.1 Relative Size of Generations

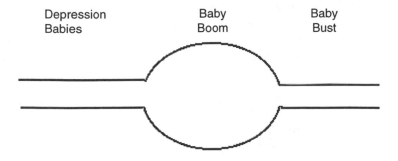

2011 they'll begin turning 65. The Baby Boomers are expected to live longer and be healthier than any previous generation. When they retire, they'll probably come back once or twice for new careers. The era of the U.S. as a nation of primarily young persons is coming to an end as we become a nation of predominantly older people who are healthy and active. This development contains tremendous opportunity for most businesses, which we'll discuss in the leadership section.

CULTURAL ASPECTS OF AGING: EMPLOYMENT ISSUES

What's it like to be an older employee? The first major difference between being perceived as a middle-aged employee in the prime of life and an older employee is the devaluation, avoidance, and discrimination that we discussed earlier. So ageism is the core issue. A related issue is the increasing likelihood of unemployment or underemployment and resulting low wages, which may result because of ageism or because of companies' downsizing strategies that focus on eliminating high-wage employees. Compounding the unemployment issue is the skills obsolescence issue. Many older persons experience a distinct communications gap with younger employees. And, older employees must make decisions about whether, when, and how to retire.

Issue: Dealing with Ageism

Once you pass what people perceive as "your prime," you'll begin experiencing the impact of ageism, the typical myths and stereotypes about older persons. The social impact of ageism can deflate your ego. The career impact can deflate your bank account. A 1980s *Harvard Business Review* study found that younger managers stereotype older workers as being rigid, too old to train, declining in competence, and less creative than younger workers. When the researchers compared the ways younger managers treat 30-year-olds and 60-year-olds, they found that:

- Managers perceive older employees to be relatively inflexible and resistant to change. They therefore make much less effort to give older persons feedback about needed changes in performance.

- Managers provide very limited organization support for the career development and retraining of older employees.

- The promotion opportunities for older people are somewhat restricted, especially when the new positions demand creativity, mental alertness, or the capacity to deal with crisis situations.

How managers withhold feedback and encouragement. In this study researchers provided a case involving customer complaints about employee performance. Most of the managers said they would have an encouraging talk with a 30-year-old employee, but they would reassign a 60-year-old. Clearly the managers saw the older employee as more resistant to their influence, even though there was nothing in the case to support such a perception. Reassigning the older employee, rather than encouraging him to improve his performance deprives the employee of the opportunity to improve his performance. Such actions make the effects of age stereotyping very difficult to overcome. By transferring older employees, managers avoid a direct test of their own assumptions about older workers' rigidity and resistance to change. Such managers cut off the opportunity to learn whether this age stereotype is valid or not.

How the too-old-to-train stereotype creates blocks. Older employees, especially those in technical positions, are vulnerable to problems of career obsolescence. Both managers and their older employees need to commit themselves to continuous career development in order to keep older workers' knowledge and skills up to date. One of the cases revealed managers' assumptions that older workers are not motivated to improve their job-related skills. These assumptions are reflected in decisions to avoid investments in the continued development of older employees. Assumptions about retirement practices can also influence these decisions. While 74 percent would allocate funds to send a 30-year-old employee to a production seminar, only 53 percent would allocate it for a 60-year-old. Managers may view investments in the development of older persons as yielding fewer organization benefits, compared with investments in younger employees. The validity of these assumptions depends on actual turnover rates among younger and older employees.

How the less-creative stereotype hinders. Managers are less likely to promote older employees. Managers in the study were asked to decide whether a marketing representative should be promoted to a marketing director position that called for fresh solutions to challenging problems. They rated the outlook for successful performance as much less favorable for a 60-year-old candidate than for a 30-year-old, and indicated very little support for promoting the older candidate.

How the declining-competence stereotype discriminates. Managers are more likely to give demanding new jobs to younger workers, reflecting the stereotype that connects age with increasing nervousness and declining mental alertness. The majority of managers viewed a 30-year-old employee as more suitable for a new role calling for poise and mental alertness. Researchers find a pattern in which older employees are seen as less able to cope with higher-level supervisory and managerial positions when role requirements conflict with age stereotypes. Therefore, the probability of a promotion is somewhat lower for an older employee than for an identically qualified younger person.

Issue: Navigating the Generation Gap

Older and younger employees often experience a communication gap that is caused primarily by the differences in their experiences and values. Understanding the key themes for each age group can build a base for understanding and reduce age discrimination.

Each generation internalizes the cultural ethos, or essence of values, typical of the larger culture at the time it was coming of age. People incorporate that cultural ethos as they deal with the issues of the day, as they respond to major historical events. For example, Table 10.2 gives one interpretation of the ethos of various American generations during this century.

TABLE 10.2 Generations and Their Cultural Ethos

Birth Years	Era	Key issues	Cultural Ethos
1900s–1920s	Swing Generation	Building an industrial nation; immigration ————>	Seizing opportunity
1930–1945	Silent Generation	Great Depression ————> World War II ————>	Surviving Defending basic freedoms
1946–1964	Baby Boomers	Postwar ————> Civil rights ————> Me generation ————>	Rebuilding Demanding personal freedoms Seeking personal fulfillment
1965–1975	Baby Bust Generation X	Information Age ————>	Spanning the global village

Based on the work of Gann and Duignan, 1986; Jackson, 1992.

Members of the Swing Generation are all older than 65 now. They survived the Great Depression and World War II and are more likely than any other group to value security and safety.

Members of the Silent Generation are in their early fifties to mid-sixties, a relatively small group that includes most of our current business and political leaders. They grew up in the 1940s and early 1950s. Most share a strong work ethic and place a premium on job and financial security. Some, especially ethnic minorities, are first- or second-generation immigrants who still retain many customs from their home cultures, such as dress, music, principles of family life, respect for authority figures, and patriotism.

Members of the Baby Boom Generation are now mostly in their thirties and early forties and some are turning 50. They grew up in the 1950s and 1960s and entered the work force in the 1970s and 1980s. Their large size gives them significant social and economic clout. In their youth they tended to be either quite traditional or iconoclastic. Some are former hippies and yippies, and many are now yuppies. Some are or were suspicious of big business and big government. A few took to the streets to demonstrate against the Vietnam war. Many have experimented with drugs, and their slogan in the 1960s was "Don't trust anyone over 30." They grew up under more permissive child-rearing practices, and they place great value on work that is self-actualizing. Some reject their parents' focus on upward mobility and dedication to work. They insist on a lifestyle that leaves ample time for the pursuit of leisure activities. Their focus on their personal development led to the designation of the "Me Generation."

Members of the Baby Bust Generation are now in their twenties with some turning 30. They are a smaller group than the Boomers. Some are children of hippies and other counter-culture types. Because this group is greatly divided between the haves and have-nots, clear statements about who they are have not yet emerged, which is one reason they're sometimes called "Generation X." Most tend to be less materialistic and more idealistic than the their Yuppie predecessors. Many are from broken homes and so tend to want marriages that work and that last. Many have adopted their parents' values of personal growth and development.

Typical Concerns

The generation gap between these groups reveals itself in their typical questions and concerns. For example:

- Swing and Silent Generation employees tend to ask, Why do these young people think the world owes them a living?
- Baby Boomer Generation employees are battling their own midlife crises and still tend to focus on discovering the meaning of life.
- Baby Bust Generation workers want to avoid burnout; they search for jobs that will let them have a personal life.

Within each generation, variety abounds, of course, based on cultural, gender, and individual differences. Between one generation and another, there tend to be large differences in beliefs, values, attitudes, and lifestyles.

Mellowing with Age

Older persons, regardless of generation, tend to grow mellow. This is what Walter Gove of Vanderbilt concluded when he explored how people view themselves at different ages (Gove 1985). His findings are supported by a variety of data that are not culture specific, suggesting that they're probably basic human tendencies. The changes in self-concept suggest that as we age:

- We become less self-absorbed, more cooperative and attentive to others, we function more effectively and become more serene and less emotional.
- We act in more socially accepted ways.
- We're more likely to see others as friendly and considerate.
- We become more community oriented.
- We focus more on spiritual concerns.

Younger people, ages 18 to 25, are more likely to see themselves as emotional, nervous, competitive, uncooperative, and not helpful or supportive of others. Having arguments that lead to physical blows occurs almost exclusively among the young men. People younger than 30 are much less likely to vote, to make charitable contributions regardless of income, or to participate in voluntary organizations.

Older persons are more likely to say that spiritual concerns are very important to them, to express a strong interest in spiritual activities, to regard themselves as spiritual or religious, to say they turn to a higher entity for help, and to indicate that spiritual beliefs comfort them. Spirituality plays a relatively minor role in the lives of most young people and takes on increasing significance as they age.

Increased Workplace Contact Among Generations

As corporate structures become more flexible and web-like, as layers of hierarchy are removed, previously segregated generations of employees find themselves working together and even rotating jobs among themselves. Another factor throwing the generations together is the entry and reentry into the workforce of middle-aged women, former retirees, and young student interns and apprentices. Four generations of workers may now find themselves working side by side (Jackson 1992). This provides rich opportunities for all of them. Younger employees have much to learn from older ones, ranging from alternative philosophies of life to practical tips gained from life experiences. Older workers can gain much from younger ones, from learning about what's new to retaining an optimistic, high-energy outlook.

How the Generation Gap Creates Walls

In one study, younger managers were less likely to support older employees' training. But managers in the over-50 age category were more likely to recommend financial support to enable an older employee to attend a technical seminar. In promotion decisions, older managers were much less likely to be influenced by the candidate's age. They were equally likely to promote both the younger and older man for a marketing position, and they favored the creation of a new supervisory position for both a younger and an older woman. We might conclude that an older employee has a better chance of fair treatment from an older boss. We might also conclude that the older boss has lived long enough to begin seeing that age stereotypes are not necessarily true. Leaders need to be aware of a possible generation gap. Perhaps including older managers on a decision-making panel would provide balance.

Issue: Facing Unemployment, Underemployment, Low Wages

Workers older than 45 had higher earnings and less unemployment than younger workers, on average, in the 1980s. In this sense, older workers have an advantage in the labor market. However, once unemployed, they experience longer periods of joblessness. And some older workers experience severe labor market problems. Managers need to understand the causes of employment problems and the policies that can improve the employment prospects of older Americans. Older workers' problems include unemployment, underemployment, and low wages.

- About 10 percent of people between 45 and 70 had labor market problems in 1980, compared to about 14 percent of younger adults.
- Older African Americans are four times as likely to have problems as older Euro-Americans, and older Latino Americans are three times as likely.
- Older women are slightly more likely than older men to have problems. While age discrimination is a part of the problem, there are other factors.
- Older men who lose their jobs on average have less education, more health problems, and stayed longer in their previous jobs than younger job losers and men with those characteristics are likely to remain unemployed longer.
- Older women who lose their jobs show a similar pattern, but also have lower wages and are distributed among occupations differently from younger women.

- Both men and women take longer to find new jobs than younger workers: for older men 20 weeks compared to 13 weeks for younger men; for older women, 21 weeks, compared with 16 weeks for younger women.

During downsizing phases, older workers are more likely to lose their jobs than their younger peers, especially if their skills are becoming obsolete, because they've usually worked up to a relative high pay scale. Unemployment is tougher for those older than 50 because of age discrimination. Some older persons who lose their jobs stay unemployed longer; for example, women and African Americans. Any person who has less education and more health problems tends to remain unemployed longer than the better educated, healthier applicants (Sandell 1987).

Lower wages. Older workers who must find new jobs are likely to accept greater reduction in their pay than younger workers. This is caused in part by the fact that many older workers gain skills in their former jobs, which they've normally held longer than the younger unemployed, skills they can't use in their new job.

Issue: Combating Skills Obsolescence

Workers older than 50 have the economic advantage of being with an organization longer and having organization-specific training. Age differences in years since schooling give an advantage to older workers up to age 50, presumably because being older means having greater work experience and therefore greater productivity. However, older workers tend to have less schooling and schooling in the less well-rewarded fields of study, such as business or science. Therefore, skills obsolescence can be a key problem for them. After age 50, age differences in years since schooling are associated with an appreciable disadvantage to older workers, suggesting the presence of skills obsolescence.

The most important factor associated with earnings and productivity changes as an employee gets older is lack of incentive on the company's part to invest in further training, leading to skills obsolescence. Older workers themselves are less likely to invest in extensive retraining. Research indicates that younger workers will make greater investments on the assumption that they have more time before expected retirement to pay back the costs and to reap the financial benefits of training. Since they earn less than older workers, their time-out from work in order to attend school costs them less (in terms of wages they would have received if they had continued working). However, in the future, training for workers older than 50 will make more sense if the worker is healthy and anticipates working for many more years.

The key disadvantages for older Euro-American male workers, compared to younger workers, are more limited schooling, schooling in less well-rewarded fields of study, skills obsolescence, lesser geographic mobility, and less incentive for further training. Older workers' earnings and productivity tend not to decline with age, but to rise less rapidly, so that younger workers tend to overtake them. This appears to be linked with lowered incentives to invest in further training, both on the part of the employer and the employee.

Training decisions often exclude older workers because they're not seen are part of a pool from which future leaders can be drawn. This may not be direct discrimination but it has the same effect. Managers assume that training for older workers has a shorter payback period. But higher turnover rates and the short half-life of many new technologies suggest that this exclusion of older persons may be more a habit and a result of stereotyping than more strict cost-benefit thinking. Many such corporate decisions are strongly influenced by negative stereotypes, such as older workers are less able to learn, more resistant to change.

Issue: To Retire or Continue Working

Older workers must overcome the myth that everyone should retire by age 65. Currently 80 percent of employees have retired by age 70, but the retirement decision is a complex one that should not be decided upon age alone. In fact, we could say the decision is a life-or-death one, and people should carefully consider the many key factors that affect retirement.

People generally view retirement as a chance to finally be free from onerous responsibility and hard work. Yet retirement means loss for many, losses that may in fact lead to decline and deterioration, such losses as:

- loss of the identity that comes from career roles
- loss of power—organizational power, earning power, prestige
- loss of challenge to keep developing abilities and potentials
- loss of inner fulfillment that is tied to work performance and achievement
- loss of the social ties and social status that are career-connected
- loss of involvement in the active mainstream

In our culture, prestige and self-worth are based largely on occupational status and income, especially for men. And women who haven't had careers of their own often bask in the reflected light of the husband's occupational status. For men and their wives, the sense of loss usually sets in a year or so into retirement. On the other hand, career women are less likely than men to be *defined* by their careers, but research indicates that retirement can be just as traumatic for them.

In 1950, 46 percent of men older than 65 were in the workforce; by 1976 the proportion had dropped to 20 percent. Laws forbidding mandatory retirement were passed shortly after. Surveys indicate that as many as a third of retirees want to stay with the company and move on to some new type of work or different work pattern, if they can. But the stereotype of age as retirement is so ingrained in our culture that most people don't even question it. In fact, researcher Betty Friedan found that most people she interviewed didn't even know there were laws against forced retirement (Friedan 1993).

Advantages for Men in Better Paying Occupations

The minority of men older than 65 who continue to work tend to be either at the bottom or the top of the occupational ladder. Most of those at the bottom are working from financial necessity. Those at the top work for the meaning, enjoyment, and vitality it gives them. Studies indicate that these men are more likely than their retired counterparts to:

- claim excellent health
- find new meaning in their work
- develop their work in new directions
- be active in a number of professional associations
- keep up with new developments and to transmit and advance them
- have a greater sense of their own identity and thus be better able to act contrary to public opinion or others' expectations

Work for a Longer Life

You may have heard that many men die soon after retirement. Does this mean you have to keep working in order to keep living? Studies are indicating that if retirement doesn't lead to new purposes, which often involve continued work or a new line of work, it often ends in early death, or is experienced as a living death. While satisfying work tends to increase longevity, unsatisfying work tends to reduce it. Depression is a typical symptom of a retirement without satisfying work. In 1980, when persons 65 and older were 11 percent of the population, they committed 25 percent of reported suicides. The male-to-female suicide rate goes from three-to-one for young men and women to ten-to-one among those 65 and older. The tendency of men to define themselves by their occupational roles is considered a major factor (Menkler 1981).

People at all ages have needs for work, involvement, intimacy, respect, and self-respect. Studies indicate that the people who experience growth, change, and aliveness in their sixties, seventies, and eighties, those who don't complain of boredom, stagnation, or loneliness, have several things in common, things that are also related to living longer (Friedan 1993).

- They're involved in work that keeps them developing and using their abilities to the fullest, either a career or vital community activity that they chose themselves.
- They're engaged in work that demands and uses the qualities that emerge in age, such as the ability to see situations as part of a bigger picture, to perceive the deeper meanings and truths, and the wisdom to speak that truth.
- They're committed to real work that is needed that brings respect.
- They don't need to pretend to be young.
- They don't expect their most valued qualities to decline with age.
- They refuse to conform to traditional old-age or gender-role stereotypes in their choice of lifestyles and friends.
- They have a wide range of friends across a variety of ages.
- They value and possess the traits of trust, risk-taking, adaptability, nonconformity, and ability to live in the present moment.

These life situations and traits are based on reality and authenticity, not pretense. However, even though the most vital persons don't pretend to be young, they probably don't view themselves as old. Gerontologists have found some evidence that people who don't think of themselves as old do better in age. Given the terrible stigma of aging in our society, viewing oneself as middle aged may actually sustain morale and physical well-being. Also, older persons who remain physically and socially active are more likely to think of themselves as younger.

Those who have it best are those who continually engage in something that is an absolute passion with them. Pretending the goals are real and the work is important are *not* the key. As in all phases of life, the goals must be the individual's, not someone else's or society's, and going through the motions of what we think we *should* do leads to resentment and depression.

Increased chance of disability. Continued good health is a key factor in the retirement decision. Disabilities cut across all age groups, but tend to increase with age. Chronic illness also becomes more prevalent, although the majority of older persons are able to carry out their daily routines. Workplace modifications for those with minor disabilities may suggest changes that are beneficial to the workforce generally, such as improving the lighting or simplifying complex controls.

Limited opportunities for part-time work. Part-time work seems the natural way to make the transition from full-time work to retirement, or to deal with certain disabilities on either a temporary or long-term basis. Survey responses indicate that older workers want to retire gradually. Yet, sudden retirement, not part-time work, is typical. Why is retirement usually sudden? Primarily because so few career options are available to older employees. While many say they would prefer modified work and schedules, flexible options are seldom available. When they are, the pay is often so low that workers choose sudden retirement (Sandell 1987).

LEADERSHIP OPPORTUNITIES

While the U.S. labor pool is shrinking, older Americans are the fastest-growing population group. It's time for employers to reassess their negative view of older workers. We all have a stake in how society will treat our future selves. Savvy business leaders see the benefits of helping older workers move into the twenty-first century. Electronic devices are replacing humans as monitors and controllers of complex machinery. Manufacturing operations are being robotized so as to eliminate routine operative jobs. Factory jobs will probably account for less than 10 percent of employment after the year 2000. New jobs are being created in fields devoted to computerization, robotization, and human services, and these jobs require radically new skills. The fundamental problem of today's older workers is occupational obsolescence. As we move from an industrial economy to an information and service economy, older workers' skills are often industry-specific and not readily transferable.

Leaders face challenges in promoting fairness and opportunities for older employees and in overcoming other employees' prejudice toward them. Other challenges include understanding older workers' needs and preventing skills obsolescence. Leaders also have rich opportunities to help bridge generation gaps, to help older employees to maintain their productivity and motivation, to retain effective older workers, and to utilize their insights and connections in marketing to older customers.

Leadership Opportunity: Promoting Fairness and Opportunity

The older population is ballooning. Baby boomers are entering their fifties now. By 2020 about one in six Americans will be older than 65. Business leaders are preparing for the changes this implies. For one thing, some sociologists are predicting that the Boomers won't be as accepting of age stereotyping and discrimination as recent generations have been. Businesses that treat them more positively will have a definite advantage.

Before the Age Discrimination Employment Act was enacted in 1976, many large companies would not hire workers older than 40. The act, designed to help overcome the effects of ageism on the careers of older persons, provides guidelines in the areas of recruiting, hiring, selection, promotion, and termination. The act has had a favorable impact on older workers, with minor negative side effects for others.

Embracing the Age Discrimination Employment Act

The Age Discrimination Employment Act (ADEA) was enacted for the purpose of:

- protecting workers age 40 to 70 from discrimination
- promoting employment opportunities for older workers capable of meeting job requirements.

It covers private employers of 20 or more persons, labor organizations, employment agencies, and all government employees.

ADEA eliminates mandatory retirement at any age. The major exception to age requirements occurs when an age requirement is a bona fide occupation qualification (BFOQ), reasonably necessary to the normal operations of a business. Also, differential treatment of employees based on reasonable factors other than age, such as physical fitness, is permitted. The ADEA does not preclude the discharge or discipline of an older worker for good cause. For example, an employer might defend a personnel decision on the ground that the older employee could not meet performance standards or that his declining functional abilities represented a potential threat to the public safety. Careful documentation of such actions are critical if an age discrimination suit is filed. The EEOC is responsible for enforcing the ADEA.

Ending recruiting discrimination. An example of recruiting discrimination is the practice of focusing on college graduates. Since age tends to be highly correlated with college graduation, the policy of recruiting future managers from the ranks of college seniors potentially discriminates against older employees with comparable credentials. A corporation would be especially vulnerable to charges of age discrimination if admission to its executive training programs were limited *exclusively* to recent college graduates.

Ending selection discrimination. Job application forms can no longer require applicants to state their age, nor can interviewers legally inquire about age. The issue is whether an applicant is capable of performing the job. An age limit is a BFOQ only when it can be shown that all, or almost all, persons over that age cannot meet the requirements of a specific job. A construction firm might be able to show that virtually no one over age 70 can meet the physical requirements for carrying 60-pound loads up a ladder. However, a restaurant chain or airline will have a difficult time showing that organization image, or even customer preferences for attractive young hostesses, is sufficient justification for rejecting an otherwise qualified over-40 job applicant.

Age limits are likely to be upheld as a BFOQ in jobs with stringent physical demands that also involve public safety. Accordingly, it is not uncommon to find age limits governing the selection and retirement of police officers, firefighters, air traffic controllers, and similar jobs where strenuous physical exertion or work under stressful conditions is required. The courts have been willing to accept age criteria for positions where the public safety is involved. It is wise, however, for companies to have statistical or medical data to back up decisions about physical incapacities associated with aging.

Ending promotion discrimination. Organizations most often get in trouble with age discrimination suits concerning promotion when they follow inconsistent promotion policies and then try to justify their decisions after an employee files a complaint. Personnel actions, including both promotion and termination decisions, are more defensible when they are based on a systematic, objective, and job-related performance appraisal system. The system should present employees with periodic feedback on their strengths and weaknesses, to help create realistic expectations about promotion opportunities. The system should also generate the documentation that would be required to prove that personnel decisions comply with the law.

Ending termination discrimination. Decisions to terminate older workers are almost always difficult because motivations for such termination can be subject to many interpretations. Perhaps the best defense against a charge of age bias is the ability to show that the decision was based on the employee's substandard performance or some similar legitimate business reason. Managers must be prepared to demonstrate that the employee's behavior was measured fairly and objectively and that the employee was given a reasonable opportunity to bring his performance up to standard. Managers should also be prepared to demonstrate that they did not harass the employee in an attempt to "run him off."

Avoiding Lawsuits

Managers must be especially sensitive to decisions that might reflect age discrimination in recruiting and selecting employees, recommending employees for training or development opportunities, and promoting employees. In each of these decisions, employee performance or potential, not employee age, should be the governing factor. Similarly, decisions about employee transfers, demotions, layoffs, and terminations should be made without regard to age.

Systematic assessment of employee performance on job-related dimensions will provide an important basis for making and defending a range of personnel actions affecting the careers of older workers. Periodic feedback to employees highlighting their strengths and weaknesses and exploring the implications of their present performance for future career moves will help dispel misconceptions and misunderstandings and create realistic expectations about the future. Effective two-way communication between employees and their managers at every level in the organization can usually prevent costly age discrimination litigation.

Understanding the Impact of the Retirement Amendments

Amendments to the ADEA first extended mandatory retirement from age 65 to 70 and later made mandatory retirement illegal at any age except for certain occupations. It was widely anticipated that raising the mandatory retirement age to 70 would force companies to place greater emphasis on assessing employee performance, so as to justify firing poor performers. In fact, three years after the amendments went into effect, no evidence was found that companies were using stricter performance assessment procedures. Substantial opposition to extending the retirement age centered on the possibility that retaining older workers would delay the promotion of some younger workers, women, and minorities. These workers are often just waiting for employees in higher positions to retire so they can move up and into their jobs. Researchers found that the amendment does affect about 4 percent of these workers.

As a result of eliminating mandatory retirement completely, government analysts predicted that by the year 2000, there would be an additional 412,000 men older than 65 in the labor force. This is an increase of about 10 percent in the labor force participation rate for males age 60 to 70, for only a "minuscule effect on the composition of the total workforce" (Rosen and Jerdee 1985, 79). Researchers concluded that most employees retire at or before age 65 and this trend is likely to continue.

Adopting Corporate Culture Norms That Appreciate Older Workers

If business leaders want to retain productive older workers, they must bring about changes in corporate culture norms. For example, managers who hold age stereotypes may be less willing to approve promotions, offer training opportunities, and work out performance problems with older workers. In fact, studies indicate that managers age 40 and over tend to be rated significantly lower than younger managers on readiness for promotion, even when education, performance, and job tenure are comparable. Such age stereotypes contribute to an organizational climate that discourages continued employment opportunities for older employees. On the other hand, when management is able to develop supportive organizational norms that encourage older workers to stay on, middle-aged and younger workers get a clear message: The contributions of senior employees are recognized and welcomed here (Cox and Nkomo 1992).

Motivating Older Employees

Managers who expect a decline in motivation among older workers might make age-based managerial decisions that in fact lead to decreased motivation for these employees. To the extent that an older employee perceives that his efforts are no longer linked to organization advancement, his motivation tends to gradually decline. Limited opportunities for development and lack of feedback about performance may further reduce the older worker's motivation. In today's relatively flat organizational structures, there are shorter ladders to climb and fewer promotions to give. Many ambitious employees reach career plateaus much earlier than in the past. Employees need to become aware of this fact and to be given opportunities for lateral moves to expand their career growth and development.

It is likely that lowered motivation may result, not from aging itself, but from managerial expectations and treatment of older employees. If this is so, then policy changes to eliminate discrimination against older employees represent only a first step. Additional efforts to help managers identify age stereotypes and eliminate their effects on everyday decisions need to be made. These efforts must also deal with all the practices that tend to support and perpetuate the stereotypes.

Leadership Opportunity: Bridging Generation Gaps

Leaders need more than a desire to help older workers. They need an appreciation of the strengths, weakness, and special needs of older employees. They must have a knowledge of special legal requirements that apply. They must know how to develop and implement specific actions plans aimed at helping them work up to their full potential in a changing work environment. Bridging the generation gap at all levels is becoming more important in the workplace because networking and relationships are more central to job performance. Many young employees may have few relationships with older persons other than their parents and grandparents.

One remedy for this experiential gap is to make assignments to teams and committees so that employees of different ages will work together. Remember, meaningful contact among diverse employees can reduce prejudice. Contact that involves working together toward meaningful goals is most likely to bridge generational differences.

Another powerful remedy is to find ways to include older workers in communication lines. Other remedies include:

- Making younger workers more aware and sensitive of older workers' needs, strengths, and potential contributions—helping them replace myths and stereotypes with facts.

- Making older workers more aware of behaviors that foster the generation gap and behaviors that bridge it. For example, a person's image is a powerful communication tool. An image that promotes rapport usually includes dressing in style, maintaining good grooming, enjoying an active personal life, showing a warm sense of humor, *not* offering knee-jerk judgmental criticisms of fellow workers or repeating the same old comments, contributing new ideas, and giving credit to co-workers.

Another remedy to generation gaps is to provide diversity training that focuses on building relationship skills with older employees. Training can focus on utilizing varied generational strengths as well as individual strengths. It can also include the advantages of hiring and retaining older employees, as indicated by various studies, as mentioned earlier, these advantages include being:

- more stable
- more reliable
- more careful
- absent less
- less likely to quit

- less likely to have accidents
- more cheerful
- more committed to the organization
- more involved with their jobs

Training seminars often start with a frank discussion of the values differences and how these differences are reflected in supervisory styles and expectations about worker loyalty, commitment, and career aspirations. Cases that present typical specific problems in the relationships between younger and older workers can be analyzed and solutions explored.

Cases can include problems that arise when young managers supervise older workers. Sociologists say that when you interact with another person, you normally define (either consciously or subconsciously) the other person's status as higher than, the same as, or lower than your own. This definition affects the way you behave with that person, what you say and do. When all the status cues are consistent, we're fairly clear about how to act. Problems may develop in status-inconsistent relationships between younger and older employees, such as when a young woman is assigned to supervise a much older man.

Be aware of communication across the generation gap. People tend to communicate within their age groups rather than between them because they seek perspectives similar to their own and support for their opinions. Also, younger workers may shun and thus isolate older workers, creating a communication gap. Training strategies can help to bridge some of the gaps.

Leadership Opportunity: Meeting Older Workers' Needs

Current changes in the nature of work can be threatening to older employees with limited skills, but they may be challenging and intriguing to other, better educated older employees. Leaders have an opportunity to help less-educated workers face their fears and make career plans for gaining new skills and knowledge. They can support better-educated workers in using and maintaining their skills.

Recognize Fears of Less Educated Older Workers

The picture as seen by many older employees with limited education and skills:

- Technological change is a threat.
- Retraining is scary or unacceptable.

- Unions are not much help because they're going along with management to eliminate the old jobs and retrain for the new jobs.
- Government is not much help because its programs are also geared toward retraining.

Support Goals of Better Educated Older Workers

Better-educated, more highly skilled older workers tend to be more flexible and to see a brighter picture:

- They often want a few minor adjustments in their work situation.
- They may desire to work a few less hours per week.
- They often want to be freed from the prison of the 5-day, 40-hour week or the arduous commute to the workplace.
- They may wish to be liberated from the controls on time and place of work implied by traditional employment contracts.
- They may want more flexibility and discretion in their work. Many may want to work at home on a full- or part-time basis, perhaps for more than one employer.

Managers need to be able to develop arrangements for time and place of work that will enable these talented older employees to continue in productive employment.

Adopt Strategies for Meeting Needs

In addition to other specific strategies mentioned in this section, some simple general strategies for understanding an individual employees' concerns include listening with awareness, developing empathy for their situation in life, and helping them to manage the changes they encounter.

Listening. Listen to older workers and be a supportive sounding board. You'll learn a great deal about their strengths and problems that way, gain insights to solutions to problems, and gain from their knowledge and experience. Consider holding small group meetings of older workers to get in touch with their interests, desires, talents, and needs.

Developing empathy. If you live long enough, you'll be an older person one day, if you're not already. Ask yourself, What will I do when I'm no longer "cute?" and then put yourself in the older person's shoes. Look for the individual personality inside the older body. Be open to many kinds of beauty. Focus on skills, experience, contribution, and performance rather than narrow ideas about physical appearance.

Managing change. Encourage older workers to stay current. Motivate and reward them to respond positively to change, to develop the new skills and acquire the information that the changing business environment requires. Many older employees need a little encouragement to help them overcome the limitations imposed by cultural myths.

Leadership Opportunity: Preventing Skills Obsolescence

Equal opportunity for older workers calls for companies to design policies that provide affordable and useful training to workers of all ages. Policies need to ensure equal access to this training and to the more secure and better-paying jobs. When older workers find themselves with obsolete skills, in dead-end jobs or career ruts, their motivation and job performance are likely to decline. The potential is still there, but it is underutilized. Leaders can remedy this situation through career planning and appropriate training.

Career Planning

In these times of rapid technological change, the most important goal of career management programs may be to identify job categories where future organizational needs are likely to be low and to help employees in these jobs to plan a new career path. Organizations can prepare employees to move into high-demand career tracks compatible with their interests, skills, and aspirations.

In addition to formal career planning programs, the day-to-day sharing of information between managers and employees provides an invaluable source of career guidance and counseling on a continuing basis. Managers can alert employees to upcoming changes that may have an impact on their careers. They can serve as a sounding board for employees' aspirations, plans, and intentions. They can give honest feedback about the likelihood of employees achieving their career goals. They may intervene directly to help employees get the training they need and to cope with job stress. They can redesign job requirements to help employees get back on track. In other words, managers can serve as day-to-day career counselors.

Given the importance of their career counselor function, managers need support from the organization in fulfilling this responsibility. Managers should be:

- informed well in advance of changes that could alter the skills and experiences necessary to fulfill job duties in their departments

- encouraged to learn more about key career issues, such as career plateaus, career burnout, and job redesign

- informed of organizational policies regarding retirement options, such as part-time status, job sharing, phaseout programs, and consulting arrangements

- given ongoing training in coaching and counseling skills, such as listening, goal setting, problem solving, and career planning

Individual career planning begins with a critical self-analysis of interests, skills, and potential. The employee should then develop short-term and long-term career goals, specific and in writing. The employee should develop written plans for achieving goals, including how to use strengths and overcome obstacles. Written plans help an individual and managers to assess progress along the way. Finally, especially important for older employees, they should make contingency plans to cover the possibility that their career progress may get seriously sidetracked.

Training to Prevent Skills Obsolescence

Technological change creates new opportunities for persons trained in technological and scientific fields. It also leads to the displacement of production workers and middle managers. Older workers' skills are likely to become obsolete.

A boom in high-tech specialties, including computer software, biomedical engineering, telecommunications, robotics, fiber optics, and laser applications are creating new employment opportunities for persons with advanced training. Meanwhile, workers in traditional manufacturing industries—and their managers—are being laid off as these functions move to lower-wage countries or are robotized.

Some companies provide in-house training to keep employees' skills and knowledge up to date. Preliminary evidence suggests that training approaches that are most compatible with the cognitive strengths of older employees:

- permit self-paced learning

- focus on experiential learning rather than abstract learning

On the other hand, *most* people probably respond best to this type of training.

Some companies provide a tuition reimbursement plan designed to help retiring workers prepare for second careers. Senior employees begin to draw from their educational fund a few years before retirement and continue to draw from it for a few years after retirement. Employees who acquire skills in the company's "critical needs areas" may be offered post-retirement, part-time, or consulting positions.

LEADERSHIP OPPORTUNITY: RETAINING PRODUCTIVE OLDER WORKERS

Currently more than half of Americans are out of the workforce before age 63, and 80 percent are out by the time they're 70. The goal of a retention strategy is to retain older workers as long as feasible. Such a strategy can benefit the organization as well as older employees and society. We'll discuss a broad outline for developing and implementing a retention strategy, along with some key factors that influence employees to retire, and some alternative options companies can offer.

An effective retention strategy can benefit the organization because it:

- lowers pension costs
- lowers turnover rates and resulting turnover costs
- provides longer and larger paybacks for investments in training
- contributes to high employee morale
- enhances the organization's reputation in the community

A good retention strategy benefits society because it:

- lowers social security costs
- adds to U.S. productivity and the tax base
- contributes to the social integration of the older population

The retention policy benefits older employees because it:

- keeps them physically and mentally active
- maintains or enhances their self-respect
- provides them with income
- satisfies their social needs by keeping them in daily touch with other active people

Understanding Factors that Affect the Employee's Decision

Before developing a retention strategy, you and other leaders need to understand why employees choose to retire. Then you can design more realistic retention strategies. The factors that have the strongest and most consistent influence on the timing of retirement are health considerations and financial well-being. Gender and educational level also appear to affect retirement intentions. The answers to the following questions will provide insight into the likelihood of an employee choosing to retire. The best way to get the answers is to ask, either through a written survey, a personal interview, or both. The key questions are:

- Can the employee afford to retire?
- Does disability or declining health make retirement desirable?
- Is the employee male or female?

Women tend to retire earlier than men, which may be related to the fact that women have been concentrated in lower-level jobs. Workers with less formal education tend to retire earlier, perhaps because they are clustered in more physically demanding and less intrinsically motivating jobs. Ethnicity has not been associated with patterns of early retirement.

Other factors that have a less significant impact on retirement plans include:

- Is the female employee married? Working married women retire earlier than their male counterparts, generally retiring when their somewhat older husbands do.
- Is the job blue collar or white collar? Blue-collar workers generally retire at an earlier age than white collar workers. The major explanation is that blue-collar jobs entail heavier physical exertion and less comfortable working conditions.

- Does the employee value work or leisure more? As we might expect, workers who attach greater importance to work as a source of life satisfaction and are generally satisfied with their jobs are less likely to retire early.

- Is the job location urban or rural? People who live in large urban areas are more likely to postpone retirement than those who live in small rural towns.

- Does the corporate culture value older employees? If the corporate culture supports older workers who delay their retirement, they are likely to stay longer. Leaders can influence the value employees generally place on the contributions of older workers and the belief that effective workers should be retained as long as possible. Some organizations actually encourage direct group pressure on people to retire. Others organizations encourage a more subtle expression of norms calling for early retirement. Such pressures do have a strong influence on employees' retirement decisions.

- Are work demands compatible with older workers' abilities? Many individual older employees are being pushed by economic realities in the direction of delayed retirement. Longer life spans and the increasing proportion of the population that is older are creating strains on social security and Medicare funds. These developments are signaling the need in the future to keep more older people working longer.

Clearly, the information economy will ease the transition to longer working lives. Working with computers in service-sector occupations such as medical diagnostics or insurance services is much less demanding physically than assembly line, construction, and other manual labor. It's unrealistic for us to expect people to spend almost a third of their lives in retirement. The challenge to traditional organization structures is tapping the knowledge of their older workers while keeping promotion opportunities open for younger employees. For newer organizational structures, where self-managing teams are replacing most of the hierarchy, such problems tend to dissolve.

- Is management supportive in helping older workers' adapt to change? Management can cooperate with older workers in many ways; for example, helping them to pace themselves and avoid burnout. Stamina may decrease for some, but they can still be productive workers. Learning time may take a little longer but will be mastered. Be flexible. Consider interactive and self-paced training, job rotation, flextime, part-time or temporary assignments, periodic sabbaticals, and phased retirement.

- Does the company offer flexible retirement options? Remember, surveys indicate that about one-third of retirees would prefer to stay with the company and move on to a different kind of work or work pattern. Offering senior employees job modifications and more flexible retirement options tends to increase their desire to postpone retirement. In addition, permitting major job modifications could launch senior employees on something of a second career, while opening career paths for younger employees.

Establishing a Retention Strategy

A broad outline for developing and implementing a retention strategy includes establishing a written policy, creating a task force to create strategies for implementing the policy, consulting with all employees, coordinating all aspects of the plan, and communicating the changed values to all employees.

Developing a written policy. An ad hoc group of top managers strategically located in the organization is given the task of researching and developing a written policy on older employees. The written policy is approved by the executive committee and the board of directors.

Developing strategies for implementation. The ad hoc group expands to create a task force to develop a retention strategy. One of the members develops a knowledge center relevant to personnel administration for older employees. A consultant with wide-ranging expertise in older worker retention is hired. Included in the task force are:

- persons with a vested interest in current personnel policies and procedures
- key people with responsibilities for such areas as pension systems, job design, and work scheduling
- people in key roles in operating departments that will be responsible for implementing the strategy
- a few older workers

Consulting with employees. The task force consults widely with people within the organization, holding meetings that contain consciousness-raising and educational components, asking key questions similar to the ones we've discussed.

Coordinating strategies, goals, and career plans. The task force establishes specific goals for the retention of employees in various age categories. Strategic goals include training and development activities. These goals are then coordinated with operating managers at the level of the individual employee. The career plans of all older employees will include plans for phasing into retirement. These career plans are kept on file in each unit. Copies of all plans are reviewed by the task force and compared with program goals. The reasons for any discrepancies are explored. Goals are brought into line with reality, or employees are encouraged to modify their plans. Commitment gained during the planning phase is reinforced.

Procedures and timetables are established. The system provides for someone to get reports on the career plans of each older employee, including plans for development, job or schedule changes, and gradual retirement. The system ties in these reports with the total human resource planning and development process. The results of the program are monitored on a unit, departmental, and divisional basis, so that the effects of the retention strategy are made visible.

Communicating changed values. The achievements of older workers are recognized and publicized. There is shift away from celebrating retirements and toward celebrating continued contributions. Some further actions to build a climate that is supportive of a retention strategy include:

- training all managers concerning the ADEA and any other legal considerations governing the employment of older workers
- helping all employees overcome deep-rooted assumptions and expectations about what senior employees can and cannot do
- raising all employees' awareness of the pervasive influence of age stereotypes on day-to-day interactions and decisions
- providing all employees with skills in confrontation and problem solving to bridge communication gaps between young managers and senior employees
- exploring value differences between younger and older workers
- examining special problems in the mentor-protégé relationship

Overcoming Barriers to a Retention Policy

Leaders must understand why managers push older workers into retirement and determine if there are ways to overcome these barriers to retaining effective employees.

Beginning in the 1980s many companies focused on cutting costs, often by downsizing. Reducing the number of highly paid senior employees and substituting cheaper younger ones became a strategy for many firms. Most companies aren't allowing senior employees the options of working part time, job sharing, tandem staffing, or other flexible scheduling, which is what most older workers say they want. Those companies who do offer such options normally make workers retire from their current level and hire them back at a much lower wage, often on a temporary basis.

Although companies can no longer force employees to retire, they can offer them tempting rewards. Failing that, they can resort to subtle pressure: lower performance evaluations, onerous job assignments, taking away responsibilities or perks, exclusion from desired projects or meetings. Finally the employee gets fed up, gives up, and retires. Studies indicate that managers are less likely to pressure employees to retire if they view them as having some of the following traits and life situations:

- younger
- higher performance ratings
- financially troubled
- likely to make a poor social adjustment to retirement
- engaging in personal activities that are compatible with business interests
- receiving union support

On the other hand, some factors that cause managers to encourage older workers to retire and therefore discourage implementation of a retention policy are:

- pension formulas that are increasingly expensive when high salaried employees work beyond age 65

- pressures to promote women and minority employees, which creates pressure for openings at higher levels

- self-interest of many managers to make more room at the top by sticking to rigid retirement ages

- evaluation avoidance—requiring everyone to retire at age 65 is easier than evaluating their fitness for employment year after year, past age 65

- weak enforcement of age discrimination laws

Providing Flexible Career Options

Many companies have only two alternatives for older employees: keep working or fully retire. More suitable options may include job changes, job sharing, part-time work, work phase-out, contract consulting, and similar creative career changes. Some companies are providing training programs that focus on alternatives to complete retirement and on post-retirement employment options and second-career opportunities.

One effective option is establishing a company temporary employee pool. Retirees who wish to work on a part-time basis sign up. Where appropriate, the company provides refresher courses to employees who have been away from the job for some time. Retirees may be called on to fill in during vacation periods or to add their expertise to special projects. At higher levels they're hired as consultants and work on a project fee basis.

Realistically Assessing Ability and Disability

Managers may be especially likely to misinterpret health information on older employees because they hold stereotypes regarding the declining health of older people. Identical health conditions may be perceived as more serious and disabling for older workers than for younger ones. One study indicated that when medical reports emphasize capacities or functions that an employee can successfully perform, manager's recommended continued employment. When medical reports emphasized disabilities, managers recommended part-time assignments, phaseouts, and termination—even when the health problems were not likely to interfere with ability to do the job, in some cases.

Disability laws could come into play in these instances. A systematic and comprehensive approach to health evaluations might include the following:

- current and complete job descriptions, with emphasis on physical and psychological demands
- medical reports that emphasizes both employee capacities and limitations associated with illness or injury and that focus on job-related implications of medical problems
- training for managers in interpreting medical reports in order to make better decisions regarding further employability
- job redesign as one strategy for meeting the needs of senior workers with health problems

Improving the Performance Review System

Good performance appraisal systems provide the accurate, objective information that managers need in order to make important decisions about motivating, rewarding, promoting, training, transferring, and terminating employees. They should be based only on job-related behaviors and achievements that are related to a job analysis, behavior standards, and agreed-upon measures. A management-by-objectives process is considered the most legally acceptable.

Leadership Opportunity: Marketing to Older Customers

The population of older persons is exploding. For one thing, people are living longer, older consumers tend to have more spending power than in the past, and the Baby Boom generation is turning 50. Older Americans offer a booming market in financial services, from insurance to estate planning. They are still a relatively untapped market in housing, clothing, travel, and investment services. Just as women professionals have an edge in understanding women's issues and relating to women customers, so older professionals and employees have an edge in understanding elders' issues and relating to older customers. And many older persons appreciate seeing that older employees are valued in the companies they do business with. It's good business to retain effective older employees.

SUMMARY

The longer we live, the more we are to be faced with cultural devaluation, for ageism has accelerated in this century. Age myths picture older employees as an increasing problem in terms of productivity, attendance and accident rates, physical and mental ability, rigidity and dogmatism, commitment to work, and physical attractiveness. Actually, older workers are just as mentally alert and productive as others and have better attendance, accident, and turnover rates. Their physical and mental ability are retained well beyond age 70 as long as they remain in good health. In fact, people reach their mental prime at about age 60. Older workers are no more likely to be rigid and dogmatic than others, but tend to have much greater knowledge and wisdom. Healthy people retain their creativity even past the age of 100.

Who are the old? The ADEA covers people older than 40, but gerontologists identify the young-old as age 65 to 75 and the old-old as older than 75. People are living longer and retaining their vitality, so even these definitions of old are likely to be extended. This fact, combined with the fact that the Baby Boom generation is turning 50, means that the older population is expanding rapidly.

Since older workers have progressed to higher pay than younger ones, this can make them a layoff target during downsizing. If they do lose their jobs, they have more difficulty finding another position. If their skills are in high demand, they may have more job security than younger workers. However, skills obsolescence and ongoing training are major issues for those past age 50. Younger managers are often unwilling to invest in their retraining, and they themselves may not be motivated. One reason is the assumption that they'll retire before the training investment pays off. Another is the myth that older people have difficulty learning and adapting to change, even though these traits are not necessarily affected by age.

At some point older employees must deal with the issue of retirement—whether to retire, what to retire to, and what impact retirement is likely to have on their lives. Unless they replace work commitment with a commitment to other meaningful activities, they're likely to decline and die. Those who live longest tend to remain mentally and physically active with a passionate purpose in life.

You as a business leader have many opportunities the appreciate and utilize the wealth of experience and talent older employees can offer your company. The ADEA provides guidelines for treating older employees with fairness and giving them equal opportunities. You can help employees overcome prejudice toward older workers through diversity training and changing corporate culture norms. You can develop strategies for understanding older workers' needs, and help them avoid skills obsolescence through career planning and training. You'll have many opportunities to help bridge generation gaps by making appropriate assignments that require workers of different ages to work together. You can help the company retain its effective older workers by finding out how older employees feel about retiring, what their work preferences are, and then developing a retention strategy. While most employees do retire by age 65, most don't necessarily want to retire earlier, many want reduced job demands, and some prefer to work well past 65 and even 75. Among the greatest opportunities older employees offer are their insights and connections in marketing to older customers.

Skill Builder 10.1: The Case of Older Worker Wendy

You're in charge of Bache Investment's college recruiting. You cannot remember a more hectic time in your life. When you were promoted to this job, your boss told you that the job would test your energy and endurance. During the past two months, you visited 24 universities and interviewed more than 200 MBA students for entry-level investment advisor positions. The experience has been exhausting. Because of your reading schedule, you have relied heavily on your assistant **Wendy** to handle many duties that you usually attend to personally.

Since returning to the office from your recruiting trips, you have become increasingly aware of Wendy's aloofness. You sense that she is purposely avoiding you. You also noted that she quickly looks away when you question her about a late travel voucher or a missing file. A little investigating revealed that Wendy is behind in her routine responsibilities and is now over a week late with an important EEO/AA report. Wendy's failure to attend a monthly staff meeting was the last straw. You are determined to get Wendy back on track or to find someone else who is capable of managing the workload. You left a note for Wendy, requesting that she meet you in your office at 8:45 Monday morning.

Now take the role of Wendy. You have been having doubts about your ability to manage the growing workload and about your future at Bache Investments. Returning to fulltime work four years ago at age 53 represented quite a change for you. Although you had worked as an executive secretary before your marriage, your previous positions had been much less demanding than this position. At home, your husband has also noticed a recent change in your behavior. He tells you that you seem tense and short-tempered and asks if you're having problems at the office. You confide that you think your boss is subtly pressuring you to quit. You explain that he told you to complete several complex monthly EEO/AA reports without reducing your regular workload.

You confess to your husband that the reports require many statistical calculations, some beyond anything you ever encountered. Completing the reports accurately seemed to take forever. You tell him how you have worked through lunch hours two and three times a week. You relate how you skipped staff meetings just to catch up on regular paperwork. You have been feeling overwhelmed and incompetent. With only six more years to go before you plan to retire, you wonder why your boss wants to force you out. Perhaps your future with the company will be resolved at the Monday morning meeting with the boss.

- In your role as Wendy's manager, what actions would you take?
- In your role as Wendy, what actions would you take?

Skill Builder 10.2: The Case of the Youthful Supervisor

Jose is 27 years old. From a Latino American family, his parents were strict and taught him that older people deserve more respect and are usually the ones in authority. His father was the undisputed head of the home, and his grandfather was the highly respected patriarch of a large clan. Jose has been transferred from a field assignment and promoted to team leader of a product promotions group. One of the team members, *Scott*, is in his fifties and has been with the company for nearly ten years. Scott reminds Jose of his father is some ways.

Jose must meet with Scott to make suggestions for improvements on his part of a current team project. Jose senses that Scott is somewhat defensive toward him and a little resistant to taking constructive criticism and suggestions from him.

- Jose asks you for advice. What would you say to him?

Skill Builder 10.3: The Case of Stock Broker John

Leigh is Human Resources Director for Goldman Funds, an investment firm. Her job is to hire stock brokers who have the ability to create wealth for Goldman clients and for the company. Leigh has been in this field for 20 years and spent many of those years as a stock broker herself, so she knows how demanding the job can be. Most of the stock brokers are young, unmarried, and devote 60 to 70 hours a week to their jobs. Most of them also spend several hours a week maintaining their physical fitness in order to deal with the stress of the job.

Leigh is interviewing applicants for a stock broker position that just opened up. The most unusual applicant is *John*, unusual because he's 67 years old while the other applicants are in their twenties or thirties. John had a long career in the insurance industry, with many years as a salesman, a few years as a claims adjuster, and the remaining years as an executive. John retired when he was 62, and within a year, he was extremely bored with retirement activities. He enrolled in the local university and has just completed a master's degree in finance. He earned grades that ranked him in the top 10 percent of his class.

John comes across as very personable in the interview. He tells Leigh, "I've always loved to sell, I've always loved dealing with calculated risks, and it's very important to me to get to know the clients I serve and to make a contribution through my work." Leigh is impressed, but she's concerned about how many years they can reasonably expect John to work. Leigh is also concerned about the high turnover rate that seems to come with the stock broker position. One of her goals is to lower the employee turnover rate.

- What are the key issues in this case?
- If you were Leigh, what would you do?

Skill Builder 10.4: A Case of Maggie's Way

Maggie, age 55, has been an office manager with the Pillsbury-Mason law firm chain for the past 15 years. She is extremely dependable, loyal, and committed to her job and the firm. She has received regular performance awards and is highly valued and respected in the firm.

Jake was hired a few months ago as an administrative assistant. He just graduated with honors and holds a brand new degree in business administration with a concentration in management. His goal is to become an office manager very quickly. He knows he has what it takes. However, he had only a few months of actual office experience before taking this job, so he's having a little difficulty adapting to his coworkers and the office environment. Jake's main frustration is that he has many good ideas, and he wants to take action on them. He knows he could run this office in a minute, but he's blocked because "Maggie's ways" control the entire office.

As the other employees say, "Maggie's Way" is sometimes confusing, but Maggie is very competent and always on top of everything. The problem is that her ways are sometimes unique, so it's difficult for new employees to understand or to find things. Her procedures generally are very simple and to the point, but sometimes they're so simple that others tend to look right over them, especially in a hectic office. On the other hand, when it comes to many procedures, Maggie insists that employees take their time, go through the proper channels, and follow her office manual. In contrast, Jake believes in getting things done efficiently, finding short cuts, avoiding time-consuming over-cautiousness, and basically getting on with it.

Jake's experience is that he has difficulty understanding many of Maggie's requests. He frequently sees the best way to handle a procedure or task, but Maggie always wants him to do it her way. When he tries to explain how a procedure could be improved upon, Maggie listens politely, but somehow it always ends up that the procedure is done her way.

Last week, Jake was under a great deal of pressure to complete a project. He took things into his own hands, did it his way, and got it out on time. When Maggie found out, she confronted him. Tempers flared and they exchanged some heated words about each other's management styles. *Stan Mason*, one of the law partners, walked by as this exchange was going on. He's concerned. Pillsbury-Mason is known for its quiet, calm, harmonious environment.

- What are the key issues in this case?
- If you were Stan Mason, what would you do?
- If you were Jake, what would you do?
- If you were Maggie, what would you do?

REFERENCES

Advertising Age. "Door Ajar to Women of All Ages in Ads." (October 4, 1993): 52.

Campbell, R.T., J. Abolafia, and G. L. Maddox. "Life-Course Analysis in Social Gerontology." *Gender and the Life Course.* New York: Aldine, 1985.

Cox, Taylor, Jr. and Stella M. Nkomo, "Candidate Age As a Factor in Promotability Ratings." *Public Personnel Management* 2 (Summer 1992): 197–210.

Friedan, Betty. *The Fountain of Age.* New York: Simon & Schuster, 1993.

Gann, L.J. and P.J. Duignan. *The Hispanics of the United States: A History.* Boulder, CO: Westview Press, 1986.

Gove, Walter R. "The Effect of Age and Gender on Deviant Behavior: A Biopsychosocial Perspective."*Gender and the Life Course.* NY: Aldine, 1985.

Hushbeck, Judith C. *Old and Obsolete: Age Discrimination and the American Worker, 1860–1920.* New York: Garland Publishing, Inc., 1989

Jackson, Susan E. *Diversity in the Workplace.* New York: Guilford Press, 1992.

Menkler, Meredith. "Research on the Health Effects of Retirement." *Journal of Health and Social Behavior* 22 (1981): 117–30.

Retirement Living (April 1976). Report of survey regarding older workers.

Rosen, Benson and Thomas Jerdee. "Managing Older Workers' Careers." *Research in Personnel and Human Resources Management* 6 (1988): 37–74.

Rosen, Benson, and T. H. Jerdee. *Older Employees: New Roles for Valued Resources.* Homewood, IL: Dow Jones-Irwin, 1985.

Ryff, Carol D. "Subjective Experience of Life-Span Transitions." *Gender and the Life Course.* New York: Aldine, 1985.

Salzberg Seminar on Health, Productivity and Aging, June 1983.

Sandell, Steven H. *The Problem Isn't Age: Work and Older Americans.* New York: Praeger, 1987.

U.S. Census Bureau. *We . . . the American Elderly.* Department of Commerce, Washington, DC, 1993.

Resources

Aging, a journal.

American Association of Retired Persons (AARP), the largest older persons' organization, which engages in research and lobbying and publishes the magazine *Modern Maturity*.

Gray Panthers, an organization.

McCabe, Jim. Consultant on Aging Workers, Technical Assistance Group, San Ramon, CA (510) 838–7277.

Older Women's League (OWL), an organization.

Waters, Elinor B. and Jane Goodman. *Empowering Older Adults.* San Francisco: Jossey-Bass, 1990. This book includes examples of corporate programs for older workers.

Working with Obese Persons

When I really look at the people on the street, I see a jungle of bodies, growing
every which way like lush plants, growing tall and short and slender
and round, hairy and hairless, dark and pale and soft and hard
and glorious. They are all loved and lovable.
Sally Tisdale

Between one and two million people are considered "morbidly obese." These people have begun organizing to fight one of the few remaining types of discrimination that has gone unchallenged. They see weight discrimination as the final frontier in the civil rights struggle and hope to eventually expand the federal Civil Rights Act to cover obese people.

> ### What's in a Name?
> The legal term *morbidly obese* refers to persons who weigh at least twice as much as the top of the medically recommended "normal weight range" for persons of their height, build, and age. For adults this means people at least 100 pounds above the normal weight range.

Before we explore the myths and facts, complete Self-Awareness Activities 11.1 and 11.2.

Self-Awareness Activity 11.1: What Do You Believe About Obese Persons?

Purpose:
- to get in touch with your beliefs and stereotypes about this group of people
- to experience how judgmental beliefs affect your thinking and feeling processes
- to experience the ways in which your beliefs create your reality regarding other persons, even before you have any interaction with them.

Part I. What Do You Believe About Obese Women?

Step 1. Associations
- Relax as deeply as you can: close your eyes and take a few deep breaths.
- Focus on the words "obese woman" and allow a mental picture to come up in your mind's eye.

- Notice the words and images that come to mind as you "see" this woman.
- Open your eyes and list 10 to 20 words in the order in which they occur to you.
- Review your list. Mark a plus beside the words that are positive, a minus beside the words that are negative, and a circle beside neutral words.

Step 2. Negative Associations

- Close your eyes and focus again on the image of the obese woman. Formulate a negative opinion or judgment, perhaps one you typically hold about such women.
- Notice your *feelings* as you see the person in this negative way. What *thoughts* come up as you focus on the image?
- Write a few sentences about your feelings and thoughts.

Step 3. Positive Associations

- Formulate a positive opinion or judgment, perhaps one you typically hold about obese women.
- Notice your *feelings* as you see the person in this positive way. What *thoughts* come up as you focus on the image?
- Write a few sentences about your feelings and thoughts.

Step 4. Insights

- Focus on the differences between your experiences when you hold negative and positive judgments or opinions. What were the differences? What meaning does this have for you, for your beliefs and feelings about people from this group, and about beliefs in general?
- Write your responses in a few sentences; include anything you like about your feelings, thoughts, and insights.

Part II. Experimenting with Opinions About Obese Men

Repeat the phrases and steps in Part I, this time focusing on the image of an obese man.

Next, determine your current knowledge about obese persons by completing Self-Awareness Activity 11.2. After you've completed this chapter, review your answers, determine whether your answers reflect cultural stereotypes and myths or personal biases, and make any corrections necessary.

Self-Awareness Activity 11.2: What Do You Know About Obese Americans?

Purpose: To see what you know about the issues covered in this chapter.

Instructions: Determine whether you think the following statements are basically true or false—and why. The answers are discussed in the following paragraph and throughout this chapter.

1. People become obese only because they overeat.
2. Anyone with sufficient willpower can lose excess weight.
3. People become excessively overweight because of personality problems.
4. Obese people have jolly personalities.
5. Obese employees are likely to cost employers more in health care and sick leave than employees who diet to keep their weight low.
6. Being overweight has no significant effect on career success.

7. Obese men suffer as much discrimination as obese women.
8. Obese persons are protected by law from workplace discrimination.
9. Extremely overweight people generally make poor workers.

MYTHS AND FACTS

Myths about obese persons are almost as abundant as the ways people in our culture have devised to belittle and exclude them. We'll discuss the fact that the process of becoming obese is complex and involves much more than just overeating. For some persons, it takes more than willpower to stay thin. And while personality problems may be a part of a "weight problem," they are not an adequate explanation in many, or even most, cases. Obese persons have all the personality variables of the general population and are no more likely to be jolly, disturbed, uncontrolled, or sloppy. Very few people who lose weight on diets keep it off for more than a few months, and this dieting syndrome may cause more health problems than just remaining at a stable, though somewhat excessive, weight. Underweight people can pose serious health risks, too. And people who become obsessed with thinness may develop such eating disorders as anorexia and bulimia, which can result in death.

Weight discrimination is rampant in our society, and being even 20 or 30 pounds overweight can result in career problems and lower income. It affects both men and women, but apparently women feel the brunt of it. Virtually all the publicized lawsuits have been filed by women, and the support groups and organizations are created and joined primarily by women. Until 1995 the "morbidly obese" had no legal protection from discrimination, then state courts ruled that they were protected under the Americans with Disabilities Act. Obese persons are on average just as productive as other workers, but some accommodation may need to be made on account of their size.

We'll discuss some typical myths that obese persons must deal with on a daily basis, along with the medical facts that are emerging about obesity. Most of the research cited is reviewed in Martin Seligman's book (1994).

Myth: People get overweight by eating too much and not exercising enough.

This may be true for most people. However, obese people consume no more calories per day than other people, according to 19 out of 20 studies on this topic. One study tells about very obese people who dieted down to only 60 percent overweight and stayed there. They needed 100 fewer calories per day to stay 60 percent overweight than normal-weight people needed to stay at normal weight. To get down to normal weight range and stay there, an obese person must eat excruciatingly less than a normal-weight person, probably for life. In 1993 a National Institutes of Health panel wrote that evidence increasingly indicates that overweight is not a simple disorder of willpower but a complex disorder of energy metabolism. The experts concluded that diets almost always are disasters, with dieters regaining the weight they had lost.

So far as exercise is concerned, it's true that overweight people are less active than thinner people. It's also true that most people eventually lose some weight by eating less and exercising more. However, greatly overweight people have a complex physical situation. Large size probably *causes* the inactivity of greatly overweight persons, and not the other way around.

Myth: People are overweight because they lack willpower.

This very basic myth says that individuals should be able to control themselves, and there is something morally wrong with them if they keep giving in to fattening foods. It says that being overweight means being a weak-willed slob. It ignores the fact that most people who use willpower and take off weight, gain it back. Also, the myth was formed before scientists discovered an "obesity gene."

Willpower doesn't work in the long run. Since we've seen plenty of people who decided to lose weight and then did it within a few weeks, we believe that willpower is the key. What we ignore is the fact that virtually everyone gains it all back within a few months or years. When Martin Seligman reviewed the studies of long- and short-term dieting, the best result he could find was one in which 13 percent of the dieters maintained their losses after three years. About a dozen respected studies of the long-term results of thousands of dieters indicate that 90 percent gain all or almost all their weight back within four or five years, many within a few months. It may be that the 10 percent who succeed over the long term:

- watch every bite they eat
- are more or less obsessed with watching their weight
- were close to their natural weight anyway and would weigh only a few pounds more if they had never dieted

The obesity gene can mutate. Scientists at the Rockefeller Institute in New York (Friedman 1995) have discovered a genetic mutation they think is responsible for at least some types of obesity. Normally, people have genes that deal effectively with central hormonal control of body weight and body fat. The system signals us when we need to eat. When we're eating, it signals us when enough food has been taken in. After we've eaten, it regulates how fast we burn up the calories.

The "obesity gene" appears to be switched on in fat tissue, where it generates a hormone-like protein that is secreted by the fat cells into the bloodstream. The messenger protein travels up to a region of the brain that controls appetite. In that way the fat stores of the body tell the brain how big or small they are, and the brain can regulate appetite, food intake, and food metabolism accordingly. Researchers believe that this gene has mutated in morbidly obese persons so that their body either fails to make the hormone or makes too little of it. Their brains don't get the proper message about how much fat is stored in the body. Also, the mutated gene may essentially keep the brain from knowing the stomach is full and alter metabolism.

Myth: Obese people just need to get on the right diet.

After years of reviewing the scientific literature on dieting and weight loss, Martin Seligman (1994), director of clinical psychology at the University of Pennsylvania, concluded that

- Dieting doesn't work; weight is almost always regained after dieting.
- Dieting may make overweight worse, not better.
- Dieting may be bad for health, comparable to or worse than overweight.
- Dieting can have negative side effects, such as repeated failure and hopelessness, depression, fatigue, bulimia, and anorexia.

A new eating disorder might be called "being 20 percent over your so-called ideal weight and ruining your life and health by dieting." An example is the 5'6" medium-frame woman who weighs 165 pounds instead of 135 or so.

Myth: Being obese poses health risks; being thin does not.

Seligman's review led to less-firm conclusions about the health risks of overweight, but he makes these suggestions:

- Underweight is clearly associated with substantially greater risk of death. Staying 20 percent or more underweight, as virtually all high-fashion models do, can greatly reduce stamina, impair the immune system, and lead to other types of health problems.
- Mild to moderate overweight, 10 to 30 percent over so-called ideal weight, may possibly be associated with a marginal increase in mortality, particularly for those at risk for diabetes.

- Substantial obesity of 30 to 100 percent overweight possibly causes health damage and may be associated with somewhat increased mortality.
- Morbid obesity, over 100 percent overweight, may well cause premature death.

He suspects, but is not yet certain, that the weight fluctuation hazard may be larger than the hazard of staying overweight. Gaining weight gradually during adulthood is normal and healthy, but going on diets dramatically increases the risk of heart attacks and strokes later on.

Myth: People who diet are healthier and live longer.

Dieting may create more stress than the added weight would create, as well as eating disorders. A 1990 study of 466 flight attendants found that 25 percent of them weigh five pounds or more than the airline's top limit. Within this "overweight" group, half either made themselves vomit or used laxatives to lose weight (Dettmar 1990).

What *does* contribute to health is moderate exercise, wholesome natural foods, minimal fat and alcohol, eating only when hungry and eating slowly and only until satisfied. In a study of 13,000 people, the least-fit 20 percent had a much higher death risk than even the next-to-least-fit 20 percent. In another study using a large sample of men, the death rate of sedentary men was 30 percent higher than those who exercised moderately (Blair et al. 1988).

Weight is not always an indicator of longevity. The major claim of the insurance companies that produce those ideal weight charts is that you'll live longer if you stay within your ideal weight range. Although people in the "normal" weight range do live longer than heavier ones, on average, how much longer is in great dispute. More importantly, large-boned, buxom women—and large-boned, unusually muscular men—may be over the ideal weight and still be at their optimal weight. Therefore, if such people were to slim down to their "ideal weight," they might shorten their lives, not lengthen them. In fact, no study has compared the longevity of people who stay within their so-called ideal weight without dieting to people who maintain it with dieting. Those who constantly diet may in fact shorten their lives.

Myth: Obese people are less productive workers.

Most jobs don't require much physical activity, and there is no reason obese persons can't be just as productive as others. Activists concede that obese people are not appropriate for all jobs, such as those performed in tight quarters or those requiring certain physical abilities. Airline attendants and ballet dancers are examples. But for most jobs, even where some physical activity is required, obese persons should not be disqualified from applying. They should have a chance to take whatever physical tests are required. If the job requires running down a track every day, let *all* the applicants show that they can run the track.

Myth: Poor persons are more likely to be obese.

The myth that poor persons are more likely to be fat implies that they are less informed and less in control of their lives. In fact, it's more likely obese persons make less because they're obese than that being poor leads to a higher incidence of obesity. This is a major workplace issue that we'll discuss in detail later.

Fat Prejudice: You Could Change If You Tried

Perhaps the cruelest aspect of obesity prejudice is that people tend to believe the obese could become slender if they simply summoned adequate willpower and self-discipline, in other words, character. The devaluing of obese persons often has the effect of invading their privacy.

The Message: You're Inferior

Obese women say that little glances and comments they receive are often more damaging than overt discrimination, wearing away at their self-esteem and confidence, reinforcing the message most have heard since childhood: "You're inferior because you're fat." Some typical humiliations obese persons have reported include:

- Frances went to see a doctor to get treatment for what appeared to be strep throat. The doctor insisted that she weigh in, then focused more on her overweight than on her illness. He insisted that she must immediately begin to lose 75 pounds.

- Joan was stopped by a policeman for speeding. He also gave her a ticket for not wearing a seat belt, even though she explained that the belt wouldn't reach around her body.

- Bill was embarrassed at the grocery checkout when the women behind him commented about two items of "fattening foods" that he was buying.

- Stephanie was trying to find a job. Time after time, she would send a resume and cover letter and the phone response was enthusiastic. When she showed up for the interview, however, she often saw shocked faces and heard, "We think you're overqualified," or "We've changed strategies."

- Karen applied for a job as a legal secretary. The attorney was impressed with her skills and told her he would hire her—if she could show a 10-pound-a-month weight loss when he weighed her in his office.

- When Jay walked into the staff meeting, two of the men jokingly grabbed their doughnuts, implying that he might scarf them down.

- Rosita was enjoying lunch at a seafood restaurant with two co-workers. One said, "You know, Rosita, that butter you just put on your bread comes to over 100 calories." The other said, "Yes, and I noticed you ordered a salad with figs, which are loaded with calories."

One activist said, "We're the last safe prejudice. The fat person is the last person employers can safely kick around."

When they leave their homes each day, one to two million obese Americans find themselves in a world built for small people, a world in which they're continually reminded they don't fit. Some of the problems they encounter:

- sitting—finding chairs anywhere that will accommodate them
- flying—fitting into tiny airplane seats
- going to a theater—fitting into tiny theater seats
- traveling in cars—fitting into small cars, dealing with seat belts that won't reach

The Assumption: You Are Your Body

The modern culture of dieting is based on the idea that the personality becomes the body, says Sally Tisdale (1993). The belief is, our size *does* change when we diet, so we must be able to choose it and therefore control it. For many overweight people, the misery is not so much about how they look, but that they feel to blame, that they've been bad to allow their bodies to get fat. Their fat is seen as perverse bad manners, and they can't walk to the corner store without risking insult.

Naturally slender Sally saw naturally obese Janice eating a cookie at lunch and commented to Aretha, "How is she going to lose weight that way?" This assumes that Janice should diet all the time, and that she *can*. It pinpoints a whole category of food that should be denied to Janice. It views Janice's unwillingness to forgo cookies as an act of rebellion. And it assumes that what Janice eats is everyone else's business.

At times obese persons feel truly reduced to being just a body and nothing more. As damaging as "conventional wisdom" about overweight has been, the more recent psychological viewpoints may be even more damaging:

- Obese people put on weight as a defense mechanism.
- They're trying to hide.
- They're trying to feed their hungry, empty hearts.
- They're seeking release from the loss of mother or father.

   . . . and on and on.

One woman who was obsessed for years with keeping her weight far below its natural point said, "By fussing endlessly over my body, I ceased to live in it." She gave up dieting and entered her body again with a whole heart. She says that by letting go of dieting she freed up mental and emotional energy and space in her life—space for more productive and joyful thoughts and activities. She will no longer pursue a thin elusive body that others say she should have. She says, "It was a terrible distraction, a sidetracking that might have lasted my whole life. By letting go, I go places" (Tisdale 1993).

Devaluation and Rejection

Devaluation and rejection are two of the biggest hurdles obese persons must overcome in achieving self-esteem and claiming a place in the world. To illustrate how extreme our culture is about thinness, consider a recent comment by reed-slim actress Shelly Long to her estranged film husband Tom Hanks. "Well, I haven't been out of the house much lately; you know I put on a few pounds." The implicit message was that she felt so bad about her appearance, she had been hiding out at home, and certainly had not had any romantic encounters!

Because of the stereotypes and myths about obesity, the government and health industry in this country have no commitment to obesity as a public health problem, according to William Dietz, director of clinical nutrition at a Boston hospital. He says, "We've ignored it and blamed it on gluttony and sloth" (Burros 1994). Many people believe that gluttony is a sin, and most believe it reflects laziness, lack of willpower, food addiction, and lack of self-esteem. Activists say that people naturally come in different shapes and sizes and that obesity is an uncontrollable genetic condition for most obese people. While most can lose weight over the short term, they cannot keep it off long term. The typical cycle is to lose weight, feel tired and starved, begin to eat more, and gain it all back.

A Cultural Obsession: Slimness and the Beauty Myth

We hear too much about how obesity is unhealthy and too little about how extreme dieting and weight obsession are unhealthy. What does it mean when more than 80 percent of U.S. women say they dislike their bodies? Coincidentally, 85 percent of them weigh more than the average fashion model, who in turn weighs 20 percent less than the average woman.

The pressure to be very thin starts quite early for little girls. Their role model since the 1960s has been the most popular American doll of all time, Barbie. It is estimated that about one in a million women would naturally have proportions similar to Barbie's, but little girls start trying at a very young age. In fact, by age 10, about 80 percent of them have been on a diet. Later we'll discuss the tyranny of the beauty myth, especially for women, and obese persons' right to challenge it.

Our entire society suffers when people are forced to fit into one appearance mold. Film maker Frederico Fellini became legendary by filling his films with many colorful characters. Diverse people make films fascinating, and they also make life fascinating and rich for us, once we give up our ego judgments and relax into the diversity. When will we start accepting diversity in size and shape, all sizes and shapes, instead of believing that beauty comes in a very narrow range of acceptable packages?

CURRENT PROFILE: WHO IS OBESE?

Most people think the term *overweight persons* refers to themselves. We've mentioned that 30 percent of Americans are considered 20 percent or more overweight, and the percentage is increasing. This means 75 million Americans could be the victim of some degree of obesity discrimination. Those who are the targets of extreme discrimination are referred to legally as the *morbidly obese*, and we mentioned that one to two million Americans fit this description.

The actual proportion of overweight Americans remained at about 25 percent from 1960 to 1980. Then in the following decade, it rose to 30 percent. Obesity is increasing even faster among young people than among adults. Twenty percent overweight means about 25 pounds over for an average 5'4" woman and 30 pounds for an average 5'10" man.)

Nearly 50 percent of African American and Mexican American women are now overweight, an increase of around 14 percent since 1980, as shown in Table 11.1. About a third of Euro-American women are overweight, a 36 percent increase since 1980.

TABLE 11.1: Americans 20 Percent or More above "Normal Weight"

	1980	1990
All Americans	25%	30%
Euro-American women	24%	33%
African American women	44%	50%
Mexican American women	44%	50%

Source: Burros, 1994.

PATTERNS AND ISSUES: A SUBCULTURE IS BORN

Obese persons are beginning to fight discrimination. The size acceptance movement has been active for about 20 years. An underlying principle is that by accepting yourself just as you are, you develop the strength, self-esteem, and confidence to fend off the insults, attacks, and discrimination the world heaps upon obese persons. One author states, "Rejection can't kill you. With the right attitude, rejection can make you stronger. Don't hide out at home. Go out in the world and risk rejection" (Wahl 1994).

Critics say that social preference for thinness is too ingrained in the culture to be legislated away. Activists reply that these same arguments were used for other forms of discrimination. "It's the same as saying you can't hire black salespersons because the customers won't like it, or that you can't hire women because they can't handle male customers' resistance to buying from women," says Art Stine of Michigan's Department of Civil Rights. His department investigates 10 to 20 cases of weight discrimination each year (Fraser 1994).

At least three national organizations have emerged in recent years to take up the cause of obese Americans. The activist group that's been most prominent in the media recently is the National Association to Advance Fat Acceptance (NAAFA). With 4,000 members in 75 chapters nationwide, NAAFA's goals include:

- improving the self-esteem of obese people
- ensuring their civil rights
- challenging our fat-rejecting culture through education, legislation, and the courts
- equal access to employment

NAAFA leaders say they like the word *fat*. They don't like *overweight*, and they ask "Over whose weight?" They say *obesity* suggests a medical disorder. NAAFA has reclaimed the label fat much as some African Americans have reclaimed "nigger" and some gays the term queer. Certainly not all obese persons agree that they want to be called fat, and most people in our culture have been conditioned to avoid calling people fat. For this reason, the most common term is obese. (Other organizations and resources are listed at the end of this chapter.)

Issue: What Rights Do Obese Persons Have?

Until recently overweight people had no legal rights for protection from employment discrimination based on weight. Those who are starting to fight back against such discrimination have been forced to resort to two related legal rights:

- protection under the ADA because obesity is treated as a disability in the workplace
- protection under the constitutional right to privacy, on the basis that personal eating habits should not affect how an employee is judged at work

"Weight is the last bastion of acceptable discrimination," according to Sally Smith, executive director of NAAFA. She notes that one person may be 100 pounds over society's ideal, and others may be just 10, and asks, "If employers can use it against the greatly overweight person today, what's to keep them from using it against the slightly overweight tomorrow?"

Right to Equal Treatment

A 1990 survey indicates that 90 percent of employees cite acceptable weight as essential for a successful career, ranking it fourth, ahead of attractiveness and youthfulness. Intelligence, job qualifications, and education were the first three essentials. Since the stereotype of the ideal woman makes her much thinner than that of the ideal man, more women than men are affected by weight discrimination.

A study of 450 employees revealed that men must be significantly heavier than women before they experience the same discrimination. As shown in Table 11.2, employers are slightly more likely to directly urge overweight men than women employees to lose weight. But even moderately overweight women are dramatically more likely than men to experience abuse by co-workers. Confirming these findings, a marketing survey indicated that 33 percent of women and 25 percent of men agree that weight matters more for women employees.

TABLE 11.2: Discrimination Experienced by Men and Women Employees

Type of Discrimination	Men (%)			Women (%)		
	Average	Moderately Overweight*	Overweight**	Average	Moderately Overweight*	Overweight**
Not being hired	—	—	42	—	31	62
Fired/pressured to resign	—	—	11	—	2	17
Urged to lose weight	15	27	69	11	33	60
Abused by co-workers	15	47	—	23	62	73
Abused by supervisors	3	13	52	2	39	45
Needed to conceal weight	—	—	17	—	10	25

*30 to 40 percent overweight
**weigh 300 lbs. or more
Source: Esther Rothblum, University of Vermont, 1993.

Right to Equal Pay

One study found that businessmen sacrifice $1,000 in salary for every pound they are overweight. Obese women tend to earn less, too. Among women who earn more than $50,000, only 13 percent are obese, while among women in the poverty category, 30 percent are obese.

In a study of women of all weights, Harvard sociologist Steven Gortmaker found that the overweight women, averaging 5′3″ and 200 pounds, had household incomes that averaged $6,710 below those of thinner women and that they were 10 percent more likely to live in poverty. The study indicates that being overweight keeps people from becoming as affluent as they might otherwise become. In the seven-year survey of more than 5,000 women, the researchers found that the obese women were more likely than thin ones to lose socioeconomic status over the course of their adolescence and young adulthood, no matter how well they did on achievement tests taken at the beginning of the study or whether they came from high-income families. The heavier the woman, the greater the job discrimination. Even women of average size or only slightly heavy were often encouraged to lose weight and are more likely to be passed over for promotion than thinner women. This phenomenon is much more common for women than men.

The problem goes beyond weight discrimination to appearance discrimination. Attractive people tend to earn about 5 percent more than those with average looks. And homely workers make about 7 percent less than those with average looks. That's a 12 percent pay gap between the homely and the attractive. Women considered to be unattractive are less likely to work than other women and tend to marry men with lower levels of education.

Attractive people are widely regarded as being more intelligent, friendly, honest, and confident than others, all traits that could influence employers and customers to discriminate in favor of them. Attractive children are rewarded with more praise from parents and teachers, influencing their self-esteem and confidence, both valued in the marketplace. Certain occupations cater to attractive employees more than others, but favoritism toward good looks and prejudice against homeliness is pervasive in most jobs. Even within any given occupation, good-looking people make more. When the appearance ratings of 700 MBA graduates were correlated with the salaries they were earning ten years after graduation, better-looking men made as much as $10,000 per year more. (Hamermesh and Biddle 1993).

Right to Challenge the Beauty Myth

Anyone has the right to challenge the beauty myth by asking such questions as, "Who says so? Who made that rule?" and by asserting their human rights to consideration and respect. It's not easy, however. The weight-loss industry now has billions at stake in Americans' obsession with slimness and dissatisfaction with their bodies. It has on its payrolls some of the most prominent weight-loss scientists, who publish journal articles recommending new, improved diets and warning of the health risks of being overweight. Instead of carefully evaluating their claims, and investigating the credibility of the sources, Americans tend to jump on every new diet bandwagon, shelling out billions each year for the privilege of depriving themselves of the foods they want when they want them. Our values set up eating conflicts; for example we love fattening foods and hate fat people. Consider these facts (Friedman 1995):

- Americans spent $40 billion a year on diet programs and diet products in the early 1990s, double the amount spent in the early 1980s.
- When we add diet-related foods sold in food stores, the amount is $80 billion.
- Advertising and commercials for calorie-rich junk foods flood the media.
- Kellogg's spent $32 million per year advertising Frosted Flakes in the early 1990s.
- Total obesity research dollars per year were $34 million.

Why the desperate search for thinness? Many say it's caused by the belief in the beauty myth. We're constantly bombarded with female role models of beauty and talent who are thinner than almost all the actual women in the population. That's what we see daily in women's clothing stores and magazines, in the movies and television. In 1980 the average Miss America contestant weighed 6 pounds less than 1960 contestants, and the average *Playboy* centerfold became noticeably thinner during those decades. Meanwhile the average woman weighed 6 pounds more in 1980 than in 1960. These trends continue in the 1990s. As a people, the more obsessed we've become with diets, the more we weigh. Defining overweight as 20 percent or more above the "normal" range, we find the U.S. leads the industrialized nations in overweight people, estimated to be about 30 percent of us (Garner, Schwartz, and Thompson 1980; Jeffrey, Adlis, and Forster 1991).

The beauty myth says that good-looking people, sexually attractive people, all look a certain way. The acceptable range of body sizes and shapes, including the sizes and shapes of key body parts, such as facial features, breasts, hips, and legs, is extremely narrow and limited, especially for women. And the ideal woman always looks and acts about 25. When they're 15, most girls are trying to look and act 25. When they're 35, 45, and 55, many women are still trying to look and act 25. When they finally give up the impossible task, many feel invisible and ignored.

Naomi Wolf, author of *The Beauty Myth* (1991), argues convincingly that people in our culture didn't hate fat until women began to join forces and reject their inferior status. She says that until women got the vote "fat rounded hips and thighs and bellies were perceived as desirable and sensual." Can it be that the more powerful women become, the more pressure we unconsciously place on them to be smaller, to get rid of the curves that make their bodies different from men's bodies? Kim Chernin (1982) theorized that we do this to women as a way of diminishing "mother power"—to wipe out the memory of the "primordial mother who rules over our childhood with her inscrutable power over life and death." Wolf adds, "A man's right to confer judgment on any women's beauty while remaining himself unjudged . . . is the last unexamined right remaining intact from the old list of masculine privilege." Recognizing that size acceptance is an issue for all women—not just large women—is a first step toward solving our nationwide eating problems. After all, it's our cultural intolerance of certain body sizes that sends us to diets in the first place. And diets often turn us into compulsive eaters or into people obsessed with food, calories, weight, and body size.

Psychotherapists Jane Hirschmann and Carol Munter (1995) use the following process to empower the obese women they work with.

- Stop hating your body by challenging those thoughts that put your body down.

- Become aware of your concerns and needs that your "bad body thoughts" mask.

- Challenge put-down thoughts, such as "My stomach's too big" by asking "Who says so? Who made that rule?"

- Make friends with your body and become its loving caretaker; give your body unconditional acceptance and love.

- Reclaim your appetite, dump diets, and learn to eat in response to stomach hunger instead of "mouth hunger" triggered by unconscious needs.

- Assert yourself when people insult your body or intrude into your business.

The process includes many strategies and tactics for dealing with the complexity of overweight. The goal is to give people a solid basis for changing the way they think about their bodies, food, and eating and to establish new, self-affirming patterns.

Issue: What Rights Do Employers Have?

Some employers who run airlines, fashion stores, restaurants, beauty salons, and real estate agencies say they have a right to establish an image and hire only employees who fit that image. Civil rights advocates counter that the only criterion should be performance. One who lost 40 pounds, said, "I did my job well before, and I do it well now. Weight has nothing to do with it." Another said, "Who are employers to play God, to judge what is professional or beautiful? Rubens painted large women who were beautiful. It seems clear to me that hiring and promotion ought to be based on your ability to do the job."

Some employers say that customers won't do business with obese persons and that co-workers won't respect them or work well with them. Activists reject the circular reasoning and the ethics of this argument, noting it was also used to resist equal rights for minorities and women. They say it's morally unacceptable for employers themselves to discriminate against obese persons just because prejudiced customers and co-workers might discriminate against them. Such actions signal that employers accept prejudice and encourage it. Just as it is the employers' responsibility to stop sexual harassment of women and ethnic discrimination toward African Americans, it's also their responsibility to stop harassment and discrimination toward obese persons.

Some employers claim that obese employees cost more in health care and sick time. Health professionals suggest that yo-yo dieting could make both obese and thinner persons less healthy. And some obese persons are reluctant to seek medical care because doctors often don't respect them, are condescending and patronizing about their weight, and harangue them to lose weight. Others don't have health care coverage. Nevertheless, there are no respectable studies showing that obese persons cost more because of health problems.

Issue: What Laws Protect Obese Workers?

Persons who suffered weight discrimination by employers have only recently gained some legal protection. Laws take two forms. The most powerful and direct are laws specifically prohibiting discrimination based on weight, height, or other aspects of physical appearance. They follow in the tradition of civil rights laws prohibiting discrimination on the basis of race, creed, color, gender, and similar characteristics. Less direct are court rulings that equate obesity with disability and require employers to make reasonable accommodation for obese employees. Most activists agree that the best protection is to add weight discrimination to the other types of discrimination prohibited by the federal and state civil rights acts.

Civil Rights Law. As of 1995, Michigan was the only state in the country with a law that specifically protects the employment rights of overweight people. Weight and height had been added to its civil rights statutes. The cities of Santa Cruz, California, and Washington, DC are among the few local governments that have added the clause to their civil rights laws. Massachusetts and New York began considering legislation in 1994 that would add height and weight to civil rights statutes covering employment and housing. A similar bill failed in Texas. California's civil rights laws, while not specifically covering weight, were the basis for a million dollar court award to a 400-pound man. He had sued the automotive parts firm that had fired him after 10 years' employment. In September 1995, after a six-week trial, he was awarded back pay and reparation for emotional distress.

Disability Law. New Jersey law regards obesity as a disability that automatically triggers discrimination protection regardless of the cause of the obesity. In most of the states where obese employees have won their lawsuits, their cases were based on the ADA. Their attorneys claimed that obesity should be viewed as a physical disability. This is risky at best since some experts still claim that obese people could lose their excess weight if they really wanted to. For example, the California Supreme Court ruled in 1993 that morbid obesity is not a medical disorder but a condition under the person's control. This case is being appealed and may end up in the U.S. Supreme Court.

The disability argument did prevail in a federal appeals court in 1993. A woman sued the Rhode Island Department of Mental Health after she was denied a state job because at 5'2" she weighed 320 pounds. Lawyers for the state agency said the law should not be interpreted to cover obesity because obesity "is caused by voluntary conduct and is not immutable." They argued that the plaintiff could lose weight and rid herself of any disability arising from her obesity at any time. But the judge and jury ruled that there was credible evidence that the metabolic dysfunction causing weight gain in the morbidly obese lingers even after weight loss. Their decision was upheld in a federal appeals court, which said that discrimination against the obese could constitute a violation of the ADA. The court further stated that:

> *In a society that all too often confuses "slim" with "beautiful" or "good," morbid obesity can present formidable barriers to employment.*

The court briefs and opinions don't indicate that obesity in itself is necessarily a disability. Instead, the reasoning is that when persons are discriminated against, either because their obesity limits their activities or because employers *perceive* obesity as a disability that limits their activities, then such persons can be protected under disability law.

EEOC Support for the Disability Approach. The EEOC filed a brief in federal appeals court in the Rhode Island case. EEOC lawyers urged the court to consider obesity just as it would view many other conditions not specifically mentioned in the ADA, based on how long the person has been affected by the condition and how difficult it would be to change. Noting that obesity isn't a "traditional" disability, the EEOC said that "although it's possible for an obese individual to lose weight, obesity is a chronic, lifelong condition." It further stated that a condition does not have to be involuntary or immutable to be covered. The EEOC did not indicate that a person must be "morbidly obese" in order to be protected from discrimination, and the ruling probably opens the door for claims from more moderately obese employees. Discrimination claims under the ADA must be filed first with the EEOC.

The idea behind the ruling is that the way persons look shouldn't affect their ability to get and keep a job. Advocates say being fat doesn't necessarily mean poor health, and it's too bad that in most states their only recourse in fighting discrimination is through laws meant to protect the disabled. Several overweight persons, when interviewed, said the predicament was offensive because most of them are not disabled and are in fact very healthy people.

Right to Privacy Law. Another legal avenue is the right to privacy, based on the principle that one's personal eating or exercise habits should not affect how one is judged in the workplace. The American Civil Liberties Union has launched a national project to fight an employer trend to meddle in employees' private lives, such as their eating, drinking, and smoking habits.

LEADERSHIP CHALLENGES AND OPPORTUNITIES

The issues obese persons must deal with present challenges to business leaders. Yet leaders can meet the needs of obese persons, and in doing this they can enrich the organization. Leaders also have an opportunity to enlighten the corporate culture and influence people to move beyond the beauty myth to an appreciation of people for their inner qualities and contributions to the organization.

Leadership Challenge: Meeting the Needs of Obese Employees

The following are some of the needs of obese employees.

- protection from discrimination and harassment by managers and employees
- respect for their privacy
- acceptance of them as they are

- appreciation of their value as human beings and of their contributions
- accommodation that will help them do their job
- fair and equal compensation

Next we'll examine some ways that business leaders can meet these needs.

Developing Policies on Obesity Harassment and Discrimination

Employers and managers have a responsibility to stop the harassment of obese employees and to stop discriminatory actions against them. The first step is to develop policies and procedures designed to provide equal opportunity and fair treatment of obese persons. Affirmative action programs and equal opportunity policies already in place for minorities and women can be used for guidance in remedying discrimination. Company policies and procedures designed to prevent sexual harassment and to handle such cases can serve as a pattern for preventing and handling cases of obesity harassment.

Making Reasonable Accommodation

Although obese persons are not necessarily disabled, those who are greatly overweight usually need some type of accommodation. The best way to find out is to ask tactfully what can be done to help them to be as productive and successful as possible on the job. Comfortable, sturdy seating arrangements are nearly always needed and appreciated, not only at a work station or executive desk but also in meeting rooms, lounges, dining facilities, and any other place the employee frequents in the course of the job. If a company car or other transportation is provided, arrange for adequate size in seats and seat belts.

A few obese persons have difficulty getting around. The same provisions that are made for other mobility-impaired employees can be made for these obese employees. These accommodations can include electric carts, ramps, elevators, and convenient parking.

Leadership Opportunity: Enlightening the Corporate Culture

Leaders can change those company practices and habits that degrade and discriminate against obese persons through their own example, through appropriate storytelling, through making them heroines and heroes when they excel, through visibly supporting them in other ways, and through providing information and training for all employees about obesity issues. Leaders can focus on the contributions of obese employees, and on their positive qualities. They can unfailingly respect their dignity and refuse to countenance disrespect in the form of wisecracks, jokes, put-downs, unsought advice, and similar behavior. Corporate diversity training programs can include a segment on obese Americans. Every employee needs to complete such a segment.

Looking Below the Surface

Leaders can move away from a focus on the superficial aspects of corporate employee image, such as size, shape, facial features, and other aspects of the beauty myth. An in-depth corporate image focuses on such inner strengths as being honest, respecting others, keeping agreements, honoring commitments, delivering the goods on time, providing top-quality service, being positive, focusing on others' strengths and contributions, seeing the humor, loving life, summoning courage, and on and on. These qualities seem old-fashioned in a way. Yet aren't they really the raw materials that leaders can skillfully draw on to create a highly motivated and committed world-class workforce?

Considering New Marketing Opportunities

Some leaders are breaking the mold and giving talented obese persons job opportunities, even in such high-profile jobs as television news reporter, talk show hostess, and situation comedy star. Some say that such media personalities seem approachable, like a "next-door neighbor," and people feel comfortable with them. Business leaders need to examine this opportunity to relate to new types of customers and perhaps open up new markets.

SUMMARY

Myths and stereotypes about obese persons cause people to judge them negatively, to reject them as friends and employees, and even to invade their privacy by telling them how to lose weight. Most studies indicate that obese persons eat no more than other people, and they often have difficulty exercising because of their size. Diets don't work for most people, especially the very obese. Nearly all dieters gain back the weight. Apparently, the metabolism of some persons is different and this may be due to a mutation of the "obesity gene." Obesity poses some health risks, but so does the dieting syndrome and so does being extremely underweight.

Most jobs are sedentary, and obese employees are just as productive as others. Because of appearance bias, however, obese persons are less likely to be hired and promoted, make less money on average, and are more likely to be poor than those considered attractive by cultural standards. These standards are more stringent for women than for men. About 30 percent of Americans, or 75 million people, are considered overweight, and between one and two million are morbidly obese.

Obese employees have had no protection from job discrimination in the past, but that's changing. Nationally, the most significant development is a case won in a federal appeals court and supported by an EEOC brief that cites morbid obesity as a condition protected under the ADA. A size acceptance movement is emerging in which obese activists declare their rights to equal treatment, to equal pay, and to challenge the beauty myth. Leadership challenges include developing policies and procedures that protect obese employees from harassment and discrimination and making reasonable accommodation for their needs. Leadership opportunities include influencing the corporate culture to value the contributions and talents of all persons, regardless of size or appearance, and responding to marketing opportunities in the obese community.

Skill Builder 11.1: The Case of Chris, a Job Applicant

Chris is 35 years old, has two years of college, and weighs 350 pounds. In response to a newspaper ad, Chris applied and interviewed for a job at Worman's Hardware Store. He didn't get the job, but when he learned of another opening, he called the chain store's personnel coordinator, *Georgia*. Georgia told Chris the store wanted more experienced people. She also told him, "There is some concern about your weight and whether you can physically handle hauling heavy items of hardware and supplies." Chris has 10 years' experience in retail selling although he has never worked in a hardware store.

- If you were Chris, what would you do?
- If you were a top manager at Worman's, how would you view this situation?

Skill Builder 11.2: The Case of Laura, Public Relations Manager

Laura was 40 years old and had successfully held several managerial positions in public relations. When she applied for a job at a major East Coast medical center, she was wearing a slenderizing dark suit and had been on a strict diet for two months. She got the job but didn't report for work until a month or so later. In the meantime, Laura relaxed her diet regime. As usual after such diets, she was starved and tired and quickly went back up to her usual 230 pounds. When she arrived for her first day on the new job, *Murray*, the director of public relations blurted out, "My God, you've put on a lot of weight since we interviewed you. I'm not sure this is the image we want for the hospital."

From that day on Laura was constantly pressured to diet and watched to see if she was slimming down. Laura felt demeaned, set apart from the others, and was subjected to humiliating comments. She had an expensive professional wardrobe, but *Jan*, her boss, told her to wear only black or navy. Laura knew that meant "camouflage your size." She says, "Every time I walked into the office, I got a quick once-over to see what I was wearing and whether I had lost weight." At a staff meeting Jan asked Laura to tell everyone about the liquid diet she was starting.

For the next year Laura was successful in her job. She got national publicity for the hospital, raised large sums of money, and developed award-winning programs. Nevertheless, she was called into Jan's office one Friday afternoon and fired. Jan didn't mention her weight directly, but said, "Things that should have changed didn't change."

- What is your opinion of the way Murray and Jan handled Laura's case?
- Do you think Laura should have done anything differently?
- What do you think she should do now?

Skill Builder 11.3: Louis' Career Goals

Louis has been working for Manko's, a privately-owned printing firm for about 5 years. The firm specializes in designing and printing forms used by automobile dealers. Louis' duties include taking phone orders and arranging for the shipping of the merchandise to clients. The shipping aspect requires lifting boxes of forms. His job calls for good customer relations skills, and over the years he has helped the firm develop and retain a loyal clientele.

Louis' doctor tells him that he's about 150 pounds over his ideal weight. This has been the case for nearly all his adult life, at least since his early twenties. Louis has dieted and lost weight several times in the past years, once even losing 125 pounds. As he says, "I've tried every dieting gimmick in the book, and I always end up at about the same weight in the long run." Louis has always been somewhat self-conscious about his weight, for he was a little "pudgy" even as a child. His mother frequently cautioned him about his eating patterns, saying, "Louis, you don't need to eat seconds; you've had enough to eat." Or, "No, Louis, you don't need to eat cookies; try an apple or an orange for a snack."

Louis' weight has not been a problem at the print shop. He gets along well with the employees, as well as the customers he relates to by phone. There are four employees: a printer, two outside salespersons, and Louis, who handles everything in the office. The owner, *Bill Manko*, relies on him to keep the office running, and the salespersons rely on him to do favors for their customers, such as shipping forms ASAP, providing information about the proper type of form a customer needs, and explaining to customers how to use certain forms.

Bill tells Louis that the firm has grown enough to need another outside salesperson. He's looking for a good person. Louis realizes that the job would be a good opportunity for him to expand his career, and he decides to apply. When Louis approaches Bill about the job, Bill seems quite surprised and says, "Well, let me think about it, Louis." A few days later, Bill says to Louis, "I think you're a better asset to the company in your present job. You don't quite fit the sales rep image, and we need your know-how and knowledge of the business and the customers to handle phone orders and shipping."

- What are the key issues in this case?
- If you were Bill, what would you do?
- If you were Louis, what would you do?

Skill Builder 11.4: The Case of Helen, Travel Agent

Helen has been working for World Points Travel Agency for about a year. World Point consists of a chain of 15 travel agencies with a total of about 100 employees. When Helen interviewed for the job, the office seemed perfectly suited to her style. People seemed to like their work and enjoy a little humor. *Franko*, the manager, was very flexible about allowing her to work only 25 hours a week and to schedule her hours around her daughter's needs. He hired her on the spot.

Helen was thrilled to get the job: all she wanted was to work part time so she could spend time with her three-year-old daughter Linda, whom she has just enrolled in a good nursery school. Helen figured that a nice part-time job at a travel agency would give her a chance to get out of the house and meet people and enough money to pay Linda's school expenses.

Everyone was friendly from the beginning, and Helen was invited to join the employee's association even though part-time workers were technically not eligible for membership. The employee's association didn't negotiate contracts or require dues, but did consult with management in making policies for the agency and the employees. Little did Helen know that the actions of the group would eventually lead to her downfall.

A few weeks ago, the group suggested to management that the company's image needed to be improved. As one of them said, "We sell so many European vacation plans, we need to present a chic, updated European image." Most of the improvements involved changing the names of vacation packages and the office decor. The trouble arose when the group decided to adopt appearance standards for employees; for example: "Employees who deal directly with the public must look attractive and professional and wear outfits that reflect current European high-fashion. Employees must keep their weight within the optimal weight range for their height and bone structure."

Helen is 5'6" tall and weighs about 200 pounds. Last week, two of the women from the employee association committee that drafted the image policy met with Helen. They asked her if she would agree to bring her weight down to 160 pounds within the next six months, saying "That seems reasonable, don't you think." Helen said, "No, I don't think it's reasonable. I gained this weight three years ago when I was pregnant and then nursing my daughter. I've tried to lose it, and it's just not that easy. I'd like to lose it on my own terms and in my own time frame. To make this kind of agreement just puts too much pressure on me."

Marge, the committee chair said, "It was the employee association's idea to do this, and you are a member of our group, so you shouldn't view this as something the company is forcing on you." Helen replied, "Do you think I don't look good enough to sell European vacation plans? Don't I have a right to look the way I want to look, so long as it isn't outrageous or harmful to business?"

Marge replied, "We all know you're a highly professional worker and an attractive representative of the company. But we think the rule should apply to everyone." The others seemed to agree with Marge.

The next day Franko approached Helen and suggested changing her job duties, saying, "Helen, let's try you out at the confirmation desk. You can keep your current salary and hours and it will probably be a better fit for you." Helen objected, "Franko, I love meeting with people and I'm good at it. I don't want a strictly telephone job behind the scenes. All I'll be doing is confirming hotel and flight reservations. It would be boring, and I would go nuts."

- What are the key issues in this case?
- If you were Helen, what would you do?
- If you were Franko, what would you do?

REFERENCES

Blair, S., et al., "Physical Fitness and All-Cause Mortality"; J. Holloway, A. Beuter, and J. Duda, "Self-Efficacy and Training for Strength in Adolescent Girls"; Paffenbarger et al., "Physical Activity, All-Cause Mortality." *Journal of Applied Social Psychology* 18 (1988): 699–719.

Brown, Laura S. and Esther D. Rothblum, eds. *Overcoming Fear of Fat.* Binghamton, NY: Harrington Park Press, 1989.

Burros, Marian. "More Americans Tipping the Scales." *New York Times* (July 15, 1994).

Chernin, Kim. *The Obsession: Reflections on the Tyranny of Slenderness.* New York: Harper & Row, 1982.

Dettmar, Lyn. Chicago clinical psychologist, study conducted in 1990.

Fraser, Laura. "The Overweight Want Their Rights." *San Francisco Chronicle* (June 22, 1994): E7.

Friedman, J. of Howard Hughes Medical Institute, Rockefeller Institute, New York, NY. *See* reports in *Nature* and *Discovery*, March 1995.

Garner, D., P. Garfindek, D. Schwartz, and M. Thompson. "Cultural Expectations of Thinness in Women." *Psychological Reports* 47 (1980): 483–491.

Grunwald, L. "Do I Look Fat to You?" *Discovery* (March 1995): 58–74.

Hamermesh, Daniel S. and Jeff Biddle. *Beauty and the Labour Market.* Cambridge, MA: National Bureau of Economic Research, 1993.

Hirschmann, Jane and Carol Munter. *When Women Stop Hating Their Bodies.* New York: Fawcett Columbine, 1995.

Jeffrey, R., S. Adlis, and J. Forster. "Prevalence of Dieting Among Working Men and Women." *Health Psychology* 10 (1991): 274–281.

Johnson, Carol A. *Self-Esteem Comes in All Sizes: How to Be Healthy and Happy at Your Natural Weight.* New York: Doubleday, 1995.

Kano, Susan. *Making Peace With Food* (a step-by-step guide to self-help in freeing yourself from diet and weight obsession). New York: Harper, 1989.

Lyons, Pat and Debby Burgard. *Great Shape.* Menlo Park, CA: Bull Publishing Co., 1990.

Olds, Ruthanne. *Big & Beautiful* (a book on overcoming fatphobia). Washington DC: Acropolis Books Ltd., 1992.

Polivy, Janet and Peter Herman. *Breaking the Diet Habit.* New York: Basic Books, 1983.

Rose, Laura, S. Brown, and E.D. Rothblum, eds. *Life Isn't Weighed on the Bathroom Scale.* Waco, TX: WRS Group, 1994.

Rothblum, Esther. University of Vermont psychologist, study conducted in 1993.

Seligman, Martin. *What You Can Change and What You Can't.* New York: Knopf, 1994.

Tisdale, Sally. "A Weight That Women Carry." *Harpers*, May 1993.

Wahl, Jan. "Taking a Female Lead." *Radiance*, fall 1994.

Wolf, Naomi. *The Beauty Myth: How Images of Beauty Are Used Against American Women.* New York: Doubleday, 1991.

Resources—Organizations and Workshops

AHELP, Association for the Health Enrichment of Large People. Annual conferences for health professionals. Joe McVoy, Ph.D., Director, AHELP, P.O. Drawer C, Radford, VA 24143.

Ample Opportunity. Organization, Portland, Oregon.

Annual Event: International No-Diet Day, May 5.

Boycott Anorexic Marketing, a Boston group founded by psychotherapist Dr. Mary Baures, who is concerned about a society that promotes eating disorders. In 1994 the group criticized the ultrathin models used by Coca-Cola and Calvin Klein and called for a boycott.

David Garner, Ph.D. Eating disorder specialist and antidiet activist.

Fed Up! Book, workshops, and support groups, by Terry Nicholetti Garrison, 233 Forest Home Drive, Ithaca, NY 14850.

Largely Positive. Workshops and support groups, manual on starting support groups, Carol Johnson, Milwaukee, Wisconsin, P.O. Box 17233, Glendale, WI 53217.

NAFAA, National Association to Advance Fat Acceptance, based in Sacramento, CA, with 4,000 members nationwide.

National Council on Size and Weight Discrimination.

Resources—Magazines and Films

Dimensions, the lifestyle magazine for men who prefer large, radiant women, and the women who want to learn about them. 7189 Capitol Station, Albany, NY 12224.

Extra!, a magazine for large persons.

Fat Chance, a documentary film sponsored by the National Film Board of Canada, to be aired on public broadcasting systems.

Healthy Weight Journal (formerly *Obesity and Health*), published by Healthy Living Institute, 402 South 14 Street, Hettinger, ND.

Radiance, the magazine for large women, a sponsored project of the San Francisco Women's Center, P.O. Box 30246, Oakland, CA 94604.

CHAPTER 12

Managing Diversity: A Multicultural Approach

A diverse company is better able to sell to a diverse world.
Microsoft executive

The best approach to managing diversity is one that includes all persons and excludes none. It provides a climate that supports all types of employees. Its goal is to include all employees in the inner circle of employees who are continuously learning to create continuous improvement—in activities that contribute to the bottom-line success of the organization.

While leaders of some companies still refer to their corporate culture as a melting pot and the company as one big happy family, a new breed of leaders is moving beyond the melting pot and legal approaches to an inclusive multicultural approach. This approach builds on the best affirmative action principles and a strong corporate culture, but it goes further. Its leaders value diversity, and they develop corporate strategies, systems, and action steps that reflect that core value. These leaders are change agents who learn how to inspire others to create the changes needed to build a productive, innovative, synergistic work force.

Before you delve into the details of this multicultural approach to managing diversity, test your knowledge of managing diversity through the multicultural approach by completing Self-Awareness Activity 12.1.

Self-Awareness Activity 12.1: What Do You Know About a Multicultural Approach?

Purpose: To see what you know about the issues covered in this chapter.

Instructions: Determine whether you think the following statements are basically true or false—and think about why. The answers will emerge in this chapter, and the summary at the end of the chapter focuses on these issues.

1. A multicultural approach to managing diversity focuses on minorities.
2. The most basic change that must take place in the organization is modifying its systems and practices to accommodate diverse employees.
3. Valuing diversity goes beyond tolerance to appreciation for all types of people.

4. The focus of employee training in the multicultural approach is on new minority employees learning about the corporate culture.

5. The multicultural approach builds upon equal opportunity principles and the current affirmative action program.

6. A key strategy for making the multicultural approach work is getting to know each individual employee.

7. The key to bringing about change is for top management to make a commitment.

THE MAJOR LEADERSHIP CHALLENGE AND OPPORTUNITY

The greatest work force challenge that business leaders face today is meeting the needs of *all* employees, people from all the diverse groups, including Euro-American men.

Leadership Challenge: Meeting Diverse Employees' Needs

Leaders with multicultural skills understand the many barriers facing ethnic minorities and women in most American corporations and develop strategies for dismantling them. The most important barriers are the policies and practices that systematically restrict the opportunities and rewards to nontraditional employees. Leaders who are most effective in formulating better policies and practices understand not only the external barriers that diverse workers face, but also some of their typical life experiences and the resulting internal barriers.

Some of the strongest barriers to the success of diverse employees are structural blocks built by the culture and the organization. Leaders with multicultural awareness and skills can help in the struggle to break down these barriers.

Changing an Incompatible Corporate Culture

To most diverse employees, the corporate culture seems unfriendly and stressful, often resulting in loneliness. At higher levels minorities, women, and employees from other diverse groups may be dramatically outnumbered by Euro-American men who treat them "differently," exclude them from social events and friendly camaraderie, and may view them as a curiosity. These newcomers sometimes report that the "insiders" watch them closely, overscrutinize their work for mistakes, withhold information, and even sabotage their work. They say they must be better than the others just to keep up. They say that when they cluster with others from their own diversity group, they may be jokingly or seriously accused of plotting against the dominant group, being divisive, or excluding others. If they remain isolated, they may be seen as arrogant or resentful. If they try to join the insiders, they may be met with stereotyping or some degree of rejection. We'll discuss this basic aspect of managing diversity in more detail later.

Changing Incompatible Organizational Systems

The most lasting and workable changes in the firm's systems and practices flow naturally from a commitment to corporate culture change. One reason AA programs have had such difficulty is that leaders rarely built them upon a commitment to corporate culture change. Once this commitment is made by a critical mass of employees, changing systems and practices becomes relatively easy. Specific suggestions are discussed later in this chapter.

Ending Historical Exclusion

Nontraditional employees have traditionally been kept out of the inner circle. The American culture has traditionally sent the message that Euro-American men take the lead role in all arenas of power. Studies indicate that a key barrier is their reluctance to share power and privilege and their natural tendency to associate with people like themselves (Carr-Ruffino 1991). Savvy leaders know it's time to break this cycle by giving everyone an equal chance.

Raising the Comfort Levels of Euro-American Men

An effective multicultural approach respects the concerns of all, including Euro-American men. It focuses on the leadership benefits of gaining multicultural skills in order to meet diverse employees halfway in cultural understanding and collaboration. Diversity training is essential.

Resistance to change results in backlash, as we discussed in chapter 1 concerning affirmative action. In fact, backlash has become so prevalent that it now is the primary barrier to the diversity efforts of many major companies. When downsizing cuts job opportunities, people become especially resentful and fearful and more likely to resent any competition from diverse employees.

People tend to be most accepting and comfortable with others who are most like them. Virtually all the emotions that block goodwill toward others spring from fear, and fear in turn often springs from the unknown, from ignorance. Studying cultural differences makes people knowledgeable, diminishes their fear of the unknown, and increases their comfort level with diverse others. Learning about stereotypes and prejudice can help also, but the instructional approach must be respectful, not blaming. It must address such concerns as reverse discrimination, lowered standards and quality, erosion of income and job security, and loss of a traditional way of life.

Removing Networking Barriers

For all nontraditional groups a major barrier is inability to create and manage networks. Individuals often cannot get the information they need about industry trends and where the company is headed, nor handle company politics adequately. Understanding the organizational culture and the barriers it may have erected can be even more important than formal degrees, according to several surveys. In fact, courses and degrees may be less relevant to success in the executive suite than they once were because most omit these soft skills (Cox 1993; Carr-Ruffino 1991).

Preventing Infighting Among Subcultural Groups

When one underrepresented group competes with another for privileges, status, and power, infighting can occur and create a barrier for all. Managers have been known to use divide-and-conquer tactics to increase friction and infighting among diverse subgroups. The dramatic increase in hate crimes, at record levels now, indicates that backlash and infighting are problems in society at large, not just in organizations. The growing diversity in the population has increased interethnic tension.

Turning Around Poor Career Development Patterns

Euro-American men are often reluctant to assign nontraditional managers to those challenging, high-profile jobs that are needed to prepare people for senior management positions. They don't want people to fail, and they want the company to look good. Such assignments include leading a major start-up, troubleshooting (sometimes overseas), serving on important task forces, taking a headquarters staff job, and taking line jobs of increasing responsibility. They involve autonomy, visibility, access to senior management, and control over significant resources. They are considered the fast track in many organizations and may be used as tests and rewards for high-potential candidates. Such career-enhancing assignments are often not available to diverse employees, who tend to be found in staff rather than line positions (Kotter 1990; U.S. Department of Labor 1991; Catalyst 1990; DiTomaso, Thompson, and Blake 1988).

Breaking the Glass Ceiling

The U.S. Department of Labor reports that 30 percent of corporate middle management is made up of women, African Americans, and Latino Americans. These groups made up less than 5 percent of senior management in 1990, even though they're about 65 percent of the work force. A major consulting firm surveyed nearly 1400 senior executives, and only 29 were women and 13 were people of color, meaning 97 percent were Euro-American males (U.S. Department of Labor 1991; Korn/Ferry 1986).

Universities such as Harvard, Yale, and Princeton, which are typically considered feeder institutions for high-paying management jobs, refused to admit women as undergraduates until the 1970s. Lack of education became a widely accepted explanation for the slow movement of nontraditional employees into and through management. It's still used today despite the fact that their educational achievement has soared. It's been more than 30 years since the passage of the 1964 Civil Rights Act. It's been more than 20 years since women and minorities entered leadership-oriented programs in significant numbers. Even if it takes 15 or 20 years to develop a general manager, more minorities and women should logically be reaching the middle- and top-level jobs. Clearly, lack of qualified candidates is not the only explanation for underrepresentation.

Leadership Opportunity: Creating an Inclusive Multicultural Approach

The multicultural approach is a diversity-within-unity approach, as indicated in Figure 12.1. Unity is provided through a strong corporate culture that focuses on the best niche for the organization to fill and on the purpose of the organization, as well as on valuing diversity. And diversity is provided for through a strong emphasis on appreciating each individual—respecting the uniqueness of every employee, including values, lifestyles, and cultural heritage. Above all, the multicultural approach is an inclusive approach. No one is excluded simply because he or she was not born a member of the ingroup—or has changed physically in ways that don't affect basic job performance.

Leaders encourage the organization to adapt in ways that support all types of employees, and they help all employees become oriented to the organization, a two-way street. Corporate leaders make certain the organization's values and norms accommodate a wide range of workers. They make sure that everyone has a chance to build multicultural skills and to update and refine them continually.

The multicultural approach aims to support and empower all employees in learning, stretching, and moving up because leaders pay attention to this issue at the individual, interpersonal, and organizational levels. Leaders develop strategies to bring all employees into the "Inner Circle" and remove barriers to inclusion, as shown in Table 12.1. The multicultural approach is also about making sure that the systems and practices of the organization support employee empowerment, through natural evolvement so that stop-and-go types of AA programs are unnecessary. It's a comprehensive managerial process for developing an environment that works for all employees. Empowering the total work force is achieved through such strategies as pushing decision making down to lower levels, organizing self-managing work teams, providing adequate education, and supporting career development.

TABLE 12.1: Managing Inclusion at All Levels

Inclusive Strategies	*Barriers to Inclusion*
Personal Level	
Become aware of prejudice and other barriers to valuing diversity Learn about other cultures and groups Serve as an example, walk the talk Participate in managing diversity	Stereotypes, prejudices Past experiences and influences Stereotyped expectations and perceptions Feelings that tend to separate, divide
Interpersonal Level	
Facilitate communication and interactions in ways that value diversity Encourage participation Share you perspective Facilitate unique contributions Resolve conflicts in ways that value diversity Accept responsibility for developing common ground	Cultural differences Group differences Myths Relationship patterns based on exclusion
Organizational Level	
All employees have access to networks and focus groups All employees take a proactive role in managing diversity and creating a more diverse workplace culture All employees are included in the Inner Circle that contributes to the bottom-line success of the company All employees give feedback to teams and management All employees are encouraged to contribute to change	Individuals who get away with discriminating and excluding A culture that values or allows exclusion Work structures, policies, and practices that discriminate and exclude

FIGURE 12.1: Diverse Groups Within a Strong Corporate Culture: Diversity Within Unity

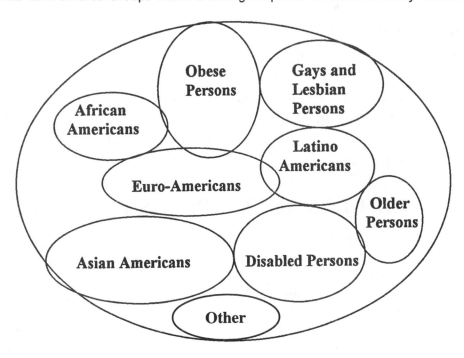

This type of diversity management is not about Euro-American males managing women and minorities, nor is it about focusing on women and minorities to the exclusion of Euro-American men. It's about all managers empowering whoever is in their work force. This inclusive approach focuses on understanding individuals and valuing each person's diversity profile. The focus is on the individual, with an understanding of each individual's background, against the backdrop of a mosaic society, as pictured in Figure 12.2 This approach views diverse employees as persons who can enrich the work team or organization, who can interact with others to create innovative sparks, entrepreneurial genius, and total-quality performance.

FIGURE 12.2: Focus on the Individual Against a Cultural Background

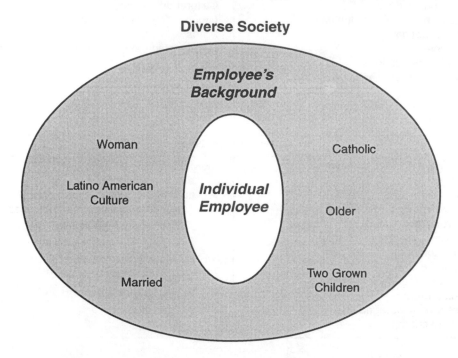

The most important aspects of the multicultural approach we suggest in this chapter are shown below.

Key Aspects of a Multicultural Approach

- Modifying the corporate culture toward a valuing-diversity culture
- Including all employees in bottom-line efforts
- Building on equal opportunity and affirmative action principles
- Adapting corporate systems and practices to reflect a valuing-diversity culture
- Addressing concerns and resistances people may have to this inclusive approach
- Building consensus for changing to a valuing-diversity culture

CREATING A VALUING–DIVERSITY CULTURE

Valuing diversity is first of all a bottom-line issue because its the first step in getting all employees contributing to bottom-line success. That's because valuing diversity is at the heart of such issues as conflict resolution, negotiation, employee relationships, employee empowerment, leadership effectiveness, continuous learning, continuous improvement, productivity, total quality management, synergistic teams, and trust building. Given the potential payoffs, companies can't afford to be satisfied with outdated corporate cultures that exclude many potential contributors.

Changing the corporate culture is most effective, of course, when top management makes a commitment to shifting the culture in ways that accommodate, motivate, and empower all employees. The ultimate goal is for everyone to grow and develop, to be effective and productive, to interact to create a synergy that sparks innovation and commitment. But any person anywhere in the organization can have an influence toward change. Wherever you are on your career path, you can accept a leadership role in this kind of change. The most powerful change starts in the basic cultural elements:

- new values that build respect for all kinds of persons and that build trust—a high value for diversity
- new stories about new kinds of heroines and heroes that become the basis for new myths and legends
- new kinds of rituals, ways of doing things and ways of interacting with each other
- new kinds of ceremonies that recognize people for their actions and attitudes that value diversity
- new kinds of symbols and slogans that touch people and communicate a valuing diversity worldview.

Culture change is the basis for all other organizational change. Lasting change must come from inside the organization. Role modeling and persuasion are the best methods, while coercion doesn't really work at all. When key leaders in all areas and at all levels become committed to change, this critical mass will bring along most other employees.

Tolerance or Appreciation?

The concept of appreciation is at the core of valuing diversity. For years Americans have been struggling toward tolerance for diverse people and groups in our society, and many have not yet achieved a feeling of tolerance. Yet mere tolerance falls short of what people must feel toward one another if they are to work together in innovative, productive teams. The type of cooperation and collaboration that creates synergy is based on mutual respect and appreciation. See if you can get in touch with the effects of tolerance versus appreciation by completing Self-Awareness Activity 12.2.

Self-Awareness Activity 12.2: Being Tolerated and Being Appreciated

Purpose: To experience the difference between tolerance and appreciation.

Step 1. Being Tolerated

a. Think of a time when you felt tolerated. In a brief paragraph describe the situation.

b. How did it feel to be merely tolerated? Describe your feelings.

c. How did feeling tolerated affect your relationship with the tolerant person(s)?

Step 2. Being Appreciated

a. Think of a time when you felt appreciated. Describe the situation in a brief paragraph.

b. How did it feel to be truly appreciated? Did you feel respected? Describe your feelings.

c. How did feeling appreciated affect your relationship with the appreciative person(s)?

Freedom to Be Authentic

Every person and every human culture needs to express who they are. The strong desire of many former communist countries and ethnic groups to claim a separate culture reflects this universal need. When groups unite to achieve certain common purposes, they can greatly increase their power. But when they can't find ways to accommodate cultural differences and blend them into a group strength, they lose their joint power. At the corporate level such groups may simply lose the opportunity to achieve greater goals, but at the societal level, they may deteriorate into anarchy and bloodshed, as happened in the Los Angeles riots and in Bosnia.

Whether in a national culture or a corporate culture, people are more productive and enthusiastic when they have the freedom to express their own values and determine their own lifestyle. The most effective organizations learn how to combine and balance the drive for individual freedom and achievement with the drive for belongingness and group affiliation. And they focus on building and maintaining trust, the essential ingredient.

Beyond the Melting Pot: Free Choice and Cultural Enrichment

Valuing diversity means dealing with cultural realities. The evidence on acculturation patterns among Asians and Latinos in the U.S. indicates that substantial identity with the root national cultures remains even after three or more generations of citizenship. The least effective policy an organization can pursue is to insist that members of any group give up some cherished belief or practice. People always resist such pressure—usually by going underground and then engaging in passive aggressive behavior. Of course covert behavior is much more difficult to deal with than open, direct behavior (Deshpande et al. 1986; Allport 1954).

Since cultural accommodation is a two-way street, the process is subtle and complex and trying to force it on any of the parties may create as many problems as it solves. The best approach is to allow people the freedom to assimilate into the mainstream culture and the corporate culture to the extent they desire and to retain their cultural heritage as they see fit. This approach must rest on appreciating differences and respecting each person's cultural heritage and their decisions about what to retain. Cultural change takes time, and a relaxed, accepting attitude allows the shifts to occur with minimal friction.

When ethnic groups retain those distinctive and colorful ways that they treasure, the organization is enriched. Each individual decides those aspects of their ethnic cuisine, art, the philosophical and spiritual beliefs, myths and stories that they want to hold dear and to express. When people are allowed and encouraged to preserve these treasures, they become more interesting and valuable to the whole organization and to the nation. They "prevent drab standardization in a culture dominated by advertising, brand names, malls, and sedative television" (Cox 1993, 84).

Leadership Traits

Unlike people who stereotype, leaders who value differences tend to:

- base beliefs about characteristics of culture groups on a systematic study of reliable sources of data
- acknowledge that people within an ethnic group vary and that they have many voices and many individual styles and patterns
- resist the tendency to evaluate differences, and avoid negative connotations

Valuing diversity is an approach that enhances acceptance, tolerance, and understanding of differences.

Education for All

The multicultural approach and valuing diversity are relatively new concepts for many employees. Training is normally needed at all levels of the organization for positive change to occur. Training usually begins at the top, since top management must thoroughly understand the concepts and apply them consistently in their own thinking and acting. Training sessions tend to focus on the ways that people differ in values, attitudes, behavior styles, ways of thinking, and cultural background. Common goals of the educational programs are for participants to:

- expand their awareness and acceptance of cultural and individual differences
- understand the nature and dynamics of cultural and individual differences
- explore their own feelings and attitudes about people who are different
- identify ways that differences might be tapped as workplace assets
- build better work relations with people who are different

This approach leads people to appreciate the value, richness, and creativity that can flow from a diverse work force. It focuses on helping everyone to better understand some key differences that tend to be common to employees from certain groups and how these differences can be valuable to the organization. It exhibits real concern and commitment to providing a corporate culture where people from all groups can thrive. When employees thrive, the company tends to thrive, as Microsoft has shown.

SHOWCASE: MICROSOFT
A VALUING DIVERSITY CULTURE

Microsoft focuses on valuing diversity and creating a corporate culture that reflects that value. This view has been productive and profitable for the firm, which grew from a start-up to the largest software firm in the world in a few short years. Microsoft has a diversity program that is proactive. Program leaders want to know when people feel unwelcome at work, when they're worried about things outside of work, or anything else that could stand in the way of top performance. A diversity staff implements diversity training programs, updates benefits policies, and investigates cases of discrimination and harassment.

The company's Diversity Advisory Council includes representatives from employee groups of gay persons, women, persons with disabilities, Jewish Americans, African Americans, Latino Americans, American Indians, and Asian Indian Americans, and it expands as new groups form. The council helps formulate policy, identify problems, and create the best possible working environment for all employees. Microsoft's diversity manager says the council helps to boost productivity and to stem turnover, adding millions to company profits.

Microsoft's management also understands that it takes more than a nondiscrimination clause and diversity groups to achieve a supportive environment for all groups. Some people are intolerant, and the company needs specific training programs to help people become more aware of the nature of prejudice, the facts about various groups, and of alternative ways of believing and interacting.

Microsoft wants to tap into the different needs and backgrounds of employees to use their talents, to use the various perspectives they bring, based on who they are. For example, a Microsoft marketing goal is to put a computer on every desk in every home. To do that, the company needs to know who these consumers are and what they're like. The philosophy:

We must make our products accessible to all types of consumers, and therefore we must market them differently to each group. A diverse company is better able to sell to a diverse world.

INCLUDING ALL EMPLOYEES IN BOTTOM-LINE EFFORTS

Continuous improvement is highly valued in most organizations these days. Although Americans tend to prefer dramatic breakthroughs, decisive victories, and clear "wins," leaders have learned that small incremental improvements are much easier to come by. They can also lead to comparable or greater success over time. One of the most powerful benefits of a continuous improvement approach and process is that it inevitably leads to continuous learning for the employees who are included in it. In fact many leaders are convinced that the successful organization these days must be a learning organization. Since organizations are people first and foremost, this means that successful organizations must be staffed by employees who are continuously learning.

The Learning Loop

The cycle of continuous learning that leads to continuous improvement and that also results from efforts to continuously improve is sometimes called the learning loop because one process feeds into the other, as shown in Figure 12.3. If you can imagine ongoing learning loops leading to ever-higher levels of learning and improvement, you would see a spiral, as shown in Figure 12.4.

FIGURE 12.3: The Learning Loop

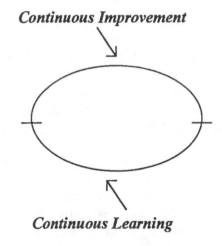

Continuous Improvement

Continuous Learning

FIGURE 12.4: Continuous Learning-Productivity Loop

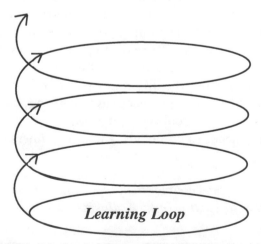

Learning Loop

Learning Loops Spiraling to Higher Levels of Improvement and Learning

ARC of Improvement

One aspect of continuous learning might be called the ARC of improvement, standing for a process of analyzing, resolving, and changing as follows.

Analyze current process, practices, and results by asking: What happened that was effective or ineffective? Why did it happen? What needs to happen?

Resolve problems and find better ways of doing things by asking: How can we bring about what needs to happen? How can we prevent problems from recurring? How can we handle the situation differently in the future?

Change. Get agreement on what will change. Give support for the change.

The story in the showcase of continuous improvement that follows helps to illustrate the concept.

SHOWCASE OF CONTINUOUS IMPROVEMENT

A Miami construction firm won a contract to "gut and rebuild the interior" of a 1930s hotel, to bring it up to modern standards but keep its Art Deco charm. The design and construction teams decided to complete one floor at a time, starting with the first floor of rooms, moving floor by floor to the tenth floor at the top, and finally to the lobby. When they finished the first floor, all were very proud of the results. The rooms looked great, and the work had been completed efficiently, effectively, and on time. It was so good they could have repeated exactly the same process for the other floors. Instead, they used the learning loop and engaged in a process of continuous improvement. They analyzed what could be done better, faster, more effectively, and more efficiently as well as how they could better coordinate tasks, combine them, reschedule them, and make similar improvements. When they finished the second floor, it was even better in quality and appearance than the first floor and had been completed more efficiently. Continuing to learn from their experiences on each floor, the teams finally surveyed the completed tenth floor, which they had done in record time. Everyone agreed that this was the best floor yet. The team leader had an idea: "Let's go back down to the first floor now and compare the results." The workers were amazed. The tenth floor was so superior to the first that they were actually a little embarrassed about the first floor.

The Inner Circle

All learning loops are not equally beneficial or productive. We all know people who become extremely efficient at filling out forms, filing papers, operating computer programs, and other activities—that are largely a waste of time. At best, these employees aren't contributing much to the bottom-line success of the organization, nor to their personal career success.

Employees who work on projects and tasks that *do* contribute directly to the quality of the organization's products and services are fortunate. The more improvement they create and the more they learn about doing the work elegantly, efficiently, and in line with customer needs and preferences, the more satisfying their jobs are. They make an important difference and they know it. That's more than fulfilling—it's exciting and motivating. It's like being a member of an inner circle.

For this reason, we'll use the Inner Circle as a metaphor of employees who are included in those learning loops directly connected to the bottom line success of the organization. Employees in the Inner Circle are in a position to grow, learn, and advance the goals of the organization. They're "where the action is," the important action, that is.

To get a clear picture of what the inner and outer circle look like in your organization, complete Skill Builder 12.4 at the end of this chapter.

Bring All Employees into the Inner Circle

An important managing inclusion principle is to bring all the employees you can into the Inner Circle and its key learning loops. Think of Figure 12.5 as your organization. Who is a part of the inner circle and who is left out? If bottom-line success is your most important priority, it makes sense to get all the employees working toward it. Learning how to do this is a key managing diversity skill. Here are some suggestions:

- Specify the skills and capabilities that are required.
- Get to know all the employees, their weaknesses and strengths.
- Develop strategies to overcome the obstacles that stand in the way, to bridge the gaps between necessary skills and capabilities and those the employee now has.
- Provide them with required knowledge and skills.

FIGURE 12.5: The Inner Circle

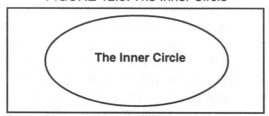

Give All Employees Quality Treatment

Leaders are focused on bringing quality to customers and through total quality management. Savvy leaders understand how to give all employees quality treatment, another key managing diversity principle. Quality treatment differs somewhat for each employee. Base your treatment on a connection with each person's humanity and individuality—and on your understanding of the requirements of the work. Here are some general actions and attitudes that constitute quality treatment:

- Believe in each employee and communicate that belief.
- Explicitly communicate high standards and high expectations.
- Promote a respect for diversity.
- Show each person that he or she is important to you and the organization.
- Provide support to *all* employees.
- Value people through your procedures and practices.
- Teach people the basis of success in the organization, including the unwritten rules; be an effective mentor.
- Lead people to engage in learning loops and bring them into bottom-line learning loops.

BUILDING ON EQUAL OPPORTUNITY PRINCIPLES

While a multicultural approach goes beyond affirmative action programs, it does not ignore equal opportunity principles or abandon AA programs. It does build on lessons business leaders have learned about how to make AA work most effectively for all groups.

Revitalizing the Affirmative Action System

The first step toward a multicultural approach is to review the company's AA policies and procedures. Top leaders can start revitalizing the AA system by communicating that it must be respected by everyone. Violation of AA policy should be treated as seriously as violation of other important corporate policies. Senior management needs to regularly monitor the organization to be sure diversity goals are being met. Employment data should be organized by gender and ethnic group status. It should show minority groups and women as a percentage of:

- total employees in each job category
- total management pool
- each level of management

The organization's grievance process for handling individual cases of discrimination should be reviewed to make sure it's fair, effective, and credible. Management needs to systematically review grievance files to detect patterns of mistreatment or discrimination.

Every aspect of an employee's career path is affected by company policies and practices regarding equal opportunity and affirmative action. In chapter 3 we discussed some of the leadership challenges for eliminating discrimination from these practices. The following checklist can guide your efforts toward revitalizing your company's practices.

Recruiting. Focus on two key principles: (1) Go where diverse employees are to recruit applicants for all types and levels of jobs. (2) Make sure that word-of-mouth recruitment reaches all types of potential applicants. In order to find diverse applicants, do the following:

- Go to universities that have large numbers of minority students. Contact all types of minority student organizations, give them job postings, go to their job fairs, speak at their meetings.

- Get lists of various types of minority organizations—community, social, professional, business, etc. Make regular and systematic contact with the formal and informal leaders of these organizations.

- Ask qualified persons from minority groups to apply for open positions. As long as a 1992 ruling of the federal Sixth Circuit Court holds up, this is legal if it helps the firm to recruit minorities as a part of an effort to fairly balance their work force. It's still illegal to take the next step and offer a job at that point (*HRM Ideas* 1992).

- Encourage your own minority employees to spread the word among their friends, family, and other contacts. Reward them for helping to recruit minority employees.

- Identify and solve applicants' transportation problems, where appropriate.

Screening. Be sure that all job criteria—such as experience, degrees, and certificates—are really good predictors of job success and don't unreasonably exclude certain groups whose members could succeed. Be sure all tests and exams are valid. Be sure that such barriers as arrest records, poor credit records, or subjective evaluations by prejudiced individuals do not unfairly discriminate against certain minorities.

Compensating. Set goals to achieve equitable salaries and perquisites across all cultural groups. Eliminate practices that lead to lower salaries and perquisites for some groups.

Integrating. Set goals to acquire a reasonably balanced staff in all corporate areas and at all levels, to eliminate "pink ghettoes," "gay ghettos," "minority jobs," etc.

Evaluating. Find ways to eliminate performance evaluation that is colored by bias, stereotyping, or prejudice. For example, have a diverse panel of employees or managers perform important performance evaluations, especially those that affect promotions.

Training and development. Monitor and track all employees' career paths and progress toward achieving their career goals. A diverse panel should make decisions about who will be offered training and development opportunities, especially those opportunities designed to prepare people for promotion.

Promoting. A panel of diverse employees is more likely to make unbiased promotion decisions than is a homogeneous panel or an individual decision maker. Publicize the criteria for promotion, demystify the process. When everyone understands what it takes, those working toward promotion can better focus their attention and energy.

Dismissing. Laying off and firing are the most difficult aspects of dealing with employees. The difficult goal is to find procedures that don't unfairly discriminate against minorities who were unable to get better jobs until recently and therefore have little seniority, older workers who have been loyal to the company and have seniority, or any other group.

Learning from Past Lessons

Among the contributions AA has made to the workplace are the lessons it has taught us about what does and doesn't work in managing diversity. Even though it's important to consider common issues, patterns, and themes of each subcultural group, it's also important to deal with each person as an individual. Everything leaders do should encourage the minority person to take an achieving, team-oriented outlook, never a victim mentality.

Set high but realistic AA goals. Progress in revitalizing AA is slow and incremental. Neither managers nor employees should expect a quick fix. Most AA programs have to be refined and refined, and some may be judged unsuccessful and terminated.

Identify job requirements as opposed to preferences, conveniences, or traditions. Creating a diverse work force is about enhancing the organization's capability to tap the potential of a diverse group of employees. Set the right goals for the AA program, and keep asking whether all systems and practices are helping to achieve those goals.

Reexamine job standards but keep them high. Ensure that hiring and performance standards are as clear and job-related as possible. They must be common across groups to be perceived as fair.

Test assumptions and support claims. Management should test the assumptions underlying personnel policies and be able to support the claims they make about the effects of systems and programs.

Encourage an achiever self-concept, not a victim self-concept. Every group in the U.S., except for Euro-American men, has been disadvantaged in the workplace by stereotypes, prejudice, and discrimination. In that sense they have been and still are victims of the system, but the victim argument produces negative side effects. Victims must have persecutors, which implies that Euro-American men are collectively guilty of oppression. Resentment grows as victim and oppressor accuse each other of injustice in the pursuit of self-interest. Relying on the status of victim to obtain rights or favors is demeaning and self-destructive to the victims because it focuses on what they don't have instead of building on what they can and do have.

A more positive approach is for minorities to focus on setting personal career goals and then on developing the strengths, talents, initiative, and contacts needed to achieve those goals. The only way to become social and economic equals is to act like and demand treatment as equals. This means building skills, showing initiative, and persevering despite real and sometimes unfair obstacles. But just as Euro-American men need some support from the system, so do minorities. While there may be a few who can muster what it takes to overcome huge barriers and climb past the middle-management level, companies should not demand or expect such superhuman efforts. Organizations must also do their share in removing unnecessary barriers and providing reasonable support.

Use leadership, not coercion. True leadership inspires positive change but doesn't force or coerce it. Coerced change usually leads to low morale, cynicism, and covert resistance. One leadership approach is to establish core groups for the purpose of bringing about change, for example to explore group differences and to promote effective communication and team building. Then management can encourage the formation of similar core groups through voluntary employee participation.

Stress uniqueness, not just common group characteristics. Be aware of the common group characteristics you're likely to encounter in different groups, but avoid a new type of stereotyping. Be open to the variance, or diversity, of individuals, and never automatically assume that a person is representative of his or her group. Be aware of the wide range of differences among individuals from a particular group.

Treat group characteristics as important, but not "special." Respect group differences in beliefs, skills, and so forth, but don't put them on a pedestal as more important than other differences among employees. An emphasis on group differences rather than individual differences can divide the work force, invite blame and resentment, and risk the development of a we/them mentality. Group differences should be handled as factors in meeting business objectives, not as ends in themselves.

Tailor treatment to individuals, not to groups. Develop individuals, not groups, but at the same time address the particular characteristics or disadvantages found disproportionately in some ethnic or gender groups. Programs to assist and develop employees should not be conditioned on group status unless there is a compelling reason to do so. Target programs to the specific strengths and weaknesses, advantages and disadvantages of individuals. Special career tracks for African Americans or women can be demeaning to them and arouse resentment among others. Flexible jobs or benefits packages may be especially important to women but must be generally available to all employees. Compensatory treatment should be provided on the basis of individual, not group, characteristics. Basing rights on ethnicity or gender should be used only as a last resort.

MODIFYING CORPORATE SYSTEMS AND PRACTICES

Top management controls the resources and has the decision-making authority to make the multicultural approach work. Top managers influence people whose prejudice is embedded in a set of beliefs and values that often includes respect for authority. They can favorably influence organization do's and don'ts that subtly guide egalitarian interpersonal behavior. All levels must support the multicultural approach, if it is to succeed. To manage the diversity, all leaders must be committed to creating unity among diverse employees. Management must include unity issues when they conduct a diversity audit to see what's needed. Then they have the basis for developing and implementing a plan that coordinates all major systems and practices (Thomas 1991; Cox 1993; Morrison 1992).

Addressing Unity Issues

Diverse organizations often have unity problems, and therefore building a strong corporate culture is essential to overcoming these problems. Typical issues are finding common ground, maintaining group cohesiveness, and communicating through cultural barriers. Any diversity audit should address these issues.

Finding common ground. Too much diversity in work teams, management groups, or any type of problem-solving group can be especially dysfunctional. When communication barriers, style conflicts, and points of view lack even a core of commonality, decision making may become impossible. Leaders can provide that core of commonality by fostering a corporate culture that's strong enough for all groups to feel connected to common values, heroes, myths, rituals, ceremonies, and other cultural anchors (Shephard 1964).

Maintaining group cohesiveness. While group cohesiveness has many advantages, higher productivity is not necessarily one of them. Research has *not* shown that cohesiveness alone improves the work performance of groups. Highly cohesive groups are just as likely to have lower productivity as they are to be more productive. The best way to improve cohesiveness *and* productivity is to find common ground and work toward common goals. Leaders can encourage this through the ways they establish and lead work teams (Arnold and Feldman 1986).

Avoiding communication breakdown. When a group becomes diverse, misunderstandings may increase, conflict and anxiety may rise, and members may feel less comfortable with being in the group. These effects may combine to make decision making more difficult and time-consuming. In these respects culturally diverse work groups are more difficult to manage effectively than homogeneous work groups. The challenge is to manage in such a way that you maximize the potential benefits of diversity while minimizing the potential difficulties.

Building a strong culture that focuses on corporate niche and also values diversity is a complex, ongoing effort. It means paying special attention to the values, norms, grapevine, heroes, rituals, and ceremonies that make up the culture. It means becoming a role model who vividly shows by actions and words what the company stands for. Two strategies that can be especially powerful in building a strong diversity culture are using self-managing teams and assigning managers as culture catalysts.

Using self-managing teams. The multicultural approach leads to a new type of organization that better suits the needs of today's workers. People are more effective when they feel in control of their destinies. The strongest motivating force for today's workers is peer-group pressure, the primary control mechanism for teams. Strong cultures, which are necessary for bonding self-managing groups into a productive whole organization, are most easily built in smaller units. The electronic equipment that links teams is far cheaper than layers of middle management.

Making managers culture catalysts. The role of managers will focus more and more on creating sparks in the corporate culture. They make culture change happen without forcing it. They build, enunciate, and promote a strong culture that bonds people together, giving people a core of common beliefs and values, a sense of common purpose.

Conducting a Diversity Audit

One of the first steps in developing a multicultural approach is to conduct a diversity audit to get feedback from employees about how they're affected by the systems and the culture. Interview questions can be based on the following types of general questions:

- Why do employees select and remain with the organization?
- What has determined their success?
- How do they assess the quality of work assignments and supervision they've received?
- What barriers hamper further upward mobility?
- How do they view the firm's overall success in managing diversity?
- Do the company's systems and practices work naturally for everyone? If not, why don't they? What must the organization do to make them work naturally for everyone?

Will the cultural assumptions of this organization allow us to take the necessary corrective action? If not, what cultural changes must we encourage?

Leaders must examine each system in detail and identify patterns that hinder multiculturalism. They must:

- determine what is generating problem patterns
- determine what to do to eliminate the undesirable patterns and convert the system to a facilitating factor
- develop a plan for implementing the system changes

The multicultural approach calls for changing the systems and then encouraging the culture to naturally change as a result. For example, we know that since companies changed their hiring and promotion systems to allow women into management positions, corporate values and norms have changed so that people no longer are disturbed or upset when women are hired or promoted into those jobs—at least at the lower management levels.

As new people join the organization, informal customs and practices that have been comfortable for Euro-American men may need modifying in order to meet the needs of new employees. Formal practices may also need change: flexible work scheduling, working at home, family leave, child-care provisions. The recurring questions should be: How can we meet the needs and preferences of diverse employees? How can we enhance their strengths and elicit the unique contributions they might make.

Do some research on what has worked for other organizations. For example, a field experiment assessed the impact of flextime use on absentee rates and worker performance. Both short-term and long-term absences declined significantly. Three out of four worker efficiency measures increased significantly under flextime (Kim and Campagna 1981).

Developing a Diversity Plan

A diversity audit can provide the company with a profile of the organization's diversity. It can inform leaders about diverse employees' values and needs through information from surveys, focus groups, interviews, task forces, and similar sources. Leaders can then describe the future state they need to create in these areas:

- matching people and jobs
- managing reward and performance
- informing and involving people
- lifestyles and life needs

The diversity audit provides information for analyzing the present state—where the company is now in each of these areas. The next step is to define the gap between this present state and desired future state. What needs to be done to bridge the gap? Leaders can then plan and manage transitions from the present state to the desired future state.

Suppose you were asked to recommend a plan for a multicultural approach to diversity for your organization. What would you include? Of course, you'd want to tailor the plan to fit your particular organization's needs, after conducting an audit. But there are certain actions that are typical of the most excellent companies for diversity. You'd want to seriously consider the following actions.

Set diversity goals. Set annual diversity goals for hiring and promotion in both staff and line jobs, for each division. To overcome the barriers inherent in being an isolated token minority, the goals should aim for a critical mass of each type of diverse worker in each area. To this end, management should consider clustering members of the same ethnic or gender group in particular work teams, departments, offices, or facilities—as a transitional procedure—in areas central to the mission of the organization, where jobs carry high status and wages. This can enhance the performance and retention of diverse employees.

The best way to ensure that diverse workers' needs and preferences are met is to promote enough members of each category up through all levels of the organization. When diverse managers gain power over significant arenas of decision making, substantive changes that meet the needs of other diverse workers will occur more naturally. For example, the managers who understand best what Asian American employees value and need are the Asian American managers, and women managers have the greatest insight into needs of women employees.

Aim for a diverse board. Encourage the board of directors to include women and minorities in proportion to the work force and customer base. Board decisions need to reflect a wide range of views.

Use diversity specialists. Make someone responsible for diversity issues. It may be an officer, a staff manager, or an entire department. In addition, establish a task force or committee that addresses diversity issues. Consider using a diversity consultant for specific needs.

Provide diversity training. Provide diversity training for every person, especially managers, every year. Incorporate appropriate diversity training into new employee orientation.

Develop for promotability. Determine what must be done to retain and promote diverse employees. The organization must first discover and then create the conditions under which women and ethnic groups can thrive at all levels of the organization. Hire entry-level people who have enough skills and experience that they have a good chance to advance. Provide a basic level of support—that is, encouragement, training, resources—to all new employees. Encourage mentoring, career tracking, and other career development strategies. Rotate supervisors in order to expose new employees to different management styles and to expose supervisors to a range of employee skills and concerns. Systematically monitor all terminations, transfers, and promotions as part of an effort to retain and promote women and ethnic employees. Provide appropriate skills training to meet the needs of minority and women employees.

Provide internships and scholarships. Set up internship programs for minority and women students, to give them some training and exposure to the company, and to enhance recruiting efforts. Consider providing scholarship programs for members of targeted groups, both as an indirect recruiting device and as part of community outreach.

Reward diversity gains. When hiring and promoting Euro-American men, include criteria that predict their contribution to the organization's AA and multicultural goals. Before hiring, look for evidence that predicts their ability to function effectively in an organization that is achieving those goals. Examples of predictive experience include experience working in multicultural settings, being supervised by a woman or ethnic manager, collaborating on multicultural work teams, having resided in a racially integrated neighborhood, providing help with child care for employees, successfully balancing job and family responsibilities. Predictive educational experience might include attending equal status, interracial schools, studying with diverse teachers, belong to school groups with diverse members, attending courses or workshops on multicultural or non-Western cultural topics, and speaking another language.

Hold every manager responsible for the progress and success of their diverse employees. Performance in this area should be part of performance evaluation and rewards. Promotion criteria can be expanded to include success in helping diverse employees thrive in the organization. Examples of specific actions include finding, hiring, promoting, encouraging, and sponsoring diverse employees.

Encourage support groups. Help minorities and women to establish support groups for purposes of networking, mentoring, supporting, and influencing company decisions. Provide some company funds to these groups for bringing in speakers, holding events, and similar activities.

Set diversity contracting goals. Create minority and women's vendor-supplier programs and use minority contractors, minority-owned banks, law firms, and other minority-owned business services for specified percentages of the annual purchasing budget.

Use community outreach. Connect with minority and women's organizations in the community. Establish a continuing dialogue for making job referrals, posting job openings, making charitable contributions, and similar activities.

Implementing a Diversity Plan: Success Factors

Key success factors of the multicultural approach center around treating people as respected individuals and giving feedback in a culturally sensitive manner. It's important to get to know people as individuals, as well as part of a particular cultural group, to give feedback sensitively based on that knowledge, and to set the tone for creativity to occur (Thomas 1991; Gottfredson 1992; Morrison 1992).

Getting to Know the Individual

Take time to get to know each employee, as well as his or her subcultural group. The more you learn about each person, the better you will be able to collaborate with that person as an individual and as part of a work team. What you don't know may keep you from doing your own job effectively. Here are some suggestions that may help.

- *Avoid appearance stereotypes.* Don't assume race or ethnicity from appearance alone. Many Latinos have Asian features, and many Blacks have Latino, Jamaican, or other origins and strongly distinguish themselves from African Americans. Bi-ethnic persons' cultural backgrounds are not easy to determine from appearance only.

- *Avoid ethnic stereotypes.* Don't assume that all foreign or minority workers are impoverished or deprived. Get to know the background of each one.

- *Put emotions in perspective.* Don't take emotional outbursts personally. Ask, are emotional outbursts a normal way of responding to the situation in that person's culture? Remember, also, that newcomers often experience a phase of frustration and anger during the adaptation phase.

- *Discover other people's values.* Watch how they behave. When someone behaves consistently in similar circumstances, it suggests a value at work.

- *Clarify which values apply in each situation.* Identify precisely which value or values are at play in a given situation. It is one thing to know that a person values family ties more than you do. It is more difficult to recognize that the family ties value is at stake when that person is absent from work for what would seem like a trivial family matter to you. Your tendency may be to judge by your standards for consistent attendance at work rather than by his standards of family loyalty.

- *Apply employee values to work enhancement.* Look for the positive side of the other person's values—not only how that value is positive in the other's culture, but also how that same value could be applied in ways that are consistent with organization values and objectives. Apply the value to the job at hand. How can you bring the person's value into play so that it helps achieve job objectives? For example, when you need teamwork to accomplish something previously done by individuals, the person from a tightly woven culture is likely to rise to the occasion.

- *Apply relevant training.* Determine each new employee's knowledge of the system, and train each one accordingly. Has this employee faced the complexities of the U.S. corporate system before? You may need to train some employees in very basic ways.

- *Determine each employee's primary thinking pattern.* Determine their primary thinking pattern. If you see that abstract and hypothetical thinking is not familiar to them, try using examples, stories, and hands-on experience.

- *Determine each employee's primary learning pattern.* Be patient while employees are in the process of gaining necessary knowledge and experience. You may have to answer more questions, even very basic ones, than you would with Euro-American male employees.

- *Reinforce successful new behavior.* Choose reinforcers, recognition, and rewards that the recipients value as such. Give them in a way that is in line with that person's values.

- *Understand cultural style differences.* For example, learn to accept compliments gracefully and without suspicion; take them in stride. Some cultures use compliments and flattery as a normal, polite way of interacting.

Giving Feedback Sensitively

People from tightly woven cultures often have some difficulty giving and getting feedback in the direct style used in most organizations and by most U.S. managers and workers. Many Asians and Middle Easterners have been taught never to confront others directly. And other European groups, such as the British, tend to be more subtle when communicating about performance. In the U.S., feedback is a standard part of performance assessment and an integral part of management and creative collaboration. Your style can either respect or violate the values of harmony and consensus as practiced in some other cultures. Here are some suggestions for giving feedback sensitively.

- *Choose the right time and place.* What is culturally appropriate for giving feedback to this employee? Shall it be in a formal or informal session? Directly or using a third party? In private or in a group? Oral or written or both?

- *Clarify your commitment to the person receiving or giving feedback.* Stress the results you are working toward and the importance of the process of asking for, giving, and getting feedback.

- *Specifically describe behavior.* Tell the other person what you have seen or understand them to have said or done. Keep in mind possible cultural differences that may affect behavior.

- *Give positive acknowledgment.* Tell what stands out for you or excites you about what the other person did or said.

- *Give supporting information.* Share information, data, or facts that you have that pertain to what the other person has done.

- *Give an I-message.* Openly and frankly share your opinions and preferences as your own. Avoid talking in terms of absolute rights and wrongs.

- *Open up possibilities.* Share ideas and suggestions you have for the other's work or performance.

- *Share your experience.* Tell about your experience with activities or work similar to the recipient's.

- *Offer clear expectations.* Be clear about what you mutually agreed upon in the past or are now asking the other person to do.

- *Use creative questioning.* Raise questions that clarify the content or direction of the recipient's performance. Questioning can bring out cultural differences.

- *Give support.* Offer support, resources, and information to enable the other person to fulfill their agreements and meet your expectations.

- *Summarize.* Recognize what each of you has contributed during and after this feedback session.

- *Ask for feedback.* Get feedback on how the other has received your feedback. Listen for clues about cultural or individual differences that may affect the situation.

Giving feedback about job performance is crucial to employees' success and can help to build trust or destroy it. Therefore, becoming aware of cultural differences concerning evaluation, appraisal, and criticism is crucial to your success as a leader.

Setting the Stage for Creativity

A key advantage of a diverse work force is the increased potential for creativity and innovation. To tap this potential, leaders must set the stage for creativity to occur. Research indicates that the following factors foster creativity in diverse groups (Miller 1992).

- Create a nonjudgmental environment that encourages people to risk exploration without having to produce a "winner" every time.
- Avoid judgmental words such as good, bad, better, best, mistake—words that kill creativity.
- Cultivate an appreciation of bizarre questions and ideas without negatively labeling them as weird or crazy.
- Produce a noncompetitive atmosphere that focuses on performance and end results, rather than on the how-tos of creative discovery.
- Foster a cooperative spirit that encourages people to learn from each other and to delight in each others' success.
- Provide reasonable, organic structure and discipline to bring out creativity.
- Have fun! Encourage people to get carried away by the sheer fun of creating something.
- Support employees in ways that allow them to release their anxieties about whether their creation is good enough.

Overcoming Resistance

Growing a multicultural organization is challenging because the barriers are many, the guidelines are still being tested, and the barriers to a particular talented employee achieving his or her full potential are complex. But when we look at the changing face of organizations today and compare that with what we saw in the 1950s, we know that many barriers have already been overcome. If we want our organizations to change and are willing to devote the energy to it, we can make remarkable progress. Success is more likely if leaders are aware of typical resistances of top managers and employees, as well as typical managerial problems in implementing a multicultural approach.

Resistance from the Top

Typical reasons top managements give for not managing diversity are rooted in lack of information about diversity, short-range planning, and a lack of commitment:

- It costs too much.
- We can't find enough qualified minorities.
- We should hire the best person.
- We don't believe in reverse discrimination.
- Enough progress has been made.
- It's time to just be gender-neutral and color-blind.

- We have too many priorities that are more crucial than diversity.
- It's too much work to make the needed changes.
- Our organization is just too large to make the needed changes.
- A focus on diversity is divisive; we focus on being one big happy family.

This "divisive" rationalization is so common and erects such a rigid barrier to multiculturalism that it's worth pursuing. Here are some variations on that theme.

Divisive Rationale 1: We shouldn't focus on differences. Some people think that if we look at how cultures differ, we won't see how they're alike and therefore we won't find a common ground of unity. But learning about other cultures and valuing cultural differences need not be a barrier to unity. We can always connect with others for many reasons, including these.

- Anthropologists assure us that humans are more alike than they are different.
- Psychologists point out that we all have needs for survival, security, belonging, recognition, and self-actualization; we differ only in the ways we go about fulfilling these needs.

Therefore, we can value diversity and still find common ground almost everywhere, if that's our intent.

Divisive Rationale 2: We don't want to stereotype people. For an opinion to be a stereotype, it must be *rigid*, not taking into account individual differences within a group. Learning about cultural patterns and typical beliefs and values should provide *flexible general guidelines* to help us understand what makes people act the way they do—to know the right questions to ask people when problems arise. We must always keep in mind that general guidelines do not apply equally to every person from a culture, just as no one of us conforms to exactly the same beliefs and behaviors within our own culture.

Divisive Rationale 3: We don't want to be racist or sexist. Actually, not admitting differences is probably more ethnocentric than is exploring and respecting differences. After all, if we're all alike, who are we like, which culture? What culture represents the norm to which we all should conform? The unconscious assumption is that it's our own, of course. It's a way of saying, "People are basically alike—like me."

Divisive Rationale 4: Focusing on similarities is easier. Life seems easier, in the short run, if we assume that everyone is alike. Dealing with diverse people means dealing with complexity and uncertainty, and it may seem easier to settle for "we're all basically alike." But if misunderstandings are based on cultural differences, then ignoring differences keeps us from getting at the root of the problem, which in turn can build and fester.

Companies that avoid addressing diversity adequately are short-sighted and in the long run will probably regret having fallen behind in the race to build and keep a staff of highly qualified people. Many just don't understand the advantages of managing diversity effectively.

Typical Implementation Problems

Some typical management problems in implementing a diversity plan include:

- top-down, directive management style, which doesn't provide for a two-way acculturation and adaptation, nor dialogue about what diverse employees need and want
- overconcern with getting tasks done and underconcern with the people doing them
- narrow view of diversity that focuses only on minorities and women rather than all employees, or only on increasing the numbers of minorities and women rather than taking a comprehensive multicultural approach

- short-term, results orientation: "We met our diversity goals for the year"
- lack of strategic perspective; a focus on daily operational concerns
- lack of leadership to develop the vision of an empowered diverse work force, to articulate a strategy to gain competitive advantage, and to build and maintain systems and practices that support the vision and strategy

Employee Resistance

Typical reasons that employees resist managing-diversity efforts include:

- lack of motivation—people not understanding the business rationale for moving ahead with managing diversity, how it will affect the productivity and viability of their departments and the organization
- belief in the melting pot, that people should adapt and be one big happy family.
- ignorance about culture, and its potential as an effective tool for empowering employees
- prejudice and stereotyping
- affirmative action backlash, and suspicion that any new diversity approach is an effort to sneak AA in through the back door
- risk aversion, unwillingness to risk the experimentation and changes that managing diversity requires
- lack of power, knowledge, or skills in managing diversity on the part of those managers and employees who want to become change agents
- responsibility overload—managers believing they don't have the time or energy for another initiative, not seeing how managing diversity can help them achieve their goals, rather than being a distraction

Knowing the resistances can help you plan for overcoming them. This knowledge can also help you analyze why the diversity efforts are not working as well as expected. The barriers list can become a checklist for figuring out why.

BUILDING CONSENSUS FOR CHANGE

Creating change is always a leadership challenge. First, build on current needs and desires for change within the organization. Second, work through your own issues around change and help others work through theirs. Third, recognize and avoid typical change traps. Finally, identify and develop conscious change agents who can in turn help you build a critical mass of people committed to making the needed changes.

Build on the Organizational Need and Desire to Change

Most organizations have many values and practices from the past, as well as current pressures and future concerns, that facilitate a multicultural approach. Among these are:

- a strong corporate culture that values diversity
- a well-planned and well-administered AA program
- awareness of limitations of AA efforts, including backlash and stigma problems—managers are looking for a better way to create equal opportunity
- a prior substantial investment in managing diversity—management has a stake in making the investment pay off

- a good track record for diversity—the company already perceives itself as diverse
- the organization's pride in being a fair and equitable employer
- legal, moral, and social responsibility concerns
- intense competition that forces managers to examine all possibilities for enhancing productivity and effectiveness
- an increasingly diverse workforce with fewer available qualified recruits
- employees' unwillingness to be assimilated and their comfort and pride with their diversity

These are the motivators that you can build on, the desires and needs for change that can help your multicultural approach become a winner.

Work Through Change Issues

Building consensus requires networking with employees who are good candidates for becoming conscious change agents. Working through your own change issues can prepare you to help others open up to positive change. What if we could address the bottom-line concerns of all the major corporate players, or stakeholders, about changing the corporation? What if you could help them clear away all their reservations to supporting the changes? Answering the provocative questions that are posed in Skill Builder 12.2 may get your creative juices flowing. Even more important, you may come up with just the right questions for your organization to address.

Avoid Typical Change Traps

Change agents need specific skills. When you venture into new territory, from the known to the unknown, the going can be rough. Most of us need some guidance from people who've been there before. Here are some typical traps you'll want to avoid (Terry 1990).

- Believing there is one best way. Focus on the end result; the paths leading there may be many.
- Adopting a label, such as "diversity manager" or "change agent" but avoiding the real struggle. We must do the work.
- Not realizing that many people are unable to comprehend and/or accept these ideas. We must deal with people according to where they are in their own development and take it one step at a time.
- Focusing only on the *reasons* change is needed or only on change actions themselves. Both theory and action are needed.
- Holding Euro-American men responsible for solving the problem of prejudice. *All* stakeholders must be deeply involved in any solution.
- Becoming self-righteous, impressed by your own virtue. Remember to look at where you've been and where you're going.
- Believing we have a choice about whether to change or not.

This last trap deserves further comment. Our choice is not whether change will take place but whether we'll make it happen, watch it happen, or ask "What happened?" Savvy leaders take a proactive stance toward change, looking for opportunities and dealing with challenges. You as a leader can help people to understand that change is the constant in life. The world keeps changing whether we approve or not. An increasingly diverse work force is a fact of life. Therefore, when we speak of creating organizational change and building consensus for change, we're talking about anticipating and recognizing changes that are already in motion and responding positively. We're speaking of making things happen in ways that build trust and cooperation rather than resisting the changing diversity of the workplace and proceeding as though it doesn't exist. A personal and organizational commitment to respect all types of employees and to support them in their career development is a proactive response to this change—one that's good for all employees and for the organization.

Develop Conscious Change Agents

If we seriously want to eliminate prejudicial injustice in America, instead of pretending to ignore color and other differences, we must be color conscious in a radically new way, according to African American consultant Robert Terry (1990). Euro-Americans must understand their ingroups' role in creating the crisis and in resolving it, taking such actions as the following:

- Become a conscious agent of change—recognize that new directions are possible.
- Seek ethical clarity—know what you want your organization, and America, to stand for and why.
- Identify the various forms and expressions of prejudice—know who we are and have been, and why.
- Develop long-range change strategies to eliminate and move beyond prejudice—to experience what a truly equitable organization might be.
- Discern the appropriate day-to-day tactics—assess your power for change.
- Experiment, test, and refine a personal lifestyle that expresses your newly affirmed values—experience who you might be.

Making a personal commitment to bring about change is the first step to becoming a conscious change agent. The next step is to become conscious of what needs changing. To be conscious is to be always actively aware of ourselves in relation to other people and things around us. Skill Builder 12.3 focuses on becoming conscious of how changes in beliefs lead to changes in actions.

Core beliefs about a situation can either lock us into limited options or solutions or they can open the door to different ways of seeing the past and present, and a different guide for future action. For example, if we see African Americans as the problem, then both our attitudes and behaviors will flow from that belief about the situation. If we believe that the Euro-American culture and privileged Euro-Americans are the problem, then it becomes possible to explore new behavior and reevaluate earlier attitudes. We may see that people from both cultures need to take responsibility for bringing about change. The most important question for each person is, "What can I do to bring about needed change?"

Once you've decided what you can do, the next step is making a personal commitment to help bring about positive change, as set out in Skill Builder 12.3. As a leader you have significant opportunities to take personal stands and to follow through with personal actions, no matter how small, toward creating positive change. You may need to go against the norms of the corporate culture, which is always challenging. But if your stands and your actions are consistently supportive of, for example, Latino American or gay employees as basically equal and valuable human beings, then your actions build a bridge over centuries of mistrust to the other side, to mutual respect and trust.

SUMMARY

Meeting the needs of all types of employees is the ultimate challenge for diversity leaders. The needs include working in a corporate culture that's comfortable for them, in an organization whose systems and practices support their career development. They need to align with a company that has ended practices that have historically excluded minorities from higher levels. Managing diversity means also meeting Euro-American males' needs for becoming comfortable with diverse persons holding leadership and peer roles. Diverse employees need to develop networks of contacts and accept career development opportunities, allowing them to break through the glass ceiling.

A successful multicultural approach must be all-inclusive and must deal with employees as individuals, taking into account their cultural and experiential background against the backdrop of a diverse society. It's crucial to move the corporate culture toward a valuing-diversity culture that goes beyond tolerance to appreciation—for all types of employees. It gives people the freedom to be themselves and to make some choices about which aspects of their culture and background they want to retain. It's based on building multicultural skills and providing diversity education for all employees.

Including all employees in the bottom-line efforts of the organization not only boosts organizational success, it also meets the needs of diverse employees. Continuous improvement feeds into continuous learning, and also results from it, creating an ongoing learning loop. Those learning loops that are directly connected to improvement of key products and services are the ones that generate excitement and satisfaction for employees. The Inner Circle is a metaphor for employees involved in such learning loops.

Building on equal opportunity principles is another key aspect of the multicultural approach. Leaders first revitalize the AA system currently in place, using past lessons we've learned about what works and what doesn't. A good diversity audit becomes the basis for developing and implementing a diversity plan. A key strategy for making the multicultural approach work is getting to know employees as individuals, taking into consideration their cultural and experiential background within the context of a diverse society. Leaders can overcome the resistance of other leaders and employees to the multicultural approach by understanding typical reasons given in the past and adopting the strategies others have used successfully to move beyond such resistance.

Building consensus for change is essential to successfully implementing the multicultural approach. While the commitment of top management is the first step, lasting change requires the consensus of a critical mass of employees. As a leader you can start the change process by building on those factors already at work within the organization that motivate people toward change. You can work through your own change issues and help others to do the same. You can anticipate some typical change traps in order to avoid them. Eventually you must develop others as conscious change agents who will in turn influence yet others toward positive change. This builds a critical mass of employees with a commitment to creating a valuing-diversity culture with a multicultural orientation.

Skill Builder 12.1: A Question of Change

Purpose: To stimulate thinking about ways to make your workplace more supportive of all employees.

Instructions: Record your responses and any additional insights, including further questions that could lead to creative solutions for your particular organization, perhaps for all organizations. If you don't work for a large organization now, think of past organizations you've worked for or have been a part of, such as a university or school.

Step 1. Consider the viewpoints of all stakeholders

Who are the stakeholders that have widely varying viewpoints in your organization? Examples might be sales employees, women in the accounting department, African American employees, Euro-American managers. A) List the stakeholders, each on a separate page. B) Under each stakeholder, write a one-line statement that you think represents that group's general viewpoint. C) Under each one-liner, list the major corporate changes you think people in that group might want.

Step 2. Develop a concept of culture

Imagine that everyone in the organization agreed that the underlying problem of prejudice and inequity is rooted in the current corporate culture. What effect would this have?

Step 3. Identify barriers to mutual respect and trust

If you and other key people conducted a long, hard, critical examination of "why we haven't been able or willing to value and appreciate our diversity," what barriers do you think you would find?

Step 4. Take responsibility for personal growth

Imagine that most of the employees worked deeply with their beliefs and feelings about prejudice and diversity. Would this eliminate most of the barriers noted in step 3? What barriers would remain?

Step 5. Influence culture change

- Would this process be enough to begin some positive change in corporate values, norms, structures, and power? What specific changes might occur? What else would be needed?

- Is there any evidence of overt or subtle paternalism, threats, or punishment in the organization? Be specific.

- Would this process be enough to begin shifting this pattern? How might this evolve? What else would be needed?

- Could this process lead to collaboration based on mutual trust, as peers committed to solving a common problem within a common framework? How might this evolve? What else would be needed?

Skill Builder 12.2: Beliefs About What Needs Changing

Purpose: To become aware of the role and power of individuals changing their beliefs.

Step 1. How can we become conscious of what needs changing? We might start by examining some core beliefs, attitudes, thoughts, feelings, decisions and day-to-day action choices. Examine this core belief:

Belief #1: *America is the great melting pot. If African Americans can't succeed in business, it's not because Euro-American managers and co-workers don't welcome them. It's because they don't have what it takes to succeed.*

Based on this belief, what needs to be done in the workplace? In society in general? What ideas come to mind? Record them.

Step 2. Now think about this alternate core belief:

Belief #2: *American culture, systems, institutions, and beliefs are what block African Americans from succeeding in business. The stereotypes, prejudice, institutionalized discrimination, and personal discrimination of Euro-Americans are the problem.*

Based on this alternate belief, what needs to be done in the workplace? In society in general? What ideas come to mind? Record them.

Step 3. Jot down your insights regarding the difference a belief makes.

Skill Builder 12.3: Making a Commitment for Change

Purpose: To make a written commitment to help change the workplace toward valuing diversity and eliminating discrimination.

Step 1. List at least three personal stands you're committed to taking:

Step 2. List at least three personal actions you're committed to taking.

Skill Builder 12.4: Who's in the Inside Circle?

Purpose: To get a clear picture of insiders and outsiders in your organization.

Step 1. Think of the organization where you work. Think about which employees are involved in continuous improvement and continuous learning—in learning loops that directly affect the success of the organization, its bottom-line results. In other words, think about which employees are included in the Inner Circle?

Step 2. Place symbols, such as triangles or circles, inside the Inner Circle that represent employees you know. You might use a different symbol, incorporating colored ink or pencil, for each employee—or a different symbol for each work team, unit, or department that's in the Inner Circle.

Step 3. Which employees are not included in the Inner Circle? They may be in learning loops, but not those that make a real difference. Draw symbols for those employees in the area outside the Inner Circle in Figure 12.5.

Step 4. What does this picture say to you about your organization?
- About its effectiveness in managing diversity?
- About its effectiveness in utilizing all its human resources.
- About its effective in developing all its employees potential for contribution?

Skill Builder 12.5 The Case of a Skills Gap at Lights Plus

Phyllis went to a Lights Plus store to buy some track lights she had seen advertised at a special reduced price. *Henry*, an African American salesperson, waited on her. Phyllis explained that the track lights were the only lighting in her home office and she needed lots of light throughout the room. Henry told her the sale track lights were very good lights, very popular. He went to the stock room to get the lights and tracks, couldn't find the tracks, and returned to tell Phyllis that they didn't have them in stock. Instead of giving up, Phyllis insisted on knowing if they could be obtained for her, so Henry asked the manager *Mark* about getting the tracks. Mark felt sure there were some tracks in the stock room and quickly found them. A sale was made. When Phyllis called in an electrician to install the lights, he pointed out that they gave small spots of very intense light and were not too effective for general lighting. In addition they were much more expensive than the general-lighting type. Phyllis decided to return them and wait for the general-lighting type to go on sale.

A month or so later Lights Plus advertised at half price the type of track lights Phyllis needed. She called the store near her to be sure they were still on sale and were in stock. When she walked into the store, Henry greeted her. He showed her the sale track lights, which were packaged in boxes, picked up a couple of boxes, and took them to the cash register. When he entered the transaction, Henry saw that the price displayed on the register was the regular price, not the sale price. Henry said, "Well, these lights are $59.99 a package." Phyllis was exasperated. She said, "Then I don't want them. I don't know why the woman who answered the phone here about an hour ago told me they were still on sale. If she had told me they were now regular price, I wouldn't have made the trip." Henry said nothing and Phyllis left the store, shaking her head.

Driving home, Phyllis recalled her last trip to Lights Plus. Henry had been uninformed about where to find merchandise in the stock room. "Maybe he's uninformed about prices too," she thought. She turned the corner, went back to the store, and asked to speak to the manager. When she explained the price problem, Mark replied, "Oh, yes, that's just one of those computer glitches. Somehow the sale information didn't get into the current computer file. No problem, you can have the track lights at the sale price." When Mark went to pick up the packets, he said, "Now some of these sets are black and some are white, even though the pictures on all the boxes show white lights." Phyllis thought, "Why didn't Henry tell me that? Without that information, I had a fifty-fifty chance of bringing home lights of the wrong color." (Note: The top management of Lights Plus has expressed the company's top-priority objective this way: "Customer satisfaction is the target.")

- In what ways did Henry fail to meet the company's target?
- Describe the gap between Henry's skills and capabilities and the required skills and capabilities. What do you think Henry should do?
- Was Mark effective in managing inclusion? Giving quality treatment? Applying the ARC of improvement? What do you think Mark should do?
- What cultural differences might explain the problems that occurred in this case?

Skill Builder 12.6: The Case of a "Diverse" Corporate Culture

Sharon is a 22-year-old college student looking for a part-time job to help pay her school expenses. She interviews for a part-time receptionist job in a medical clinic. When *George*, the office manager, meets Sharon, he feels that she will "melt right into the company culture." The support staff is diverse, consisting of 11 Asian Americans, 6 African Americans, 4 Euro-Americans, and 8 Latino Americans. George believes that given her enthusiasm, Sharon will get along well with her co-workers, and given her educational background, he's sure she can perform the job duties. He offers her the job and she accepts.

Her first day on the job Sharon is introduced to all the staff members. She immediately feels as if she's part of the family. Her co-workers are very friendly, and each of them makes her feel welcome and comfortable. Sharon is assigned to report to *Tiffany*, an African American supervisor. From the first day Sharon notices that the staff in fact does not act like a family when it's time for coffee breaks and lunch. Actually the staff is pretty segregated. The African Americans sip and munch together, while the Asian Americans form their own group, speaking Cantonese. Meantime, the Latino Americans get together and speak Spanish. Tiffany leads Sharon straight to the African American group and they welcome her.

As Sharon and Tiffany get to know each other, Sharon reveals that her father is African American and her mother is Asian American. They divorced when Sharon was only three and Sharon has not seen much of her father since the divorce. Sharon doesn't have many African American friends. "Most of them seem to take the attitude that I'm not black enough," she says. "I think they're referring to the way I express myself rather than my skin color. I know I look more African American than Asian American. But I do speak Cantonese and of course my thinking is much like my mom's."

One day Sharon asks Tiffany, "Why do people go off into their own little ethnic groups all the time? They never seem to intermingle except on the job, only enough to get the work done." Tiffany replies, "Just human nature, I guess, We don't try to get people to intermingle. We just leave well enough alone. People get along pretty well now. If we try to get more interaction, they might start fighting, who knows?"

Now, a few weeks later, Sharon feels ignored by her African American co-workers and a little uncomfortable with them. She knows it's because she seems withdrawn and reserved to them, like she's holding back. But it's just the Asian way. Sharon tries a few times to join the Asian American group, even speaking Cantonese with them. At first they're surprised and interested in knowing more about her. But now they too tend to ignore her. Somehow she doesn't quite fit in with them either.

Sharon is feeling lonely. Every day she sits at the front desk, taking incoming calls, recording messages, and greeting patients. Sometimes Tiffany helps her out. But even when they're working side by side, they don't have many personal conversations any more. When her afternoon shift is over, Sharon goes home with few interesting stories to tell her mother—a few about patients, but none about co-workers. Sharon is thinking about looking for another job. Tiffany notices that Sharon is not as enthusiastic as she was when she first took the job. Even George has noticed a difference in Sharon's attitude.

- What are the key issues in this case?
- If you were Sharon, what would you do?
- If you were Tiffany, what would you do?
- If you were George, what would you do?

A CONCLUDING ACKNOWLEDGMENT OF YOUR ACHIEVEMENT

Congratulations! If you've worked your way through this book, you now have a solid foundation for becoming a diversity leader and a conscious change agent. You've begun building a most valuable set of multicultural skills. In Chapter 1 you learned that you would proceed through five skill-building steps, and now you've completed those steps.

Steps You've Completed in Building Your Multicultural Skills

Step 1. You've become aware of culture and its pervasive influence.

Step 2. You've learned more about your own culture.

Step 3. You recognize your own ethnocentricity, the ways in which you stereotype, judge, and discriminate, and your emotional reactions to conflicting cultural values.

Step 4. You've learned about other cultures you encounter in the workplace so you can recognize when cultural differences may be at the root of problems and so you can appreciate the contributions people from diverse cultures can make to the work situation.

Step 5. You've built your interaction skills and practiced new behaviors through the self-awareness activities and skill builders in this book.

Being a diversity leader can be difficult and complex. You often must intuit your way into the murky unknown as change in the workplace accelerates. But the effort is so worthwhile, and success is so rewarding.

Managing diversity is the challenge of the new millennium—for our communities and our planet as well as for our workplaces. Do we want a world of prejudice, bigotry, hatred, rage, riots, terrorism, and war? Or do we want to work through our differences so we can work together in peace and harmony? If we want harmony, then common sense tells us that workplace and community discrimination against whole groups of people must come to an end.

Managing diversity is also the opportunity for the new millennium. It offers opportunities to grow personally and collectively, to learn new ways of collaborating, to create a synergy that sparks innovation and accelerates human knowledge and achievement. Let's welcome these changes for the opportunities they open up and for the challenges that motivate us to keep sharpening our multicultural skills.

REFERENCES

Allport, G.W. *The Nature of Prejudice.* Boston: Addison-Wesley Publishing Company, Inc., 1954.

Arnold, H., and D. Feldman. *Organizational Behavior.* New York: McGraw-Hill, 1986.

Ashenfelter, Orley. "Racial Discrimination and Trade Unions." *Journal of Political Economy* 80 (1972): 435–464.

Blanchard, F.A., and F.J. Crosby, eds. *Affirmative Action in Perspective.* New York: Springer-Verlag, 1989.

Carr-Ruffino, N., et al. "Legal Aspects of Women's Advancement." *Woman Power.* Thousand Oaks, CA: Sage, 1991.

Carr-Ruffino, Norma. "U.S. Women: Breaking Through the Glass Ceiling." *Women in Management Review* 6, no. 5, 1991.

Catalyst. *Women in Corporate Management.* New York: Catalyst, 1990.

Cox, Taylor. *Cultural Diversity in Organizations.* San Francisco: Berrett-Koehler, 1993.

Deshpande, Hoyer, and J. Donthu. "The Study of Ethnic Affiliation." *Journal of Consumer Research* 13 (1986): 214–220.

DiTomaso, N., D.E. Thompson, and D.H. Blake. "Corporate Perspectives on the Advancement of Minority Managers." *Ensuring Minority Success in Corporate Management.* New York: Plenum, 1988.

Gottfredson. "Dilemmas in Developing Diversity Programs." *Diversity in the Workplace.* New York: Guilford, 1992.

HRM Ideas & Trends in Personnel, no. 272. Commerce Clearing House (April 1992): 53.

Kim, J.S., and A.F. Campagna. "Effects of Flextime on Employee Attendance and Performance." *Academy of Management Journal* 24 (1981): 729–741.

Kotter, J.P. "What Leaders Really Do." *Harvard Business Review,* (May–June 1990): 103–111.

Miller, Brian. "Adult Sexual Resocialization." *Sociology of Homosexuality.* New York: Garland, 1992.

Morrison, Ann, R.P. White, and E. Van Velsor. *Breaking the Glass Ceiling.* Reading, MA: Addison-Wesley, 1987.

Morrison, Ann. *The New Leaders.* San Francisco: Jossey-Bass, 1992.

Shephard, C.R. *Small Groups.* San Francisco: Chandler Publishing, 1964.

Terry, Robert W. (Detroit Industrial Mission). *For Whites Only.* Grand Rapids, MI: William B. Eerdmans Publishing Company, 1970, 1990.

Thomas, Roosevelt. "From Affirmative Action to Affirming Diversity." *Harvard Business Review* 68, no. 2 (1990): 107–117.

Thomas, Roosevelt. *Beyond Race & Gender.* New York: AMACOM, 1991.

U.S. Department of Labor. *A Report on the Glass Ceiling Initiative.* 1991.

Other Resources

The following materials address the political correctness issue:

Gates, H.L., Jr. *Loose Canons.* New York: Oxford University Press, 1992.

Graff, Gerald. *Beyond the Culture Wars: How Teaching the Conflicts Can Revitalize American Education.* W.W. Norton, 1992.

The diversity training materials that follow are available from:

Managing Diversity, JALMC, P.O. Box 819, Jamestown, NY 14702.

Banks, G. *The Human Diversity Workshop.*

Dickerson-Jones, Terri. *50 Activities for Diversity Training.*

Dickerson-Jones, Terri. *50 Activities for Managing Cultural Diversity.*

Directory of Diversity Recruitment.

Fyock, C. *Cultural Diversity: Challenges and Opportunities.*

Gardenswartz, L. and A. Rowe. *Managing Diversity: A Complete Desk Reference and Planning Guide* and *The Diversity Tool Kit.*

Managing Diversity, a monthly newsletter.

Myers, S. and J. Lambert. *Diversity Icebreakers: A Trainer's Guide.*

Turkewych, C. and H. Guerreiro-Klinowski. *Intercultural Interviewing.*